THEGREENGUIDE
French Riviera

House in Île de Porquerolles © Monika Lewandowska/iStockphoto.com

General Manager   Cynthia Clayton Ochterbeck

THEGREENGUIDE **FRENCH RIVIERA**

Editor   Rachel Mills, Alison Coupe
Principal Writer   Heather Stimmler Hall
Production Manager   Natasha G. George
Cartography   Stéphane Anton, John Dear
Photo Editor   Yoshimi Kanazawa
Interior Design   Chris Bell
Layout   Alison Rayner
Cover Design   Chris Bell, Christelle Le Déan
Cover Layout   Michelin Apa Publications Ltd.

Contact Us   The Green Guide
                                 Michelin Maps and Guides
                                 One Parkway South
                                 Greenville, SC 29615
                                 USA
                                 www.michelintravel.com
                                 michelin.guides@us.michelin.com

                                 Michelin Maps and Guides
                                 Hannay House
                                 39 Clarendon Road
                                 Watford, Herts WD17 1JA
                                 UK
                                 ℘01923 205240
                                 www.ViaMichelin.com
                                 travelpubsales@uk.michelin.com

Special Sales   For information regarding bulk sales,
                                 customized editions and premium sales,
                                 please contact our Customer Service
                                 Departments:
                                 USA   1-800-432-6277
                                 UK   01923 205240
                                 Canada 1-800-361-8236

HOW TO USE THIS GUIDE

PLANNING YOUR TRIP

The blue-tabbed PLANNING YOUR TRIP section at the front of the guide gives you **ideas for your trip** and **practical information** to help you organise it. You'll find tours, practical information, a host of outdoor activities, a calendar of events, information on shopping, sightseeing, kids' activities and more.

INTRODUCTION

The orange-tabbed INTRODUCTION section explores the French Riviera's **Nature** and geology. The **History** section spans 1500 BC through the Revolution to the modern day. The **Art and Culture** section covers architecture, art, literature and music, while the **Region Today** delves into the modern French Riviera.

DISCOVERING

The green-tabbed DISCOVERING section features Principal Sights by region, featuring the most interesting local **Sights**, **Walking Tours**, nearby **Excursions**, and detailed **Driving Tours**. Admission prices shown are normally for a single adult.

ADDRESSES

We've selected the best hotels, restaurants, cafes shops, nightlife and entertainment to fit all budgets. See the Legend on the cover flap for an explanation of the price categories. See the back of the guide for an index of where to find hotels and restaurants.

Sidebars

Throughout the guide you will find blue, peach and green-colored text boxes with lively anecdotes, detailed history and background information.

😊 A Bit of Advice 😊

Green advice boxes found in this guide contain practical tips and handy information relevant to the sight in the Discovering section.

STAR RATINGS★★★

Michelin has given star ratings for more than 100 years. If you're pressed for time, we recommend you visit the ★★★, or ★★ sights first:

★★★	**Highly recommended**
★★	**Recommended**
★	**Interesting**

MAPS

- 🖐 National Driving Tours map, Places to Stay map and Sights map.
- 🖐 Region maps.
- 🖐 Maps for major cities and villages.
- 🖐 Local tour maps.

All maps in this guide are oriented north, unless otherwise indicated by a directional arrow. The term "Local Map" refers to a map within the chapter or Tourism Region. A complete list of the maps found in the guide appears at the back of this book.

PLANNING YOUR TRIP

INTRODUCTION TO THE FRENCH RIVIERA

DISCOVERING THE FRENCH RIVIERA

CONTENTS

Welcome to the French Riviera

The French Riviera stretches along the Mediterranean coast in southeastern France between the Italian border and the Rhône Valley. It's an amazingly diverse region of sunny beaches and prestigious ports as well as dramatic mountain peaks and secluded perched villages. Aside from its natural beauty, visitors will also discover a rich artistic, cultural and architectural heritage from Roman times and the Middle Ages up through the Belle Époque and continuing today.

Îles des Embiez

©Camille Moirenc/Hemis/Photoshot

TOULON & AROUND (p98–125)

The oft-overlooked city of Toulon at the western edge of the French Riviera is well worth a stop for its historic naval harbour and newly restored old town. The surrounding villages produce some of the best wines of the region, and the beaches on the Iles des Embiez offer a sunny retreat from the summer crowds.

GOLDEN ISLANDS (p126–169)

For those who dream of unspoiled islands, sandy beaches and chic resorts, this Eden-like stretch of the Riviera won't disappoint. The natural beauty of the Maures Massif and the Golden Islands has been fiercely

Île de Porquerolles

©Luca Chiartano/Dreamstime.com

protected from overdevelopment. And even after the summer crowds of St Tropez and Hyères disappear, the Provençal-style fishing villages and Belle Époque palaces make for pleasant sightseeing.

INLAND PROVENCE (p170–195)

Far from the showy splendour and busloads of tourists found on the coastal resorts, the villages, valleys and prehistoric monuments of Inland Provence are given to peaceful

Cotignac

exploration. The 12C Abbaye du Thoronet is worth a detour of its own, and wine collectors won't want to miss the vineyards around Brignoles. Aups and Cotignac remain two of the most charming villages in the region.

FRÉJUS & THE ESTEREL MASSIF (p196–221)

The most Provençal area of the French Riviera is known for the unspoiled forests and red rock hills of the Massif de l'Esterel, while the lively twinned towns of Fréjus and St-Raphaël attract

Esterel Massif viewed from Fréjus

©Guillaume Besnard/Fotolia.com

visitors who prefer a more discreet resort experience to its beaches. History *aficionados* won't want to miss the impressive Gallo-Roman remains found in and around Fréjus.

CANNES & THE GRASSE REGION *(p222–281)*

Don't forget to pack your bathing suit and sunglasses! The most popular beaches on the French Riviera are found in the dynamic resort towns of Cannes, Antibes and Juan-les-Pins, while the hills further inland are home to the world-famous perfume-making town of Grasse and its surrounding perched villages. The fashionable palace hotels and private yachts are a surprising contrast to the Provençal-style villages with their shady squares and ancient churches, making this an ideal place to experience both worlds.

NICE, THE RIVIERA & MONACO *(p282–339)*

This glamorous stretch of the Riviera features the glittering Principality of Monaco, with its Belle Époque casino

View of Grasse

S. Sauvignier/ MICHELIN

and fairytale castle, and the bustling big city of Nice, known for its colourful Carnival parades, old town market, and world-class art collections. While cruising between the two on the scenic corniche roads, visitors will find more tranquil coastal paths along Cap Ferrat and Cap d'Ail, and amazing views from the perched village of Èze.

Charming village of Èze

©Peter Adams/AWL Images

THE PRE-ALPS OF NICE *(p340–373)*

The most dramatic landscape on the French Riviera is found in the hinterlands above Nice, where the sunny Mediterranean meets the

Rock cliffs of La Colmiane

©Michel Megret/Robert Harding

snow-covered Alps. The rocky peaks and deep river valleys attract hikers, rock climbers, rafters and mountain bikers in summer, as well as skiing in winter. The Mercantour National Park, which shares a border with Italy, offers glimpses of rare flora and fauna as well as prehistoric engravings in the Vallée des Merveilles. Sturdy shoes and reliable maps are a must!

Promenade des Anglais and Hôtel Negresco, Nice
©Romain Cintract/Hemis/Photolibrary

Michelin Driving Tours

For an overall impression of these various driving tours, consult the map on the inside back cover.

1 VAR COASTLINE AND THE GOLDEN ISLANDS

Round tour of 235km/146mi starting from Toulon

The city of Toulon should be visited in the local tradition, in other words at a leisurely pace, taking time to explore the intricate streets shaded by century-old plane trees. After dropping by the lively marché Lafayette and choosing a few fresh vegetables and mouthwatering local treats, set out to discover "the most beautiful harbour" on the Riviera, passing by Pointe du Fort Balaguier and Cap Sicié. Nestled between land and sea, Sanary and Bandol, and their islands of Bendor and Embiez, will seduce you by their heavenly setting. Further on, the perched villages of Le Castellet, Beausset and Evenos compose the perfect picture of Provençal bliss. Then admire the harbour from atop Mont Faron. Continue to the bird sanctuary at La Londe for an escape to the tropics. Treat yourself to a stay on the gorgeous islands of Port-Cros and Porquerolles; the underwater sightseeing trail offers incomparable views of the sea's fauna and flora for divers and snorkelers. A tour of the Mine de

Citadel of St-Tropez
S. Sauvignier/MICHELIN

Cap-Garonne at Le Pradet is the perfect way to round off your outing.

2 LE HAUT-VAR

Round tour of 245km/152mi starting from Draguignan

This itinerary will take you across the upper stretches of the Var Valley, characterised by rolling wooded countryside dotted with old abbeys and remarkable sites: Tourtour nestling on the crest of a hill overlooking olive groves; Cotignac perched precariously on a cliff; Villecroze and Seillans enhanced by hardened volcanic ash rock formations; Entrecasteaux, whose château is graced by gardens attributed to Le Nôtre. You may be surprised by the diversity of the villages and towns you will encounter. Some clearly enjoy perpetuating local tradition while others promote a more dynamic artisan culture. Don't miss the colourful markets offering truffles, goat's cheese or olives, depending on the season, and the restaurants, where you will be served tasty regional cuisine pleasantly seasoned with aromatic herbs.

3 LE MASSIF DES MAURES

Round tour of 275km/171mi starting from Fréjus

Far away from the coast and its bustling crowd, this tour will take you through refreshingly cool forests of cork oak and the pretty Gratteloup arboretum, where eucalyptus, chestnut, maple, cedar and juniper trees exude their intoxicating aroma. Visit the superb Domaine du Rayol, designed at the turn of the 20C, and rediscover regional arts and crafts: the cork industry in Gonfaron; *marrons glacés* in Collobrières; pipe-making and carpet weaving in Cogolin. The hill villages of Ramatuelle, Grimaud and Gassin command panoramic views of the coast, as do the Moulins de Paillas. Before having a swim in one of the many sheltered inlets, you may want to settle on the terrace of the Sénéquier in St-Tropez alongside the rich and famous or you may prefer to browse among the market stalls in the old port in the hope of chancing upon a fake Picasso...

4 MASSIF DE L'ESTEREL AND THE FAYENCE REGION
Round tour of 285km/177mi starting from Cannes
Whatever the season, this itinerary will prove an enchanting experience on many counts: the rich, luxuriant vegetation, the chirping of the cicadas, the delicately fragrant mimosa blossoms, the warm embrace of the sun and the red rock of the Esterel heights. Running between La Napoule and Agay, the Corniche d'Or offers stunning views of the sea. You will succumb to the charms of St-Raphaël, a lively seaside resort, and Fréjus with its prestigious military past, not to mention Fréjus-Plage, which boasts the longest sandy beach on the Riviera. Further inland, the Fayence area will introduce you to a host of perched villages huddled on mountain slopes, dominated by vestiges of their medieval citadels: Caillan, Fayence, Tourrettes, Seillan, Tanneron and Auribeau-sur-Siagne.

5 FRAGRANCES AND COLOURS OF THE PRE-ALPS
Round tour of 215km/134mi starting from Grasse
The Pre-Alps of Provence, extending to the foot of the Alpine range and cut across by steep ravines, offer a delightful combination of colours and fragrances, where the heady smells of olive and cypress tree vie with the more subtle scent of rose, jasmin, oleander and violet. Flowers have given Grasse its reputation, so your first stop in this city must be the International Museum of Perfume and the different *parfumeries* explaining the secrets of the trade. The entrance to the Gorges du Loup is the perfect place to stop and admire the hill village of Gourdon, jealously guarding its abyss, and the Caussols Plateau, a curiously barren stretch of land riddled with chasms. After observing the geological formations in the caves of St-Vallier and St-

Cézaire, continue to St-Paul-de-Vence, a typical medieval village known for its arts and crafts, and to the delightful hamlet of Tourrettes-sur-Loup, where terraced violet fields have been cultivated from generation to generation. The Baou of St-Jeannet dominating the Var River is a sheer rocky cliff popular among seasoned climbers. Lastly, the coastal road stretching between Cagnes-sur-Mer and Antibes offers pretty views of the Baie des Anges and access to a number of contemporary art museums.

6 L'ARRIÈRE-PAYS NIÇOIS
Round tour of 270km/168mi starting from Nice
This driving tour will provide you with a fascinating selection of natural sites and architectural riches: quaint perched villages, chapels decorated by famous painters or unknown artists from the Middle Ages, steep cliffs overlooking gorges echoing with the swirling of crystal clear waters, and lush forests rustling with the sounds of local fauna. Running alongside the lower Var Valley, bordered to the west by the Baou of St Jeannet, you will start to approach the heights beyond Nice, dominated by Mont Chauve. After driving through Aspremont, Levens and Duranus, you will reach the breathtaking Vésubie Gorges. From there, brace yourself for the long series of steep hairpin bends leading up to the Madone d'Utelle sanctuary, a popular place of pilgrimage, and the nearby belvedere commanding a splendid panorama of the Alpes-Maritimes and Mediterranean Sea. Proceeding upstream along the Vésubie River in the direction of Col de Turini, you will come to Bollène-Vésubie, precariously nestling on the mountain slope. On reaching L'Authion, go round to Pointe des Trois-Communes to feast your eyes on the sweeping landscape. Continue towards the Gorges of Piaon. After the curious Notre-Dame-de-la-Menour Chapel, with its two-storey Renaissance façade, you will come to Sospel, springing from its verdant

setting, where tasty regional dishes can be sampled. Drive through several passes before rejoining Lucéram Valley, famed for its Christmas festivities attended by local shepherds. Finally, three belvederes, each home to a small village, Berre, Falicon and Tourrettes, will complete this charming tour of the Nice hinterland.

7 THE CORNICHES OF THE RIVIERA

Round tour of 250km/155.5mi starting from Nice.

If you have seen Hitchcock's thriller *To Catch a Thief,* then you will know that it is advisable to hug the road winding its way between Nice and Monte-Carlo as closely as possible. This route, which features a series of vertiginous viewpoints, goes past some of the prettiest spots on the Côte d'Azur. Set out from Villefranche, famous not only for its Chapelle St-Pierre decorated by Jean Cocteau, but also for its pretty harbour and succulent seafood dishes. Follow the Grande Corniche up to Roquebrune, with forays downhill to Beaulieu (Villa Kérylos), St-Jean-Cap-Ferrat (Villa Rothschild) and Èze, clinging to its rocky spur, where a tour of artists' workshops can be pleasantly rounded off by a visit to the Jardin Exotique. Enjoy the view from the Vistaero before descending towards Roquebrune with its medieval castle and venerable olive tree believed to be over 1,000 years old. After Menton, the road will take you through the perched villages of Ste-Agnès, Peille and Peillon, where the steep alleyways *(calades)* lead to chapels adorned with fine frescoes.

When and Where to Go

WHEN TO GO
SEASONS

The **tourist season** on the French Riviera lasts virtually all year round. The **winter months** are characterised by a mild, sunny climate and are ideal for those who seek to avoid the peak influx of tourists. However, some hotels, restaurants and attractions are closed between November and February.

Spring and **autumn** can sometimes bring heavy rainfalls and the infamous *mistral* wind, but neither overshadows the magnificent display of flora in full bloom at these times.

Summer is of course the best season for bathing and working up a suntan, not to mention taking part in the energetic nightlife. Traffic on the coast is, however, always very congested during this period; it can also be difficult to find accommodation, so it is advisable to book well in advance, particularly in August.

WEATHER FORECASTS
Recorded report

- for the Alpes-Maritimes: ☎08 92 68 02 06
- for the Var: ☎08 92 68 02 83
- for conditions at sea: ☎08 92 68 08 77
- for the region: ☎08 92 68 00 00
- for the mountains: ☎08 92 68 04 04

Online weather reports
- www.meteo.fr
- www.meteo123.com

Road conditions
- www.ViaMichelin.com (itineraries and updates)
- snow and avalanche reports: ☎08 92 68 10 20

WHAT TO PACK

As little as possible! Cleaning and laundry services are available everywhere. Most personal items can be replaced at reasonable cost. Try to pack everything into one suitcase and a tote bag. Porter help may be in short supply, and new purchases will add to the original weight. Take an extra tote bag for packing new purchases, shopping at the market, carrying a picnic, etc. Be sure luggage is clearly labelled and old travel tags removed. Do not pack medication in checked luggage, but keep it in your carry-on. **Tourist Information Centres – The Michelin Guide France** gives the addresses and telephone numbers of the Tourist Information Centres *(Syndicats d'Initiative)* to be found in most large towns and many tourist resorts. They can supply large-scale town plans, timetables and information on local entertainment, accommodation, sports and sightseeing.

WHERE TO GO
WEEKEND BREAKS
Two itineraries for those who want to spend a long weekend in the Riviera:

NICE

Day 1	Visit the seafront and the Vieux Ville in the morning, then Cimiez and a museum or gallery.
Day 2	Spend the morning in **Monaco**★★★, then see **Eze**★★ and **Cap Ferrat**★ via the corniche roads.
Day 3	Drive up to the **Gorges de la Vésubie**★★★, with a detour to see the **Madone d'Utelle Panorama**★★★, returning via **Sospel**★.

CANNES

Day 1	Visit the Marché, Le Suquet and the port in the morning, with lunch, sunbathing and shopping on the Croisette.
Day 2	Drive to **Antibes**★★ via the **Cap**★ to stroll the **Old Town**★, followed by a tour of **St-Paul-de-Vence**★★, returning via **Grasse**★ and **Mougins**★.
Day 3	Drive the **Corniche de l'Estérel**★★★ to **St-Raphaël**, then visit the ruins of **Fréjus**★.

ONE-WEEK ITINERARY
For a seven-day visit, make Nice your base for the first three days. Visit the Old Town and its notable museums, then the towns along the Corniche roads from Villefranche up to Menton for the best views, including an evening in Monte Carlo.

Move down to Antibes and Cannes for the next three days, with time for a trip to the Ile des Lérins, an afternoon at the beaches of Juan-les-Pins, and a drive up the Loup Valley to St-Paul-de-Vence or Gourdon. Use the last day to drive the scenic Corniche de l'Estérel, with a detour to St-Tropez if the traffic isn't too bad, or to Le Thoronet to escape the heat and crowds.

View of the Massif de l'Estérel

J. Malburet/MICHELIN

Promenade des Anglais, Nice

TWO-WEEK ITINERARY

Two weeks on the French Riviera will allow time to explore each area in-depth, to enjoy the many opportunities for water sports or hiking, or to visit the museums or explore the ancient churches off-season. To the one-week itinerary add a day in the hinterlands of Nice, hiking in the Mercantour to see the Vallée des Merveilles or rafting down the Roya Valley. Add an extra day for shopping in the artisan villages of Eze, Vence or Valbonne, or the fashionable boutiques of Monaco or Cannes. The remaining two days can be spent diving in the Iles de Porquerolles or hiking along the nature trails at Port Cros, with a guided tour of the historic naval harbour at Toulon and a drive up to Mont Faron for exceptional panoramic views.

THEMED TOURS
FOREST PARKS

All along the Alpes-Maritimes coast there are islands of greenery *(parcs forestiers départementaux)* provided for walkers of all ages.

- **Parc de la Grande-Corniche** in Èze (access from Col d'Èze on the Grande Corniche)
- **Parc de Vaugrenier** (access by N 7 between Antibes and Marina Baie des Anges)
- **Parc de la Vallée de la Brague** (at the eastern end of Biot village)
- **Parc du San Peyre** (from La Napoule towards A 8 motorway and a left turn onto Route du Cimetière), a former look-out post (alt 131m/430ft) which offers a superb panorama of Cannes Bay
- **Parc de la Pointe de l'Aiguille** (car park on N 98 at the edge of Théoule).
- **Route Historique des Hauts-Lieux de Provence** – A circuit from St-Maximin-la-Ste-Baume via Draguignan and Les Arcs to Fréjus returning along the coast to Toulon, organised by an association at the Office de Tourisme, 83460 Les Arcs-sur-Argens ℘04 94 73 37 30.
- **Route des Côtes de Provence**

SCENIC VIEWS
Riviera Caves

The limestone region of the Pays Grassois (especially the Caussols Plateau) features many interesting geological features dating from different periods – the caves *(grottes)* at St-Cézaire (*see GRASSE*), the gigantic limestone crevices such as the original caves consisting of a succession of natural dams *(gours)* such as the Grotte de Baume Obscure (*see ST-VALLIER-DE-THIEY*). The **Grottes de Villecroze** near Draguignan (*see VILLECROZE*) are formed of tufa (hardened volcanic ash). Other caves, which are accessible with adequate equipment and some technical knowledge, belong in the caving category (🔔see p25). People with no caving experience can get an idea of the activity in the first section (about 12m/39ft) of the **Embut de Caussols** (*embut* is the Provençal word for swallowhole).

Military Fortifications of the Alpes-Maritimes

The strategic significance of the frontier zone in the southeast was developed in 1880 by Sérés de Rivières. The project was completed and improved in 1929 by its integration into the Maginot Line which defended the eastern frontier from Dunkirk to Menton.
The whole construction gives an interesting view of military architecture in the 19C and 20C. Some of the buildings have been disarmed, restored, and are accessible to visitors:

- **Fort de Ste-Agnès**
  (🔔*see MENTON*)
- **Fort du Barbonnet**
  (🔔*see Forêt de TURINI*)
- **Fort Suchet (19C)**, the only one that can be visited
  (🔔*see Forêt de TURINI*).
- **Fort St-Roch** (🔔*see SOSPEL*)

Other less interesting forts make pleasant destinations for walks with fine views.

🔔Visitors should bear in mind that although the buildings of the Maginot Line appear to be in good condition, they may conceal indoor wells or dangerous passages. Some properties are private, as they have been acquired by individuals.

In the highly strategic sector of L'Authion, near Col de Turini (🔔*see Forêt de TURINI*), several structures designed by Sérés de Rivières have survived and can be reached by the loop road encircling the massif:

- Fort des Mille-Fourches
- La Forca
- Redoute des 3 Communes (1897), the first building constructed of reinforced concrete.

From Mont Chauve d'Aspremont (🔔*see NICE*) there is a brilliant view of the whole coast under clear skies. On the summit (854m/2 802ft) is a Sérés de Rivières fort with a monumental south façade, typical of the period; it is occupied by the Service des Télécommunications. Mont Chauve de Tourette is visible further north, capped by a fort from a similar period. The section near Col de Tende, which was Italian from 1860 to 1947, is an impressive example of the Italian system of defence. The remarkable central fort is set on top of the col and approached by the narrow road, which branches off by the entrance to the road tunnel; each of its façades has a different architectural style. The interior (🔔*difficult access*) resembles a small town, self-sufficient in supplies.

On the Track of Macaron

The old rail bed of one of the dismantled sections of the pinecone train *(train des pignes)*, which linked Toulon to St-Raphaël from early in the 20C to 1950, is open to walkers. Although the track and stations have mostly disappeared, owing to the effects of time and events such as the Allied Landings at the end of the Second World War, works of art and some stations (Carqueiranne) have survived. The tunnels are often used by walkers as short cuts, providing unusual and surprising glimpses of the Maures coast.

What to See and Do

OUTDOOR FUN
BOAT TRIPS

There are regular ferries to the Île de Bendor, Île des Embiez, Île d'Hyères and Île de Lérins, and also boat trips from the following resorts:

Bandol
- Les Embiez to Toulon via Cap Sicié, Gare Maritime (*04 94 32 51 41*), Cassis and the Calanque d'En-Vau via Lla Ciotat – whole day to the Château d'If and Le Frioul – underwater exploration with l'Aquascope (Cie Atlantide)

Sanary
- Îles des Embiez to Toulon Anchorage and Cap Sicié to Calanques de Cassis

Le Lavandou
- Île du Levant

Cavalaire
- Îles d'Hyères

St-Tropez
- Îles d'Hyères.

Ste-Maxime
- Les Issambres, Port-Grimaud (navettes), Baie des Cannebiers.

Ste-Maxime
- St-Tropez (shuttle) to Îles d'Hyères

Cannes
- Îles de Lérins – excursion to St-Tropez and Monaco on a catamaran

Juan les Pins
(departure from Ponton Courbet)
- Underwater viewing cruise off Cap d'Antibes

Nice
- La Riviera

Menton
- The Riviera to Monaco (with and without stopping)

Toulon
- La Seyne-sur-Mer, Les Sablettes, Tamaris, St-Mandrier *(navettes)*. Harbors of Toulon.

St-Raphaël
- St-Tropez
- Îles de Lérins

SAILING

Most of the seaside resorts on the French Riviera, from Lecques to Menton, have well-equipped marinas, making this coast arguably the best in France for sailing. Although nearly every port has moorings with good facilities, the enthusiasm for sailing is such that enormous marinas have been constructed with extensive services to satisfy even the most exacting yachtsman. Ports providing over 1 000 berths are Bandol, Toulon, Hyères (Port-St-Pierre), La Londe (Port Miramar), Le Lavandou, St-Raphaël (Ste-Lucia), Cannes (Pierre Canto and the Vieux Port), St-Laurent-du-Var and Antibes (Port-Vauban), which is the largest to date.

Another great place for sailing and other water sports is Mandelieu-La-Napoule, which has six ports *(www.mandelieu.com)*.

The marinas open to visiting crafts are marked on the Places to Stay map on pp50–51.

There are sailing clubs which provide lessons in most resorts; during the summer it is possible to hire craft with or without a crew.

Further information is available from each port authority and from the **Fédération Française de Voile** (*17 Rue Henri-Bocquillon, 75015 Paris; *01 40 60 37 00; www.ffvoile.org)*.

Sailing into the Blue

S. Sauvignier-MICHELIN

SCUBA DIVING

There are many clubs providing scuba diving lessons. The main centres are Bendor (Centre Padi is one of the largest in Europe), Le Pradet (Garonne beach), Giens (La Tour Fondue), Sanary, Cavalaire, Ramatuelle (L'Escalet), St-Tropez, Ste-Maxime, St-Raphaël, Mandelieu-La-Napoule, Cannes and Villefranche.
A brochure listing all the local clubs is available from **La Maison du Tourisme du Golfe de St-Tropez** in Gassin (℘04 94 43 42 10; www.st-tropez-lesmaures.com).
Excursions to explore the Mediterranean flora and fauna are provided by the Centre du Rayol-Canadel and the Parc National de Port-Cros.
The **Fédération Française d'Études et de Sports Sous-Marins** (24 Quai de Rive-Neuve, 13007 Marseille; ℘04 91 33 99 31; www.ffessm.fr) is an umbrella organisation, comprising 100 local clubs, which publishes a comprehensive yearbook covering all underwater activities in France.
Information also available from the **Comité Régional Côte d'Azur des Sports Sous-Marins** (Cap Blanc, Port de Bormes, 83230 Bormes-les-Mimosas; ℘04 94 71 63 43; www. ffessmcotedazur.com).

Finest Underwater Landscapes

The coves of the Maures and the Esterel on the Var coast and the clear water around the Îles d'Hyères are invitations to discover the charm of the Mediterranean *(La Grande Bleue)* and of the silent underwater world. The volume of marine traffic over the centuries has turned the seabed into a museum of shipwrecks – about 100 ships and upwards of 20 aircraft have sunk along this coast. Most of them are lying in more than 20m/65ft of water, accessible only to experienced divers who are members of specialist clubs. Other wrecks, lying in shallower waters, can easily be visited by amateurs. Information about underwater centres near such wrecks is available from the Fédération des Sports Sous-marins in Marseille.
The wrecks of the Provençal coast and their history are described in *Naufrages en Provence* by J-P Joncheray.

UNDERWATER FISHING

The abundance of creeks along the coast should satisfy all demands. The sport is strictly regulated; the essential regional regulations are given below. Underwater fishing is forbidden in certain areas of the coastline from early November to the beginning of March. It is essential to check with the

Exploring the underwater world

H. Le Gac/MICHELIN

local maritime authority – Toulon, 244 Avenue de l'Infanterie-de-Marine ℘04 94 46 92 00 and Nice, 22 Quai Lunel ℘04 92 00 41 50.

Some areas are out of bounds to fishing all the year round – south coast of St-Mandrier Peninsula, part of Porquerolles Island, Port-Cros Island and its neighbouring islets. There are underwater nature reserves, marked by buoys, near Golfe-Juan, Beaulieu and Roquebrune-Cap-Martin. Villefranche harbour is a protected area. Underwater anglers must comply with general fishing regulations and bear in mind that in the Mediterranean Sea:

- it is illegal to catch or fish for grouper and oysters (for mother-of-pearl)

- it is illegal to fish for sea urchins from 1 May to 30 September

- it is illegal to pursue or catch marine mammals (dolphins, porpoises), even without intending to kill them

- the minimum size of catch is 12cm/4.7in (except for sardines, anchovies), 18cm/7.1in for crayfish.

- whatever the circumstances, it is illegal to be in possession of both diving equipment and an underwater gun.

Underwater safety
Enthusiasm for exploring the superb underwater landscape of the Riviera should not blind the occasional diver to the need to observe certain regulations:

- never go diving alone, nor after eating a heavy meal, nor after drinking alcohol or fizzy drinks, nor when tired

- avoid shipping lanes and areas used by windsurfers

- when signalling for help, make it known that it is a diving accident so that the rescuers can prepare a decompression chamber, which is the only effective aid in the case of diving accidents, even minor ones.

SEA FISHING
In Sanary, in the Cogolin Marina and in Ste-Maxime there are organisations through which visitors may hire out boats and professional fishermen for sea fishing or join a sea fishing party (usually in summer from 6am to 10am). Contact these local tourism offices for more information.

OTHER SEASIDE ACTIVITIES
The long stretches of the Var coast, consisting of beaches where the *mistral* blows, have become some of the most popular locations in the Mediter-

ranean for those who enjoy riding the waves on a **sail board** (windsurfing) or a **funboard**; the shorter board used for the latter makes acrobatics possible. Almanarre beach on the west side of the Giens peninsula has become a mecca for funboarders and played host to the World Championships. More technical skill is required on other beaches such as Six-Fours-les-Plages and the two sides of Cap Nègre. For a different view of their favourite beaches, holidaymakers can indulge fearlessly in the joys of **parascending**: flying over the water below a parachute towed by a motorboat. The aim is to stay in the air for as along as possible and as high as possible. Instruction in this sport is available on nearly all the organised beaches, where there is enough wind.
Jet-skiing is practiced on certain stretches of coast, which have been carefully chosen and are not accessible from the land. The sport provides a superb experience of moving at speed. It is, however, strictly regulated

- machines must be 150m/ 164yd apart
- machines may operate only during the day
- machines may operate between 300m/328yd outside the channels and up to 1 nautical mile
- pilots must hold a proficiency certificate.

Most of the large resorts offer jet-ski rentals by the hour or the half day. It is also possible to hire sea canoes in Salins d'Hyères and certain resorts on the Var coast. Motor vessels are forbidden within 300m/328yd of the shore (except in the access channels) and must not exceed 5 knots in certain restricted areas (Îles d'Hyères, Îles de Lérins and Villefranche harbour). Elsewhere the top speed is 10 knots.

COASTAL WALKS

Before the late 20C building boom the famous Customs Path ran all along the Riviera coast; some particularly picturesque sections still survive and have been developed by the Coast Conservancy (*Conservatoire du Littoral*).
There are several signed country footpaths along the Var coast, of which about ten, from Bandol to St-Aygulph, are described in a topo-guide published by the **Fédération Française de la Randonnée Pédestre** (*www.ffrandonnee.fr*).

HIKING

A network of waymarked paths covers the region described in this guide.
GR (Grande Randonnée) paths, which are fully open only from the end of June to early October, are for experienced hikers accustomed to mountain conditions.

- **GR 5:** the oldest and most majestic, which terminates in Nice after crossing Europe; the last section from Nice to St-Dalmas-Valdeblore passes through Aspremont, Levens, the Vésubie gorge and Madone d'Utelle.
- **GR 52:** from St-Dalmas-Valdeblore to Menton via Le Boréon, La Vallée des Merveilles, Turini Forest, Sospel and Val Rameh Tropical Garden.
- **GR52A:** among the peaks in the eastern part of the Parc National du Mercantour beyond the Col de Tende.

Hiking on a GR path

B. Kaufmann / MICHELIN

Other paths, open all year, for walkers of all levels of competence:

- 🚶 **GR 4:** from Grasse via Gréolières and Entrevaux to the Verdon Gorge.
- 🚶 **GR 51:** nicknamed "the Mediterranean balcony", from Castellar (east of Menton) to Col de la Cadière (Estérel) providing panoramic views of the coast from the first ridge.
- 🚶 **GR 510:** entirely in the Alpes-Maritimes region, from Breil-sur-Roya via Sospel, Villars-sur-Var, Puget-Rostand, Roquestéron, St-Auban and Escragnolles to St-Cézaire-sur-Siagne, discovering another valley dotted with hill villages at each stage of the 10-day hike.
- 🚶 **GR 9:** from Signes through the Massif des Maures to St-Pons-les-Mûres.
- 🚶 **GR 99:** from Toulon through the Brignolais country to the Verdon Gorge.
- 🚶 **GR 90:** the shortest, from Le Lavandou through the Massif des Maures to Notre-Dame-des-Anges, where it meets the GR 9.

Topo-guides for the **Grandes Randonnées** (long hikes) and **Petites Randonnées** (short hikes) are published by the Fédération Française de la Randonnée Pédestre – Comité National des Sentiers de Grande Randonnée, and are obtainable from the Centre d'Information, 64 Rue de Gergovie, 75014 Paris; ✆01 45 45 31 02 (or order the catalogue of 170 publications online at the association's site – in French – www.ffrandonnee.fr).

NATURE PARKS
Wildlife – Parc National du Mercantour

Mercantour National Park, the last of the French National State Parks, was created in 1979 and covers an area of 68 500ha/169 267 acres in the Alpes-Maritimes and Alpes-de-Haute-Provence *départements* (encompass-ing 22 and 6 *communes* from each respectively).

The park, which was once the French part of Italian royal hunting grounds and extended over both sides of the Alps prior to 1861, has been twinned since 1987 with the Italian Argentera Nature Park with which it shares a border along 33km/20.5mi.

These two organisations are in charge of introducing and monitoring animal species in the whole of this protected region. In this way, ibexes which have wintered in the Argentera arrive to spend the summer months in the Mercantour, while wild sheep *(moufflons)* do the opposite.

The Mercantour is a high, mountainous park, with terraces from 500–3 143m/1 640–10 312ft in altitude, offering breathtaking views of natural amphitheatres, glacial valleys and deep gorges.

It contains a rich variety of flora; over 2 000 species have been counted there, including **Saxifraga florulenta**, which was for a time the park's emblem. All levels of vegetation are present, from olive trees to rhododendrons and gentians, which make such a splendid display of colour in the spring.

Fauna includes some 6 300 chamois, nearly 300 ibexes and 1 250 moufflons, which are well adapted to the Mediterranean climate.

The wooded slopes at medium altitude are home to various deer and smaller mammals such as hares, ermines and marmots. Feathered members of this community include black grouse, ptarmigans and splendid examples of birds of prey such as the short-toed eagle *(circaëtus)* and the golden eagle.

The reintroduction of the bearded vulture was achieved successfully in the summer of 1993. There are now five birds in the park. For the first time in France since 1942, wolves have returned of their own accord to live in the park. They come from Italy, where this protected species is now growing.

Wolves have returned to live in the Parc National du Mercantour

Deborah Waller/stock.xchng

The 600km/373mi of footpaths laid out within the park's boundaries enable tourists to discover the park on foot. These include the **GR5** and the **GR52A** ⚐, or the Mercantour panoramic footpath, which crosses the Vallée des Merveilles, as well as footpaths at L'Authion, Le Boréon and Madone de Fenestre.

This guide describes the regions of the Vésubie and Merveilles valleys, the Authion Massif and Turini Forest. ⚐Mountain bikes are not allowed in the central area of the park.

OTHER PARKS

The old royal hunting ground of the Sardinian monarchy extended until the Second World War over the two slopes of the Mercantour and the Marguareis. Since then the Italian section has been administered as a nature reserve with an active policy for the conservation of species and habitats. Two large natural parks have been created: **Parco dell'Argentera**, the largest, and Alta Valle Pesio, further east. Together with the Parc du Mercantour they have conducted a campaign for the reintroduction of endangered species – the bearded vulture and the ibex. In the Parco dell'Argentera there are many "royal" botanical paths easily accessible to hikers from the French side of the border by the frontier passes – Col de la Lombarde

and Col de Tende. From the latter pass two paths *(each about 3hr)* follow the peaks towards Rocca dell'Abisso (2 755m/9 039ft – west) and Cima di Pepino (2 335m/7 661ft – east).

The **Alta Valle Pesio** park, in the Marguareis, is the wildest and least easy to reach from France. Hikers should branch into the northeast route from Limone-Piemonte or go up the valley from Savone.

The Vermenagna Valley which extends from Col de Tende to the Cuneo Plain is still within the range of the Provençal culture; Provençal spectacles *(Roumiage de Provenço)* are held in the Grana Valley in July. Among the specialities of the district is a famous cheese, Castelmagno, and handmade cutlery, such as the Vernantino pocket knife.

Parco Naturale Regionale dell'Argentera
Corso Dante Livio Bianco 5 – 12010 Valdieri (CN) ☎39 171 97 397

Parco Naturale Regionale Alta Valle Pesio e Tanaro
Via Sta Anne 34 – 12013 Chiusa Pesia (CN) ☎39 171 73 40 21

Tourist office in Limone-Piemonte
Via Roma (CN) ☎39 171 92 101.

Heading Off-Piste at 1,500m

Michael Collier/stock.xchng

HORSE RIDING

♦ Comité National de Tourisme Équestre

🐎 9 Boulevard Mac-Donald, 75019 Paris, ✆01 53 26 15 50. www.tourisme-equestre.fr. They produce an annual guide (in French) called "Tourisme et loisirs équestres en France".

♦ Comité Régional de Tourisme Équestre Pays d'Azur

🐎 Immeuble le Weldom, 2 rte de Nice, 06650 Le Rouret, ✆06 81 58 84 70. http://cheval.d.azur. crte.free.fr.

♦ Association Varoise de Développement du Tourisme de Randonnée (AVDTR)

🐎 1 Boulevard Foch, 83000 Draguignan; ✆04 94 68 97 66 – which publishes the brochure *Guide Annuaire de Cavalier Varois*.

♦ Exploring the Border on Horseback

This is an unusual way of exploring the Massif du Mercantour. There is a waymarked route on the **Franco Italian Natural Spaces Equestrian Itinerary** *(Itinéraire Équestre des Espaces Naturels Franco-Italiens – Itinerario Equestre degli Soazi Naturali Franco-Italiani)* from St-Mar-

tin-Vésubie through the Italian parks – Argentera and Alta Valle Pesio – to Certosa di Pesio; there are ten staging posts with facilities for riders and their mounts.

Practical information is available from the Parc du Mercantour and the Parco dell'Argentera information offices *(⊙see Hiking)*.

The Parc du Mercantour publishes a brochure containing various bridle routes and staging posts in the Argentera and Mercantour highlands.

WINTER SPORTS

It is only a short distance *(less than 2hr by car)* from the coast to a range of winter sports stations:

- ⛷ La Colmiane-Valdeblore
- ⛷ La Gordolasque-Belvédère
- ⛷ Boréon-St-Martin-Vésubie
- ⛷ Turini-Camp d'Argent
- ⛷ Peïra-Cava
- ⛷ Gréolières-les-Neiges
- ⛷ L'Audibergue

There are off-trail runs near La Haute-Roya – La Brigue (alt 900m/2 953ft) and Tende-Val Casterino (alt 1 500m/ 4 921ft).

The proximity of the Italian ski resort, Limone-Piemonte, which can be reached by rail, means that many types of snow sport are available.

MOUNTAINEERING

There is a large variety of climbing in the highlands from the Pre-Alps of Nice via the steep faces of the *baous* in the Var Valley and the Rock in Roquebrune-sur-Argens to the rock faces of the Verdon Gorge. Guided excursions in rock-climbing, mountaineering, rambling, downhill skiing and overland skiing are organised by:

◆ the **Club Alpin Français**
   41 Rue Charles-Poncy,
   83000 Toulon
   ℘04 94 62 19 16
   http://clubalpin.toulon.online.fr

◆ the **Club Alpin Français**
   14 Avenue Mirabeau, 06000 Nice
   ℘04 93 62 59 99
   www.cafnice.org

◆ the **Association des Guides et Accompagnateurs des Alpes Méridionales**
   Roquebillière
   ℘04 93 03 44 30
   St-Martin-Vésubie
   ℘04 93 03 26 60

◆ **Bureau des Guides de la Côte d'Azur**
   71 Bd. de la Rocade,
   06250 Mougins
   ℘04 93 75 27 39/06 08 47 55 07
   www.altitude06.com

◆ **Bureau des guides du Mercantour**
   75 Rue du Dr-Cagnoli, 06450
   St-Martin-Vésubie
   ℘04 93 03 28 28

CAVING

The Var has many sites of original configuration; the Siou Blanc Plateau is a catalogue of variants of chasms and potholes which the amateur can explore. Among these is the deepest pothole in the region (350m/1 148ft). The Grotte de Mouret, near Draguignan, is useful for practice. In the Alpes-Maritimes, both the Pays Grassois and the Caussols Plateau offer many opportunities for seasoned cavers. The legendary Massif du Marguareis (northeast of Tende), the site of the exploits of the potholer Michel Siffre in the 1960s, is still a paradise for the experienced caver. This immense chalky plateau is peppered with sinkholes, with vertiginous rock faces overhanging the Italian slopes, and contains deep chasms (more than 900m/2 953ft). Information available from:

◆ **Comité Départemental de Spéléologie du Var**
   l'Hélianthe, Rue Émile-Olivier,
   83000 Toulon
   ℘04 94 31 29 43
   www.cdspeleo83.fr

Massif du Marguareis

- **Comité Départemental de Spéléologie des Alpes-Maritimes**
  Chez M. Madelaine, 10 chemin de Cambarnier-Nord, 06650 Opio
  ✆06 77 14 75 20/06 87 47 99 80
  http://cds06.ffspeleo.fr

- Speleology divisions of the Club Alpin Français in Nice or Toulon.

WATER SPORTS

Canoeing

Some of the rivers in the Alpes-Maritimes can be explored by canoe throughout the year but the best time is in spring. In any season beware of sudden floods caused by heavy rain upstream. The most attractive stretches of river are to be found just inside the boundaries of the Mercantour or near St-Martin-Vésubie. Shooting rapids excursions through gorges accompanied by experts are organised by the Toulon division of the Club Alpin Français. Those offering the best services are awarded the title **Point-Canoë-Nature** by the **Fédération Française de Canoë-Kayak** *(87 Quai de la Marne, 94340 Joinville-le-Pont; ✆02 48 89 39 89; www.ffcanoe.asso.fr)*.

Canyoning

The most attractive stretches of water provided by the Alpes-Maritimes for this activity, which combines rock-climbing, potholing and swimming in running water, are to be found within the Parc du Mercantour and in St-Martin-Vésubie. There are also two exceptional sites in the valley of the Haute-Roya near Saorge – La Maglia (through caves) and La Bendola (two days in the water). Canyoning is strictly forbidden in the central part of the Parc du Mercantour.
Between St-Martin-Vésubie and its confluence with the Var, the River Vésubie offers a variety of canyons – Duranus, the agreeable site at L'Imberguet, La Bollène and Gourgas, which is technically demanding.

The Estéron, an eastern tributary of the Var, provides classic stretches in exceptional settings between Roquestéron and St-Auban.
The network of rivers in the Var provides many opportunities for canyoning, with 11 authorised sites of varying difficulty suitable to all levels of competence. The Destel Gorge, between Caramy and Carcès, the lower stretches of the Jabron (downstream of Trigance) and the Pennafort Gorge are suitable for beginners. Seillans-la-Cascade, the Nartuby and the Destéou in the Maures demand greater skill. At all times of the year there is a risk of sudden increases in the volume of water following a storm upstream and the sudden release of retained water. Canyoning trips with guides are organised by the Toulon branch of the Club Alpin Français. Information is also available from the **Comité Départemental de Spéléologie du Var** *(✆04 94 87 42 72)* and a guide called "Clues et Canyons" by the Conseil Général des Alpes-Maritimes *(www.randoxygene.org)* available in tourism offices throughout the Alpes-Maritimes.

Lakes

The largest lake in the Estérel, **Lac de St-Cassien** (430ha/1 062 acres), not only supplies electricity and water to the eastern Var and provides water for the fire-fighting aircraft, but also has a nature reserve at the west end with a reed-bed where more than 150 species of over-wintering migrating seabirds have been recorded.
There are facilities for windsurfing and pedalo – tuition from the base and equipment for hire from the open-air cafés along the sometimes steep banks; motorised vessels are forbidden.

- **Aviron St-Cassien-Club Inter communal du pays de Fayence**
  Lieu-dit Biançon
  83440 Montaurous
  ✆04 94 39 88 64/04 93 42 20 91

The **Lac de Carcès** (100ha/247 acres) is a reservoir formed by a dam and fed by the River Argens. There is a pleasant wooded road along the eastern bank; the opposite bank, more rural, is much used by fishermen. Canoeing in kayaks is permitted.

Game Fishing

Local and national fishing regulations apply to fishing in lakes (Carcès and St Cassien) and in rivers (Gapeau, Réal Martin, Argens, Roya, Bévéra, etc.). It is also advisable to join the Association de Pêche et de Pisciculture in the area in question by paying the annual fees appropriate to the form of fishing practised and then by buying a daily permit from an authorised vendor. Trout fishing is permitted from the 2nd Saturday in March to the 3rd Sunday in September; pike fishing is allowed only between 31 January and 15 April. Fishing for common grayling in the Siagne is banned year round. Up-to-date information available from

- **Fédération Départementale du Var**
  ℘ 04 94 69 05 56
  www.fedepechevar.com

- **Fédération Départementale des Alpes-Maritimes**
  ℘ 04 93 72 06 04
  www.peche-cote-azur.com

- **Conseil Supérieur de la Pêche**
  Immeuble Le Péricentre,
  16 Av. Louison-Bobet, 94132
  Fontenay-sous-Bois Cedex
  ℘ 01 45 14 36 00, which provides a leaflet called *Pêche en France*.

CYCLING AND MOUNTAIN BIKING

The diversity of terrain inland and the network of cycle tracks along the coast and in the massifs of the Estérel and the Maures are popular for mountain biking. Many organisations, hotels and clubs hire out this kind of bicycle and provide details of local cycle tracks. Lists of suppliers are also available from local tourist offices.

Main Railway Stations

Antibes, Bandol, Cagnes-sur-Mer, Cannes, Hyères, Juan-les-Pins, and St-Raphaël hire out various types of bicycles, which can be returned to a different station.

The regulations concerning admission to the Parc du Mercantour apply also to cyclists; details available from the Maisons du Parc and the headquarters (*23 Rue d'Italie, Nice*).

The **Comité Départemental du Tourisme du Var** distributes a leaflet describing more than 20 signed routes for cyclists; among the principal ones are:

Fishing in Lac St-Cassien

©Francesco Ridolfi/Bigstockphoto.com

Pushing Pedals from Sea to Sea

EuroVelo is a venture funded by the European Union and about 60 local organisations in 22 countries. Visit **www.EuroVelo.org** to find out about the 12 cycling routes that will eventually trace more than 60 000km/37 282mi throughout Europe. Routes include Moscow to Galway, Ireland, and another from northern Norway to the tip of Sicily. The Mediterranean route traces the coastline from Cadiz, Spain, to Athens, via the French Riviera and Monaco.

- Roof of the Var (*Toit du Var*) (70km/43mi)
- Bauxite Road (*Route de la Bauxite*) (80km/50mi)
- North face of the Maures (*l'Ubac des Maures*) (80km/50mi)
- Maures chestnut woods (*Châtaign-eraies des Maures*) (90km/56mi)

One of the most famous mountain biking events in Europe is the Roc d'Azur at Ramatuelle with a height difference of nearly 200m/656ft (50km/31mi long) (*see Calendar of Events*).

- **Comité Départemental de Cyclotourisme des Alpes-Maritimes:** 2 Bd. Settimelli Lazare, 06230 Villefranche-sur-Mer
  ☎04 93 01 81 85
  www.cyclotourisme06-ffct.org

- **Comité Départemental de Cyclotourisme du Var:** L'Hélianthe, Rue Émile-Ollivier, 83000 Toulon
  ☎04 94 36 04 09
  www.cyclotourisme83-ffct.org

- **Fédération Française de Cyclotourisme:** 12 Rue Louis-Bertrand, 94207 Ivry-sur-Seine Cedex.
  ☎01 56 20 88 87
  www.ffct.org

AERIAL SPORTS

Hang-gliding, parachuting and ultra-light craft

There are about 20 suitable sites for parachuting, hang-gliding (*vol libre*) and ultra-light craft (*planeur ultra léger motorisé*).

- **Envol de Provence:** 7 Ave du Cheval Blanc, 83870 Signes
  ☎04 94 90 86 13 or 06 07 28 93 41
  www.envol-parapente.com

- **Fédération Française de Vol Libre:** 4 Rue de Suisse, 06000 Nice
  ☎04 93 88 62 89
  www.ffvl.fr

- **Fédération Française de Planeur Ultra-Léger Motorisé:** 96bis Rue Marc-Sangnier, 94700 Maisons-Alfort
  ☎05 49 81 74 43
  www.ffplum.com

Gliding

The main gliding centre, which is run by the **Association Aéronautique Provence-Côte d'Azur**, is near Fayence where aerological conditions are exceptional. It has become the leading gliding centre in Europe and has contributed to the rapid development of glider aerobatics. Each year champions from all over the world demonstrate their skill at the *Open de France de Planeur*.

- **Association Aéronautique Provence-Côte d'Azur** 83440 Fayence
  ☎04 94 76 00 68.
  www.aapca.net.

ACTIVITIES FOR CHILDREN

For a change from the beach, on cloudy days, there are many attractions all along the Riviera – leisure pools, animal parks to name two. In this guide, sights of particular interest to children are indicated with a KIDS symbol. Some attractions offer discount fees for children.

LEISURE POOLS

🛝 **Parc Nautique Niagara**
Route du Canadel,
83310 La Môle
📞04 94 49 58 87
www.parcniagara.com

🛝 **Aquasplash**
RN7, 06600 Antibes
📞04 93 33 49 49
www.marineland.fr

🛝 **Aqualand Fréjus**
RN98, 83600 Fréjus
📞04 94 51 82 51
www.aqualand.fr

🛝 **Aqualand**
559 Chemin Départemental,
83270 St-Cyr-sur-Mer
📞04 94 32 08 32
www.aqualand.fr

ANIMAL PARKS

◆ **Sanary-Bandol** – Zoo
◆ **Toulon** – Zoo du Mont-Faron
◆ **La Londe-les-Maures** –
  Jardin d'Oiseaux Tropicaux
  (&see HYÈRES)
◆ **Gonfaron** – Village des Tortues
  (&see Massif des MAURES)
◆ **Fréjus** – Zoo
◆ **Antibes** – La Jungle des Papillons,
  La Petite Ferme, le Golf Adventure-
  land and Marineland
◆ **St-Jean-Cap-Ferrat** –
  Chimpanzee shows at the Zoo
◆ **Monaco** – Jardin Animalier

SHOPPING

Most of the larger shops are open
Mondays to Saturdays from 9am to
6.30 or 7.30pm. Smaller, individual
shops may close during the lunch
hour. Food shops – grocers, wine
merchants and bakeries – are
generally open from 8am to 6.30
or 7.30pm; some open on Sunday
mornings. Many food shops close
between noon and 2pm and on
Mondays. Bakery and pastry shops
sometimes close on Wednesdays.
Hypermarkets usually open until 9pm
or later. People travelling to the USA
cannot import plant products or fresh
food, including fruit, cheeses and
nuts. It is acceptable to carry tinned
products or preserves.

RECOVERING THE VALUE ADDED TAX

There is a Value Added Tax in France
(TVA) of 19.6% on almost every
purchase (some foods and books are
subject to a lower rate). However, non-
European visitors who spend more
than 175€ in any one participating
store can get the VAT amount
refunded. Usually, you fill out a form
at the store, showing your passport.
Upon leaving the country, you submit
all forms to customs for approval
(they may want to see the goods, so if
possible don't pack them in checked

Market day in Lorgues

D. Pazery/ MICHELIN

PROVENÇAL MARKETS	
Aups	Wednesdays, Saturdays
Bargemon	Thursdays
Le Beausset	Fridays (fair)
Bormes-les-Mimosas	Wednesdays
Brignoles	Saturdays
Callas	Tuesdays, Saturdays
Cogolin	Wednesdays, Saturdays (fair)
La Croix-Valmer	Sundays
Draguignan	Wednesdays, Saturdays
Fayence	Tuesdays, Thursdays (fair)
Fréjus	Wednesdays, Saturdays (fair)
La Garde	Tuesdays, Saturdays (fair)
Grimaud	Thursdays (fair)
Hyères	Tuesdays, Thursdays (fair)
Le Lavandou	Thursdays
Lorgues	Tuesdays
Le Luc	Fridays
Ramatuelle	Thursdays, Sundays (fair)
St-Tropez	Tuesdays, Saturdays (fair)
Ste-Maxime	Thursdays (fair)
Toulon	daily
Tourtour	Tuesdays, Saturdays
Trans-en-Provence	Sundays
Villecroze	Thursdays (fair)

two or more countries within the European Union, you submit the forms only on departure from the last EU country. The refund is worthwhile for those visitors who would like to buy fashion wear, furniture or other fairly expensive items, but remember, the minimum amount must be spent in a single shop (though not necessarily on a single day).

PROVENÇAL MARKETS

Provençal markets, fragrant with thyme, tarragon, lavender and garlic, are part of the traditional image of the South of France.
A list of traditional craft markets, where the products of the Var region are sold, is published annually by the **Chambre des Métiers** (BP 69 – 83402 Hyères Cedex; ℘04 94 21 00 57).
As a rule, during the summer season, stalls selling fruit and vegetables and craftwork can be found under the plane trees of even the smallest village. They typically open at about 8am or 9am, and finish at lunch or about 1pm.
The most picturesque and lively markets of the Var and the days on which they are held are listed opposite.

CRAFTS AND SOUVENIRS

In high season many villages and resorts organise courses focusing on local arts and crafts – painting on porcelain in Le Cannet, weaving and woodwork in the Cannes district and regional cuisine in St-Martin-Vésubie. Certain villages are designated "Ville et Métiers d'Art" such as Biot, Cagnes-sur-Mer, Fréjus, Ollioules and Vallauris. For more information on these, call ℘01 48 88 26 56 or visit www.vma.asso.fr.

REGIONAL SPECIALITIES

The main areas where craftwork and local produce can be bought by visitors from the producers are shown on the map – Specialities & Vineyards (see pp68–9).

luggage). The refund is usually paid directly into your bank or credit card account, or it can be sent by mail. Big department stores that cater to tourists provide special services to help you; be sure to mention that you plan to seek a refund before you pay for goods (no refund is possible for tax on services). If you are visiting

Biot glasses

S. Sauvignier/ MICHELIN

Further information on specialist products:

Sweets

Confiserie des Gorges du Loup, Le Pont-du-Loup, 06140 Tourrettes-sur-Loup. ℘04 93 59 32 91. Also find nougat in Roquebrune-sur-Argens and honey in Bandol, Cotignac, or the Massif du Tanneron.

♦ **Marrons glacés and preserved chestnuts**
Nouvelle Confiserie Azuréenne, Boulevard Koenig, Collobrières ℘04 94 48 07 20. www.confiserieazureenne.com.

Glassware

Verrerie de Biot in Biot where it is possible to watch master glassblowers at work.

Perfume

Scents for the home or body are made in Grasse, Eze and Gourdon.

Ceramics

Biot, Vallauris, and Salernes (☉*see AUPS*) specialise in pottery as well as ceramics.

Liqueur de Lérina

This is made on the Îles de Lérins, by the monks of the Abbaye St-Honorat.

Leather

The *sandale tropézienne* is the same model that has been made by the same company since 1927 (☉*see SAINT-TROPEZ*).

WINE TASTING

Wine Cooperative Cellars

The **Côte de Provence wine road** winds its way through the vineyards; the wine cellars which are open for tasting are advertised on the roadside signs (look for *dégustation*). To organise tours and tastings of particular wines, contact these organisations:

℘ **Vins de Bandol**
La Maison des Vins du Bandol, 22 allée Alfred-Vivien, 83150 Bandol ℘04 94 29 45 03. http://maisondesvins.free.fr.

℘ **Coteaux varois**
La Maison des Vins Coteaux Varois, inside the Abbaye Royale de la Celle. 83170 La Celle. ℘04 94 69 33 18. The Coteaux Varois AOC is spread out over 28 communes around Brignoles, and Sainte-Baume to Bessillons.

℘ **Côtes-de-Provence**
La Maison des vins des Côtes de Provence, RN 7, 83460 Les Arcs-sur-Argens. ℘04 94 99 50 20. www.cotes-de-provence.com. This is the most popular wine of the Provence-Alpes-Côte d'Azur region. There are three vineyards on Île de Porquerolles producing an AOC (*Appellation d'Oriqine Contrôlée*) Côte de Provence wine. All offer wine tasting sessions:

Vallauris pottery

S. Sauvignier/MICHELIN

Bottles of Côte de Provence

S. Sauvignier/ MICHELIN

SUMMER AÏOLI FESTIVALS IN THE VAR	
8-11 July	Châteauvieux
8 August	Mazaugues
9 August	Entrecasteaux (one of the largest)
12 to 15 August	La Motte-du-Var
12 to 15 August	La Celle
12 to 16 August	Collobrières
14 to 16 August	Ampus
20 to 22 August	Solliès-Ville
26 to 28 August	Fayence

(Reserve and pay entrance fees at the local tourist office).

- Domaine de l'Île, the oldest
- Domaine Perzinsky
- Domaine Courtade

Other Côte de Provence wines are made in Les Arcs, Draguignan (organic wine), Fréjus, Gassin (see RAMATUELLE), Le Luc (organic wine) and Lorgues. This Maison des Vins also offer classes on wine tasting.

Vins de Bellet

Syndicat des vignerons de Bellet, 06200 St-Roman-de-Bellet
04 93 37 81 57
www.vinsdebellet.com
Vin de Bellet is produced on the hillsides behind Nice around St-Romain-de-Bellet; it is on sale in the cellars which are open to the public; further information from the Nice tourist office.

Santon Fairs in the Var

Clay figures *(santons)* became popular during the French Revolution, when many churches were closed. A craftsman in Marseille decided to market these figurines, so that people could set up nativity scenes at home. The term comes from the Provençal *santoun*, meaning "little saint". Originally, these statuettes were confined to religious or biblical themes, but they have come to represent traditional aspects of the region (arts, crafts, folklore, animals).

Domaine de Lauzade

Route de Toulon, 83340 Le Luc
04 94 60 72 51
www.lauzade.com
Tastings of Provençal wines
Mon–Sat morning.

La Cave du Moulin

50 Avenue Mallet, 06250 Mougins
04 92 92 06 88
Oenologie courses and wine tasting.

COOKING CLASSES

The Comité Régional du Tourisme Provence-Côte d'Azur *(www.decouverte-paca.fr)* provides information on cooking classes throughout the region, and publishes an annual brochure on local gastronomy, *Terre de Saveurs*.

Lenôtre Côte d'Azur

63 Rue d'Antibes, Cannes.
04 97 06 67 62. www.lenotre.fr.
Classes for children, teens, and adults on everything from pastries to prefectly prepared vegetables.

SIGHTSEEING
TOURIST TRAINS

The single-track main railway line between Nice and Cuneo in Italy crosses the old County of Nice, passing through Peille, L'Escarène, Sospel, Breil-sur-Roya, Fontan-Saorge, St-Dalmas-de-Tende, Tende, Vievola and finally Limone in Italy. The track was built from 1920 onwards and incorporates some spectacular engineering feats as it twists and turns through the tortuous mountain landscapes, sometimes even spiralling to change level. This train affords wonderful views that are always visible from the road, particularly between L'Escarène and Sospel and between Breil and Tende along the rugged gorges of the River Roya. On the Italian side of the border, the line descends less steeply down to Cuneo through the charming Vermegnagna Valley. The frequent service enables skiers to reach the Massif du Mercantour and spend the day skiing in the Italian winter sports resort of Limone-Piemonte.

There are at least four daily return services to and from Nice-Ville station, but check the schedule, which can be downloaded from the website, carefully. For timetable information: ℘08 91 70 30 00. www.ter-sncf.com/Regions/paca/fr.

The **Train des Merveilles** is a scenic tourist train between Nice and Tende that runs daily July-October through Sospel, Peille, Breil-sur-Roya, and La Brigue. The winter service, known as the **Train des Neiges Castérino**, runs weekends January-March. For times and ticket information, www.trainstouristiques-ter.com.

Provençal Railway

The famous pine-cone train **(Train des Pignes)** is named after the pine cones which were used as fuel to stoke the engines. It runs between Nice and Digne-les-Bains (150km/93mi) passing through Puget-Théniers, Entrevaux, Annot, St-André-les-Alpes. The single track was constructed from 1890 to 1911 and comprises 60 remarkable feats of engineering – metal bridges, viaducts, tunnels (one of which is 3.5km/2.3mi long). It is a relic of a vast regional network which early in the 20C served the whole inland area from Toulon to Draguignan. The journey, 2hr by train, 3hr by omnibus, passes through five valleys, offering fine views of the landscape and perched

villages which are often difficult to reach by car.

All year round it is possible to take the train to Lac de Castillon, the Verdon Gorges and the winter sports stations in the Alpes-Maritimes *département*. From Plan-du-Var there is a service to the walking country in the Vésubie Valley. In summer the Alpazur service runs from Nice as far as Grenoble and there is a tourist steam train on the Puget-Théniers section. There are wayside halts at which walkers can leave or rejoin the train at the beginning and end of a day's hike.

Chemins de Fer de Provence: Gare du Sud, 4 Rue Alfred-Binet, 06000 Nice ℘04 97 03 80 80. www.trainprovence.com. Other address: Station/Gare, Avenue P.-Sémard, 04000 Digne-les-Bains. ℘04 92 31 01 58.

FROM THE AIR

There are about two dozen locations in the region conducive to aerial sightseeing, including hang-gliding, para-gliding, kite-surfing, and ultra-light high-altitude gliding:

♦ **Envol de Provence** – 7 Ave du Cheval Blanc, 83870 Signes. ℘04 94 90 86 13 or 06 07 28 93 41. www.envol-parapente.com.

♦ **Fédération Française de Vol Libre** – 4 Rue de Suisse, 06000 Nice. ℘04 97 03 82 82. www.ffvl.fr.

♦ **Association Aéronautique Provence-Côte d'Azur** – Aérodrome, 83440 Fayence-Tourrettes. ℘04 94 76 00 68. www.aapca.net.

♦ **Fédération Française de Vol à Voile** – 29 Rue de Sèvres, 75006 Paris. ℘01 45 44 04 78. www.ffvv.org.

For helicopter sightseeing and transfers:

♦ **Héli Air Monaco** – Ave des Ligures ℘00 377 92 05 00 50 www.heliairmonaco.com

♦ **Héli Sécurité** – 83310 Grimaud ℘04 94 55 59 99 www.helicopter-saint-tropez.com

BOOKS

Les Misérables by Victor Hugo (1862). A historic look at the slave-galley days of Toulon from the point of view of the convict Jean Valjean, who spent 19 years in the Bagne of Toulon for stealing bread to feed his starving family.

Tender is the Night by F Scott Fitzgerald (1934). Inspired by the Boston art collectors Gerald and Sara Murphy, as well as by his own wife, Zelda, Fitzgerald's classic story of Americans adrift on the French Riviera describes the slow demise of Dick Diver, a psychiatrist who marries his patient Nicole.

The Rock Pool by Cyril Connolly (1936). Originally rejected by publishers in England on grounds of obscenity, this book examines the decadent side of the expatriate community in Juan-les-Pins and Antibes.

Bonjour Tristesse (Hello Sadness) by Françoise Sagan (1954). A classic of French literature, the heroine, Cécile, is a precocious 17-year-old (the author's age when she wrote the story), who grapples with her widowed father's second marriage and her own coming-of-age on the Esterel Coast.

Letters from Colette by Colette. (1980). The letters of this renowned French author document the change of St-Tropez from a secluded, peaceful fishing village where artists and writers would retreat, to a glitzy tourism destination.

Voices in the Garden by Dirk Bogarde (1981). The British actor, who resided in Grasse for many years during the latter part of his life, wrote this fascinating novel about a middle-aged couple living on the Riviera, whose life is irrevocably changed after meeting a young English tourist and his girlfriend and offering them hospitality in their sumptuous villa.

The Garden of Eden by Ernest Hemingway (1986). The story, published after the author died, unfolds on the Riviera and involves a young writer, his glamorous wife, and the pressures of a destructive love triangle.

Maigret on the Riviera by Georges Simenon (1988). Only mildly distracted by the balmy weather and lush vegetation, the famous, pipe-smoking Inspector Jules Maigret must discover how an inoffensive, down-at-heel Australian came to be murdered in this idyllic setting.

Perfume by Patrick Süskind (1989). A dramatic thriller set in the 18C perfume-making industry in Grasse.

Artists and their Museums on the Riviera by Barbara Freed, Alan Halpern; Harry Abrams (1998). A useful paperback guide for exploring the art museums in the region, placing the artists and their work in context.

Art-Sites France: Contemporary Art & Architecture Handbook by Sidra Stich (1999). Invaluable for those interested in contemporary artwork, this book covers the whole of France with detailed descriptions of galleries, museums, film and video centres, specialised bookstores, sculpture parks and many architectural sites.

Once Upon a Time: The Story of Princess Grace, Prince Rainier and Their Family by J Randy Taraborrelli (2003). A biography of the Monégasque Royal family, which starts with the history of the principality to the life of Grace Kelly and, finally, Monaco today.

FILMS

Max in Monaco (1913).
A silent comedy, featuring Max Linder, is set in the Principality of Monaco.

Fleur d'Amour (1927).
Maurice Vandal portrays the formerly "hot" district of "Chicago" in Toulon.

À Propos de Nice (1929).
Jean Vigo's classic focused on the contrast between holidaymakers loafing around on the beach in Nice and the working-class districts.

César (1936).
The colourful pre-war setting of Toulon appears in this locally-made Marcel Pagnol film with Provençal actor Raimu (see COGOLIN).

Les Visiteurs du Soir (1942).
Tourrettes-sur-Loup was the Medieval setting for Marcel Carné's period drama.

Les Démons de l'Aube (1945).
Yves Allégret's film set in the Var is about the Provençal landings in the Second World War.

To Catch a Thief (1955).
The impressive drops of the Grande Corniche provided a marvellous backdrop (before urban development changed the look of Monaco) in this thriller by Alfred Hitchcock starring Cary Grant and Grace Kelly.

And God Created Woman (1956).
Roger Vadim launched both Brigitte Bardot and **St-Tropez** with this provocative film.

The Collector (1967).
Eric Rohmer's love triangle takes place in a vacation villa in St-Tropez.

Le Gendarme de St-Tropez (1964).
The absurd side of the glitzy St-Tropez lifestyle are shown in six episodes of this celebrated comedy detective series.

Monte Carlo or Bust! (1969).
A comedy set in 1920s Monte Carlo, starring Tony Curtis, Dudley Moore, Peter Cook and Eric Sykes.

La Nuit Àméricaine (1973).
Partly filmed at the Studios de la Victorine, François Truffaut's film used several locations including Nice and the Vésubie Valley.

Herbie Goes to Monte Carlo (1977).
The comic adventures of the *Love Bug* throughout the world had to include an episode in Monaco, starring Dean Jones.

La Cage aux Folles (1978).
The original version of this comedy is set within a transvestite club in St-Tropez.

Dirty Rotten Scoundrels (1988).
Con-artists portrayed by Steve Martin and Michael Caine compete for the sunny territory of Beaulieu-sur-Mer among other locations on the Riviera.

French Kiss (1995).
The pretty village square in Valbonne is the setting for the Southern France scenes in this romantic comedy starring Meg Ryan and Kevin Kline.

Festival in Cannes (2002).
An insider look at the movie industry from the international film festival in Cannes by Ron Silver.

Ocean's Twelve (2004).
The Monte Carlo casino is the high-stakes setting for this drama starring George Clooney, Brad Pitt, Matt Damon, Julia Roberts, Catherine Zeta-Jones and Vincent Cassel.

Brigitte Bardot in And God Created Woman (1956)

©STARSTOCK/Photoshot

Calendar of Events

FÊTES, FESTIVALS & SPORTING EVENTS

JANUARY

Barjols — Festival of St Marcel. Celebrated since 1350, with a religious procession and the roasting of a cow for the villagers. http://barjols.net/saintmarcel.htm

Valbonne — Grape and Olive Festival (last weekend).

Monaco — International Circus Festival. www.montecarlofestival.mc

Monaco and hinterlands — Monte-Carlo Rally (end of the month)

27 JANUARY

Monaco (La Condamine) — Festival of St Dévote. A torchlight procession, symbolic burning of a boat, and fireworks to honor their patron saint. www.visitmonaco.com

FEBRUARY

Menton — Lemon Festival

Villefranche-sur-Mer — Flowered Naval Parade

Bormes-les-Mimosas — Mimosa Procession/Corso (third Sunday), a procession of flower-covered floats to celebrate the mimosa blossoms. www.bormesles mimosas.com

TWO WEEKS AROUND SHROVE TUESDAY (MARDI GRAS)

Nice — Carnival and Flower Festival (*Batailles de Fleurs*). *www.nicecarnaval.com.*

EVENING OF GOOD FRIDAY

Roquebrune-Cap-Martin — Evening Procession of the Entombment of Christ. Reenacted annually since the time of the White Penitents, with snail shell candles and symbols of the Passion carried by costumed participants.

EASTER SUNDAY AND MONDAY

Vence — Provençal Folklore Festival. A joyous village festival commemorating their resistance to the Huguenot siege during the Wars of Religion in 1592.

THIRD SUNDAY AFTER EASTER

Fréjus — Bravade St-François. A popular costumed military processional through town in honour of the patron St-Francis-de-Paul, who saved the town from the Plague.

MARCH

Golfe-Juan — Reenactment of Napoléon's landing (first weekend)

Nice (Cimiez) — Feast of the Gourds (with dried and painted gourds) (end of the month)

Nice — Arrival of the Paris–Nice Cycling Race

APRIL

Mouans-Sartoux — Honey Festival (last Sunday)

Monaco — Printemps des arts. The Spring Arts Festival celebrating the latest in theatre, dance and music. www.printempsdesarts. com. (through May)

Monaco, Nice — International Tennis Tournament (one week)

Lemon Festival, Menton

©Sean Nel/Bigstockphoto.com

Parade at Nice Carnival

J.L. Gallo/ MICHELIN

MAY

Cannes — International Film Festival ☎05 45 61 66 00 (reserved for professionals) www.festival-cannes.com

Nice (Cimiez) — La Fête des Mai. The oldest folk festival in Nice, with dancing and picnics in the Cimiez gardens (weekends). www.nicetourisme.com

Grasse — Rose Festival (penultimate weekend). A 3-day cut rose festival with a market, concerts and rose competition. www.ville-grasse. fr/exporose/

Monaco — Formula One Grand Prix in the centre of Monaco. www.formula1.com

LATE MAY TO MID-JULY

Toulon — Music Festival and International Music Competition (wind instruments)

JUNE

St-Tropez — Spanish Procession (Bravades) (15th). A colourful Provençal festival and procession honouring the town's patron saint since the 15C. www.ot-saint-tropez.com

EARLY JULY TO LATE SEPTEMBER (EVEN YEARS)

Vallauris — Biennial International Festival of Ceramic Art. www.vallauris-golfe-juan.fr

JULY

Cannes (Le Suquet) — Musical evenings featuring famous virtuosos and young talent. www.palaisdesfestivals.com

Cap d'Antibes (La Garoupe) — Seamen's Festival. Barefoot procession of seamen carries the gilded statue of Notre-Dame de la Garoupe from the cathedral in Antibes to the chapel in La Garoupe.

Vence — Fête de la Conque. Traditional music festival (first weekend) with concerts and a village-wide country-style buffet. http://pagesperso-orange. fr/locepon

Villefranche-sur-Mer — Feast of St Peter, fishermen's festival (first weekend)

Tende — Feast of St Eligius, patron saint of muleteers (second Sunday).

FIRST FORTNIGHT IN JULY

Vallées de la Roya et de la Bévéra — Les Baroquiales festival of baroque art. ☎04 93 04 12 55. www.lesbaroquiales.org

SECOND FORTNIGHT IN JULY
Juan-les-Pins-Antibes —
World Jazz Festival.
www.jazzajuan.fr
Ramatuelle — Classical Music
Festival. ℘04 98 12 64 00
Toulon — Jazz Festival
℘04 94 09 71 00
www.jazzatoulon.com
Nice (Cimiez: Amphitheatre) —
Jazz in Nice: ℘04 93 87 16 28
www.nicejazzfestival.fr
Îles des Embiez — Les Voix du Gaou:
salsa, rock, soul, reggae, Raï, etc.
www.voixdugaou.com.
Abbaye du Thoronet — Medieval
music festival. ℘04 93 52 26 38.

JULY AND AUGUST
St-Tropez — Music, Dance & Theatre
Festival at the Château de la
Moutte (evenings). www.lesnuits
duchateaudelamoutte.com.
Cotignac — Open-air Cinema Festival
(evenings). "Toiles du Sud" take
place at the Théâtre du Rocher.
www.lestoilesdusud.fr
Abbaye du Thoronet — Medieval
and Traditional Music Festival.
www.musique-medievale.fr

AUGUST
Villeneuve-Loubet — Shingle Castle
Competition (third Sunday).
Castle buiding competition with

Royal Regattas, Cannes
©Serge Villa/Dreamstime.com

the "galets" from the beach,
followed by fireworks show.
www.villeneuveloubet.fr
Vallauris — Pottery Festival (13th)
Entrecasteaux — Chamber Music
Festival: ℘04 94 04 44 83
Grimaud — Wool Festival (Ascension
Day). With sheep shearing
contests, market, and village feast.
www.mairie-grimaud.fr.
Hyères — Festival'Hyères, a three
week music festival on the
beachfront. www.festivalhyeres.fr
Menton — Chamber Music Festival
about 13 concerts are held in front
of the Church of St-Michel)
Grasse — Jasmine Festival
(first weekend). Flowered float
parade and fireworks.
www.ville-grasse.fr/jasminade
Fréjus — Grape Festival (first Sunday).
Celebration of the first grapes
harvested, with tastings,
traditional dancing and a special
mass.
www.frejus.fr
Roquebrune-Cap-Martin —
Passion Procession through the
old village streets (5th).
Bendor — Fishermen's Festival (15th)
Barjols — Leatherwork Fair (17-18th)

FIRST FORTNIGHT IN AUGUST
Ramatuelle — Theatre Festival
℘04 94 79 20 50
www.festivalderamatuelle.com

SEPTEMBER
Cannes — Royal Regattas (last week).
www.regatesroyales.com
Peille — Folk Festival *Festin des
Baguettes* in honour of a young
dowser-shepherd, who during a
drought found water with a diving
rod made from an olive branch
(first weekend).
Monaco — Vintage Car Rally
(third weekend)
Many villages — Michaelmas
Celebrations (29th)
Throughout France — Heritage
Days (third weekend). All listed
historic buildings throughout
France are open to the public

during the weekend of the Fête du Patrimoine. www.journeesdu patrimoine.culture.fr.

OCTOBER
Gonfaron — Chestnut Festival. Grilled chestnuts and a market of local products made from *chataignes* (chestnuts). www.journal.gonfaron.net
Ollioules — Olive Festival (first weekend)
Collobrières Chestnut Festival (last three Sundays). Local produce market, activities for children and chestnut products to celebrate the harvest. www.collobrieres-tourisme.com.
Roquebrune-sur-Argens — Honey Festival (first weekend)

La Garde-Freinet — Chestnut Festival (last two Sundays)
Vence — Folk festival of music, dancing (beginning of the month)

NOVEMBER
Monaco — Monaco's National Day (19th)
Taradeau — New wine festival (third Sunday).

DECEMBER
Bandol — Wine Festival (first Sunday).
Lucéram — The Shepherds' Christmas Offering and Provençal Mass.
Vallée de la Roya — Santon Festival (Nativity Scenes).
Cannes — International Dance Festival.

Know Before You Go

USEFUL WEBSITES
www.ambafrance-us.org
The French Embassy in the USA has a Website providing basic information (geography, demographics, history), a news digest and business-related information.
It offers special pages for children, and pages devoted to culture, language study and travel, and links to other selected French sites (regions, cities, ministries).

www.franceguide.com
The French Government Tourist Office/Maison de la France site is packed with practical information and tips for those travelling to France. The home page has a number of links to more specific guidance, for American or Canadian travellers for example, or to the FGTO's London pages.

www.FranceKeys.com
This sight has plenty of practical information for visiting France. It covers all regions, with links to tourist offices and related sites. Very useful

for planning the details of your tour across France!

www.ferryoffers.co.uk
This British site offers information and bookings for ferries, Eurostar, Eurotunnel, and train tickets throughout France .

www.visiteurope.com
The European Travel Commission provides useful information on travelling to and around 27 European countries, and includes links to some commercial booking services (e.g. vehicle hire), rail schedules, weather reports and more.

VIRTUAL RIVIERA
Here are a few selected websites devoted to Cote d'Azur:

www.beyond.fr
Beyond the French Riviera is a site in English with lots of links, information on places, sports, history, accommodation and more; practical and comprehensive.

www.provenceweb.fr
Provence on the Web includes an on-line magazine with featured villages,

upcoming events, recipes and touring suggestions (thematic tours, bike tours and others) for surfers.

www.rivieratimes.com
The online edition for the monthly English newspaper *The Riviera Times* includes the latest news, classified ads, and a link to the sister newspaper *The Monaco Times*.

http://riviera.angloinfo.com
AngloINFO is a popular website for the English-speaking expatriate community along the Côte d'Azur. It includes a directory of local businesses and organisations, particularly those run by or catering to English speakers, and lively community Forums .

www.riviera-reporter.com
This is the website for the monthly printed English magazine *Riviera Reporter*. It has archived articles that are helpful for both visitors and English-speaking locals on the Riviera.

TOURIST OFFICES
Information from **France on Call**:
℘(514) 288-1904.

INTERNATIONAL
Australia – New Zealand
Sydney
Level 13, 25 Bligh Street,
Sydney, New South Wales 2000
℘(02) 9231 5244
Fax: (02) 9221 8682

Canada
Montreal
1981 Avenue McGill College,
Suite 490, Montreal PQ H3A 2W9
℘(514) 288-2026
Fax: (514) 845 4868

Eire
10 Suffolk Street, Dublin 2
℘(353) 16 790 813

South Africa
P.O. Box 41022, Craig Hall 2024
℘(011) 880 8062
Fax: (011) 770 1666

United Kingdom
London
Lincoln House, 300 High Holborn,
London WC1 V7JH
℘(0207) 061 6639
Fax: (020)7493 6594

United States
East Coast – New York
444 Madison Avenue,
16th Floor, NY 10022-6903
℘(212) 838-7800
Fax: (212) 838-7855

Mid West – Chicago
676 North Michigan Avenue,
Suite 3360, Chicago, IL 60611-2819
℘(312) 751-7800
Fax: (312) 337-6339

West Coast – Los Angeles
9454 Wilshire Boulevard,
Suite 715,
Beverly Hills, CA 90212-2967
℘(310) 271-6665
Fax: (310) 276-2835

LOCAL/REGIONAL
Visitors may also contact local tourist offices for more detailed information, to receive brochures and maps. The addresses and telephone numbers of tourist offices for individual towns in this guide are located in that town's listing after the symbol ⬚.

Below, the addresses are given for local tourist offices of the *départements* and *régions* covered in this guide.

Comité Régional du Tourisme de Provence-Alpes-Côte d'Azur
10 Pl. de la Joliette, Les Docks,
Atrium 10.5, BP 46214
13567 Marseille, Cedex 02
℘04 91 56 47 00
www.decouverte-paca.fr

Comité Régional du Tourisme Riviera-Côte d'Azur
55 Promenade des Anglais,
BP 602, 06011 Nice Cedex 1
℘04 93 37 78 78
www.guideriviera.com

Comité Départemental du Tourisme du Var
1 Boulevard Foch, BP 99,
83003 Draguignan Cedex
☎04 94 68 58 33
www.tourismevar.com

Office de Tourisme et des Congrès de la Principauté de Monaco
2A Boulevard des Moulins,
98000 Monaco
☎04 93 50 60 88
www.visitmonaco.com

Parc Naturel National du Mercantour
23 Rue d'Italie, 06000 Nice
☎04 93 87 86 10
www.parc-mercantour.com

Parc Naturel National de Port-Cros
Castel Ste-Claire, Rue Ste-Claire,
83400 Hyères
☎04 94 65 32 98
www.portcrosparcnational.fr

Fédération Nationale des Comités Départementaux de Tourisme
2 Rue Linois, 75015 Paris
☎01 45 75 62 16
www.fncdt.net

Tourist Information Centres
The **Michelin Guide France** gives the addresses and telephone numbers of the Tourist Information Centres (Syndicats d'Initiative) to be found in most large towns and many tourist resorts. They can supply large-scale town plans, timetables and information on local entertainment, accommodation, sports and sightseeing.

INTERNATIONAL VISITORS
DOCUMENTS
Passport
Nationals of countries within the European Union entering France need only a national identity card (a passport for UK nationals). Nationals of other countries must be in possession of a valid national passport. In case of loss or theft, report to your embassy or consulate and the local police.

Visa
No entry visa is required for Canadian, US, or Australian citizens travelling as tourists and staying for up to 90 days, except for students planning to study in France. If you think you may need a visa, apply to your local French Consulate.
US citizens are advised to consult www.travel.state.gov for entry requirements, security and other information including contact numbers of US embassies and consulates. In an emergency call the **Overseas Citizens Services**: ☎1-888-407-4747 (☎1 202 501 4444 from overseas).

CUSTOMS
In the UK, **HM Revenue & Customs** (www.hmrc.gov.uk) publishes A Guide for Travellers on customs regulations and duty-free allowances. **US citizens** should view Tips for Traveling Abroad online (travel.state.gov/travel/tips/brochures/brochures_1225.html) for general information on visa requirements, customs regulations, medical care, etc.
There are no customs formalities for holidaymakers bringing their caravans into France for a stay of less than six months. No customs document is necessary for pleasure boats and out-

DUTY-FREE ALLOWANCES	
Spirits (whisky, gin, vodka, etc.)	10l/2.6gal
Fortified wines (vermouth, port, etc.)	20l/5.2gal
Wine (not more than 60 sparkling)	90l/23.7gal
Beer	110l/29gal
Cigarettes	800
Cigarillos	400
Cigars	200
Smoking Tobacco	1kg/2.2lb

EMBASSIES AND CONSULATES IN FRANCE

Australia	Embassy	4 rue Jean-Rey, 75015 Paris ℘01 40 59 33 00. www.france.embassy.gov.au
Canada	Embassy	35 avenue Montaigne, 75008 Paris ℘01 44 43 29 00. www.international.gc.ca
Eire	Embassy	4 rue Rude, 75016 Paris ℘01 44 17 67 00. www.embassyofireland.fr
New Zealand	Embassy	7 rue Léonard-de-Vinci, 75016 Paris ℘01 45 00 24 11. www.nzembassy.com/france
South Africa	Embassy	59 quai d'Orsay, 75007 Paris ℘01 53 59 23 23. www.afriquesud.net
UK	Embassy	35 rue du Faubourg St-Honoré, 75008 Paris ℘01 44 51 31 00. http://ukinfrance.fco.gov.uk/en
	Consulate	16 bis rue d'Anjou, 75008 Paris ℘01 44 51 31 00
	Consulate	353 boulevard du Président Wilson, 33073 Bordeaux ℘05 57 22 21 10
USA	Embassy	2 avenue Gabriel, 75008 Paris ℘01 43 12 22 22. http://france.usembassy.gov
	Consulate	2 rue St-Florentin, 75001 Paris. ℘01 43 12 22 22

board motors for a stay of less than six months but the registration certificate should be kept on board.

Americans can bring home, tax-free, up to US$ 800 worth of goods (limited quantities of alcohol and tobacco products); Canadians up to CND$ 750; Australians up to AUS$ 900; and New Zealanders up to NZ$ 700.

Persons living in a member state of the European Union are not restricted with regard to purchasing goods for private use, but the recommended allowances for alcoholic bevarages and tobacco are listed in the table entitled "Embassies and Consulates in France" (&see box).

HEALTH

First aid, medical advice and chemists' night service are provided by chemists/drugstores (pharmacie), identified by the green cross sign. Since the recipient of medical treatment in French hospitals or clinics must pay the bill, it is advisable to take out comprehensive insurance coverage. Nationals of non-EU countries should check with their insurance companies about policy limitations.

Reimbursement can then be negotiated with the insurance company according to the policy held.

All prescription drugs should be clearly labelled, and it is recommended that you carry a copy of the prescription.

British and Irish citizens, if they are not already in possession of an **EHIC** (European Health Insurance Card), should apply for one before travelling. The card entitles UK residents to free or reduced-cost medical treatment. Apply at UK post offices, call ℘0845 606 2030 or visit www.ehic.org.uk. You pay upfront but can reclaim most of the money (see website for details).

Americans concerned about travel and health can contact the International Association for Medical Assistance to Travelers, which can also provide details of English-speaking doctors in different parts of France: ℘(716) 754-4883. www.iamat.org.

The American Hospital of Paris is open 24hr for emergencies as well as consultations, with English-speaking staff (63 Bd. Victor Hugo, 92200 Neuilly sur Seine; ℘01 46 41 25 25; www.american-hospital.org).

The hospital is accredited by major insurance companies.

The British Hospital is just outside Paris in Levallois-Perret *(3 r. Barbès; ℰ01 46 39 22 22; www.british-hospital.org)*. This facility is registered as a charity in the UK and provides English-speaking medical staff to the British community in France.

ACCESSIBILITY

The sights described in this guide that are easily accessible to people of reduced mobility are indicated by the symbol ♿. Many of France's historic buildings, including musems and hotels, have limited or no wheelchair access. Older hotels tend to lack lifts (elevators). Tourism for All UK *(℘0845 124 9971; www.tourismforall.org.uk)* publishes some handy information about accessibility in various accommodation types and places.

Information about accessibility is available from French disability organisations such as **Association des Paralysés de France** *(17 bd Auguste Blanqui, 75013 Paris; ℘01 40 78 69 00; www.apf.asso.fr)*.

Useful information on transport, holidaymaking, and sports associations for the disabled is available from French-language website www.handicap.fr. In the UK, www.radar.org.uk is a good source of info and support and US website www.access-able.com provides information on travel for mature travellers or those with special needs, including lists of experienced travel agents and useful internet links. The **Michelin Guide France** and **Michelin Camping & Caravanning France** both indicate hotels and campsites with facilities suitable for travellers with physical disabilities.

Getting There and Getting Around

BY PLANE

The French domestic network operates frequent services from Paris (Charles de Gaulle and Orly), covering the whole country. The main holiday destinations in the south of France are Nice, Marseille, Toulon and Monaco.

Air France is the leading airline for domestic flights but there are also flights available on the European carrier, **easyJet**.

Direct flights from England can be booked with easyJet, **British Airways**, **British Midland** and **Ryan Air**. There are transfer buses to town terminals and to rail stations. The **RER-B** regional rail links to the centre of Paris from both Roissy and Orly. There are also package tour flights with a rail or coach link-up. Information, brochures and timetables are available from airlines and travel agents.

easyJet
℘08 25 08 25 08 *within France*
www.easyjet.com

British Airways
℘0870 8509 850 *from England*
℘0825 825 040 *from France*
www.britishairways.com

British Midland
℘0870 6070 222 *from England*
℘01 55 69 83 06 *from France*
www.flybmi.com

Air France
℘0 820 820 820 *within France*
www.airfrance.com

Ryan Air
℘08 92 55 56 66 *within France*
www.ryanair.com

BMI Baby
℘08 90 71 00 81 *within France*
www.bmibaby.com

Aéroports de Paris
℘08 36 681 515
www.adp.fr

Aéroport de Nice-Côte d'Azur
℘04 89 88 98 28
www.nice.aeroport.fr

Aéroport international de Toulon-Hyères
☏0825 01 83 87
www.toulon-hyeres.aeroport.fr

BY SEA
FROM THE UK OR IRELAND

There are numerous **cross-Channel services** from the United Kingdom and Ireland. To choose the most suitable route between your port of arrival and your destination use the **Michelin Tourist and Motoring Atlas France**, **Michelin map 726** (which gives travel times and mileages) or **Michelin Local maps** from the 1:200 000 series.

P&O Ferries	In the UK: ☏08716 645 645.
	In France: ☏0825 120 156
	www.poferries.com
Norfolk-line	In the UK: ☏0844 847 5042
	Outside the UK: ☏+44 208 127 8303
	www.norfolkline-ferries.co.uk
Brittany Ferries	In the UK: ☏0871 244 0744
	In France: ☏08 25 82 88 28
	In Ireland: ☏021 427 7801
	www.brittany-ferries.com
Irish Ferries	In the UK: ☏08717 300 400
	In Ireland: ☏0818 300 400
	In France: ☏01 70 72 03 26
	In the US: ☏(772) 563 2856
	www.irishferries.com
Seafrance	In the UK: ☏0871 423 7119
	In France: ☏0825 082 505
	www.seafrance.com

BY TRAIN/RAIL

Eurostar runs via the Channel Tunnel between London St Pancras and Paris in 3hr *(bookings and information ☏0345 303 030 in the UK; ☏1-888-EUROSTAR in the US; www.eurostar.co.uk)*. In Paris it links to the high-speed rail network **(TGV)** which covers

☺ Practical Information ☺

The French railway company SNCF operates a telephone information, reservation and prepayment service in English from 7am to 10pm (French time). In France call ☏08 36 35 35 39 *(when calling from outside France, drop the initial 0)*.

most of the country and which has recently been extended to the South of France *(for details call ☏0836 676 869)*. The main towns served by the TGV network are Lyon, Avignon, Valence, Montpellier, Aix-en-Provence, and Marseille. As far as the Riviera is concerned, there are 6–8 trains leaving daily from Paris-Gare de Lyon for Nice station, running roughly between 8am and 10.30pm (night train). The fastest schedule takes 5hr.

Eurail *(www.eurail.com)* offers travel passes that may be purchased by residents of countries outside the European Union. In the US, contact your travel agent.
☺*Tickets must be validated (composter) by using the orange automatic date-stamping machines at the platform entrance (☺failure to do so may result in a fine).*

Eurailpass, **Flexipass** and **Saverpass** are three of the travel passes which may be purchased by residents of countries outside the European Union. In the US, contact your travel agent or Rail Europe *(2100 Central Avenue, Boulder, CO, 80301; ☏1-800-4-EURAIL)* or **Europrail International** *(☏1 888 667 9731; www.europrail.net)*. If you are a European resident, you can buy an individual country pass, if you are not a resident of the country you are buying it for. In the UK, contact Europrail *(179 Piccadilly London W1V 0BA; ☏0990 848 848)*. Information on schedules can be obtained on websites for these agencies and the **SNCF**, respectively: www.raileurope.com, www.voyages-sncf.com. At the SNCF site, you can

TGV Méditerranée

In June 2001, former President of the Republic, Jacques Chirac, officially inaugurated France's southern high-speed rail link, bringing Provence within three hours of Paris and six of London. The streamlined blue and silver train now reaches Marseille after a mere 3hr, leaving from Paris. The 12-year campaign to complete the route followed by the TGV Méditerranée was fraught with difficulties. Besides the opposition shown by local residents, there were a number of geographical, architectural and ecological constraints. Considerable care was taken to preserve the natural environment and to avoid disturbing protected species. Moreover, new bridges and viaducts had to be built with local stone in order to blend in with the surrounding landscape. Indeed, on the journey from Valence to Marseille you will see no fewer than 23 bridges! Today the line carries over 60 000 passengers every day.

The line travels from Paris–Lyon-Saint Exupéry Airport, Paris–Valence, Paris–Avignon, Paris–Aix-en-Provence, Paris–Marseille, Paris–**Toulon**, Paris–**Hyères**, Paris–**Fréjus**, Paris–**Nice**, Paris–Nîmes, Paris–Montpellier, Paris–Béziers and Paris–Perpignan.

The trains provide a very good service to passengers: more legroom, a central luggage rack, an area set aside for bicycles, family and disabled facilities, telephone booths, plug sockets for European 2-pin plugs (first class), a wide range of light snacks or meals and even a free newspaper with your breakfast in first class.

book ahead, pay with a credit card, and receive your ticket in the mail at home free of charge (seven days minimum before leaving in the case of foreign countries, four days for France).

DISCOUNTS

There are numerous **discounts** available when you purchase your tickets in France, from 25–50% below the regular rate. These include discounts for using senior cards and youth cards (the nominative cards with a photograph must be purchased beforehand), and lower rates for 2–9 people travelling together (no card required, advance purchase necessary).
There is a limited number of discount seats available during peak travel times, but the best discounts are available during off-peak periods.

The French railway company **SNCF** operates a telephone information, reservation and prepayment service in English from 7am to 10pm (French time). In France call ℘*08 36 35 35 39.*

Line no 1
Marseille, Toulon, Hyères

Line no 2
Marseille, Toulon, Les Arcs-Draguignan

Line no 3
Les Arcs, Draguignan, Fréjus, St-Raphaël, Cannes, Nice

Line no 4
Mandelieu, Cannes, Nice, Ventimiglia

Line no 5A
Nice, Breil-sur-Roya, Cueno, Torino

Line no 6
Marseille, Toulon, Nice, Ventimiglia

Line Grasse-Cannes
Grasse, Le Bosquet, Cannes, Nice

From July to September the **Carte Isabelle** is an unlimited day-pass between Fréjus and Vintimille, Cannes and Grasse, and Nice and Tende.

BY COACH/BUS

- **Eurolines (London)**
  4 Cardiff Road, Luton, Bedfordshire
  LU1 1PP. ☎08717 818 181.
  www.eurolines.co.uk.
- **Eurolines (Paris)** ☎08 92 89 90 91.
  www.eurolines.fr.
- **www.eurolines.com**
  The international website with
  information about travelling
  all over Europe by coach (bus).

BY CAR

The area covered in this guide is easily
reached by main motorways and
national routes. **Michelin map 726**
indicates the main itineraries as well as
alternative routes for avoiding heavy
traffic during busy holiday periods,
and gives estimated travel times. The
latest Michelin route-planning service
is available on Internet, **www.Via
Michelin.com**. Travellers can calculate
a precise route using such options
as shortest route, route avoiding
toll roads, Michelin-recommended
route, as well as gain access to tourist
information (hotels, restaurants,
attractions). The service is available
on a pay-per-route basis or by
subscription. The roads are very busy
during holiday periods (particularly
weekends in July and August) to avoid
traffic congestion it is advisable to
follow the recommended secondary
routes (signposted as *Bison Futé –
itinéraires bis*). The motorway network
includes rest areas *(aires d'autoroute)*
and petrol/gas stations, usually with
restaurant and shopping malls attached,
about every 40km/25mi, so that long-
distance drivers have no excuse not to
stop for a rest every now and then.

DOCUMENTS

Driving licence

For British drivers unaccustomed to
driving on the right, extra care will
be needed. Road signs generally use
easy-to-understand international
visual symbols instead of words.
When driving in France, EU nationals
must have their own valid **national
driving licence**. Travellers from other
EU countries and North America can
drive in France with a valid national
or home-state **driving licence**.
An **international driving licence**
is useful because the information
on it appears in nine languages
(keep in mind that traffic officers
are empowered to fine motorists).
A permit is available (US $15) from the
National Automobile Club
*(1151 East Hillsdale Blvd., Foster City,
CA 94404;* ☎*650-294-7000;
www.nationalautoclub.com)*; or
contact your local branch of the
American Automobile Association
(www.aaa.com). All drivers must
also have with them the vehicle's
registration papers and a current
insurance certificate.
The originals of all documents are
required. Copies are not acceptable.

INSURANCE

Many motoring organisations offer
accident insurance and breakdown
service schemes for members. Check
with your current insurance company
regarding cover while abroad. If you
plan to hire a car using your credit
card, check with the company, which
may provide liability insurance
automatically (and thus save you having
to pay the cost for optimum coverage).

ROAD REGULATIONS

The minimum driving age is 18.
Traffic drives on the right. All passengers must wear **seat belts**. Children
under the age of 10 must ride in the
back seat. Headlights must be swit-
ched on in poor visibility and at night;
use side-lights only when the vehicle is
stationary. In the case of a **breakdown**,
a red warning triangle or hazard
warning lights are obligatory, as well
as a luminous jacket. In the absence of
stop signs at intersections, cars must
yield to the right. Traffic on main roads
outside built-up areas (priority indicated
by a yellow diamond sign) and on round-
abouts has right of way. Vehicles must
stop when the lights turn red at road
junctions and may filter to the right only
when indicated by an amber arrow.

RENTAL CARS – RESERVATIONS IN FRANCE		
Avis France:	☎ 0820 05 05 05 (UK)	www.avis.fr
Europcar:	☎ 0825 35 83 58 (UK)	www.europcar.com
Budget France:	☎ 0825 00 35 64 (UK)	www.budget.com
Hertz France:	☎ 0825 861 861 (UK)	www.hertz.com
SIXT:	☎ 0820 00 74 98 (UK)	www.e-sixt.com
CITER:	☎ 0825 16 12 20 (UK)	www.citer.fr
Thrifty:	☎ 01494 751 500 (UK)	www.thrifty.com
Nova Car Hire:	☎ 0800 018 6682 (UK)	www.novacarhire.com

The regulations on **drinking and driving** (limited to 0.50g/l) and **speeding** are strictly enforced, usually by an on-the-spot fine and/or confiscation of the vehicle.

Speed Limits
Although liable to modification, these are as follows:

- Toll motorways *(autoroutes)* 130kph/80mph (110kph/68mph when raining);
- Dual carriageways and motorways without tolls 110kph/68mph (100kph/62mph when raining);
- Other roads 90kph/56mph (80kph/50mph when raining) and in towns 50kph/31mph;
- Outside lane on motorways during daylight, on level ground and with good visibility – minimum speed limit of 80kph/50mph.

Parking Regulations
In town there are zones where parking is either restricted or subject to a fee; tickets should be obtained from the ticket machines *(horodateurs)* and displayed inside the windscreen on the driver's side; failure to display may result in a fine, or towing and impound.

Tolls
In France, most motorway sections are subject to a toll *(péage)*.
You can pay in cash or with a credit card (Visa, MasterCard).

CAR RENTAL

There are car rental agencies at airports, railway stations and in large towns. Drivers must be over 21; between ages 21–25, drivers are required to pay an extra daily fee; some companies allow drivers under 23 only if the reservation has been made through a travel agent. It is relatively expensive to hire a car in France; Americans in particular will notice the difference and should make arrangements before leaving.

MOTORHOME RENTAL
Worldwide Motorhome Rentals
Offers fully equipped camper vans for hire.
☎ 888- 519-8969 *US toll-free*
☎ 530-389-8316 *outside the US*
Fax 530-389-8316
www.mhrww.com

PETROL/GASOLINE
French service stations dispense:
- *sans plomb 98* (super unleaded 98)
- *sans plomb 95* (super unleaded 95)
- *diesel/gazole* (diesel)
- *GPL* (LPG).

For US citizens: gasoline is more expensive in France than in the USA. Prices are listed on signboards on the motorways; it is usually cheaper to fill up after leaving the motorway; check hypermarkets on the outskirts of town. You can pay at the pump using credit/debit cards.

Where to Stay and Eat

WHERE TO STAY
FINDING A HOTEL

Turn to the **Addresses** within individual sight listings for descriptions and prices of typical places to stay **(Stay)** with local flair. The key on the front cover flap of the guide explains the symbols and abbreviations used in these sections. The French Riviera offers a wide array of accommodation options, from simple bed and breakfasts (known as *gîtes* or *maisons d'hôte*) in charming villages to palatial hotels overlooking the Mediterranean.

Prices tend to rise in proximity to the beaches and in the larger cities such as Nice, Cannes, Toulon and Monte Carlo, while some of the best deals can be found in the smaller perched villages and quiet country inns in the hinterlands.

Use the **Map of Places to Stay** to identify recommended places for overnight stops. For an even greater selection, use the **Michelin Guide France**, with its famously reliable star-rating system and hundreds of establishments all over France.

Book ahead! The French Riviera is a very popular holiday destination. For further assistance, **Loisirs Accueil** is a booking service that has offices in some French *départements* – contact tourism offices for further information. A guide to good-value, family-run hotels, **Logis et Auberges de France**, is available from the French tourist office, as are lists of other kinds of accommodation such as hotel-châteaux, bed-and-breakfasts, etc. **Relais et Châteaux** provides information on booking in luxury hotels with character: 15 Rue Galvani, 75017 Paris; ℘08 25 323 232.

Economy Chain Hotels

If you need a place to stop en route, these can be useful, as they are inexpensive (around 45€ for a double room) and generally located near the main road. While breakfast is available, there may not be a restaurant; rooms are small, with a television and bathroom. Central reservation numbers:

- 🕿 **Akena** ℘01 69 84 85 17 www.hotels-akena.com
- 🕿 **B&B** ℘01 72 36 51 06 www.hotel-bb.com
- 🕿 **Etap Hotel** ℘0892 688 900 www.etaphotel.com
- 🕿 **Hotel Formula 1** ℘0892 685 685 www.hotelformule1.com
- 🕿 **Accor Hotels** ℘0825 88 00 00 www.accorhotels.com/fr
- 🕿 **Villages Hôtel** ℘03 80 60 92 70 www.villages-hotel.com

The chain hotels listed below are slightly more expensive (from 58€) and offer a few more amenities and services. Central reservation numbers:

- 🕿 **Campanile** ℘01 64 62 59 70 www.campanile.com
- 🕿 **Etap** ℘0892 688 900 www.etaphotel.com
- 🕿 **Ibis** ℘0892 686 686 www.ibishotel.com

COTTAGES, BED & BREAKFASTS

The **Maison des Gîtes de France** is an information service on self-catering accommodation on the French Riviera (and the rest of France). *Gîtes* usually take the form of a cottage or apartment decorated in the local style where visitors can make themselves at home, or bed and breakfast accommodation *(chambres d'hôtes)* which consists of a room and breakfast at a reasonable price. Contact the Gîtes de France office in Paris *(59 Rue St-Lazare, 75439 Paris Cedex 09; ℘01 49 70 75 75; www.gites-de-france.com)* or their representative in the UK, **Brittany Ferries** *(⟡see p44)*. You can also contact the local tourist offices which may have lists of available properties and local bed and breakfast establishments.

Terraced restaurants on the streets of Cannes

E. Baret/ MICHELIN

HOSTELS, CAMPING

To obtain an **International Youth Hostel Federation card** (there is no age requirement, and there is a senior card available too), you should contact the IYHF in your own country for inform-ation and membership applications (US ☎1 301 495 1240; UK ☎01629 592 700; Australia ☎61 2 9283 7195). There is a booking service online *(www.hihostels.com)*, which you may use to reserve rooms as far as six months in advance.

There are two main youth hostel *(auberges de jeunesse)* associations in France, the **Ligue Française pour les Auberges de Jeunesse** *(6/ r. Vergniaud, 75013 Paris; ☎01 44 16 78 78; www.auberges-de-jeunesse.com)* and the **Fédération Unie des Auberges de Jeunesse** *(27 r. Pajol, 75018 Paris; ☎01 44 89 87 27; www.fuaj.org).*

The Féderation's informative website provides an online booking service. There are numerous officially graded **campsites** with varying standards of facilities on the French Riviera. The **Michelin Camping & Caravanning France** guide lists a selection of camp sites. The area is popular with campers in the summer months, so it is wise to book in advance.

WHERE TO EAT

A selection of places to eat **(Eat)** in the different locations covered in this guide can be found in the **Addresses** appearing in the *Discovering The French Riviera* section. The key at the back of the book explains the symbols and abbreviations used in the Addresses. We have highlighted an array of eating places primarily for their atmosphere, location and regional delicacies. Prices indicate the average cost of a starter, main dish and dessert for one person.

Use the red-cover **Michelin Guide France**, with its well-known star-rating system and hundreds of establishments throughout France, for an even greater choice. If you would like to experience a meal in a highly rated restaurant from **The Michelin Guide**, be sure to book ahead. In the countryside, restaurants usually serve lunch between noon and 2pm and dinner between 7.30 and 10pm. It is not always easy to find something in between those two mealtimes, as the "non-stop" restaurant is still a rarity in the provinces. However, a hungry traveller can usually get a sandwich (usually a filled baguette) in a café, and ordinary hot dishes may be available in a brasserie. Throughout France, the culture leans more towards sitting and eating than to grabbing a sandwich on the go, so plan ahead.

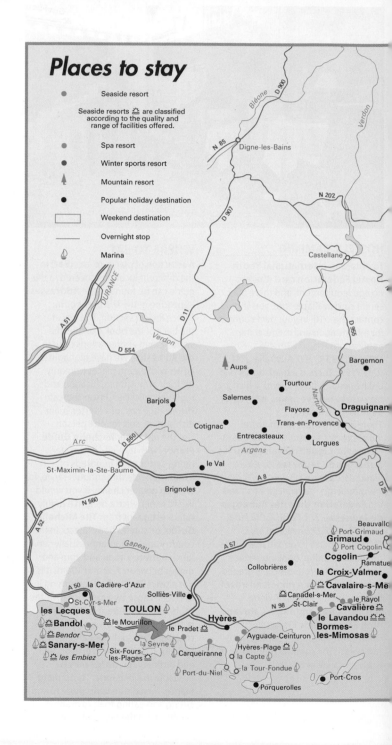

Places to stay

●	Seaside resort

Seaside resorts ☝ are classified according to the quality and range of facilities offered.

●	Spa resort
●	Winter sports resort
🜨	Mountain resort
●	Popular holiday destination
▭	Weekend destination
—	Overnight stop
⛵	Marina

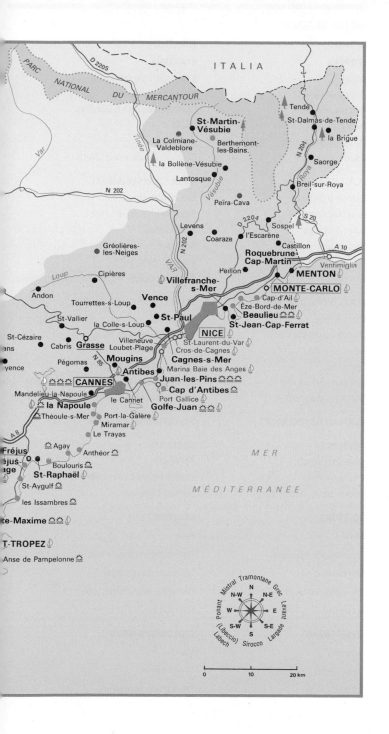

ITALIA

PARC NATIONAL DU MERCANTOUR

D 2205

Var

Tende
St-Dalmas-de-Tende

St-Martin-Vésubie

La Colmiane-Valdeblore

Berthemont-les-Bains

la Brigue

Saorge

la Bollène-Vésubie

Lantosque

Tinée

Vésubie

Breil-sur-Roya

Roya

N 204

Peira-Cava

N 202

Levens

S 20

Sospel

Gréolières-les-Neiges

Coaraze

l'Escarène

Castillon

Loup

Cipières

Peillon

A 10

Roquebrune Cap-Martin

Ventimiglia

Andon

Villefranche-s-Mer

MENTON

Tourrettes-s-Loup

Vence

MONTE-CARLO

St-Vallier

St-Paul

Cap-d'Ail

la Colle-s-Loup

Éze-Bord-de-Mer

Beaulieu

St-Cézaire

Villeneuve Loubet-Plage

NICE

St-Jean-Cap-Ferrat

Cabris

Grasse

St-Laurent-du-Var

Pégomas

Mougins

Cros-de-Cagnes

Antibes

Cagnes-s-Mer

Marina Baie des Anges

CANNES

Juan-les-Pins

Mandelieu-la-Napoule

le Cannet

Cap d'Antibes

la Napoule

Port Gallice

Théoule-s-Mer

Port-la-Galère

Golfe-Juan

Miramar

Le Trayas

Fréjus

MER

Agay

Anthéor

Fréjus-Plage

Boulouris

MÉDITERRANÉE

St-Raphaël

St-Aygulf

les Issambres

Ste-Maxime

ST-TROPEZ

Anse de Pampelonne

Ponant Mistral Tramontane Grec Levant

N
N-W   N-E
W   E
S-W   S-E
S

(Libeccio) Sirocco Largade
Labech

0   10   20 km

51

MENU READER

La Carte

ENTRÉES
Crudités

Terrine de lapin

Frisée aux lardons

Escargots

Cuisses de grenouille

Salade au crottin

PLATS (VIANDES)
Bavette à l'échalote

Faux filet au poivre

Côtes d'agneau

Filet mignon de porc

Blanquette de veau

Nos viandes sont garnies

PLATS (POISSONS, VOILAILLE)
Filets de sole

Dorade aux herbes

Saumon grillé

Coq au vin

Poulet de Bresse rôti

Omelette aux morilles

PLATEAU DE FROMAGES

DESSERTS
Tarte aux pommes

Crème caramel

Sorbet: trois parfums

BOISSONS
Bière

Eau minérale (gazeuse)

Une carafe d'eau

Vin rouge, vin blanc, rosé

Jus de fruit

MENU ENFANT
Jambon

Steak haché

Frites

The Menu

STARTERS
Raw vegetable salad

Rabbit terrine (pâté)

Curly lettuce with bacon bits

Snails

Frog's legs

Goat cheese on a bed of lettuce

MAIN COURSES (MEAT)
Sirloin with shallots

Sirloin with pepper sauce

Lamb chops

Pork filet

Veal in cream sauce

Our meat dishes are served with vegetables

MAIN COURSES (FISH, FOWL)
Sole fillets

Sea bream with herbs

Grilled salmon

Chicken in red wine sauce

Free-range roast chicken from the Bresse

Wild-mushroom omelette

SELECTION OF CHEESES

DESSERTS
Apple pie

Cooled baked custard with caramel sauce

Sorbet: 3 flavours

BEVERAGES
Beer

(Sparkling) mineral water

Tap water (no charge)

Red wine, white wine, rosé

Fruit juice

CHILDREN'S MENU
Ham

Ground beef

French fried potatoes

Basic Information

BUSINESS HOURS

National museums and art galleries are closed on Tuesdays; municipal museums are generally closed on Mondays. Shops hours are usually Monday to Saturday 10am to 6pm. In smaller towns, shops may also close for lunch and off-season. Churches, especially in secluded areas or small villages, are often only opened for services or on request.

DISCOUNTS

Significant discounts are available for senior citizens, students, under 25-year-olds, teachers, and groups for public transportation, museums and monuments and some leisure activities such as films (at certain times of day). Bring student or senior cards with you, and bring along some extra passport-size photos for discount travel cards.

The **International Student Travel Conference** (www.istc.org), global administrator of the International Student and Teacher Identity Cards, is an association of student travel organisations around the world. ISTC members collectively negotiate benefits with airlines, governments and providers of other goods and services for the student and teacher community, both in their own country and around the world. The non-profit association sells international ID cards for students, youngsters under the age of 25 and teachers (who may get discounts on museum entrances, for example).

The ISTC is active in a network of international education and work exchange programes. The corporate headquarters address is:

◆ Herengracht 479,
  1017 BS Amsterdam,
  The Netherlands
  ☎31 20 421 28 00
  Fax 31 20 421 28 10.

ELECTRICITY

The electric current is 220 Volts/50Hz. Circular two-pin plugs are the rule. Adapters and converters (for hairdryers, for example) are best bought before you leave home. If you have a recharge-able device, read the instructions carefully. Sometimes these items only require a plug adapter, in other cases you must use a voltage converter.

EMERGENCIES

Police:	17
SAMU (Paramedics):	15
Fire (Pompiers):	18

INTERNET ACCESS

Internet access is often easiest to find in hotels in larger towns such as Nice, Monaco, Cannes and Antibes, where WiFi is becoming standard (often free) and dial-up access is virtually nonexistent. These towns have many wireless hotspots in cafés, bars and libraries, as well as a few internet cafés for those travelling without a computer. The villages and mountain valleys inland have less reliable access; always call hotels or local tourist offices to confirm in advance.

You can look online at **www.easy internetcafe.com** to find your nearest internet café.

 Museum Passes

The Comité Régional du Tourisme Riviera Côte d'Azur has three different museum passes available: City of Nice Pass (municipal museums), Museums of Menton pass (eight sights in and around Menton), and the French Riviera Museum Pass, which offers unlimited free priority access to museums, monuments, gardens on the Riviera from Fréjus to Menton. For more information contact any of the tourist offices within the region, or visit **www.guideriviera.com**.

MAIL/POST

Main post offices open Monday to Friday 8am to 7pm, Saturday 8am to noon. Smaller branch post offices generally close at lunchtime between noon and 2pm and at 4pm.

Postage via airmail:
- ✉ UK: letter (20g) 0.70€
- ✉ North America: letter (20g) 0.85€
- ✉ Australia, NZ: letter (20g) 0.85€

Stamps are also available from news agents and *bureaux de tabac*. Stamp collectors should ask for *timbres de collection* in any post office.

MEDIA

With a large Anglophone expatriate population living on the Côte d'Azur year-round in addition to the seasonal tourists, there are several news sources available in English.

NEWSPAPERS

Local print media in English include the bi-monthly Riviera Reporter magazine, the monthly Riviera Times newspaper, and the Var Village Voice. Newsstands in major towns carry the daily editions of the International Herald Tribune, the FInancial Times and the London Times the day they are printed. Other newspapers often arrive on the Riviera a day later.

RADIO

Riviera Radio

Feeling pangs for your native language? Desperately seeking an English-speaking doctor or nanny? Looking for rented accommodation? Riviera Radio is the answer to all your problems. The only 100% English-speaking radio in the area, it broadcasts on FM *(106.5 in the Alpes-Maritimes, 106.3 in Monte-Carlo; ℘00 377 97 97 94 94 from France)* and covers the stretch of coastline running between St-Tropez and the Italian resort of San Remo. This Monaco-based radio station provides useful tips for tourists and residents alike and presents a great many regular programmes: business and financial news, local traffic and weather reports, guide to English-speaking films in VO *(Version Originale)*, job offers, updated news bulletins in conjunction with the BBC World Service, calendar of major fairs and conferences, etc. One of Riviera Radio's most popular features is their weekday morning Community Chest *(9.20am)*, when listeners call in to buy or sell miscellaneous items.

TELEVISION

French channels Canal+ and Arte often air American and British programs in their original language, however most English-speaking residents and hotels subscribe to satellite for channels such as BBC and CNN.

MONEY
CURRENCY

There are no restrictions on the amount of currency visitors can take into France. Visitors carrying a lot of cash are advised to complete a currency declaration form on arrival, because there are restrictions on currency export.

Notes and coins

Since January 2002, the **euro** is the official currency of France and other participating EU Member Sates. One euro is divided into 100 cents, or *centimes*. Franc notes can be exchanged only at the Banque de France (until 2012).

BANKS

Banks are open from 9am to noon and 2pm to 4pm and branches are closed either on Monday or Saturday. Banks close early on the day before a bank holiday. A passport is necessary as identification when cashing traveller's cheques in banks. Commission charges vary and hotels usually charge more than banks for cashing cheques. One of the most economical ways to use your money in France is by using

American Express ☎01 47 77 72 00	
Visa ☎08 36 69 08 80	
MasterCard/Eurocard ☎01 45 67 84 84	
Diners Club ☎01 49 06 17 50	

ATM/cash machines to get cash directly from your bank account or to use your credit cards to get cash advances. Be sure to remember your 4-digit PIN, you will need it to use cash dispensers and to pay with your card in most shops, restaurants, etc. ATM code pads are numeric; use a telephone pad to translate a letter code into numbers. Visa is the most widely accepted credit card, followed by MasterCard; other cards (Diners Club, Plus, Cirrus) are also accepted in most cash machines. American Express is more often accepted in premium establishments.

Most places post signs indicating the cards they accept; if you don't see such a sign, and want to pay with a card, ask before ordering or making a selection. Cards are widely accepted in shops, hypermarkets, hotels and restaurants, at tollbooths and in petrol stations. If your card is lost or stolen in France, call one of the following 24-hour hotlines:

You must report any loss or theft of credit cards or traveller's cheques to the local police who will issue you with a certificate (useful proof to show the issuing company).

PUBLIC HOLIDAYS

There are 11 public holidays in France. In addition, there are other religious and national festivals days, and local saints' days, etc. On all these days, museums and monuments may vary their hours of admission.

In addition to the usual school holidays at Christmas and in the spring and summer, there are long mid-term breaks (ten days to two weeks) in February and early November.

1 January	New Year's Day (*Jour de l'An*)
March/April	Easter Day and Easter Monday (*Pâques*)
1 May	May Day (*Fête du Travail*)
8 May	VE Day (*Fête de la Libération*)
Thurs 40 days after Easter	Ascension Day (*Ascension*)
7th Sun–Mon after Easter	Whit Sunday and Monday (*Pentecôte*)
14 July	France's National Day (*Fête de la Bastille*)
15 August	Assumption (*Assomption*)
1 November	All Saint's Day (*Toussaint*)
11 November	Armistice Day (*Fête de la Victoire*)
25 December	Christmas Day (*Noël*)

SMOKING

Smoking is banned inside all public spaces, including hotel rooms, bars, and clubs, since January 2008. It is still permitted on outdoor café terraces and in specially-built fumoirs.

TELEPHONES
PUBLIC TELEPHONES

Most public phones in France use pre-paid phone cards (*télécartes*), rather than coins. Some telephone booths accept credit cards (Visa, MasterCard/Eurocard). *Télécartes* (50 or 120 units) can be bought in post offices, branches of France Télécom, *bureaux de tabac* (cafés that sell cigarettes) and newsagents and can be used to make calls in France and abroad. Calls can be received at phone boxes where the blue bell sign is shown; the phone will not ring, so keep your eye on the small digital screen.

NATIONAL CALLS

French telephone numbers have ten digits. Paris and Paris region numbers begin with 01; 02 in northwest France; 03 in northeast France; 04 in southeast France and Corsica; 05 in southwest France.

INTERNATIONAL DIALLING CODES *(00 + code)* 📞			
Australia	61	New Zealand	64
Canada	1	United Kingdom	44
Eire	353	United States	1

WHEN IT IS NOON IN FRANCE, IT IS	
3am	in Los Angeles
6am	in New York
11am	in Dublin
11am	in London
7pm	in Perth
9pm	in Sydney
11pm	in Auckland

In France "am" and "pm" are not used but the 24-hour clock is widely applied.

INTERNATIONAL CALLS

To call France from abroad, dial the country code (33) + 9-digit number (omit the initial 0). When calling abroad from France dial 00, then dial the country code followed by the area code and number of your correspondent.
International information:
US/Canada: 00 33 12 11
International operator:
00 33 12 + country code
Local directory assistance: 12

MOBILE/CELL PHONES

In France these have numbers that begin with 06. Two-watt (lighter, shorter reach) and eight-watt models are on the market, using the Orange, Bouygtel or SFR networks. *Mobicartes* are prepaid phone cards that fit into mobile units. Mobile phone rentals (delivery or airport pickup provided):
World Cellular Rentals:
www.worldcr.com

TO USE YOUR PERSONAL CALLING CARD	
AT&T	📞 0-800 99 00 11
Sprint	📞 0-800 99 00 87
MCI	📞 0-800 99 00 19
Canada Direct	📞 0-800 99 00 16

TIME

France is one hour ahead of Greenwich Mean Time (GMT). Even though the Prime Meridian (0°) passes through Spain and France, both countries use the mean solar time of 15 degrees east (Central European Time) rather than 0 degrees (GMT).

Sundial in Borme-les-Mimosas

TIPPING

Since a service charge is automatically included in the price of meals and accommodation in France, any additional tipping is up to the visitor, generally small change, and generally not more than 5%. Hairdressers are usually tipped 10–15%.

As a rule, prices for hotels and restaurants as well as for other goods and services are significantly less expensive in the French regions than in Paris.

Restaurants usually charge for meals in two ways: a *forfait* or *menu*, that is a fixed price menu with two to three courses, sometimes a small pitcher of wine, all for a set price, or *à la carte*, the more expensive way, with each course ordered separately.

Cafés have very different prices, depending on where they are located. The price of a drink or a coffee is cheaper if you stand at the counter *(comptoir)* than if you sit down *(salle)* and sometimes it is even more expensive if you sit outdoors *(terrace)*. In some big cities, prices go up after 10pm in the evening.

CONVERSION TABLES

Weights and Measures

1 kilogram (kg) 6.35 kilograms 0.45 kilograms	**2.2 pounds (lb)** 14 pounds 16 ounces (oz)	**2.2 pounds** 1 stone (st) 16 ounces	*To convert kilograms to pounds, multiply by 2.2*
1 metric ton (tn)	**1.1 tons**	**1.1 tons**	
1 litre (l) 3.79 litres 4.55 litres	**2.11 pints (pt)** 1 gallon (gal) 1.20 gallon	**1.76 pints** 0.83 gallon 1 gallon	*To convert litres to gallons, multiply by 0.26 (US) or 0.22 (UK)*
1 hectare (ha) **1 sq. kilometre (km²)**	**2.47 acres** 0.38 sq. miles (sq.mi.)	**2.47 acres** 0.38 sq. miles	*To convert hectares to acres, multiply by 2.4*
1 centimetre (cm) **1 metre (m)**	**0.39 inches (in)** 3.28 feet (ft) or 39.37 inches or 1.09 yards (yd)	**0.39 inches**	*To convert metres to feet, multiply by 3.28; for kilometres to miles, multiply by 0.6*
1 kilometre (km)	**0.62 miles (mi)**	**0.62 miles**	

Clothing

Women					Men			
		35	4	2½			40	7½	7
		36	5	3½			41	8½	8
		37	6	4½			42	9½	9
Shoes		38	7	5½	**Shoes**		43	10½	10
		39	8	6½			44	11½	11
		40	9	7½			45	12½	12
		41	10	8½			46	13½	13
		36	6	8			46	36	36
		38	8	10			48	38	38
Dresses		40	10	12	**Suits**		50	40	40
& suits		42	12	14			52	42	42
		44	14	16			54	44	44
		46	16	18			56	46	48
		36	06	30			37	14½	14½
		38	08	32			38	15	15
Blouses &		40	10	34	**Shirts**		39	15½	15½
sweaters		42	12	36			40	15¾	15¾
		44	14	38			41	16	16
		46	16	40			42	16½	16½

Sizes often vary depending on the designer. These equivalents are given for guidance only.

Speed

KPH	10	30	50	70	80	90	100	110	120	130
MPH	6	19	31	43	50	56	62	68	75	81

Temperature

Celsius (°C)	0°	5°	10°	15°	20°	25°	30°	40°	60°	80°	100°
Fahrenheit (°F)	32°	41°	50°	59°	68°	77°	86°	104°	140°	176°	212°

To convert Celsius into Fahrenheit, multiply °C by 9, divide by 5, and add 32.
To convert Fahrenheit into Celsius, subtract 32 from °F, multiply by 5, and divide by 9.
NB: Conversion factors on this page are approximate.

Villefranche-sur-Mer
S/PHOTOGRAPHER MICHELIN

The Region Today

LIFE ON THE RIVIERA
THE COAST

A Holiday Destination – Visitors seeking fashionable and elegant resorts can choose between the bustle of Cannes and Monte-Carlo or the quieter and more discreet setting of Hyères, Beaulieu, Menton, Cap Ferrat or Cap Martin. Those longing for the appeal of a big city with all its amusements will undoubtedly turn to Nice. Lively St-Tropez will attract a large number of summer visitors; the seeker of solitude will find isolated inlets and localities; and a full range of hotels will cater to every budget.

The Riviera region features charming country houses, built in Provençal rustic style, with pink or ochre-coloured façades, overhanging red-tiled roofs and arbors covered with wisteria and climbing plants. There are also beautiful gardens in which great earthenware jars, which once contained olive oil or wine, are now purely decorative. Magnificent parks offer fine views from their terraces, and everyone can enjoy the light and colour in a charming and relaxed atmosphere.

Numerous constructions are invading the coast and one can see here and there towns built over water, such as the lake town of Port-Grimaud, the Cogolin Marina and the marine city of Port-la-Galère.

Ambitious building projects, some of which are totally out of proportion, have sprung up on all sides; a great number of private properties have appeared at the water's edge, although the public has right of access all along the coast.

Ports and Fishing – The naval port of Toulon is in a league of its own on the popular recreational coast. Cannes, Monaco and Antibes are long-established pleasure boat ports: beautiful yachts with polished wood and gleaming steelwork lie at anchor in the bay or are moored to the quays.

Fishing on the Riviera is confined to the coast and, as the catch is insufficient for the area, it has to be supplemented by shipments from the Atlantic.

There are no large fishing ports but numerous little harbours along the coast: Bandol, St-Tropez, St-Raphaël, Villefranche-sur-Mer, for example, have adapted to the demands of tourists and equipped themselves with moorings for pleasure boats.

For some years now the Nice region has made efforts to modernise the fishing industry and increase the number of boats in use. This has been achieved through the use of very large running nets known as *lamparos* and *seinches* and the construction of fish canneries.

The Markets – Most of the coastal towns have their own open-air markets where, to the colourful banks of flowers, fresh produce, and stalls of gleaming fish, are added the noisy bustle and the warmth of the local accents of buyers and sellers, creating a true Côte d'Azur scene.

INLAND

The interior reveals the last vestiges of what was once a rough and precarious way of life: valley sides and hill slopes terraced with stone walls retaining small strips of soil for growing cereals or two or three rows of vines and a few olive and almond trees.

The *garrigue*, where small flocks of sheep and goats were put to graze, formed a sharp contrast with the fertile valleys and irrigated plains of the lowlands and the coast, where cereals, early vegetables and flowers were harvested and vines and fruit trees flourished. The lonely villages clinging to solitary ridges and small farms lying abandoned among their terraced walls bore no resemblance to the market towns of the plains, spread along the main roads, or to the farms *(mas)* scattered in the midst of large cultivated areas.

The centre of the village is the little square *(cours)* shaded by plane trees round a small fountain. This is where the cafés are to be found, always full in this region, where people love social life, conversation and politics and where much of the day is spent away from the houses, which are left with the shutters closed to keep out the heat and insects.

21ST CENTURY

While the museums, old town markets, quaint perched villages and sandy beaches keep the continuous influx of tourists occupied for most of the year, the French Riviera economy doesn't solely depend on tourism, an industry vulnerable to international politics and economic slumps. Nice, Monaco and Cannes have invested heavily to become important business travel destinations, hosting conferences and trade shows year round, and Toulon continues to develop its thriving port, while technology and research centres have been booming throughout the region.
The French Riviera will always preserve and promote its colourful history and natural beauty, but in the 21C it has shrugged off its sleepy resort reputation to embrace a dynamic and internationally minded identity.

POPULATION

The population on the French Riviera was just 200 000 in 1860, and now has 1.8 million residents, with a 3% growth rate since 1990, more than twice the national average. Over 90% of this population is concentrated on the coastal cities of Menton, Nice, Antibes, Cannes, Hyères, Fréjus, and Toulon. International residents make up 12% of the population, with half of them coming from the European Union and almost 45% from North Africa.

LIFESTYLE

The French Riviera lifestyle is perfectly summed up as *Art de Vivre*, or the Art of Living. Everything from the lush Mediterranean landscape to the sun-drenched Provençal cuisine contribute to the overall sense of good living … and taking the time to enjoy it. The region runs at the leisurely pace typical of Latin countries, where afternoon siestas and Sunday boules games around

the town square with a glass of chilled rosé or pastis are still common.

RELIGION

Like much of France, Catholicism is the most widespread religion on the French Riviera, with Catholic churches, chapels, abbeys and monasteries found throughout the region. Other religions, including Judaism, Islam, and Christian faiths such Protestantism and Orthodox Catholic are also represented here, often with architecturally fascinating places of worship, thanks to the large international communities from North Africa, Russia, northern Europe and the Middle East.

LOCAL GOVERNMENT

The French Riviera is made up of 316 *communes* (town, village or city) and two administrative *départements* (the Var and the Alpes-Maritimes), within the larger Provence-Alpes-Côte-d'Azur (PACA) region. This guide covers the Riviera from Bandol to Menton, including the mountainous inland regions of the Provençal Tableland, the Pre-Alps of Grasse and the high country north of Nice. Also covered in this guide is Monaco, a small principality on the Riviera surrounded by the Alpes-Maritimes. Adjacent regions described in the Michelin Green Guides are *Provence* and *French Alps*.
Since the early 1980s, the government of the French Republic has decentralised its legislative authority, so that now each *commune*, *département* and *région* has its own locally elected council and mayor or president. Nice is the *prefecture*, or administrative capital, for the Alpes-Maritimes, and Toulon is the *préfecture* for the Var. Since 2008, both Nice and Toulon elected mayors from the Union for a Popular Movement (UMP), the party of President Nicolas Sarkozy.

INDUSTRY

Economic activities on the French Riviera have evolved significantly over the centuries, from shipping and fishing to farming and wine-making. The first major shift happened in the 18C with the arrival of the first tourists. Since the 1970s, the region has evolved once more into a region of technology, science, and international business.

TOURISM

The French Riviera is second only to Paris for tourism. It represents 1% of the worldwide tourism industry (€12million in revenue), with ten million visitors annually, 52% of them from outside France. One in five visitors is a business traveller, and today the region is home to the largest concentration of conference and trade show facilities in Europe. In addition to an attractive setting and enviable climate, the region is ultimately successful because of its highly developed infrastructure and accommodation for all budgets. The pleasure ports of the French Riviera are the largest in Europe, hosting 50% of the world's yachts and cruise ships each year.

CRAFTS

Numbers of craftmakers have moved into the old inland villages, which they have often restored with care, and are producing traditional objects made by the old methods or highly original creations.

Biot – The production of large earthenware jars in Biot goes back to the days of the Phoenicians. In the Middle Ages Biot was an important centre for ceramics and it was not until the 19C that it was eclipsed by Vallauris. There are several modern workshops specialising in traditional earthenware jars, pottery, ornamental stoneware and metalwork.

Since the 1960s Biot has owed its growing international reputation to its glass craftsmanship. By visiting a glass workshop one can see how the various pieces are made using early techniques. Exhibits include carafes, bottles, glasses, small oil lamps and traditional Provençal jugs with long spouts *(calères, ponons)* for drinking without touching the vessel with one's lips.

Vallauris – Ceramics from Vallauris enjoy a worldwide reputation. In 1947 Picasso came to work in a studio in the town and attracted a crowd of followers. Nowadays it is difficult to distinguish between the mass-produced pot and the hand-made article, in the shop windows.

Many of the potters – whether they use old methods (wood firing) or new techniques – produce attractive work: glazed kitchenware (tureens, bowls, jugs), handsome stoneware, various glazed or unglazed articles and clay pipes. Besides pottery, many other interesting activities have been introduced, including the production of hand-crafted puppets, handsome furniture and decorative sculpture made from olive wood, colourful painted chests and cupboards, fine hand-woven linen and furnishings.

Tourrettes-sur-Loup – Tourrettes has been revived by its crafts industry. It was an important weaving town in the Middle Ages and renewed its connection with this craft after the Second World War, becoming a renowned centre for hand-woven fabrics. The weavers produce very high quality goods in small quantities.

Several of the workshops in the winding streets offer a very varied range of cloth: reproductions of old Provençal fabrics, shot material for the high fashion market or furnishings, and hand-woven ties. Tourrettes also houses potters (making earthenware sheep using a Mexican process, engraving in vivid enamels), painters and sculptors in olive wood.

AGRICULTURE

Cut Flowers – Alphonse Karr *(see ST-RAPHAËL)*, a political refugee living in Nice before the annexation, is generally credited with having founded the flower trade. With the help of an associate, Karr began large-scale cultivation and had the idea of sending bunches of fresh violets and small packets of mixed seeds to Paris. From this modest start the trade in cut flowers and mimosa has developed considerably owing to irrigation and hothouses.

Hill Villages

The Riviera has attracted man since the earliest times, who built their strongholds on isolated hills. Many old villages may be seen perched like an eagle's nest on a hilltop or set on the flank of a hill; some are practically deserted, while others have been restored, such as the villages of Gourdon, Èze, Utelle, and Peille. For centuries the peasants built their villages in this way, at a distance from their lands and water supplies, and surrounded them with ramparts.

This was a wise precaution in the days of the great Germanic invasions, the Moslem pirates, and the attacks by the mercenaries of the Middle Ages and the Renaissance. The coming of security, better communications and the development of farming techniques in the 19C ended this isolation. Villages began to expand in the plains, sometimes doubling in size, and country dwellers were able to live on the land they cultivated and build their houses there.

These secluded villages are picturesque to visit. Built with stones from the hillsides, they seem to blend in with the countryside. The winding streets and alleyways *(calades)*, which are steeply sloped and only to be traversed on foot, are paved with flagstones or cobbles, intersected by tortuous stairways and crossed overhead by vaults and arches. Sometimes arcades follow one another at ground level, affording the passerby shelter from the sun and rain.

The houses, roofed with curved clay tiles, have high narrow fronts, worn by the centuries. They buttress each other and surround the church or château, which dominates the village. Old nail-studded doors, wrought-iron hinges and bronze knockers still adorn the more prosperous residences.

Sometimes the little townships, which have attracted many craftsmakers, are still enclosed by ramparts, with a fortified gate as the main entrance.

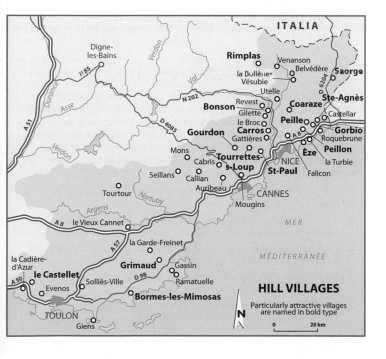

HILL VILLAGES

Particularly attractive villages are named in bold type

0   20 km

Flowers and Scented Plants of the Grasse Region – The two main flower crops of this area are roses and jasmine. The May tea-rose is the same as that grown in the east but the Mediterranean variety has a fine scent. Jasmine is of the large flowering variety which has been grafted onto jasmine officinalis. It is a particularly costly and delicate plant which flowers from the end of July to the first winter frosts.

The orange blossom used for perfume is obtained from the bitter fruit tree, known as the Seville orange *(bigaradier)*. Orange-flower water is made from direct distillation. The cherry laurel, eucalyptus and cypress are distilled both for essence and for *eau de toilette*. Mimosa is used for the production of essence by extraction.

Sweet basil, clary (sage), tarragon, melissa or balm mint, verbena, mignonette, peppermint and geranium all yield products used in perfumery, confectionery and pharmaceuticals. Scented plants include wild lavender, aspic, thyme, rosemary, sage etc.

Le Bar-sur-Loup, Golfe-Juan, Le Cannet and Vallauris as well as Seillans (Var department), are major centres for the production of natural aromatic raw materials, although Grasse is number one in this domain.

This luxury industry, which caters mostly to the export market, is supplemented by the synthetic perfume industry. The French perfume industry's exports exceed €5.9 billion, the most important customers being the United States, Japan, Germany and the United Kingdom.

First Vegetables – After North Africa, Spain and Italy, the region of Toulon and Hyères provides the first seasonal vegetables and fruit. The Var is noted for the cherries of Solliès-Pont and the peaches from the region around Fréjus.

Olive Trees and Oils – Traditionally, the northernmost place where olive trees (symbol of Southern agriculture) are grown, is also the limit of the Midi or South of France.

Production of olive oil in the region accounts for more than two-thirds of that of the whole country, and is spread throughout the Var, around Draguignan and Brignoles, and in the Bévéra and Roya valleys. Following the frosts of 1956, when nearly a quarter of the olive trees died, the olive groves have

How to Recognise a Good Olive Oil

The essential characteristic of virgin olive oil is its extraction by a mechanical process from the first cold pressing without being refined. Six further operations are necessary before the oil is ready to be marketed: grading *(calibrage)* and washing in cold water *(lavage)*, crushing *(broyage)* in a traditional mill, after which the resulting paste is pressed on fibre mats *(scourtins)*. The oil thus obtained is purified by centrifuge (by natural settling and decanting if the traditional process is followed throughout).

Regulations define several categories of oil which must be mentioned on the label:

- Extra-virgin oil *(huile vierge extra)* which is easily digested, has most flavour and very low acidity (less than 1%)

- Virgin oil *(huile vierge)* which also has a very good flavour but can have double the acidity of extra-virgin oil

- Olive oil *(huile d'olive)* which has an acceptable taste for local cooking but fairly high acidity (about 3%)

- Refined oil *(huile d'olive lampante)* which is mixed with virgin oil as its acidity (nearly 4%) makes it unfit for consumption.

Bouillabaise

S. Sauvignier/MICHELIN

been replanted progressively with two more hardy species: the **aglandau** and the **verdale**. There are many other varieties, with flavours which vary according to the soil and the date of harvest. Traditionally, several varieties are grown in one olive grove. Harvest is from the end of August, depending on the area; table olives are picked by hand, while those destined for miling are shaken off the tree and collected in nets.

Around Nice, shaking *(gaulage)* is always used. Olives from Nyons *(tanches)* are the only ones to be designated AOC *(Appellation d'origine contrôlée – of guaranteed quality)*. The **belgentiéroise** olive, harvested at the end of August, can be eaten within the month; the **grossane** is a fleshy black, salted olive; the **salonenque** is a green variety also known as *olive des Baux*. The **cailletier**, or little Nice olive, is stored in brine for six months before being eaten. All of these can be eaten as an apéritif or made into oil.

SHIPPING

Toulon is the largest commercial shipping port on the French Riviera, and also serves as the largest naval base in France. It's the primary port for shipments of cargo and passengers to Corsica. There is a smaller commercial shipping port in Nice, but the regional shipping activity is largely for cruise ships, ferries and pleasure yachts.

FISHING

Most of the fishing along the French Riviera is done on a small *artisanale* scale for local consumption, much as it has for centuries. Despite its relatively small contribution to the region's economy, it nevertheless touches many coastal communities where fishing has been an important way of life for the locals for many generations.

TECHNOLOGY

The high-tech industry has grown significantly since the 1970s, encouraged by the establishment of science parks such as Sophia-Antipolis near Valbonne. Today, information technology and telecommunication represents €4.2million in annual revenue, and biotechnology and chemical research (cosmetics, scents, flavourings) accounts for another €2.1million annually. Aerospace research and development have also grown in importance, both in the public and private sectors, while Toulon has begun investing in naval technology tied to national defence.

FOOD AND DRINK

The main features of Provençal cooking are garlic and frying in oil (preferably olive oil). Garlic has inspired many poets who have written of the "Provençal truffle", the "divine condiment", "man's friend". Olive oil is used wherever butter would be used further north. "A fish lives in water and dies in oil" according to a local proverb.

Bouillabaisse – Here we salute the most celebrated of Provençal dishes. The classic *bouillabaisse* must consist of the "three fishes": scorpion fish *(rascasse)*, red gurnet and conger eel. Several other kinds of fish and shellfish are usually added – it is essential that the fish be freshly caught and cooked in good quality olive oil. The seasoning is just as important: salt, pepper, onion, tomato, saffron, garlic, thyme, bay leaves, sage, fennel and orange peel. Sometimes a glass of white wine or brandy gives the final flavour to the broth, which is poured onto thick slices of bread.

Aïoli – *Aïoli* is another Provençal speciality: a mayonnaise made with olive oil, strongly flavoured with crushed garlic. Comparing the northern variety of mayonnaise with *aïoli*, Mistral dismissed it as insipid "jam". *Aïoli* is served with *hors-d'œuvres*, or with *bourride* (a soup of angler fish, bass and whiting, etc.), among many other dishes.

Fish – One of the Mediterranean's tastiest fish is the red mullet *(rouget)*, which the famous gastronome, Brillat-Savarin, called the "woodcock of the sea" probably because gourmets cook it without first scaling or cleaning it. The *loup* (local name for bass) grilled with fennel or vine shoots is another delicious dish. *Brandade de morue* is a purée of pounded cod mixed with olive oil, some garlic cloves and truffle slices.

Aromatic herbs – Considered with garlic and olive oil to be one of the basics of Southern cooking, aromatic herbs, cultivated or growing naturally on sunny hillsides, perfume gardens and markets and enhance local cuisine. Known as *herbes de Provence,* the mixture includes **savory** *(sarriette)*, used to flavour goats' and ewes' milk cheeses; **thyme** *(thym)* cooked with most vegetables and also grilled meat; **basil** *(basilic);* **sage** *(sauge)*, **wild thyme** *(serpolet)*; **rosemary** *(romarin)* which is good for the digestion; **tarragon** *(estragon);* **juniper** *(genièvre),* used to flavour game; **marjoram** *(marjolaine);* and **fennel** *(fenouil)*. It

is used in many dishes and can, according to taste, be a main constituent or just a trace.

Thirteen desserts – Provençal tradition presents diners at Christmas with 13 desserts (representing Christ and the 12 Apostles): raisins, dried figs, walnuts, hazelnuts, almonds, grapes on the vine, apples, pears, black nougat (made with honey), *fougasse* (sort of brioche), prunes stuffed with almond paste, melons stored in straw and dry cakes flavoured with orange blossom.

At Epiphany, a **galette des rois** is served in the form of a brioche filled with almond paste and topped with a paper crown which goes to whoever finds the china figurine in their slice.

Wines – Vines have been cultivated in Provence since Antiquity.

The **rosé wines**, their glowing colour achieved by a special process from black grapes, are gaining increasingly widespread popularity; pleasant and fruity to the palate, they go well with any dish.

The **white wines** are generally dry in character but have a good bouquet and are an excellent accompaniment to shellfish and Mediterranean fish.

There is a wide variety of full-flavoured **red wines**: full-bodied or subtle and delicate depending on whether they come from Bandol or the southern slopes of the Maures or, on the other hand, from the Argens Valley or St-Tropez.

The most popular wines are from the region of Bandol, Ollioules, Pierrefeu, Cuers, Taradeau and La Croix-Valmer, from the Niçois area and particularly the wines of Bellet, La Gaude, St-Jeannet and Menton (& *see Planning Your Trip: Wine Tasting and Regional Produce*).

SPECIALITIES FROM NICE

Niçois cuisine, a lively expression of the character of Nice, is inspired by the cooking of Provence and of Liguria in Italy as it is the meeting point of the two traditions.

The narrow streets of Old Nice, clustered at the foot of the castle hill, overflow with opportunities to try the best-known specialities as well as seasonal variations.

Two well-known examples of the cooking of Nice are an **onion tart** *(pissaladière)*, garnished with a thick anchovy sauce *(pissala)* and black Nice olives, and **salade niçoise**, a tasty combination of local tomatoes, cut into four, lettuce leaves, beans, radishes, peppers, onions, hard-boiled eggs and Nice olives, garnished with anchovy fillets and basil leaves and moistened with olive oil.

For a snack to be eaten in the street there is a large chickpea flour pancake *(socca)*, divided into portions and accompanied by a small glass of local wine *(pointu)*; it is sold in and around place St-François.

At lunchtime recharge the batteries for more sightseeing with a round sandwich *(pan bagnat* – soaked bread) containing tomatoes, lettuce, onions, anchovies and olives, moistened with olive oil and flavoured with garlic.

Salad or soup or omelette may accompany a marinade of young fish *(poutina)* which are caught with the permission of the local authorities between Antibes and Menton in February. During the rest of the year gourmets may console themselves with a **fish soup** *(soupe aux poissons de roche)* made with little crabs *(favouilles)*.

The evening menu may be enlivened by a slice of **suckling pig** *(porchetta)* stuffed with herbs and its own offal, served with a mixed salad *(salade de mesclun* in the local dialect) composed of 14 types of young salad plants picked in the area.

The dishes on offer in the tiny restaurants in the villages inland include stuffed squash blossoms *(fleurs de courgette farcies)*; a vegetable stew *(ratatouille)* made of tomatoes, eggplant *(aubergines)*, peppers and courgettes *(zucchinis)* gently cooked in oil; shell-shaped pasta *(gnocchi)* made of wheat and potato flour and served with a thick sauce *(daube)*; deep-fried pastry parcels *(barbajouan* – Uncle John) filled with rice, squash, garlic, onion and cheese; a stockfish dish known as **estocaficada** (see opposite).

Pissaladière

©Tips Images

The convivial family dish, known as **pistou**, is a vegetable soup to which is added an unctuous concoction of basil, garlic, tomatoes and unstinted olive oil.

For dessert there is a sweet tart *(tourte de blea)* garnished with chopped chard leaves, pine kernels and currants.

Halfway through Lent the pastry cooks' windows display small sweet pastry cushions known as **ganses**. A cake flavoured with orange flower water *(fougasse)* is sold all year round; in Monaco it is decorated with aniseed in the national colours of red and white.

One may resist the torpor of midday by sitting in the shade with a glass of crushed ice flavoured with mint *(gratta queca)*.

Estocaficada – This is the local version of the stockfish of Marseille, known for short by old hands as "estocafic". As it takes a whole day to prepare, it has become a dish for special occasions. To fillets of stockfish (dried cod), flaked with a fork and lightly browned, are added peeled and de-seeded tomatoes, the tripes of the stockfish cut into strips, chopped olives and bouquets of herbs including fennel, marjoram, parsley, thyme, bay and savory. The dish is braised for three to four hours, generously laced with brandy *(la brande)*. When the liquor has reduced to a level which only the vigilance of the cook can determine, a good measure of stock is added to the pot.

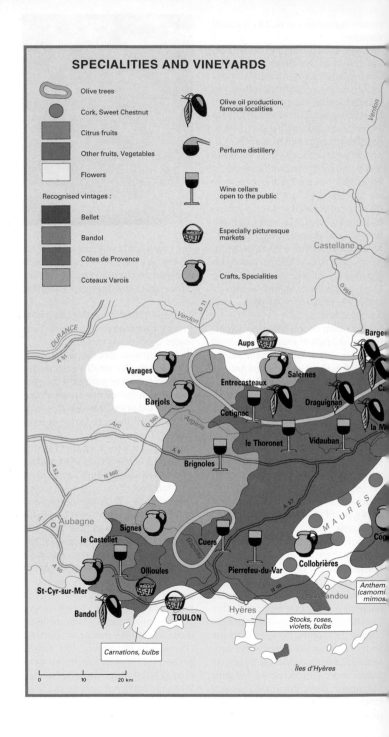

SPECIALITIES AND VINEYARDS

Olive trees

Cork, Sweet Chestnut

Citrus fruits

Other fruits, Vegetables

Flowers

Recognised vintages :

Bellet

Bandol

Côtes de Provence

Coteaux Varois

Olive oil production, famous localities

Perfume distillery

Wine cellars open to the public

Especially picturesque markets

Crafts, Specialities

Verdon

Castellane

DURANCE

A 51

Verdon

D 11

D 985

Aups

Varages

Salernes

Entrecasteaux

Barjols

Draguignan

Cotignac

Arc

D 560

Argens

A 8

le Thoronet

Vidauban

la M

Ca

Barger

Brignoles

A 52

N 560

A 57

M A U R E S

Aubagne

Signes

Cuers

Cog

le Castellet

Collobrières

A 50

Ollioules

Pierrefeu-du-Var

St-Cyr-sur-Mer

Anthem (camomi mimos

Bandol

TOULON

Hyères

le andou

Stocks, roses, violets, bulbs

Carnations, bulbs

Îles d'Hyères

0   10   20 km

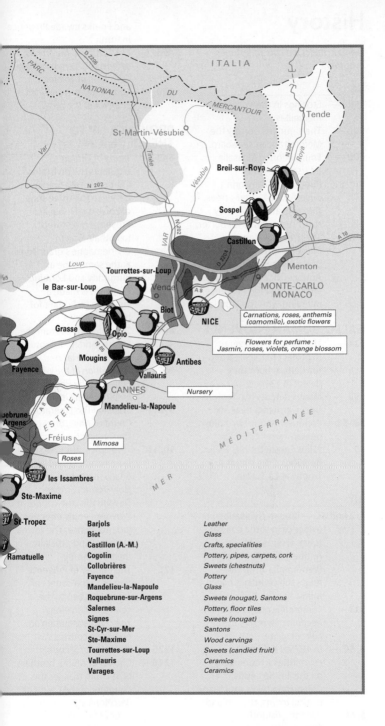

ITALIA

Tende

St-Martin-Vésubie

Breil-sur-Roya

Sospel

Castillon

Menton

MONTE-CARLO
MONACO

Tourrettes-sur-Loup

le Bar-sur-Loup

Vence

Biot

NICE

Carnations, roses, anthemis
(camomile), exotic flowers

Grasse

Opio

Flowers for perfume :
Jasmin, roses, violets, orange blossom

Mougins

Antibes

Fayence

Vallauris

CANNES

Nursery

Mandelieu-la-Napoule

uebrune-
Argens

ESTEREL

Fréjus

Mimosa

Roses

les Issambres

Ste-Maxime

St-Tropez

Ramatuelle

MÉDITERRANÉE

MER

Barjols	Leather
Biot	Glass
Castillon (A.-M.)	Crafts, specialities
Cogolin	Pottery, pipes, carpets, cork
Collobrières	Sweets (chestnuts)
Fayence	Pottery
Mandelieu-la-Napoule	Glass
Roquebrune-sur-Argens	Sweets (nougat), Santons
Salernes	Pottery, floor tiles
Signes	Sweets (nougat)
St-Cyr-sur-Mer	Santons
Ste-Maxime	Wood carvings
Tourrettes-sur-Loup	Sweets (candied fruit)
Vallauris	Ceramics
Varages	Ceramics

History

Events in italics indicate milestones in history.

BC

1500 — Etchings in the Vallée des Merveilles.

900 — The Ligurians occupy the Mediterranean seaboard.

600 — Foundation of Massalia (Marseille) by the Phocaeans. They bring olive, fig, nut, cherry trees, the cultivated vine; they substitute money for barter.

5-4C — The Greek settlers in Marseille introduce trading posts: Hyères, St-Tropez, Antibes, Nice and Monaco. The Celts invade Provence, mingling with the Ligurians.

GALLO-ROMAN PROVENCE

122 — The Romans intervene to protect Marseille from the Celts, whom they defeat in 124.

102 — Marius defeats the Teutons from Germania near Aix.

58–51 — Conquest of Gaul by Julius Caesar.

49 — Julius Caesar founds Fréjus.

6 — Building of the Alpine Trophy at La Turbie.

AD

1, 2 and 3C — Roman civilisation in evidence in some coastal towns (Fréjus, Cimiez, Antibes); the Via Aurelia (Ventimiglia-Brignoles-Aix) is the country's main highway.

313 — *Constantine grants Christians freedom of worship by the Edict of Milan.*

4, 5C — In 410 St-Honorat establishes a monastery on the Iles de Lérins. Christianity takes root in the coastal towns, then inland.

5, 6C — Vandals, Visigoths, Burgundians, Ostrogoths and Franks invade Provence in turn.

496 — *Clovis, King of the Franks, defeats the Alemanni from Germania at Tolbiac.*

800 — *Charlemagne is crowned Emperor of the West.*

PROVENCE UP TO THE "REUNION"

843 — *Treaty of Verdun* regulates the division of Charlemagne's Empire between the three sons of Louis the Debonair. Provence is restored to Lothair (one of Charlemagne's grandsons) at the same time as Burgundy and Lorraine.

855 — Provence is made a kingdom by Lothair for his son, Charles.

884 — The Saracens capture the Maures and for a century terrorise the land.

962 — *Restoration of the Western Empire as the Holy Roman Empire under Otto I.*

974 — William «The Liberator», Count of Arles, drives out the Saracens.

10, 11C — Provence, after passing from hand to hand, is finally made part of the Holy Roman Empire. Despite this, the counts of Provence enjoy effective independence. The towns are freed and proclaim their autonomy.

12C — The County of Provence passes to the counts of Toulouse, then to the counts of Barcelona. The counts maintain an elaborate court at Aix.

1226 — *Accession of St Louis.*

1246 — Charles of Anjou, brother of St Louis, marries the daughter of the Count of Barcelona and becomes Count of Provence.

The Wars of Religion – 1562–1598

This is the name given to the 36-year-long crisis marked by complex political and religious conflict. During the latter half of the 16C, the French monarchy was in poor shape to withstand the looming hegemony of Spain, with political life in chaos and debt reaching incredible dimensions. The firm stand taken on religion by Spain and Italy on the one hand and by the Protestant countries on the other was missing in the France of Catherine de' Medici's regency, where both parties jostled for favour and a policy of appeasement applied.

The nobility took advantage of the situation, seeking to bolster their power base in the provinces and, under cover of religion, to grasp the reins of government. The Catholic League was formed by the Guise and Montmorency families, supported by Spain and opposed by the Bourbon, Condé and Coligny factions, Huguenots all, with English backing.

Though historians distinguish eight wars separated by periods of peace or relative tranquility, the troubles were continuous: in the country, endless assassinations, persecutions and general lawlessness; at court, intrigues, volte-faces and pursuit of particular interests. Actual warfare, threatened ever since the Amboise Conspiracy, began at Wassy in 1562, following a massacre of Protestants. The names of Dreux, Nîmes, Chartres, Longjumeau, Jarnac, Montcontour, St-Lô, Valognes, Coutras, Arques, Ivry follow in bloody succession.

The Peace of St-Germain in 1570 demonstrated a general desire for reconciliation, but only two years later came the St Bartholomew's Day Massacre.

The States General were convened at Blois at the request of the supporters of the League who were opposed to the centralisation of power into royal hands. Fearful of the power enjoyed by Duke Henri of Guise, head of the Catholic League and the kingdom's best military commander, King Henri III had him assassinated in the château at Blois one cold morning in December 1588, only to be cut down himself by a fanatical monk the following year.

This left the succession open for the Huguenot Henry of Navarre, the future Henri IV. By formally adopting the Catholic faith in 1593 and by promulgating the Edict of Nantes in 1598, this able ruler succeeded in rallying all loyal Frenchmen to his standard, putting at least a temporary end to the long-drawn-out crisis.

1254 — Landing of St Louis at Hyères on return from the seventh Crusade.

1295 — Charles II establishes the village and port of Villefranche.

1308 — Overlordship of Monaco is bought from the Genoese by a member of the Grimaldi family.

1343–82 — Queen Jeanne becomes Countess of Provence. Plague decimates the population.

1388 — Nice hands itself over to the Count of Savoy.

1419 — Nice is officially ceded to the Duke of Savoy.

1434 — René of Anjou, "Good King René", becomes Count of Provence. He sets up court in Aix and helps revive the economy of the region.

1481 — Charles of Maine, nephew of René of Anjou, bequeaths Provence (except Nice, which belongs to Savoy) to Louis XI.

1486 — Reunion of Provence with France ratified by the "Estates" of Provence (assembly of representatives of the three orders); Provence attached to the Kingdom "as one principal to another".

1489 — The independence of Monaco is recognised by regional powers, Provence and the county of Nice, both of whom attempt to increase the population with favourable immigration incentives.

PROVENCE AFTER THE "REUNION"

1501 — Establishment of Parliament at Aix (Parliament of Provence), sovereign court of justice, which later claims certain political prerogatives.

1515 — *Accession of François I.*

1524 — During the wars between François I (1515-1545) and Emperor Charles V, Provence is invaded by the Imperialists, commanded by the High Constable of Bourbon.

1536 — Invasion of Provence by Emperor Charles V.

1539 — Edict of Villers-Cotterêts decrees French as the language for all administrative laws in Provence.

1543 — Nice besieged by French and Turkish troops. Catherine Ségurane instrumental in causing the Turks to withdraw.

1562–98 — *Wars of Religion. Promulgation of the Edict of Nantes.* Henri IV builds the first military port in Toulon.

1622 — Louis XIII visits Provence.

1639 — Richelieu establishes the French Royal Navy, with the a fleet in Toulon.

1643–1715 — *Reign of Louis XIV.*

1691 — Nice taken by the French.

1696 — France returns Nice to Savoy.

1707 — Invasion of Provence by Prince Eugene of Savoy.

1718 — County of Nice becomes part of the newly created Kingdom of Sardinia.

1720 — The great plague decimates the population of Provence.

1746 — Austro-Sardinian offensive is broken at Antibes. Austrian War of Succession.

1787 — Reunion of the "Estates" of Provence.

1789 — *The French Revolution.*

REVOLUTION–EMPIRE

1790 — Provence divided into three *départements*: Bouches-du-Rhône, Var, Basses-Alpes.

The French Revolution

The Revolution, opening up the continent of Europe to democracy, was the outcome of the long crisis affecting the Ancien Régime.

Hastened along by the teachings of the thinkers of the Enlightenment as much as by the inability of a still essentially feudal system to adapt itself to new social realities, the Revolution broke out following disastrous financial mismanagement and the emptying of the coffers of the state. In 1789 the commoners created the National Assembly, the Bastille prison was stormed, aristocratic and church privileges were abolished (night of 4 July) and the Rights of Man were proclaimed. The royal family tried to flee in 1791, and after being captured were tried as traitors and guillotined in 1793.

The main events unfolded in Paris but their repercussions were felt throughout France and Europe. In 1792 the French Revolutionary Army captured Nice, which had been under Sardinian rule (to whom it would return 1814–1860). In 1793 a counter-revolution broke out in several southern cities, including Toulon, where Royalists handed the city to a Anglo-Spanish fleet. The Revolutionary Army laid siege to Toulon for four months, ultimately driving the British away under the command of the young artillery commander, Napoleon Bonaparte, who was then promoted to Brigadier General.

19C print depicting the Siege of Toulon in 1793

Wealthy French aristocrats buy property in Nice.

1793 — Siege of Toulon, in which Bonaparte distinguishes himself. Nice is reunited with France.

1799 On 9 October, Bonaparte lands at St-Raphaël on his return from Egypt.

1804 — *Coronation of Napoleon.* The Riviera economy suffers from his Continental Blockade. Completion of the **Grande Corniche** from Nice to Menton.

1814 — *Abdication of Napoleon at Fontainebleau, 6 April.* Embarkation of Napoleon at St-Raphaël, 28 April, for the Island of Elba. The County of Nice is restored to the King of Sardinia.

1815 — Landing of Napoleon at Golfe-Juan, 1 March. He reaches Paris in record time by crossing the Alps. *Battle of Waterloo, 18 June.*

19TH CENTURY
THE DEVELOPMENT OF THE FRENCH RIVIERA

In the 19C, the French Riviera slowly transformed from the isolated, impoverished, and somewhat unwelcoming corridor between Provence and Italy, to a chic resort destination. Early travel guides by Tobias Smollet (*Travels through France and Italy*) and Stephen Liégeard (*La Côte d'Azur*) offered glowing descriptions of flowering gardens and sparkling blue sea, but the popularity of the region really took off after the British Lord Brougham and Queen Victoria began coming on a regular basis for the curative climate. Aristocrats and royal courts from Europe and Russia were the first to build their palaces along the coast in Cannes, Nice and Monaco, where the casino was booming. The arrival of the railroad in 1864 brought the affluent bourgeoisie and famous artists, many who shocked the locals by sunbathing and swimming in the Mediterranean. By the turn of the century the French Riviera was an internationally renowned resort for the rich and famous.

1830 — *Accession of Louis-Philippe.*

1832 — The Duchess of Berry lands at Marseille, hoping to raise Provence in favour of a legitimist restoration.

1834 — Ex-Chancellor Lord Brougham "discovers" Cannes.

1852-1870 — *Reign of Napoleon III.*

1860 — County of Nice restored to France.

1865 — Roquebrune and Menton, who declared their independence from Monaco in 1848, become part of France.

1865 — The railroad links Marseille to Nice, reaching Monaco in 1868.

Allied soldiers in a landing craft travel through Marseilles Harbour, August 1944.

© Corbis

1878 — Opening of the Monte-Carlo Casino. Development of the winter tourist season of the Riviera.

1887 — The journalist Stephen Liégeard coins the phrase, "Côte d'Azur", or Azure Coast.

late 19C — Artists such as Paul Signac establish the St-Tropez School of Painting.

20TH CENTURY
THE SUMMER SEASON DEBUTS

In the late 19th and early 20C, most of the tourism on the French Riviera was still reserved for the winter months. Ski resorts began appearing in the snowy mountains above Nice as early as 1909. The summer season, popularised by American artists and writers, officially launched in 1931, when hotels and resorts remained open throughout the year and Coco Chanel made tanning fashionable. In France, the first paid vacations made the French Riviera accessible for the average worker.

After the interruption by WWII, the French Riviera saw exponential growth and development in infrastructure, with high-speed trains, highways, and an international airport opening up the region to the mass tourism that the region enjoys to this day.

1911 — First Monte Carlo Rally

1914–18 — Many village populations depleted by First World War.

1920 — Moyenne Corniche built.

1931 — Resorts open in summer.

1940 — The Italians occupy Menton.

1942 — The Germans invade the Free Zone. The scuttling of the French Fleet in Toulon harbour.

1944 — Liberation of Provence.

ALLIED LANDING IN PROVENCE (1944)

Operation "Dragon" – This was the aftermath of operation "Overlord" which had liberated Normandy three months earlier. At a critical moment in the battle of Normandy the Allies landed on the coast of Provence fortified by the Germans under the name "Südwall" with the American 7th Army under **General Patch**, of which the French Ist Army (composed mostly of African soldiers) formed the principal part.

"Nancy a le torticolis" (Nancy has a stiff neck) – This laconic message, broadcast on the BBC in the evening of 14 August announcing the landings in Provence, raised the hopes of the Resistance groups which had been on alert since the projected landings reported on 6 June 1944. Between June and August, the dropping of arms by parachute was stepped up, notably in the *pouvadous* (dry and stony moors); these arms were destined for the Maquis (Resistance) in the Maures, the Alps, Bessillon and Ste-Baume. In the early hours of 15 August, airborne Anglo-American troops were dropped around Le Muy to take control of the strategic communications route, RN 7. The village of **La Motte** became the first Provençal village to be liberated. At the same time, French commandos from Africa landed at Cap Nègre, and Esquillon Point, while American Special Forces attacked the Îles d'Hyères. Thus protected, the main army, assembled on the 2 000 ships, including 250 warships, landed at 8am on the beaches of Cavalaire, St-Tropez, Le Dramont and the Esterel. Despite a rapid advance, the two sectors were still separated at the end of the day by pockets of German resistance at St-Raphaël and Fréjus which fell only the following day. On 16 August the B Army under General De Lattre landed at Cavalaire Bay and in the gulf of St-Tropez and, having relieved the Americans, attacked the defences of Toulon.

General Montsabert outflanked the town to the north to fall on Marseille. After the fall of Hyères and Solliès, Toulon was reached on 23 August but fighting continued until 28 August with the surrender of the St-Mandrier peninsula. On the same day, after five days of fighting, Marseille was liberated.

To the east, the Americans of the First Special Force advanced to the Alpes-Maritimes to back up the Resistance forces and drive the Germans back into the Italian Alps: Nice fell on 30 August and Menton on 6 September. In the hinterland, the Massif de l'Authion, transformed into an entrenched camp by the Germans, was the site of hard fighting for 8 months. L'Authion was overcome on 13 April 1945, Saorge on 18 April but Tende was liberated only on 5 May, three days before the general armistice! Provence had been liberated in less than 15 days. The Allies pursued the Germans, who retreated up the Rhône Valley; the 1st French Army under De Lattre de Tassigny effected a link-up with the 2nd Amoured Division under Leclerc in Côte d'Or south of Châtillon-sur-Seine.

1946 — First International Film Festival in Cannes.

Since 1946 — Development of summer tourist trade on the Riviera. Harnessing of the River Durance and River Verdon.

1947 — Upper valley of the Roya incorporated into France.

1960–1963 — Modern art flourishes in the region with the New Realism and the School of Nice artists.

1970 — International technology park opened at Sophia Antipolis near Valbonne reflects increasing emphasis on development of the region into a hi-tech industrial belt.

1980 — The Provençal Motorway (A8) links the Rhône and Italian networks.

1989 — Law passed to strengthen measures against forest fires which pose an increasing threat to the region.

1989 — The **TGV** (*train à grande vitesse* – high-speed train) arrives on the Riviera.

August 1994 — Celebration of the 50th anniversary of the Liberation of Provence.

1996 — A high-speed boat service (NGV) between Nice and Corsica.

21ST CENTURY

2000 The naval base at the Toulon Arsenal becomes home to the French nuclear-powered aircraft carrier, the *Charles De Gaulle*.

June 2001 — The *TGV Méditerranée* is inaugurated, reducing the Paris–Marseille trip to three hours.

April 2005 — Prince Albert succeeds his father, Prince Ranier III, who died after ruling the Principality of Monaco for 57 years.

2007 — Construction completed on the first line of the Nice tramway.

2008 — Thales Alenia Space, in the Centre spatial de Cannes Mandelieu becomes the biggest employer in the Alpes-Maritimes.

2009 — Planning begins for the new LGV PACA high-speed train linking Marseille to Nice, for 2020.

Art and Culture

ABC OF ARCHITECTURE

Roman Era

LA TURBIE – The Alpine Trophy (1stC BC)

This monument was erected in homage to Augustus' victory in the Alps. Damaged and despoiled over the years, it was finally restored by the architect Formigé in the 1930s.

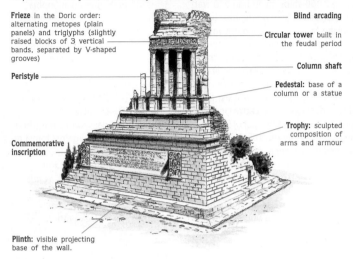

Frieze in the Doric order: alternating metopes (plain panels) and triglyphs (slightly raised blocks of 3 vertical bands, separated by V-shaped grooves)

Peristyle

Commemorative inscription

Plinth: visible projecting base of the wall.

Blind arcading

Circular tower built in the feudal period

Column shaft

Pedestal: base of a column or a statue

Trophy: sculpted composition of arms and armour

Early Christian Era

FRÉJUS – Interior of the baptistery (5C)

This is one of the few edifices from the Early Christian Era visible in the region. Some parts date from the Roman Era. An early 20C restoration restored the building to its former appearance.

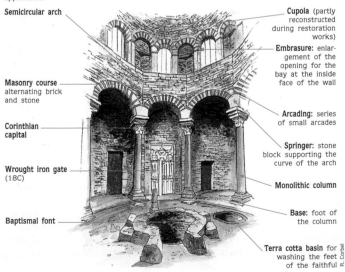

Semicircular arch

Masonry course alternating brick and stone

Corinthian capital

Wrought iron gate (18C)

Baptismal font

Cupola (partly reconstructed during restoration works)

Embrasure: enlargement of the opening for the bay at the inside face of the wall

Arcading: series of small arcades

Springer: stone block supporting the curve of the arch

Monolithic column

Base: foot of the column

Terra cotta basin for washing the feet of the faithful

R. Corbel

Religious architecture

LE THORONET – Ground plan of the abbey church (11C)

Because it did not serve a parish, the church in Thoronet does not have a central doorway. The rounded east end is typical of the region of Provence, in contrast to the flat chevet usually preferred by the Cistercian order.

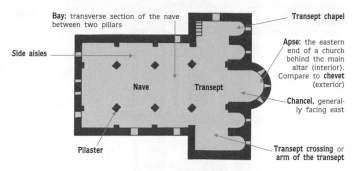

Bay: transverse section of the nave between two pillars

Transept chapel

Side aisles

Apse: the eastern end of a church behind the main altar (interior). Compare to **chevet** (exterior)

Nave **Transept**

Chancel, generally facing east

Pilaster

Transept crossing or arm of the transept

Cross-section of a Romanesque Provençal church

The right and left-hand sides of the drawing show two main variations of this type of church.

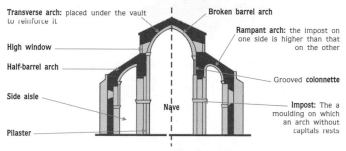

Transverse arch: placed under the vault to reinforce it

Broken barrel arch

Rampant arch: the impost on one side is higher than that on the other

High window

Half-barrel arch

Grooved colonnette

Side aisle

Nave

Impost: The a moulding on which an arch without capitals rests

Pilaster

GRASSE – Doorway of the Chapelle de l'Oratoire (14C)

The Gothic doorway and windows of this chapel were recovered from the old Franciscan church. In 1851, they were moved to this chapel, set on a hill in the old town centre.

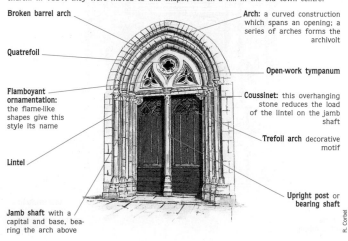

Broken barrel arch

Arch: a curved construction which spans an opening; a series of arches forms the archivolt

Quatrefoil

Open-work tympanum

Flamboyant ornamentation: the flame-like shapes give this style its name

Coussinet: this overhanging stone reduces the load of the lintel on the jamb shaft

Trefoil arch decorative motif

Lintel

Upright post or bearing shaft

Jamb shaft with a capital and base, bearing the arch above

R. Corbel

NICE – Cathédrale Sainte-Réparate (17C)

Sainte-Réparate was originally a chapel, built in the 13C. The current Baroque façade and ground plan are the work of the local architect Jean-André Guilbert.

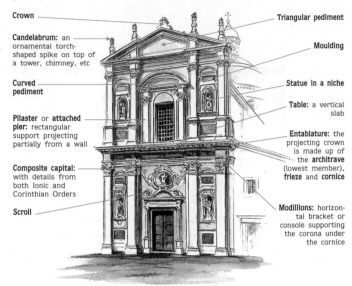

Crown

Candelabrum: an ornamental torch-shaped spike on top of a tower, chimney, etc

Curved pediment

Pilaster or attached pier: rectangular support projecting partially from a wall

Composite capital: with details from both Ionic and Corinthian Orders

Scroll

Triangular pediment

Moulding

Statue in a niche

Table: a vertical slab

Entablature: the projecting crown is made up of the architrave (lowest member), frieze and cornice

Modillions: horizontal bracket or console supporting the corona under the cornice

LES ARCS – Altar screen of the Sainte-Roseline chapel (early 16C)

Baroque altar screens in Nice and the surrounding region are mostly made of coloured marbles and stucco; gilded wood is more common on the other side of the Var.

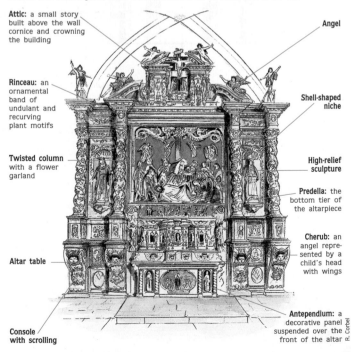

Attic: a small story built above the wall cornice and crowning the building

Rinceau: an ornamental band of undulant and recurving plant motifs

Twisted column with a flower garland

Altar table

Console with scrolling

Angel

Shell-shaped niche

High-relief sculpture

Predella: the bottom tier of the altarpiece

Cherub: an angel represented by a child's head with wings

Antependium: a decorative panel suspended over the front of the altar

R. Corbel

Traditional architecture

SAINT-TROPEZ – Houses on the harbour

The houses typically found in a village on the Riviera, known in France as the Côte d'Azur, are narrow and high, packed together along the waterfront or the winding streets of a hillside town; they are enlivened by colourful façades.

Louvered shutters: the slats filter out the sun and let in the air

Curved tiles

Chimney cap: crowning termination

Dormer cheek: the side of a dormer

Modern **dormer window**

Shade

Roof with **two slopes**

Tile creasing: two courses of tiles project beyond both faces of the wall to throw off rainwater

Canvas awning

Balcony

LE VIEUX-CANNET – Campanile

Campaniles appeared in the 16C, atop bell towers or belfries. Of various sizes, some are quite elaborate.

Metal frame withstands wind

Masonry course: the height of the regular rows is variable

Ressaut (projecting part)

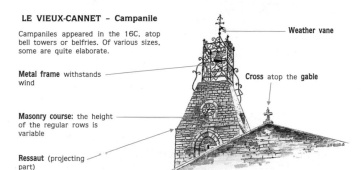

Weather vane

Cross atop the **gable**

LORGUES – Fontaine de la Noix (1771)

Each town or village has one or more fountains, whether a simple spigot or a sculpted, dated monument.

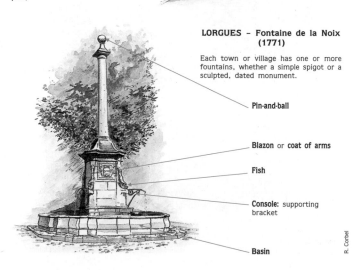

Pin-and-ball

Blazon or **coat of arms**

Fish

Console: supporting bracket

Basin

R. Corbel

79

Seaside architecture

HYÈRES – Villa Tunisienne (1884)

Seaside architecture of the 19C was inspired by Moorish culture. Chapoulart, the architect who designed the Villa Mauresque in Hyères, built this variation on the theme for himself, with a patio. Previously, it was also known as the "Algerian Villa".

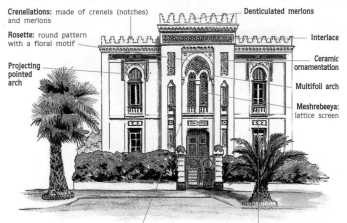

Crenellations: made of crenels (notches) and merlons

Rosette: round pattern with a floral motif

Projecting pointed arch

Denticulated merlons

Interlace

Ceramic ornamentation

Multifoil arch

Meshrebeeya: lattice screen

Fore part of the building, projecting from the façade and as high as the main building

Balustrade: railing with balusters

MONTE-CARLO – Game room in the casino (late 19C)

Monte-Carlo grew up around the casino, which typifies the eclectic style of seaside architecture at the end of the 19C. The luxurious decoration inside echoes the elaborate ornamentation on the outside.

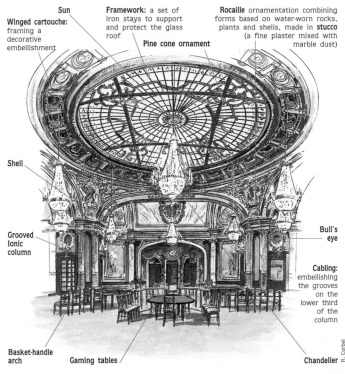

Sun

Winged cartouche: framing a decorative embellishment

Framework: a set of iron stays to support and protect the glass roof

Pine cone ornament

Rocaille ornamentation combining forms based on water-worn rocks, plants and shells, made in **stucco** (a fine plaster mixed with marble dust)

Shell

Grooved Ionic column

Basket-handle arch

Gaming tables

Bull's eye

Cabling: embellishing the grooves on the lower third of the column

Chandelier

R. Corbel

Military architecture

ANTIBES – Fort Carré (16C)

The ramparts of Antibes were demolished in 1895. All that remains is this fort, completed in 1585; the bastion design is a precursor of the star bastion defensive system developed by Vauban in the century following.

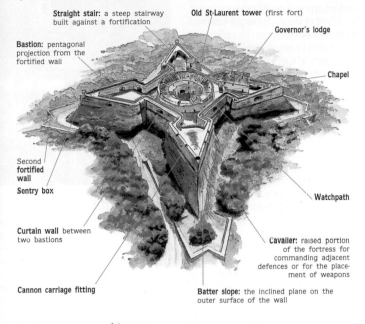

Straight stair: a steep stairway built against a fortification

Old St-Laurent tower (first fort)

Governor's lodge

Bastion: pentagonal projection from the fortified wall

Chapel

Second **fortified wall**

Sentry box

Watchpath

Curtain wall between two bastions

Cavalier: raised portion of the fortress for commanding adjacent defences or for the placement of weapons

Cannon carriage fitting

Batter slope: the inclined plane on the outer surface of the wall

Contemporary architecture

SOPHIA ANTIPOLIS – Commercial building (1978)

The buildings in the Valbonne business park were constructed beginning in 1970. They have been designed to fit into the natural shape of the landscape. Some are equipped to use solar energy.

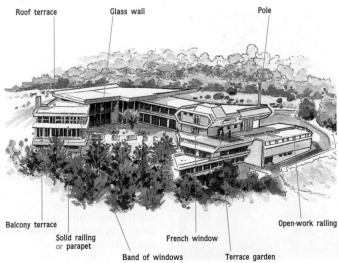

Roof terrace

Glass wall

Pole

Balcony terrace

Solid railing or **parapet**

French window

Open-work railing

Band of windows

Terrace garden

R. Corbel

HISTORY OF ARCHITECTURE

Although the Riviera has fewer monuments than Provence, the visitor will discover a rich heritage of art in its earliest forms side by side with its most modern expressions. Whether exploring the alleys of the picturesque perched villages or strolling on the coast, you will be able to appreciate the top representations of every major architectural current throughout the centuries.

GALLO-ROMAN ANTIQUITIES

Provence and particularly the Riviera have been thriving areas since Roman times. As later generations took the materials used by the Romans for the construction of their own new buildings, only a few fragments of the ancient civilisation have survived. In the districts of Fayence, Fréjus and St-Raphaël, Roman canals are still being used to carry water.

The Roman ruins at Cimiez (☞see NICE) are extensive. At Fréjus (☞see FRÉJUS), as well as the arena, there are traces of the harbour installations. The Alpine Trophy at La Turbie (☞see LA TURBIE) is of special interest; it is one of the few such Roman trophies still in existence. Buildings from the Merovingian and Carolingian periods include the baptistry at Fréjus and the chapels of Notre-Dame-de-Pépiole and La Trinité at St-Honorat de Lérins

Remains of the Roman aqueduct in Fréjus

E. Baret/MICHELIN

Abbaye du Thoronet

ROMANESQUE PERIOD

In the 12C an architectural renaissance in Provence blossomed in the building of numerous churches. The Romanesque style here is more eclectic than innovative, resulting not in large buildings, such as those in Burgundy, but rather in unpretentious churches, remarkable for the bonding of their evenly cut stones with fine mortar work.

The churches are plain outside, their façades being often poor in style; the only break in the flatness of the sides comes from powerful buttresses. The square belfry and the east end are sometimes decorated with applied blind arcades, known as **Lombard bands**, evidence of northern Italian influence.

On entering, the visitor is struck by the simplicity and austerity of the interior which often consists of a single nave and a shallow transept. If aisles form part of the plan, the apse ends in a semicircle flanked by two apsidal chapels.

The interesting abbey of Le Thoronet (☞see Le THORONET) contains a church of the Cistercian Order with the wide transept and bare appearance characteristic of the churches built by the Benedictines. In contrast, however, the roof of broken barrel vaulting and the semicircular apse show the influence of local craftsmen.

GOTHIC TO BAROQUE

There are few Gothic buildings in the region. Provençal Gothic is a transitional style which depends heavily on Romanesque traditions. The style is represented in the powerful groined vaulting at Grasse and the remarkable cloisters at Fréjus.

In the 15C, Good King René brought numerous Italian craftsmen to Provence. But even though Provençal painting was influenced by the Renaissance, the architecture remained unaffected.

Classical buildings, however, abound (17C and 18C). Design lost its original style and became more severe and majestic. In the towns the wealthier citizens built town houses. The development of Baroque is to be seen in ecclesiastical buildings in the County of Nice at Sospel, Menton, Monaco, La Turbie and Nice. Façades are adorned with pediments, niches and statues; inside, the architectural lines are often concealed by highly ornate altarpieces, panelling and baldaquins.

MODERN PERIOD

The 19C showed little originality and Baroque continued to be favoured for new constructions and restorations. The Romanesque-Byzantine style was employed in the church of Notre-Dame-de-la-Victoire-de-Lépante, St-Raphaël, the neo-Gothic on the west front of the church at Cimiez and neo-Romanesque for Monaco's cathedral. Slightly later, the Casino in Monte-Carlo and the Hôtel Negresco in Nice were designed in an ostentatious style borrowed from the Belle Epoque (c 1900).

Examples of 20C works include the church of Ste-Jeanne-d'Arc in Nice, the country church of St-Martin-de-Peille and the Chapelle du Rosaire des Dominicaines in Vence (also known as the Chapelle Matisse). The Fondation Maeght in St-Paul, the Musée Marc-Chagall in Nice, and the striking property development at the Baie des Anges Marina in Villeneuve-Loubet or Port-Grimaud are other fine examples of modern architecture.

Baroque-syle house (1890), Place l'Île-de-Beauté, Nice

ART
PAINTING
Primitives

From the middle of the 15C to the middle of the 16C a school of painting, at first purely Gothic then influenced by the Italian Renaissance, flourished in the County of Nice. It is best-known through the works of **Louis Bréa** and **Durandi**. It is said of Bréa that he was a "Provençal Fra Angelico", praise justified by the sincerity and sobriety of his brushwork and his gift for stressing the humanity of his subjects. However, his simplicity is a far cry from the mysticism of Fra Angelico, and his colours and dull tones lack the sparkle of the great Italian genius.

These Provençal artists worked mainly for the Penitent brotherhoods, which explains why their paintings are scattered in many churches and pilgrim chapels. They can be seen in Nice (where Brea's brother Antoine and nephew François are represented), Gréolières, Antibes, Fréjus, Grasse and Monaco.

During the same period, the humblest churches of the County of Nice were decorated with the most striking mural paintings. These are to be seen at Coaraze, Venanson, Lucéram, Saorge and Notre-Dame-des-Fontaines where Renaissance Primitive **Giovanni Canavesio**, working beside **Jean Baleison**, created Gothic-inspired works of exceptional quality.

The Classical Period

The 17C and 18C were marked by the fine pictures of the Parrocles, the Van Loos, Joseph Vernet and Hubert Robert. It is **Fragonard**, however, who is the pride of Provence. Rakish scenes were his favourites; he painted them with great enthusiasm and exquisite style. He often used as background to his jubilant party scenes the landscapes flooded with light and the gardens full of flowers seen round his native town of Grasse.

Love Letter (c. 1770)
by Jean-Honoré Fragonard

Modern Painting

At the end of the 19C numerous artists, representing the main trends in modern painting, were fascinated by the radiant light of the Mediterranean South of France.

Impressionism

The return of **Cézanne** to Provence (1881) was followed by many Impressionists such as **Berthe Morisot** (in Nice), **Monet** (in Antibes) and **Renoir** (in Cagnes), who sought to portray the subtle effects of light on Mediterranean landscapes. Monet's works mark the first appearance of the Riviera in painting: "I fence and wrestle with the sun" (letter

Amphorae

From ancient times, the Provençal coasts have been visited by numerous merchant ships often of imposing size (more than 30m/98ft long) and heavily laden (up to 8 000 amphorae, or two-handled jars). The problems of manoeuvring these heavy boats with oar, sail and a lack of knowledge of the reefs led to innumerable shipwrecks. The wrecks salvaged with their cargoes of amphorae bear witness to the busy commercial exchanges between areas of production and the consumers in urban centres. Navigation took place between April and September, when the weather conditions were most favourable. Foodstuffs such as wine, oil and fish were also transported.

The cargo on these boats was arranged at right angles to the keel; the pointed ends of the amphorae were wedged in place by the branches of trees, and the empty spaces between their necks were filled with the next row, thus assuring that the whole cargo was stable. Some holds contained up to four levels of amphorae.

⊚ Regulations concerning underwater archaeological finds:

⊚ All cultural goods from the sea (amphorae, etc.) found on public property belong to the State. Therefore, anyone diving who finds any archaeological remains must leave them in place and untouched.

⊚ In the event of objects being brought up by chance (e.g. in nets), it is forbidden to dispose of them and the find should be reported to the nearest Affaires Maritimes within 48hr. Offenders are dealt with in the High Courts.

⊚ Lastly, a small consolation, divers who have declared a find of a wreck or archaeological remains could benefit from a reward fixed by the government.

from Monet to Rodin, January 1888). It's from this period, with the "series", that Monet begins recording the variations of light on the same subject. Renoir spent the last years of its life in Cagnes, painting flowers and fruits, landscapes and people of the South.

Impressionism gave birth to a new school, **Pointillism**, a method of painting created by **Seurat**, which consisted of dividing shades into tiny dots of pure colour, distributed so as to intensify the effect of light.

Paul Signac, Seurat's disciple, established himself in St-Tropez in 1898 and many of his friends followed him, namely Manguin, Bonnard and Matisse.

Fauvism

Matisse and Dufy, who had settled in Nice, reacted against Impressionism and, through the use of pure and brilliant colours, juxtaposed in simplified forms and perspectives, tried to express not just the fleeting sensation evoked by the spectacle of nature but the very thoughts and emotions of the artist.

Contemporary Movements

Picasso, co-founder with Braque of Cubism – an art concerned above all with form – was in his turn seduced by

Pierre Puget (1620–94)

This native of Marseille was one of the greatest French sculptors of the 17C. He began by carving the prows of ships and later developed huge carved poops. During a journey in Italy, he developed his many talents by working as a pupil of Pietro da Cortona.

After the fall of Fouquet, his patron, he established himself away from Versailles and was appointed director of Toulon harbour by Colbert, who thought well of him. Jealousy and conspiracy soon brought him into disgrace, so he threw himself into the embellishment of Toulon.

His best-known works are the atlantes supporting the balcony of Toulon Town Hall and the *Milo of Croton*, which is exhibited in the Louvre in Paris. His Baroque style could express power, movement and pathos.

the Riviera, and lived in Vallauris in 1946, then in Cannes and finally in Mougins. **Braque** spent his last years painting in Le Cannet, while **Fernand Léger**, another Cubist painter, lived in Biot.

Port St-Tropez by Paul Signac

©Photo Scala, Florence/Musee de l'Annonciade

Pablo Picasso in his studio in Vallauris in 1957

©Underwood & Underwood/Corbis

Dunoyer de Segonzac was tireless in his portrayal of St-Tropez.

Chagall found the light and flowers of Vence a marvellous stimulus to his multicoloured dreams.

Other artists, such as **Kandinsky** in La Napoule, **Cocteau** in Menton, **Van Dongen** in Cannes, **Magnelli** in Grasse and **Nicolas de Staël** in Antibes, although not spending much time in the region, nevertheless marked their stay in an unforgettable manner.

At the same time in Nice in the 1960s a group of artists including **Arman**, **César**, Dufrêne, Hains, **Klein**, Raysse, Rotella, Spoerri, Tinguely and Villeglé formed the **Nouveau Réalisme** joined later by Niki de Saint Phalle, Deschamps and Christo. They were reacting against **Abstraction**, which was the prevailing artistic trend after the war, and experimented with new approaches to reality making use of objects found in the modern industrial and consumer world. Alongside these innovators were the members of the **Nice School**, who each sought his own vision (**Ben**, Bernar Venet, Sacha Sosno); and **Bernard Pagès** and **Claude Viallat**, who, closely linked to the theories of Conceptual Art, led to the creation of the Support-Surface in the 1970s *(for more on contemporary movements ⓒ see NICE – Musée d'Art Moderne et d'Art Contemporain)*.

LITERATURE

The fine climate and natural beauties that so appealed to artists throughout the centuries also worked their magic on writers and poets from around the world. Tobias Smollett, whose *Travels Through Italy and France* was published in 1766, was an early visitor who helped put the Riviera on the literary map. In the second half of the 19C, the area acquired its other name when French author Stephen Liégeard published his guide to the Provençal coast called *La Côte d'Azur.*

By now, the tide of visiting authors had become a flood. Some came for the sake of their health, others to escape unhappy marriages or persecution or heavy taxes, and still more for the way of life. These literary refugees include some of the art's greatest names: D H Lawrence, James Joyce, Vladimir Nabokov, Berthold Brecht, Katherine Mansfield, W B Yeats, Graham Greene, Anthony Burgess, W Somerset Maugham, Aldous Huxley, H G Wells, Ernest Hemingway, F Scott Fitzgerald, Dorothy Parker and James Thurber.

For some, the Riviera provided a comfortable place in which to write about distant places; the list of titles written along the stretch of coastline is vast. Others, such as F Scott Fitzgerald in his tragic *Tender is the Night* (1934), were inspired by the people and landscapes they found there.

Not all the writers who flocked to the Riviera were foreign, however. Jean Cocteau arrived on the Côte d'Azur at a young age, spending much of his life around Menton, while Colette lived in St Tropez for ten years in the 1920s and 1930s.

CINEMA

The Riviera's association with moving pictures is almost as long as the history of film itself. In 1895, the pioneering brothers Auguste and Louis Lumière shot several of their first works in and around their summer residence, the Villa du Clos des Plages in La Ciotat, including *L'Arrivée d'un Train en Gare de La Ciotat*

(The Arrival of a Train at La Ciotat Station), which so alarmed early audiences. The seaside town's cinematic credentials stop there; the Eden Theatre, which opened soon after, is the world's oldest surviving movie theatre.

During the early decades of the 20C, the 'seventh art' put down firm roots in the Riviera, with stars and directors alike lured by the light, the climate and the way of life. The Victorine, the area's first film studio, opened in Nice in 1919, around the same time that Hollywood was setting up shop. Its acquisition six years later by Hollywood director Rex Ingram established it as the focus of the burgeoning European film industry, with local film-makers such as Jean Cocteau, among others, setting works in the area.

The launch of an international film festival in Cannes in 1946, originally planned for 1939, served to confirm the Riviera's place in the cinematic universe and heralded a 'golden era' for film-making in the region. The following decades produced US and French classics such as Alfred Hitchcock's To Catch A Thief (1956) starring Cary Grant and Grace Kelly, while Roger Vadim's Et Dieu... créa la femme of the same year catapulted both Brigitte Bardot and the fishing port of St Tropez into the limelight.

Since the 1970s, increasing competition from other parts of Europe – particularly after the fall of Communism in eastern Europe from the late 1980s – has helped to create a more challenging era. However, the industry's leading lights still flock to Cannes each May for the festival; more than 300 of them have added their handprint and signature to the Pavement of the Stars in front of the Palais des Festivals since its inception in 1985. Nice's Victorine studio still attracts international as well as local stars: Robert de Niro in Ronin, John Travolta in Swordfish and Jean-Claude van Damme in Maximum Risk among them.

MUSIC

Though eclipsed by a starrier literary and cinematic heritage, the Riviera has a musical tradition, too. The gaboulet-tambourin, a cross between a flute and a tambourine thought to date from the 13C, is an intrinsic element of the local traditional songs and dances, in particular the farandole. On the classical side, Nice's Opera opened in 1776, and hosted many of the south's most famous concerts; the lyric society of Nice was founded in the 19C, and still organises private concerts as well as weekly open-air free concerts in the Albert 1er garden.

Cannes Film Festival

In 1939, Jean Zay, the French Minister of Fine Arts, founded the International Film Festival at Cannes. Cannes was chosen as the location due to its sunny climate. The inauguration, planned for September, was cancelled when the Second World War broke out. The real launch of the festival took place on September 20, 1946 in the former Casino Municipal near the Old Port; the festival returned to this site 40 years later at the time of the inauguration of the Nouveau Palais des Festivals in 1983.

In 1949 the festival moved to the Palais de la Croisette (demolished in 1988). In spite of its suspension in 1948 and 1950 for financial reasons and an interruption in May 1968, the fame of the festival has grown over the years, with a star-studded jury presided over by celebrities.

During the ten days of the event, several competitions take place: the Selection Officielle (competing for the prestigious **Palme d'Or**); Hors-Compétition (not in competition); Semaine de la Critique (critics' picks); Quinzaine des Réalisateurs (film directors' programme); Caméra d'Or (first films); Un Certain Regard (independent productions). The great media interest in the various ceremonies of the festival offers a unique springboard to all films, whether mainstream or fringe, and confirms its role in uncovering talent in the so-called seventh art.

Nature

TOPOGRAPHY

CONTRASTS

This is a country of contrasts:

...in coastline

Extending from Bandol to Menton, the Riviera is extremely varied (&see The Coast, p91). The sheltered inlets between the red rock promontories of the Esterel differ markedly from the great sweeping bays and flat shores which gently punctuate the coastline; while elsewhere on the coast, such as at Cap Sicié, mountains plunge steeply into the sea, sheer as a wall.

...in relief

A countryside just as varied lies inland. The fertile plains and foothills of Provence are typically Mediterranean in their vegetation but among them are barren, rugged heights like those to the north of Toulon. The mountain masses of the Maures, which rise to no more than 800m/2 600ft, are crisscrossed by valleys and ravines and covered with fine forests of cork oak and chestnut; while the Esterel, massif is dominated by the outline of Mont Vinaigre and the peaks of Pic de l'Ours and Pic du Cap Roux. The country behind Cannes and Nice is one of undulating hills stretching to the Pre-Alps of Grasse, where gorges have been cut into the plateaux and the mountain chains are split by rifts (clues), particularly in Haute-Provence.

Behind the Riviera the peaks of the Pre-Alps of Nice rise to more than 2 000m/6 560ft, while further to the north and northeast the true Alpine heights tower on the Italian border.

...in climate

There is a winter warmth on the Nice coast (the average temperatures for January in Nice are max 13°C/55°F; min 4°C/39°F) and, less than two hours away by car, the icy air of the ski slopes; the summer heat of the coast and the exhilarating coolness of the mountain resorts; the cold *mistral* wind and the burning *sirocco*; long days of drought, dried-up rivers and, suddenly, tremendous downpours and overflowing torrents.

...in vegetation

The forest of Turini, with its centuries-old beeches and firs, resmbles that of a northern land; the woods of the Maures and the Esterel are typically southern with their cork oaks and pines, periodically ravaged by forest fires. The wild scrub and underbrush of the *maquis* is far from the orderly rows of the orange and lemon groves; the lavender and thyme growing wild from the vast cultivated fields of flowers; the palm trees, agaves and cacti of the coast from the firs and larches of the highlands.

Baie de Briande, St-Tropez Peninsula

F. Baret/MICHELIN

NATURE

...in activity

The coast attracts all the activity of the area: the busiest roads, the most important towns and the best equipped resorts are concentrated there. Inland, however, there is peace and quiet, even complete solitude; sleepy little towns and old villages, perched like eagles' nests high up on the hillsides but now almost deserted (see HILL VILLAGES).

...in economy

Nice is the coast's tourist capital; Monte-Carlo, a great gambling city. The busy flower trade and the production of perfume exist side by side with new research centres dealing with oceanography and data processing.

Land of the Sun

Such a multiplicity of impressions has one common factor – the Mediterranean climate. In the Land of the Sun, the sun shines continually (2 725 hours annually in Nice compared with 1 465 hours in London).

Except in high summer, outlines are sharpened and natural features acquire an architectural aspect in the clear air. The shining blue of the sea and sky blends with the green of the forest, the silver-grey of the olive trees, the red porphyry rock and the white limestone.

TERRAIN

Provence was formed from two mountain systems: one very old – the Maures and the Esterel – the other much younger – the Provençal ranges of Pyrénéan and the Pre-Alps of Alpine origin.

The Maures

This crystalline mountain mass spreads from the River Gapeau in the west to the Argens Valley in the east, from the sea in the south to a long depression in the north, beyond which are the limestone Pre-Alps. Long low parallel ranges, covered with fine forests which have not escaped the forest fires, make up the Maures Massif; the highest point is La Sauvette (779m/ 556ft).

The Esterel

The Esterel, separated from the Maures by the lower Argens Valley, has also been eroded by time, and is therefore of low altitude. Its highest peak is Mont Vinaigre at 618m/2 027ft. The deep ravines cut into its sides and its jagged crests dispel any impression of mere hills.

The Esterel, like the Maures, was once entirely covered with forests of pine and cork oak but these have been ravaged periodically by forest fires.

Shrubs and bushes grow beneath the trees: tree heathers, arbutus, lentisks and lavender, while scrub (maquis) covers the open ground. In spring the red and white flowers of the cistus, yellow mimosa and broom, and white heather and myrtle form a brilliant floral patchwork.

Provençal Ranges

These short limestone chains, arid and rugged, rise to heights of 400–1 150m/1 200–3 500ft. Of Pyrenean origin with a highly complex structure, they do not have the continuity of those of Alpine origin such as the Southern Pre-Alps. The most southerly peaks, just north of Toulon, are the Gros Cerveau (429m/1 407ft), which is bisected by the Ollioules gorges, Mont Faron (542m/1 778ft), which dominates the town; and Le Coudon; Montagne de la Loube rises 28km/17.4mi to the north. Between the ranges are fertile valleys where the traditional crops of cereals, vines and olives are cultivated.

Maritime Alps and Mercantour

The northeast the horizon is dominated by a vast mountainous mass (altitude: 1 500–2 900m/4 922–9 515ft), which is dissected by the upper valleys of the Var, Tinée, Vésubie and Roya. On the Italian border these mountains meet the great crystalline massif, Le Mercantour, the peaks of which exceed 3 000m/9 842.5ft.

Pre-Alps

This region contains a large part of the Southern Pre-Alps. Between the River Verdon and River Var the **Pre-Alps of**

River Loup

Grasse are formed by a series of parallel east-west chains, with altitudes varying between 1 100-1 600m/3 609-5 249ft which are frequently indented by wild and narrow rifts *(clues)*.

The **Nice Pre-Alps** rise from the coast in tiers to a height of 1 000m/3 281ft, affording a wide variety of scenery inland from Nice and Menton. These ranges, which are Alpine in origin, run north-south before changing direction abruptly to finish up parallel with the coast.

Provençal Tableland

From Canjuers plateau to the Vence pass, the Pre-Alps are rimmed with a tableland of undulating limestone plateaux, similar to the *causses*, into which water infiltrates, penetrating through rifts to feed resurgent streams like the Siagne. The River Loup has carved out a very picturesque gorge.

Below lies a **depression** or "lowland" where the towns of Vence, Grasse and Draguignan are situated. Beyond the River Argens, the depression extends east down the river to Fréjus and west towards Brignoles; the main axis, however, is southwest to Toulon to the northern slopes of the Maures and Le Luc basin.

RIVERS

Mediterranean rivers are really torrents and their volume, which varies considerably from a mere trickle to a gushing flood, is governed by melting snow, rainfall and evaporation, depending on the season.

The lack of rain and the intense evaporation of the summer months reduce the rivers to little dribbles of water along their stony beds.

In spring and autumn the rains fall suddenly and violently and even the smallest streams are immediately filled with rushing water.

The flow of the Argens varies from 3-600m3/60-132 000gal a second and that of the Var from 17-5 000m3/3 790 to over a million gallons. At the height of its spate the Var is more than half a mile wide and the stain of its muddy waters can be seen in the sea as far away as Villefranche on the far side of Nice.

The water level in rivers in limestone regions is always very uneven. The rains seep into the ground through numerous fissures to reappear often a considerable distance away as large springs gushing out from the sides of valleys. Some of the springs rise in riverbeds, such as the gushers *(foux)*, which cause the River Argens to flood. Most of the rivers with torrential rates of flow transport material but the River Argens is the only one to have built up an alluvial plain comparable to those of the Languedoc coast. All the torrential rivers have created beautiful valleys, deep gorges (the Loup and the Siagne gorges) or rifts (*clues* – the Clue de Gréolières), which are among the attractions of inland Provence.

CAVES AND CHASMS

In contrast to the deeply dissected green valleys, such as the gorges of the Loup and the Siagne, the Caussols plateau (&see *ST-VALLIER-DE-THIEY*) rolls away to the far horizon, stony and deserted, a typical karst relief. The dryness of the soil is due to the calcareous nature of the rock which absorbs rain like a sponge.

Water Infiltration

Rainwater, charged with carbonic acid, dissolves the carbonate of lime to be found in the limestone. Depressions, which are usually circular in shape and small in size and are known as **cloups** or **sotchs**, are then formed. The dissolution of the limestone rocks, containing especially salt or gypsum, produces a rich soil particularly suitable for growing crops; when the *cloups* increase in size they form large, closed depressions know as **dolines**. Where rainwater infiltrates deeply through the countless fissures in the plateau, the hollowing out and dissolution of the calcareous layer produces wells or natural chasms which are called **avens**. Little by little the chasms grow, lengthen and branch off, communicating with each other and enlarging into caves.

Underground rivers

The infiltrating waters finally produce underground galleries and collect to form a more or less swiftly flowing

Le Boréon in the upper valley of Vésubie

E. Baret/MICHELIN

river. The river widens its course and often changes level, to fall in cascades. Where the rivers run slowly they form lakes, above natural dams, known as **gours**, which are raised layer by layer by deposits of carbonate of lime. The dissolution of the limestone also continues above the water-level in these subterranean galleries: blocks of stone fall from the roof and domes form, the upper parts pointing towards the surface of the earth. When the roof of the dome wears thin it may cave in, disclosing the cavity from above and opening the chasm.

THE COAST

The mainly rocky coastline reflects the different types of mountain and plateau to be found inland emerging as cliffs and rocks where they meet the sea.

The Toulon Coast

This highly indented section of the coast provides well-sheltered harbours, Bandol and Sanary bays and the outstanding Toulon port. The stretches of almost vertical cliffs are interrupted by some fine beaches.

The Maures Coast

Between Hyères and St-Raphaël, the Maures Massif meets the sea and the coastal scenery

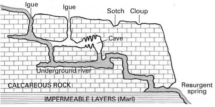

Development of a resurgent spring

offers charming sites and enchanting views.

The Giens Peninsula, formerly an island, is now joined to the mainland by two sandy isthmuses. Nearby are the Hyères islands, densely covered with vegetation, and the Fréjus plain, once a wide bay but now filled by alluvial deposits brought down by the Argens. Characteristic also of this particular section of the coast are great promontories such as Cap Bénat and the St-Tropez Peninsula, narrow tongues of land such as Cap Nègre and Cap des Sardinaux and wide bays like the Bormes harbour and the gulf of St-Tropez.

The Esterel Coast

The red porphyry rocks of the Esterel Massif, steep and rugged, make a striking contrast with the blue of the sea. Along this stretch of coast the mountains thrust great promontories into the sea, between inlets *(calanques)* and small bays. Offshore, the surface of the sea is scattered with thousands of rocks and small, green moss-covered islets, and submerged reefs can be seen beneath the clear water. The Corniche d'Or (*see Massif de l'ESTEREL*) is reputed internationally for its breathtaking scenery, superb viewpoints and resorts.

The Antibes Coast

The vista changes once again between Cannes and Nice. The shore is no longer eaten away by the sea; it is flat and opens into wide bays. It is a smooth, unbroken coast on which the Cap d'Antibes peninsula is the sole promontory.

The Riviera Proper

From Nice to Menton the Alps plunge abruptly into the sea. Here the coastline forms a natural terrace, facing the Mediterranean but isolated from its hinterland. Cap Ferrat and Cap Martin are the two main promontories along this stretch of coast. The term Riviera, which has already passed into the language of geography, is applied to this type of coast line. A triple roadway has been cut over the steep slopes, lined with villas and terraced gardens.

THE MEDITERRANEAN SEA

The Mediterranean is Europe's bluest sea. The shade – cobalt blue to artists – comes from the clarity of the water. Visitors soon realise that the colour often changes depending on the nature of the sky, the light, the seabed and the depth of water so that at times the "blue Mediterranean" is opal or a warm grey.

The water

The temperature of the water, governed on the surface by the sun's heat, is constant (13°C/55.4°F) from 200–4 000m/650–13 000ft downwards, whereas in the Atlantic it drops from 14–2°C/57.2–35°F. This is an important factor in the climate, for the sea cools the air in summer and warms it in winter. Rapid evaporation makes the water noticeably more salty than that of the Atlantic. The waves are small, short and choppy; storms come and go quickly.

The Tides

Tides are almost non-existent (about 25cm/10in). Sometimes when the wind is very strong the tide may reach as much as 1m/3ft. These figures are markedly different from the tides of the Atlantic or from the tides of 13–15m/40–50ft round Mont-St-Michel off the Normandy coast. This relative tidal stability has resulted in the Mediterranean being chosen as the base level for all French altitudes.

The Provençal coastline drops sharply into water that becomes relatively deep a short distance from the shore. Between Nice and Cap Ferrat soundings indicate a depth of 1 000m/3 281ft about half a mile out.

THE SEASONS

A superb climate

Crowds come flocking in summer and the tourist season lasts almost the whole year.

The Côte d'Azur is one of the most inviting names in the world! Properly speaking, the name Riviera applies to the French coast between Nice and Menton and to the Italian coast between Ventimiglia and Genoa. English visitors, at first for the sake of health but later more and more in search of pleasure, were attracted to the Riviera (especially Nice) in the 18C. The Côte d'Azur (Bandol to Menton) has become widely known as the French Riviera.

Winter
The proverbial mildness of the French Riviera is due to a number of factors: a low latitude, the presence of the sea, which moderates temperature variations, a wholly southern aspect, and the screen of hills and mountains, which protects it from cold winds. The average temperature for January in Nice is 8°C/46°F. Icy winds blow from the east and from the southeast bringing rain. Fog and sea-mists appear only on the coast in the height of summer, and harsh winters with ice and snow are rare.

The thermometer may rise to 22°C/72°F but at sunset and during the night the temperature drops suddenly and considerably. There is little rainfall; it is the dew that keeps the vegetation fresh. The hinterland is cold and often snow-covered but the air is limpid and the sun brilliant – an ideal climate for winter sports.

Spring
Short but violent showers are characteristic of springtime on the Riviera. This is when the flowers are at their best and a joy to look at. The only drawback is the *mistral*, which blows most frequently at this season, especially west of Toulon. The mountains, however, act as a buffer and the wind is never as intense as it can be in western Provence and the Rhône Valley.

The Romans made a dreaded god of this fearsome wind. It comes from the northwest in cold gusts; after several days this powerful blast of clean air has purified everything and the wind-swept sky is bluer than ever.

Summer
The coast offers an average temperature of 26°C/79°F throughout July and August. The heat, however, is bearable because it is tempered by the fresh breeze that blows during the daytime. This is not the season for flowers: over-

whelmed by drought the vegetation seems to sleep. When the hot breath of the *sirocco* comes out of the south everyone grumbles.

The hinterland offers a wide variety of places to stay at varying altitudes up to 1 800m/5 905ft; the higher one climbs the more invigorating the air.

Autumn
There are plenty of perfect days during the Mediterranean autumn, punctuated by violent storms after which the sun reappears, brilliant and warm. In the whole year, there is an average of only 86 days of rain in Nice (150 in London), but the quantity of water which falls is higher (863mm/34in in Nice against under 609mm/24in in London).

FLORA AND FAUNA
Plants and trees do not grow in the same way on the Riviera as they do further north. New shoots appear, as they do elsewhere, in the spring but a second growth begins in the autumn and continues throughout most of the winter. The dormant period is during the summer when the hot, dry climate favours only those plants that are especially adapted to resist drought. These have long tap roots, glossy leaves which reduce transpiration, bulbs acting as reservoirs of moisture and perfumes which they release to form a kind of protective vapor.

TREES
Olive Trees
2 500 years ago, the Greeks brought olive trees to Provence where they grow equally well in limestone or sandy soils. The olive has been called the immortal tree for, grafted or wild, it will always grow from the same stock. Those grown from cuttings die relatively young, at about 300 years old. Along the coast, the trees reach gigantic dimensions, attaining 20m/65.6ft in height, their domes of silver foliage 20m/65.6ft in circumference and trunks 4m/13ft round the base. The olive tree, which has more than 60 varieties, is found up to an altitude of 600m/1 968.5ft and marks the

Umbrella pines of Porquerolles

limit of the Mediterranean climate. It grows mainly on valley floors and on hillsides. The trees begin to bear fruit between their sixth and twelfth year and are in full yield at 20 or 25. The olives are harvested every two years. Olive groves are numerous in the areas around Draguignan, Sospel and at Breil, in the Roya Valley.

Oak Trees

The oaks native to the Mediterranean region are evergreen. The durmast and holm oaks grow in chalky soil at altitudes below 800m/2 624.5ft. As scrub-oaks, they are a characteristic feature of the *garrigue* (rocky, limestone moors). In its fully developed state the holm oak is a tree with a short thick-set trunk covered in grey-black bark and with a dense, rounded crown. The cork oak is distinguished by its large dark-coloured acorns and its rough bark. Every eight to twelve years the thick cork bark is stripped off, exposing a reddish brown trunk.

Pine Trees

The three types of pine to be found in the Mediterranean region have unmistakable silhouettes.
The maritime pine, which grows only on limestone soil, has dark, blue-tinged green needles and deep red bark.

The **umbrella pine** is typically Mediterranean and owes its name to its easily recognisable outline. It is often found growing alone.

The **Aleppo pine** is a Mediterranean species that thrives on chalky soil along the coast; it has a twisted, grey trunk and lighter, less dense, foliage.

Other Provençal Trees – The smooth-trunked **plane tree** and the **lotus tree** shade the courtyards, streets and squares and also line the roads.

The dark silhouette of the coniferous, evergreen **cypress** is a common feature of the countryside; planted in rows, the pyramidal cypress forms an effective windbreak.

The common **almond tree**, a member of the Rosaceae, is widespread in Provence and blossoms early. The robust **chestnut** flourishes in the Maures Massif. Certain mountain species of **fir** and **larch** are to be found in the Alps; the forest of Turini is a fine fir-growing region.

Exotic Trees

In parks and gardens and along the roads stand magnificent **eucalyptus trees**. This hardy specimen is particularly suited to the climate. In winter another Australian import, **mimosa**, covers the slopes of the Tanneron Massif with a yellow mantle.

The greatest concentration of **palm trees** is to be found in the Hyères district. The two types most common to the Riviera are the date palm with its smooth, tall trunk sweeping upwards and the Canary palm which is much shorter and has a rough, scaly trunk. **Orange** and **lemon groves** flourish on the coastal stretches between Cannes and Antibes, and Monaco and Menton.

BUSHES AND SHRUBS

The **kermes oak** is a bushy evergreen shrub, which rarely grows more than 1m/3.3ft in height. Its name comes from the kermes, an insect halfway between a cochineal fly and a flea, which lives throughout its existence attached to the stems of the oak.

The **lentisk** is an evergreen shrub with paired leaves on either side of the main stem and no terminal leaf. The fruit is a small globular berry, which turns from red to black when it is mature.

The **pistachio** is a deciduous shrub which can grow to a height of 4–5m/ 13–16.4ft. The leaves grow in groups of five to eleven, one of which is terminal. The fruit is a very small berry, red at first, ripening to brown.

The Mediterranean **thistle** is a perennial, which attains a height of 1m/3.3ft. The irregular pointed leaves are bright green on top and covered with white down on the underside.

The Garrigue

Some of the limestone areas are so stony (Vence pass road and D 955 from Draguignan to Montferrat) that even thorns (kermes oak, gorse and thistle) and aromatic plants (thyme, lavender and rosemary) can survive only here and there in between the bare rocks; this is the *garrigue*.

The Maquis

Scrub *(maquis)* thrives on sandy soil and forms a thick carpet of greenery, which is often impenetrable. In May and June when the cistus is in flower it is a marvellous spectacle, especially in the coverts of the Esterel.

Lavandin

Lavandin is a hybrid plant resulting from the cross of true lavender with spike lavender. Its flowers may be blue, like true lavender or grey, like aspic. The plants are used for landscaping but they also produce oil of an excellent quality. In France, lavandin has been grown in Provence on a large scale for many years. Thanks to its camphoraceous smell with strong eucalyptus overtones, it is often used to scent soaps and detergents.

SUCCULENTS

Some varieties of succulents are African in character: Barbary figs, agaves, cacti and aloes grow in open ground. Ficoids with large pink and white flowers cling to old walls. The **aloe** has thick and fleshy leaves, from which a bitter juice is extracted for medicinal use.

The **Barbary fig** is an unusual plant from Central America, which grows in arid soil in hot climates; its broad, thick, fleshy leaves bristle with spines. The Moroccans call it the Christian fig; it is also known as the "prickly pear".

For a wider knowledge of exotic flora, take a stroll in:
♦ *Jardin Exotique in Monaco*
♦ *Jardin de la Villa Thuret in Cap d'Antibes (see ANTIBES)*
♦ *Several botanic gardens in Menton*
♦ *Domaine du Rayol (including Val Rameh, see CAVALAIRE)*
♦ *Jardin Olbius Riquier in Hyères*

FOREST FIRES

From time immemorial the scourge of the Provençal woodland, especially in the Maures and the Esterel, has been the forest fire, which causes more damage than deforestation by man, now carefully monitored, and destruction by goats which live on the tender young shoots. During the summer the dried-up plants of the underbrush, pine needles, resins exuded by leaves and twigs are highly combustible and sometimes catch fire spontaneously. Once started,

The Three Musketeers of the "Silent World"

In August 1937, two young divers with homemade equipment based on recycled tubes, attempted to beat a harpooning record. In the absence of any substantial booty, J Y Cousteau and P Taillez found that their dive in the midst of shoals of grouper and bass revealed the potential of underwater exploration.

A third leading harpoonist, J Dumas, soon joined them and the hunt for pictures superseded the hunt for sea-bass. In the autumn of 1943, Dumas, experimenting with an aqualung, dived to a depth of 62m/203ft and was affected by nitrogen narcosis (rapture of the deep). After the Second World War the underwater explorers' odyssey was immortalised on film and their craft, *Calypso*, was seen all around the world.

a fire may spread to the pines with disastrous results in a strong wind. Great walls of flame, sometimes 10km/6mi in length and 30m/100ft high, spread at speeds of 5-6km/2-3mi per hour. When the fire has passed, nothing remains standing except the blackened skeletons of trees while a thick layer of white ash covers the ground.

The Riviera still bears the scars of the particularly severe forest fires that raged during the summer of 2003, fueled by the worst drought and heatwave in 15 years, and it will be many years before regeneration of its natural habitat is complete.

Preventive measures include the removal of undergrowth near residential areas, creation of fire-breaks and the appointment of fire-watchers and patrols. Active

intervention is provided by the fire brigade and the airborne water carriers based in Marignane. In the event of a major fire risk, the ALARME plan enables access roads to private homes to be cleared for firefighters and limits the movements of walkers.

For information on the closures in forests, there is a recorded message service (*04 94 47 35 45*) for the use of hikers.

MEDITERRANEAN MARINE LIFE

Life in the Mediterranean Sea resembles a house full of animal tenants with astonishing characteristics living one above the other. During an underwater dive, the following species may be observed.

Cacti in the Jardin Exotique, Èze

Brown Grouper

Depending on its age and size, the grouper is first female, then male. It changes sex at about nine years old when it weighs 10kg/22lb. Since the fish can live for about 50 years, it spends most of its life as a male.

The young female grouper lives on rocky seabeds in shallow water (less than 10m/33ft deep), which makes it an easy prey for underwater hunters and other predators. As it reaches adulthood it makes its home in holes in the rocks at a depth of at least 50m/164ft, where it lives as a formidable carnivore at the extremity of the marine food chain. It may eventually reach a length of 1.2m/4ft and weigh 30–40kg/66–88lb. This fish, which had become very rare in the Mediterranean, has benefited from a 5-year moratorium prohibiting the catching of groupers.

The Parc Naturel de Port-Cros is now designated to protect the grouper within an area around the island.

Jellyfish

Jellyfish, which appear seasonally in coastal waters, sometimes cause problems for holidaymakers. The most common species, **pelagia**, can sting with its mouth, tentacles and umbrella. The poison, which is intended to immobilise prey, is powerful enough to cause redness and burning of the skin. The population of pelagia follows a 12-year cycle, depending on climatic conditions, and their arrival is usually preceded by a very dry spring. Another species of jellyfish, the Portuguese Man-of-War, has long tentacles (up to 10m/33ft), which are invisible to swimmers and have a very powerful sting. They are fortunately rare in the Mediterranean.

Posidonia

This flowering plant, which has bunches of long dark-green leaves, plays an essential role in the Mediterranean environment. Its rhizomes grow slowly, thus allowing it to fix the sediments from the coast and create a habitat rich in oxygen and favourable to many animal species.

Pelagia noctiluca

©Planctonvideo/Dreamstime.com

When the posidonia dies, these animal species either die out or migrate.

A dive into the colourful world of the posidonia provides the possibility of seeing many amazing species. The **sea cucumber**, also known as holothurian, is the dustbin of the sandy seabed and lives only in the posidonia. The **sea-slug**, found all over the Mediterranean, is a white mollusc with brown spots, which contrasts with the red sponges. The **striped weever fish** lives on the seabed near the posidonia, buried in the sand with just its head visible. It has a very poisonous dorsal fin, the sting of which can be serious. The **sea-horse** likes to hide near its relative, the **pipe-fish**, whose amazing threadlike form, with trumpet-shaped mouth, mimics the leaves of the posidonia among which it lives.

In the last few decades harbour works and construction along the coast have caused much sedimentation and the resultant pollution is endangering the fragile habitat. Since 1989, a genetically altered strain of algae, the non-toxic **taxifolia**, has spread rapidly along the French Riviera. It is feared that the spread of this alga, originally created to decorate aquariums, may be harmful to the posidonia as well as other marine life in the Mediterranean, although experts still haven't agreed on the best way to eradicate the alien species.

Roquebrune-Cap-Martin
David Noble/Pictures Colour Library

TOULON AND AROUND

The city of Toulon, and the smaller villages which surround it on the western border of the French Riviera, are often overlooked by travellers who pass through on their way to Provence. But this dynamic region has done much to restore its image over the past decade, and offers pleasant surprises throughout the year to curious visitors who take the time to explore its mountain views, charming seaside resorts, and historic naval harbour.

Highlights

1 Visit the famous harbour of **Toulon**, home of the French navy since the 16C (p121)

2 Take in the spectacular views from the top of **Mont Faron** (p120)

3 Explore the Gallo-Roman villa at the **Musée de Tauroentum** (p107)

4 Go for a wine tasting in the prestigious **Bandol Vineyards** (p102)

5 Snorkel in the blue waters off the **Îles des Embiez** (p110)

The Largest Naval Base in France

As the third largest city in the Provence-Alpes-Côte-d'Azur region (after Nice to the east and Marseilles to the west), Toulon and its immense harbour have sustained the local economy since the Middle Ages. Aside from being one of the major commercial shipping ports in the Mediterranean, it has also served as a defensive port for Provence, a departure point for maritime exploration, a renowned centre for ship-building and fishing, and today houses the French military in the largest naval base in France. While traditionally not considered a tourist destination, the city has restored much of its old town and public areas of the port used for local sightseeing cruises.

Resort Towns

The arrival of the railway in the mid-1800s ended much of the maritime passenger traffic, but brought the seasonal tourism that would rejuvenate sleepy fishing villages such as Bandol, Six-Fours-les-Plages, and Ile des Embiez. Not just popular with French tourists seeking vacation homes, it was also a popular region for writers, filmmakers and artists such as Thomas Mann, Katherine Mansfield, Aldous Huxley and Marcel Pagnol.

Marine explorers Philippe Tailliez, Jacques-Yves Cousteau and Frédéric Dumas perfected their scuba-diving equipment in the waters off Bandol, Sanary, and Embiez.

Today these resorts are carefully monitored to protect local flora and fauna, with botanical coastal trails and thriving marine preserves.

Toulon naval harbour

Bandol vineards in Le Castellet with a view to the perched village

©David Noble/Pictures Colour Library

The Mountains

Toulon and the coastal towns are dominated by the towering Mont Faron, Le Gros Cerveau, and Mont Caume. Steep and winding roads lead up to the rocky peaks where you can enjoy panoramic views over Toulon and the entire Mediterranean. Those avoiding the vertiginous drive take the cable car from Toulon to the top of Mont Faron, topped by a monument commemorating the 1944 Allied landings in Provence. One of the more charming perched villages in this area is Le Castelet, which offers views over the Bandol vineyards from its historic ramparts.

The Climate

Toulon has the warmest temperatures in metropolitan France, averaging 8.8°C/48°F in winter; however, though the *mistral* winds make it seem cooler when they blow with legendary ferocity. Sunny days predominate, with short but heavy rainfall in early spring and late autumn. The relatively mild climate and sheltered inlets in the resorts make it a popular destination year round. This climate also helps produce one of the most prestigious appellations of Côte de Provence, the strong red wines of Bandol, which can be tasted in many of the cellars and wine shops in the region.

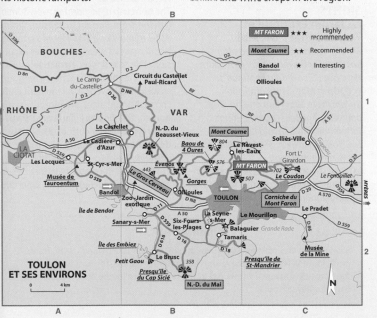

Bandol★

Var

Bandol is a pleasant resort lying inside a pretty bay, sheltered from the north winds by high wooded slopes. It has always been a popular holiday destination among artists and literary celebrities.

RESORT LIFE
The Marina
Enjoy the bracing sea air by following the **Allée Jean-Moulin**★ and Allée Alfred-Vivien along the port, both bordered with pines, palms and flower beds.

The Beaches
This seaside resort has four sandy beaches: the east-facing Lido, the well-sheltered Rènecros facing west and the Centrale and Casino beaches facing due south.
The rest of the coast (towards ST-CYR-SUR-MER) offers smaller beaches alternating with rocky areas.
Chemin de la Corniche skirts the little peninsula with Bendor Island lying off shore, affording a fine view of the coast from Cap de l'Aigle to Cap Sicié.

SIGHTS
Jardin Exotique et Zoo de Sanary-Bandol
3km/2mi north; 500m/550yd after passing over the motorway (A50), turn right (sign "Zoo-Jardin Exotique").
Open May–Sept 8am–noon, 2–7pm (from 10am Sun and holidays; open Oct–Apr 8am–noon, 2–6pm (afternoon only Sun and holidays). 8.50€ (child 6€). ℘04 94 29 40 38. www.zoosanary.com.
In these shaded gardens cacti and tropical plants are grown to remarkable sizes. Among hundreds of rare plants, animals

- **Population:** 8 647.
- **Michelin Map:** 340 J7.
- **Info:** Allée Alfre-Vivien. ℘04 94 29 41 35. www.bandol.fr.
- **Location:** Accessible by the A 50, the resort town of Bandol lies 18km/11mi west of Toulon.
- **Timing:** Allow a full day for a stroll around the port, visits to the exotic gardens and zoo, and a drive through the perched villages. An excursion to Bendor Island takes about 45 minutes, or a half day for a swim at the beach.
- **Kids:** The zoo and exotic gardens are particularly child friendly.

from all over the world can be seen – monkeys, coatis, lemurs, peccaries, deer, ponies, miniature goats and llamas. You can also observe the colourful parrots, peacocks, pink flamingoes and cranes.

Île de Bendor
The **boat trip** (*departures every 30min leaving from Bandol in season, 7min; 8€ round trip; ℘04 94 29 44 34*) to the island makes a pleasant summer excursion. The island is an attractive tourist centre offering fine beaches, a harbour, as well as a Provençal village with craft shops. Named after the famous *pastis* maker, the **Espace Culturel Paul-Ricard** features a curious **Exhibition des Vins et Spiritueux** (*no charge; ℘04 94 29 44 34; www.euvs.org*). Set up in a large hall decorated with frescoes, it covers the production of wine, aperitifs

---

Bandol AOC

Beyond the villas scattered in groves of pine and mimosa behind the seafront are fields of flowers and vineyards which produce Bandol, the best-known of the Côtes-de-Provence wines. Ask at the tourist office for the brochure detailing Bandol vineyard tours.

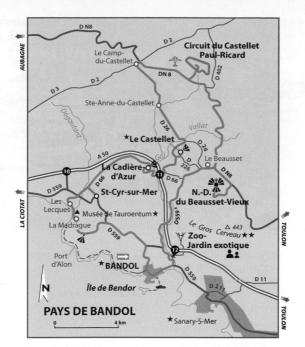

PAYS DE BANDOL

and liqueurs in 51 different countries, with 8 000 bottles on display.

🚗 DRIVING TOUR

Perched Villages★
Round trip of 55km/29mi –
allow a half day.

▷ *From Bandol take D 559 northeast;*
go left on D 559B towards Le Beausset.

Just after Le Beausset (where you should stop on market days), turn right on N 8 towards Toulon. The narrow road winds its way through olive groves, orchards and vineyards.

Chapelle Notre-Dame-du-Beausset-Vieux
Leave the car below the chapel. 🕐*Open 2–6pm (until 7pm in summer, 5pm in winter).* 📞*04 94 98 61 53.*
This stark Provençal Romanesque chapel with barrel vaulting in the nave and oven vaulting in the apse has been restored by volunteers. The Virgin and Child in the choir comes from Pierre Puget's

studio. In the left niche a group of 400-year-old **santons** illustrates the Flight to Egypt. Some of the votive offerings *(side aisle)* date back to the 18C.
From the terrace above the chapel a **sweeping panorama**★ takes in Le Castellet, Ste-Baume, Gros Cerveau and the coast from Bandol westwards to La Ciotat.

▷ *Return to N 8 and continue north towards Aubagne.*

Circuit du Castellet Paul-Ricard
▷ *8km/5mi north of Beausset by N 8.*

This track (6km/3.7mi long) was officially opened in 1970 on the occasion of the first Grand Prix de France, won by Jacky Stewart. Since then, many international F1 and F3 drivers, such as Alain Prost in 1976, have attended the driving school on the circuit.
Popular events include the **Grand Prix Historique de Provence**, the **Deux Tours d'Horloge** (shows and races for vintage cars in April), and the colourful truck show, the **Grand Prix International de Camions**.

Port of Bandol

▷ *On leaving the circuit, turn left on RN 8 towards Aubagne. At Camp-du-Castellet crossroads, turn left and left again on D 26, then right on D 226 towards Le Castellet.*

Le Castellet★

Nestled on a woody hill dominating the vineyards, this remarkable stronghold has well-preserved ramparts, a carefully restored 12C church and a castle, parts of which date back to the 11C. From beyond the gate on Place de la Mairie there is an attractive **view** inland towards Ste-Baume. Many houses were originally built in the 17C and 18C. There are art and craft workshops – painting, pottery, weaving and leatherwork.

▷ *Leave Le Castellet going downhill towards D 66.*

La Cadière-d'Azur

This very old hill town produces Bandol wine. Some of its former defences are still standing. The 13C Peï Gate, in front of the town hall leads to a maze of picturesque old streets. From the eastern end of the village there is a fine **view**★ inland over Le Castellet to Ste-Baume.

▷ *Follow D 66 to St-Cyr-sur-Mer.*

St-Cyr-sur-Mer – *see ST-CYR-SUR-MER.*

▷ *Follow the D559 back to Bandol.*

ADDRESSES

🏠 STAY

🛏 **Golf Hôtel** – *10 Corniche Bonaparte, on Rénecros Beach by Bd. Louis-Lumière. ✆04 94 29 45 83. www.golfhotel.fr. Closed Nov–Feb. 24 rooms.* 👪 📅 . 🍴8.50€. *Restaurant* 🛏🛏. A seaside hotel, complete with deckchairs and beach restaurant in summer. Most of the cosy rooms give onto the sea; some are fronted by a small balcony. Dinner served only in July and August.

🛏🛏 **Auberge La Cauquière** – *Puits d'Isnard, Le Beausset. ✆04 94 98 42 75. www.lacauquiere.com. 10 rooms.* 📅 🍴6€. *Restaurant* 🛏🛏. A charming inn with garden and swimming pool in the centre of Le Bausset. Just ten minutes by car from the beaches and Route des Vins de Bandol. Rooms are arranged around a cosy courtyard.

🛏🛏 **Chambre d'Hôte Les Cancades** – *1195 Chemin de la Fontaine de Cinq-Sous, Le Beausset. 3km/2mi E of Le Castellet, take Chemin de la Fontaine de Cinq-Sous (across from Casino supermarket). ✆04 94 98 76 93. www.les-cancades.com. 4 rooms.* 🍴 🍴. A steep, narrow path leads to the wooded, residential area and this charming Provençal mas. The fine, handsomely furnished rooms, park, swimming pool and summer kitchen are all blissfully quiet and relaxing.

⍩ EAT

🍽 **Snack Bar Le Souco** – *1 Rue de la Poste, Le Castellet. ☎04 94 32 67 94.* 🗐. This café-restaurant frequented by the locals is open year round. Terraces at the front and back.

🍽🍷 **L'Oasis** – *15 Rue des Écoles. ☎04 94 29 41 69. www.oasisbandol.com. Closed Dec, Sun eve off season.* Delightful dining room painted in warm Mediterranean tones. In summer, enjoy the charming terrace looking out onto the garden. Smallish but impeccably kept rooms are available for overnight stays.

🍽🍷 **Le Clocher** – *1 Rue Paroisse. ☎04 94 32 47 65. Closed Wed.* In an ancient stone house at the foot of the church belltower in Vieux Bandol, this tiny restaurant serves typical regional dishes of the Midi. Small terrace on the street.

☞ ON THE TOWN

Tchin Tchin – *11 Allée Jean-Moulin. ☎04 94 29 41 04. www.tchintchin.fr.* This prestigious bar saw its golden age in the 1970s, when it attracted many celebrities from the entertainment world, namely Jacques Brel and Richard Antony, who coined the title of the club. A good selection of cocktails and regular jazz concerts.

Casino de Bandol – *2 Pl. Lucien-Artaud. ☎04 94 29 31 31. www.partouche.com.* Not only does this casino have 120 slot machines, a traditional gaming room and a piano bar, it's also a popular Place in the region for its nightclub and special events.

⍩ SHOPPING

Beausset Market – Friday and Sunday in the centre of town: fresh produce, gourmet specialities, flowers, local crafts and clothing.

Le Tonneau de Bacchus – *296 Avenue du 11-Novembre. ☎04 94 29 01 01. www. tonneau-de-bacchus.com. Closed Mon.* This cellar offers a wide selection of wines from France and especially the Bandol area. The cellarman is extremely knowledgeable about wine and he will be delighted to introduce you to the vintage bottles. Regular oenology courses and thematic evenings. Fine gastronomic specialities from Provence are also on sale.

Domaine de Souviou – *RN 8, Le Beausset. ☎04 94 90 57 63. www.souviou.com. Closed Sun from Oct–Easter.* Producer and seller of both wine and olive oil. Tastings and tours of the ancient farm available.

Miellerie de l'Oratoire – *Rte. des Oratoires, 987 Quartier de l'Estagnol, Ste-Annedu-Castelet. ☎04 94 32 65 78. www.miel2lor.com.* Virginie and Olivier love to share all they know about beekeeping and honey. heir boutique offers fresh honey and pollen products, soaps, candles, candies and spice bread.

Moulin de St-Côme – *D 266 between St-Cyr and Bandol, Quartier St-Côme, La Cadière-d'Azur. ☎04 94 90 11 51. www.moulinstcome.com. Closed Sun.* Free visit to the mill and olive oil tastings. The boutique has olive oils from France and elsewhere, soaps, perfumes, pottery, fabrics, and Provençal specialities.

OUTDOOR ACTIVITIES

Bandol is classified as a *station nautique*, with a diverse offering of water sports and a renowned diving centre on the Ile de Bandol. ▯*Ask for more information at the tourist office or visit www.france-nautisme.com.*

👥 **Aquascope** – *608 chemin du Grand, If. ☎06 03 44 59 63 (high season). Closed Oct–Apr, Mon.* ☜*15€ (child 8€).* Thirty-minute tours on a boat with transparent hull for underwater observation of marine flora and fauna.

EVENTS

Fête du Millésime – *☎04 94 90 29 59. www.vinsdebandol.com.* A wine and gourmet food festival at the Port the first Sunday in December.

Circuit du Castellet Paul-Ricard – historic car races, every April.

Le Pradet

Var

This charming resort nestling below the Massif de la Colle Noire has a good selection of small, easily accessible beaches tucked between the rocky outcrops. Its minerology museum and botanical trail make this a pleasant excursion from Toulon.

> **Population:** 10 603.
> **Michelin Map:** 340 L7; local map: *see NICE.*
> **Info:** Pl. Général-de-Gaulle. 𝒫04 94 21 71 69. www.ot-lepradet.fr.
> **Location:** Pradet sits on the eastern edge of Toulon, at the foot of the Colline de Paradis and Mont des Oiseaux, on route D 559.

RESORT LIFE

Beaches

La Garonne Bay is punctuated by several attractive creeks. Some are accessible by car, but the best way to explore them is to take the coastal walking path which can be followed between each beach accessible by road.

Coastal Footpath★

7km/4.2mi. Allow at least 3hr.
🔼 *The winding path is very steep in places. Access to the beaches is often by steep steps cut out of the rock. The route signposted in yellow runs from the car park at the lovely Crique du Pin de Galle to Bau Rouge.*

The steep slope above **Pin de Galle** beach offers magnificent views over Toulon harbour. The numerous cabins in the pine wood add to the bucolic charm of the setting. The shaded path joins the road through the park before descending steeply to **Monaco Beach**. At the end of this beach, part of which is used by nudists, the path begins beyond a low wall and climbs a cliff covered by superb *maquis* vegetation.

A little further on there is a lovely **view**★ of the inlets along the coast. A well-marked path goes down to **Les Bonnettes Beach** at the foot of a remarkable rocky inlet. In season there is a lifeguards' post and an open-air café here. The path then links **La Garonne Beach** with **Les Oursinières Beach**. Beyond Oursinières Port a footpath to the right leaves the road to Le Pradet. It leads past panoramic viewpoints on the cliffs to **Bau Rouge**.

SIGHTS

👥 Musée de la Mine de Cap-Garonne★

In Le Pradet take D 86 south towards Plage de la Garonne. After the beach, take the road which climbs to the left, signposted "La Mine".
♿ 👥 *Guided tours (1hr) 2–5pm.* 🕐 *Closed 1 Jan, 24–25, 31 Dec.* 👜 *6.20€ (child 3.80€). 𝒫04 94 08 32 46. www.mine-capgaronne.fr.*

Botanical Walking Trail

Situated at the heart of the town, the **Bois de Courbebaisse** (5ha/124 acres) is a pleasant way to discover local botanical species.

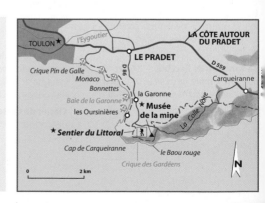

Wearing a hardhat, visitors get to explore the old copper ore mines used here since the 16C. It went on until 1917, when the reduction in copper content of the ore no longer produced a profit. The tour focuses on the redeveloped part of the galleries and, through several reconstructions and presentations, illustrates the long-standing evolution of working methods and the daily lives of miners at Cap Garonne. At the end of the tour, in a **great hall**★, there are tables with magnifying glasses showing the various colours of copper ore.

Saint-Cyr-sur-Mer

Var

This seaside resort lies in a sheltered harbour with beaches of fine sand bordering fertile plains of grapevines and olive trees. Popular for its mild climate, St-Cyr-sur-Mer is home to the only surviving Roman villa on the Mediterranean coast.

- ▶ **Population:** 8 898.
- ⏱ **Michelin Map:** 340 J6.
- ⓘ **Info:** Pl. de l'Appel-du-18-Juin. ℘04 94 26 73 73. www.saintcyrsurmer.com.
- ▶ **Location:** Located 6km/3.7mi northwest of Bandol. A long avenue of residential buildings leads to the coastline, with the Port de Lecques to the west, and Port de Madrague to the east.

SIGHTS
Musée de Tauroentum★

131 Rte de La Madrague, in the direction of Port de Lecques. ⏱*Open Wed–Mon Jun–Sept 3–7pm; Oct–Mar Sat–Sun and school holidays 2–5pm; Apr–May Thu–Sun 2–5pm.* ⬅*3€.* ℘*04 94 26 30 46.* The museum is built on the foundations of a Roman villa, featuring wreathed columns with Corinthian capitals from the villa's peristyle and a granite column from a pergola that adorned the seafront. The museum also contains 1C mosaics, fragments of frescoes and amphora.Behind the museum a path leads to a pottery kiln and remains of houses bearing traces of frescoes.

Centre d'Art Sébastien

12 Bd. Jean-Jaurès. ⏱*Open Wed–Mon Jun–Sept 9am–noon, 3–7pm; Oct–May 9am–noon, 2–6pm.* ⏱*Closed public holidays.* ⬅*1€.* ℘*04 94 26 19 20.* Set up in a former factory in 1993, this arts centre hosts temporary exhibitions and a permanent collection of works by the artist Sébastien (1909–90), who was friends with Picasso, Matisse, and Jean Cocteau.

Mosaics in Musée de Tauroentum

E. Baret / MICHELIN

EXCURSION
The Coastal Path

Take D 87 from St-Cyr to la Madrague. The path starts at Pointe Grenier. 🚶*4.5km/3mi to port d'Alon (yellow trail markers) or 6km/3.7mi to Bandol. The walk is not a difficult one, but wear sturdy shoes and bring drinking water.* 👶*Be careful with children as there are some dangerous drop-offs.*
This path from la Madrague to Bandol offers hikers an opportunity to enjoy a view of the sea from far above. At the peak of Pointe Grenier is a Napoleon III military battery and chapel. On the inland side you can look over vineyards and if you are a fan of flora, you may sight a local species of violet or mushroom.

ADDRESSES

🛏 STAY

🍽 **Le Petit Nice** – *Les Lecques.* 🕿*04 94 32 00 64. www.hotelpetitnice.com. Closed 15 Nov–15 Mar. 31 rooms.* 🅿. 🍴*8.50€.* The calm and beautiful garden makes this a pleasing stay. Small rooms with contemporary decor; those of the annexe are simpler but more roomy. The bay windows of the restaurant open onto the swimming pool and greenery.

🍽🍽🍽 **Grand Hôtel des Lecques** – *Les Lecques.* 🅿 🕿*04 94 26 23 01. www.grand-hotel-lecques-st-cyr-mer. cote.azur.fr. Closed 16 Nov–22 Mar. 58 rooms.* 🍴. *Restaurant🍽🍽🍽.* The paths cutting across the luxuriant park surrounding this hotel are bordered with palms, pine trees and morning glory. A most appealing setting for the formidable 19C mansion. Cheerful rooms appointed in Provençal tradition. Outdoor pool.

🛍 SHOPPING

Markets – Traditional market held on Sunday mornings; regional specialities at La Madrague Port (Mon and Thu mornings), on Place Gabriel-Péri (Tue and Fri mornings) and at Les Lecques (Wed and Sat mornings).

🏃 SPORT AND LEISURE

Beaches – 2km/1mi of sandy beaches line the semicircular bay running from Les Lecques to La Madrague. Further west *(10min by car)* the **Calanque de Port-d'Alon**, nestling in a pine forest, affords greater privacy.

Port de la Madrague – *Port authority.* 🕿*04 94 26 39 81.* 400 moorings including 37 set aside for tourist traffic.

Golf de Frégate – *D 559, Route de Bandol.* 🕿*04 94 29 38 00. www.fregate. dolce.com.* Beautiful 18-hole, world-class court and 9-hole model court offering pretty views of the sea.

👫 **Aqualand** – *ZAC des Pradeaux.* 🕿*08 92 68 66 13. www.aqualand.fr. Closed Oct–May.* 🎫*24€ (child 17€).* Water park with slides, wave pool, and swimming pools.

Lecques Aquanaut Centre – *Nouveau Port des Lecques.* 🕿*04 94 26 42 18. www.lecques-aquanaut.fr.* Diving club.

Sanary-sur-Mer★

Var

The charming resort, all pink and white, is lively year round. It has a little fishing port bordered by palm trees and a bay with fine beaches well-protected from the Mistral winds by the wooded hills. During the rule of Nazism in the 1930s, German intellectuals and writers took to living here, including Berthold Brecht and Thomas Mann.

SIGHTS

Chapelle Notre-Dame-de-Pitié
Access via Bd. Courbet.
The 16C chapel on a hillock west of the town is decorated with votive offerings, mostly naive paintings. Outside is a **view**★ of Sanary Bay.

▶ **Population:** 18 023.
🗺 **Michelin Map:** 340 J7; local map: *see Excursions.*
ℹ **Info:** 2 quai du Général-de-Gaulle. 🕿*04 94 74 01 04.* www.sanarysurmer.com.
▶ **Location:** Located 5km/3mi from Bandol; 13km/8mi from Toulon.

Tour Romane
On the port. 🕐*Open 10am–12.30pm, 3–6.30pm.* 🎫*No charge.* 🕿*04 94 74 01 04.*
This 13C watchtower (21.5m/70.5ft tall), enclosed by a hotel, houses a museum dedicated to F Dumas, one of the pioneers of deep-sea diving. The collection includes old tools of underwater hunting, diving, and objects coming from the ancient wrecks in the bay of Sanary.

Sanary port

E. Barel/ MICHELIN

 DRIVING TOURS

1 GROS CERVEAU★★ *13km/8mi – about 1.5hr.*

◐ *From Sanary take Av. Europe-Unie, at Ollioules turn left onto D 20.*

The drive begins through terraced gardens and vineyards, with views over the inner harbour of Toulon. Gradually the panorama extends southeast over Toulon and Cap Sicié Peninsula. Farther on is a **view**★ of the Grès de Ste-Anne (enormous rocks riddled with caves), Beausset Plain, the Ste-Baume Massif, the Évenos hills, the Ollioules Gorges, and the sweeping coastline.

◐ *8km/5mi after Ollioules (sign) make a U-turn to a platform.*

A short walk reveals a marvellous **view**★★ of the coast from the Giens Peninsula to Île Verte off La Ciotat.

2 MONT CAUME★★
23km/14.3mi northeast – allow 2hr.
◐ *Leave Sanary on Av. de l'Europe-Unie going east on D 11 to Ollioules.*

Ollioules
Old arcaded houses and a Provençal Romanesque church stand at the foot of the 13C castle.

◐ *Beyond Ollioules turn left onto N 8 which enters the gorges.*

Gorges d'Ollioules★
The arid and sinuous gorges were formed by the Reppe which tumbles into the sea in Sanary Bay. As the road emerges at the northern end there is a view on the left of the Grès de Ste-Anne, a curious mass of sandstone rocks.

◐ *In Ste-Anne-d'Évenos, turn right onto D 462. Turn right towards Évenos and park near a cross set in a rock.*

Évenos★

15min round trip.

The village is a jumble of half-ruined and abandoned houses, built of grey basaltic stone, clinging to the steep rock slopes beneath the ruins of a 16C castle. Its keep stands on the edge of a volcano from which the lava slag is still visible. The platform has **views** of Destel and Ollioules Gorges and Gros Cerveau.

▷ *Continue east along D 62 turning left at Col du Corps de Garde onto D 662.*

Mont Caume

Mont Caume rises to 801m/2 628ft, and its steep approach road offers fine viewpoints. From the top *(climb the mound)* there is a magnificent **panorama**★★ of the coast.

③ PRESQU'ÎLE DU CAP SICIÉ★

Round tour of the peninsula
25km/15.5mi. Allow 2hr

▷ *From Sanary take Av. d'Estienne-d'Orves.*

The road skirts Bonnegrâce Beach and Pointe Nègre with views of Sanary Bay and Bandol.

Le Brusc

Fishing village and resort; ferries to Île des Embiez *(see opposite)* leave from the port.

Petit Gaou

The rocky promontory pounded by the sea, once an island, resembles a Breton seascape. Good **views** of the coast.

Grand Gaou

Accessible by a pedestrian bridge, this island was designated as a nature preserve in 2000 to keep its wild aspect. There's a botanical path and designated areas for picnics.

▷ *Return to Le Brusc and take D 16 towards Six-Fours; in Roche-Blanche bear right.*

The road runs parallel to the coast about 1km/0.6mi inland but gives glimpses of La Ciotat, Bandol and Sanary. At the crossroads there is a **view**★★ of the Toulon harbour, Cap Cépet, the Giens Peninsula and the Îles d'Hyères.

▷ *Turn right; park at the radio station.*

Chapelle Notre-Dame-du-Mai★★

Behind radio station. ⊙*Call for hours.*
☎*04 94 25 50 39.*

The chapel is a place of pilgrimage (14 September) dedicated to Our Lady of the May Tree, also known as Our Lady of Good Protection, and contains many votive offerings. From the top of Cap Sicié there is a dizzying drop to the sea and a splendid **panorama**★★ of the coast from the Îles d'Hyères to the calanques lying east of Marseille.

▷ *Return to the crossroads continuing straight ahead.*

The narrow road cuts through **Forêt de Janas,** a fine plantation of conifers, before rejoining D 16 (turn left).

Six-Fours-les-Plages

 see SIX-FOURS-LES-PLAGES.

▷ *Return to Sanary on D 559.*

EXCURSION

ÎLES DES EMBIEZ★

Separated from the Port du Brusc by a lagoon, the five islands making up the Embiez archipelago are surrounded by rich fishing banks popular with anglers and divers. The islands of kitsch statues, Provençal houses, pleasant beaches and oceanographic museum belong to the Ricard empire *(see BANDOL).*

The biggest of the five islands (95ha/235 acres), Île de la Tour Fondue, is commonly known as Les Embiez. The second largest one, Grand Gaou, is linked to the mainland by a footbridge. The Île du Grand Rouveau has an automatically manned lighthouse, and Petit Rouveau is a bird sanctuary. The smallest isle, Petit Gaou, serves as a 🅿 car park on the road from Le Brusc.

Access to the Island – *Société Paul Ricard.* ℘*04 94 10 65 20 or 0 890 711 183. www.paul-ricard.com.* 🚢*10€ round trip (child 6€).* This company operates 13 to 24 crossings per day *(8min)* from the embarkment Brusc at Six-Fours.

👥 **Aquascope** – *Île des Embiez, Brusc, Six-Fours-les-Plages.* 🕐*Open Jul–Aug 9am–6pm; Apr–Jun and Sept 2.30–5pm.* 🕐*Closed public holidays.* 👣*Guided tours (30min).* 🚢*16€ (child 9€).* ℘*04 94 34 17 85.* An unusual way to observe underwater life through the transparent hull of a boat.

👥 **Aquavision** – *Île des Embiez, Quai St-Pierre, Six-Fours-les-Plages.* 🕐*Open Apr–Sept Tue–Sun 10am–4pm.* 🚢*12€ (child 8€).* ℘*04 94 10 65 29.* A 40-minute tour of the port and seal-ife preserve in a glass-bottom boat.

VISIT

Île des Embiez

This island boasts fine gravel beaches, rugged coastline with many coves, salt marshes, umbrella pine woods and vine-yards yielding rosé wine. There is a busy **marina** overlooked by the ruins of the medieval Château de Sabran. Divers will find the waters teeming with fish**.** For the less adventurous there is the small **tourist train** *(*℘*06 88 69 76 78;* 🚢*4€, 2.50€, children 6–18),* which tours the island, as well as an opportunity to view the underwater world from on board the *Aquascope.*

👥 Institut Océanographique Paul-Ricard★

Aquarium Museum: 🕐*open daily 10am–noon, 1.30–5.30pm.* 🕐*Closed Sat afternoon Sept–Jun, Wed and Sun mornings Nov–Mar, 24 Dec–1 Jan.* 🚢*4.50€ (child 2€).* ℘*04 94 34 02 49. www.institut-paul-ricard.org.*

The old naval gun site on St-Pierre prom-ontory houses an oceanographic insti-tute devoted to the Mediterranean Sea. The **Observatoire** is fitted with high-tech laboratories where research is car-ried out on marine biology, fish farming and sea pollution. The **museum** has 30 sea-water **aquariums** and 100 species of aquatic animals.

ADDRESSES

🏠 STAY

🛏 **Chambre d'Hôte Villa Lou Gardian** – *646 Rte. de Bandol.* ℘*04 94 88 05 73. www.lou-gardian.com. 4 rooms.* 🛁. 🍴. Despite its location near a main road, the colourful, minimalist deco-rated rooms of this recently renovated hotel are comparatively quiet. Choose one nearer the pool. A large garden, a tennis court and a table d'hôte set up in the summer patio await your arrival.

🍴 EAT

🍽 **Chez Mico** – *18 Rue Barthélémy-de-Don.* ℘*04 94 74 16 73. Closed Mon–Tue off season.* A local institution for over 35 years, this restaurant serves Meditarranean cuisine in an eclectic dining room decorated with old cooking utensils, travel souvenirs, carnival masks and witches.

🍽 **Restaurant du Théâtre** – *Impasse de l'Enclos, near the theatre.* ℘*04 94 88 04 16. Closed Sun eve, Mon.* Take a few steps down and enter this U-shaped restaurant appointed with rustic furnishings. Your attention will soon be caught by the mouthwatering sight of salmon, meats, prawns and skewered game roasting in the open fireplace!

🎭 ENTERTAINMENT

Centre National de Création et de Diffusion Culturelles – *Chateauvallon. www.chateauvallon.com. Closed Sun.* Indoor and open-air amphitheatre with a diverse programme of theatre, music, dance, circus, and arts shows through-out the year.

CALENDAR

St-Pierre et de la Lavande – Festival of the sea, every June.

Fête de la St-Nazaire – Every August, with Provençal games.

Six-Fours-les-Plages

Var

Sandy beaches, wild coastline and an ancient fortified village attract many summer visitors to Six-Fours.

OLD SIX-FOURS
▷ *Access via Av. du Maréchal-Juin; turn left onto a narrow road.*

Fort de Six-Fours★
From the platform at the entrance to the 19C fort (⛔ *closed to the public*), a **panorama**★ extends from east to west over Toulon harbour and coastline.

Collégiale St-Pierre
🕐*Open Wed–Mon Jun–Oct 3–7pm; Nov–May 2–6pm. 📞04 94 34 24 75.*
At the foot of the fortress stands the church of the now abandoned village of old Six-Fours, where early Christians persecuted for their religious views fled and sought refuge. The monks of Montmajour and St-Victor established the priory and chapel in the 11C.

Coastal Trails
To follow this by road, *see Driving Tour* ③*Cap Siciéa in SANARY-SUR-MER.*
The first of the two hikes here is easy (6km/3.7mi), the second more difficult (10km/6mi).

- **Population:** 32 742.
- **Michelin Map:** 340 K7; local map: *see SANARY-SUR-MER: Excursions*
- **Info:** Promenade Charles-de-Gaulle. 📞04 94 07 02 21. www.six-fours-les-plages.com.
- **Location:** The *commune* of Six-Fours-les-Plages encompasses 125 hamlets and districts around the central town of Reynier.

🚶 *1.5hr. Start at Bonnegrâce beach.*
The path runs along the beaches through low thorny vegetation and over the Cap Négre to the fishing port of Le Brusc.

🚶 *4hr. Start from Brusc.*
From the roundabout, go up the Chemin de Gardiole and, via the Chemin de Lèque, the Haute Lecques. You leave the pavement at the end of the Rue de Gargadoux. This part of the coastal trail is called the *Corniche Merveilleuse.* Climb up to the **Chapel Notre-Dame-de-Mai**. The trail continues to Cap Sicié's Fabrégas beach.

ADDRESSES

🏨 STAY
🛏🍽 **Hôtel du Parc** – *112 Rue Marius-Bondil, Le Brusc. 📞04 94 34 00 15. www.locana.com. Closed Jan–Feb. 17 rooms.* 🛏*7.50€.* Just 200m/650ft from the port of Brusc and its beaches. The hotel is situated in a large house, its dining room overlooking the back garden.

🍴 EAT
🍽 **Le Ligure** – *60 Av. John-Kennedy, Route de Plages. 📞04 94 25 63 87. Closed 15 Nov–15 Dec, Sun eve, Mon off season.* Outstanding views can be had of Sanary Bay from the panoramic terrace of this restaurant. Fish, seafood and freshly cooked pizzas.

🏃 SPORT AND LEISURE
HIKING & CYCLING
In addition to the coastal walking trails, the massif of the Cap Sicié has five hiking itineraries *(about 2hr each)* to explore on your own or with a guide. Six-Fours has five circular bike trails from 10km/6mi to 25km/15mi.

EVENTS
Fête de la Bouillabaisse – Held in June, this festival celebrates the popular local dish *bouillabaillse*, with tastings and live entertainment.

Toulon★★

France's largest naval port sits in one of the most secure and most beautiful harbours of the Mediterranean, surrounded by pastel building façades and tall hills crowned by forts. Although cruise ships and military freighters have long since replaced the galleys of yesteryear, this modern town hasn't lost its nautical heritage, which can be found throughout the narrow streets of the old town and the quays of the old port.

A BIT OF HISTORY

The Age of the Galleys (17C and 18C) – One of the attractions for travellers of the 17C and 18C was to visit the galleys moored in the old port. The majestic vessels, whose triangular sails were decorated by the master sculptors and painters of the arsenal, seemed to fly across the surface of the water. The galley slaves had a different point of view. Four men were needed to pull each of the 25 or 26 oars. They were criminals of various ilk, Turkish slaves, politcial and religious prisoners, and "volunteers" driven by extreme poverty, who stayed with their oars at all times, even to eat and sleep.

One of the Painted Walls of Toulon

D. Pazery/ MICHELIN

▶ **Population:** 167 816.

⌖ **Michelin Map:** 340 K7; local map: *see Excursions*.

🛈 **Info:** Pl. Raimu. ℘04 94 18 53 00. www.toulontourisme.com.

▶ **Location:** The Old Town of Toulon is located on the Old Port, or Vieille Darse, bounded to the east by Cours Lafayette, to the west by Rue Anatole-France and to the north by Rue Landrin. The greater Toulon area includes the towns surrounding the harbours as well as the Bay of Lazaret formed by the peninsula of the Presqu'île de St-Mandrier. The Old Town is accessible to pedestrians only.

🅿 **Parking:** The largest parking areas are located on Place d'Armes, Place de la Liberté/Palais Liberté, and at the Centre Mayol.

⊛ **Don't Miss:** The most appealing areas of Toulon are the winding streets of the Old Town and the old port around the Arsenal and Quai Cronstadt. If you have access to a car, don't miss the views from the top of Mont Faron.

⏱ **Timing:** Plan on a half day for the walking tours, more if you plan to do some shopping along the Rues d'Alger, Jean-Jaurès, Hoche and Place Victor-Hugo. The afternoon can include a boat tour of the harbour and Presqu'île de St-Mandrier, then driving excursions up to Mont Faron.

👥 **Kids:** Children fascinated with model-making will find plenty to keep them occupied in Toulon's arsenal and naval museums.

In 1748, the system of galley slaves was abandoned, and the oarsmen became forced laborers, buiding ships and maintaining the harbour. This penal colony, the Bagne de Toulon, is described in detail by Victor Hugo in his novel *Les Misérables*. At its peak the colony held nearly 4 000 convicts, each permanently attached to a chain weighing 7kg/15lb. The Bagne de Toulon closed in 1874.

Bonaparte's First Feat of Arms – On 27 August 1793, Royalists handed Toulon over to an Anglo-Spanish fleet.
A Republican army was sent to Toulon, with an artillery under the command of an obscure junior captain called Bonaparte. A battery was installed facing the British fort, called "little Gibraltar", but was subjected to such terrible fire that the gunners faltered. The young Corsican set the example; he laid the guns and manned the sponge-rod, and soon had enough fearless volunteers. "Little Gibraltar" fell on 17 December. The foreign fleet withdrew after burning the French ships, the arsenal, and the provision depots, as well as taking along part of the population.

Second World War – In November 1942, in response to the Allied Landings in North Africa, Hitler decided to invade the French free zone and sink the French fleet. On 19 August 1944, four days after the Allied Landing on the Maures beaches, French troops attacked the Toulon defences, a plan of which had been smuggled out in 1942 by sailors in the Resistance. The city was liberated on 26 August.

Post-war – Up to 1939 Toulon had been too dependent on the naval dockyard and very isolated by its geographic position. After the war efforts were made to diversify: the Arsenal broadened the scope of its production, commercial trade in the port was developed and new industries were introduced. The construction of holiday homes in the region sustained the building trade in the period after the post-war reconstruction boom, while road improvements made the town more accessible.

🐾 WALKING TOUR

As you stroll through town, keep an eye out for the distinctive painted walls (Rue du Noyer, Rue Micholet, Av. Franklin Roosevelt) that illustrate the life and times of the town.

1 FROM THE STATION TO THE ARSENAL

Place de la Liberté

This square is the heart of the modern town, with a monumental Fontaine de la Fédération erected in 1889 to celebrate the centenary of the Republic. The superb Grand Hôtel (1870) in the background is the last remaining building of the Edwardian era.
On either side of the square, Boulevard Strasbourg and Avenue du Général-Leclerc form the main axis of the town. The Opéra Municipal (1862) was the centre of attraction in the evenings until just before the Second World War. Today, the cafés and cabarets give this district a festive atmosphere.

Toulon Purple

In Roman times Toulon was celebrated for the manufacture of the imperial purple. The dye was obtained by steeping the colour glands of the pointed conches (genus *Murex*) which proliferate along the coast in salt solution previously brought to boiling point for ten days in lead vats. The purple obtained was used to dye silk and woollen materials. This sumptuous colour was initially reserved for emperors but later its use spread, though the imperial treasury maintained a monopoly over its manufacture. The foundations of the old Toulon dye-works were uncovered during reconstruction work in the arsenal.

PRACTICAL INFORMATION
GUIDED TOURS OF THE CITY
Guided theme tours *(2hr)* starting out from the tourist office are a great opportunity to discover the old town of Toulon. *Reservations necessary:* ✆*04 94 18 53 00.*

Petit Train Touristique: Departs (Jul–Aug) from the Carré du Port for a tour with commentary *(50min)* of the Old Town to the beaches at Mourillon and the Tour Royale. ✆*06 20 77 44 43.* 👛*5€ (child 3€).*

TRANSPORT
Pedestrian area: The district in the old part of town bordered by Rue Anatole-France, Avenue de la République, Avenue de Besagne and Boulevard de Strasbourg is closed to traffic.

Buses: The RMTT (✆*04 94 03 87 03, www.reseaumistral.com)* provides an efficient bus service covering Toulon and its outskirts. Plans, timetables and tickets can be obtained from the newsstand at 11 Rue Revel.

Boat shuttle service: *SITCAT/RMTT on Quai Cronstadt or 720 Av. du Colonel-Picot.* ✆*04 94 03 87 03.* There are several daily services to and from La Seyne-sur-Mer, Tamaris and St-Mandrier-sur-Mer. These lines are part of the local transport system.

Pass Téléphérique: This day pass is good for the entire RMTT network (bus and boat) and allows RT access to the téléphérique on Mont Faron. 👛*6.60€ (child 4.60€)*

Place Victor-Hugo
Farther on you will discover one of the façades belonging to the Théâtre de Toulon, one of France's finest regional theatres. Its principal façade faces Place Victor-Hugo and its lively pavement cafés.

▷ *Take Rue Jean-Jaurès and turn left on Rue-Anatole France.*

Place d'Armes
Colbert commissioned the building on this square as a venue to review his troops, originally called Champ de Bataille. It soon became a popular meetingplace among nobility and officers leaving on overseas assignments.

Corderie
To the south of Place d'Armes.
🚫 *Military property, closed to the public.*
Designed by Vauban to house the naval rope factory (*corderie*), this building now houses the navy's administrative offices. The fine **door**★ (1689) came from the former Jesuit college and was added in 1976.

▷ *Continue on Rue-Anatole France.*

👥 Musée de la Marine★
♿*Pl. Monsenergue.* 🕐*Open daily Feb–Dec 10am–6pm.* 🚶*Guided tours (1hr) possible Jul–Aug 2.30pm, 3.30pm.* 🕐*Closed 1 May, 25 Dec.* 👛*5€ (children under 18 free).* ✆*04 94 02 02 01. www.musee-marine.fr.*
Entrance to the Naval Museum is through an impressive 18C doorway flanked by statues of Mars (left) and Bellona (right). On entering, the visitor is transported straight into the Quai de l'Artillerie and the old arsenal – the subject of this large, life-like fresco was taken from a painting (18C) by Joseph Vernet. Note the sky painted in gold leaf. On the ground floor there are large-scale models of a frigate, La Sultane, and of an 18C vessel, the *Duquesne*. Fine paintings, drawings and other exhibits recall Toulon's seafaring history and its prison. There is also an interesting collection of model ships and submarines.

Arsenal Maritime
Covering 240ha and employing around 6 300 civilians, this arsenal mainly maintains the Mediterranean fleet: frigates, carriers, sloops, subs and minesweepers. Some of the dry docks are 17C.

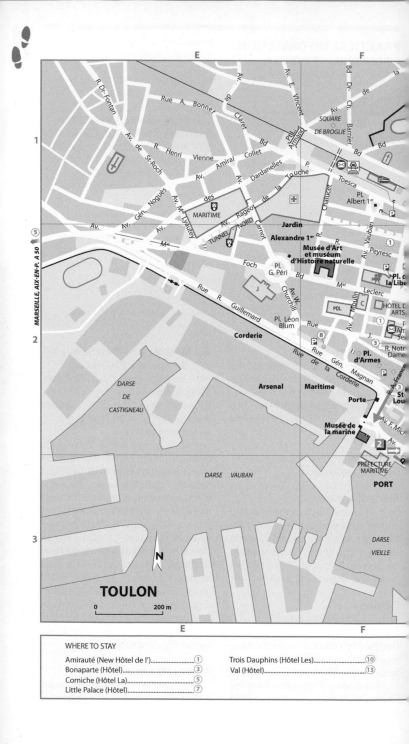

TOULON

0   200 m

WHERE TO STAY

Amirauté (New Hôtel de l')............................①
Bonaparte (Hôtel)..③
Corniche (Hôtel La).......................................⑤
Little Palace (Hôtel).......................................⑦

Trois Dauphins (Hôtel Les)........................⑩
Val (Hôtel)...⑬

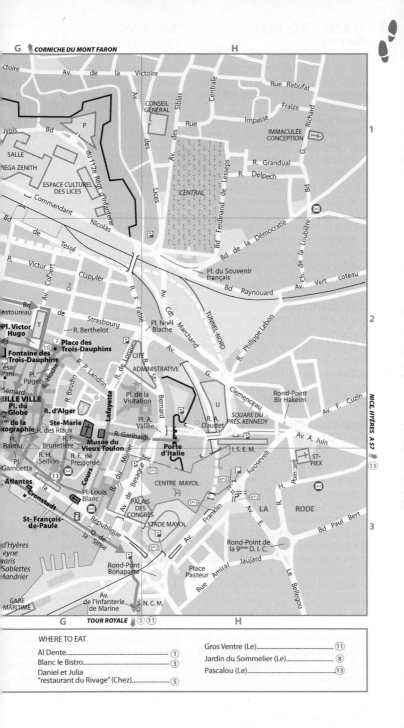

WHERE TO EAT

Al Dente.. ①
Blanc le Bistro..................................... ③
Daniel et Julia
"restaurant du Rivage" (Chez)................... ⑤

Gros Ventre (Le)................................... ⑪
Jardin du Sommelier (Le)..................... ⑧
Pascalou (Le).. ⑬

② A MILITARY PAST
The Port★

Construction of the old port (Vieille Darse or Darse Henri-IV) began in 1589 under the Governor of Provence. The two breakwaters on the south side were completed in 1610.

At that time there was no royal fleet; when the king required ships, he leased them from lords and captains who had them built, armed and equipped. It was Richelieu who created a military arsenal to build and repair warships. Under Louis XIV the port proved too small and Vauban had the new port (Darse Neuve) excavated between 1680 and 1700. To accommodate further growth, an annex was built In 1836 at Mourillon, and two harbours added under Napoleon III at Castigneau and Missiessy.

Quai Cronstadt

Shops and cafés create an animated waterfront. The tall modern buildings with their many-coloured windows form a screen between the old port and the old town. The only reminders of the past are the famous **atlantes**★ by Pierre Puget, on the old town hall balcony.

Boat Tour of the Rade★

Bateliers de la Côte d'Azur, landing-stage on Quai Cronstadt, beside the Préfecture Maritime. ⚓*Guided, commentated tours (1hr), hourly departures Feb–Oct.* ⚓*9.50€. Reservations* ℘*04 94 93 07 56. www.bateliersdelacotedazur.com.*

The Toulon Rades are home to the Force d'Action Navale, which includes aircraft carriers, minesweepers, anti-submarine or missile-launcher frigates and the slender, dark contours of a nuclear submarine.

The Tamaris coast rade leads to two forts, Balaguier and l'Ayguillette. The tour returns via Lazaret Bay, along the St-Mandrier Peninsula and the long sea wall, which affords excellent **views**★ over Toulon.

▷ *At the roundabout Gen. Bonaparte, follow the Av. de la Tour-Royale.*

Tour Royale

◷*Enquire at the tourist office about visits.* ℘*04 94 02 02 01.*

Known also as the Grosse Tour or Mitre Tower, this built by Louis XII in the early 16C for defensive purposes (its walls are 7m/23ft thick at the base). It then served as a prison. From the watch-path there is a lovely **panorama**★ of Toulon and Mont Faron.

③ OLD TOWN★

The ancient heart of Toulon is characterised by its confusion of streets. A long-term renovation plan started in 1985 has already restored many of the charming façades and fountains.

▷ *Enter Pl. de l'Amiral-Senès then turn right onto Rue Notre-Dame.*

Église St-Louis

Rue Louis-Jourdan.

This church is a fine example of Neoclassical architecture, built in the late 18C in the form of a Greek temple.

▷ *Continue on Rue Vezzani.*

The 18C reproduction of a ship's prow seems to sprout out of a wall, in homage to the shipbuilding of the town.

▷ *Take Rue Pomet on the right.*

The curious fountain on Place du Globe evokes the Bagne of Toulon.

Maison de la Photographie, Musée de la Figurine

Pl. du Globe, Rue Nicolas-Laugier. ◷*Open Jul–Aug daily 10am–12.30pm, 1.30–6pm; Sept–Jun Tue–Sat noon–6pm.* ⚓*No charge.* ℘*04 94 93 07 59.*

Two museums in the former public bath house include the Musée de la Photographie, which hosts regular temporary exhibitions, and the Musée de la Figurine, with 3 000 figurines on display in dioramas of historic scenes, such as Bonaparte's campaign in Egypt.

Atlantes by Puget on the old town hall, Toulon

▷ *Take Rue du Noyer, just off Pl. Raimu. On the right is a mural painting on Rue Micholet. Return to Rue de la Glacière and turn left, then follow Rue Andrieux.*

Fontaine des Trois-Dauphins

The character of Place Puget is embellished by this curious fountain sculpted in 1780 by two local artists with plants growing in its basins. The three intertwined dolphins are covered in moss and calcium deposits, on which grow ferns, a fig tree, a medlar and an oleander! The cafés of Place Puget are pleasantly shaded.

▷ *Go down Rue Hoche.*

Rue d'Alger

This modernised pedestrian precinct is the main commercial street leading to the old port, Vieille Darse.

▷ *Turn left onto Rue Seillon, then follow Rue de la Fraternité.*

Église St-François-de-Paule

This small church was built in 1744 by the Recollects. Its double-arched façade and Genoan bell tower identify it with the Nice Baroque style.

▷ *Backtrack to the square and turn right at the first street.*

Rue Méridienne and Place à l'Huile lead to Place de la Poissonnerie which for several centuries accommodated the old Fish Marke, demolished in 1898.

▷ *Go up Rue Pressensé, then Rue des Boucheries.*

Cathédrale Ste-Marie

◔ *Open daily 9am–noon, 2–6pm.*
The cathedral was constructed in the 11C and restored in the 12C. In the 17C it was enlarged and given a Classical façade. The interior mixes Romanesque and Gothic, with several works of art by Puget and Van Loo.

▷ *Continue to Cour Lafayette.*

Cours Lafayette

The colourful, bustling vegetable and flower **market** is held here on Tuesdays to Sundays.

Musée du Vieux Toulon

◔ *Open Tue–Sat 2–6pm.* ◔ *Closed public holidays.* ⊜ *No charge.* ☎ *04 94 62 11 07. www.avtr-org.*
This museum, located in the headquarters of the old bishopric, has two galleries displaying maps, engravings and paintings recalling great moments in the history of the city since the Middle Ages. The display cases contain ceramics, statuettes, costumes and exhibits

of Provençal traditions. In the second gallery, there is a lovely relief map of the city, made in 1880.

▷ *Leave the Old Town by Rue Garibaldi.*

Porte d'Italie
This bastioned gate, built in 1790 on the site of ancient fortifications, is the only remnant of the defences which surrounded Toulon.

SIGHTS
Musée de Toulon et du Var
113 Bd. du M.-Leclerc. ⊙Open Mon–Fri 9am–6pm; Sat–Sun 11am–6pm. ⊙Closed public holidays. ⊗No charge. ℰ04 94 36 81 10. www.museum-toulon.org.
This natural history museum occupies the right wing of a Renaissance-style building. The left wing is reserved for the Museum of Art (*see below*). Two galleries on the ground floor house the stuffed zoological collection.

Musée d'Art
113 Bd. du M.-Leclerc. ⊙Open Tue–Sun noon–6pm. ⊙Closed public holidays. ⊗No charge. ℰ04 94 36 81 01.
The Flemish, Dutch, Italian and French Schools (16C–18C) are all represented in the museum's collections, which feature works by 19C artists, including a large number of Provençal painters, such as the Toulon landscapist Vincent Courdouan. The museum also possesses an eclectic contemporary art collection.

Jardin Alexandre-I
This garden is home to some attractive trees, including magnolias, palms and cedars. Look for the water fountain by Hercule called, appropriately, *Fontaine du Buveur* (Drinker's Fountain).

EXCURSIONS
Mont Faron★★★
This small limestone massif of Mont Faron (*alt 584m/1 916ft*), bordered by deep valleys, dominates the city of Toulon. It is a pleasant drive in summer over pine-clad slopes, providing good

views★ of Toulon, the harbours, the St-Mandrier and Cap Sicié Peninsulas.

Téléphérique du Mont Faron★
▷ *Take Bd. Ste-Anne and follow signs (Téléphérique du Mont Faron) to the cable-car station in Av. Perrichi. At busy periods it is possible to park below the station on the left.*

⊙Operates Feb–Nov; see website or call for precise details; ticket office closes 15min before closure. ⊙Closed public holidays. ⊗6.30€. ℰ04 94 92 68 25. www.telepherique-faron.com.
The cable-car ride (*6min*) offers fine **views★** over the town, the harbour and the limestone cliffs circling Toulon. To the left the remains of many small forts can be seen. A pleasant view can also be had by walking about 10m/33ft to the left along the road to Mont Faron.

Musée-Mémorial du Débarquement en Provence★
Sommet du Mont Faron. ⊙Open May–Sept daily 10am–1pm, 2–6.30pm; Oct–Apr Tue–Sun 10am–1pm, 2–5.30pm. ⊗3.80€. ℰ04 94 88 08 09.
Installed in the Beaumont Tower, left of the road, is this memorial commemorating the liberation of southeast France by the Allies in August 1944.
The first section is devoted to the memory of the English, American, Canadian and French who took part. In the second part, there is a diorama of the liberation of Toulon and Marseille and a cinema (*15min documentaries, filmed during the landing*).
From the terrace (*accessible during a tour of the museum*) there is a magnificent sweeping **panorama★★★** (*three viewing tables*) of Toulon, the harbours, the Mediterranean, and the islands and mountains all around Toulon.

Zoo du Faron
Mont Faron. ⊙Open Jul–Aug 10am–6.30pm; Sept–Jun 2–5.30pm. ⊙Closed when raining. ⊗8€ (child 5€). ℰ04 94 88 07 89.
This zoo specialises in the reproduction of endangered animals such as snow

panthers and ocelots. There are also lions, tigers, bears and monkeys.

Solliès-Ville

▶ *15km/9mi northeast – 1.5hr.*
From Toulon take A 97 motorway.
Follow directions to La Farlède and then D 67 to Solliès-Ville.

The old town of Solliès-Ville clings to the side of a hill overlooking the rich Gapeau Plain. Below lies Solliès-Pont, a busy market town in a region famous for its cherry orchards and its fig trees. The **church** (ⓒ*same hours as the Maison Jean-Aicard, below*) with two naves combines Romanesque traits with Gothic arches. The monolith at the high altar is thought to be a 15C ciborium, the walnut organ case from 1499, and the crucifix on the pillar from the 13C.

Maison Jean-Aicard

ⓒ*Open Tue–Sat noon–6pm.* ⓒ*Closed public holidays.* ⊗*No charge.* ℘*04 94 33 72 02. www.solliesville.fr.*
This is the house of the poet, novelist and dramatist Jean Aicard (1848–1921) which has been converted into a small museum. On **Esplanade de la Montjoie**, the ruined castle of the Forbins, lords of Solliès, commands a beautiful **view**★ of the Gapeau Valley and the Maures Massif.

🚗 DRIVING TOURS

The roads used in these excursions serve military installations; traffic is permitted up to the entrance of these installations, but the military authorities forbid entrance to certain places indicated by notices.

① TOUR OF THE HARBOURS★★

17km/10.5mi south. Allow 1hr.
▶ *Leave Toulon by highway A 50, then D 559 and turn left towards La Seyne.*

La Seyne-sur-Mer

Built beside the bay which bears its name, La Seyne has a port for fishing boats and pleasure craft but is basically an industrial town that depended on the naval shipyards for its livelihood. A small bay, bordered by the forts of Éguillette and Balaguier, allows a good overview of Toulon, Le Faron and Le Coudon.

Fort Balaguier

ⓒ*Open Tue–Sun Jul–Aug 10am–noon, 3–7pm; Sept–Dec and Feb–Jun 10am–noon, 2–6pm.* ⓒ*Closed 1 May, 25 Dec.* ⊗*3€.* ℘*04 94 94 84 72.*
The fort was recaptured from the English in 1793 by the young Napoleon. Set up in the fort's rooms, with walls 4m/13ft thick, is a naval museum with a collection of model ships and memorabilia from the Napoleonic era. The 17C chapel contains objects from the Toulon galleys and naval prisons: registers, chains and works of art made by the prisoners.
From the terrace overlooking the fort's garden and its aviary, there is a remarkable **view**★ of the coastline from Toulon to the Île du Levant.

Tamaris

George Sand wrote several of her novels in this shaded resort on the hillside.

Villa Tamaris-Pacha

Av. de la Grande Maison. ♿ⓒ*Open Tue–Sun 2–6.30pm.* ✎*Guided tours Wed all day, Thu–Fri 4–5.30pm.* ⓒ*Closed public holidays.* ⊗*No charge.* ℘*04 94 06 84 00. www.villatamaris.fr.*
The history of this magnificent residence, still unfinished, is worthy of the *Arabian Nights*. Towards the middle of the 19C, Marius Michel, a native of Sanary-sur-Mer, became the concessionnaire of the lighthouses, quays and warehouses of Constantinople and created the modern port of Istanbul under the Ottoman administration. He built his wife a palace inspired by the Florentine villas in Tamaris in the Var, but after three years of hard work his wife was stabbed and killed by a mentally ill person in 1893, and all work was stopped. The palace remained unoccupied for a century. Now redeveloped, it houses a cultural institution.
Beside the bay, a luxurious house (private property), also the work of Michel

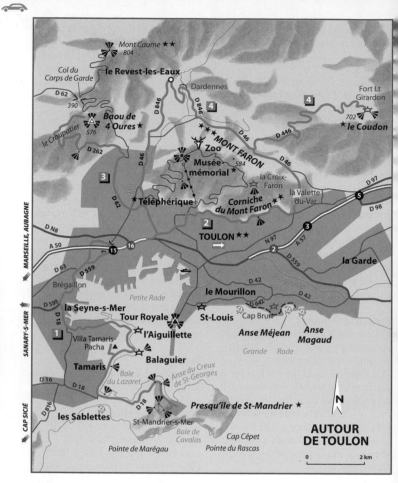

AUTOUR DE TOULON

Pacha, as he was known, displays the ornately carved Mauresque style.

Les Sablettes

This long, wide beach of fine sand looks out to the open sea. The houses were rebuilt after the last war in neo-Provençal style.

Take the road along the narrow sandy isthmus, which links the peninsula to the land mass, where you'll find a fine view of Toulon surrounded by mountains.

Presqu'île de St-Mandrier★

The road round the peninsula offers a **view**★ of the whole harbour and of Toulon and its setting before skirting the bight of St-Georges, which houses an aeronaval base and training centre

for marine engineers as well as the fishing and leisure port of **St-Mandrier-sur-Mer**. A right-hand turning at the entrance to the town climbs steeply to a small cemetery with a **panorama**★★ of Toulon and the Îles d'Hyères.

2 CORNICHE DU MONT FARON★★

Allow 30min.

The Corniche du Mont Faron, a panoramic road, provides the best view of the whole of Toulon harbour. The best time to visit is late afternoon, when the light is ideal.

▷ *To reach the Corniche du Mont Faron take Pont de Ste-Anne, Av. de la Victoire and Bd. Ste-Anne (left).*

Mont Faron cable-car

D. Pazery/ MICHELIN

The drive along the magnificent **Corniche Marius-Escartefigue** and the slopes of Mont Faron provides views of Toulon and its surroundings. The **view**★ of the harbours includes the Petite Rade between Le Mourillon and La Seyne backed by the cliffs of Cap Sicie, and the Grande Rade, partially enclosed *(south)* by the St-Mandrier Peninsula and its low narrow isthmus and *(east)* by Cap Carqueiranne, Giens Bay and Giens Peninsula.

③ BAOU DE QUATRE OURES★
11km/7mi northwest – 1hr.
▷ *From Toulon take Av. St-Roch, Rue Dr-Fontan, Av. Général-Gouraud and then turn left on Av. des Routes; on Pl. Macé turn right to D 62 (Av. Clovis), then turn left onto D 262.*

About 3km/2mi further on is a platform offering a magnificent **view**★★ of Toulon.

▷ *The narrow road to the top (4km/2.5mi) crosses a firing range (open to traffic).*

At the top there is a fine **panorama**★★ of the coast from Cap Bénat to La Ciotat and inland from Ste-Baume to the Maures.

④ LE COUDON★
Round trip 36km/22– about 1.5hr.
▷ *From Toulon take Pont de Ste-Anne and Av. de la Victoire; turn left onto Bd. Ste-Anne and right onto Bd. Escartefigue. Then turn left onto Av. de la Canaillette, which leads to D 46. Turn right and right again onto D 446.*

The Unusual Military Career of the St-Mandrier Peninsula

The hill of La Croix aux Signaux, a secret German naval base, was from September 1943 to August 1944 an assembly base for midget submarines which left via an access tunnel ending up on Cavalas beach. In 1929, however, the Marine Nationale Française had buried there (14m/46ft deep) two enormous gun turrets each holding two 340 guns, 17m/56ft long, covering a sector from Le Lavandou to La Ciotat! Shelling preparations for the landing in Provence in 1944 brought an end to development of this base.

It was from the rifle range at St-Mandrier that the first French liquid-powered rocket was launched in March 1945, inaugurating the European space race.

Le Coudon★

Alt 702m/2 303ft.

At the start of the climb you can see Mont Coudon in its entirety and also La Crau and the surrounding plain. The road finally comes out onto a wasteland scattered with evergreen oaks. The **view**★ widens continuously until at the entrance to Fort Lieutenant-Girardon the entire coast from the Giens Peninsula to the former island of Gaou near Le Brusc is visible.

▷ *Return to D 46 and turn right. After 2.5km/1.5mi – D 846 crosses a dam to Le Revest-les-Eaux.*

Le Revest-les-Eaux

This is a delightful old village with a 17C church at the foot of Mont Caume overlooked by a "Saracen tower". Its 17C château, with two pepperpot towers, now houses a café-bar. The church is from the same era.

▷ *Return to Toulon through the Las Valley (D 846) between the mountains of Faron and Croupatier.*

ADDRESSES

🏠 STAY

🛏 **Hôtel Little Palace** – *6-8 r. Berthelot.* 📞*04 94 92 26 62. www.hotel-littlepalace. com. 23 rooms. ⬛8€.* A charming and simple hotel, decorated in warm earth tones. Known for its copious breakfast buffet.

🛏 **Hôtel Bonaparte** – *16 r. Anatole-France.* 📞*04 94 93 07 51. www.hotel bonaparte.com. 19 rooms. ⬛8€.* Provençal-style hotel in the centre of town, with small but well-appointed rooms. Air conditioned on top floor.

🛏 **Les 3 Dauphins** – *9 Pl. des 3 Dauphins.* 📞*04 94 92 65 79. 14 rooms. ⬛8€.* The windows of this hotel give onto a tiny square. The smallish rooms have been tastefully appointed and decorated in cheerful shades.

🛏 **Val'Hôtel** – *Av. René-Cassin, ZA Paul Madon, La Valette, take exit 5 off the A 57, follow signs to ZI de Toulon-la-Valette.* 📞*04 94 08 38 08. www.monalisahotels. com. 42 rooms. ⬛7€. Restaurant 🛏.* This hotel offers several advantages: a lush garden setting; tlarge, colourful rooms with balcony or terrace; and inexpensive weekend rates. A bit close to the motorway exit.

🛏🛏 **New Hôtel de l'Amirauté** – *4 Rue Adolphe-Guiol.* 📞*04 94 22 19 67. www.new-hotel.com. 58 rooms. ⬛9€.* In the centre of town, the decor is reminiscent of the large luxury liners of bygone times. Functional, efficiently soundproofed rooms.

🛏🛏🛏 **La Corniche Best Western** – *17 littoral Frédéric-Mistral across from the Port St-Louis and near the Mourillon beaches.* 📞*04 94 41 35 12. www.best westernhotelcorniche.com. 25 rooms. ⬛14€. Restaurant 🛏🛏.* This hotel just two steps from the beaches at Mourillon has views over the sea, perfect for those looking for a seaside holiday atmosphere.

🍴 EAT

🍽 **Al Dente** – *30 Rue Gimelli.* 📞*04 94 93 02 50. Closed Sat, Sun lunch.* The main reason for coming here is the remarkable choice of pasta dishes and Italian specialities, with additional menus at highly affordable prices.

🍽 **Le Pascalou** – *3 Pl. à l'Huile.* 📞*04 94 62 87 02. Closed Mon.* The lunchtime restaurant of the fish market of the same name, serving the catch of the day on a tiny square.

🍽🍽 **Blanc le Bistro** – *290 r. Jean-Jaurès.* 📞*04 94 10 20 40. Closed 25 Jul–10 Aug, Sat lunch, Sun, Mon eve.* A contemporary restaurant serving generous French dishes with a modern touch.

🍽🍽 **Le Gros Ventre** – *279 Littoral Frédéric Mistral.* 📞*04 94 42 15 42. www.legrosventre.net. Closed Wed–Thu,*

Fri lunch). A family-run establishment serving the day's catch and grilled meats, as well as fine wines from their cave, in an elegant setting just off Le Mourillon beach.

🍲🍲🍷 **Chez Daniel "Restaurant du Rivage"** – *La Seyne-sur-Mer, 4km/2.5mi south of La Seyne by Rte. de St-Mandrier and country lane.* ☎*04 94 94 85 13. Closed Nov, Sun eve, Mon Sept–Jun.* A small rocky inlet is the choice setting for this seafood restaurant that knows the true meaning of Provençal life. The freshly caught fish offered to diners may come from the sea or from the big fish tank set up on the premises.

🍲🍲🍷 **Le Jardin du Sommelier** – *20 Allées Courbet.* ☎*04 94 62 03 27. www.le-jardin-dusommelier.com. Closed Sat lunch, Sun.* Gourmet cuisine served in an elegant setting. Try the lobster with any wine from their first-rate *cave.*

🎭 **ON THE TOWN**

Café-Théâtre de la Porte d'Italie – *Pl. Armand-Vallée.* ☎*04 94 92 99 75. Check the programme of events. Closed Jun–Sept.* This café-théâtre presents clarinet and jazz concerts, stand-up comedy and pantomime shows.

Opéra de Toulon – *7 Rue Racine.* ☎*04 94 92 58 59. Closed Aug. www. operadetoulon.fr.* Built in 1862, the Opéra de Toulon is ranked second in France on account of its seating capacity and remarkable acoustics.

🍴 **CULINARY SPECIALITIES**

The natives of Toulon particularly enjoy *l'escabèche de sardine, la cade* (a flat cake made from chickpeas, similar to *socca* in Nice), *la pompe à l'huile* (a hard cake, oiled and flavoured with orange water) and the famous sweet doughnut *(chichifregi)* which can be bought from the stalls in the Lafayette market.

🛒 **SHOPPING**

The best place to go shopping is the area around Rue Jean-Jaurès, Rue Hoche, Place Victor-Hugo and Rue d'Alger. Rue Lamalgue (near the Port St-Louis) is a good market street for gourmet treats.

Provençal Market – Tue–Sun mornings on the Cour Lafayette.

Les Navires de la Royale – *30 Rue des Riaux.* ☎*06 11 18 55 61. Closed Mon.* Amateur sailors should make a point of visiting this shop, owned an enthusiastic lover of all things maritime. His days are spent making and restoring all sorts of boats, ranging from yachts to schooners to catamarans.

🏃 **SPORT AND LEISURE**

Mourillon beach – *To the east, along Littoral Frédéric-Mistral, between Fort St-Louis and the water sports centre.* The long Toulon beach, separated from the road by a large park, consists of four curved stretches of coastline covered with fine sand or gravel.

Méjean and Magaud beaches – *From Le Mourillon, follow directions to La Garde-Le Pradet.* At the entrance to La Garde, Chemin de la Mer leads to two natural sandy beaches, Magaud and Méjean.

EVENTS

Bacchus, Fête des Vins et de la Gastronomie – ☎*04 94 91 56 87.* Wine and gastronomy festival, last weekend in March on Place d'Armes.

Toulon Music Festival ☎*04 94 93 55 45.* From mid-June to mid-July, this classical music festival takes place in three exceptional locations: Fort Lamalgue in Toulon, Châteauvallon in Ollioules, and la Collégiale in Six-Fours-les-Plages.

Toulon Jazz Festival – ☎*04 94 09 71 00.* Ten-day jazz festival in July in locations throughout Toulon.

Festival de Noël – Christmas festivities throughout the month of December, including a nativity scene, crafts market, and ice skating.

Fête de la Mer et des Pêcheurs – A sea and fishing festival in the port of La Seyne-sur-Mer the last weekend in June.

...of Hyères and the Maures Massif

When most people think of the French Riviera, they imagine tanning on secluded beaches of stunning beauty, discovering local crafts in the cobblestone streets of historic villages and partying in glitzy clubs surrounded by celebrities. And that's exactly what visitors to the Golden Islands of Hyères and the Maures Massif will find. This part of the Mediterranean coastline is an Eden-like paradise of unspoiled islands and sandy beaches framed by the forested mountains. Chic resorts full of luxury yachts share a decidedly Provençal spirit with the tiny perched villages that haven't changed in centuries. And while humans have made their mark with their lush gardens, Belle Époque mansions, imported palm trees and ancient forts, the natural beauty of the region has been fiercely protected from the unchecked development plaguing less fortunate corners of the French Riviera.

Highlights

1   Hire a boat for the day to visit the beautiful Golden Islands of **Hyères** at your own pace (p136).

2   Snorkel along the underwater nature trail at the **Île de Port-Cros** (p160).

3   Escape the crowds of St Tropez with a coastal hike around the **St Tropez Peninsula** (p164).

4   Drive through the scenic forested hills along the **Corniche des Maures** (p150).

5   Enjoy panoramic views from the 11C ramparts of the perched village of **Grimaud** (p133).

The Green Department

The locals in the Golden Islands and Maures Massif take the protection and preservation of their environment seriously. It's located in the heart of the Var department, which, with 62% of its lands still undeveloped, is the second greenest department in France.

Maritime pines, cork oaks, chestnut trees and maquis scrub make up most of the Maures Massif flora, thriving on the ancient geological formations that form rocky peaks. Forest fires are a constant threat, and after the partial devastation of the Maures Massif during the heat-wave of 2003 authorities have cracked down on barbecuing and smoking along forest trails.

Aerial view of Petit Langoustier, Île de Porquerolles

D. Pazery/ MICHELIN

Environmental Preservation

The biggest threat, however, is the inevitable development by humans, so much of the land, coastline and even the waters around the Golden Islands are protected as part of the French National Park of Port Cros. Ile de Port-Cros is the only 100% car-free island of the Golden Islands of Hyères, named for the mica and quartz rock that catch the sun. Its clear waters and underwater nature trail are popular with divers. The fauna of the region are also preserved from extinction, with sanctuaries for tropical birds, fish and even the endangered Hermann tortoise.

Clean and Accessible Coastline

Coastal hiking trails, known as the sentier littoral, have their own special protection agency, the Conservatoire du Littoral. Not only do they keep the coastline clean, they also make sure it stays open to the public. Since 1976, any new properties built on the beach have to leave a 3m/9.8ft path closest to the water accessible for hikers. This law covers over 200km/125mi of the Var coast, including the scenic St-Tropez peninsula. While there are many sandy, family-friendly beaches such as Lavandou, Ste-Maxime, and Pampelonne, much of the coastline is made up of rocky inlets perfect for fishing or finding a bit of privacy from the crowds.

Historic Moments

Like most of the French Riviera, the Golden Islands of Hyères were once the stronghold of pirates up until the French kings chased them out in the 17C and replacing their lairs with military forts, many of which still dot the coastline today. The early perched villages and monasteries were often given their lands and allowed to cultivate them tax-free in return for keeping an eye on the horizon for invaders.

The arrival of the railroad in the mid-1800s brought Queen Victoria and wealthy Anglophone travellers hoping to escape from consumption, or tuberculosis, in Hyères' mild climate.

Cap Lardier, St Tropez Peninsula

J. Malburet/MICHELIN

The chic crowds eventually moved eastward to Cannes and Nice, leaving this area to the writers, artists and filmmakers like Colette, Anaïs Nin, Matisse, Jean Cocteau, Paul Signac, and Roger Vadim, whose 1956 film "And God Created Woman" starring Brigitte Bardot launched St-Tropez into the limelight it still enjoys.

Local Industry

Tourism is the principal industry in this region, with over 25% of the properties used as second homes for holidaymakers. They also cultivate flowers, fruits, the vineyards that produce Côte de Provence wines, and the natural cork from cork oak trees. Before becoming part of the nature preserve in 1995, the marshland ponds of the Giens Peninsula were used to harvest over 30,000 tons of sea salt each year.

Although the Var department is named after the river which runs through the Côte d'Azur region, administrative juggling after the French Revolution redrew the boundaries, and the river no longer flows through the department that bears its name.

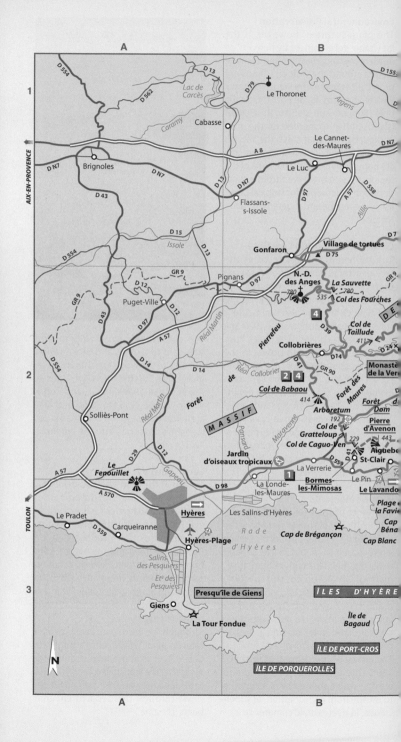

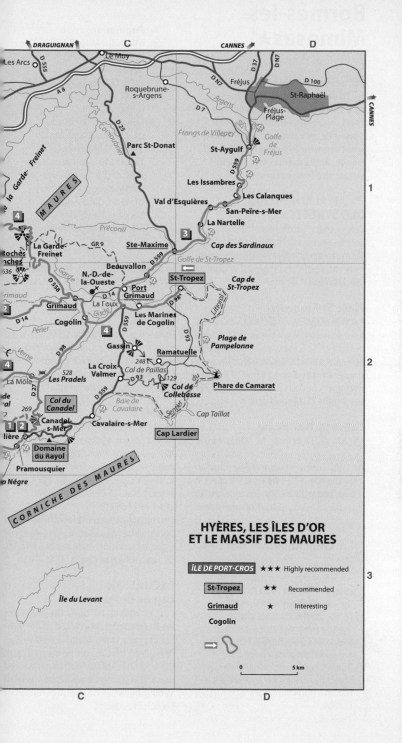

DRAGUIGNAN C **CANNES** D

Les Arcs
D 555
A 8
Le Muy
D 37
DN7
D 100
Roquebrune-
s-Argens
DN7
Fréjus
St-Raphaël
D 7
Argens
Fréjus-
Plage
CANNES
Étangs de Villepey
Golfe
de
Fréjus
Parc St-Donat
St-Aygulf
D 25
Corniche
D 559
Les Issambres
1
Les Calanques
Val d'Esquières
San-Peïre-s-Mer
4
Préconil
La Nartelle
Cap des Sardinaux
La Garde-
Freinet
MAURES
la Garde- Freinet
GR 9
Ste-Maxime
3
Golfe de St-Tropez
Roches
ches
536
Beauvallon
D 559
St-Tropez
Cap de
St-Tropez
N.-D.-de-
la-Oueste
D 558
Garde
Port
Grimaud
rimaud
Grimaud
D 14
La Foux
D 98
Littoral
3
D 14
Gisde
Les Marines
de Cogolin
Cogolin
D 559
Périer
D 98
Gassin
D 93
Plage de
Pampelonne
Verne
4
248
Ramatuelle
4
La Croix
Valmer
Col de Paillas
129
al
528
Les Pradels
D 93
Col de
Collebasse
Phare de Camarat
D 27
La Môle
269
D 559
Baie de
Cavalaire
Sentier
Cap Taillat
Col du
Canadel
1 **2**
Canadel-
s-Mer
Cavalaire-s-Mer
Cap Lardier
lière
Domaine
du Rayol
Pramousquier
o Nègre
CORNICHE DES MAURES

HYÈRES, LES ÎLES D'OR
ET LE MASSIF DES MAURES

ÎLE DE PORT-CROS ★★★ Highly recommended

St-Tropez ★★ Recommended

Grimaud ★ Interesting

Cogolin

→

Île du Levant

0   5 km

C D

Bormes-les-Mimosas★

Var

Bormes-les-Mimosas stands in an enchanting **setting**★ near the sea, on a steep slope at the foot of the Forêt du Dom. Colourful oleander, camomile, eucalyptus, and mimosa scent the winding streets of the old village, and a marina and beaches attract the sun seekers.

- ▶ **Population:** 7 051.
- **Michelin Map:** 340 N7; local map: *see Massif des MAURE.*
- **Info:** Pl. Gambetta. ℘04 94 01 38 38. www.bormesles mimosas.com.
- **Location:** The beaches of this Var village stretch 17km/10.5mi from Le Lavandou to the bay of Brégançon: La Favière with its pleasure port, the Bay of Gaou, Cabasson, and Léoube. The Massif des Maures flank the village.

WALKING TOUR

OLD STREETS★

Below the church the streets of old Bormes are typical of a Provençal village. Many steep alleyways tumble down from the castle, the steepest known as "neck-breaker" *(Rompi-Cuo)!*

Place St-François

A statue of Francesco di Paola, who saved Bormes from the plague in 1481, stands in front of the massive 16C **Chapelle St-François**. The terrace fronting the chapel affords a good **view** of Bormes port and Cap Bénat. The round tower seen in the distance is an old mill.

Église St-Trophyme

> ▶ *200m/218 yd from the Hôtel de Ville.*

An 18C Romanesque-style church near the town hall bears a sundial on the façade with a Latin inscription: *Ab Hora Diei ad Horam Dei* (from daily time

to divine time). Inside, 14 oil paintings by Alain Nonn (1980) depict Stations of the Cross.

Château

Follow the *Parcours Fleuri*, a flower-lined walk round the partially restored castle. Beyond, the terrace provides a fine **view**★ over Bormes, the port, Cap Bénat and the islands of Port-Cros.

SIGHTS

Musée Arts et Histoire

65 Rue Carnot. ⓞ*Open Jul–Aug 10am–noon, 3.30–6.30pm, Sun 10am–noon; Sept–Jun Tue–Sun 10am–noon, 2.30–5pm, Sun 10am–noon.* ⓞ*Closed 1 Jan, 1 May, 25 Dec.* ⓢ*No charge.* ℘*04 94 71 56 60.*
This museum presents local history and personalities *(see above).* A century of regional painting includes landscapes by **Jean-Charles Cazin** (1841–1901).

EXCURSION

Cap de Brégançon

East of Hyères harbour the 16C **Fort de Brégançon** *(closed to the public)* sits on a small island linked to Cap Bénat by a footbridge. Neglected from the beginning of the 18C, then restored under the young General Bonaparte, in 1968 it became the summer retreat of French Presidents.

Latin American Ties

Two inhabitants of Bormes played an important part in the Wars of Independence in Latin America in the 19C: **Hippolyte Mourdeille** (1758–1807) lost his life chasing the Spaniards out of Montevideo; **Hippolyte Bouchard** (1780–1837) organised the Argentinian navy. Bormes honours their achievements by celebrating Argentina's National Independence Day (9 July).

ADDRESSES

🛏 STAY

Le Grand Hôtel – *167 Rte du Baguier, exit noth of Bormes, towards Collobrières.* ℘*04 94 71 23 72. www.augrandhotel.com. Closed Oct–Mar.* 🅿 *45 rooms.* ⏢*8.50€. Restaurant* ⊜. For a whiff of Victoriana, check in at this hillside grand hotel built in 1903. Large, soundproofed rooms, most with a balcony overlooking the sea.

Hôtel Les Palmiers – *Chemin du Petit-Fort, 8km/5mi south of Bormes.* ℘*04 94 64 81 94. www.hotel-palmiers.com. Closed Nov 15–31 Jan.* 🅿 *17 rooms.* ⏢*14€. Restaurant* ⊜⊜. Lying in a residential district halfway between the beach and Brégançon Fort, this hotel is a haven of peace. Most of the rooms have large balconies. The dining room opens out onto a flowered terrace. Half-board only in summer.

🍴 EAT

La Ferme des Janets – *378 Chemin des Janets, Route d'Hyères.* ℘*04 94 71 4511. www.fermedesjanets.fr. Closed 2 Jan –15 Feb.* A footpath wending its way past vineyards and cyprusses leads to a charming mas where poultry are raised. After a hearty meal of traditional country food, relax on the leafy terrace or play a game of boules.

Lou Portaou – *Rue Cubert-des-Poètes.* ℘*04 94 64 86 37 – Closed 15 Nov– 20 Dec, Mon eve and Tue off season, lunch in season. Reservations required.* Set up in a 12C watchtower overlooking the village, this restaurant exudes an unpretentious atmosphere, enhanced by stone walls and antique furniture. Local cuisine is served in the dining room or on the terrace.

🛒 SHOPPING

Markets – Wednesdays in the old village, Saturdays at La Favière (in summer) and Marché Provençal at Pin-de-Bormes (last weekend in September).

TOURS

Guided Tour – *Apr–Sept Thu 5pm.* ⊜*Tickets 5€.* A 90min walking tour of the old town architecture and flora. Sign up at the tourist office.

Brochures – The tourist office has a map of the old village sights, and sell a guide to the local flora, *Guide des Fleurs*, for around *5€*.

Wine – Ask at the tourist office for the brochure "Route des Vins de Bormes-les-Mimosas" for information on the 12 local Côtes-de-Provence vineyards.

CALENDAR

Mimosalia – *Last weekend in January.* Open market for show plants.

Corso – *Between end of January and March.* Bormes celebrates Mardi Gras with a Corso parade and floats throughout the village streets.

Foire aux Santons – *First weekend in December.* Display and sale of the Provençal dolls called Santons.

Cogolin

Var

This typical Provençal village in the Gulf of St-Tropez lies at the foot of an ancient tower. Cogolin is a wine-growing centre, also known for its artisan crafts and hand-made pipes.

🚶 WALKING TOUR

At the top of the village behind Hôtel de Ville are alleyways joined by medieval vaulted passages.

▶ **Population:** 11 066.
🧭 **Michelin Map:** 340 O6; local map: *see Massif des MAURES*.
ℹ **Info:** Pl. de la République. ℘04 94 55 01 10. www.cogolin-provence.com.
▶ **Location:** Located south of Grimaud on the D 558and west of St-Tropez on the N 98 (beware seasonal traffic jams).

Nuts about them!

Pine nuts, also called *pignons*, are delicately flavoured seeds taken from the cones of the stone pine. Their presence in Provençal cooking is by no means recent as the Romans are believed to have used them to make wine and mustard. Today pine nuts are a common feature of Mediterranean cuisine. In savoury dishes, they add texture to green vegetables and lend a crunchy consistency to stuffings. They are also used in pastries, preferably toasted, notably in the delicious almond tarts known as *amandines*.

Pipes from Cogolin

D. Pazery/ MICHELIN

▶ From the tourist office, pass Hôtel de Ville, turn left on Rue du 11-Novembre 1918.

Église St-Sauveur
Dating back to the 11C, with a fine Renaissance serpentine gateway, the church has an altarpiece by Hurlupin (1540) depicting St-Antony. Don't miss the ancient fountain on Place Abbé-Toti.

Rue Nationale
Along this street are more Renaissance doorways, some from the 12C; the bourgeois building at no 46 is the Château Sellier (&*see Sights*). At Place Bellevue is the **Chapelle St-Roch**, decorated with contemporary art, while further up on the hill, via Montée Aloes, is the **clock tower** (14C), from the fortified castle.

SIGHTS
Musée Sellier
46 Rue Nationale ◷*Open Tue–Sat Jun–Sept 10am–1pm, 3–6pm; Oct–May 10am–12.30pm, 2.30–5.30pm.* ◉*2.30€.* ℘*04 94 54 63 28.*
This château houses temporary arts exhibitions, the Musée de Coq "Rooster Museum", the town's emblematic symbol, and the **Medieval Templars Museum**, with documents and uniforms that illustrate the history of the religious order of knights from the 11C–14C.

Marines de Cogolin

▶ *5km/3mi northeast by N 98 & D 98A.*

Near Cogolin lies a fine sandy beach and a marina with regular boat shuttle services to the nearby ports.

ADDRESSES

🛏 STAY
◉ **Le Coq'Hôtel** – *Pl. de la Mairie.* ℘*04 94 54 63 14. www.coqhotel.com. Closed Jan. 24 rooms.* ▣ ⊑*9€. Restaurant* ◉◉. The hotel's mascot is the rooster, whose emblem can be found on the façade or perched inside the lounge. Gay, lively colours adorn the rooms, with an eclectic selection of furnishings. Double-paned windows overlook the square; other rooms face the inner courtyard where breakfast is served.

🍴 EAT
◉ **Côté Jardin** – *Rue Pasteur, facing Pl. du Marché, aka Pl. des Boules; also by the passage at 1 Rue Gambetta.* ℘*04 94 56 80 40. Closed Oct–Mar.* This open-air restaurant in the heart of Cogolin serves grilled meats, sandwiches, snacks, and ice cream in a leafy garden.

🛒 SHOPPING
Provençal Market – There is a lively market every Wednesday and Saturday, and on Friday nights in July-August.

Fabrique de M. Rigotti – *Zone Industrielle, 5 Rue François-Arago.* ℘*04 94 54 62 05. Closed Aug.* This workshop *(guided tours available)* manufactures and sells locally made reeds and parts for musical instruments.

Cogolin Pipes – *Maison Courrieu, 42/58 Avenue Georges-Clémenceau.* ℘*04 94 54 63 82. www.courrieupipes.fr.* Briar roots from the nearby Maures Forest have been providing the raw material for the manufacture of pipes in Cogolin for more than 200 years. Visitors can see the manufacturing techniques as well as beautiful collections of the finished product.

Manufacture de Tapis de Cogolin – *10 Bd. Louis-Blanc (off Avenue Georges-Clemenceau). Exhibition gallery open weekdays 8.30am–noon, 2–5.30pm (Fri 5pm). Closed 15 days in Aug, 24 Dec–2 Jan.* ℘*04 94 55 70 65. www.tapis-cogolin.com.* In the early 1920s, Armenian refugee weavers settled in Cogolin, and the carpet factory was established in 1928. A tour demonstrates hand weaving (using low warp looms – *la basse lisse*) and hand tufting.

Grimaud★

Var

Isolated from the summer crowds of the coast, the perched village of Grimaud has retained its Provençal character, while the modern Port-Grimaud is a lively and bustling summer destination.

🐾 WALKING TOUR
OLD TOWN★
1hr.

▶ *Tour marked by arrows. Map with commentary at the tourist office.*

The 12C **Eglise St-Michel** is a small Roman church in the form of a Latin cross, with restored 19C frescoes. Nearby are the imposing ruins of the 11C **château**, whose three enclosures and four three-storey towers were demolished in 1655. From the upper ramparts there are fine **views★** of the Maures and the Golfe de St-Tropez.

Go down to the **Chapelle des Pénitents** *(to the east)*, which houses the relics of St. Theodore, then join the Route Départementale *(county road)* where you'll find the **Musée d'Art et Traditions Populaires** (🕐open Mon–Sat May–Sept 2.30–6pm, Oct–Apr 2–5.30pm, 🕐closed public holidays; ✍no charge; ℘04 94 55 43 83), which retraces the history of the village in an ancient olive mill.

▶ **Population:** 4 181.
▶ **Michelin Map:** 340 O6
▶ **Info:** Bd. des Aliziers. ℘04 94 55 43 83. www.grimaud-provence.com
▶ **Location:** The old town is 10km/6mi west of St-Tropez on the N 98A, then D 61.
▶ **Parking:** In high season it's best to leave your car near the cemetery *(Parking du Château)*, on the north side of the town near the Pont des Fées.

▶ *Pass by the tourist office and go up the street to the Pl. Neuve.*

A fountain here commemorates the installation of running water in Grimaud in 1886. On the Rue des Templiers leading back to the church stop to admire the arcades and serpentine doorway on the Maison des Templiers.

EXCURSION
Port-Grimaud★

▶ *Follow signs for Port-Grimaud (Nord) 5km/3mi to the car park.*

Port-Grimaud is a 1960s complex of luxury housing with a fully equipped

Port-Grimaud

marina and a fine beach designed to look like a Mediterranean fishing village. Public transport is available in passenger barges *(coches d'eau)*.

Église St-François-d'Assise

This is an ecumenical church, conceived as part of the overall plan and resolutely modern, although inspired by the Provençal Romanesque style. The tower affords a pretty **view**★ of Port-Grimaud, St-Tropez Bay and the Maures Massif.

ADDRESSES

🏠 STAY

⊜⊜ **Chambre d'Hôte La Toscane** – *Route départementale, Villa la Toscane, 4km/2.5mi from Grimaud Village.* ☎04 94 43 24 11. www.la-toscane.com. 4 rooms. 🍴. 🛏. The rooms of this Tuscan-style villa are cheerfully decorated with Provençal furnishings and tiled floors. Nice garden. Swimming pool.

⊜⊜⊜ **La Bastide de l'Avelan** – *Quartier Robert, 2km/1mi from Grimaud Village by the D 94.* ☎04 94 43 25 79. www.bastideavelan.com. 4 rooms. 🍴. 🛏. Simple but charming rooms in this typical Provençal house, all facing the gardens and swimming pool.

🍽 EAT

⊜⊜ **L'Écurie de la Marquise** – *3 Rue Gacharel.* ☎04 94 43 27 26. Closed lunch Jul–Aug. Reservations recommended. Located on a small pedestrian street in the old town, this unpretentious restaurant has a rustic decor and tasty Provençal cuisine.

⊜⊜ **Auberge La Cousteline** – *2.5km/ 1.5mi outheast on D 14.* ☎04 94 43 29 47. www.aubergelacousteline.fr. Closed 10 Nov –15 Dec, Tue Sept–Jun, Mon Oct–May, lunch Jul–Aug. This converted farmhouse set in lush vegetation has a cozy country atmosphere and a menu that changes with the seasonal market.

GUIDED TOURS

👥 **Coches d'Eau de Port-Grimaud** – *12 Pl. du Marché.* ☎04 94 56 21 13. 🚤run mid-Jun– mid-Sept 9am–10pm; mid-Sept–mid-Jun (call for hours). Boat tours on Port-Grimaud and electric boat rental.

👥 **Petit Train Touristique** – *Apr–Oct.* ☎04 94 97 22 85. 🎫6€ (children 3€). This train circles between Grimaud *(place Neuve)* and Port-Grimaud *(main entry to Port-Grimaud Nord, near the car park).*

CALENDAR

Markets– Thursdays on Place Vieille. Thursdays, Sundays in Port-Grimaud.
Fête du Moulin – June.
Les Grimaldines – Festival of World Music, mid-July to mid-August (Tuesday eves).

Hyères★

Var

The palm trees and mild climate of this southernmost Riviera resort are a good indication of what has attracted winter visitors to Hyères (aka Hyères-les-Palmiers) for more than a century. Its magnificent villas and Belle Epoch palace hotels reveal the faded glory of the town once populated by wealthy aristocrats.

A BIT OF HISTORY

Early History – Excavations on the coast reveal that Greeks from Marseille set up a trading station called **Olbia**, which was succeeded by a Roman town **Pomponiana**, and then a convent called **St-Pierre-d'Almanarre** during the Middle Ages, when the inhabitants moved further up the hill. The port of L'Aygade (subsequently silted up) was a base for Crusaders; **St Louis** disembarked there in 1254 on returning from the Seventh Crusade. In the 17C Hyères declined in favour of Toulon.

Modern Revival – The town became a well-known resort in the 19C, particularly among the English, Irish and Americans. In the 20C tourism led to the development of the beaches, although Hyères is a lively town throughout the year. The surrounding plain is extensively cultivated to produce early fruit (strawberries, peaches) vegetables, and great vineyards.

BEACHES

Hyères is blessed with 20km/12.4mi of beaches under lifeguard watch in the summer, and wild coastline on the Giens Peninsula.

L'Almanarre

Long sandy beach near the ancient site of the Greek town of Olbia, used by many surfing schools. The salt road (Route du Sel; accessible only in summer) leads along the peninsula, passing a vast salt-marsh (400ha/988 acres) and then the Étang des Pesquiers, home to many aquatic birds.

▶ **Population:** 55 007.

◔ **Michelin Map:** 340 L7; local map: *see Massif des MAURES*.

▯ **Info:** 3 Av. Ambroise-Thomas. ℘04 94 01 84 50. www.hyeres-tourisme.com.

◉ **Location:** The greater Hyères area is divided into two by the Voie Rapide (Olbia, or N 98), with the old quarters on the slope to the north, and the airport, beaches and harbour to the south.

℗ **Parking:** No charge for parking in the harbour or on Place Louis-Versin. Underground car parks *(fee)* can be found outside the Casino, in the Olbia shopping mall and in the Denis gardens on Place du Maréchel-Joffre.

◌ **Don't Miss:** A tour of the Belle Epoch villas and hotel palaces in summer, available through the tourist office.

◔ **Timing:** An entire day should be reserved for Hyères. Start with walking the scenic streets of the old town *(vieille ville)*, shopping on the Rue Massillon and tours of the palm-lined streets and 19C villas. The afternoon can be spent exploring the Giens peninsula, with a few hours at one of the sunny beaches and ports.

♔ **Kids:** Young children will enjoy the zoo at the Jardins Olbius-Riquier, while older children might prefer karting or watching a race at the hippodrome.

Hyères-Plage

A small forest of umbrella pines shelters this area, which includes the shallow

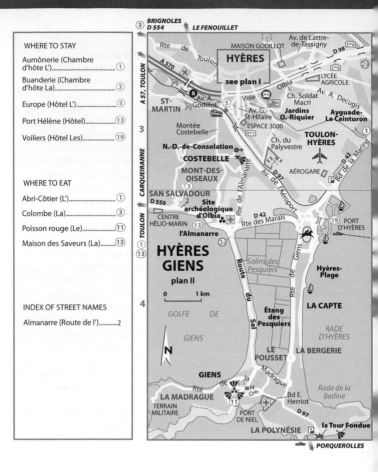

beaches of the Hippodrome, La Capte and La Bergerie up to Giens. Boats leave from the **port** for the Îles d'Hyères.

Ayguade-le Ceinturon
This is the old port of Hyères, where St Louis disembarked on his return from the Seventh Crusade. It is now a pleasant resort area with two sand beaches.

▶ *Continue via Berriau-Plage to Port-Pothuau, a picturesque little fishing port.*

Gardens
👪 Jardins Olbius-Riquier
Av. Ambroise-Thomas. 🕐*Open daily 7.30am–5pm; summer until 8pm.* ⮌*No charge.*
The extensive gardens (6.5ha/16 acres) grow a rich variety of tropical plants, palms and cacti. In the **greenhouse**

the more fragile species can be seen together with a few rare animals. The gardens include a small **zoo**.

Parc St-Bernard (Jardin de Noailles)
Next to the Villa Noailles (⭐ See Sights). The park encloses the castle ruins and has a remarkably wide range of Mediterranean flora. The terraces command a picturesque **view**★ from the old town to the peninsula and the islands.

Parc du Château Ste-Claire
Av. Edith-Warton. 🕐 *Open summer 8am–7pm; winter 8am–5pm.* ⮌*No charge.*
A fine villa built in 1850 by Colonel Voutier, the man who discovered the *Venus de Milo*, sits in the middle of this park filled with exotic plants. The château houses administrative offices.

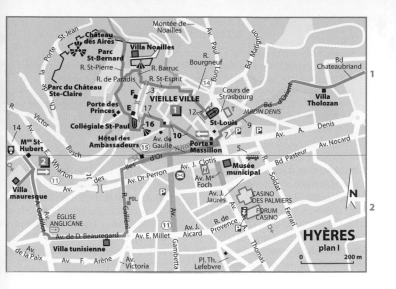

HYÈRES
plan I

0   200 m

🚶 WALKING TOUR
1 A STROLL IN THE OLD TOWN
Allow 1.5hr.

▷ *Leave from Pl. Georges-Clémenceau.*

Porte Massillon
The gate leads onto Rue Massillon, a bustling shopping street, once the main street of the old town, with many Renaissance doorways.

In **Place Massillon,** where the daily market is held, stands the 12C tower, **Tour St-Blaise,** last remnant of a Knights Templar commandery, which now houses temporary art exhibitions (ⓘopen Apr–Oct Wed–Sun 10am–noon, 4–7pm; Nov–Mar Wed–Mon 10am–noon, 2–5.30pm; ∅no charge; ✆04 94 35 22 36).

▷ *From Pl. Massillon take the steps to the Rue Ste-Catherine and Pl. St-Paul.*

Place St-Paul
From this terrace square, once the site of the cloisters of the **Collégiale St-Paul** (ⓘ see Sights), is a good **panorama**★ (viewing table) over the peninsula.

Old Streets
Porte St-Paul (gateway) near the collegiate church is incorporated into a handsome **Renaissance house** with a turret at one corner. Pass beneath and follow Rue St-Paul to Rue Ste-Claire where Porte des Princes stands framing the chevet and bell tower of the Collégiale St-Paul. Retrace your steps to Rue de Paradis where there is a fine **Romanesque house** (no 6), which has been restored.

▷ *From the Rue St-Bernard, walk to the top of the old town until you reach the Villa Noailles (ⓘsee Sights). A large path on the left leads to the ruins.*

A Touch of Exoticism

Hyères is famous for palm trees. The cultivation of palms began to expand in 1867 and reached its peak in the 1930s. There are no less than 10 varieties named Hyères palms. The renown of these trees has brought about their export as far as Saudi Arabia. In Hyères itself, strollers can enjoy the exotic charm of the palms in Avenue Godillot, one of the most attractive roads in France, and in three public gardens: the Casino gardens, Roy gardens and Denis gardens. In the fine Olbius-Risquier gardens there is a complete range of existing species.

Château des Aires Ruins

The ruins can also be reached by car along Montée de Noailles (car park). The Château d'Hyères passed from the Lords of Fos to the Counts of Provence, who rebuilt it in the 13C. The ruins are quite extensive, with panoramic **views**★ from the towers and crenellated keep.

◖ *Return to Rue St-Bernard, taking a right on Rue Barbuc and down Rue Bourgneuf. Before the bottom of the street take a right to Pl. Bourgneuf, then left onto Rue St-Louis.*

Église St-Louis

Pl. de la République. ℘04 94 00 55 50. This former church of the Franciscan convent brings to mind the Italian Romanesque style. It's a good example of the transition from Romanesque to Provençal Gothic.

2 THE 19C TOWN

By car.

The development of winter tourism in Hyères dates back to the mid-19C, including many celebrities: Queen Victoria, the novelist RL Stevenson, and great French figures such as Victor Hugo and Maupassant. Luxury hotels were built to cater to these wealthy visitors.

The "Godillot" District

This is the name of the western part of the town developed by Alexis Godillot, arms supplier to the Second Empire and owner of a quarter of the town.

◖ *Go down Av. Godillot and turn left on Av. de Beauregard.*

Across from the Anglican St Paul's Church is the **Villa Tunisienne** in Moorish style, once home to Godillot's architect, Chapoulart. Go left on Rue Gallieni you'll find the ex-**Hôtel des Palmiers** (1884). On the Avenue des Îles-d'Or, the **Hôtel des Ambassadeurs** still displays a grand entrance.

◖ *At Pl. Georges Clemenceau, follow the Rue Dr-de-Seignoret.*

Quartier Chateaubriand

The beautiful Classic-style villas in the Quartier d'Orient, developed from 1850, have a touch of fantasy. On Boulevard Chateaubriand and Boulevard d'Orient, you can admire the Villa Léon-Antoinette, La Favorite and Villa Ker-André.

SIGHTS
Villa de Noailles

Montée de Noailles. ⌂Guided tours on request. ◷Open Jul–Sept Wed–Thu and Sat–Mon 10am–noon, 4-7.30pm, Fri 4–10pm; Oct–Jun Wed–Sun 10am–noon, 2–5.30pm. ⊗No charge. ℘04 94 01 84 40. www.villanoailles-hyeres.com. In 1923 the Noailles, a rich couple of art patrons, commissioned ths winter villa from the Belgian architect Mallet-Stevens. With its covered swimming pool and 60 or so rooms, it was one of the first modern homes on the Riviera, and quickly became a favourite rendezvous for avant-garde artists of the 1920s (Picasso, Giacometti, Man Ray, Picasso, Dali). The city restored the villa in 1986, and temporary exhibitions are held on the first floor. The Cubist garden was designed by Gabriel Guévrékian.

Musée Municipal

Rotonde Jean Salusse. &. ○*Open Apr–Oct Wed–Mon 10am–noon, 4-7pm; Nov–Mar Wed–Sun 10am–noon, 2–5.30pm.* ○*Closed public holidays.* ◎*No charge.* ℘*04 94 00 78 42.*
Greek and Roman archaeological specimens from Olbia, and a gallery of local artists and furnishings from Louis XV and Louis XVI.

Ancienne Collégiale St-Paul

Pl. Saint-Paul. ○*Open Apr–Sept Wed–Mon 10am–noon, 4–7pm; Oct–Mar Wed–Sun 10am–noon, 2–5.30pm.* ◎*No charge.* ℘*04 94 00 55 50 (Église St Louis).*
The Romanesque bell tower of this former collegiate church goes back to the 12C. A fine Renaissance door and monumental stairway lead to a narthex covered with votive offerings (some dating from the 17C).

Olbia Archaeological Site

Access from Hyères on the D 559, direction Carqueiranne, located at the northernmost point of L'Almanarre. ⊶*Closed for renovation until 2011.*
Defensive village and maritime market port in the 4C BC, Olbia was a stopping point along shipping routes. It's one of the only conserved sites of its kind still existing on the Mediterranean coast.

Chapelle Notre-Dame-de-Consolation

Access from Hyères on the D 559, direction Carqueiranne, to the summit of the Colline de Costebelle. ℘*04 94 57 75 93.*
There has been a sanctuary on the top of Costebelle hill since the 11C. The present chapel was built in 1955. A huge coloured sculpture of Our Lady against the cross forms the bell tower's vertical axis. Sculptures in cement and stone depict events in the Virgin's life. The stark architecture of the interior is enhanced by the monumental blue and gold **stained-glass windows**★. The neighbouring promenade gives a **view**★ of the Hyères and Toulon ports.

Tour Fondue, Gien peninsula

S. Sauvignier/ MICHELIN

🚗 DRIVING TOUR

TOURING THE COAST
Giens Peninsula★★

The Gien Peninsula is a rare natural phenomenon, created when strong currents and the mouths of the two rivers straddling the former island of Giens created a double isthmus on the rocky seabed, linking it to the mainland.
The parallel bars enclose a lagoon, the **Étang des Pesquiers**, that provides an ideal habitat for water fowl. Up to 1 500 flamingos migrate here in mid-September.
The small seaside resort village of **Giens** has castle ruins that form a mound from which there is a magnificent **panorama**★★. To the south lies the little port of Niel, surrounded by a lovely pine wood.

○ *Drive east to the Tour Fondue.*

Tour Fondue

The name comes from a 17C fort that stood here. Boats sail to the Île de Porquerolles, and there is a beautiful view of the islands and peninsula.

Tour of the peninsula on foot

🚶 *18km/11mi – allow 5hr.*

😊 Restricted Access 😊

The western tombolo at Giens, under the protection of the Conservatoire du Littoral, is subject to strict regulations:

- 🚗 Road traffic is permitted from Easter to All Saints' Day on the tombolo road, with no parking en route; the road is closed the rest of the year.

- 🚗 Parking allowed only in the two car parks at each end of the western tombolo.

- 🚗 To reach the beaches, use only the marked paths, without walking on the dunes or vegetation, and avoiding the marked protected zones.

- 🚗 Drying sails or any canvas on the vegetation is not allowed.

The partly signed route links the port of La Madrague to Badine beach through mountainous and pine-forested coastline of hidden beaches and inlets.

EXCURSIONS
Sommet du Fenouillet
4km/2.5mi. From Hyères take Av. de Toulon, turn right onto road to Le Fenouillet. 🚶 *30min round trip.*
From the neo-Gothic **chapel** there is a path to Le Fenouillet, the highest point of the Maurettes (291m/955ft) with a very good **panorama**★ of the Hyères and Toulon harbours and surrounding mountains.

ADDRESSES

🛏 STAY

🍴 **Hôtel l'Europe** – *45 av. Édith-Cavell.* 📞*04 94 00 67 77. www.hotel-europehyeres.com. 25 rooms.* 🛏*7.50€.* A restored 19C mansion close to the train station, with bright rooms.

🍴 **Hôtel Port Hélène** – *D 559, at L'Almanarre.* 📞*04 94 57 72 01. www. hotel-port-helene.fr. 12 rooms.* 🛏*9€.* A cute hotel fronted by a pink façade,

lost among umbrella pines and palms. The rooms are well kept and have balconies offering views of the sea. Very reasonable prices for the area.

🍴–🍴🍴 **Hôtel Les Orangers** – *64 Av. Îles d'Or.* 📞*04 94 00 55 11. www.orangers-hotel.com. 16 rooms.* 🛏*7€.* Charming, comfortable and cosy hotel set in the medieval part of Hyères.

🍴🍴 **Chambre d'Hôte L'Aumônerie** – *620 av. de Fontbrun, Carqueiranne.* 📞*04 94 58 53 56. www.laumonerie.com. 4 rooms.* 🚭🛏 *Reservations recommended.* Away from the bustling crowd, this blissfully quiet pink house among the maritime pines has simply appointed rooms. A private path leads directly to the beach.

🍴🍴 **Chambre d'hôte La Buanderie** – *36 Av. des Colibris, le Mont des Oiseaux, Hyères, 4km/2.5mi south of Almanarre.* 📞*04 04 94 38 30 98. www.la-buanderie. com. Closed 24 Dec–2 Jan. 3 rooms.* 🚭🛏. On a hillside overlooking the sea, this bed and breakfast is tastefully decorated with clean lines and minimal fuss. The swimming pool has a teak deck for sunbathing.

🍴🍴 **Hôtel Les Voiliers** – *Av. du Dr-Robin, port St-Pierre.* 📞*04 94 38 72 24. www.yachtclubhyeres.fr. 36 rooms.* 🛏*7.50€.* A nautical theme decorates this hotel on the port, with reasonably priced doubles and more expensive rooms with harbour views.

🍴🍴–🍴🍴🍴 **Hôtel Le Soleil** – *4 Rue du Rempart.* 📞*04 94 65 16 26. www. hotel-du-soleil.fr. 36 rooms. 20 rooms.* 🛏. Old house with lots of character in the upper part of the old town, near the Nouailles villa-museum. Small but clean rooms; Provence-style breakfast room.

🍴 EAT

🍴 **L'Abri-Côtier** – *Pl. David_di, Plage de l'Ayguade.* 📞*04 94 66 42 58.* 🚭. *Closed Oct–Mar.* In a beach cabana on the Port de l'Ayguade and decorated in bright, cheerful colours, this restaurant offers up tasty Mediterranean dishes such as marinated sardines, roasted camembert with pesto and octopus stew. Sporty types can impress diners at the sand volleyball court.

⊜⊜ **Le Poisson Rouge** – *Port du Niel, Giens Peninsula.* ✆*04 94 58 92 33. www.restaurantlepoissonrouge.com. Closed Mon off season, Sun eve, Nov–Mar.* An enchanting old stone building with a terrace shaded by olive trees overlooking the Port Niel gives this seafood restaurant a pleasant atmosphere.

⊜⊜ **La Colombe** – *663 Route de Toulon, 2.5km/1.5mi west, in La Bayorre.* ✆*04 94 35 35 16. www.restaurantlacolombe.com Closed Sat lunch, Mon, Sun off season, Tue lunch Jul–Aug.* Carefully prepared local cuisine is served in a traditional Provençal house. The spacious, sundrenched terrace and friendly service make it a popular establishment.

⊜⊜ **La Maison des Saveurs** – *18 av. Jean-Jaurès, Carqueiranne (town centre).* ✆*04 94 58 62 33. Closed Mon off season.* Set up in a local building in the town centre, this cosy restaurant decorated in Provençal tradition has two undeniable assets: a lovely terrace sheltered from the beating sun by a plane tree and a menu offering extremely attractive prices.

⊜⊜⊜–⊜⊜⊜⊜ **Les Jardins de Bacchus** – *32 Av. Gambetta.* ✆*04 94 65 77 63. www.bacchushyeres.com. Closed 2–28 Jan, Sat lunch, Sun eve, Mon.* A pleasant stop in the town centre, serving reional wines and local-style meals in a renovated and modern-style dining area or on the summer terrace.

⊜⊜⊜–⊜⊜⊜⊜ **Joy** – *24 Rue de Limans.* ✆*04 94 20 84 98. Closed 5–20 Nov, Sun–Mon off season.* A quiet location in a pedestrianised street, an elegant setting and contemporary cuisine make this restaurant, run by a Dutch couple, a popular choice.

🛒 SHOPPING

Pastor – *86 Avenue Gambetta.* ✆*04 94 01 46 46. www.jlpastor.fr. Closed Mon.* One of the most popular bakery-pastry boutiques in Hyères, with olive or bacon fougasses, lavendar bread in summer, Christmas pastries with anisette, and sorbet sold by the half-litre (0.13gal) in amazing flavors: try the hot wine of Provence!

MARKETS

Provençal – Tuesdays mornings on Place de la République and Saturday mornings along Avenue Gambetta.

Organic – Tuesday, Thursday and Saturday mornings on Place Vicomtesse de Noailles.

Antiques – Every first Sunday of the month on Place Clémenceau and République.

🏃 SPORTS AND LEISURE

Hyères is considered on of France's *stations nautiques*, meaning there are endless opportunities for water sports of all kinds. Ask at the tourist office for more information or visit *www.france-nautisme.com.*

Diving – There are many excellent underwater delights to explore with one of the many diving clubs in the area: in Hyères, La Londe; in the Porquerolles, Porquerolles Plongée; at Port-Cros, Sun Plongée; and in Levant, Levant-Plongée.

Casino – *Casino des Palmiers, Av. Ambroise-Thomas.* ✆*04 94 12 80 80. www.casinodespalmiers.fr.* Slot machines, roulette, blackjack, restaurant and nightclub.

Hyères-Port Saint-Pierre – ✆*04 94 12 54 40 (Hyères).* ✆*04 94 58 02 30 (La Capte, 125 moorings),* ✆*04 94 66 33 98 (l'Ayguade, 500 moorings). www.ville-hyeres.fr.* Four basins able to accommodate 1 350 moorings, 120 of which are for temporary stays.

TRANSPORT

Buses – *Bus station on Pl. Joffre.* ✆*0825 000 650.* Hyères and the Giens Peninsula are served by several bus lines, particularly going to the beaches (Almanarre, Ayguade), and links with boat trips headed for the Îles d'Or.

CALENDAR

Almanarre Funboard Festival – Almanarre beach stretches (6km/3.7mi) along the Étang des Pesquiers, facing the Golfe de Giens. On still days it is popular with families, but when the *mistral* blows, it becomes a mecca for "funboarding" and spectators who come to marvel at the acrobatics. Schools along the beach offer windsurfing lessons.

Îles d'Hyères★★★

Var

These popular Côte d'Azur islands off the Hyères harbour are just a short sea crossing from the coast, and offer many beautiful scenic walking trails, sandy beaches and the rocky inland hills. These islands -- Le Levant, Port-Cros and the Porquerolles -- are also known as the Îles d'Or (Golden Islands) due to the fact that in certain lights their mica shale rocks cast golden reflections.

A BIT OF HISTORY

A Land of Asylum

In the 5C the monks of Lérins arrived, succeeding the Ligurians, the Greeks and the Romans as the islands' lords. In the following centuries they were repeatedly attacked by pirates until François I put the islands of Port-Cros and Levant under the protection (and rule) of the Marquis of the Îles d'Or, provided that the Marquis kept them under cultivation. Despite exemption from taxes, the islands lacked manpower until a right of asylum was established, granting criminals immunity if they remained on the islands.

Jailbirds swarmed ashore, where they turned to piracy, even attempting the capture of one of the king's ships from Toulon. Only under Louis XIV did the last of these dubious characters leave the area.

◔ **Michelin Map:** 340 M/N7/8; local map: *see Massif des MAURES*.

▨ **Info:** Bureau d'Information at the port, Porquerolles. ℘04 94 58 33 76. www.porquerolles.com. Parc National de Port-Cros, Castel Ste-Claire. ℘04 94 12 82 30. www.portcros parcsnationaux.fr.

◑ **Location:** The three islands of the Îles d'Hyères are accessible by ferry boats. Île de Porquerolles is the largest, closes to the Giens peninsula. The best way to get around here is by bike. The Île de Port-Cros, smaller and more mountainous, is a nature preserve: bicycles not allowed. To the east is the Île du Levant, occupied primarily by a military base and private nudist beaches. No matter which island you visit, be sure to take along plenty of drinking water.

👫 **Kids:** A bike ride on Île de Porquerolles and, for children who swim, a snorkeling trip to the underwater trail at Port-Cros. A glass-bottom boat makes trips from Giens to Porquerolles (◔*see Addresses*).

Mexico-sur-Mer

For 60 years this island was the private property of a single family. In 1911, a Belgian engineer, F Joseph Fournier, having made his fortune in Mexico, decided to give Porquerolles as a wedding gift to his young bride. Once settled on the island with his family and an army of gardeners, he attempted to re-create the atmosphere of a Latin American hacienda by importing exotic plants. He began with the cultivation of several exotic fruits then unknown in France, pineapples and kumquats. Along the walks are plants such as the bellombra with its massive roots. Also witness to this replanting, the 180ha/445 acres of vines originally planted have been reduced to half the quantity but continue to produce a reputable rosé. This was the first vineyard to gain the AOC Côtes de Provence *appellation*.

GETTING THERE

The islands are accessible from several ports, with many companies offering half-day or full-day excursions or links. Be sure not to miss the last boat back to the mainland!

From La Tour Fondue (Giens Peninsula) – *TLV (Transports Littoral Varois), Port de La Tour Fondue. ℘04 94 58 21 81. www.tlv-tvm.com.* Regular daily service to the Porquerolles. Circuits of the Porquerolles and Port-Cros available weekdays Jul–Aug.

From Hyères – *TLV, Port Saint-Pierre. ℘04 94 57 44 07. www.tlv-tvm.com. 1 to 4 departures per day depending on the season.* Trips to Port-Cros (1hr), Le Levant (1.5hr); circuit of Port-Cros and Levant available Jul–Aug.

From Le Lavandou, Cavalaire – *Vedettes des Îles d'Or. ℘04 94 71 01 02. Operates mid-Apr–Sept.* Departures for Port Cros, Le Levant, Porquerolles, and St-Tropez.

A FEW GUIDELINES

Fire – During periods of major fire risk, the ALARME plan comes into force (announced before embarkation); it means that access is limited to the beaches, the coastal path and the villages. A recorded message is available by phone from 7pm the evening before, ℘04 98 10 55 41.

Rules – At Porquerolles and Port-Cros, it is forbidden to smoke, make fires, camp, pick the plants or flowers, leave the marked paths, litter or walk pets (outside the village); at Port-Cros it is forbidden to use bicycles, collect seashells, or fish.

Water – There are few or no places to find water on the island (but it can be purchased in the village shops), so bring plenty on your own and be sure to fill up before going on long hikes.

A British Coup

In 1793, after the capture of Toulon by the Revolutionaries (*see TOULON*), British and Spanish squadrons anchored off the Îles d'Hyères. The commander of Fort Ste-Agathe at Porquerolles, forgot ten on his island by the French authorities, had only the vaguest idea of what was happening on the mainland. The British admiral invited him on board his flagship and the commander went unsuspectingly. While the whisky was circulating, British sailors landed, surprised the garrison and destroyed the fort (it was rebuilt in 1810). The ships then raised anchor taking with them, as prisoner, the crestfallen commander.

Allied Landing (August 1944)

During the night of 14 to 15 August 1944, American troops landed on the islands of Port-Cros and Levant to eradicate the German batteries that threatened the Allied Landing.

DRIVING TOUR

TOURING THE ISLANDS

Île de Porquerolles★★★

Porquerolles measures 7km/4.3mi long by 3km/2mi wide, and was called Protè (First) by the Greek settlers who came to live along its shores. The best way to discover the island is by bicycle (hired in the village). The north coast has sandy beaches bordered by pine trees, heather, and scented myrtle; the south coast is steep and rugged with one or two inlets that are easily accessible. There are few inhabitants inland, where you'll find vineyards, pine and eucalyptus woods and thick Mediterranean vegetation.

The Village

The small village of Porquerolles, which lies at the end of a minute port now used as a harbour for pleasure boats, has given its name to the whole island. The village was built by the military in the mid-19C and consists of a main square, a humble church containing an unusual Stations of the Cross carved by a soldier

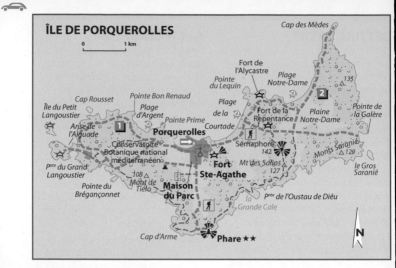

ÎLE DE PORQUEROLLES

with his penknife and a few fishermen's cottages, as well as more recently constructed hotels and private houses.

Fort Ste-Agathe

🕐 *Open May–Sept 10am–noon, 2–5.30pm.* 💶*4€.* ☎*04 94 12 30 40.*

This fort occupyies a strategic position on a mound overlooking the port. Its walls in the shape of a trapezium are surmounted by a massive corner tower, all that remains of the original structure built by François I in 1532. It was rebuilt in 1810 (after the English burned it down in 1793) to meet new military requirements. The round tower is constructed on a massive scale: walls 4m/13ft thick, 20m/66ft in diameter and 15m/49ft high, where the Parc de Port-Cros organises educational exhibitions. From the terrace on top of the tower, with its five embrasures for large-bore cannon, there is a magnificent **view**★.

▶ *At the exit of the village of Porquerolles, follow the Route du Phare, then turn right at the Carrefour des Oliviers to the Hameau Agricole.*

Conservatoire Botanique National Méditerranéen

🕐 *Open Apr–Jun and Oct 9.30am–12.30pm, 1.30–5pm; Jul–Aug 9.30am–12.30pm, 1.30–6pm.* 💶*No charge.* ☎*04 94 12 30 32.*

Since 1985 the major part of the island has been managed by the National Park of Port-Cros, which owns the land. Created in 1979, the Conservatoire was set up to preserve the area and to protect the Mediterranean fauna and flora thriving in the basin. Educational displays.

Walks on the Porquerolles
Lighthouse Walk★★
🚶 *1.5hr round trip.*

This walk to the lighthouse *(phare)* is a "must" even for tourists with only a few hours to spend on the island. The **lighthouse** (☞*guided tours 10am–noon, 2–4pm;* 💶*no charge)* stands on the most southerly point of the island, and has a beam which carries 54km/34mi. From the top a **panorama**★★ extends over most of the island.

Beach Walk★★
🚶 *2hr round trip.*

This pleasant walk along sandy paths, in the shade of the pine trees, starts from Fort Ste-Agathe *(bear left)* and skirts the Plage de la Courtade. After Pointe du Lequin the path dips towards the sea, revealing the **Plage Notre-Dame,** a beautiful sandy beach bordered by pine trees. The **signal station** *(sémaphore)*, Plage d'Argent, **Pointe du Grand Langoustier** and **Cap des Mèdes** all make excellent walks.

La Palud Cove,
Port-Cros Island

B. Kaufmann/ MICHELIN

Île-de Port-Cros★★★

Port-Cros Island is hillier, more rugged, and higher above the sea than its neighbours, and Its lush vegetation is unrivalled on the coast. The island is 4km/2.5mi long by 2.5km/1.5mi wide and its highest point, Mont Vinaigre, reaches 194m/679ft.

A few fishermen's cottages, a bunch of shops and a small church adorn the area around the bay, which is commanded by Fort du Moulin (aka the "Château").

Port-Cros, together with Île de Bagaud and the neighbouring islets has been designated a **Parc National,** covering 700ha/2.7sq mi on land and 1 800ha/7sq mi at sea.

▷ *The principal walks are signed at the quayside; variations are shown by a broken line in red on the map.*

Plage de la Palud★
🚶 *1.5hr round trip.*

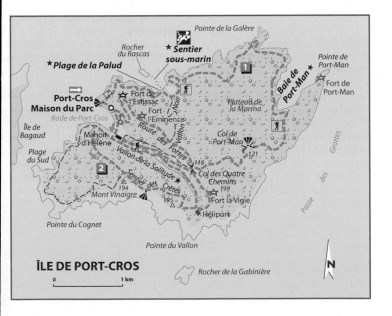

Pointe de la Galère

Rocher
du Rascas

★ **Sentier
sous-marin**

★ **Plage de la Palud**

Pointe de
Port-Man

Baie de
Port-Man

Fort de
Port-Man

**Port-Cros
Maison du Parc**

☆ Fort de
l'Estissac

Fort
l'Eminence

Plateau de
la Marma

Rade de Port-Cros

Île de
Bagaud

Manoir
d'Hélène

Route des Fortes

Col de
Port-Man

Plage
du Sud

Vallon de la Solitude

Sentier des Crêtes

194
195

Col des Quatre
Chemins
199

des Grottes

Mont Vinaigre

Fort la Vigie

Passe

Pointe du Cognet

Héliport

Pointe du Vallon

ÎLE DE PORT-CROS

0   1 km

Rocher de la Gabinière

N

Climb up to the castle for a view of the neighbouring Île de Bagaud. A **botanical path** with Mediterranean specimens winds its way along La Palud Bay before reaching the beach. It passes by **Fort de l'Estissac** (🕐open Jun–Sept; ⊘no charge; 📞04 94 01 40 72), which houses exhibitions on the marine environment.

👥 Underwater Trail★
🕐*Open mid-Jun–Sept. Guided tours by one of the park attendants (except in bad weather). ⊘No charge.*
An underwater observation point, no deeper than 10m/33ft, is located in the section between the little island of Rascas and La Palud beach, marked by yellow buoys. Here anyone who can swim – diving is not necessary – can observe a great variety of typical Mediterranean species that live at this depth. Numbered buoys mark the best viewpoints.
A preliminary visit to the park office in the port is strongly recommended. In the case of a solitary dive (bring along your own mask, breathing apparatus and flippers), a plastified aquaguide is provided to identify marine life.

▷ *Return to the village, passing between the forts of L'Éminence and L'Estissac.*

Vallon de la Solitude★
🚶 *2hr round trip (marked path).*
This is the ideal walk for visitors spending half a day on the island. At the beginning of the valley stands the Manoir d'Hélène–a manor house converted into a hotel – so called after the heroine in Melchior de Vogüé's novel *Jean d'Agrève* which is set on Port-Cros. The path is in deep shade for almost all its length. Once within sight of Fort de la Vigie start back along the cliff walk (Route des Crêtes), with **views** of the sea.

▷ *At Mont Vinaigre bear right into the Vallon de la Fausse Monnaie (Valley of False Currency).*

Port-Man★ – *Round tour of 10km/6mi.*
🚶 *4hr round trip (marked paths).* This pleasant excursion is made along a shaded and nearly level path from which, at the end of the Col de Port-Man, there is a pretty **view** of the Île du Levant. It ends in the **Baie de Port-Man**, a wonderful sheltered green bay.

▷ *Return via Pointe de la Galère, Plateau de la Marma and Plage de la Palud.*

Other Walks
Indicated by the dotted orange line on the map, these include the Plage du Sud (sand) and its impressive cliff, the Route des Forts, the Vallon Noir and the Col des Quatre Chemins.

Île du Levant
Local map 🧭 see Massif des MAURES.
The island consists of a rocky spine 8km/5mi long but only 1 200m/1 300yd wide rimmed by vertical cliffs inaccessible except at two points: the Avis and Estable *calanques*. You disembark at the Aiguade landing and follow the path to Héliopolis. The Lérins monks used to use the Île du Levant as the abbey's garden and granary.
Today 90% of the island is occupied by the Marine Nationale (🚫*access is forbidden*).

Héliopolis
In the western part of the island, the village of Héliopolis and the Grottes area *(private property)* have one of the oldest nudist camps in Europe, opened in 1931. In season local clubs organise diving activities which are open to the general public (🧭 *see Planning Your Trip*).

ADDRESSES

🏠 STAY

🍽🛏 **Hôtel Manoir** – *Port-Cros.* *📞04 94 05 90 52. Closed 4 Oct–9 Apr. 22 rooms.* 🍴*12€. Restaurant*🍽🛏. Charming 1830s hotel in an exceptional garden setting near the port. Minimalist rooms, swimming pool. Half-board only.

🍽🛏 **Mas du Langoustier** – *West of the port, Porquerolles. 📞04 94 58 30 09. www.langoustier.com. Closed Oct–Apr. 45 rooms, half-board.* 🍴. *Restaurant*🍽🛏. The prices are usually high on the Porquerolles, but at least in this chic hôtel-restaurant the quality and service are worth it. The dining room overlooks the sea and the Fort du Langoustier. The cuisine is gourmet Mediterranean and French classics.

🍽🛏 **L'Auberge des Glycines** – *22 Pl. d'Armes, Porquerolles. 📞04 94 58 30 36. www.auberge-glycines.com. Closed at lunch. 11 rooms, half-board.* 🍴*7€. Restaurant* 🍽🛏. This adorable cottage with lavender-blue shutters has rooms overlooking a shaded patio or the village square. The restaurant serves Provençal cooking.

🍴 EAT

ÎLE DE PORQUEROLLES
Bakery – *Pl. d'Armes.*
Convenience Store – *Pl. d'Armes. Closed afternoons off season.*

🍽 **Villa Sainte Anne** – *Pl. d'Armes. 📞04 98 04 63 00. www.sainteanne.com.* 🚪 *Closed Nov–25 Dec, Jan–Feb.* This restaurant near the church has a shady terrace and cuisine that makes the most of the fresh catch of the day. Real Provençal atmosphere and great people-watching. 22 rooms available🍽🛏.

🍽🛏–🍽🛏 **Le Mas du Langoustier** – *F - 83400 Île De Porquerolles. 📞04 94 58 30 09. www.langoustier.com. Closed early Oct–late Apr.* Modern, inventive cuisine with a fabulous sea view. 50 rooms available🍽🛏.

ÎLE DE PORT-CROS
Deli – *Off the main quay (look for signs for épicerie). Closed Dec–Mar.*

🍽 **Sun Bistrot** – *At the port. 📞04 94 05 90 16. Closed Nov–Dec.* Brasserie and snack bar frequented by students from the diving school, selling pizzas, salads, fish and patés.

ÎLE DE LEVANT
Héliopolis – Outside the floating snack boats on the port, this is the only place to eat.

🏃 SPORTS AND LEISURE

Diving – The great depths and the lack of strong currents around the islands and in the Baie de Carqueiranne provide ideal conditions for diving as well as for underwater photography of the many wrecks. There are several diving clubs in Hyères and La Londe; *Sun Plongée* in Port-Cros and *Porquerolles Plongée* in Porquerolles.

👥 **Marabel Aquascope** – *Île de Port-Cros. 📞06 08 26 91 99.* 👁*15€ (4–12 years, 10€). Closed Nov–Mar.* Guided tours *(30min)* in a boat specially designed to observe underwater life. Departures every 40min. Only 10 seats available (rest standing).

👥 **TMV** – *Port de la Tour-Fondue, Giens. 📞04 94 58 95 14. www.tlv-tvm.com. Jun 5 departures per day –* 👁*12.50€ (children 4–10 9.50€).* Glass-bottom boat tours of the underwater flora and fauna *(35min).*

Île de Levant – The accessible areas of the island are in the west and north; in the north a channel is reserved for water sports and an area is set aside for windsurfing. 🏖*The main beaches, reached by the coast path on each side of the landing-stages, are exclusively for nudists.*

🍷 LOCAL WINES

Domaine de la Courtade – *Porquerolles. 📞04 94 58 31 44. www.lacourtade.com. Closed Sat–Sun.* This reputable vineyard can be reached after a pleasant 15-minute walk. Call ahead if you would like to purchase wine at the domaine.

Domaine Perzinsky – *Porquerolles. 📞04 94 58 34 32.* Created in 1989, this vineyard is the closest to the village. Tastings and tours available.

Le Lavandou★

Var

This charming family resort sheltered by the Cap Bénat has preserved its Provençal character. Its port, one of the most important fishing centres in the Var up to the 1930s, is now home to pleasure yachts.

THE TOWN

The main square, **Place Ernest-Reyer**, is laid out like a garden and has pretty **views** of the islands of Levant and Port-Cros. **Boulevard de-Lattre-de-Tassigny** is a pleasant promenade along the beach, with **views** of the port and the coast eastwards to Cap Lardier. There are lively, colourful **markets** on Place du Marché and Avenue du Président-Vincent-Auriol on Thursdays and in Cavalière on Mondays (June to September).

BEACHES

All the beaches at Le Lavandou are sand, placed under constant surveillance and equipped with emergency signals. Standards of comfort, hygiene and sporting facilities vary from one

▶ **Population:** 5 780.

Michelin Map: 340 N7; local map: *see Massif des MAURES*.

Info: Quai Gabriel-Péri. ℘04 94 00 40 50. At Cavalière : La Rotonde, Av. du Golf. ℘04 94 05 80 50. www.lelavandou.com.

Location: Le Lavandou sits on the Corniche des Maures (*see Massif des MAURES*), east of Bormes-les-Mimosas. The centre of town overlooks the port, while most hotels are situated near the beaches to the southwest.

beach to the other. Adventurous tourists can take up windsurfing in St-Clair and canoeing in La Fossette. There is nude sunbathing on Plage du Rossignol and a nudist beach in Le Layet.

BOAT TRIPS
Îles d'Hyères★★★
Allow one day. (For maps and description see ÎLES d'HYÈRES.

ADDRESSES

🏠 STAY

➭➭ **Hôtel Les Alcyons** – *In Aiguebelle, 4.5km/3mi from Lavandou.* ℘04 94 05 84 18. www.beausoleil-alcyons.com. *Closed Oct 16-Apr. 24 rooms.* 🅿 ⛲. At the foot of the Maures Massif, barely 20min from the beach, this friendly establishment is perfect both for swimming and hiking. Each of the rooms, decorated with rattan furniture, has a balcony and air-conditioning.

➭➭➭ **Roc Hôtel** – *In St-Clair, 2km/1mi from Le Lavandou.* ℘04 94 01 33 66. www.roc-hotel.com. *Closed 24 Oct–26 Mar. 29 rooms.* 🅿 ⛲9€. An ochre building houses this hotel lying on a handsome sandy beach. Most of the light, modern rooms have balconies facing the sea. Breakfast is served on the terrace during the summer.

🍴 EAT

➭ **Chez Zète** – *41 Av. du Général-de-Gaulle.* ℘04 94 71 09 11. *Closed Dec, Mon, and Sun evening (except Jul–Aug).* In Le Lavandou's main shopping street, this family business draws large crowds year round with succulent Provençal cooking, an unpretentious setting and a shaded terrace.

➭ **Hélios Plage** – *In Aiguebelle, Av. du Général-Bouvet, then take the footbridge.* ℘04 94 71 49 79. *Closed mid-Nov–Apr and evenings.* ⛲. If you want to lounge around on the sand and enjoy views of Levant Island, sit down in this charming cabin with white wainscoting and choose between a salad, the chef's special or a tasty dish of pasta.

🛒 SHOPPING

Domaine de l'Anglade – *Av. Vincent-Auriol.* ℘*04 94 71 10 89. www.domaine delanglade.fr. Call for hours or check website.* This attractive vineyard, located in the town of Le Lavandou, produces red, white and rosé wine, wine for apéritifs and vinegar. Tasting sessions and shop.

Markets – Thursday morning *(all year)* at Av. Vincent-Auriol, and Monday morning *(Jun–Sept)* in Cavalière.

OUTDOOR THEATRE

Théâtre de Verdure – *Cinéma Plein Air, Av. du Grand-Jardin.* ℘*04 94 00 41 71. Closed Sept–Jun. See the programme for events.* This outdoor theatre puts on summer plays and organises concerts of classical and pop music.

🏃 SPORT AND LEISURE

École de Voile de Cavalière – *Av. du Cap-Nègre.* ℘*04 94 05 86 78. www.ecole voilelavandou.com. Closed Nov–Mar.* This club gives sailing lessons and rents various sailing boats (catamaran, dinghy, optimist) and windsurfing boards.

Seascope – *Gare Maritime.* ℘*04 94 71 01 02. www.vedettesilesdor.fr.* 🎟*12€ (children 9.20€).* The Seascope's transparent hull affords wonderful views of the sea depths, marine flora and many Mediterranean fish species.

CIP Lavandou – *Le Lavandou Port, Quai Gabriel-Péri.* ℘*04 94 15 13 09. www.cip-lavandou.com.* Local diving club with a friendly atmosphere.

The Song of Summer

The image of the Mediterranean is invariably associated with the song of the cicada, together with the game of boules *(pétanque)* and a siesta under the pine trees.
The song of the cicada is stimulated by a combination of particular conditions – the temperature must be at least 25°C/77°F in the shade and there should not be too much noise. A tiny change – such as a cloud passing in front of the sun or the wind rustling in the trees – is enough to upset the insect. Only the male cicada sings, since the noise is a mating call to females. The dawn serenade is produced when the insect contracts two rigid plates, cymbals, on its abdomen which vibrate at 500 times a second. The sound is amplified by a ventral cavity full of air which acts as a resonance chambre. When the female has located the sound using ears on her abdomen, she joins her suitor in the tree.

Lavandou Scuba Diving School – *New Port, underneath the restaurant Le Barracuda.* ℘*04 94 71 83 65. www.lavandou-plongee.com.* Lessons for both beginners and experienced divers and various other services (equipment rental, tours of shipwrecks, exploring sites around Port-Cros, etc.). *Call to reserve a time.*

Yachting harbour

B. Kaufmann/ MICHELIN

Massif des Maures★★

Var

The emerald forests of the Massif des Maures stretch along the coastline from Hyères to St-Raphaël and up into the Gapeau and Argens river valleys. A drive along the **Corniche des Maures** reveals glimpses of the colbalt blue sea against rocky inlets, contrasting with the wilder landscape of the inland hillside.

A BIT OF HISTORY

Maures has Provençal origins that mean "dark forests", used to describe this densely wooded mountain range. Traditionally the name is an allusion to the Moorish pirates from Spain (they were really Saracens) who drove the inhabitants from the shore into the hills from where they could watch the horizon.

The 20C vogue for sea-bathing brought this magnificent coast back to life and ended the economic isolation of the region. On 15 August 1944 the Allied and French armies landed on the Maures beaches to liberate the south of France.

🚗 DRIVING TOUR

Corniches des Maures★★
From Le Lavandou to St-Tropez on D 559

Le Lavandou★
🕭 *see Le LAVANDOU.*

St-Clair
Small resort a short distance from the main road with a beautiful beach.

Aiguebelle
A peaceful seaside resort.

Cavalière
Cavalière has a fine views and a beach sheltered from the *mistral*.

- 🕭 **Michelin Map:** 340 M/P5/7 or 528 folds 47 to 49.
- 🚩 **Info:** Maison du Tourisme Golfe de St-Tropez/Pays des Maures, Carrefour de la Foux, Gassin. ✆ 04 94 55 22 00. www.golfe-infos.com.
- ◖ **Location:** The Maures is made up of four parallel chains of geographical relief, two along the coast (including the Îles d'Hyères) and two inland (La Verne and La Sauvette), separated by the River Grimaud and the River Collobrières.

Pramousquier
A modest resort with a sheltered beach of fine sand. The road leaves the shore to wind through pines and gardens.

Canadel-sur-Mer
Canadel, lying at the base of the last foothills of the Pradels range and flanked by superb pine woods, possesses one of the most sheltered beaches on the Maures coast. A monument on the beaches commemorates the **Allied Landings** here on 14 August 1944.

Cavalaire-sur-Mer
A perfect holiday destination, with a fine sandy beach, scuba diving, and a port with 1 200 moorings. Just beyond are the beaches of Le Rayol (🕭 *see Domaine du RAYOL*).

La Croix-Valmer
This village has been a winter retreat and spa since the early 1900s. Today it is known for its reputable Côtes de Provence wines. The site of La Croix village is said to be where Constantine had his vision while on his way to Rome to claim the Empire.

According to legend he saw a cross in the sky with the words *In hoc signo vinces* "in this sign you will conquer", a prediction of his forthcoming victory. After the battle Constantine converted to Christianity. A stone cross erected on

GENERAL ADVICE ABOUT VISITING THE MASSIFS

Cars – Roads belonging to the DFCI (Défense Forestière Contre l'Incendie – forest fire-fighters) are closed to public traffic. They count as private roads; an open barrier does not indicate that access is permitted. Parking in front of these barriers is prohibited and cars should be parked well to the side of narrow roads to allow the passage of emergency vehicles. Pedestrian access is always possible.

Fire Risk – Fires are prohibited at all times, and smoking is prohibited Mar–Oct. During periods of high fire risk, the ALARME plan is put into action and certain public roads (classed as major

fire risks) may be closed to vehicles. Offenders are liable for heavy fines. Walkers are strongly advised to avoid such areas for reasons of safety. To check for closures call ☎04 98 10 55 41.

Camping – Camping is prohibited in the massif and within 200m/656ft of any of the forests.

Animals – Pets must be kept on a leash; do not disturb the wild animals.

Plants and chestnuts – Do not stray from marked paths or pick plants or fruit, in particular chestnuts, as you may be requested to pay a fine.

Litter – Use the rubbish bins provided or take any rubbish with you.

---

the pass commemorates the story and gives the village its name.

St-Tropez to Fréjus★★
On the opposite side of the peninsula, the Massif des Maures slopes gently down towards the Mediterranean. On the sunny coast running along N 98, these cheery seaside resorts boast fine beaches, with clusters of rocks breaking the clear surface (& see Driving Tour ③).

Beauvallon
Beauvallon is on the north shore of St-Tropez Bay, well shaded by pines and oaks.

Ste-Maxime★ & see STE-MAXIME.
The road, which skirts the coast closely as far as St-Aygulf, circles Cap Sardinaux.

The coastline between La Nartelle and St-Aygulf is broken up into several inlets (calanques) with small beaches.

Massif des Maures

D. Pazery/ MICHELIN

Les Issambres

This pretty resort is associated with Val d'Esquières, San Peïre and Les Calanques and forms a rapidly expanding holiday centre.

EXCURSION
La Garde-Freinet

🛈 1 Pl. Neuve. ✆04 94 43 67 41. www.lagardefreinet-tourisme.com.

In the heart of the Maures Massif, between the Argens Valley and St-Tropez Bay, lies the quiet village of La Garde-Freinet. A flourishing crafts centre, the town is also known for its scenic cork-oak and chestnut forests, perfect for a day of hiking, biking or horseback riding.

La Garde-Freinet is 10km/6mi north of Grimaud (🔖 see GRIMAUD) on the D 558. The tourist office has marked out a promenade through the steep, winding streets of the village (1hr) with arrows and an accompanying map.

After a walk through the perched village, visit the ruins of the Fort Freinet. A Provençal market takes place on Place Neueve Sunday and Wednesday mornings.

A Bit of History

Owing to its strategic location La Garde-Freinet suffered over a century of occupation by the Saracens. In local tradition the name Saracen is applied collectively to the Moors, Arabs, Turks and Berbers who harassed the country from the 8C to the 18C. After being defeated by Charles Martel at Poitiers in 732, the Arabs drifted down into Provence. Although driven back several times, they managed to hold on to the region around La Garde-Freinet. On the height which dominates the present village they built a fortress from which they used to descend to pillage inland Provence. It was only in 973 that Count William, the Liberator, managed to expel them.

In contrast to the damage they caused, the Saracens taught the Provençal people about medicine, how to use the bark of the cork oak and how to extract resin from pine trees. They also introduced the flat house tile and the tambourine.

Ruins of Fort Freinet
1km/0.6mi.

▷ *Take GR 9 on the south side of the village. Leave the car in the parking area leveled out at a bend in the road and follow the signs painted on a rock. This rough trail is not recommended for small children.*

🚶 *1hr round trip.*

There is a good view of the Le Luc Plain and the first Alpine foothills. A path leads first to a mission cross (Croix des Maures) and then climbs quite steeply to the fortress ruins (12C–16C) of the feudal castle attributed to the Saracens. It blended in for many years with the rocky site.

Excavation work carried out has resulted in the discovery and uncovering of the foundations of a 15C fortified village. From the summit, the **panorama**★ extends out to sea and a long way inland.

▷ *Take the path running along the moat, leading back to the village.*
Or go back to the car park and follow the forest track for 5km/3mi until you reach the sign for Roches Blanches.

Panorama des Roches Blanches★

At this spot, known as White Rocks *(for access, walk round the barrier)*, there is a view in all directions: *(left)* Garde-Freinet Forest and the valley of the River Argens *(right)* over the slopes of the north Maures and *(east)* the bay of St-Tropez.

🚗 DRIVING TOURS

1 IN MAURES COUNTRY
70km/44mi leaving from Hyères – allow one day. 🔖 *See map pp128–9.*

▷ *Leave Hyères northeast on N 98.*

After crossing the Gapeau, the road passes salt-marshes near Hyères, with good views of Cap Bénat and the Île du Port-Cros.

Guided Nature Hikes

The ten communes of the Massif des Maures organise hikes of 1-2.5hr with different themes (flora-fauna, the forest life, cultural heritage, night walks, etc.). The calendar of walks is available from the Comité Départemental du Tourisme du Var *(www.tourismevar.com or www.webvds.com/sorties)*. Information and registration at the following tourist offices: Bormes-les-Mimosas ℘04 94 01 38 38; Hyères ℘04 94 01 84 50; La Londe-les-Maures ℘04 94 01 53 10; Le Muy ℘04 94 45 12 79; Le Pradet ℘04 94 21 71 69; Pierrefeu-du-Var ℘04 94 28 27 30; Ramatuelle ℘04 98 12 64 00; Roquebrune-sur Argens ℘04 94 45 72 70.

Jardin d'Oiseaux Tropicaux
At La Londe-les-Maures.
🕐*Open Jun–Sept 9am–7pm; Feb–May 2–7pm, Oct–Nov 2–6pm.* 🕐*Closed Dec–Jan.* ✍8€ *(child 5€).* ℘04 94 35 02 15. www.jotropico.com
In a large natural park full of palms and exotic plants from Australia, Mexico and Asia, are tropical birds of all sizes and colours, many in danger of extinction, from all corners of the world.

▷ *Take the D 559 towards Canadel-sur-Mer. Turn left onto D 27.*

Col du Canadel★
Alt 267m/876ft.
Suddenly the sea comes into view and there is a superb **panorama**★★ of Canadel, Pramousquier beach, Cap Nègre, the Bormes harbour and Cap Bénat.
🚶*Park your car on the col and follow the forest track on the right to the Col de Caguo-Ven, 1hr.*
This is a picturesque route with magnificent **views**★ of the Maures Massif and, to the south, the coast and the Îles d'Hyères. Vieux-Sauvaire is reached after one hour's walk *(restaurant open here in season)* after which the path goes back down to Col de Barral (372m/1 220ft).

▷ *Continue along D 27 then turn left onto N 98, heading towards La Môle, then straight to Dom Forest.*

Forêt Domaniale du Dom★
This state forest, composed mainly of pines, cork oaks and chestnuts, spreads over the Les Pradels and La Verne ranges. **Jean Aicard** (1848–1921), poet and nov-elist, set his work *Maurin des Maures* in this area.

Arboretum de Gratteloup
🅿*Car park beside the N 98, by the Maison Forestière.* 🕐*Open daily.* ✍*No charge.* ℘04 97 71 06 07.
This arboretum (3ha/7.4 acres), created in 1935, contains mostly Mediterranean species (cypress, pines, juniper, yoke elms and hop hornbeams), and an area devoted specifically to chestnut trees.

▷ *At Col de Gratteloup, take D 41 heading for Bormes-les-Mimosas.*

Col de Caguo-Ven
Alt 237m/778ft.
From the pass, there is a **view** of the Hyères and Bormes ports and the Île de Porque-rolles.
🚶*At the peak, another 45min walk towards Col de Barral and Col du Canadel.* You'll arrive at the giant boulders of **Pierre d'Avenon** (alt 443m/1 450ft), where the circular **view**★ encompasses the whole Maures coastline from Cap Lardier to Hyères with the port of Le Lavandou and Bormes.

▷ *Return to Hyères via Le Pin and the D 559.*

② PASS ROAD★★
109km/67mi leaving from Le Lavandou – one day. 🚶*See map pp128–9.*
This beautiful, circular tour along very hilly but unfrequented roads, goes over at least seven passes *(cols)* and penetrates deep into the heart of the massif.

> *From Le Lavandou take D 559 west to Le Pin and turn right onto D 41.*

The road winds uphill, with a fine **view** ahead of Bormes and its castle.

Bormes-les-Mimosas★
see BORMES-LES-MIMOSAS.

> *Continue on D 41 to Col de Caguo-Ven. Continue downhill to Col de Gratteloup (alt 199m/656ft).*

The road passes over wooded slopes of cork oak and chestnut – deep valleys *(east)* and glimpses of the sea and the mountains around Toulon *(west)*.

> *Continue along D 41.*

Col de Babaou★
Alt 415m/1 362ft. There is an attractive **panorama**★ of the Giens peninsula and the Îles d'Hyères. Beyond the pass rise the tallest of the Maures summits, wooded by magnificent chestnuts and cork oaks.

> *Turn right onto D 14.*

Collobrières
The picturesque houses of this shaded town overlook the river swirling beneath an old humpback bridge. The local specialities are *marrons glacés* (sugared chestnuts) and other delicacies made with chestnuts. The *confiserie* (confectionery) is open to the public.

> *Continue east on D 14. After 6km/3.7mi turn right.*

A narrow road leads to the ruins of the former Carthusian monastery of La Verne, in its majestic forest setting.

Monastère de la Verne★★
Open Wed–Sun Feb–Mar and Oct–Dec 11am–5pm; Apr–Sept until 6pm. Closed public holidays. ⊚6€. ℘04 94 43 48 28.
The monastery was founded in 1170 on an isolated wooded slope in the

Maures. Rebuilt several times, it survived until the monks abandoned it during the Revolution. Since 1983 it has been occupied by the religious Order of Bethlehem.

Porch
The huge doorway is built of blue-green serpentine stone. Two ringed columns flank the door, surmounted by a triangular pediment resting on two pilasters.

Guesthouse
A path on the right of the porch leads to the reception room, a large courtyard with a fountain at the centre, and buildings where guests were received. A passage leads to the scullery and the 12C **kitchen** with rib vaulting, while the wooden staircase in the courtyard leads to the remains of the **little cloisters:** six barrel-vaulted serpentine bays. The **great cloisters** have depressed vaulting and serpentine decoration.

> *Return to D 14 and proceed east.*

After Col de Taillude the road looks across La Verne Valley to the ruins of the charter house crowning the opposite slope and then, after passing high above the hamlet of Capelude, makes its way into the upper valley of the Le Périer stream. From the centre of the valley there is a **vista** of the Grimaud Plain and St-Tropez Bay.
Abruptly the road turns into the valley of the Giscle (or the Grimaud rivulet) from where Grimaud can be spotted in the distance.

Grimaud★ *see GRIMAUD.*
> *From Grimaud take D 558 south, crossing the Grimaud Plain.*

Cogolin *see COGOLIN.*
> *N 98 follows the Môle Valley upstream. 8km/5.1mi from Cogolin, just before La Môle, the winding D 27 strays from the valley to cut across the coastal range. Go back to Le Lavandou by the coast road.*

③ FROM ST-TROPEZ TO ST-RAPHAËL

39km/24mi – half a day not including tours of St-Tropez and St-Raphaël.
See map pp128–9.

St-Tropez ★★ *see ST-TROPEZ.*

▷ *Leave St-Tropez to the southwest on D 98A. After 4km/2.5mi turn right.*

Port-Grimaud ★ *see GRIMAUD.*

▷ *Return to N 98, which skirts the north shore of the bay, overlooking St-Tropez. Follow N 98 up to St-Aygulf.*

St-Aygulf *see FRÉJUS.*
Beyond St-Aygulf the view sweeps over the lower Argens Plain. The splendid rocks of the Montagnes de Roquebrune stand out from the Maures Massif. Turning towards the Esterel range, you can see the Dramont Signal with the peak of Cap Roux looming in the background.

Further north is **Fréjus**★ *(not marked as part of route p129).* *see FRÉJUS.*

▷ *Take Bd. S.-Decuers south.*

Fréjus-Plage *(not marked as part of route p129).* *See FRÉJUS: Port-Fréjus.*

▷ *Take N 98 by the sea to St-Raphaël (not marked as part of route p129).*

④ THE SUMMITS ROUTE★

120km/74.5mi – allow one day.
See map pp128–9.

Round trip starting from St-Tropez

This excursion passes through wooded countryside to the lower slopes of the twin peaks of Notre-Dame-des-Anges and La Sauvette.

▷ *Leave St-Tropez to the southwest on D 98A along the bay of St-Tropez. At La Foux turn left onto N 98 to Cogolin.*

Cogolin *see COGOLIN*

▷ *Stay on N 98 towards Môle Valley.*

Shortly before the village of La Môle stands a château *(right)* with pepperpot towers where **Antoine de Saint-Exupéry** (1900–44), aviator and writer, lived as a child *(see Massif de l'Esterel).* Vineyards give way to forest-covered slopes of **Dom Forest**★.

▷ *Continue along N 98. At Col de Gratteloup turn right onto D 41, up to Collobrières, then after La Rivière turn right onto D 14. After 3km/2mi to the east of Collobrières, turn left onto D 39.*

The road winds through wooded countryside overlooking a steep-sided stream and affords the occasional glimpse of La Sauvette peak to the right. Shortly before Col des Fourches the road to the left leads to the Notre-Dame-des-Anges Hermitage, pinpointed by the television relay mast.

Notre-Dame-des-Anges★
The priory near the summit (780m/ 2 559ft) stands in an attractive **setting**★

Hermann's Tortoise

This tortoise, the only species native to France, appeared in Mediterranean Europe about one million years ago. It lives in the scrub *(maquis)* which provides all its food – oak leaves, fruit and molluscs. After hibernating in a tree stump until about June, the female lays her eggs in a nest which she immediately abandons. If they survive the first two months of life as well as predatory badgers, the baby tortoises can look forward to a life of 60 to 100 years.

Falling victim to man-made alterations in its habitat and unregulated collecting, the tortoises now survive only in Corsica and in the Massif des Maures, where a tortoise village has been established to protect the species.

Admiring the view from Notre-Dame-des-Anges

amid schist rocks and chestnut trees. The Merovingian foundation may have superseded an earlier pagan site. Remodelled in the 19C, the buildings included accommodation for pilgrims and a chapel, covered with votive offerings.

Beyond the screen of trees surrounding the chapel there is a remarkable **view**★ *(north)* of the Argens depression backed by the Alps; *(west)* Ste-Baume; *(south)* over the Maures heights to the sea, the Hyères islands, the Giens Peninsula and Toulon.

◗ *Return to Col des Fourches and turn left towards Gonfaron.*

The road passes by **La Sauvette** (779m/2 556ft), the highest point in the Maures Massif, before descending to Le Luc Plain.

Gonfaron

This village set within the Massif des Maures is still an active centre of cork manufacturing. At the north edge of the village rises an isolated hill, crowned by a chapel dedicated to St Quinis.

Cork Oak

The cork oak is an evergreen that requires heat and humidity. It grows near the sea up to a height of 500m/1 640ft and has proved to be particularly resilient in the case of fire. It is easy to spot on account of its large blackish acorns and scored bark.

Gathering the bark *(démasclage)* takes place for the first time when the tree is 25 years old; this is known as the male bark. Subsequent harvests, which take place in July and August when the sap is rising, occur every nine or ten years, which is the time it takes for a new layer of cork to form; this is known as the female bark, which is highly prized by industry (manufacture of chipboard at Le Muy) and craftsmen (boards, ornamental objects and materials for ceramicists).

By the mid-1960s the Maures area was producing 5 000t of cork yearly, supplying 100 or so local firms. In 1994 the foresters of the Var department produced 500t of cork, but the local firms had disappeared. Nowadays, few cork oak trees are harvested in the Var..

⚐⚑ Village de Tortues de Gonfaron
In Gonfaron turn right onto D 75. The best times to visit are during the morning (11am) and in the late afternoon (4pm). ♿⏰*Open Mar–Nov 9am–7pm.* ⬛*9€ (child 6€).* ☎*04 94 78 26 41. www.villagetortues.com.*
The village is a breeding centre for the Hermann tortoise species *(Testudo hermanni hermanni)*, a one-million-year-old herbivore threatened with extinction. Courtship occurs in April, May and September, egg-laying mid-May and hatching in early September. The village is also home to France's freshwater turtle and the common or European tortoise *(Testudo graeca).*

▷ *Continue on D 75; at the crossroads turn right onto D 558 towards La Garde-Freinet.*

La Garde-Freinet
⬙*see La GARDE-FREINET.*

▷ *Take D 558 south.*

Still descending, the road passes cork oak and chestnut-covered slopes and affords glimpses of the bay and peninsula of St-Tropez.

Grimaud★ ⬙*see GRIMAUD.*

▷ *Return to St-Tropez by D 14 and D 98A at La Foux.*

ADDRESSES

⌂ STAY

⬙ **Chambre d'Hôte Le Mas des Oliviers** – *Chemin les Ferrières, Puget-Ville, 2.5km/1.5mi by N 97 Route de Cuers.* ☎*04 94 48 30 89. www.masdesoliviers. com. 3 rooms.* ⬛*Meal* ⬙⬙. This charming Provençal *mas* seems lost among vineyards and olive groves. Large, carefully kept rooms are decorated in Mediterranean style. Sauna and fitness room. Horse riding and cycling nearby.

⬙ **Golfe Bleu** – *Rte. de La Croix-Valmer, Cavalaire-sur-Mer, 1km/0.6mi from the wayside cross on D 559.* ☎*04 94 64 07 56. Closed Nov–Jan. 15 rooms.* 🅿 ⬛*7€. Restaurant* ⬙. Neat, homey establishment away from the town centre. The rooms are soundproofed and air-conditioned. The simply decorated restaurant opens out onto a small terrace.

🍴 EAT

⬙ **Alizés** – *Promenade de la Mer, Cavalaire-sur-Mer.* ☎*04 94 64 09 32.* ⬛*12€.* A lively atmosphere and the undeniable charisma of the owners are the main assets of this modern-hotel and restaurant offering pretty views of the sea. Family cooking with an emphasis on fish and homemade desserts. 18 guest rooms available.

⬙⬙ **Maures** – *19 Bd. Lazare-Carnot, Collobrières.* ☎*04 94 48 07 10.* This village inn enjoys a well-deserved reputation among its regular clientele on account of the excellent quality/price ratio and the warm welcome. In summer meals are served on the terrace beneath the plane trees.

🛒 SHOPPING

Confiserie Azuréenne – *Bd. Koenig, Collobrières.* ☎*04 94 48 07 20. www.confiserieazureenne.com.*
This confectionery is entirely devoted to chestnuts. It makes and sells marrons glacés, chestnut jam, sugared chestnut purée etc. Visitors can also be shown around the factory museum.

MARKET
Marché de la Croix Valmer every Sunday morning.

🏃 SPORT AND RECREATION CENTRE

Smash Club – *Av. du Golf, Cavalière.* ☎*04 95 05 84 31. Closed mornings Nov–Mar.* A sports centre with six tennis courts, golf links, a weight room, an archery gallery, a sauna, mountain bikes for rental. Tennis tournaments and badminton, beach-volley, football and boules competitions are organised during the summer season.

Village of Ramatuelle

Ramatuelle★

Var

Set among vineyards halfway up a slope, this pink-roofed village possesses all the features of an old Provençal town with its narrow winding streets, vaulted arches and old house huddled against the ancient town wall. Although quite isolated, Ramatuelle is a popular summer destination close to the Pampelonne Beach.

- ▶ **Population:** 2 271.
- **Michelin Map:** 340 O6; local map: *see Massif des MAURES*.
- **Info:** Pl. de l'Ormeau. ☎04 94 12 64 00. www.golfe-infos.com.
- **Location:** Ramatuelle lies 11km/7mi east of La Croix-Valmer (*see Massif des MAURES*) and south of St-Tropez on the D 93.
- **Parking:** There are parking areas around the church, the cemetery and the Town Hall (*Mairie*).

VISIT
The Village
The narrow, winding roads passing beneath arches and flowery window boxes make for an enjoyable stroll through the village. The Romanesque **church** with its flat east end opens through a 17C serpentine door. Inside are two 17C Baroque altarpieces of magnificent gilded wood. Many door lintels, including that on the entrance to the church, mention the year in which the village was rebuilt: 1620.

At the bottom of the village, on Rue du Moulin Roux, you'll find prisons built under Napoleon III (late 1800s) that are often wrongly attributed to the Saracens because of their Arabic style.

An Unlucky Past

In spite of its isolated location, the village fell under the occupation of the Saracens who had otherwise made their lair in La Garde-Freinet. During the Wars of Religion in 1592, having opted to side with the Catholic League, Ramatuelle was destroyed after a siege.

Monument to the Resistance
Opposite the cemetery stands a memorial to the members of the Special Services who died in the Second World War. The submarines that stayed in contact with the members of the Resistance during the occupation used to wait offshore by the Roche-Escudelier.

Domaine du Rayol★★

Var

The Domaine du Rayol is a reminder of the Riviera's period of luxury, created at the beginning of the 20C when European industrial and banking families built holiday seaside resorts on the lush virgin landscape. Rayol itself enjoys an exceptional site on the coast, forming an amphitheatre on wooded slopes surrounded by cork oaks, mimosas and pines. The beach at Rayol-Canadel-sur-Mer *(2km/1mi west via D 599)*, a sheltered cove bordered by pines, is one of the nicest on the Maures coastline.

- **Michelin Map:** 340 N7.
- **Info:** Pl. du Rayol, Rayol-Canadel-sur-Mer. &04 94 05 65 69. www.domainedurayol.org.
- **Location:** Coming from St-Tropez, the road into the domaine branches off to the left at the entrance of the village Rayol-Canadel-sur-Mer (*see Massif des MAURES*).

SIGHTS
The Domaine★★

Av. des Belges. Open Jul–Aug 9.30am–7.30pm; Apr–Jun and Sept–Oct 9.30am–6.30pm; Nov–Mar 9.30am–5.30pm. 8€. &04 98 04 44 00. www.domainedurayol.org.

In 1910 a Parisian banker named Courmes had a house built here surrounded by exotic gardens. The stock market crash in 1929 put an abrupt end to the development of the estate.

The aeronautics engineer Potez, who took refuge on the coast in 1940, reno-vated the property and returned the garden to its former glory. He had a belvedere built by Patek, with a circular pergola, linked to the coast by a magnificent flight of steps. In 1989 the Conservatoire du Littoral acquired the whole estate (20ha/49.5 acres) after several decades of neglect, in order to preserve some of the last wild shores of the Corniche des Maures.

Magical Summer Nights

During the summer season, there are evening concerts of classical music in the Domaine du Rayol, with the opportunity to stroll through the illuminated gardens during the intervals.

Domaine du Rayol

D. Pazery/ MICHELIN

Posidonia, the Lungs of the Mediterranean

This flowering plant, which looks like bunches of long green leaves, is an essential element of marine life in the Mediterranean. It grows on sandy seabeds on the narrow coastal fringes.

Posidonia plays the same role as forests: it provides a habitat for animal and plant species, a source of oxygen and stabilises the seabed. It is threatened with damage and extinction by man's intervention: unpurified sewage discharge, uprooting by boats mooring, building on the coast and by the invasion of another species (*Caulerpa taxifolia*).

The landscape gardener Gilles Clément has created a patchwork of gardens planted with rare and exceptional vegetation found growing in Mediterranean climates around the world. Winding paths offer glimpses of the turquoise sea and a headland carpeted with pines.

Sentier Marin★

🕐 *Open Jul -Aug. Guided underwater tours of Mediterranean flora and fauna (1.5hr) Tue–Sun, advance reservation and payment required.* ⊚15€.

All equipment is supplied on the premises (diver's suit, mask, fins and snorkel).

A trip from the little beach at Rayol offers an unusual view of underwater life in the Mediterranean. This tour, accompanied by wardens from the Conservatoire, is preceded by an introduction to the species most likely to be seen, their description and the best place to look for them among the posidonia.

St-Tropez★★

Var

After almost a half-century of fame, St-Tropez, or St-Trop' as the locals say, is still in fashion. Its attraction lies both in its stunning location on the southern shore of one of the most beautiful bays of the Riviera, and its continuous stream of celebrities, artists, musicians, journalists and photographers who meet here every summer. The contrast of modern luxury yachts and the scruffy but colourful Provençal facades of the little port of St-Tropez is what makes the Riviera so alluring to the throngs who visit here year after year.

A BIT OF HISTORY

The Legend of St Tropez – The town is named after the Christian centurion **Torpetius** (Torpès), whose body, beheaded by Nero, was cast adrift in a boat with a cock and a dog, who were meant to

▶ **Population:** 5 612.
🧭 **Michelin Map:** 340 O6; local map: *see Massif des MAURES*.
🛈 **Info:** Quai Jean-Jaurès. ☎04 94 97 45 21. www.ot-saint-tropez.com.
◗ **Location:** Unless you arrive by yacht, access is slow and frustrating, with infamous summer traffic jams on the only road to the town (D 98a) in July and August; try to get there early in the morning, or stay on the less crowded southeastern coasts of the St-Tropez Peninsula.
🅿 **Parking:** Parking in the village, even in parking garages, is difficult. The map designates free, covered, and paying parking areas on the peninsula.

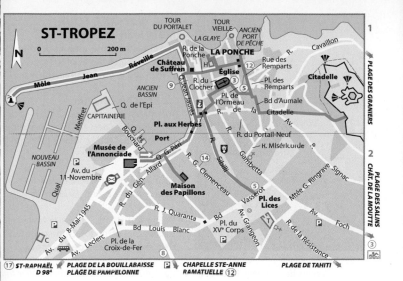

ST-TROPEZ

devour his remains. Instead it arrived ashore intact where St-Tropez stands.

Republic of St-Tropez (15C–17C) – In 1470 the Grand Seneschal of Provence accepted the offer of a Genoese gentleman, Raffaele de Garezzio, to settle with 60 Genoese families in St-Tropez, which had been destroyed by war at the end of the 14C. De Garezzio rebuilt and defended the town. St-Tropez became a sort of small, prosperous republic administered by the heads of the families and later, by elected consuls.

Judge Suffren (18C) – Among the St-Tropézian navigators who contributed to the rise of the city and the defence of the kingdom in the 17C, the most famous is Pierre-Andre de Suffren (1729–1788), a judge with the Knights of Malta who became a captain of the royal navy *(you will see his statue on the quay)*. He was sent to the Indies, where he won several victories over the British.

The "Bravades" – Two *bravades* or "acts of defiance" take place every year. The first of these acts, a simple religious procession in honour of St Tropez, has maintained its local importance since the end of the 15C. On 16 and 17 May the gilded wooden statue of St Tropez

is carried through the festive town, where red and white (the colours of the corsairs) prevail. The second act celebrates the victory of the St-Tropez militia who, on 15 June 1637, fended off 22 Spanish galleys attempting to take the town by surprise.

A Popular Resort among Intellectuals – At the turn of the 20C, St-Tropez was a charming little village unknown to tourists and poorly served by a small rail line. It was then that Maupassant discovered it. The painters who followed Signac's example made it more widely known. Between the two World Wars, Colette used to spend the winter here, as did Jean Cocteau. Starting with the 1950s, St-Tropez was fashionable with the literary set from St-Germain-des-Prés in Paris and then with the cinema stars, together with their fans, gaining the town an international reputation that hasn't faded.

RESORT LIFE
The Port★★
The harbour is the hub of village life in St-Tropez. Fishing boats, commercial vessels and excursion craft share the mooring with a crowd of yachts, from humble to luxurious. On the waterfront and in the neighboring streets, the old

St-Tropez

S. Sauvignier/ MICHELIN

pink and yellow houses have been converted into cafés and pastry shops, cabarets and restaurants, luxury boutiques, galleries and antique shops.

The Beaches

The beaches around St-Tropez are truly heavenly, with their fine sand and charming rocky coves. The nearest is Bouillabaisse Beach (perfect for windsailing when the *mistral* is blowing). To the east of the town lies **Graniers Beach** *(access from Rue Cavaillon)*. Further east round the headland stretches **Les Salins Beach** *(on Avenue Foch)*. But by far the most appealing and the most fashionable are the **Pampelonne Beaches**, well sheltered from the *mistral* winds. Cannebiers Bay affords glimpses of the superb villas of the rich and famous.

WALKING TOUR

Môle Jean-Réveille

The attractive **panorama**★ from the top of the jetty includes all of St-Tropez, the Esterel and in fine weather, the Alps.

La Ponche Quarter

Tucked between the port and the citadel, this is the oldest and most charming district of St-Tropez, where fishermen and artists used to live.

> *Turn right at the seaward end of Quai Jean-Jaurès onto Pl. Hôtel-de-Ville.*

On the left stands a massive tower, all that remains of the 16C **Château de Suffren des Seigneurs de St-Tropez**.

> *Turn left beyond the Hôtel de Ville to reach the bay of La Glayel.*

Rue de la Ponche leads through the old gateway to a beach overlooked by the Vieille Tour *(old tower)* where fishing boats ride at anchor.

> *Follow the street to the adorable Pl.des Remparts, then to Bd d'Aumale.*

Citadelle★

The citadel stands on a hillock at the east end of town. The hexagonal keep with three round towers was built in the 16C.
In the 17C a fortified wall was added *(© open Apr–Sept 10am–6.30pm, Oct–Mar 10am–12.30pm, 1.30–5.30pm; 2.50€ (5.50€ Jun–Sept); ℘04 94 97*

La Nioulargue, a Sailing Festival

Since its first meeting in 1981, more than 250 competitors rush here in early October to take part in this race which has become the great European meeting for old boats.

The course starts at the Tour du Portalet, goes round the shallows marked by the Nioulargue (sea nest, in Provençal) buoy and returns to the harbour. The skillful dances performed by ketches (recognisable by the small mast at the stern) and schooners (with the small mast in the bows) call for miraculous feats in anticipating manœuvres and great strength to move the enormous sails (the stress at the foot of the main mast can be as much as 500t!). Watch the race from a boat shuttle service in the gulf (*see Addresses*), or share the rental of a small boat. A more peaceful view of the scene is possible from the citadel; take binoculars.

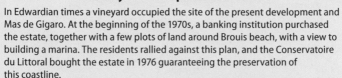

History of the Cap Lardier Estate

In Edwardian times a vineyard occupied the site of the present development and Mas de Gigaro. At the beginning of the 1970s, a banking institution purchased the estate, together with a few plots of land around Brouis beach, with a view to building a marina. The residents rallied against this plan, and the Conservatoire du Littoral bought the estate in 1976 guaranteeing the preservation of this coastline.

The Customs Officers' Footpath – This footpath, which follows 200km of the Var coastline, dates from the First Empire (early 19C). It was commissioned by Fouché when he was Minister and was intended to facilitate the patrolling of armed customs officers looking for smugglers. Since 1976 the path has been restored and all private properties adjoining the shore are obliged to allow a passage (at least 3m/10ft wide) across their land.

---

54 37). The ramparts command a fine **panorama**★ of St-Tropez to the Maures.

◯ *Retrace your steps to the Rue d'Aumale then to Pl. de l'Ormeau.*

Church
Rue du Cdt Guichard.
◷*Open 9.30am–noon.*
The 19C church was built in the Italian Baroque style. The interior contains some finely carved woodwork and to the left of the high altar, a bust of St Tropez, and several old blunderbusses which exploded without hurting anyone during a bravade.

◯ *From Rue du Clocher, turn left on Rue Commerçants, and left on Rue Marché.*

The charming **Place aux Herbes** is the backdrop to a small market open in the mornings. Walk past the animated fish stalls underneath Porte de la Poissonnerie and proceed to Quai Jean-Jaurès.

◯ *Leaving the port, take Rue Laugier, then Rue Gambetta.*

These two lively shopping streets are lined with renowned boutiques.

Place des Lices
A popular meetingplace with cafés, market and leafy plane trees.

SIGHTS
L'Annonciade, Musée de St-Tropez★★
Pl. Grammont. ◷*Open Jul–Oct 10am–1pm, 2–7pm; Dec–Jun Wed–Mon 10am–noon, 2–6pm.* ◷*Closed 1 Jan, 1 May, Ascension, 25 Dec.* ⊕6€ Jul–Oct, 5€ Dec–Jun. ☎04 94 17 84 10.
The chapel of Our Lady of Annonciade, built in 1510 and deconsecrated during the Revolution, was split into two levels and set up as a museum in 1937 with artworks dating from 1890. Included are works by **Pointillists** Paul Signac, H-E Cross, Théo van Rysselberghe, Maximilien Luce and Picabia. The **Fauves** are represented by Matisse, Braque, Manguin, Vlaminck, Kees Van Dongen and Dufy. The **Nabis** group are represented by Bonnard, Vuillard and Félix Vallotton. **Expressionists** include Rouault, Chabaud, Utrillo and Valadon.

⚎ Maison des Papillons (Musée Dany-Lartigue)
9 Rue Étienne-Berny. ◷*Open Mon–Sat 2.30–6pm.* ⊕3€ *(children under 8 free).* ☎04 94 97 63 45.
This charming Provençal house is the former home of painter and entomologist Dany Lartigue, son of the photographer J.-H. Lartigue. It houses a collection of nearly 5 000 butterflies – all the diurnal species existing in France, caught by the artist himself – as well as a donation of 20 000 exotics.

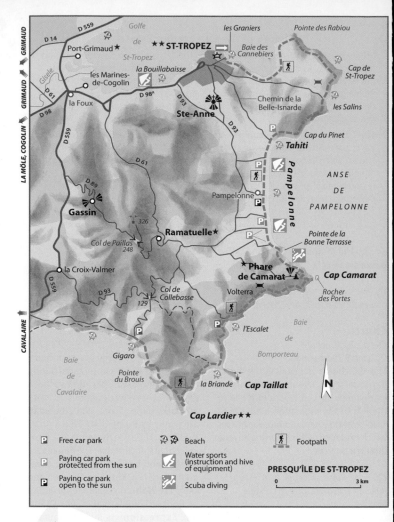

Map legend:

🅿	Free car park	🏖🏖	Beach	🚶	Footpath
🅿	Paying car park protected from the sun	🏄	Water sports (instruction and hive of equipment)		**PRESQU'ÎLE DE ST-TROPEZ**
🅿	Paying car park open to the sun	🤿	Scuba diving		0 3 km

🚗 DRIVING TOUR

Moulins de Paillas and Gassin★

Round trip 28km/17.3mi
This countryside tour offers extensive views of the coast and the Maures hinterland and pictureque old villages.

▷ *1km/0.7mi. Take Avenue Paul-Roussel and Route de Ste-Anne.*

Chapelle Ste-Anne

Standing on a volcanic rock spike in the shelter of huge trees, this attractive Provençal chapel is a place of pilgrim-

age for seafarers and *bravadeurs"*with a **view**★ of the sea in all directions. The road passes through the vineyards above Pampelonne Bay.

▷ *Turn right onto D 61 for Ramatuelle.*

Ramatuelle★
🐌*See RAMATUELLE.*
▷ *Turn right onto D 89 for Col de Paillas.*

Moulins de Paillas★★

Beyond three ruined olive mills (*one restored,* 🕐*open Mar–Oct, ask at tourist office;* 📞*04 98 12 64 00*), there is a radio beacon on a circular platform. Follow the signs to get a glimpse through the trees of a **panoramic view**★★ over the rough peaks of the Esterel, the coast of the Maures Massif, St-Tropez Bay, Cap Camarat lighthouse, the Île du Levant and Île de Port-Cros, Gassin, the Pradels range *(southwest)* and the Sauvette chain *(northwest)*, as well as Cogolin and Grimaud in the valley.

▷ *Right, back at junction, for Gassin.*

Gassin *Alt 201m/659ft.*
In contrast to modern resorts, this village has proudly retained its Provençal character, with its network of alleyways. The **Terrasse des Barri,** planted with lotus trees and exuding delightful Mediterranean fragrances, provides a **view**★ of St-Tropez Bay, the Îles d'Hyères and the Alps on clear days.

▷ *Take D 559, then D98 for St-Tropez.*

HIKING TOURS
Presqu'île St-Tropez★★
Although in high season tourism takes over St-Tropez, the surrounding country presents a traditional landscape of vineyards, cypress trees and immaculate farmhouses *(mas)* shaded by umbrella pines. The **St-Tropez Peninsula**★★ consists of the rocky headlands of Cap Camarat, Cap Taillat and Cap Lardier and the long ribbon of fine sand in Pampelonne Bay.

St-Tropez to Tahiti Beach
🚶 The path, with superb views of the foothills of the Maures and red rocks of the Esterel, leaves from Graniers Beach at the west end of the harbour. The path reaches Les Salins beach, the first stopping point where refreshment is available in the open-air cafés *(guinguettes)* during the summer season. The path then rounds Cap Pinet and ends at Tahiti beach on Pampelonne Bay. *Allow 3hr.*

Tahiti Beach to Cap Camarat
🚶 The path runs parallel with the long sandy stretch of Pampelonne Beach *(5km/3mi)* to Bonne-Terrasse Point. At Bonne-Terrasse Bay the path climbs the rocks through thicker vegetation. Near Rocher des Portes there is a footpath *(right)* towards Camarat lighthouse. *Allow 2hr.*

▷ *From Ramatuelle take D93 east; turn right on the road "Route du Phare" along the promontory beyond Les Tournels camp site; park outside the lighthouse pedestrian area.*

Phare de Camarat★
This magnificent **lighthouse** commissioned in 1831 was converted to electricity after the Second World War and automated in 1977. At 129.8m/425.8ft above sea level, it is one of the tallest in France, with a 60km/37mi range. From the summit there are **views** ★★ over the whole of the peninsula and St-Tropez Bay.

Cap Camarat to Cap Taillat
No refreshments, except in L'Escalet.
🚶 After skirting Rocher des Portes, the path leads to the beach at L'Escalet passing a series of isolated, accessible coves with rock slabs ideal for sunbathing. The walk offers views of the imposing **Château de Volterra** *(closed to the public)*. The path ends at Cap Taillat. *Allow 2hr.*

▷ *Join the route from the customs cabin at the Escalet's parking.*

The path cuts across the base of the headland and disappears into scrub vegetation until l'Escalet Beach. Beyond the woods the countryside is carpeted with vineyards. **Cap Taillat** is a growing sand bar connecting the reef to the coast, turning it into a peninsula. At the very end stands a semaphore signal.

🚶 Cap Taillat to Gigaro via Cap Lardier★★
Most of the route falls within the **protected site**★★ of Cap Lardier, run by the Conservatoire du Littoral. The path follows a series of cliffs with views of Briande Bay. It is possible to return to Gigaro from Briande Beach by the inland path (route DFCI). *Allow 2hr.*

ADDRESSES

🛏 STAY

Hôtel Lou Cagnard – *Av. Paul-Roussel. ℘04 94 97 04 24. www.hotel-loucagnard.com. Closed 6 Nov–27 Dec.* 📓*19 rooms. ⌂9€.* Enjoy breakfast seated in the shade of a mulberry tree in the tiny garden of this Provençal house, just off Place des Lices. At night you'll be lulled to sleep by the chirping of cicadas. Very reasonable prices.

Bello Visto – *Pl. deï Barri, Gassin. ℘04 94 56 17 30 or 04 94 56 47 33. www.bello-visto.fr. 9 rooms. ⌂8€. Restaurant*🍽🍽. A small family-run hotel and restaurant posted on Place des Remparts *(barri)*, at the top of Gassin. The majority of the rooms, like the terrace, profit from views over the Massif des Maures and the gulf of St-Tropez. Dining room with fireplace and Provençal cuisine.

Bastide des Salins – *4km/2.5mi southeast of St-Tropez. ℘04 94 97 24 57. www.bastidedessalins.com.* 📓*13 rooms. ⌂27€.* You will be greeted like friends of the family at this old Provençal house surrounded by extensive leafy grounds. Barely 5 minutes from Place des Lices and yet totally isolated, this hotel offers large rooms decorated in the Provençal spirit, appointed with great simplicity.

Hôtel Ponche – *Pl. Révelin. ℘04 94 97 02 53. www.laponche.com. Closed Nov– Mar.* 📓*18 rooms. ⌂19€. Restaurant*🍽🍽🍽. The rooms of this cosy hotel occupy four village houses formerly belonging to fishermen; the blue one was a favourite of Romy Schneider's. The warm, bright hues and considerate service make the Hôtel Ponche an absolute must.

🍴 EAT

La Cantina – *16 Rue des Remparts. ℘04 94 97 40 96. Closed Nov–Mar.* After sipping your tequila, savour generous helpings of Mexican cuisine in this typical setting characterised by religious statues, and painted wood furnishings. Youngish clientele. Relaxed ambience.

La Table du Marché – *38 Rue Georges-Clemenceau. ℘04 94 97 85 20. www.christophe-leroy.com.* A temple of gastronomy located near Place des Lices, open at all hours of the day. In addition to the restaurant offering traditional French cuisine, La Table du Marché also sells homemade pastries: croissants, cakes and the legendary "gendarme de St-Tropez" – mouthwatering chocolate mousse filled with vanilla crême brûlée.

Au Vieux Gassin – *Pl. deï Barri, Gassin. ℘04 94 56 14 26. Closed mid-Oct–mid-Mar.* A ravishing little hilltop village serves as the backdrop for this popular restaurant. A terrace with panoramic views is partially enclosed and heated in cooler weather, taking over a large section of the charming Place deï Barri. The regional menu had a few "exotic" specialities.

Le Banh Hoï– *12 r. Petit St-Jean. ℘04 94 97 36 29. Closed 12 Oct–3 Apr.* Low lighting, black lacquer walls and Asian artworks decorate this restaurant specialising in Thaï and Vietnamese cuisine.

Chez Camille – *Quai de Bonne Terrasse. ℘04 98 12 68 98. Closed 12 Oct–8 Apr, Tue.* A family-run restaurant on the waterfront serving **bouillabaisse** (spicy fish stew) and grilled fish since 1913. Ask about boat shuttle service.

Le Girelier – *quai Jean-Jaurès. ℘04 94 97 03 87. www.legirelier.fr. Closed Nov–mid-Mar.* A harbourside fishermen's hut converted into a stylish, contemporary dining room with simply cooked shellfish platters and bouillabaisse.

🍸 ON THE TOWN

St-Tropez has two facets. In summer, it is a town for the rich and wealthy and is given over to sailing, bathing, entertainment and nightlife. However, in winter, it looks more like a ghost town. Most businesses close down between November and April and the swinging bars, restaurants and hotels are completely deserted.

Bar du Château de la Messardière – *Route de Tahiti. ℘04 94 56 76 00. www.messardiere.com.Closed mid-Oct–mid-Mar.* This bar belongs to one of the Riviera's most prestigious hotels. Hushed, cosy ambience in the piano bar of this former 18C private residence. The terrace commands nice views of St-Tropez Bay.

Bar Sube – *15 quai de Suffren. ℘04 94 97 30 04. www.hotel-sube.com. Closed 5–31 Jan.* This is one of the most beautiful bars of the city. Model boats decorate the interior, where the leather armchairs and fireplace make for a cordial and comfortable place. Small tables are installed on the balcony, with prime views of the old port.

SHOPPING

Markets – Tuesdays and Saturdays on Place des Lices.

Foire de la Ste-Anne – Fair on Place des Lices, every 26 July.

Shopping streets – The most lively shopping streets are Rue Clemenceau, Rue Gambetta and Rue Allard, offering an impressive selection of local arts and crafts: pottery, glassware etc.

Les Sandales Tropéziennes – *16 Rue Georges Clemenceau. ℘04 94 97 19 55. www.rondini.fr. Closed Nov–Feb.* The Rondini house has been crafting natural leather St-Tropez sandals since 1927.

Le Petit Village – *La Foux, near the commercial centre just outside Gassin. ℘04 94 56 32 04. www.mavigne. com. Closed Sun.* This showroom brings together the wines from eight prestigious vineyards on the St-Tropez peninsula just off the busy La Foux intersection. Includes the famous Château de Pampelonne vineyard. Free tastings and many regional products for sale.

FOR YOUR SWEET TOOTH
La Tarte Tropézienne – *Pl. des Lices. ℘04 94 97 71 42. www.tarte-tropezienne.com.* It was in this pâtisserie that the famous tarte tropézienne saw the light of day, invented in 1955 by Polish baker Alexandre Micka: a round delightfully moist, brioche cake flavored with orange blossom, filled with custard and sprinkled with crystallised suger.

Sénéquier – *Quai Jean-Jaurès. ℘04 94 97 00 90. www.senequier.com. Closed 4 Jan–19 Feb.* The pavement terrace and crimson chairs of this tea room are famous throughout the world or so

say the locals! Renowned personalities such as Jean Marais, Errol Flynn and Colette would come here for a cup of delicately fragrant tea, an iced coffee, a delicious ice cream or a few squares of homemade nougat.

SPORTS & LEISURE

Octopussy Plongée – *Capitainerie du port. ℘04 94 56 68 71 or 06 83 25 34 83. www.octopussy-plongee.fr. Closed Dec–Mar.* Scuba diving lessons and excursions for all levels in the blue waters around St-Tropez.

Maison du Tourisme du Golfe de St-Tropez – *Carrefour de la Foux, Gassin. ℘04 94 55 22 00. www.st-tropez-lesmaures.com.* This tourist office issues a list of all the companies based in St-Tropez Bay that specialise in deep-sea diving. Or, see the website.

TRANSPORT

Les Bateaux Verts – *14 Quai Léon Condroyer, Ste-Maxime. ℘04 94 49 29 39. www.bateauxverts.com.*

Return Trip from St Tropez to Ste Maxime (20min) 12€ (children 6€)

Return Trip from Ste Maxime to Baie des Canoubiers (45min) 13.40€ (children 7€)

Return Trip from St Tropez to Baie des Canoubiers 9€ (children 5€)

Tarte Tropézienne

Sainte-Maxime★

Var

The fashionable resort of
Ste-Maxime lies along the north
shore of St-Tropez Bay. It has a fishing
harbour, well-appointed marina and
beautiful beach of fine sand.

VISIT
Seafront
From the beach to the port, the shaded
Promenade Simon-Lorière commands
fine views of St-Tropez. It is accessible
to cars under the name Avenue Charles-
de-Gaulle. A marker designates the route
taken by the Allied forces in 1944.

Tour Carrée des Dames
A square defensive tower, built in the
16C by the Lérins monks, has been
transformed into a **Museum of Local
Tradition** (Musée des Traditions
Locales – ☾open Wed–Sun 10am–
noon, 3–6pm; ⊜2.30€; ℘04 94 96
70 30). Ste-Maxime and its surrounding area are presented with exhibits
on nature (sea), history and regional
customs (arts and crafts, Provençal
dress).

Church
The doorway of this church is decorated
with modern ceramic tympanum. Inside
is a fine Baroque (17C) green and ochre

- ▶ **Population:** 13 739.
- ⚲ **Michelin Map:** 340 O6;
  local map: *see Massif des
  MAURES.*
- ℹ **Info:** Promenade Simon-
  Loriere. ℘04 94 55 75 55.
  www.sainte-maxime.com.
- ▶ **Location:** Ste-Maxime
  sits on the edge of the
  Massif des Maures and
  14km/8.7mi across the bay
  from St-Tropez on the N 98.

marble altar from the Chartreuse de la
Verne. Note the 15C choir stalls.

EXCURSION
Parc St-Donat
10km/6mi – allow 1hr.
▶ *From Ste-Maxime take Bd. Georges-
Clemenceau, D 25 north.*

A leisure park has been laid out in the
woods between Col de Gratteloup and
St-Donat Chapel. The main attraction
is the Museum of Mechanical Musical
Instruments (**Musée du Phonogra-
phe et de la Musique Mécanique**
– ⚲☾open May–Sept Wed–Sun 10am–
noon, 4–6pm; ⊜3€; ℘04 94 96 50 52).
The building, which recalls a turn-of-
the-century barrel organ, houses an
astonishing collection of 350 musical
instruments and sound recording
machines.

Sainte-Maxime harbour

D. Pazery/MICHELIN

ADDRESSES

🛏 STAY

L'Auberge Provençale – *19 Bd. Aristide-Briand.* ☎*04 94 55 76 90. Closed 20 Dec–10 Jan. 15 rooms. ⊡5.50€. Restaurant⊝☺☻.* Despite its unprepossessing façade, this inn close to the beach offers charming accommodation in keeping with Provençal tradition. The bedrooms have been given warm, earthy hues and the southern cuisine relies on fresh market produce.

Le Chardon Bleu – *29 Rue de Verdun.* ☎*04 94 55 52 22. www.aubergedu chardonbleu.fr. 25 rooms. ⊡6.50€.* Conveniently situated at the heart of the resort, barely 150 yards from the sea, this hotel offers air-conditioned rooms with small balconies. Two rooms have a big terrace.

🍴 EAT

Chez Sophie – *4 Pl. des Sarrasins.* ☎*04 94 96 71 00. Closed Nov–Dec.* Charming restaurant that epitomises the Provençal spirit: colourful decoration, wooden furnishings, terrace shaded by a plane tree, menu inspired by regional cuisine. The dishes and tasty homemade desserts are served by charming locals with a Mediterranean drawl.

La Maison Bleue – *6 Nov–27 Dec.* A Provençal house entirely dedicated to pasta and its history: early advertising posters, enamelled plaques and old wrappers adorn the ochre walls of this restaurant, whose terrace is pleasantly shaded by plane trees.

🎭 ON THE TOWN

Café de France – *Pl. Victor-Hugo.* ☎*04 94 96 18 16.* A whiff of the past permeates this brasserie, opened in 1852 when Ste-Maxime was a fishing village. Old-time photographs and an ancient mirror evoke this bygone era. The big terrace sheltered by plane trees faces the marina. Fresh oysters in season.

Bar de l'Amarante Golf Plaza – *Av. Célestin.* ☎*04 94 56 66 66. www.golf-plaza.fr.* Prestigious hotel bar set against a backdrop of cork oaks and Mediterranean scrubland, overlooking Ste-Maxime and St-Tropez Bay. Additional facilities include a golf course, a fitness club and a large-scale game of chess.

🛒 SHOPPING

MARKETS

Artisan Market – Daily 5am–11pm on the pedestrian streets mid-June to mid-July.

Food Market – In a covered venue near Place du Marché every morning (except Monday in winter); open market Thursday morning on Place des Sarrasins.

Fair – Lively fair every Friday at Place Jean Mermoz.

🎪 OUTDOOR PERFORMANCES

Théâtre de la Mer – *Promenade Simon Lorière.* ☎*04 94 55 75 55/04 94 49 20 01. www.ste-maxime.com. Closed Oct–May.* Every summer this open-air theatre stages concerts of classical music and contemporary pop, folk dance, and firework displays.

🏃 SPORTS AND LEISURE

Héli Sécurité – *Quartier Perrat, Z.A. Grimaud.* ☎*04 94 43 39 30. www. helicopter-saint-tropez.com.* Recreational flights in helicopters and shuttle services between airports or resorts.

Club Nautique de Sainte Maxime – *Bd. Jean-Moulin.* ☎*04 94 96 07 80. www.cnsm83.fr.st. Open school holidays.* This water sports club organises sailing courses during the school holidays.

Golf de Sainte-Maxime – *Rte. du Débarquement.* ☎*04 94 55 02 02. www.bluegreen.com. Closed winter.* Superb, undulating golf course laid out over the heights of Ste-Maxime, dominating St-Tropez Bay. Bar with terrace facing the sea.

Les Bateaux Verts – *14 Quai Léon-Condroyer.* ☎*04 94 49 29 39. www.bateauxverts.com.* Coastal excursions from Easter to October: tours of the Gulf of St-Tropez, the inlets of the Esterel, Îles d'Hyères.

INLAND PROVENCE

Inland Provence is made up of small villages and towns in what the French call the *arrière pays*, the back country, which does not touch the coastline of the Var administrative department. Apart from the stunning 12C Abbaye du Thoronet and the lively town of Draguignan, few sites attract busloads of tourists. Rather, it is an area conducive to leisurely exploration, where visitors can find vestiges of history around every corner, from prehistoric funeral monuments to 17C château ruins. Secluded in pine forests, perched on rocky cliffs, hidden in deep valleys, or simply located on the fertile plains, these towns offer visitors a welcome respite from the crowded coastal cities of the French Riviera.

Villages of Character

Since 1999, eight French regions including the Var have designated certain towns as "Villages de Caractère", whose historical, natural, architectural and cultural treasures are carefully preserved and promoted. To qualify as a Village of Character, a town must have a harmonious blend of historic architecture, have fewer than 3 500 residents, and have at least one registered monument or sight. In the Var department, Aups and Cotignac are two of the eight villages which have been awarded this prestigious designation, and are well worth a detour.

Historic Riches

There are more than 70 megaliths in this region, making it one of the richest in prehistoric treasures in the country. One of the most famous is in Lorgues, where visitors can see the Peyrcervier Dolmen, a type of megalithic tomb resembling a

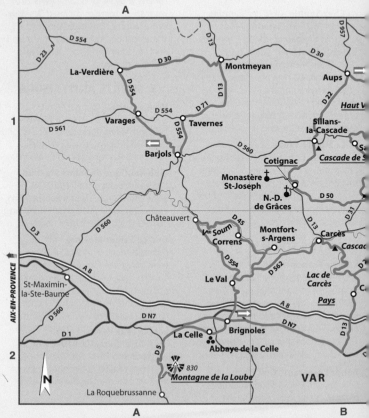

stone table. Gallo-Roman ruins can be found in many villages, including vestiges of the Roman road from Spain to Italy in Draguignan, the Gayole Tombstone in Brignoles and artefacts from the Bouverie caves in the Musée du Patrimoine of Roquebrune-sur-Argens. From the Middle Ages and the Ancien Régime through the Empires and World War II, the villages of Inland Provence are marked by history at every turn

Local Economy

Inland Provence has been producing wine and olive oil since the Roman times, as ancient stone mills attest. Today the heart of the regional winemaking is in Brignoles, while Draguignan is predominantly an administrative centre where a third of the population work for the military, hospital, prison and regional government offices. Pottery, faïence and

Highlights

1 Listen to medieval music at **Abbaye du Thoronet** (p193).

2 Take a tour of the cave dwellings in **Villecroze** (p195).

3 Visit the perched village of **Châteaudouble** (p185).

4 Take part in the colourful *Fête de St-Marcel* in **Barjols** (p176).

5 Taste the local wines in and around **Brignoles** (p178).

terracotta Santon dolls are produced in the region, and Aups is famous as the Black Truffle capital of Provence. Tourism, however, is not as predominant in this part of the French Riviera, despite its ideal location between the sea and the Gorges de Verdon.

C

LA PROVENCE INTÉRIEURE

Le Thoronet	★★	Recommended
Cotignac	★	Interesting
Aups		Worth seeing
		Driving tour with departure town

Les Arcs

Var

Also known as Arcs-sur-Argens, this town dominated by the ruins of Château Villeneuve is nestled in Côtes de Provence vineyards.

OLD TOWN

▶ *From Pl. de l'Église take Rue de la Paix up to the dungeon keep.*

The old town streets and alleys surround the ruins of the medieval castle. In the Middle Ages a watch from the keep warded off Saracen invasions. Set within a miniature setting of Les Arcs, an **automated nativity scene** attracts many visitors to the church (*Pl. Ferré*). The side chapels are painted with frescoes: *(left)* the miracle of St Roseline's roses; *(right)* and a **polyptych**★ in 16 sections by Louis Bréa (1501) of the Virgin and Child surrounded by Provençal saints.

EXCURSION

Chapelle Ste-Roseline★

4km/2.5mi east of Les Arcs by the D91.
🕐*Open Wed–Sun Jun–Sept 3–7pm; Mar–May 2–6pm; Oct–Feb 2–5pm.*
🎟*No charge.* ☎*04 94 73 330 13.*
The Provençal-style Romanesque chapel in the country outside Les Arcs was part of the 11C abbey La Celle-Roubaud.

The Legend of Sainte Roseline

The young Ste Roseline (1263–1329) of Château de Villeneuve, daughter of the Lord Arnaud de Villeneuve, would hide food in her apron to distribute to the poor. One day a palace guard stopped her and asked what she was carrying. "Roses," she replied, and when she opened her apron the roses miraculously appeared. The shrine of St Roseline in the church holds her body. Pilgrimages take place five times a year, including Trinity Sunday and first Sunday in August.

▶ **Population:** 6 108.
ὁ **Michelin Map:** 340 N5.
🗓 **Info:** Pl. du Général-de-Gaulle. ☎04 94 73 37 30.
▶ **Location:** The town is located in the Var, 25km/15.5mi west of FREJUS on the RN7 and D57. The modern part of Les Arcs is at the foot of the old town, separated by the Tour d'Horloge (clock tower).

Interior★

A Renaissance chancel and statue of St Catherine of Alexandria divides the nave; on the high altar stands a superb early 16C Baroque altarpiece. Contemporary works of art inspired by the legend of Ste Roseline include a large mosaic by Chagall and a bronze low relief.

ADDRESSES

🛏 STAY 🍽 EAT

🍽**Aurélia** – *Route nationale 7, Le Pont-d'Argens.* ☎*04 94 47 49 69. Closed Jan, Restaurant closed off season Sun eve, Mon, holidays. 20 rooms.* 🅿 ⊏*9€. Restaurant* ⊖⊜. Located on the outskirts of the village, this hotel is protected from the noise of the nearby RN7, and many rooms have their own balcony. The restaurant has a fireplace and terrace overlooking the Argens River.

🛒 SHOPPING

Maison des Vins côtes-de-Provence – *Route nationale 7.* ☎*04 94 99 50 20. www.caveaucp.fr. Closed Oct–Mar.*
This country estate along the Argens River is the headquarters of the Côtes-de-Provence appellation wines, with 700 different winemakers, a modern tasting area*(free)* and a gourmet restaurant.

Aups

Var

With its soothing stone fountains, fortress ruins, picturesque old streets and squares shaded by magnificent plane trees, Aups is a charming place to stroll.

VISIT
Collégiale St-Pancrace
Pl. Frédéric Mistral. ℘04 94 70 00 80.
A Provençal Gothic church with a Renaissance doorway and 15C churchbell, restored in 2006. For three days in midMay the locals celebrate St-Pancrace. The church treasury houses some interesting 15C-18C gold and silverplate tableware.

Musée Simon-Ségal
Av. Albert I. ◷*Open Jul–Aug Wed–Mon 10am–noon, 4-7pm.* ⇌*No charge.* ℘*04 94 70 00 07.*
This museum of modern art in the former Ursuline Convent's chapel contains 280 paintings, including 175 from the Paris School.

Musée de Faykod
3.5km/2mi on the Rte. de Tourtour (D 77). Look for arrows on the right and a long driveway. ◷*Open Wed–Mon Jul–Aug 10am–noon, 3–7pm; Sept–May 2–6pm (7pm in Jun).* ⇌*6€ (child 2€).* ℘*04 94 70 03 94. www.musee-de-faykod.com.*
Collection of white marble sculptures by Maria de Faykod in a park set within the *garrrigue* scrubland.

🚗 DRIVING TOUR

Le Haut Var★
53km/33mi – about 5hr.

▷ *From Aups take D 77 east.*

After Château de la Beaume bear left on D 51 through **Tourtour**★ (ⓒ*see TOURTOUR*) , passing the olive trees, pines and vineyards on the way to **Villecroze** (ⓒ*see VILLECROZE*).

▶ **Population:** 2 029.
⚙ **Michelin Map:** 340 M4.
🛈 **Info:** Pl. F.-Mistral. ℘04 94 84 00 69.
◐ **Location:** Aups sits at the foot of the Espiguières hills in the Var, bordered to the northwest by the steep highlands of HauteProvence with the Massif des Maures dominating the horizon to the south.
🅿 **Parking:** Parking can be found just off the Avenue Verdun, near the tourist office.

▷ *From Villecroze continue along the D 51, then turn right at the D 560.*

Salernes
Salernes is known for the manufacture of pottery and the hexagonal russet-coloured Provençal tiles known as *tomettes*. The **church**, set among 17C houses, boasts a belfry at both ends. The openair market takes place every Wednesday and Sunday.
🚶 A fold-out map detailing six walking and mountain biking trails is available from the tourist office in Salernes. 🛈 *Pl. Gabriel-Péri* ℘*04 94 70 69 02. www.villesalernes.fr.*

▷ *Take D 31 south by Bresque Valley.*

Black Gold of the Haut-Var

The truffle (called *rabasse* in Provence) is a fungus which grows on the secretions which seep out of diseased oak trees. There are two categories of truffle: the white and the black, which are recognisable by their distinctive smell. They are harvested from November to February by dogs or by sows that take two years to train. The largest truffle market in the Var takes place in Aups every Thursday during the gathering season.

Entrecasteaux ☞*See ENTRECASTEAUX*

▶ *Take D 31 south; turn right on D 50.*

Cotignac ☞*See COTIGNAC*

▶ *Take D 22 north.*

Cascade de Sillans★
Before the village turn right onto a path.
🚶 *30min round trip.*
In an enchanting setting the Bresque cascades over a 42m/138ft drop into an emerald pool.

Sillans-la-Cascade
Surrounded by forests, this attractive village has ancient ramparts and picturesque streets. The 18C château hosts regular art and artisan exhibitions (🕐*open Apr–Dec Wed–Sun; ★no charge*).

▶ *Continue on D 22 to return to Aups.*

ADDRESSES

🛒 SHOPPING
Specialities – Here, the famous truffle reigns supreme and can be found in many dishes. The area is also known for its production of honey and goat's cheese made in the Upper Var Valley.

Moulin à Huile Gervasoni – *Montée des Moulins*. ☎*04 94 70 04 66. Closed Oct–Mar.* This 18C olive mill still manufactures and sells olive oil alongside other regional specialities such as tapenade, Provençal fabrics, artisan soap and carved olive wood items.

Markets – Wednesdays and Saturdays on Place Frédéric-Mistral. Truffle market on Thursday *(Nov–mid-Mar)*. Artisan market evenings *(Jul–Aug)*.

🚶 SPORT AND LEISURE
Office du tourisme de Salernes – ☎*04 94 70 69 02. www.officetourisme-salernes.fr.* A brochure with six hiking and mountain biking trails is available at the tourist office.

Barjols
Var

Set within a natural amphitheatre, this small town is known for its many fountains, the unusual St-Marcel Festival (mid-January), and the traditional Provençal tambourines and flutes *(galoubets)*.

🚶 WALKING TOUR
THE OLD TOWN
🗺*Maps detailing the circuit of 30 fountains are available from the tourist office.*
Old Barjols contains 12 wash-houses and 30 **fountains**. The most remarkable one, near the town hall, is a limestone-encrusted mushroom-shaped fountain, known locally as the *Champignon*. A magnificent **plane tree** (circumference 12m/39ft), said to be the largest in Provence, dominates the town hall square.

▶ **Population:** 2 963.
☞ **Michelin Map:** 340 L4.
ℹ **Info:** Boulevard Grisolle. ☎04 94 77 20 01. www.ville-barjols.fr.
▶ **Location:** The town of Barjols is in the Var, 22km/13.6mi north of Brignoles off the D 554.
🕶 **Parking:** Parking can be found to the west of the village, near the tourist office.

In the lower town, the **Pontevès House**, named after an old Provençal family from a nearby village, is enhanced by a Renaissance doorway.
Clinging to the hillside, north of the church, lies **Réal★**, the town's oldest quarter. Inhabited since the 12C it has been occupied for the most part by tan-

ners as water is an essential tool of their trade; three levels of partial troglodyte (16C–17C) basins for tanning hides were uncovered in the 1980s. The text of the Déclaration des Droits de l'Homme et du Citoyen, has been carved on a glazed stelae beneath a vault.

Church
Av. de la République.
The original Romanesque structure was rebuilt in the 16C with a Gothic nave. The organ loft, choir panelling and carved misericords are 17C. To the right of the entrance, behind a 12C font, is the original carved tympanum of Christ with angels and symbols of the Evangelists.

▲▲ Maison Régionale de l'Eau
Bd. Grisolle. ⏰*Open Mon–Fri 9am– noon, 2–6pm.* ⏰*Closed public holidays.* ⊜*No charge.* ✆*04 94 77 15 83.*
Built within an 18C hospice, this Regional House of Water is both an educational centre and an aquarium with fish found in local rivers.

EXCURSIONS
Source d'Argens
15km/9mi to the southwest.

▷ *From Barjols take D 560.*

Vallon de Font-Taillade
The road plunges into a green valley of forests and vineyards, following a wind-ing stream.

▷ *500m/547yd after Brue-Auriac a path to the left leads to a chapel.*

Chapelle Notre-Dame
Next to a graveyard stands an aban-doned Romanesque chapel built from the local red stone. Its pleasant façade topped by a wall-belfry with twin win-dows is obscured by undergrowth.

▷ *Return to D 560 and turn left. Stop in front of the bridge, after 3km/2mi.*

Source d'Argens
🏃 On the right of the road a path leads through the bushes to a spring which feeds the River Argens.

🚘 DRIVING TOUR

Plateaux du Haut-Var
52km/32mi – half a day.

▷ *Leave Barjols just before the public pool, following a small street northwest towards Varages.*

Varages
This village once vied with Moustiers in the production of faience. The produc-tion continues today in Varages, prima-rily for export. A fair dedicated to faience takes place each summer.

Church
Built in the 17C in Provençal Gothic style, the church has a bell tower covered in glazed multicoloured tiles. Inside, the altar of St Claude, patron saint of faïence-makers, is decorated with medallions and crosses made locally.

Musée des Faïences
12 Pl. de la Libération. ⏰*Open Jul–Aug 10am–noon, 3–7pm (Mon 3–7pm); Sept–Jun Wed–Sun 2–6pm.* ⏰*Closed 23 Dec–Jan.* ⊜*2.50€.* ✆*04 94 77 60 39.*
This museum in the Maison Gassendi tells the history of faience in Varages from the end of the 17C, with a remark-able 19C faience fountain by Mazières.

▷ *Take D 554 north from Varages*

La Verdière

This hillside village is dominated by its church and a dilapidated 10C fortress.

▷ *East of La Verdière take D 30 towards Montmeyan.*

Montmeyan
This medieval perched village domi-nates the mouth of the Verdon Gorge. There is a fine **view**★ from the southern

Festival of St Marcel

Since time immemorial the people of Barjols have slaughtered an ox every year to celebrate their survival during a siege. In 1350 a group of pious citizens, rescuing the relics of St Marcel (a 5C bishop) from the abandoned abbey near Montmeyan, fell in with the other celebrants and religious and secular festivities were thus combined. Each January St Marcel's bust is carried in procession throughout the town while a decorated ox is led round the town on its way to the abattoir. On the following day after High Mass, the escorted statue joins the float bearing the ox on a spit and proceeds to the main square where the ox is roasted whole. A Provençal style celebration with flutes, tambourines, music and dancing ends with the roast ox distributed to the crowd (&see Calendar of Events).

entrance to the village over the Castellane Pre-Alps to the east. Pass the Tour Charlemagne, vestiges of the 14C castle, for more views.

○ D13, then D 71 to Tavernes.

Tavernes

Set in the midst of olive groves and vineyards, this attractive village has the remains of typically Provençal architecture: there is a square belfry with an 18C wrought-iron campanile on top, and the remains of medieval walls.
🚶 2hr. At the top of the village sits Notre-Dame-de-Bellevue, a chapel dedicated to Our Lady of Bellevue.

○ The D 554 back to Barjols crosses then runs along a charming brook called the Ruisseau des Écrevisses.

Brignoles

Var

Brignoles is in the lower Carami Valley, its old town clings to the north side of a hill and the new town in the plain below. The narrow twisting streets of old Brignoles form a dense hillside labyrinth below the venerable castle, once home to the counts of Provence. This rich market town produces peaches, honey, olives and oil, but its modern prosperity is due to the annual wine fair.

ADDRESSES

🛏 STAY

🍽 **Logis Hôtel du Pont d'Or** – *Rue Eugène, Payan, Rte. St-Maximin.* &04 94 77 05 23. *Closed early Dec–mid-Jan.* 🅿. *15 rooms.* ⚏7.50€. *Restaurant* 🍽.
A former coach house with modern decor. Each cosy room is decorated differently. Traditional Provençal cuisine.

🍴 EAT

🍽 **La Remise** – *5 Rue Boeuf.* &04 94 77 29 87. *Closed Nov–mid-Jan, Wed–Thu in winter.* This small, contemporary restaurant has a shady terrace overlooking the famous *Champignon* fountain.

🛒 SHOPPING

Market – Sat and Thu (flower market), Leather Market every weekend in Aug.
Local arts – Traditional artisans can be found in the old tannery district to the east of town.

▶ **Population:** 14 963.
◔ **Michelin Map:** 340 L5.
🛈 **Info:** Syndicat d'Initiative, 10 Rue Palais. &04 94 69 27 51. Office intercommunal de tourisme de la Provence Verte, carrefour de l'Europe. &04 94 72 04 21. www.la-provenceverte.org.
🅿 **Parking:** Large parking area in town and at Place des Augustins.

VISIT

South of Place Carami, picturesque old streets lead to the church of St-Sauveur and to the castle of the counts of Provence. Walk along the covered Rue du Grand-Escalier, Rue du St-Esprit and Rue des Lanciers, where there is a **Romanesque house** with twin windows.

Église St-Sauveur

⊙ Open Jul–Aug Wed–Sat 8.30am–7pm, Sun 9am–1pm, 5.30–7pm.
℘04 94 69 10 69.
This church has a fine Romanesque doorway (12C) and a Provençal Gothic style nave. The south chapel contains a **Descent from the Cross** by Barthélemy Parrocel, who died at Brignoles in 1660.

Musée du Pays Brignolais

Palais des Comtes de Provence.
⊙ Open Apr–Sept Wed–Sat 9am–noon, 2.30–6pm, Sun 9am–noon, 3–6pm; Oct–Mar Wed–Sat 10am–noon, 2.30–5pm, Sun 10am–noon, 3–5pm.
⊙ Closed public holidays. ⊜4€. ℘04 94 69 45 18. www.museebrignolais.com.
This regional museum is housed in the former castle of the 12C Counts of Provence. The chief exhibit is the **La Gayole tombstone**★ (late 2C–early 3C) illustrating the transition from pagan to Christian iconography. Also see the reproduction of an 18C Provençal kitchen and a cement boat by Joseph Lambot.

EXCURSION
Abbaye de la Celle

Leave Brignoles by the D 554 going south and turn right on the D 405.
•••Guided tours (45min) Apr–Sept Mon–Fri 9am–12.30pm, 2–6.30pm, Sat–Sun 9am–1pm, 2.30–6.30pm; Oct–Mar Mon–Fri 9am–noon, 2–5pm, Sat 9am–noon, 2–5pm (from 10am Sun). ⊙ Closed 1 Jan, 1 May, 11 Nov, 25 Dec. ⊜2.30€. ℘04 94 59 19 05. www.la-celle.fr.
In the 13C the Benedictine convent attracted the daughters of the Provençal nobility, but by the 16C standards had fallen so low that the nuns openly visited their lovers so it was closed in 1660. The cloisters, chapter house and refectory can be visited. The austere Romanesque abbey church, now a parish church, contains a 15C Crucifixion.

🚗 DRIVING TOURS

1 BRIGNOLES COUNTRY★
56km/35mi – allow 3hr –
ⓒ see local map below.

▷ *Leave Brignoles north on the D 554.*

The dark green of the pines in this undulating countryside contrasts with the vineyards and red-stained earth (from the bauxite mines).

Le Val
The village lies beside the Roman Via Aurelia, with narrow houses clustered around an elaborate, 18C wrought-iron campanile. Despite development, the site has preserved its Provençal character.
On the way into the village is the **Hôtel des Vins,** with a fresco by one of Dali's pupils. The Romanesque church still has some beautiful 18C frescoes as well as some 16C polychrome statues.

Detail of the doorway, Église St-Saveur

Musée du Santon

2 Rue des Fours. ♿ ⏰ *Open 9am–noon, 2–6pm.* ⏰ *Closed 1 Jan, 25 Dec.* 💶 *2€ (child 1€).* ☎ *04 94 86 48 78.*

Housed in the old communal oven (12C) the museum features a collection of Provençal santons as well as Nativity scenes from around the world.

Musée d'Art Sacré

North of the village. ♿ ⏰ *Same times and charges as for the Musée du Santon.*

Located in a 16C Penitents' Chapel is a religious art collection of commemorative plaques dating from the 17C, statues and embroidered pastoral robes.

Musée des Jouets

Southeast of the village.
⏰ *Open Tue–Sun Jul–Aug 3.30–6pm; Sept–Jun 3–5pm.* 💶 *2€ (child 1€).* ☎ *04 94 86 32 95.*

This museum features antique toys, old figurines, antique military uniforms, remarkable dioramas of the Napoleonic period and sheets of paper soldiers.

▷ *Take the D 562 northeast to Carcès.*

Carcès

The town produces oil and honey and has extensive wine cellars. The colourful glazed roof tiles of Carcès afford protection against the strong *mistral* winds.

▷ *Head towards Cabasse on the D 13 to the Pont Carami.*

Carami Falls

🚶 *2.5hr.* Park at the bridge and follow the trail 8km/5mi to a tiered waterfall (7m/22ft).

▷ *Continue along the D 13.*

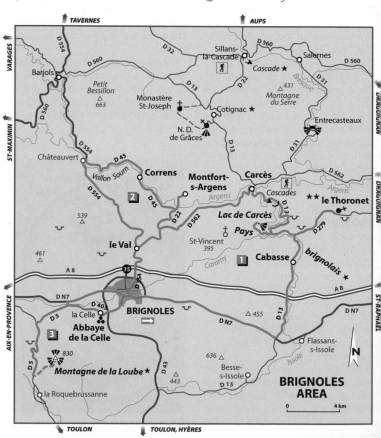

Lac de Carcès

The pine-clad shores of this lake are a favourite haunt of fishermen (*swimming not allowed*).

Continue on D 13; turn left onto D 79 for the Abbaye du Thoronet.

Abbaye du Thoronet★★ –
see Abbaye du THORONET.

Return to D 13 and turn left towards Cabasse along the Issole Valley.

Cabasse

The village on the Côtes de Provence wine road is dotted with dolmens, standing stones and Gallo-Roman ruins. The 16C **Église St-Pons** has a noteworthy **high altar★** of carved and gilded wood in Spanish Renaissance style (1543). Gallo-Roman milestones stand near a 2C funerary inscription set in the outside wall.

Proceed along D 13 then turn right onto N 7, back to Brignoles.

2 VALLON SOURN
Round trip 39km/25mi – about 1hr – see local map

Take D 554 north to Le Val. Turn right onto D 562, then left onto D 22.

Montfort-sur-Argens

The ruins of a forbidding feudal castle mark this Templar commandery, which now produces grapes and peaches. Two square towers remain, with mullioned windows, and a 15C spiral staircase.

Return to the crossroads and turn right onto D 45, following the Argens.

Correns

A riverside village beneath the towering Gros Bessillon, known for its white wine. The castle has interesting gargoyles.

Vallon Sourn

In Provençal *sourn* means somber, describing the valley between steep cliffs riddled with caves where people hid during the Wars of Religion.

In Châteauvert turn left onto D 554 to return to Brignoles.

3 MONTAGNE DE LA LOUBE★
14km/8.7mi southwest – about 3hr, including hike – see local map.

Take D 554 south. Turn right onto D 405; turn left onto D 5. Park on a road 1km/0.6mi before La Roquebrussanne.

Montagne de la Loube★
2hr on foot round trip.

The narrow road up this mountain passes strangely shaped rocks resembling animals and human beings.

Climb the final steps to the telecommunications mast.

From the summit (830m/2 723ft) is an interesting **panorama★**. In the valleys, the farmland is hemmed in by barren ridges and on the hillsides the bauxite mines cast red gashes in the green covering of pine and holm oak.

Return to Brignoles by D 5 and N 7.

"A Stacada"

This unusual and highly colourful event takes place every four years *(next 2013)* to commemorate the abolition of the *droit de seigneur*, brought about by the rebellion of the Breil inhabitants, who had been subjugated by a local tyrant. Some of the villagers, adorned in rich medieval costumes, parade through the town, stopping along the way to re-enact scenes from this historical event. The unexpected arrival of the lord allows the inhabitants to demand reparation. After many races between the lord's Turkish guard and the nobles, the latter are finally captured and put in chains *(a stacada)*.

ADDRESSES

🏠 STAY

🛏🛏 **Chambre d'Hôte Château de Vins** – *Vins-sur-Caramy, 9.5km/6mi from Brignoles on D 24, Rte du Thoronet. ℘04 94 72 50 40. www.chateaudevins.com. Closed Nov–Apr. ⬚. 5 rooms.* Listed 16C building with four turrets whose austere yet imposing rooms carry the names of famous musicians.

🛏🛏 **La Cordeline** – *14 Rue des Cordeliers. ℘04 94 59 18 66. www.lacordeline.com. Reservations a must. 4 rooms. Meal🍽🍽.* Handsome 17C mansion providing accommodation in tastefully furnished rooms, complete with fully equipped bathroom and small salon. A haven of tranquillity at the heart of the town.

🍴 EAT

🍽 **La Remise** – *4 Avenue de la Libération, Besse-sur-Issole, 15km/9mi southeast of Brignoles on N 7 towards Le Luc and right on D 13. ℘04 94 59 66 93. Closed Mon Jul–Aug.* Small, unpretentious establishment discreetly located at the entrance to the village. The white walled decor has a simple, minimalist feel.

Outside is a shaded courtyard. Simple fare with a Mediterranean touch.

🍽 **Le Val Bohème** – *3 Pl. du 4-Septembre, Le Val. ℘04 94 86 46 20.⬚.* The special of the day at this small restaurant depends on the seasonal produce found at the local market. A charming terrace overlooks the church.

🛒 SHOPPING

Open-Air Markets – Every Wednesday on Place Carami and Saturday on Place Général du Gaulle and Place du 8 Mai.

Maison des Vins Coteaux Varois – *Abbaye de la Celle, La Celle. ℘04 94 69 33 18. Closed Sun in winter.* This boutique is in a 12C abbey, with 80 different wine producers. There's also a small vineyard on the premises open to visits.

🎉 EVENTS

Agricultural Fair – Dedicated to wines from Provence and the Var region, as well as honey, olives, and olive oil. Held for ten days in April.

Foires à la Saucisse au Val – Sausage festival the first weekend in September.

Cotignac★

Var

This peaceful Provençal village seems to flow down from a cliff (80m/262ft high) above the Cassole River, riddled with caves and chasms. Atop the cliff sit two 14C tower remains of Castellane Castle.

VISIT
The Old Village
🗺 *A detailed walking tour map is available at the tourist office.*

Shaded by the plane trees, the **cours centrale** (main square) has beautiful 16C–18C façades and an ancient fountain. On the Grande Rue, look up to see the three caryatids at no 7, and the 18C Hôtel de Ville with its 15C belfry at Place de la Mairie. The **Théâtre de Verdure** hosts summer arts events. Follow the

▸ **Population:** 2 146
🕐 **Michelin Map:** 340 L4.
🚩 **Info:** Rue Bonnaventure, ℘04 94 04 61 87.
◗ **Location:** Cotignac is 15km/9mi south of Aups on the D 22.
🅿 **Parking:** Parking is available near the main square and the exit of the village (in the direction of Carcès).

path up to the clifftop overlooking the countryside to a two-storey **grotto** (👁 *guided tours Tue–Sat Jul–Aug 10am–noon, 3–7pm; 15 Apr–Sept 2–5pm; Mon morning only; ≈2€*) where the village inhabitants used to hide their provisions from pillagers during invasions.

Return via Place de la Mairie, passing by the ancient olive oil mill on your way.

Chapelle Notre-Dame-des-Grâces

1km/0.6mi south on D 13 via a road to the right. ◷*Open daily 8am–7pm.* ✆*04 94 69 64 92.*
The chapel, surmounting Mont Verdaille, is associated with an appearance of the Virgin in the 16C, which is depicted in a painting above the altar. In 1660 young Louis XIV came here on a pilgrimage with his mother Anne of Austria. From the esplanade around the church, there is a pleasant **panorama** of the Argens Valley and the Brignoles region.
🏃 *45min round trip.* A wooded path from the chapel leads to **St-Joseph Monastery**. Only the church is open to the public.

ADDRESSES

🏠 STAY

◒◓ **Chambre d'Hôte Domaine de Nestuby** – *5km/3mi south of Cotignac towards Brignoles.* ✆*04 94 04 60 02. www.nestuby-provence.com. Closed 15 Nov –1Mar. 5 rooms.* 🍴🛏. *Restaurant*◒◓.
Lying at the heart of a vineyard, this welcoming cottage contains fine, comfortable rooms furnished with antiques. The owner will introduce you to the wine made on the estate at his table d'hôte in the former stables.

🍽 EAT

◒◓ **Restaurant Le Clos des Vignes** – *Route de Montfort, 5km/3mi south of Cotignac towards Brignoles.* ✆*04 94 04 72 19. Closed Mon–Tue, Sun eve Oct–Jun. Reservations recommended.*
This former sheep barn surrounded by vineyards has been restored with a dining room-verandah and a summer terrace. Succulent cuisine made with fresh regional produce.

🛒 SHOPPING

Local Specialities – The village is famed for its wine, oil, honey and pine nuts *(pignons)*. In the bakeries you'll find the delicious *croissants aux pignons*.

Markets – *Cours Gambetta and Pl. Joseph-Sigaud*– Provençal market on Tuesday, and agricultural market on Fridays *(mid-Jun–mid-Sept)*.

Les Ruchers du Bessillon – *5 Rue de la Victoire.* ✆*04 94 04 60 39. www.les ruchersdubessillon.com.* This boutique sells a large selection of organic honey.

Draguignan

Var

The town of Draguignan developed from a Roman fort built on an isolated knoll where the 17C Tour d'Horloge (clock tower) now stands. Known for its colourful festivals and popular Provençal markets, the town is at the centre of the Var's wine-growing region. An ideal hub for visiting the surrounding villages.

A BIT OF HISTORY
From the Middle Ages
In the 13C the town grew at the foot of the hill, where a defensive wall with three gates, two of which remain (Porte

▶ **Population:** 37 088.
◔ **Michelin Map:** 340 N4.
🛈 **Info:** Av. Carnot. ✆04 98 10 51 05. www.dracenie.com. Guided tours of the town available through the tourist office. Call for more information.
◉ **Location:** The town is in the Var off the N 555, 30km/18.6mi northwest of Fréjus.
🅿 **Parking:** Park between the tourist office and the Old Town is at the Allées d'Azémar *(first hour free)*.

des Portaiguières and Porte Romaine), and a keep (on the bluff) were built. Louis XIV ordered the keep to be razed in retribution for the conflict between local factions in 1649.

In 1797 the town became the administrative centre *(préfecture)* of the Var by order of Napoleon; in 1974 Toulon took over. In the 19C barons Azémar and Haussmann, both prefects of the Var, laid out tree-lined walks and straight boulevards throughout the town.

An American Cemetery, to the east of the town, and a memorial to the Liberation on the corner of Avenue Lazare-Carnot and Avenue Patrick-Rosso, recall the fighting that took place in August 1944. The town has been home to an artillery school since 1976.

St Hermentaire and the dragon

The name Draguignan is derived from Draconio, from the Latin root *draco* meaning dragon. Legend has it that, in the 5C, pilgrims on their way from Ampus to the renowned Lérins Abbey via Lentier encountered a dragon roaming the marshes, now meadows watered by the Nartuby.

The terrified pilgrims appealed for the help of the hermit Hermentaire, who lived in the area. He slayed the

dragon and built a chapel dedicated to St Michael the Archangel. The existing church of **St-Michel**, north of Place du Marché, contains an 18C statue of St Hermentaire in gilded wood.

WALKING TOUR
THE OLD TOWN

▷ *Begin at Pl. du Marché.*

The Rue des Marchands opens onto Old Draguignan (pedestrian district), where the 14C gates, **Porte Romaine** and **Porte des Portaiguières**, frame an intricate maze of charming streets lined with ornate doorways and houses at odd angles. The marketplace is set with fountains and shaded by plane trees.

▷ *Follow the Rue de l'Observance and turn left on the Montée de l'Horloge.*

Tour de l'Horloge

The clock tower replaced the keep pulled down in 1660. It has four flanking turrets and an ornate wrought-iron campanile. The **view** from the top encompasses the town and the Nartuby Valley.

▷ *Double back to the Rue des Tanneurs, to the Porte de Portaiguières, which pierces a 15C square tower.*

Clock tower, Draguignan

D. Pazery/MICHELIN

Don't miss the vast façade of an old 13C **synagogue** in Rue de la Juiverie and the old mansion at no 42.

▷ *At the end of the street turn right to the church and return to the Pl. du Marché.*

SIGHTS
Musée Municipal

9 Rue de la République. &⊙*Open Mon–Sat 9am–noon, 2–6pm.* ⊜*No charge.* ℘*04 98 10 26 85. www.ville-draguignan.fr.*

This 17C Ursuline convent was remodelled in the 18C by the Bishop of Fréjus. It now displays interesting and rare artworks, antique furniture, sculpture, ceramics from France (Vallauris, Moustiers, Sèvres) and the Far East.

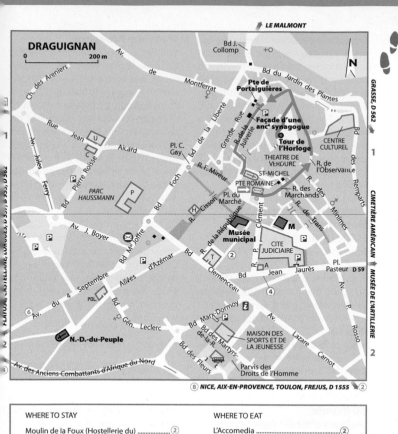

Noteworthy pieces include paintings by Van Loo, 16C parade armour, and a composition sculpted by Camille Claudel (1903). One room is devoted to 17C French and Dutch painting, and other to archaeology, with items discovered during Gallo-Roman excavations.

Musée des Arts et Traditions Populaires de Moyenne Provence★

15 Rue Joseph-Roumanille. ⓘ*Open Tue–Sun 9am–noon, 2–6pm.* ⓘ*Closed Sun morning, public holidays.* ⏺*3.50€.* ℘*04 94 47 05 72. www.dracenie.com.* This museum highlights traditional activities of the region. Exhibits display everyday objects from the region's farming (cereals), wine growing, olive and cork cultivation, bee-keeping, sheep-raising, hunting, arts and crafts (floor tiles from Salernes, glassworks from the area around Fayence to Fréjus) and silkworm raising.

Musée de l'Artillerie

Av. de la Grande-Armée, 3km/2mi east of Draguignan by Bd. J.F.-Kennedy and D 59; at the artillery school's main entrance. ⓘ*Open mid-Jan–mid-Dec Sun–Wed 9am–noon, 1.30–5.30pm.* ⓘ*Closed public holidays.* ⏺*No charge.* ℘*04 98 10 83 86. http://musee-artillerie.chez-alice.fr.* The artillery school (founded in 1791) was transferred to Draguignan in 1976; it merged in 1983 with the anti-aircraft school from Nîmes. The museum presents the evolution of weaponry and military strategy from ancient times up to the contemporary period. The ground floor contains displays of heavy arms and old-fashioned small arms represented by various types of guns and rockets. The display of modern artillery comprises field weapons, trench equipment, fortifications, mountain weapons and anti-aircraft defence equipment. The mezzanine has been laid out as a Second Empire military camp.

Cimetière Américain et Mémorial du Rhône

553 Bd. J.F.-Kennedy. ⚓🕒*Open daily 9am–5pm.* ⚓*No charge.*
☏*04 94 68 03 62.*

In the landscaped cemetery (5ha/12 acres) are the graves of 861 American soldiers belonging to General Patch's 7th Army who fell in Provence during the campaign of 15 August 1944 in support of the Normandy landings. The chapel is decorated inside with mosaics by the American Austin Purves.

Chapelle Notre-Dame du Peuple

Southwest of the Old Town; see map.
This chapel was originally built in the 16C in Flamboyant Gothic style and enlarged in 19C. It contains votive offerings dedicated to the Virgin who saved the town from the Plague *(pilgrimage 8 September)*. On the north wall is the central panel of a 16C altarpiece.

EXCURSIONS
Pays Dracénois
Malmont Viewpoint (Table d'Orientation du Malmont)★
6km/3.7mi – about 45min.

▷ *From Draguignan take Bd. Joseph-Collomp north 6km/4mi to a pass. Turn left onto a narrow road for 300m/330yd.*

An extensive **view**★ covers Mont Vinaigre in the Esterels, Agay port, the Argens Valley, the Maures hills and Toulon.

Trans-en-Provence
5km/3mi south of Draguignan by N 555.
Up to the Second World War, this lively village was renowned for its silk spinning. The town hall, built in 1779, with its lovely Louis XV **façade**★ decorated in *trompe-l'œil*, is a rare example of 18C civic architecture. There is a fine reredos in **St-Victor** (14C church). A path leads from Place de la Mairie in front of the town hall to the **waterfalls and gorges of the Nartuby**. This outstanding **site**★ is best viewed from between Pont Vieux and Pont Bertrand.
On the Chemin du Cassivet is a Puit Aérien *(look for the signs on the left when entering the village; path passes under the D 555)*. This "aerial well" was designed by the Belgian engineer Knapen in 1930. The well works by recovering moisture during the night in order to water crops.

Flayosc – *7km/4.3mi – about 45min.*

▷ *From Draguignan take D 557 west.*

This charming Var village overlooking vineyards, meadows and orchards has retained its 14C fortified gates. The typically Provençal **Place de la Reinesse** has plane trees, a mossy fountain and a small wash-house; the Romanesque **church** has a massive square bell tower.

Chapelle Ste-Roseline★
10km/6mi. South of Draguignan on N 555 and turn right onto D 91.
🕒*See Les ARCS.*

🚗 DRIVING TOUR

Gorges de Châteaudouble★
41km/25.4mi – about 1hr.

▷ *Leave Draguignan on Av. de Montferrat and follow D 955.*

Pierre de la Fée
This 'fairy's stone' is a fine dolmen, with a table 6m/19.7ft long, 4.5m/14.7ft wide and weighing 40t resting on three raised stones more than 2m/6.5ft high.

Gorges de Châteaudouble★
This serpentine gorge was carved by the Nartuby, a tributary of the Argens.

▶ *Return to Le Plan and turn right onto D 51 to the village of Châteaudouble.*

Châteaudouble village occupies a cliff overhanging the gorges of the Nartuby by 100m/330ft. Its medieval passages are interspersed with little squares and fountains.
The Saracen Tower offers a superb **view**★ over the whole village. Steep paths lead from the gorges to the pre-

historic caves of Mouret, Chèvres and Chauves-Souris.

▶ *From Châteaudouble drive north towards Ampus. D 51 crosses a plateau through the Bois des Prannes.*

Ampus
The village church is a well-restored Romanesque building. Just behind it, a path marked by modern Stations of the Cross (1968) leads to a rocky outcrop.

▶ *Return to Draguignan on D 49 for a good view of the town.*

ADDRESSES

STAY

⊜ **Chambre d'hôte La Pergola** – *192 Av. du 4-Septembre.* ℘*04 94 99 18 54. www.draguicity.com/lapergola. 4 rooms.* ⊒*7.50€. Restaurant* ⊜. A bed & breakfast in the centre of town, with a pretty terrace and fountain at the entrance. The comfortable rooms have en suite bathrooms and air conditioning.

⊜ **Hostellerie du Moulin de la Foux** – *941 chemin St-Jean-de-la-Foux – 3km/2mi south on D 1555, rte de Fréjus.* ℘*04 98 10 14 14. www.hotel-dumoulin-de-la-foux.com.* ▣*. 27 rooms.* ⊒*7€. Restaurant* ⊜. This charming inn inside an ancient olive mill has a large leafy terrace overlooking the river. Rooms are comfortable, the renovated ones have more conveniences.

⊜ **Hôtel Les Oliviers** – *4km/2.5mi West of Draguignan by D 557 (Route de Flayosc).* ℘*04 94 68 25 74. www.hotel-les-oliviers.com. Closed 5–25 Jan. 12 rooms.* ▣*.* ⊒*8€.* Roadside hotel conveniently situated on the way to Flayosc. The rooms, all on the ground floor, are light and neatly arranged.

⊜⊜ **Chambre d'Hôte St-Amour** – *986 Rte. de la Motte, Trans-en-Provence, 5km/3mi S of Draguignan.* ℘*04 94 70 88 92. www.domainedesaintamour.com. 3 rooms.* ⊟*.* ⊒*.* A large, rambling park and a curious swimming pool are the backdrop to this 18C stone house

offering a self-contained flat and several rooms, each decorated in a distinctive style.

⍩ EAT

⊜ **L'Accomedia** – *13 Rue des Endronnes.* ℘*04 94 50 72 72. Closed 7–31 Aug.* An Italian restaurant opposite the local theatre, and embellished with a fresco evoking the Carnival. In a light, modern setting, typical Mediterranean specialities are prepared and attractively served.

⊜⊜ **Lou Galoubet** – *23 Bd. Jean Jaurès.* ℘*04 94 68 08 50. Closed mid-Jul– mid-Aug, Sun and Tue eves, Mon.* Classic French dining with fine, contemporary decor in a sunny dining room.

⊳ SHOPPING

Markets – Place du Marché hosts a lively, colourful market on Wednesday and Saturday mornings.

Moulin du Flayosquet – *Rte. d'Ampus, Le Bastidon, Flayosc.* ℘*04 94 70 41 45. Closed Sun–Mon Sept–Jun, Sun Jul–Aug, two weeks in Mar and Nov.* This superb 13C mill has preserved its original equipment and still uses its traditional blades for pressing. The boutique sells a selection of regional products in addition to olive oils.

Domaine Rabiega – *Route de Lorgues.* ℘*04 94 68 44 22. www.rabiega.com. Closed Sun.* A beautiful property situated amongst the olive trees and vineyards, the domain produces 20 000 bottles per year of organic wines (mostly reds).

GETTING AROUND
Buses – ℘*0 800 651 220*. There are 4 local lines. Single tickets available from bus drivers, books of tickets from the bus station on Rue des Martyrs-de-la-Résistance *(closed Sun)*. Coaches will take you to St-Raphaël *(60min)*, Toulon *(120min)*, and to the SNCF train station Les Arcs-Draguignan *(25min)*. ℘*04 94 68 15 34*.

Entrecasteaux
Var

Built on the slopes of a hill overlooking the banks of the River Bresque, this village prides itself on its public gardens designed by Le Nôtre. The streets are shaded by hundred-year-old plane trees.

VISIT
The town's narrow streets wind around an old fortified church with a buttress spanning the road. From the church esplanade, head down to the Pont St-Pierre and the wash house *(lavoir)*, where you'll see the château's round ice house. Go around the back through the the the ancient entance gate. Cross the gardens and exit by the pretty horseshoe shaped staircase, to the **Chapelle des Pénitents** (now home to the Town Hall). Finally, follow the pleasant path up to the **Chapelle Ste-Anne** where you'll find a fine view.

Château
◖◖Guided tours (1.5hr) Easter–Oct Sun–Fri 4pm (and 11.30am in Aug). ⊜7€. ℘04 94 04 43 95.
This austere 17C building dominating the valley of the Bresque has a high façade topped by a double row of tiles and wrought-iron balustrades. The château was the stronghold of the Castellane, followed by the Grignan before passing to the Bruni family. After a long period of neglect, the château was restored by the British painter Ian McGarvie-Munn who turned part of it into a museum before his death in 1981. The tour includes the castle kitchen, outbuildings, guardrooms and salons.

▶ **Population:** 1 016.
Ġ **Michelin Map:** 340 M4.
🖪 **Info:** Cours Gabriel-Péri. ℘04 94 04 40 50.
◖ **Location:** The town sits 24km/15mi south of Aups on D 31. There's a map on the square next to the garden that highlights all of the places of interest in the village.

ADDRESSES

🛏 STAY
⊜⊜ **Chambre d'hôte Bastide Notre-Dame** – *Au Bourg*. ℘04 94 04 45 63. http://bastidenotredame.free.fr. *4 rooms. Closed 1 month in winter. 4 rooms.* ⊟⚏. This hillside B&B estate has four simple rooms, a pool and veranda.

🍴 EAT
⊜⊜ **La Fourchette** – *Le Courtil, near the château.* ℘04 94 04 42 78. *Closed mid-Dec–mid-Feb, Sun eve–Tue.* Light and refined cuisine made from fresh market produce. The tiny, tiled dining room with a fresco of the village provides an intimate place for winter meals.

🏃 SPORT AND LEISURE
Provence Canoë – *New Évasion, on the D 562 between Lorgues and Carcès.* ℘04 94 29 52 48. www.new-evasion.fr. *Closed Dec–Mar.* Discover the Argens River by canoe or kayak. Half-day excursions.

CALENDAR
Local patron saints – Ste-Anne is celebrated on July 26 and St-Sauveur during the first weekend in August.
Pesto soup banquet – Last Sun in July.
Floralies – Plant and flower fair, third weekend in April.

Lorgues

Var

Lorgues is a small medieval town with a beautiful market square, graced with splendid plane trees originally planted in 1835. Beyond the village are wooded hilltops, cultivated with vines and olives.

- ▶ **Population:** 8 550.
- ⊙ **Michelin Map:** 340 N5.
- ℹ **Info:** Pl. d'Antrechaux. ℘04 94 73 92 37. www.ot-lorgues.com.
- ◐ **Location:** Lorgues is 13km/8mi southwest of Draguignan on the D 557 and D 562. At the centre, the medieval city stretches along the main shopping street. The more modern, 20C buildings lie to the west.

THE OLD QUARTER
A Touch of Medieval Charm

The tourist office provides maps of the village walking tour.

The streets of the town radiate from a central square, dotted with fountains, fortified 12C gateways, and many interesting old houses with their attractive façades, lintels, and wrought-iron.

Collégiale St-Martin

The 18C church was built by Bishop Fleury of Fréjus, who later became Louis XV's minister. It is unusually large with a dressed stone façade, and a **Virgin and Child** attributed to Pierre Puget. Don't miss the fine organ and carved pulpit.

EXCURSIONS
Ermitage de St-Ferréol

1km/0.6mi. Follow the signs to the northeast of the town. The chapel stands on a low wooded hill with traces of a Roman settlement.

Chapelle Notre-Dame-de-Benva

3km/2mi northwest (D 50) on the Entrecasteaux road. Open Jul–Sept Thu 10am–noon, 3.30–5pm. ℘04 94 73 92 37.

The chapel of Our Lady of Benva (corruption of the Provençal *ben vai* "good journey") stands on a hillside with its porch astride the old Entrecasteaux road. Inside and outside are 15C frescoes in the Naïve tradition.

Monastère Orthodoxe St-Michel

8km/5mi north by D 10 or 10km/6mi by D 77. Guided tours (40min) Thu and Sat–Tue 10am, 2pm, 3pm, 4pm, Wed afternoon only, Fri morning only. ℘04 94 73 75 75.

These stone buildings of Byzantine inspiration were once home to an Orthodox community founded under the authority of the Patriarch of Antioch. The crypt, refectory and church are adorned with frescoes in the Romanesque and Byzantine styles.

Taradeau

9km/5.6mi – southeast on D 10.

A "Saracen" tower and a ruined Romanesque chapel crown the bluff dominating the village of Tardeau, which produces reputable wines.

◐ *Take D 73 north. Turn right into a path marked "Table d'Orientation 800m".*

🚶 From the top there is a vast **panorama**★ over Lorgues, Les Arcs, the Provençal tableland and the Grasse Pre-Alps, the Esterel and the Maures.

Abbaye du Thoronet ★★

13km/8mi southwest. From Lorgues take D 562 towards Carcès. Bear left onto D 17 and turn right onto D 79. See Abbaye du THORONET.

ADDRESSES

🛏 STAY

🍽 **Les Pins** – *3630 Rte. de St-Antonin.* *04 94 73 91 97. www.le-clos-de-tiffanie. com. Closed mid-Nov–mid-Mar. 5 rooms. (at dinner). Restaurant* 🍽🍽.
This grand villa under the pines is surrounded by vineyards. Three suites with a terrace next to the pool are in the annex. Two other rooms, in the main building, are decorated in the same Provençal style.

🍽 EAT

🍽🍽 **Le Chrissandier** – *18 Cours de la République. 04 94 67 67 15. http:// lechrissandier.com. Closed Tue eve, Wed.* Nestled in the old medieval quarter, this rustic-style restaurant attracts a regular clientele at lunchtime and caters for tourists in the evening. The menu changes every day, dictated by the fresh market produce.

🛒 SHOPPING

Marché – Tuesdays, and small producers on Friday.
Wine – A dozen vineyards can be found around Lorgues, many offering tastings and sales of their Côtes-de-Provence and Vins de Pays du Var and d'Argens. Ask at the tourist office for a list.

Le Luc

Var

Old Luc seems almost like a film set of an old Provençal village, with its romantic scruffiness, mossy fountains, impossibly narrow streets, uneven cobblestones and a cat sleeping in the sun of a flowered courtyard. Despite its sleepy atmosphere, Le Luc is an important farming centre, serving as the collection point for the regional harvests of grapes and olives in the Var plain.

▸ **Population:** 8 711.
⚲ **Michelin Map:** 340 M5; local map: *see Massif des MAURES*.
ℹ **Info:** Château des Vintimille, Pl. de la Liberté. 04 94 60 74 51.
▷ **Location:** Le Luc serves as an important Var crossroads at the centre of the A 8 (the viaduct is high above the village), the RN 7, Brignoles and Draguignan.

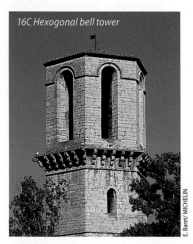
16C Hexogonal bell tower

E. Baret/ MICHELIN

THE OLD VILLAGE
An Imposing Belfry

Le Luc lies in the shade of a 16C hexagonal bell tower (27m/89ft high) built in the style of Italian campaniles. An identification table on the main buildings provides a description of the village.

View from the Oppidum de Fouirette

🚶 *1.5hr round trip.*
Walk towards Vergeiras, then follow a signposted path.
From the top of the hill (300m/984ft high) is a wonderful **view**★ over the Maures plain, from Gonfaron to Rocher de Roquebrune.

SIGHTS

Musée Historique du Centre-Var

24 Rue Victor-Hugo. ○*Open mid-Jun–mid-Sept Mon–Sat 3–6pm.* ○*Closed public holidays.* ☞*No charge.* ℘*04 94 60 70 12. www.coeurduvar.com.*
This museum about local history is housed in the 17C Chapelle Ste-Anne and displays collections of historical artefacts uncovered during local excavations: fossils (dinosaur eggs), a carved Roman sarcophagus, medieval sculptures, minerals from the Maures Massif and ancient weapons. There is also a historical display on Le Luc and the life of the local marine engineer Jean-Baptiste Lebas (1797-1873), who transported the famous obelisk from Luxor to Place de la Concorde in Paris.

Musée régional du Timbre et de la Philatélie

Pl. de la Convention. ○*Open Wed–Thu 2.30–5.30pm, Fri–Sun 10am–noon, 2.30–5.30pm.* ○*Closed 1 Jan, 1 May, 25 Dec.* ☞*2€.* ℘*04 94 47 96 16. www.lemuseedutimbre.com.*

Campaniles in the Var	
Les Arcs	Clock Tower (18C)
Aups	Clock Tower
Carcès	Campanile atop a fortified gate (18C)
Carnoules	Belfry (17C)
Cotignac	Campanile (16C)
Draguignan	Tower (17C)
Flassans	Atop the belfry (18C)
Le Luc	Tower (16C)
St-Tropez	Campanile (19C)
Salernes	Belfry (18C)
Tavernes	Campanile (18C)
Toulon	Arsenal tower (18C)

This regional museum devoted to the history of postage stamps and philately is housed in the Château de Vintimille, a striking 18C building. The display follows the different stages in the traditional manufacture of postage stamps and philatelic counterfeiting.

ADDRESSES

☞ STAY

☞ **La Haute Verrerie** – *Rte. de St-Tropez, Le Cannet-des-Maures, 6km/3.7mi east of Le Luc by D 558.* ℘*04 94 47 95 51. 4 rooms.* ⊟ ☲. A lively brook flows at the foot of this charming 1839 Provençal house, once used as a glass-making workshop. The rooms, housed in several outbuildings, are each decorated in their own style. The prettiest has a solarium.

☞ **Chambre d'hôte Le Hameau de Charles-Auguste** – *Rte. de Baraouque.* ℘*04 94 60 79 45. 4 rooms.* ⊟ ☲*10€.* Set within a group of outbuildings constructed around the original 18C farmhouse, this bed and breakfast has been lovingly decorated with flea-market finds and antiques.

☞ EAT

☞☞ **Le Gourmandin** – *Pl. L.-Brunet.* ℘*04 94 60 85 92. www.legourmandin.com. Closed 23 Aug–20 Sept, 20 Feb–10 Mar, Sun and Thu eves, Mon.* This *auberge* in the heart of the village has a convivial atmosphere and a rustic dining room. Traditional cuisine is served.

☞ SHOPPING

Provençal Market – Friday mornings.

Domaine de la Lauzade – *Route de la Lauzade.* ℘*04 94 60 72 51. www.lauzade.com. Closed Sun.* Guided tours, tastings and direct sales of Côtes-de-Provence at this small vineyard. There are also regular art exhibitions.

Domaine de la Pardiguière – *Rte. des Mayons, Fontaines aux Grives.* ℘*04 94 60 75 37. Open by request.* There are excellent views over the countrysde from this family-run organic vineyard and olive orchard. Olives, olive oil and wine sold on-site.

Roquebrune-sur-Argens

Var

The small town of Roquebrune, perched on a rocky peak at the foot of the Rocher de Roquebrune, was most likely founded in the early 11C. There still exist vestiges of the original ramparts and many 16C houses.

SIGHTS

The Village

Originally a stronghold, the castrum was surrounded by a curtain wall (destroyed in 1592 during the Wars of Religion) whose traces are visible, particularly in Boulevard de la Liberté. Across from the clock tower is the picturesque Rue des Portiques, lined with ancient houses, many from the 16C. Inside the fortifications, the narrow, winding streets recall Roquebrune's medieval legacy.

Église St-Pierre-St-Paul

The 16C Gothic church features an unusual 18C façade, and 11C remnants of two chapels with thick quadripartite vaulting of rectangular-shaped diagonal and transverse arches. The first chapel contains a wooden altarpiece (1557) of John the Baptist flanked by St Claudius and St Bridget, while the second chapel houses an altarpiece from the same period depicting the Last Judgement. In the nave is a 16C altarpiece composed of carved panels depicting the Passion.

Musée du Patrimoine

Impasse Barbacane, the continuation of Rue des Portiques. &🕐*Open Jul–Aug daily 9am–noon, 2.30–6.30pm; rest of the year Tue–Sun 9am–noon, 2–6pm.* 👓*3€.* ✆*04 94 19 89 89.*
Located in the old St-Jacques Chapel, the museum houses Prehistoric and Roman finds excavated in the Bouverie caves *(nearby)* which were inhabited from 30 000 to 8 000 BC by the **Bouverian** culture unique to southeastern France. Also displayed are fine objects from the Neolithic Era, and remarkable Roman remains in a reconstruction of a tomb.

▶ **Population:** 11 405.
& **Michelin Map:** 340 O5.
🗊 **Information:** 1 Rue Jean-Aicard. ✆04 94 19 89 89. www.roquebrunesur argens.fr.
◔ **Location:** The town lies 12km/7.5mi west of Fréjus on the D 8, then the D 7. From the A 8, exit Puget-sur-Argens and take the N 7 west, then left on D7.
🅿 **Parking:** At the foot of the village.

Chapelle St-Pierre

From Roquebrune take D7 southeast.
🕐*Open during exhibitions.*
The chapel has preserved a Carolingian apse but was rebuilt in the Romanesque style in the 11C, with a recessed tomb on the façade. To the east is an old cemetery with tombs carved into the rock.

🚗 DRIVING TOUR

Rocher de Roquebrune

14km/8.5mi round trip – 1hr, excluding the climb.
The proud silhouette of Roquebrune rock (composed of red sandstone) forms a small, solitary massif between the Maures and Esterel. Its jagged silhouette dominates the lower Argens Valley.

▷ *From Roquebrune-sur-Argens, take the small road to the south opposite the cemetery.*

Chapelle Notre-Dame-de-Pitié

The chapel stands on rising ground amid pine and eucalyptus trees at the foot of a majestic red cliff. Beyond the screen on the high altar stands a 17C retable framing a Pietà. Next to the chapel, there is a **view** ★ of the Argens Plain, Fréjus, St-Raphaël and the Esterel heights.

▷ *Return to Roquebrune and turn left onto D 7. After 500m/547yd bear left; 1km/0.6mi further on turn left again onto a forest road. After 2km/1mi park where a path veers right.*

Roquebrune Summit★

🚶 *2hr on foot round trip; a difficult walk; keep to the path.*

From the summit (alt 372m/1 073ft), there is an extended **view**★ of the Maures, Fréjus Bay, the Esterel and the Alps on the horizon.

At the rock's summit stand three crosses by the sculptor Vernet in memory of three famous Crucifixions painted by Giotto, Grünewald and El Greco. The summit symbolises Golgotha.

⊙ *Drive down the south face of Roquebrune rock and turn right onto D 25. After 1km/0.6mi, turn right along the north face. Drive through the hamlet of La Roquette.*

Chapelle Notre-Dame-de-la-Roquette

🚶 *30min on foot round trip. Park in the car park by the road and take the path on the right.*

The ruined chapel, an ancient place of pilgrimage and meeting place for hikers is located in an attractive **setting**★ of lotus, chestnut and holly trees beside a great rock chaos of red sandstone. From the terrace (alt 143m/470ft) the **view** includes the lower Argens Valley and the Provençal tableland.

ADDRESSES

🛒 SHOPPING

L'Amie Ailée – *36 Rue St-Éloi. 𝒫04 94 45 30 20. www.lamieailee.fr. Closed Sun.* Sale of honey, pollen, nougat, Royal Jelly.

LOCAL TREATS

Local markets Monday morning on Place San Peïre, Friday morning on Place Alfred-Perrin. The delicious Honey Fair takes place in late October.

🏃 SPORT AND LEISURE

Activities – Quad-bikes, canoeing, kayaking, diving, fishing, guided nature walks, leisure parks, Zen Océane, a health outfit/spa, and much more.

Abbaye du Thoronet★★

Var

Le Thoronet, the oldest of the three Cistercian abbeys in Provence (along with Sénanque and Silvacane) is surrounded by wooded hills in a tranquil, isolated spot, in keeping with the strict rules of the Cistercian Order.

A BIT OF HISTORY

From foundation to the present – In 1136 monks from the abbey of Mazan (Haut-Vivarais) moved to Le Thoronet near Lorgues and established themselves on land presented to them by Raymond Bérenger, Count of Barcelona and Marquis of Provence. The abbey soon became prosperous from the many donations it received, particularly from the lords of Castellane. The church, the

⌖ **Michelin Map:** 340 M5; local map: *see BRIGNOLES*

🛈 **Info:** 𝒫04 94 60 43 90.

⊙ **Location:** The abbey is situated between Lorgues and the Lac de Carcès (⌖ *see Driving Tour in BRIGNOLES).* From the A 8, exit Le Cannet.

cloisters and the monastic buildings were built between 1160 and 1190. Like many other Cistercian abbeys in the 14C, Le Thoronet sank into decline. First internal dissension and later the Wars of Religion caused the monks to desert the premises. In 1787 it was attached to the See of Digne, then abandoned once again during the Revolution. In 1854 it was bought by the State and saved from ruin at the instigation of Prosper Mérimée.

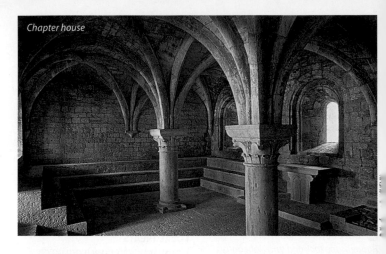

Chapter house

ABBEY TOUR 1hr

⏱ *Open Apr–Sept Mon–Sat 10am–6.30pm, Sun 10am–noon, 2–6.30pm; Oct–Mar Mon–Sat 10am–1pm, 2–5pm, Sun 10am–noon, 2–5pm.* ⊘*Closed public holidays.* ⊕*7€.* ☎*04 94 60 43 90. http://thoronet.monuments-nationaux.fr.*

Thanks to the quality of the surviving buildings (church and cloisters), and their simple but rigorous style, the abbey of Le Thoronet is widely considered one of the jewels of Cistercian architecture.

Church★

This was built in the style of the Provençal-Romanesque School: squat, austere and rigorously geometric, with stonework blocks accurately cut and assembled without mortar. The square bell tower of stone is an exception to the architectural rules of the order, which required simple wooden structures, due to violent winds and the risk of fire.

The nave is covered with barrel vaulting, slightly pointed, supported on tranverse arches. It consists of three bays, prolonged by a fourth of the same height at right angles to the transept: only the raised arches indicate the presence of two arms of the transept which are vaulted like the nave.

The chancel ends in an oven-vaulted apse and is lit through three windows. It is preceded by a shallow bay, featuring a triumphal arch surmounted by an oculus. The aisles are lower than the nave and covered with rampant pointed vaulting resting on transverse arches.

Cloisters★

The cloisters on the north side of the church are austere and solidly built in the form of a trapezium. The south gallery is at about the same level as the church, but the west (exhibition of manuscripts and illuminated texts) and the north and east (which once supported another storey beneath a pitched roof) are lower because of the uneven ground; in all, seven steps were needed to compensate for the change of level. The galleries have transverse arches and

The Poet Abbot

In the late 12C, the abbey's most famous abbot was appointed: **Folquet de Marseille**. His family came from Genoa but he gave up a career in trade to devote himself to poetry. He became a famous troubadour, quoted by Dante, and then in 1196 decided to become a Cistercian monk. In 1201 he was appointed Abbot of Le Thoronet and then Bishop of Toulouse in 1205.

barrel vaulting. The solid, round headed arches which open onto the cloisters' garth (now a garden) are each divided in two by a stout column. Opposite the refectory door, projecting into the garth, is the **lavabo** where the monks washed their hands before meals. The hexagonal structure has been restored, and the water container is provided with holes and spouts through which the water ran into the basin below.

Conventual buildings
These stand on the north side of the church near the cloisters. The door of the **library** (armarium), which is on the ground floor, is surmounted by a triangular lintel.
The **chapter house**★ dates from the early Gothic period. The ogival vaulting, in which the ribs fan out like palm trees, is supported by two columns with roughly sculpted capitals, ornamented with leaves, pine cones, palm fronds and a hand gripping a staff. These are the only carvings in the abbey. The stone benches have been partially reconstructed. Next to the chapter house is the **parlour** which also serves as a passage between the cloisters and the outer garden. The **dormitory** over the chapter house is reached by a vaulted stairway and roofed with pointed vaulting supported on transverse arches. The 18 windows with double embrasures have been reglazed. At the southern end, jutting out above the cloisters, is the Abbot's chamber. The doors in the north gallery opened into the monks' room, the warming room, the refectory and the kitchen, which have all disappeared.
The **store room**, on the west side of the cloisters, has pointed vaulting and contains 18C vats for wine and olive oil as well as the remains of a press.
The lay-brother building, at the northwest corner of the store room, provided

Monastic Austerity
There is hardly any sculpture or carved decoration in the church to detract from its majestic proportions and purity of line. There is, however, a gentle curve on the imposts on the pillars and the half-columns supporting the transverse arches rise to only 2.9m/9.5ft above the ground according to Cistercian tradition.

separate housing for the lay-brothers, who carried out manual labour for the monks and who lived a less restrained monastic life. It has been partially restored and comprises a refectory on the ground floor and a dormitory above.

Outbuildings
Beside the stream, the foundations of the **guesthouse** have been excavated. The tithe barn on the south side of the church was later converted into an oil mill and contains some mill stones and a mortar.

ADDRESSES

⌘ EAT
⌘ **Le Tournesol** – 9 Rue des Trois-Ormetox, Le Thoronet, 4km/2.5mi from the Abbey. ☎04 94 73 89 81. Closed Jan. This tiny 17C house in a village alley will surprise you with its colourful walls and furniture, its homey cooking and its charming terrace giving onto the street.

CALENDAR
Rencontres de Musique Médiévale – A medieval music festival takes place in and around the abbey and church the last two weeks of July. www.musique-medievale.fr.

Tourtour★

Var

This village, set within a wooded region, is flanked on each side by ancient castles. Remains of the 12C Abbaye de Florielle, founded by the Cistercian monks before they moved to Thoronet, can still be seen.

▶ **Population:** 533.
Michelin Map: 340 M4.
Info: Av. des Ormeaux, ℘04 94 70 54 36. www.tourisme-tourtour.com.
Location: Located east of Aups at the foothills of the Pre-Alps, facing the Varois plain.

WALKING TOUR
OLD VILLAGE★

The village has retained its medieval character with the remains of fortifications, attractively restored houses and narrow, sloping streets, linked by vaulted passages, which converge on the central square.

A vaulted passageway leads from the square beside the **clock tower** *(tour de l'horloge)* to an old mill, which now houses the Fossil Museum *(see Sights).*

Beside the museum building *(left)* are the ruins of a 12C castle which has been restored and now houses an art and antiques gallery. Further up the road, you'll pass by a charming wash house on the way to a two-storey medieval tower, the **Tour Grimaldi.**

The town hall occupies the former **Château des Raphelis**, a solid 16C building with pepperpot towers.

Église St-Denis

This 11C church, standing on the southeastern edge of the ridge, was extensively modified in the 20C.

Viewpoint★

From the church esplanade there is a wide **panorama**★★ *(viewing table)* over the Argens and Nartuby valleys, extending *(east)* to the Maures and *(west)* to Ste-Baume, Mont Ste-Victoire and the Luberon.

SIGHTS
Musée des Fossiles

Rue des Moulins. Guided tours *(15min) mid-Jun–mid-Sept Wed–Mon 11am–12.30pm, 3.30–7pm.* Guided tours by request. No charge. ℘04 94 70 59 47. www.tourisme-tourtour.org. This museum contains local fossils including ammonites, dinosaur eggs and reptilian teeth.

Moulin à Huile

Rue des Moulins. Guided tours *(1hr) mid-Jun–mid-Sept 11–12.30pm, 3.30–7pm; mid-Dec–mid-Jan depending on temporary exhibitions.* No charge. ℘04 94 70 59 47. www.tourisme-tourtour.com.

Église St-Denis

This communal oil mill has been in service since the 17C and has three presses. During the summer, the mill houses exhibitions of paintings.

ADDRESSES

STAY

Auberge St-Pierre – *3km/2mi east of Tourtour on the D 51 and secondary road. ℘04 94 70 57 17. www.guideprovence.com/hotel/saint-pierre.*

Closed mid-Oct–Apr. ☐*16 rooms.* ☐*12€. Restaurant* ☐☐. Nature lovers will enjoy this hotel hidden within the vast grounds of a Provençal estate. Not far from the village of Tourtour, the rooms are calm and bright, handsomely furnished. The estate has a pool, tennis, fitness room, and mountain biking trails.

SHOPPING

MARKETS
Wednesday and Saturday on Place des Ormeaux.

Villecroze

Var

Villecroze lies in wooded Provençal tableland surrounded by vineyards, orchards and olive groves. The village has developed around caves, partly converted into dwellings.

> **Population:** 1 093.
> **Michelin Map:** 340 M4.
> **Info:** Rue Ambroise-Croizat. ℘04 94 67 50 00.
> **Location:** Situated 8km/5mi south of Aups.

VISIT
The Village
The Middle Ages atmosphere lingers in the village's streets, its 15C clock tower, the surprising Rue des Arcades and the the 18C Romanesque church, Église Notre-Dame, with its wall belfry.

Parc Municipal
▶ *Entrance via Route d'Aups, then a right-hand turn leading to a car park.*

A waterfall cascades 40m/130ft down the cliff face and forms a stream in an oasis of greenery beside a rose garden. A marked path leads to the caves *(grottes).*

SIGHTS
Caves
Guided tours (30min) Jul–Aug Tue–Sun 10am–noon, 2.30–6.30pm; Feb–Apr and Nov Sat–Sun during school holidays 2–5pm; May–Jun Wed and Fri–Sun 2–5.30pm; Sept–mid-Oct Sat–Sun 2–5pm. 2€. ℘04 94 70 63 06.
In the 16C the caves were partially converted into dwellings by the lords of Villecroze. The tour includes several little chambers with attractive concretions.

Belvédère de Villecroze
From Tourtour take D 51 towards Villecroze.
The little road winds through woods which soon give way to strangely shaped rocks and caves. About 1km/0.6mi before Villecroze is a belvedere with a circular **panorama**★ of Tourtour, Villecroze, Salernes, Gros Bessillon and the Maures.

ADDRESSES

EAT
La Cascade – *Chez Martine, Av. Ambroise-Croizet, village centre. ℘04 94 67 57 10. Closed Sun eve, Mon.*
Country-style cuisine with a Provençal touch is served in this family-run restaurant on the vilage's main road above Place du Général-de-Gaulle. The dinng room is simple, but always has a convivial atmosphere.

SHOPPING
Market – Thursday morning on Place du Général-de-Gaulle.

FRÉJUS AND THE ESTEREL MASSI

This area of the French Riviera is the furthest corner of Provence, on the eastern edge of the Var department (county). Although it doesn't have the "flash and cache" of Cannes to the east or St-Tropez to the west, it nevertheless impresses visitors with its natural beauty of unspoiled forests and red rock mountains framing the azure-blue sea. Many come to this part of the Riviera to escape the summer crowds, while lively towns like Fréjus and St-Raphäel as well as the convenient proximity to Nice (less than an hour from Nice international airport) keep it from feeling overly secluded. For those who enjoy sweeping panoramic views, coastal hikes, ancient history and sandy beaches, this is an ideal area to explore.

Highlights

1 Drive the Corniche d'Or to the **Pic de l'Ours** (p206).

2 Take a guided tour of the ancient cloisters and baptistery of the **Groupe Episcopal** (p212).

3 Attend a musical concert in Fréjus's **2C Roman arena** (p210).

4 Explore underwater wrecks with the diving club at the **Port-Fréjus** (p214).

5 See the works of Dada artist Max Ernst in **Seillans** (p221).

History

Like much of the French Riviera, Fréjus and the Esterel Massif were inhabited by the Romans, invaded by pirates, cultivated by monks, discovered by 19C travellers and then liberated in the Second World War when the Allies landed on its beaches. What makes this area remarkable is how many historic sites still stand.

As one of the most important settlements of the Gallo-Roman era, Fréjus is home some of the oldest buildings in France, including the 2C Roman ruins such as the Amphitheatre and the 5C Baptistery at the Groupe Episcopal. France's foreign troops from colonies in Africa and Asia acclimatised to French weather in Fréjus in the early 20C, leaving behind colourful examples of their religious devotion, including a Buddhist pagoda and a Sudanese mosque.

Other historic treasures dating back to pre-historic times can be found at the archaeological museum in Saint Raphäel.

View of the Massif de l'Esterel from the coast

View from the Pic du Cap-Roux

The Fréjus-Saint Raphäel Hub

The dynamic centre of this area is found in the twinned cities of Fréjus, known for its prestigious history dating back to the Romans, and Saint Raphäel, a modern resort town which became popular during the Belle Epoch. Here, approximately 85 000 residents (and visitors) benefit from the cities' combined municipal services, coordinated environmental preservation, and complementary cultural development.

Natural Beauty

The red porphyry rocks that define the Massif de l'Esterel have made it one of the most beautiful sites on the French Riviera. It remained relatively unspoiled throughout the 19C since the scenic road known as the Corniche d'Or wasn't constructed until 1903, connecting the coastline to the peaks that allow for panoramic views over the entire region.

The rocky inlets, interspersed with natural sand beaches, are framed by the gently sloping mountains covered in green pine, oak, heather, and arbousiers (wild strawberry trees). Inland are rivers and lakes such as Lac de St-Cassien in Fayence and the Villepey marshes outside Fréjus. Nature-lovers will find many outdoor activities in the region, from snorkelling and windsurfing to hiking and mountain biking.

Resort Living

Sun-seekers have a variety of sandy beaches, secluded inlets, and picturesque pleasure ports to explore, particularly around Fréjus Plage and Saint Raphael's historic riverfront walk. Water sports, underwater sightseeing cruises and boat rentals can be arranged through the local tourist offices.

For a bit more peace and quiet, several high-end resorts such as the Four Seasons have opened inland around Fayence.

Local Economy

The main economic activity of the Fréjus and Massif de l'Esterel area is tourism, like most of the French Riviera.

Fishing and production of wine, honey, olive oil, and fruits and vegetables has continued throughout the centuries, although agriculture in general is not very significant. Visitors will also find many local artisan crafts such as the clay *santon* figurines.

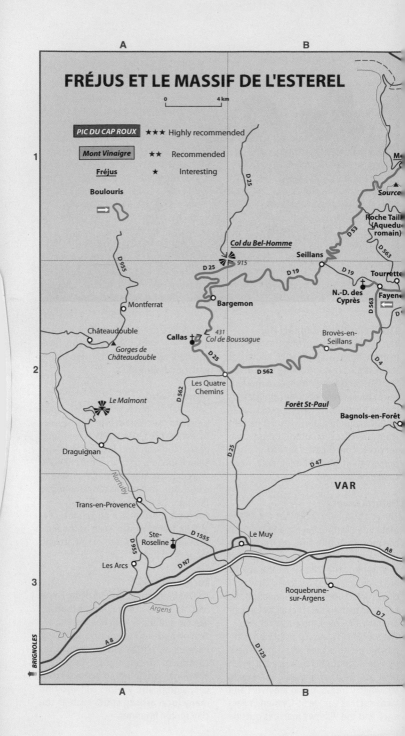

FRÉJUS ET LE MASSIF DE L'ESTEREL

0   4 km

PIC DU CAP ROUX   ★★★ Highly recommended

Mont Vinaigre   ★★   Recommended

Fréjus   ★   Interesting

Boulouris

D 25

Col du Bel-Homme

D 53

Source

Roche Tail
(Aqueduc
romain)

D 563

Seillans

D 25   915

D 19

D 19   Tourrette

Fayen

N.-D. des
Cyprès

D 563

Montferrat   Bargemon

Châteaudouble

Gorges de
Châteaudouble   Callas   431
Col de Boussague

Brovès-en-
Seillans

D 25

D 562

Le Malmont

D 562   Les Quatre
Chemins

D 25

Forêt St-Paul

Bagnols-en-Forêt

Draguignan

D 47

VAR

Nartuby

Trans-en-Provence

Ste-
Roseline   D 1555

Le Muy

A 8

D 955   D N7

Les Arcs

Roquebrune-
sur-Argens

D 7

Argens

A 8

BRIGNOLES

D 125

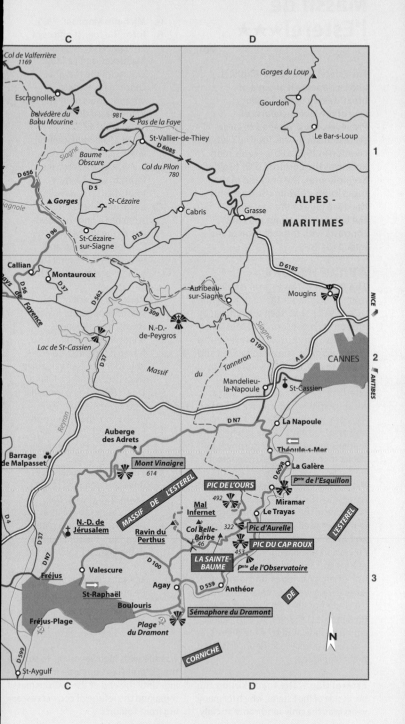

C
D

Col de Valferrière
1169

Escragnolles

Belvédère du
Babu Mourine

981

Pas de la Faye

St-Vallier-de-Thiey

Gorges du Loup

Gourdon

Le Bar-s-Loup

D 6085

Siagne

Baume
Obscure

Col du Pilon
780

1

D 656

Gorges

D 5

St-Cézaire

Cabris

Grasse

ALPES -

MARITIMES

agnole

D 96

St-Cézaire-
sur-Siagne

D 13

Callian

Montauroux

D 56
Pays de Fayence

D 37

D 562

Auribeau-
sur-Siagne

D 309

N.-D.-
de-Peygros

D 6185

Mougins

NICE

Lac de St-Cassien

D 37

Massif

du

Tanneron

Siagne

D 199

A 8

CANNES

2

ANTIBES

Reyran

Mandelieu-
Napoule

St-Cassien

Auberge
des Adrets

D N7

La Napoule

Théoule-s-Mer

Barrage
de Malpasset

Mont Vinaigre
614

MASSIF DE L'ESTEREL

PIC DE L'OURS

D 6098

La Galère

Pⁿᵗᵉ de l'Esquillon

D 4

N.-D. de
Jérusalem

Ravin du
Perthus

Mal
Infernet

492

Col Belle-
Barbe
46

322

Miramar

Le Trayas

Pic d'Aurelle

LESTEREL

D 37

D 100

LA SAINTE-
BAUME

453

PIC DU CAP ROUX

Pⁿᵗᵉ de l'Observatoire

D N7

Fréjus

Valescure

Agay

D 559

Anthéor

DE

3

St-Raphaël

Boulouris

Sémaphore du Dramont

Fréjus-Plage

Plage
du Dramont

N

D 599

St-Aygulf

CORNICHE

C
D

Massif de l'Esterel★★★

Var

The Esterel between St-Raphaël and La Napoule is an area of breathtaking natural beauty. One of the loveliest parts of Provence, it was opened to large-scale tourism by the Touring Club's creation in 1903 of the scenic road known as the Corniche d'Or (Golden Scenic Route). The fiery red of the rocks forms a strong contrast with the deep blue of the sea, while the bustling life along the coast contrasts with the seclusion of the inland roads.

A BIT OF HISTORY

The Massif – The Esterel, separated from its neighbour the Maures by the Argens Valley, has been worn down by erosion; its highest point, Mont Vinaigre, is just 618m/2 027ft. However, in this mountain mass, the deep ravines and broken skyline dispel any impression of this being mere hills.

The Esterel is made up of volcanic rocks (porphyry), which give the range its characteristic profile, its harsh relief and vivid red tints. Agay is where the Romans found the blue porphyry particular to their Provençal monuments.

Via Aurelia – The Esterel was bordered to the north by the Via Aurelia (Aurelian Way), one of the most important routes of the Roman empire, connecting Rome and Arles via Genoa, Cimiez, Antibes, Fréjus and Aix. Paved, cambered, and more than 2.5m/8ft wide, the road made use of many bridges and other civil engineering works to create the shortest route possible. At the end of each Roman mile (1 478m/1 617yd) distances would be indicated by a tall milestone – one is on display in St-Raphaël (Musée Archéologique).

Esterel Gap – The road skirting the north side of the Esterel, which for many years was the only land route to Italy,

- **Michelin Map:** 340 P/Q5.
- **Info:** The tourist offices of St-Raphaël-Agay, Fréjus, Mandelieu and Le Muy work with the National Office of Forestry to organise tours of the forests in the Massif de l'Esterel. ℘04 94 19 52 52 (St-Raphaël tourist office). www.saint-raphael.com, www.agay.fr, www.ville-frejus.fr, www. lemuy-tourisme.com, www.onf.fr.
- **Location:** The Esterel stretches along the coast-line of the Var between Cannes and Fréjus, and encompasses several small villages and resorts such as St-Raphaël.
- **Parking:** Except in high season around the major towns, free parking is relatively easy to find near hiking trailheads. It is advisable to remove all valuables from your car when hiking.
- **Don't Miss:** The panoramic view from the Pointe de l'Esquillon, the scenic port in Agay, and for the robust hikers, the views from the Pic de l'Ours.
- **Timing:** You could easily drive through the Esterel along N 98 coastal road from Cannes to Fréjus in less than an hour, with a pause for a short hike at Dramont or the Point d'Esquillon. For the longer hikes plan for at least a half day, and to be prepared with enough drinking water, food and appropriate footwear.

was rife with highwaymen; "to survive the Esterel Gap" became a local saying. Until the end of the 19C the massif remained the refuge of convicts escaping from Toulon.

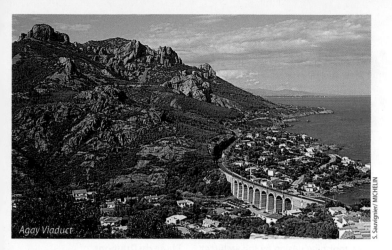

Agay Viaduct

S. Sauvignier/ MICHELIN

RESORTS

Stretching more than 30km/18.6mi between St-Raphaël and La Napoule, the striking landscape of the Corniche de l'Esterel is punctuated by several pleasant seaside resorts.

Boulouris

This small resort, where villas are dotted among pines in beautiful gardens, has several little beaches and a harbour.

Agay

The resort borders a deep port, the best in the Esterel, used in earlier times by the Ligurians, the Greeks and the Romans. The scenic bay of the **Rastel d'Agay** is lined by a large, sunny beach.

Anthéor

The resort of Anthéor is dominated by the three peaks of the Cap Roux range. Just before the Pointe de l'Observatoire, is a **view** inland of the red rocks of St-Barthélemy and Cap Roux. *The road to the summit is described under* 4.

Le Trayas

The resort is divided into two parts: one terraced on wooded slopes, the other by the seashore. The creeks and inlets which mark the coast include many small beaches, the largest of which lies at the end of Figueirette Bay.

Miramar

This elegant resort, with its private harbour, lies in Figueirette Bay.

Antoine de St-Exupéry

Born in Lyon in 1900, Antoine de St-Exupéry attended the Jesuits College and completed his education in Fribourg, Switzerland. Interested in flying from an early age, he joined the French Army Air Force in 1921 but resigned five years later to become a civilian pilot. He soon turned to literature and began writing in 1928. His second novel *Vol de Nuit* was awarded a prize by the French Academy in 1931. However, the book for which he will always be fondly remembered is *Le Petit Prince* (1943), a charming fable for children. In the Second World War, he served as an instructor and would carry out reconnaissance flights. On 31 July 1944, he set out for the Alps on one of these assignments and never returned.

A few days later, he was officially reported missing. His body was never recovered from the ocean waters, but the remains of his Lockheed Lightning P-38 were discovered off the coast of Marseille in 2004.

The Kingdom of Auguste I

Off Dramont beach is a small island of red porphyry, l'Île d'Or, marked by a strange tower which appears to grow out of the rock. This Medieval-style tower was built in 1897 by an eccentric Parisian doctor, Auguste Lutaud, who transformed the island into his own private kingdom, proclaiming himself King Auguste I of the Île d'Or. He became the darling of fashionable Riviera society and organised lavish receptions during the Belle Époque. The monarch died in 1925; his island remains private property.

La Galère

The resort is built on wooded terraces on the slopes of the Esterel where it forms the western limit of La Napoule Bay. Below the road, the seaside development of **Port-la-Galère** *(private port)*, an astonishing design by the architect Jacques Couelle, seems to merge into its rocky environment.

Théoule-sur-Mer

This resort, which is sheltered by the Théoule promontory, has three small beaches. The crenellated building on the shore, now a château, used to be a soap factory in the 18C.

🚗 DRIVING TOURS

1 CORNICHE DE L'ESTEREL★★★
40km/25mi – about 5hr.

▷ *From St-Raphaël (☝️see ST-RAPHAËL) take N 98 south.*

The road skirts the St-Raphaël marina. On the seafront is a memorial to the French Army campaigns in Africa.

▷ *Drive through Boulouris to the N 98.*

Plage du Dramont
☝️*See ST-RAPHAËL.*

A stele erected to the right of the road commemorates the landing of the US Army, 36th Division, on August 15, 1944. Running alongside the lovely Camp-Long beach and Dramont Forest, the road leads to the resorts of Agay and Anthéor. Shortly before reaching the Pointe de l'Observatoire, enjoy the **view** to the left, encompassing the red rocks of St-Barthélemy and Cap Roux.

Pointe de l'Observatoire★
The ruins of a blockhouse command a stunning **view**★ of blood-red porphyry rocks standing out against the cobalt blue of the sea, and vews of the Anthéor, Cap Roux, Esquillon Points and La Napoule Bay.

Cap Esterel

B. Kaufmann/ MICHELIN

> Drive through Le Trayas. On a bend near the Hôtel Tour de L'Esquillon, pull off the road into the car park. A path (sign) leads up to Pointe de l'Esquillon.

Pointe de l'Esquillon★★
🚶 15min round trip.
A beautiful **panorama**★★ (viewing table) of the Esterel heights, the coast, Cap Roux, the Îles de Lérins and Cap d'Antibes. After La Galère, the road skirts Pointe de l'Aiguille, opening up a **view**★ of La Napoule Bay, Cannes, the Îles de Lérins and Cap d'Antibes.
On reaching La Napoule, the N 98 crosses the River Siagne and then follows the curve of the bay up to Cannes (👁see CANNES).

2️⃣ VIA AURELIA★
46km/28.3mi – about 6hr.

> From Cannes★★ (👁see CANNES) take the N 7.

This route runs through Esterel Forest, then passes through the industrial zone of La Bocca and across the alluvial plain of the River Siagne.

> Turn left onto the road leading to Cannes-Mandelieu airport, then right.

Ermitage de St Cassien
The 14C chapel set on a low rise in an oak plantation with a few cypress trees

was once the site of a Roman temple; it is now a place of pilgrimage.

> Return to N 7.

Mandelieu-la-Napoule
👁See MANDELIEU-LA-NAPOULE.
The N 7 runs along the valley between the Esterel and Tanneron Massifs.

Auberge des Adrets
This inn was the favourite haunt of the notorious 18C highwayman **Gaspard de Besse**. At the crossroads, Carrefour du Logis-de-Paris, the road skirts the foot of Mont Vinaigre, the highest peak in the Esterel (618m/2 027ft).

> At Carrefour du Testannier, turn left onto a road marked "Forêt Domaniale de l'Esterel". At Le Malpey forester's lodge, follow signs to Mont Vinaigre.

Mont Vinaigre★★
🚶 30min round trip.
A path leads to the top which offers a splendid **panorama**★★★ on all sides: on the coast Cap d'Antibes, Pointe de la Croisette, Cannes and La Napoule Bay, Pic de l'Ours with its tower and TV mast, Pic du Cap Roux and Fréjus Bay, inland the Massif des Maures, the Argens Valley, and the limestone hills of Provence.

> Return to the N 7.

Visiting the Massif

- Roads marked as "RF" on the map are open to traffic under certain conditions: speed limited to 40kph/25m, no vehicles weighing over 3.5t and no traffic between 9pm and 6am. The roads marked in a red dotted line are closed to public traffic, but pedestrian access is possible.
- During periods of high fire risk, the ALARME plan is put into action and some roads may be closed to vehicles. Hikers are advised to avoid such areas.
- Camping is prohibited throughout the massif.
- When walking in the massif, respect plants and wild animals, do not litter the grounds, stay on the paths and keep dogs under control. Mountain bikers must not stray from the signposted paths and tracks laid out in the forests.
- For up-to-date information concerning the massif, call ☎04 98 10 55 41.

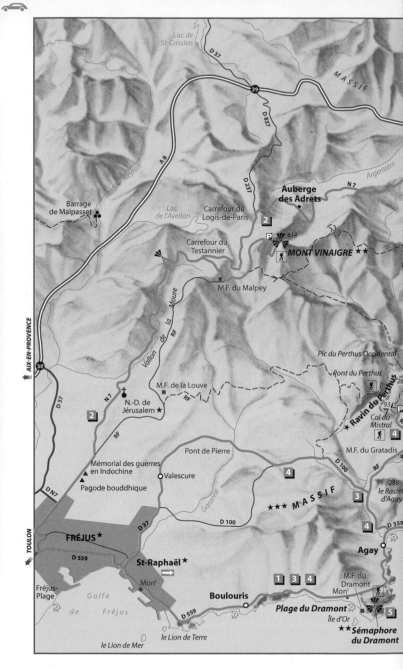

At the bend, there is a **view** on the right towards Fayence; then the road follows the the Moure Valley. The original Via Aurelia followed the line of the forest road on the opposite bank.

Fréjus★ *See FRÉJUS.*

▶ *Return to St-Raphaël by Bd. S.-Decuers.*

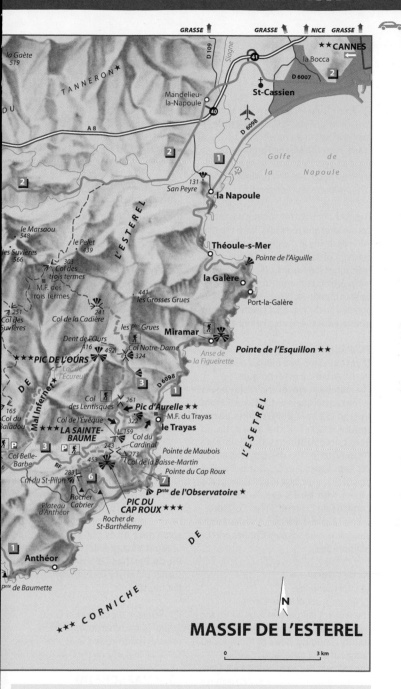

MASSIF DE L'ESTEREL

N

0   3 km

Hiking Map

The ONF (National Office of Forestry) has a trail guide and hiking map available for sale at local tourist offices. *www.onf.fr.*

③ PIC DE L'OURS★★

57km/35.4mi along steep, narrow roads that are not always surfaced – allow one day.

◐ *From St-Raphaël take N 98 southeast. Leaving Agay, take the Valescure road and bear right towards Pic de l'Ours. After the Maison Forestière du Gratadis bear right and, having crossed the River Agay, bear left towards Pic de l'Ours (Moutrefrey crossroads).*

The road climbs to the summit past oaks, barren land and red rocks, with the Mal Infernet ravine in the distance. The road reaches Col de l'Évêque and then Col des Lentisques *(one-way traffic between the two passes: take the road to the east of the peak on the outward journey, and the interior road on the way back),* with frequent **glimpses** of the sea to the right.

Pic d'Aurelle★★

🔺 *1hr round trip by a marked path starting from Col des Lentisques.*
The Aurelle is one of the major peaks in the coastal chain of the Esterel. From the top (323m/1 060ft) a fine **panorama**★★ takes in the area running from Cap d'Antibes to the Pointe de l'Observatoire. The stretch between Col des Lentisques and Col Notre-Dame is one of the most beautiful drives in the Esterel, with **bird's-eye views**★ of the Corniche de l'Esterel. From Col Notre-Dame (323m/1 060ft), a remarkable panorama extends over Cannes and La Napoule Bay.

Pic de l'Ours★★★

🔺 *1.5hr round trip.*
🅿 *Car park at Col Notre-Dame.*
The series of hairpin bends by which the path reaches the summit affords constantly changing views of the wooded ranges of the Esterel and coastline. The remarkable **panorama**★★★ from the summit (496m/1 627ft) where there is a television transmitting station, includes the coast and the Var countryside.
From Col Notre-Dame, continue to the Col de la Cadière on foot, where the

view★ opens to the north towards La Napoule and the Massif du Tanneron. At Col des Trois Termes, take the track on the right (almost hairpin back on yourself) to join N 7.

◐ *Return to St-Raphaël on N 7.*

④ ROUT DU PERTHUS★

20km/12.4mi – 3hr – see local map.

◐ *Leave St-Raphaël by N 98 south, as far as the Gratadis Masion Forestière, then turn left towards the Belle-Barbe Pass. Parking at the pass.*

Ravin du Mal Infernet★

🔺 *2hr round trip.*
Follow the footpath which leads into the wooded ravine of Mal Infernet, a majestic setting overlooked by many jagged rocks. The path goes as far as the Lac de l'Écureuil. It is possible to continue on foot as far as Col Notre-Dame.

◐ *Return to Col de Belle-Barbe. Take the road heading northwest towards the Maison Forestière de Roussivau. Leave the car in the Col du Mistral car park and take the left-hand path.*

Ravin du Perthus ★

🔺 *1.5hr.*
The road skirts the Perthus summits to the south. At Pont du Perthus a marked footpath leads off into the Perthus ravine. It offers a pretty setting for some easy hikes before the foothills of Mont Vinaigre. To the right stands **Pic du Perthus** (266m/887ft), with its scarlet porphyry rocks towering above the forest.

◐ *Return to the car park at Col du Mistral by the same path and head towards Valescure and St-Raphaël by the Col de Belle-Barbe on the D 100 and D 37.*

⑤ SÉMAPHORE DU DRAMONT★★

🔺 *1hr round trip; the path is paved and signposted. Immediately after the Dramont campsite, turn right. 100m/110yd further, leave the car and take the path*

to the signal station.
From below the signal station there is a **panorama**★★: to the southwest of the Maures, the two porphyry rocks guarding the entrance to the Gulf of Fréjus (*Lion de Mer* and *Lion de Terre*), and Île d'Or with its tower. To the north lies Mont Vinaigre. Walk back along the signposted path leading to the little port.

6 PIC DU CAP-ROUX ★★★

🏃 *2hr round trip from the Ste-Baume parking area. You can reach the parking area from St-Raphaël by taking tour 3 by N 98 and the forest road.*
The footpath leads to the Cap-Roux pass. From the summit (452m/1 483ft), there is a superb **sweeping panorama**★★★. If you continue on to the Col de l'Evêque, you can see as far as the Lérins Islands, before continuing on to the Sainte-Baume spring.

7 LA SAINTE-BAUME★★★

🏃 *5.5hr round trip from the Ste-Baume parking area.*
This longer and steeper version of the previous walk leads to the Col du Saint-Pilon. As you progress through meadows of wild rosemary, the view from the high road unfolds. The path follows the coastline on a sloping trail. You meet a railway tunnel, then reach the Col de la Baisse-Martin and Col du Cardinal. Then, it's all downhill, and at the bottom is a heavenly spring.

ADDRESSES

🏨 STAY

😴😴 **France-Soleil** – *206 Av. Pléiades, Agay. ✆04 94 82 01 93. Closed Nov–Easter. 18 rooms.* 🅿️. ⛽*10€.* This modest, family-run hotel has basic rooms spread out over three buildings, most overlooking the sea.

🍽️ EAT

😴😴 **L'Arbousier** – *6 Av. de Valescure, St-Raphaël. ✆04 94 95 25 00. www. arbousier.fr. Closed mid-Dec–mid-Jan, Mon–Tue.* This restaurant in a house in the old town centre serves Mediterranean cuisine in a bright dining room or on the shaded terrace, with its wrought-iron furniture.

Fayence

Var

Fayence enjoys a privileged setting half-way between the mountains and the sea, surrounded by charming villages and only 10km/6mi from the Lac de St-Cassien. Artisans and artists ply their trade in the narrow, picturesque streets, and a lively market is held on place de l'Église Tuesdays, Thursdays and Saturdays.

🐾 WALKING TOUR
OLD TOWN

Below the church, steep streets and a 17C gateway lead to the town gates. The Porte Sarrasine is still crowned by machicolations.
The **18C church** has a Classical interior. The high altar, Baroque in style, is the

▶ **Population:** 4 790.
🚗 **Michelin Map:** 340 P4.
🏠 **Info:** Pl. Léon-Roux. ✆04 94 76 20 08. www.paysdefayence.com.
◐ **Location:** Fayence lies on the edge of the Provençal tableland in the Var, opposite its twin village, Tourrettes (◐*see Driving Tours*), on the road from Draguignan to Grasse.

work of the Provençal marble mason Dominique Fossatti (1757).
From the terrace, to the right of the church, the **view** ★ extends beyond the hang gliding field to the Maures and Esterel heights.

From the top of the hill, where the ancient chateau used to be, is a **view** of the Pre-Alps of Castellane and Grasse.

EXCURSIONS
Bagnols-en-Forêt
14km/8.7mi south by the D 563 and then the D4.
Beyond the Pic de la Gardette, this charming hilltop village appears as you round a bend. Abandoned in the 14C, it was empty until 1447 when a group of Italian immigrants from Liguria settled and manufactured millstones for making oil *(see some originals in the* **Musée Archéologique** *in the tourist office on place de la Mairie,* ✆*04 94 40 64 68).* The town is a departure point for the **forêt domaniale de Saint-Paul**★.

Callian
7.5km/4.6mi east by D 19.
Streets lined with old houses wind round the castle in a delightful setting. **Views** from the main square look southwest over flower fields to the Lac de St-Cassien beneath the Tanneron heights. The famous French designer Christian Dior is buried in the local cemetery

Montauroux
21km/13mi east by D 19.
This pretty village, known for its fountains and old houses from the 16C and 17C, was once home to Christian Dior. He paid for the restoration of the **Chapelle St-Barthélemy,** built in the 17C by the Pénitents Blancs.

Lac de St-Cassien
10km/6mi east by D 19 and D 563.
This scenic lake is nestled at the foot of the Tanneron (♨*see Massif du TAN-NERON).* Fishing, swimming and water sports are allowed on the lake.

Tourrettes
1.3km/0.8mi east by D 563.
This quiet village is lined with pretty houses decorated with flower boxes. The **castle** (⚬⚊ *closed to the public),* modelled on the St Petersburg Cadet School, was built around 1830.

🚗 DRIVING TOURS

Col du Bel-Homme
64km/40mi – about 2hr
▷ *From Fayence take D 563 south.*

Notre-Dame-des-Cyprès
In a setting of tall cypress trees, this Romanesque chapel (12C) looks out over Fayence and Tourrettes.

▷ *Return to D 563 past Fayence airport, turn right on D 562. At Les 4 Chemins turn right on D 25 to Callas.*

Callas
Grouped round the castle ruins against a hillside, Callas is still a typical village of the Haut-Var with its 17C belfry, porches and dovecote. The Romanesque **church** displays a 17C altarpiece above nine hooded penitents

▷ *Continue along D 25 over Col de Boussague.*

Bargemon
An old stronghold at the foot of the Provençal Tableland, Bargemon still recalls its past in its old streets, broken ramparts, ruined castle and 12C fortified gateways.
The 15C **church** near the town gateway was incorporated into the town's fortifications, with a 17C square bell tower and a flamboyant **doorway**. The angel heads on the high alter are by Pierre Puget. Note the 16C triptych portraying St Antoine, St Raphaël and St Honorat.
Chapelle Notre-Dame-de-Montaigu
The village is dominated by the spire of this chapel, a place of pilgrimage since the 17C when a miraculous statue of the Virgin was brought here from Belgium by a monk who was a native of the village.
Musée-Galerie Honoré Camos
🕐*Open Jun–Oct Tue–Sun 10am–12.30pm, 3.30–7pm, Mon 2–5pm; Dec–Apr daily 10am–12.30pm, 2.30–6pm.* ✆*No charge.* ✆*04 94 76 72 88.*

Situated in the Chapelle St-Etienne, this museum highlights the local history, traditional activities, and the work of the painter Honoré Camos (1906–91).

▷ *From Bargemon take D 25 west.*

Col du Bel-Homme★

A path on the left leads to the top *(alt 951m/3 210ft)*. From the viewing table a **panorama★** extends south to the coast, northeast to Grasse, and north to the Castellane mountains.

▷ *Return to Bargemon and take D 19 towards Seillans.*

Seillans★
See SEILLANS.

▷ *Leave Seillans and travel northeast along D 53; on your right you will see a Roman aquaduct.*

Aqueduc de la Roche Taillée

The Romans built this aqueduct to bring drinking water to Fréjus from the Siagnole, still in service today.

▷ *Another 5km/3mi on, you'll come to the village of Mons.*

Mons★

At an altitude of 800m/2625ft.
Pl. St-Sébastien. ℰ04 94 76 39 54.

This old village is perched between earth and sky on a wild and sunny mountain plateau flourishing with every single type of sub-Alpine Provençal plant. Mons was repopulated after several plagues in the Middle Ages by Genoan families who rebuilt the village and cultivated the land with olives and wheat.

Place St-Sébastien

Set off by an 18C fountain, the square has a terrace that looks out over the Siagne and Siagnole Valleys and provides an exceptional **view★★**, which on a clear day, extends from Le Coudon (north of Toulon) via the Lérins islands and to the Italian Alps *(viewing table)*.

Church

*Guided tours 2–6pm by request. Apply to the tourist office.
ℰ04 94 76 39 54.*

The building, which was started in the Upper Provençal Romanesque style, was greatly altered in the 15C and 17C. It is fitted with unusually uniform furnishings: five Baroque altarpieces including a huge triptych dating from 1680 on the high altar. To the right stands a beautiful 15C silver processional cross. The bell in the belfry was cast in 1438.

ADDRESSES

🛏 STAY

⊜⊜🖫 **Moulin de la Camandoule** – *2km/1mi west of Fayence by D 19 Route de Seillans and a country lane. ℰ04 94 76 00 84. www.camandoule.com. Closed autumn school holidayas, Feb holiday. Thu (except eve in high season), Wed. 12 rooms. 🅿 �æ12€. Restaurant⊜⊜🖫.* An old olive mill at the foot of the village has been converted into a quaint Provençal stopping-place decorated in warm, southern colours. The grounds are home to a pool, a Gallo-Roman aqueduct and a terrace.

🍽 EAT

⊜⊜🖫 **Le Temp des Cerises** – *Pl. République. ℰ04 94 76 01 19. Closed Tue, lunch Mon–Sat, 1–27 Dec.* A typical Fayence restaurant serving regional specialities in an ochre and red dining room or the shady terrace.

🛍 SHOPPING

LOCAL MARKETS

Fayence – Pl. de l'Église, Tuesday, Thursday and Saturday.

Bargemon – Pl. St-Étienne, Thursday.

Callas – Saturday mornings.

Mons – Pottery market the first weekend in August.

🚣 SPORT AND LEISURE

Aviron St-Cassien-Club Intercommunal du Pays de Fayence – *In Biançon, by D 37. Montauroux. ℰ04 94 39 88 64. Closed Sat–Sun, Aug.* Introductory rowing courses on the lake.

Fréjus★

Var

Known primarily as a popular beach resort, Fréjus still carries the vestiges of its colourful past as an important Roman settlement and a prosperous medieval town. Today its historic port vestiges, Roman ruins and ancient cathedral contrast with a unique military base, Buddhist pagoda and African mosque, giving Fréjus a rare cosmopolitan air.

A BIT OF HISTORY
Birth and Heyday (1C BC)
Fréjus takes its name from **Forum Julii,** a trading and staging post on the **Via Aurelia** founded by Julius Caesar in 49 BC. Octavian, the future Emperor Augustus, turned the market town into an important naval base (39 BC), and established a colony of his veteran soldiers. The prosperous city expanded until it numbered 40 000 inhabitants.

Fréjus 2 000 Years Ago
See map pp212–213.
Ramparts surrounded the town, pierced by four gateways corresponding to the two broad streets, quartering the town in the tradition of Roman settlements. An aqueduct 40km/25mi long brought fresh water to the town.
Among the naval bases of the Roman world only Fréjus and Ostia, in Italy, offer sufficient remains to be reconstructed: from the eastern end of the Esplanade Paul-Vernet (Roman forum), one can look down on the plain and see the vestiges where the port lay 2 000 years ago. It measured 22ha/54 acres, a considerable area for those times. It was linked with the sea by means of a canal and guarded by two large symmetrical towers, of which one, bearing Augustus' Lantern, still stands.

Decline
During the long years of Roman peace, the military aspect of the port declined and in the late 2C AD the fleet was moved away but the port remained a lively commercial centre until the 4C.

▶ **Population:** 51 537.
Michelin Map: 340 P5; local maps: *see Massif de l'ESTEREL* and *Massif des MAURES.*

The harbour and canal were neglected and began to silt up. At the beginning of the 10C the town was destroyed by the Saracens.
In 990 under Bishop Riculphe, the city rose again on a much smaller scale; the medieval town walls followed the line of Rue Jean-Jaurès and Rue Grisolle. Henri II turned Fréjus into a large naval base, and during the French Revolution the port was sold as a national estate.

⚓ WALKING TOURS
AN EARLY ROMAN SETTLEMENT★

○ *The Roman ruins are scattered over a large area; allow 1.5–2hr.*
P *Park at Pl. Agricola.*

From place Agricola you can see one of the two remaining towers of the **Porte des Gaules**, the old gateway through the Roman ramparts.

○ *Go down the Rue H. Vadon.*

Amphithéâtre (Arènes)★
Rue Henri-Vadon ○*Open Tue–Sun 9.30am–12.30pm, 2–6pm (until 5pm Nov–Apr).* ○*Closed public holidays.* ∞*2€.* ℘*04 94 53 58 75. www.ville-frejus.fr.*
Built outside the city in the 2C, the amphitheatre could accommodate approximately 10 000 spectators.
Destined primarily for the pleasure of soldiers and veterans, it was clearly built with an eye to austerity and economy. In this respect it differs from the larger amphitheatres erected in Arles and Nîmes.
On the esplanade stands *Le Gisant*, a sculpture commemorating the Malpasset disaster, which claimed more than 420 lives (*see Excursions*).

PRACTICAL INFORMATION

Guided tours – The Fréjus tourist office and Ministry of Culture organise **8 itineraries** *(2hr ☞5€)* covering the old city and the Roman ruins, as well as a **special tour** of a different site or monument each month *(1hr ☞3€)*. In partnership with the ONF (National Office of Forestry), the tourist office also organises **forest hikes** in the Esterel.

Fréjus'Pass – *On sale at each site.* ☞*4.60€ (12–18 years 3.10€)*. This pass allows access to the Amphithéâtre, Archaeology Museum, Notre-Dame-de-Jérusalem, Jean Cocteau Chapel and Roman Théâtre with one ticket.
Buses – *Information and tickets on Pl. Paul-Vernet.* ℘*04 94 53 78 46.* The 10 lines of Esterel Bus serve Fréjus, St-Raphaël, Draguignan, and Roquebrune.

▷ *Take Rue Joseph-Aubenas, then Av. du Théâtre Romain. A detour via Rue Gustave-Bret leads to the medieval ramparts.*

Theatre

Av. du Théâtre-Romain.
◷*Same conditions as the Arènes.*
This theatre is far smaller than the amphitheatre; it consists of only the radial walls on which the arches supporting the tiers of seats once rested. It measures 84m/92yd by 60m/66yd. Inside, the orchestra pit is clearly visible, together with the stage foundations and the slot into which the curtain was lowered.

▷ *Return to the top of the street, taking a right and then a left to the Aque duct on Av. Quinzième-Corps-d'Armée.*

Aqueduct

Only pillars and ruined arcades remain of the aqueduct that reached the city level with the ramparts. The water was then channeled beneath the northern parapet as far as the water tower *(castellum)* from which the distribution conduits started. Nearby are traces of a Roman **platform**, which served as the military headquarters *(praetorium)*: offices, storerooms, lodgings and baths. To the south lay the naval dockyard.

▷ *Go down the Av. du Quinzième-Corps-d'Armée to the Pl. Paul-Vernet, and take a right on Rue Raynaude, then a left to Pl. Castelli. Across the square take the vaulted passage of the Rue du*

Portalet to reach the Porte d'Orée, down the Rue des Moulins.

The Old Port

The Porte d'Orée consists of a fine archway, most likely the remains of a chamber formerly attached to the harbour baths. Follow the path skirting the **Butte St-Antoine** to the southern quay, where a tower known as **Augustus' Lantern** was built in the Middle Ages atop Roman ruins as a landmark for sailors entering the port. The wall marking the line of the sea canal stretches away to the southeast.

THE OLD CITY

45min from Place Formigé.
Walk down the Rue du Beausset to see the ancient Episcopal Palace (now housing the Town Hall), with its original 14C façade in pink Esterel sandstone.

▷ *Return to Pl. Formigé, and go north on Rue de Fleury.*

At no 58, the Maison du Prévôt (also called Capitou) has an interesting façade and doorway pierced into a fortified tower, now the entrance to the Groupe Episcopal *(◷see Sights)*. At the end of the street *(no 92, right)* there is a doorway in green serpentine from the Maures.

▷ *Turn left onto Rue Jean-Jaurès, following the medieval rampart ruins.*

The old 18C town hall *(no 112)* features an unusual façade embellished with a curved balcony and a loggia.

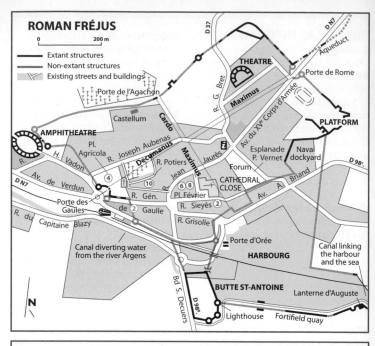

ROMAN FRÉJUS

0   200 m

— Extant structures
— Non-extant structures
▨ Existing streets and buildings

WHERE TO STAY	WHERE TO EAT	
Aréna (L').......... ②	Amandier (L').............. ②	Micocouliers (Les).......... ⑥
	Grand Café de l'Estérel (L').......... ④	Poivrier (Le)..................... ⑧
		Potiers (Les).................... ⑩

◐ *Take a right on the Rue Sleyès.*

At no 53 is a doorway framed by two 17C stone atlantes is all that remains of the former mansion of Abbé Sieyès.

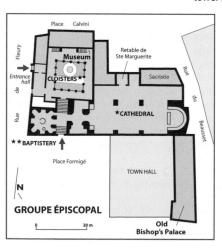

GROUPE ÉPISCOPAL

0   20 m

◐ *Continue past Pl. Liberté to Rue Grisolle.*

This street follows the line of the medieval enclosure, with a handsome round tower *(no 71)* and a medieval façade *(no 84, right)*. The picturesque **Passage du Portalet** connects a string of little squares leading to Place Formigé.

SIGHTS
Groupe Épiscopal★★ *1hr.*
Pl. Formigé. At the bottom of the steps the Basptistery is to the left, the cathedral to the right and the cloisters straight ahead. ◷*Open Jun–Sept daily 9am–6.30pm; Oct–May Tue–Sun 9am–noon, 2–5pm.* ◷*Closed public holidays.* ⊜*5€.* ℘*04 94 51 26 30. www.monum.fr.*

Portal

Guided visits only.

Under an ogee arch are two **panels**★ carved in the 16C to illustrate scenes from the life of the Virgin, St Peter and St Paul, portraits and military motifs.

Baptistery★★

Guided visits only.

This baptistery, one of the oldest buildings in France, is thought to date back to the 5C. Separated from the cathedral by the porch, it has an octagonal-shaped interior featuring alternate curved and rectangular niches separated by black granite columns. These are topped by

capitals of marble taken from Fréjus' ancient forum.

Cathedral★

The cathedral, an early example of Provençal Gothic art, is dedicated to Our Lady and St Stephen. Some parts of the building may date back to an earlier basilica. The porch supporting the 16C belfry was erected some 200 years later. Over the apse rises the battlemented tower which once defended the Episcopal Palace. The lovely **choir stalls** date from the 15C and the high altar of white marble from the 18C. There are also two 14C tombs; at the end of the

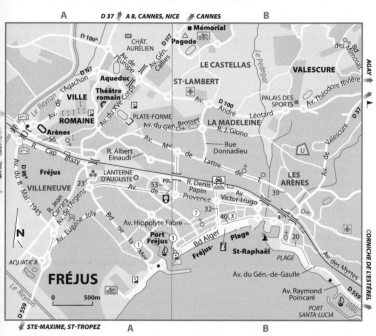

Cloisters, Groupe Épiscopa

aisle, near the tombs of the bishops of Camelin (17C), is a remarkable Renaissance crucifix in wood.

Cloisters★

The 12C–13C cloisters were intended for the chapter canons and comprised two storeys; only one upper gallery remains. The groined vaults which once covered the galleries were replaced by a pine-wood ceiling with exposed beams, decorated in the 15C with curious little **painted panels**★ of animals, chimerae, grotesques and characters from the Apocalypse.

Archaeological Museum

Pl. Calvini (first floor of the Cloisters).
◷*Open Tue–Sun 9.30am–12.30pm, 2–6pm (until 5pm Nov–Apr).* ◉*2€.* ℘*04 94 52 15 78.*

This museum presents a fine collection of Gallo-Roman antiquities recovered from local excavations. Finds include a rare Roman mosaic, a two-headed Hermes in marble (uncovered in 1970), a head of Jupiter (1C BC) and several statues in marble and bronze.

ON THE WATER
Port-Fréjus

In 1989, after ten years' work, Fréjus paid tribute to its long-standing maritime traditions by opening a yachting pleasure port whose style recalls the town's Roman origins. The different areas are

joined by gangways, which in summer are the scene of much colourful and lively activity.

Fréjus-Plage

The magnificent beach of fine sand that extends this new area runs several miles from the Port-Fréjus to the Pont du Pédégal. Further west, the Plage d'Aviation is another fine sand beach. Beside the sea (at Bd. de la Libération) stands a memorial recalling the sacrifice of Senegalese infantrymen (L'Armée Noire).

MILITARY HISTORY

In 1910 Fréjus resumed an active military role with the creation of the first air and sea base in France. At the beginning of the First World War this became a centre for colonial troops from Africa and Asia, who established a rest and recreation base here as a gentle acclimation to the European climate. Their different cultures left a legacy of exotic buildings.

Mosquée de Missiri

▷ *Leave Fréjus by Av.de Verdun, then proceed towards Fayence on D 4. After 3km/2mi turn left (⊶ closed to the public).*

In a pine wood stands a large, ochre Sudanese mosque, a concrete replica of the celebrated Missiri de Djenné mosque in Mali, built in the 1920s by Senegalese soldiers.

▷ *Continue in the same direction. 1km/0.6mi after D 4 joins motorway A 8, past the bridge, on the right.*

Musée des Troupes de Marine

21 Rue de Bagnols. ◯*Open Wed–Fri and Sun–Mon mid-Jun–mid-Sept 10am–noon, 3–7pm; mid-Sept–mid-Nov 2–6pm; mid-Nov–mid-Jun 2–5pm.* ◯*Closed 24 Dec–2 Jan.* ✍*No charge.* ✆*04 94 17 86 55. www.aamtdm.net.*

This museum retraces the history of the Marine Corps since 1622. The expeditions during the great colonial period from the Second Empire (1852–70) to 1914 (Africa, Indochina, Madagascar) are re-created with arms, uniforms, pennants, dioramas, drawings, and photographs. In the crypt are buried unknown marines from the Infantry Division who fell when fighting the Bavarians at Bazeilles (Ardennes) in 1870.

▷ *Take Av. du Quinzième-Corps and then Av. du Général-Callies towards Nice. Turn right after the roundabout. Leave car in the car park between the two monuments and continue on foot.*

Mémorial des Guerres en Indochine

862 Av. du Gén.-d'Armée-Jean-Calliès, via the Av. du Quinzième-Corps-d'Armée, ◯*Open Wed–Mon 10am–5pm.* ◯*Closed 1 Jan, 1 May, 25 Dec.*

✍*No charge.* ✆*04 94 44 42 90. www.memorial-indochine.org.*

At the foot of a hill this imposing circular necropolis symbolically faces the sea. Since 1987, the remains of 24 000 soldiers and civilians who died in active service in former Indochina have been repatriated here. Illuminated maps and models are used to describe the historic events and battles.

Pagode Bouddhique Hông Hiên

Near the Memorial. ◯*Open daily 9am–5pm; Apr–Oct 9am–7pm.* ✍*2€.* ✆*04 94 53 25 29.*

Traditional Vietnamese architecture was the inspiration for this Buddhist Pagoda, built in 1917 by Vietnamese soldiers who had come to fight for France. The grounds surrounding the pagoda are planted with exotic flowers, including lotus, and contain representations of sacred animals and spirits .

EXCURSIONS
Chapelle Notre-Dame de Jérusalem★

Av. Nicolaï, 5km/3mi north of Fréjus by the RN 7. Park, then 5min on foot. ◯*Open Wed–Mon 9.30am–12.30pm, 2–5pm.* ◯*Closed public holidays.* ✆*04 94 53 27 06.*

This tiny chapel, situated in the Tour de Mare district, was the last building to be

Missiri Mosque, Fréjus

E. Barel/ MICHELIN

designed by Jean Cocteau. He had finalised the layout and the interior decor as early as 1961 but the chapel remained unfinished until two years after the poet's death, in 1965. The exterior mosaics were added in 1992.

👪Parc Zoologique★
In Capitou, 5km/3mi north of Fréjus on Av. de Verdun (N 7), then right onto D 4 towards Fayence. ♿🕐*Open daily Mar–Oct 10am–5pm (until 6pm Jun–Aug); Nov–Feb 10.30am–4.30pm.* 👁*14€ (child 3–9 years 9.50€).* 📞*04 94 40 70 65. www.zoo-frejus.com.*
The Zoological Park covers about 20ha/49 acres in the foothills of the Esterel Massif. Visitors may walk or drive beneath the pines, oaks and olive trees to observe a variety of birds (pink flamingoes, vultures and parrots) and wild animals (African elephants, zebras and lemurs). Regular animal shows.

Étangs de Villepey
5km/3mi. From Fréjus take N 98 west towards St-Tropez. Parking on the premises (fee charged at the entrance).
Fed by both sea water and by freshwater streams, these protected wetlands include reed-beds, umbrella pine groves and brackish stretches along N 98. More than 200 species of birds, thrive here. Spring is the best time to see pink flamingoes, herons and egrets.

Remains of Malpasset Dam
From Fréjus follow signs to "Nice par l'autoroute A 8". At the last roundabout before the motorway sliproad, take D 37 signposted "Barrage de Malpasset" for 5km/3mi. Park the car under the motorway viaduct. 🚶*1hr round trip.*
The arch dam, built in 1954 with a capacity of 49 million cu m/1 730 million cu ft, was intended to relieve the scarce water supplies in the Var coastal region during the summer months. On the evening of December 2, 1959 the torrential rains of previous weeks caused the abutments of the arch to collapse. Within 20 minutes, a 55m/180ft high wave surged through Fréjus, claiming 400 victims.
A footpath goes up the Reyran Valley through sparse *garrigue* vegetation and huge scattered blocks of concrete, which were torn off the dam. Follow it down to the foot of the dam, where the size of the breach in the arch makes a striking impression. The turbine still lies in the middle of it.

ADDRESSES

🛏 STAY
🏕 **Camping La Baume la Palmeraie** – *4.5km/2mi north on D 4, Rte. de Bagnols-en-Forêt.* 📞*004 94 19 88 88. www.la baumelapalmeraie.com. Closed Oct–Mar.*
Campsite set in lush surroundings with swimming pool and 👪play equipment. Bungalow rentals possible.

🛏 **Chambre d'hôte les Vergers de Montourey** – *Ferme St Jean, Quartier Montourey.* 📞*04 94 40 85 76. 4 rooms, 2 suites.* 🛏. Beautiful 18C farmhouse with six good-sized rooms, each named after a fruit.

🛏🍽 **Hôtel L'Aréna** – *145 Bd. du Général-de-Gaulle.* 📞*04 94 17 09 40. www.arena-hotel.com. Closed Dec 15–1 Jan. 36 rooms.* 🅿🛏*14€. Restaurant* 🛏🍽.
A former staging post with a colourful front provides pleasant accommodation in carefully kept rooms arranged in the Provençal style. Relax sipping your cocktail on the terrace or reclining by the pool.

🛏🍽 **Hôtel Atoll** – *923 Bd. de la Mer.* 📞*04 94 51 53 77. www.atollhotel.fr. 30 rooms.* 🛏*6.50€.* Just 100m/109yd from the beach, and near a theme park, stands this renovated hotel. Simply decorated rooms.

🛏🍽 **Hôtel L'Oasis** – *impasse Charcot.* 📞*04 94 53 01 04. www.hotel-oasis.net. Closed mid-Nov–Jan. 27 rooms.* 🛏*7€.*
Built in the 1950s, this hotel stands back from the promenade nestling in a quiet street in a wealthy neighbourhood. Family atmosphere. Pergola in the middle of the pine trees.

🛏🍽–🛏🍽 **Chambre d'hôte Mas du Centaure** – *2281 Bd. du Général Leclerc, Puget Sur Argens, 7km/4.3mi northwest of Fréjus.* 📞*04 94 81 58 25.*

www.lemasducentaure.com. 1 room, 2 suites (reduced fees for children). ☐. Set in stunning natural surroundings, rooms are beautifully decorated and well equipped. Separate room for children. Swimming pool and private terrace.

ⵛ⫽ EAT

☐ **Grand Café de l'Estérel** – *14 Pl. Agricola.* ☎*04 94 51 50 50. Closed Sun.* A single menu offered at rock-bottom price, written on a board and renewed every day, will satisfy your appetite at lunchtime in this convivial and popular brasserie.

☐ **Les Micocouliers** – *34 Pl. Paul-Albert Février.* ☎*04 94 52 16 52.* This restaurant set up on the square opposite the Groupe Espiscopal has a most appealing summer terrace (covered and heated in winter). Inside, the brightly coloured tablecloths and rustic-style decoration blend in well with the owner's Provençal cooking.

☐☐ **L'Amandier** – *19 r. Marc-Antoine Desaugiers.* ☎*04 94 53 48 77. Closed 26 Oct–12 Nov, 1-14 Jan, Mon lunch, Wed lunch, Sun.* Restaurant located along a pedestrianised street, close to the town hall. Charming welcome, trendy, tasty and carefully prepared cuisine, and very reasonable prices.

☐☐ **Le Mérou Ardent** – *157 Bd. de la Libération.* ☎*04 94 17 30 58. Closed 4–12 Jun, 19 Nov–18 Dec, Sat–Sun, Thu lunches in season, Wed–Thu off season. Restaurant* ☐☐–☐☐. A small restaurant with a nautical decor, located on the beachfront Boulevard. Good service, fish specialities.

☐☐ **Le Poivrier** – *52 Pl. Paul-Albert Février.* ☎*04 94 52 28 50. Closed Nov, Mon Sept–May, Sun.* The tasty homemade cuisine is a mix of Mediterranean tradition and a pinch of exotica, served in a small, vaulted cellar going back to Roman times. In summer, have your meals out on the terrace on Place Paul-Albert Février or on the patio shaded by reed screening.

☐☐ **Les Potiers** – *135 Rue des Potiers.* ☎*04 94 51 33 74. Closed 1–20 Dec, lunch Jul–Aug, Wed lunch, Tue Sept–Jun. Reservations required.* In a tiny street near the Église St-François and Place

Agricola, this friendly, family-run restaurant serves French classics and seafood dishes with a Mediterranean touch. The deco is rustic and cosy, but with only a few tables reserve early!

☐☐☐ **Autres Ray'Son** – *Quai Marc Antoine.* ☎*04 94 17 11 21. Closed Mon. Reservations required.* Traditional yet creative French cuisine is served at this restaurant situated right on the quay.

🛒 SHOPPING

Fréjus Markets – Wednesdays and Saturdays in the old quarter; Sundays on the Bd. d'Alger and Bd. de la Libération; Tuesday and Friday on the Pl. de la République.

🏃 LEISURE ACTIVITIES

CIP Port Fréjus – *Aire de Carénage, Port Fréjus Est.* ☎*04 94 52 34 99. www.cip-frejus.com.* A deep-sea diving centre for both beginners and experienced swimmers will take you round the celebrated shipwrecks dotted along the Var coastline.

Aqualand – *RN 98, Le Capou.* ☎*04 94 51 82 51. www.aqualand.fr. Closed Sept–May.* ≈*24.50€ (child 3–12, 18€).* Water sports enthusiasts will love this theme park, with its amazing waterslides *Rapid Rafting* and *White Hole*, its swimming pool with waves (the biggest in Europe) Miniature golf course, as well.

Marina – *Capitainerie/Harbour Authority.* ☎*04 94 82 63 00. www.portfrejus.fr.* The 220m/722ft pier can accommodate more than 750 boats.

Base Nature – *Bd. de la Mer.* ☎*04 94 51 91 10. Closed mornings off season.* This nature park welcomes hikers, cyclists (80ha/198 acres) as well as swimmer and sun-bathers over a 2km/1mi stretch of beach. Additional activities include sand-yachting, flying kites, playing boules and roller-skating.

CALENDAR

Bravade Saint-François – Third Sunday after Easter, a traditional religious procession through the historic centre of town.

Fête du Raisin – Celebration of the first wine grapes, harvested the first week in August. Wine tasting from the local producers on Pl. Formigé.

St-Raphaël★

Var

A fashionable summer and winter resort situated on Fréjus Bay, St-Raphaël has a well-sheltered beach at the foot of the Esterel. The railway brought prosperity to this town under the Second Empire, and a century later it has transformed into one of the great modern cities of the Riviera.

▶ **Population:** 33 084.
🚗 **Michelin Map:** 340 P5; local map: *see Massif de l'ESTEREL*.
🅸 **Info:** Rue Waldeck-Rousseau. ℘04 94 19 52 52. www.saint-raphael.com.
◗ **Location:** St-Raphaël stretches along the coast of the Esterel for 35km/21mi.

A BIT OF HISTORY

Origins – St-Raphaël, like Fréjus, is a daughter of Rome. A Gallo-Roman holiday resort stood on the site now occupied by the large Casino, built in terraces with mosaics, thermal baths and a *vivarium* (fish reserve), where rich Romans came here to enjoy the sea air.

In the Middle Ages the villas were plundered by Saracen pirates. After their expulsion (end of the 10C), the Count of Provence left these deserted lands to the monks of Lérins and St-Victor, who built a village around the church.

Bonaparte in St-Raphaël – On 9 October 1799 the small village was suddenly brought into the limelight when Bonaparte, returning from Egypt, landed there after a voyage of 48 days (a pyramid standing in Avenue Commandant-Guilbaud commemorates this event). In 1814 St-Raphaël received Napoleon once again, this time as a defeated man leaving for exile in Elba.

The Resort is Developed – **Alphonse Karr** (1808–90) was an extravagant personality who used his talents as journalist and pamphleteer to oppose Napoleon III from Nice, where he was in exile. He settled in St-Raphaël in 1864 in a villa named "Maison Close." Writing to a Parisian friend, he said: "Leave Paris and plant your stick in my garden: the next morning, when you awake, you will see that it has grown roses." Writers and artists responded to his invitation: Alexandre Dumas, Maupassant, Berlioz and Gounod, among others.

Félix Martin, local mayor and civil engineer, followed Karr's lead and transformed the village into a smart resort, encouraging building, and linking St-Raphaël with Hyères by means of a small railway along the coast. Illustrious guests marked their stay in St-Raphaël with works of art: Gounod composed *Roméo et Juliette* in 1869, Scott Fitzgerald wrote *Tender is the Night*, and Félix Ziem painted here.

THE TOWN CENTRE

The original town centre consists of an important and quite rare collection of seaside architecture dating from the beginning of the Third Republic (in the late 19C).

Seafront

The bustling waterfront by the old harbour is lined with cafés and shops along the Cours Jean-Bart and Quai Albert-Ier. From beneath the palms and plane trees of Promenade René-Coty and Avenue du Général-de-Gaulle is a fine **view** of the sea and the twin rocks known as the Land Lion and the Sea Lion.

Tours

Guided Tours – Discover St-Raphaël's heritage, every Thursday 10am. ⊸*2.30€*. For information contact the tourist office, ℘*04 94 19 52 52*.

Nature Walks – The tourist office can also organize nature walks along the coastal footpaths or in the Esterel hills, in partnership with the ONF.

Villas

Among the exotically decorated historic villa façades is the Villa Roquerousse (1900) on the Promenade René-Coty with its lavish ornamentation. Along Boulevard Félix-Martin is the charming oriental Villa Sémiramis, Villa Paquerettes decorated with ceramics, and a little farther on the shadow of Gounod still haunts *l'Oustelet dou Capelan* ("The Priest's House") in Provençal).

Both Plateau Notre-Dame and St-Sébastien hill are full of remarkable villas.

Notre-Dame-de-la-Victoire-de-Lépante

This **church**, in neo-Byzantine style, was built in 1883 by Pierre Aublé, the architect of many of St-Raphaël's villas.

QUARTIER DE VALESCURE

This district was once much patronised by foreign visitors. The director of the Paris Opera in 1880, Carvalho, laid out, with advice from Charles Garnier, a park decorated with vestiges from the Palais des Tuileries in Paris, including a fountain at the crossroads of Rue Allongue and Rue Maréchal-Leclerc.

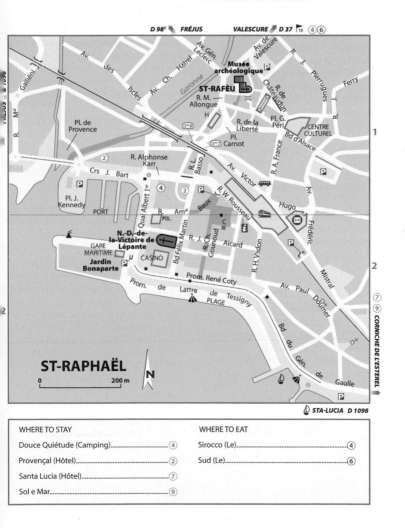

WHERE TO STAY		WHERE TO EAT	
Douce Quiétude (Camping)	④	Sirocco (Le)	④
Provençal (Hôtel)	②	Sud (Le)	⑥
Santa Lucia (Hôtel)	⑦		
Sol e Mar	⑨		

Musée Archéologique

🕐*Open Dec–Oct Tue–Sat 9am–12pm, 2–6pm.* ✆*No charge.* 📞*04 94 19 25 75. www.ville-saintraphael.fr.*

This archaeology museum is situated at the ancient crossroads of Roman land and sea routes, and is thus endowed with a rich heritage of archaeological remains. It houses a remarkable collection of **amphorae**★ dating from the 5C BC to the 5C AD. A gallery displays the evolution of scuba diving equipment and finds from local Prehistoric sites from the Palaeolithic Era to the Bronze Age. The church, built in the 12C in the Romanesque-Provençal style, served as a fortress and a refuge for the population during pirate attacks. In one of the side chapels, a red sandstone pagan monolith supports the altar table. The gilded wooden bust of St Peter is carried by the fishermen in procession to the Sea Lion in August.

ADDRESSES

🏠 STAY

🍽 **Camping Douce Quiétude** – *3435 Bd J.-Baudino – 3km/2mi via northeast exit towards Valescure.* 📞*04 94 44 30 00. www.douce-quietude.com. Closed Nov– late Mar. Reservations advisable. 400 pitches.* atering. The shade of the pine trees will keep you cool during your siesta, before you go to the beach located a few minutes from this campsite reserved for caravans. Children and parents can enjoy many physical activities together. Mini-club for young children. Rental of bungalows and mobile homes.

🍽🍽 **Hôtel Provençal** – *197 Rue Garonne.* 📞*04 98 11 80 00. www.hotel-provencal.com. Apartments with 3 beds.* 🛏*9€.* Slightly away from the busy port, an entirely renovated building containing modern, functional rooms with good soundproofing.

🍽🍽 **Hôtel Santa Lucia** – *418 Route de la Corniche.* 📞*04 94 95 23 00. www.hotelsantalucia.fr. Closed 20 Dec–mid-Feb. 12 rooms.* 🛏. 🅿. Beautiful, recently renovated hotel. Each room recreates the atmosphere of a different country (England, Morocco, Italy, Japan…). Choose one at the back, overlooking the sea.

🍽🍽–🍽🍽 **Hôtel Sol e Mar** – *Rte de la Corniche d'Or, 83530 Agay, 6km/3.7mi east along D 559.* 📞*04 94 95 25 60. www.monalisahotels.com.* 🅿. *45 rooms. Restaurant* 🍽🍽. Authentic seaside hotel: most rooms look out towards the Îles d'Or ; swimming pool open to the sky, beach-solarium and seawater pool with overflow dug out of the rocks on the shore. Panoramic restaurant with opening roof and fine terrace.

🍴 EAT

🍽🍽 **Le Sud** – *16 Bd. Darby.* 📞*04 94 44 67 86. Closed 1–10 Jun, Tue–Wed except Jul–Aug, Sat–Mon lunches.* Located in an open-air shopping centre, this sunny restaurant is decorated with paintings and old photographs. Terrace surrounded by a garden. Appetising, trendy provençal menu.

🍽🍽 **Le Sirocco** – *35 quai Albert-1er.* 📞*04 94 95 39 99. www.lesirocco.fr. Closed 15 Dec–15 Jan. Reservations recommended.* The hot dry Sahara wind may guide you towards this restaurant. Located for the past 20 years opposite the old harbour, it has been consistently serving a tasty cuisine with a seaside flavour. Carefully laid tables, small summer terrace in front. Seaside atmosphere.

Seillans

Var

Seillans is a surrealist village, where Dadaist illustrator **Max Ernst** (1891–1976) chose to live towards the end of his life, and the ivory and pink houses cascade down the steep slope of the Canjuers Plateau at an even steeper angle than the average perched village. Quaint cobbled lanes lead up to the church and the old castle.

▶ **Population:** 2 489.
  Michelin Map: 340 O4.
  Info: Rue du Valat. ☎04 94 76 85 91. www.seillans.fr.
  Location: Seillans is in the foothills of the Canjuers plain (*see FAYENCE Driving Tours: Le col du Bel-Homme*).
  Parking: Park at the top of the village, before the chateau.

SIGHTS
Church
The rebuilding of the church in 1477 incorporated a few sections dating from the 11C. From the church there is a fine view over Fayence.

Chapelle Notre-Dame de l'Ormeau
1km/0.6mi southeast on the Fayence road. *Guided tours with commentary year round (mid-Sept–mid-Jun by reservation at Seillans tourist office).*
This Romanesque chapel, dedicated to Our Lady of the Elm Tree, is flanked by a bell tower of dressed stone, but marred by the subsequent addition of a porch. The interior contains a remarkable 16C **altarpiece**★★. In the centre, a crowd of people climb the tree of Jesse. The predella, beneath a wooden peristyle, illustrates (left to right) the life of Ste Anne, the birth and marriage of the Virgin, and the Annunciation. To the left of the altarpiece is a fine low-relief

E. Baret/ MICHELIN

Shepherds' Adoration in the Chapelle N.-D. de l'Ormeau

scuplture of the Assumption (17C); to the right, in a recess, an early statue of Our Lady of the Elm Tree.
To the left of the entrance there is a Roman tombstone with an inscription, and the walls are adorned with numerous votive offerings dating from around 1800.

The Dada Master

Max Ernst settled in Seillans with his wife, the painter Dorothea Tanning, in 1964. A small **museum** *(Collection Max Ernst – Dorothea Tanning: open Jul–Aug Mon–Sat 2.30–6pm; Jun and Sept Tue–Sat 3–5.30pm; closed public holidays; 2€; ☎04 94 50 45 54)* displays over 70 of his lithographs and engravings, remarkable for their sense of humour.

ADDRESSES

STAY
  Les Deux Rocs – *Pl. Font-d'Amont.* ☎*04 94 76 87 32. www.hoteldeuxrocs. com. Closed Jan–Feb. 14 rooms.* ⚏*12€. Restaurant* ⓈⓈ. Imposing inn housed in an old village building. The original staircase leads to the rooms, appointed with colourful wall hangings and antique furniture. Enjoy your meal by the fireplace or in the welcome shade of plane trees on the summer terrace near the village fountain.

CANNES & THE GRASSE REGION

As the true heart of the French Riviera, Cannes and the Grasse region have been enchanting visitors from around the world for centuries. It's an area that encompasses the legendary perfume-making town of Grasse and its surrounding perched villages, as well as three of the most dynamic resort towns and beaches in France. Travellers can enjoy the quiet Provençal atmosphere of the Lerins Islands and inland villages like Biot and Gordon, or take advantage of the lively nightlife and window shopping in Cannes, Juan-les-Pins, or Antibes. This is where prestigious art museums and chic galleries easily coexist with ancient fortified ramparts and centuries-old ruins. The proximity to Nice International Airport, easy access to major coastal and inland routes, and service by the regional train lines also makes this an ideal base for exploring the rest of the French Riviera.

Highlights

1 Visit the newly restored Musée Picasso in **Antibes** (p229)

2 See panoramic views from the **Baou de St-Jeannet** (p239)

3 Rent a *chaise-longue* on one of the private beaches in **Cangnes-sur-Mer** (p240)

4 Watch the sunset from the fortified ramparts in **St Paul de Vence** (p270)

5 Dine in the monk's seaside restaurant on **Île St-Honorat** (p262)

Lively Year Round

While many people think of the French Riviera first and foremost as a summer vacation destination, Cannes and Grasse Region are bustling throughout the year.

A large population of "locals" from around the world work in the various technology parks, in the greenhouses that produce the region's flowers and fruits, on the superyachts that require constant upkeep, and in the conferences and fairs that attract international visitors. Cannes, Antibes, Villeneuve-Loubet and Grasse are the liveliest, with most hotels and restaurants remaining open year round.

Illustrious Cultural History

Almost every town in this part of the French Riviera has attracted a loyal following of artists, writers and musicians. Antibes was home to the writer Nikos Kazantzakis, the cartoonist Peynet, and Picasso during one of his more prolific periods. Renoir lived in Cagnes-sur-Mer until his death, Fernand Leger left his mark forever on the tiny village of Biot, and Modigliani and Soutine made

Boulevard de la Croisette, Cannes

© Davide_60/Fotolia.com

x

Musée Picasso, Antibes

St-Paul-de-Vence a trendy place for artists. Many of these towns have dedicated museums to their artists. Juan-les-Pins, however, dedicated an event – the Jazz Festival – to commemorate great jazz artists who once lived there such as Cole Porter and Sydney Bechet. Today the start of the big screen continue to visit for the Cannes Film Festival, making their temporary homes at the palace hotels on the Croisette and the Cap d'Antibes.

Military Reminders

The forts in Antibes and the Île Ste-Marguerite are no longer active military sites, but the greatest French general of them all, Napoleon Bonaparte, left his mark on the region forever with the Route Napoleon, which traces his triumphant (albeit brief) return to power from Juan-les-Pins to Grenoble. Museums throughout the region attest to the military importance of this coastline throughout the centuries, from Greek and Roman times through the Middle Ages and up through the 17C when Antibes was still protecting the eastern frontier from the Sicilians. The only invasion today comes in the form of summer sun-seekers to the beaches.

Nautical Fans

Visitors with a nautical interest will find their heart's delight in the ports of Cannes, and Antibes, where sleek private super yachts as big as cruise ships line up at the quays alongside more humble fishing boats and stunning sailing yachts. Sailors won't want to miss the ancient chapel next to La Garoupe lighthouse in the Cap d'Antibes to pay their respects to their patron saint, and water sport enthusiasts can pay homage to the man who invented water-skiing in Juan-les-Pins.

Several sailing events take place here throughout the year and, of course, the local museums provide a detailed history of every aspect of shipping, sailing and boating on the Mediterranean back to the Roman times.

Natural Wonders

This part of the Riviera has no shortage of natural beauty and sights of interest to nature lovers. Explore the stalactites of the Baume Obscure or peek at the stars in the observatory in Saint-Vallier-de-Thiey.

See the sharks and the performing dolphins at Marineland and discover rare plants in the botanical gardens of Antibes. Ski down the slopes at Gréolières-les-Neiges or cool off in the waterfalls at the Gorges du Loup. Hiking trails offering stunning cliff views around Gourdon or peaceful contemplation of the sea on the Îles des Lérins.

Tourist offices in the region can provide special maps for those interested in the local flora and fauna.

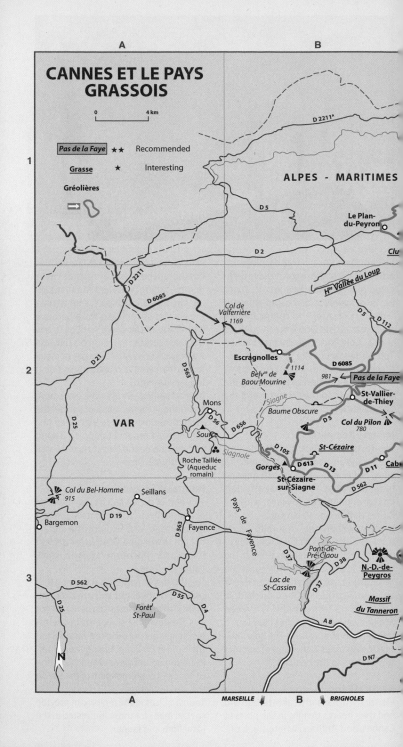

CANNES ET LE PAYS GRASSOIS

0   4 km

Pas de la Faye ★★ Recommended

Grasse ★ Interesting

Gréolières

ALPES - MARITIMES

D 2211ᴬ

Le Plan-
du-Peyron

D 5

D 2

Clu

D 2211

D 6085

Hte Vallée du Loup

Col de
Valferrière
1169

D 5

D 112

Escragnolles

1114

Belvᵉ de
Baou Mourine

981   Pas de la Faye

D 6085

St-Vallier-
de-Thiey

Siagne

Mons

Baume Obscure

D 5

Col du Pilon
780

D 56

D 656

Source

St-Cézaire

D 105

Siagnole

D 13

Cab

Roche Taillée
(Aqueduc
romain)

Gorges

D 613

St-Cézaire-
sur-Siagne

D 11

D 562

VAR

D 21

D 563

Col du Bel-Homme
915

Seillans

D 25

D 19

Bargemon

D 563

Fayence

pays de Fayence

Pont-de-
Pré-Claou

N.-D.-de-
Peygros

D 37

D 38

Lac de
St-Cassien

D 37

Massif
du Tanneron

D 562

D 25

Forêt
St-Paul

D 55

D 4

A 8

D N7

N

A   B

MARSEILLE ⬇   B   ⬇ BRIGNOLES

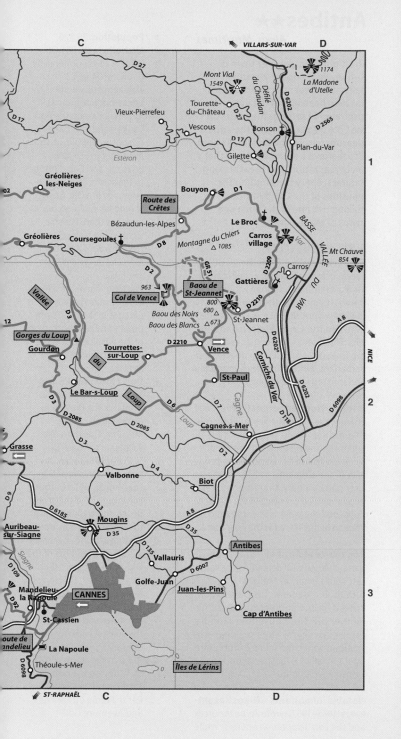

VILLARS-SUR-VAR

D 27

Mont Vial
1549

Défilé
du Chaudan

La Madone
d'Utelle

1174

D 6202

Vieux-Pierrefeu

Tourette-
du-Château

D 27

Vescous

Bonson

D 2565

D 17

Esteron

Gilette

D 17

Plan-du-Var

1

Gréolières-
les-Neiges

02

Bouyon

D 1

Route des
Crêtes

Le Broc

BASSE

Bézaudun-les-Alpes

Carros
village

Gréolières

Coursegoules

D 8

Montagne du Chiers
△ 1085

VALLÉE

Mt Chauve
854

Carros

D 2

GR 51

963

Col de Vence

Baou de
St-Jeannet

D 2209

Gattières

DU

Vallée

D 3

800
680 △

St-Jeannet

D 2210

VAR

Baou des Noirs
Baou des Blancs △ 673

A 8

NICE

12

Gorges du Loup

du

Gourdon

Tourrettes-
sur-Loup

D 2210

Vence

D 6202

Corniche du Var

D 6202

Le Bar-s-Loup

Loup

St-Paul

D 3

D 6

D 7

Cagne

D 118

D 6098

2

D 3

D 2085

D 2085

Loup

Cagnes-s-Mer

D 2

Grasse

D 3

D 4

Valbonne

Biot

D 9

D 6185

D 3

A 8

Auribeau-
sur-Siagne

Mougins

D 35

D 35

Antibes

Siagne

D 135

Vallauris

D 6007

D 109

Golfe-Juan

Juan-les-Pins

D 92

Mandelieu-
la Napoule

CANNES

Cap d'Antibes

St-Cassien

oute de
ndelieu

La Napoule

D 6098

Théoule-s-Mer

0

Îles de Lérins

3

ST-RAPHAËL

C

D

225

Antibes★★
Alpes-Maritimes

The highly popular port town of Antibes, hugging the coastline halfway between Nice and Cannes, has long been one of the most inspirational settings for artists on the Côte d'Azur. Home to the largest pleasure port on the Riviera, Antibes also features a scenic old town that's lively year round, and breathtaking natural scenery surrounding the mansions of the Cap d'Antibes, making this one of the must-see towns of the region.

A BIT OF HISTORY

Greek Antipolis – From the 4C BC the Greeks of Massalia set up a chain of trading posts with the Ligurian tribes along the coast. Antipolis, the new Greek city that grew opposite Nice, was contained between the Cours Masséna and the sea. The Greeks were succeeded by the Romans, and then by pirates and Barbarians, whose invasions gradually undermined the city's prosperity.

Antibes, frontier outpost – The kings of France realised the key military role that Antibes could play from the 14C when the town stood on the Franco-Savoyard frontier. It became the property of the Grimaldis in 1386 and was later purchased by King Henri IV. Each reign improved or enlarged the fortifications until the work was completed by Vauban in the 17C with the Fort Carré.

Bonaparte at Antibes – In 1794 Bonaparte, charged with defending the coast, settled his family in Antibes. Although a general, his pay seldom arrived on the appointed day, so his mother did the household laundry herself in a nearby stream. Bonaparte was imprisoned for a time in Fort Carré after the fall of Robespierre during the French Revolution.

Notable inhabitants – **Nikos Kazantzakis** (1885–1957) wrote *Zorba the Greek* and the *Last Temptation of Christ* while

▶ **Population:** 75 820.
⚙ **Michelin Map:** 341 D6
ℹ **Info:** 11 Pl. du Général-de-Gaulle. ℘04 97 23 11 11. www.antibesjuanlespins.com.
▷ **Location:** Antibes has four major areas: the Port Vauban and Fort Carré to the north, the Old Town *(vieil Antibes)*, La Salis beaches, and Cap d'Antibes to the south. The narrow streets of the Old Town should be explored on foot, but there is also a sightseeing train (⚙ *see Le Petit Train d'Antibes; Mar–Oct daily; ℘06 03 35 61 35).*
🅿 **Parking:** There are a few underground parking garages in the Old Town, but it's easier to park in one of the vast lots along the Port Vauban *(fee in high season).*
👁 **Don't Miss:** The Picasso Museum in the Château Grimaldi, the Provençal market at the Cours Masséna, the immense yachts on the Quai de la Grande Plaisance, the panoramic views of the coastline from La Garoupe lighthouse, and the scenic beach and walking trail at the Plage de la Garoupe.
🕐 **Timing:** Antibes deserves a full day. The sights of the Old Town and port should be visited first, then any museums or the Fort Carré. Then drive around the Cap d'Antibes and hike along the coastal path *(sentier)* or the sandy beaches.
👪 **Kids:** At the northeast end of Antibes is the popular Marineland waterpark, La Petite Ferme du Far West and Aventure Golf.

Port Vauban and the Fort Carré

J. Malburet/MICHELIN

living in Antibes. **Nicolas de Staël** (1914–55) painted his last canvases in Antibes, before taking his own life. A young, glamorous American couple, **Sara** and **Gerald Murphy**, fell in love with Antibes in the mid-1920s, and their villa became a favoured holiday haunt for their many American friends, including the **Fitzgeralds** and **Hemingways**.

🐾 WALKING TOUR
OLD ANTIBES★
Allow 2hr (see town map).
◗ *Begin at Avenue de Verdun.*

Port Vauban
Avenue de Verdun commands a good view of the marina and the 16C **Fort Carré** *(see Sights)*, with the heights of Nice in the background. The **Port Vauban**, one of the largest in the Mediterranean, is used by luxury cruise yachts, the largest that can be found along the Quai de la Grande Plaisance (also known as *Quai des Millionaires*).

◗ *Enter the old town by the sea gate and follow Rampe des Saleurs on the left to the Promenade Amiral-de-Grasse.*

Promenade Amiral-de-Grasse
This former seafront promenade runs along the vestiges of 17C ramparts below the old cathedral and **Grimaldi Château** (Musée Picasso, *see Sights*). It gives a fine **view**★ of the coastline stretching towards Nice and the Alps.

PRACTICAL INFORMATION
MUSEUM PASS A 7-day pass is available at any of the participating museums: Peynet, Picasso, de la Tour, Archéologique, Napoléonien, and Fort Carré. 10€.
TOURS The tourist office provides a fold-out map with four walking itineraries called "Balades au Coeur d'Azur". They can also help arrange mini-bus excursions.
TOURS AND PUBLIC TRANSPORT
Buses: *EnviBus – Gare Routière, Pl. Guynemer.* ℘04 89 87 72 00. *www.*

envibus.fr. 1€ *(3hr),* 8€ *(10 tickets).*
The most convenient lines are 1 and 3 (going to Juan-les-Pins), 2 (around the Cap d'Antibes), 10 (to Biot and Valbonne), and 5 (to Vallauris). Most buses run between 7am and 9pm.

Train: The **TER line 4** connects Antibes and Juan-les-Pins.

Boat Trips: Small **power boats** can be rented by the hour from Port Vauban's Quai des Pêcheurs, just outside the Porte Marine *(see JUAN-LES-PINS for glass-bottomed boat tours of the CAP d'ANTIBES).*

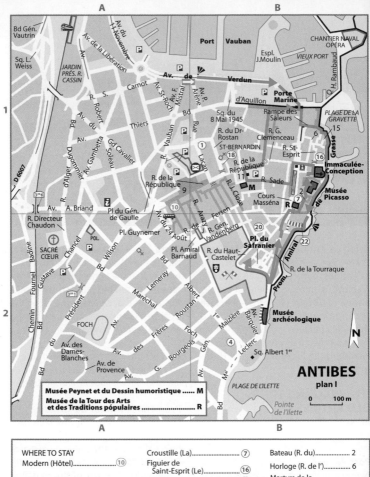

ANTIBES
plan I

0   100 m

Musée Peynet et du Dessin humoristique ...... M
Musée de la Tour des Arts
  et des Traditions pópulaires .... R

WHERE TO STAY				Croustille (La)	⑦		Bateau (R. du)	2
Modern (Hôtel)	⑩			Figuier de Saint-Esprit (Le)	⑯		Horloge (R. de l')	6
				Oscar's	⑱		Martyrs de la Résistance (Pl. des)	9
WHERE TO EAT				Sucrier (Le)	⑳			
Appart Thé	①			Vieux Murs (Les)	㉒		Nationale (Pl.)	11
Bistrot 44 (Le)	④						Revely (R. du)	15

◐ *Turn left on Rue du Haut Castelet and follow it to Pl. du Safranier.*

Place du Safranier

This square is the heart of the free commune known as "Le Safranier", set up in the wake of the Second World War. The writer Nikos Kazantzakis lived at 8 Rue du Bas-Castellet. The plaque on the façade encapsulates his philosophy: "I fear nothing. I expect nothing. I am a free man".

◐ *Double back and take a left onto Rue de la Touraque.*

Old streets

To the left and right are picturesque side streets, bright with flowers in season.

◐ *You'll arrive at the Cours Masséna market place; turn right on Rue de l'Orme, then on Rue du Bateau.*

Église de l'Immaculée-Conception

Of the original Romanesque church, which served as a cathedral in the Middle Ages, only the east end remains. The belfry is a converted 12C watchtower. The art treasures feature a wooden Crucifix (1447) in the choir, a former pagan

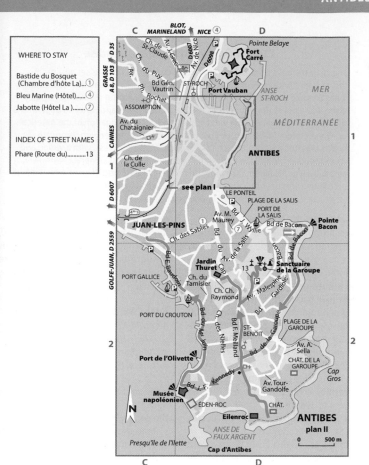

Map labels: GRASSE A8, D 103 D 35 · BLOT, MARINELAND · NICE ④ · Ch. de St-Claude · Av. de Nice · Pointe Belaye · Fort Carré · Ch. du Puy · Bd Gén. Vautrin · ST-ROCH · Port Vauban · ANSE ST-ROCH · MER · Rochat · CANNES · ASSOMPTION · Av. du Chataignier · MÉDITERRANÉE · 1 · Ch. de la Culle · ANTIBES · D 6007 · see plan I · LE PONTEIL · PLAGE DE LA SALIS · Av. M. Maurey · Bd J. Wyllie · PORT DE LA SALIS · Bd de Bacon · Pointe Bacon · JUAN-LES-PINS ① · Ch. des Sables · GOLFE-JUAN, D 2559 · Jardin Thuret · Bazou · Sanctuaire de la Garoupe · 13 · PORT GALLICE · Ch. du Tamisier · Ch. Ch. Raymond · PORT DU CROUTON · Maltespine Gardiole · PLAGE DE LA GAROUPE · Bd du Val Julin · Ch. des Nielles · Bd F. Meilland · ST-BENOÎT · Bd de la Garoupe · Av. A. Sella · CHÂT. DE LA GAROUPE · Cap Gros · 2 · Port de l'Olivette · Bd J. F. Kennedy · Av. Tour-Gandolfe · CHÂT. · Musée napoléonien · ÉDEN-ROC · Eilenroc · CHÂT. · ANTIBES plan II · ANSE DE FAUX ARGENT · Presqu'île de l'Ilette · Cap d'Antibes · 0 500 m · N · C · D

stone altar in the south apsidal chapel, a 16C **Recumbent Christ** carved in lime wood, and a 1515 **altarpiece** by Louis Bréa in the south transept.

▶ *Take Rue de l'Horloge (right), Rue du Revely (left) and Rue Aubernon (right) for a picturesque route to the port.*

SIGHTS
Château Grimaldi (Musée Picasso)★★

Pl. Mariejol. ♿ ⏰*Open Tue–Sun Oct–May10am–noon, 2–6pm; Jun–Sept 10am–6pm; Jul–Aug open late Wed and Fri until 8pm.* ⏰*Closed 1 Jan, 1 May, 1 Nov, 25 Dec.* ⊜6€ *(3€ students).* ☏*04 92 90 54 20. www.antibes-juan-lespins.com.*

The original 12C castle overlooking the sea was built on the foundations of a Roman camp situated on the Antipolis acropolis. It was reconstructed in the 16C but the square Roman tower, battlement walk and pairs of windows remain from the original structure. The castle was home to the Grimaldi family until the 17C.

In the **chapel** of Château Grimaldi is the **Deposition from the Cross**★ (1539) by Antoine Aundi, with the earliest known view of Antibes.

Donation Picasso★

Soon after his arrival on the Riviera in the autumn of 1946, **Pablo Picasso** (1881–1973), who had part of the castle at his disposal, started work on some large-scale paintings. His output was

EDEN-ROC, an Edwardian Paradise

This majestic palace surrounded by an estate (8ha/20 acres) is set on a promontory of Cap d'Antibes. Famous for its quaint huts *(cabanes)* and its private beach, it has become an essential port of call for film stars visiting the Riviera. A party given by Russian princes in spring 1870 launched the Grand Hôtel du Cap. After a slack period the Grand Hôtel was resuscitated at the instigation of the American Gordon Bennett. In 1914 an annexe, the Eden Roc, together with its private beach, was built. Since then it has known unflagging success, with a varied and cosmopolitain clientele featuring such eminent figures as General Eisenhower, who used it as his winter quarters, the painters Picasso and Chagall, who worked here, and a number of rich eccentrics like the oil magnate Gulbenkian *(Mister 5%)*.

remarkable; the majority of the paintings, lithographs and drawings in the collection are from one season's work. Due to post-war canvas shortages, he painted on fibro-cement and plywood. His **paintings** are joyful works bursting with imagination, inspired by the marine and mythological life of the Mediterranean: *Ulysses and the Sirens, Fish, La Joie de Vivre, Watermelon, The Oak Tree* and an imposing triptych – *Satyr, Faun* and *Centaur with Trident*. The showcases hold an impressive collection of Picasso's **ceramics**, created at Vallauris between 1948 and 1949.

On the second floor, works by Nicolas de Staël, who spent his last winter in Antibes, are on display in Picasso's old studio. Note in particular *Still Life with Chandelier, Fort Carré* and the gigantic canvas entitled *Grand Concert*.

The **stairwell** presents modern artworks by Arp, Magnelli, Ernst. In the **courtyard** there is a composition by the sculptor Arman depicting guitars, inspired by Picasso's *À ma Jolie*. In the **terrace** garden are statues by Germaine Richier and works by Miró, Pagès, Amado Spoerri and Poirier. The Musée Picasso also has a Roman **archaeological collection**.

Musée Peynet et de la Caricature★

Pl. Nationale. &Open Tue–Sun Oct–May 10am–noon, 2–6pm; Jul–Aug open late Wed and Fri until 8pm. Closed public holidays. ∞3€ (under 18s free). ☎04 92 90 54 30.

Located in an old 19C school are lithographs, ink drawings, watercolours, sculptures, and greeting cards by Ray-

mond Peynet (1908–1999). The cartoonist, who moved to Antibes in 1950, is known for his two young lovers, Les Amoureux, whose adventures were published in *Paris Match, Marie-Claire*, and *Elle*.

Fort Carré

Av. du 11-Novembre. Open Tue–Sun Oct–May 10am–4.30pm; Jun–Sept 10am–6pm). Guided tours (30min) Jun–Sept. Closed 1 Jan, 1 May, 1 Nov, 25 Dec. ∞3€. ☎06 14 89 17 45. www.antibes-juanlespins.com.

Built atop an isolated outcrop in 1550, the central St-Laurent tower was consolidated by four surrounding citadels 15 years later. Thanks to the fortification work carried out by Vauban, this stronghold braved many an assault during its existence, yielding only to the Duke of Epernay and Napoleon's enemies.

Musée Archéologique

1 Av. Maizière (Bastion Saint-André). &Open Tue–Sun 10am–noon, 2–6pm (until 8pm Wed and Fri in Jul–Aug). Closed 1 Jan, 1 May, 1 Nov, 25 Dec. ∞3€. ☎04 92 90 54 35. www.antibes-juanlespins.com.

The 17C Bastion St-André contains an **archaeological collection** illustrating 4 000 years of history, including the reconstruction of a Roman ship used for transporting amphorae and an ornamented lead sarcophagus. The back of a large vaulted room, built on a reservoir, houses a bread oven and objects salvaged from shipwrecks from the Middle Ages to the 18C.

Musée de la Tour

2 Rue de l'Orme ◐*Open Wed and Fri–Sun 2–6pm.* ◒*Closed 1 Jan, 1 May, 1 Nov, 25 Dec.* ◉*3€.* ✆*04 93 34 13 58. www.antibes-juanlespins.com.*

Housed in the Tour de l'Orme, this museum has exhibitions of everyday objects, costumes and crafts from 18C and 19C. A pair of water skis from **Léo Roman**, who invented the sport in 1921 in Juan-les-Pins, are also on display.

EXCURSIONS

♣♠ Marineland★

4km/2.5mi north towards Nice.
&◐*Open Jul–Aug daily 10am–midnight; spring 10am–7pm; autumn and winter (except Jan) 10am–5pm.* ◉*32€ (23€ children 3–12), combined entrance for AquaSplash.* ⓟ ✆*04 93 33 49 49. www.marineland.fr.*

This marine zoo has many large pools with **killer whales**, dolphins, elephant seals, seals and sea lions. There are regular acrobatic shows. and a spectacular **"Sharks"** exhibit takes visitors down a 30m/98ft tunnel with a view of a dozen grey sharks and tiger sharks. Marineland also houses a small museum of models, marine instruments and other items, including a reconstitution of the 1944 **allied landings** in Provence.

♣♠ Parc Aqua-Splash

Entrance via Marineland. ◐*Open mid-Jun–early Sept daily 10am–7pm.* ◉*32€ (23€ children 3–12), combined entrance for Marineland.* ✆*04 93 33 49 49. www.marineland.fr.*

This water leisure park features a swimming pool with waves, water slides, giant pool, and kiddie pool.

♣♠ La Petite Ferme du Far West

Entrance via the Marineland car park.
&◐*Open Feb–Dec daily 10am–dusk.* ◉*10€ (8€ children 3–12).* ✆*04 93 33 49 49. www.marineland.fr.*

This Wild West town re-creates the spirit of the frontier with a fort, Mississippi riverboats, friendly horses and cattle.

♣♠ Adventure Golf

Entrance via the Marineland car park.
&◐*Open Feb–Dec daily 10am–dusk.* ◉*9€ (7€ children 3–12).* ✆*04 93 33 49 49. www.marineland.fr.*

Miniature golf featuring three different 18-hole courses with a Jules Verne theme.

🚗 DRIVING TOURS

Cap d'Antibes★

10km/6mi – allow 2hr.

The garden-like peninsula, known as the Cap d'Antibes, is dotted with sumptuous hotels and villas catering to both summer and winter visitors.

▷ *Begin at the Pointe Bacon, just past La Salis beach on Bd. de Bacon.*

Pointe Bacon

This point gives a **view**★ of Antibes and Fort Carré, sweeping across the Baie des Anges opposite Nice and the surrounding countryside to Cap Ferrat.

▷ *Continue on Bd. de La Garoupe; right onto Bd. Francis Meilland; signs for Phare de La Garoupe.*

Sanctuaire de la Garoupe

635 Rte du Phare. &◐*Open 10am–noon, 2.30–7pm (winter 10am–noon, 2.30–5pm).* ✆*04 93 67 36 01.*

Two 17C wrought-iron gates form the entrance to this small church and its two chapels. Inside is an interesting **collection of votive offerings**; the oldest dates back to 1779. Over the high altar is the **Sebastopol icon**, a magnificent Russo-Byzantine work, believed to date from the 14C. There are 60 naval votive offerings, maritime souvenirs and a gilded wood statue of **Notre-Dame de Bon-Port** (Our Lady of Safe Homecoming), patron saint of sailors. Every year in July the statue of Our Lady, taken to the old cathedral in Antibes on the previous week, is brought back in procession to La Garoupe by the seamen. Beside the sanctuary stands the curious Oratoire de Ste-Hélène, first patron of Antibes, who has been worshipped here since the 5C AD in the original pagan shrine.

Phare de la Garoupe

The **lighthouse**, one of the most powerful on the Mediterranean coast, with a beam that carries 52km/32mi out to sea and 100km/33 000ft up to aircraft.

▷ *Double back and turn right on Bd. Meilland; follow Bd. du Cap to the INRA - VIlla Thuret.*

Jardin Thuret★

90 Chemin Raymond. ⏰*Open Mon–Fri Apr–Oct 8am–6pm; Nov–Mar 8am–5.30pm.* ⏰*Closed public holidays.* 👓*No charge.* ✆*04 93 67 88 66. http://jardin-thuret.antibes.inra.fr.*

These **botanical gardens**, covering 4ha/10 acres, were created by the scientist Gustave Thuret in 1857. He sought to acclimatise plants and trees from hot countries: the first eucalyptuses from Australia were planted here. Bequeathed to the state, these gardens are currently administered by the National Institute of Agronomic Research. They contain a magnificent collection of 3 000 rare plant and tree species. Villa Thuret, the gardens' botanical centre, contains offices and research labs.

▷ *Return to Bd. Meilland and continue along Av. L.H. Beaumont.*

Villa Eilenroc

♿ *Av. L.-H.-Beaumont. Villa:* ⏰*open Sept–Jun Wed 9am–noon, 1.30–5pm; Gardens and eco-museum: open*

Tue–Wed and Sat 9am–5pm. ⏰*Closed public holidays.* 👓*No charge.* ✆*04 93 67 74 33.*

This beautiful seaside estate built in 1867 was designed by Charles Garnier, architect of the Paris Opera. It was left to the city of Antibes, which uses it for receptions and the annual "Musiques au Cœur d'Antibes" lyrical arts festival (early July). The interior retains its 1930s decor. The villa grounds include a rose garden and olive tree conservatory.

🚶 *1hr.* Follow the street around the back of the gardens to join the "Sentier Littoral" walking path that leads back to La Garoupe beach.

▷ *Return to the Avenue Beaumont and turn left onto Bd. J F. Kennedy.*

Musée Napoléonien

Bd J.-F.-Kennedy, Juan-les-Pins. ⏰*Open Tue–Sat mid-Sept–mid-Jun 10am–6pm; mid-Sept–mid-Jun 10am–4.30pm).* ⏰*Closed public holidays.* 👓*3€.* ✆*04 93 61 45 32.*

The former Le Grillon battery has been converted into a museum devoted to Napoleon's reign. At the entrance are two magnificent replicas of Louis XIV-era bronze canons. Also on display are **Napoleon's bust** sculpted by Canova in 1810, model soldiers and officers of the Great Army, Napoleon's autograph and imperial proclamations.

From the roof, there is a fine **view**★ over the wooded headland to the Îles de Lérins and to the distant Alps.

ADDRESSES

🛏 STAY

🍽🍽 **Modern Hôtel** – *1 Rue Fourmilière.* ✆*04 92 90 59 05. www.modernhotel06. com. 17 rooms.* ⊋*6€.* At the entrance of a pedestrian zone, this small hotel has simple, minimalist decor.

🍽🍽 **Hôtel Bleu Marine** – *Chemin des 4-Chemins (north Antibes, near hospital).* ✆*04 93 74 84 84. www.bleumarine antibes.com. 18 rooms.* 🅿. ⊋*7€.*

A contemporary hotel near Marineland and the pebble beaches, with easy access to the A8 and N7. Rooms on the top floors have sea views, some have air conditioning.

🍽🍽 **Hotel La Jabotte** – *13 Avenue Max-Maurey, Cap d'Antibes.* ✆*04 93 61 45 89. www.jabotte.com. 10 rooms.* 🅿. ⊋. *Restaurant*🍽🍽🍽. On a street perpendicular to La Salis beach, this charming little hotel features individually decorated rooms overlooking a sunny patio. The owner's decorative calligraphy work is on display throughout the hotel.

⊜⊜🛏 **Chambre d'Hôte La Bastide du Bosquet** – *14 Chemin des Sables, (Domaine des Mûriers), Cap-Antibes. ☎04 93 67 32 29. www.lebosquet06.com. Closed mid-Nov-Dec 20. 4 rooms.* 🍽. Attractive 18C country house at the heart of a residential area that will guarantee you a peaceful stay. Cool, pleasing rooms of different sizes with colourful Provençal furnishings. Leafy garden and terrace.

⍟ EAT

⊜ **Appart Thé** – *24 Rue Lacan. ☎04 93 34 08 24. Closed Sun.* This small and stylish tea room just off the pedestrian square serves salads, quiches and ice cream in addition to 15 types of tea. A small terrace in front during warmer weather.

⊜ **La Croustille** – *4 Cours Masséna. ☎04 93 34 84 83.* Settle on the charming terrace of this creperie-salad bar in old Antibes and soak up the lively, colourful atmosphere of the local market. The cosy interior is decorated with family photographs and models of sailing boats. Reasonable prices.

⊜⊜ **La Bonne Table – Bistro 44**– *44 Bd Albert-1er. ☎04 93 34 43 08. Closed Nov, eves in winter.* A family restaurant near the Archaeological Museum, just off the seafront, serving traditional French dishes to loyal clientele.

⊜⊜ **Le Figuier de St-Esprit** – *14 Rue St-Esprit. ☎04 93 34 50 12. Closed Tue, Wed lunch, 23 Nov–21 Dec.* A modern, stylish restaurant on the ramparts recently taken over by chef Christian Morriset. Contemporary French cuisine and a terrace shaded by a fig tree.

⊜⊜ **Oscar's** – *8 r. Rostan. ☎04 93 34 90 14. www.oscars-antibes.com. Closed Sun–Mon. Reservations required.* Italian-inspired Provençal cuisine is served in an elegant dining room decorated with marble cherub statues and exposed stone walls.

⊜⊜ **Le Sucrier** – *6 Rue des Bains. ☎04 93 34 85 40. Closed Tue.* Tucked down a tiny side street, this cosy restaurant features contemporary French cooking based on the fresh market produce of the season. Exposed stone walls and wooden beams give the dining room an authentic Provençal feel.

⊜⊜⊜ **Les Vieux Murs** – *25 promenade Amiral-de-Grasse. ☎04 93 34 06 73. www.lesvieuxmurs.com.* Red stone walls, Murano chendeliers and silk fabrics give the dining room of this seafront restaurant a refined atmosphere. The cuisine is Mediterranean, with emphasis on fish and fresh market produce.

🛒 SHOPPING

Marché Provençal – *Cours Masséna – Closed afternoons, Mon in low season).* This colourful, covered market features regional produce and speciality items such as honey, lavender, cheeses, jams, spices, olive oil and dried meats.

Rue Sade – This picturesque street stretching from the Cours Masséna to Place Nationale is full of charming boutiques and gourmet food shops.

🏃 SPORT AND LEISURE

Beaches – The long pebble beach of Antibes extends way beyond Fort Carré. Four other public beaches are covered in fine sand: La Gravette (south of the old port), the Îlette, La Salis and La Garoupe.

Water Sports – Antibes is a *station nautique*, with a wide variety of water sports on offer from water-skiing and scuba diving to sailing and windsurfing. *Contact the tourist office for more information or visit www.france-nautisme.com.*

AMC Croisères – *1228 Bd de la Garoup, Cap-d'Antibes. ☎04 92 93 16 39. www.am-catamaran.com. ⌚From 40€.* Catamaran cruises leave from Antibes, St-Raphael or St-Tropez, with diving and sea-kayaking equipment on board.

Biot★

Biot (the final 't' is voiced) is a picturesque hillside village famous for its pottery, blown glass and the artist Fernand Léger.

SIGHTS
Old Village

To appreciate the authentic charm of the picturesque streets, start from the tourist office *(syndicat d'initiative)* and following the arrows, through the town gates, Porte des Migraniers (Grenadiers) and Porte des Tines (both 16C), emerging into the beautiful **Place des Arcades** with its rounded and pointed arches.

Church

Set back from Place des Arcades with a mosaic stone pavement, the church is actually below street level, with stairs leading down from the entrance. Rebuilt in the 15C it was decorated with murals which the bishop of Grasse considered crude and had painted over.
On the west wall is the **altarpiece**★ of the Virgin of the Rosary in red and gold attributed to Louis Bréa. At the far end of the church is another altarpiece, attributed to Canavesio, who married a local girl: an **Ecce Homo** with two cherubs and the instruments of the Passion.

2 500 Years of History

There is evidence of settlement by the Celto-Ligurians, Greeks and Romans from finds made in the area and in the La Brague plain. In 1209 the Templars took over from the local lords and unified the village. In 1312 the deeds passed to the Hospitallers of St John of Jerusalem and order reigned.
In the 14C Biot suffered from the Black Death and warring factions; the decline was reversed following an edict in 1470 by Good King René, allowing 40 families from the Ligurian coast to settle in the village.

▶ **Population:** 8 791.
◈ **Michelin Map:** 341 D6.
▣ **Info:** 46 Rue St-Sébastien. ℘04 93 65 78 00. www.biot.fr.
◑ **Location:** Biot lies 4km/2.5mi inland, about 7.5km/4.6mi from Antibes on the N 7 then the D 4.
🅿 **Parking:** Only residents can drive into the village, but there are several free parking areas around the town with regular shuttles to the village centre.

Musée National Fernand-Léger★★

Southeast of the village, just off D 4 (signposted). ♿🕐*Open Wed–Mon Jun–Oct 10am–6pm; Nov–May 10am–5pm.* 🕐*Closed 1 Jan, 1 May, and 25 Dec.* ⊙*7.50€; no charge 1st Sun of each month, or for those under 26.* 🅿℘*04 92 91 50 30. www.musee-fernandleger.fr.*

Built in 1960 by local architect **Andreï Svetchine**, this museum of 348 works by Léger (1881–1955) and the gardens were donated to the State by Nadia Léger and Georges Bauquier.
The façade is decorated by a vast **mosaic** (500sq m/5 382sq ft) celebrating sports, designed for the Hanover Stadium.
The ground floor gallery presents original ceramics produced between 1950 and 1955 in the Brice workshop in Biot and **paintings** reflecting the artist's evolution from 1905 to his death.
Portrait of the Uncle (1903) and *My Mother's Garden* are Impressionist in style, while Cézanne's influence is evident in *Study of a Woman in Blue* (1912–13) and *14 July*. After 1945 the artist painted large canvases praising the virtues of hard work and industrial civilization – *Builders*, 1950, marks a significant achievement in style and inspiration – relaxation and *joie de vivre (Campers)*. *The Great Parade* (1954) pays homage to the fabulous world of the circus.

A Story of Success

The architect Andreï Svetchine was the son of a Russian general; he was born in Nice, where he grew up and attended the Academy of Decorative Arts. He soon demonstrated remarkable skills as an architect and was to design some of the most prestigious private residences and museums on the Riviera, notably the Fernand Léger Museum in Biot (🔎 *see Sights*). In the early 1960s, the painter Marc Chagall asked him to build a house and adjoining studio. The result, "La Colline", was a splendid construction in white Provençal stone arranged in rectangular shapes. He also undertook to refurbish La Colombe d'Or, the famous hotel in St-Paul-de-Vence that caters to an exclusive international clientele. In 1984, towards the end of his life, he supervised the challenging task of restoring St-Nicolas, the superb Russian Orthodox Cathedral in Nice.

Musée d'Histoire Locale et des Céramiques Biotoises

9 Rue Saint-Sébastien. 🕐*Open Wed–Sun summer 10am–6pm; winter 2–6pm.* 🎫*2€; no charge 1st Sun of each month.* 📞*04 93 65 54 54.*

This museum of local history and ceramics is situated in the restored **Chapelle des Pénitents-Blancs**, topped by a three-sided pinnacle. It was under the Phocaeans that the production of ceramic jars originated in Biot, and in the Middle Ages the large jars were used for olive oil. In addition to ancient ceramics is a reconstructed local kitchen.

👪 Bonsai Arboretum

Chemin du Val de Pôme, 100m/110yd south of Musée Fernand Léger. 🕐*Open Wed–Mon 10am–noon, 2–6pm.* 🎫*4€ (2€ children).* 📞*04 93 65 63 99.*

This sloping garden (53 000sq m/ 32 300sq ft), displays a large collection of bonsai trees against the backdrop of a reconstructed Japanese garden.

For those interested in Modern Art

- **Antibes:** Musée Picasso
- **Biot:** Musée Fernand-Léger
- **Cagnes-sur-Mer:** Musée Renoir and Musée d'Art Moderne Méditerranéen
- **Menton:** Musée du Palais Carnolès, the Salle des Mariages in the town hall and the Musée Jean-Cocteau
- **Nice:** Musée Marc-Chagall, Musée des Beaux-Arts, Musée Matisse and the Musée d'Art Moderne et Contemporain
- **St-Paul:** Fondation Maeght
- **St-Tropez:** Musée de l'Annonciade
- **Vallauris:** Musée National "La Guerre et la Paix" and the donation Magnelli
- **Vence:** Chapelle du Rosaire (Chapelle Matisse)
- **Villefranche:** Chapelle St-Pierre (Chapelle Jean-Cocteau)

Where to see the works of the Great Masters

- **Chagall:** Musée National du Message Biblique in Nice
- **Cocteau:** Chapelle St-Pierre in Villefranche-sur-Mer, Musée Jean-Cocteau and the Salle des Mariages in the Menton town hall, Chapelle Notre-Dame-de-Jérusalem in Fréjus
- **Dufy:** Musée des Beaux-Arts in Nice
- **Léger:** Musée National Fernand-Léger in Biot
- **Matisse:** Musée Matisse in Nice and the Chapelle du Rosaire in Vence
- **Picasso:** Musée Picasso in Antibes and Musée National "La Guerre et la Paix" in Vallauris
- **Renoir:** Musée Renoir in Cagnes-sur-Mer

ADDRESSES

¶/ EAT
◻◻ **Le Café de la Poste** – *24 Rue St-Sébastien.* ✆*04 93 65 19 32. Closed 11 Nov–11 Dec.* One of the oldest cafés on the Riviera, the decor of this bistro-type restaurant features a pretty wooden counter, a huge fresco on painted ceramics and a collection of humorous paintings. Traditional cuisine.

⌂ SHOPPING
Verrerie de Biot – *Chemin des Combes, at the foot of the village, along D 4.* ✆*04 93 65 03 00. www.verreriebiot.com.* ♿.

This small factory founded in Biot in 1956 features several workshops that demonstrate the successive stages of the art of glass blowing, characterised by a bubbly texture peculiar to the Biot production. The different shops sell all kinds of glassware: vases, glasses, etc.

TOURS
Several themed self-guide maps to the village are available at the tourist office. For exploring the area, purchase a copy of their Vallée de la Brague hiking map with 11 trails along the Brague River (♨*see VALBONNE*).

Cagnes-sur-Mer★

Alpes Maritimes

The hills surrounding Cagnes-sur-Mer are cultivated with roses, mimosas, roses, citrus and and olive trees. The picturesque upper town has become home to many painters, attracted by the beautiful setting.

A BIT OF HISTORY
The Grimaldis of Cagnes – Originally a fortress built in 1309 by Monaco's Lord Rainier Grimaldi, the Cagnes castle was converted in 1620 by Henri Grimaldi into a finely decorated palace. Loyal to the king of France, he persuaded his cousin, Honoré II of Monaco (♨*see MONACO*), to place himself under French protection (Treaty of Péronne, 1641). When the Revolution broke out, the reigning Grimaldi was driven out by the inhabitants and sought refuge in Nice.

THE VILLAGE
Haut-de-Cagnes★
▷ *Take the free shuttle from the central bus station or walk up to Haut-de-Cagnes along Montée de la Bourgade.*

This quaint old town circled by ramparts and dominated by its medieval castle has steep paved streets and vaulted

▸ **Population:** 48 313.
♿ **Michelin Map:** 341 D6.
▯ **Info:** 6 Bd. Maréchal-Juin. ✆04 93 20 61 64. www.cagnes-tourisme.com.
◗ **Location:** Cagnes is on the coast between Nice and Antibes. It comprises Haut-de-Cagnes, crowned by a medieval castle; Cagnes-Ville, the modern quarter; and Cros-de-Cagnes, a fishing village and beach.
▣ **Parking:** The largest car park *(fee)* is at Place St-Luce (♨*see map*) in Cagnes-Ville near the bus station. There are also some spaces in Haut-de-Cagnes at the Parking *Boule de Château.*
◉ **Don't Miss:** The ancient streets of Haut-de-Cagnes, the views from the Château Museum, and jet-skiing at the beach.

passageways featuring 15C and 17C houses. The **Porte de Nice** near the church tower dates back to the 13C.

Église St-Pierre
The entrance to the church, unpredictably, is through the gallery. Inside, the early Gothic nave contains the Grimaldi

tombs, while a larger nave added in the 18C houses a statue of the Virgin and Child and an altarpiece of the 18C Spanish School portraying St Peter receiving the keys to Paradise.

SIGHTS
Château-Musée★
Pl. Grimaldi. ◷*Open 10am– noon, 2–5pm (May–Sept until 6pm).* ◷*Closed public holidays.* ⌑*4€.* ℘*04 92 02 47 30.*
A double staircase and a Louis XIII doorway give access to this imposing castle crowned with machicolations.
The Renaissance **patio**★★ has an agreeable elegance in contrast to the feudal castle's austere façades. Eight low-vaulted medieval rooms open onto the patio galleries, featuring exhibits of medieval history, 2C Roman sculpture discovered in Cagnes, and a **museum**. The former boudoir of the Marquise of Grimaldi on the first floor houses 40 paintings donated by the famous singer **Suzy Solidor**. The ceiling of the banqueting hall represents the 17C **Fall of Phaeton**★, a *trompe-l'œil* painted by the Genoese, Carlone.
The **Musée d'Art Moderne Méditerranéen** on the second floor pays tribute to contemporary Mediterranean art, with a rich collection of works by 20C painters such as Dufy and Vasarely.

From the top of the tower there is a fine **view**★ over the roofs of Old Cagnes from the Ailps to the sea.

Musée Renoir
Chemin de Collettes. ◷*Open Wed–Mon Oct–Apr 10am–noon, 2–5pm; May–Sept 10am–noon, 2–6pm.* ⌑*4€.* ☐*Free.* ℘*04 92 20 61 07. www.cagnes-tourisme.com.*
Pierre-Auguste Renoir (1841–1919) spent the last 12 years of his life in this artist's house and studio, which has been preserved just as it was. Ten of his **canvases** are exhibited on the ground floor; they belong to his last, especially sensual period *(Bathers,* 1901–02). It is also at Cagnes that he attempted sculpture: in front of the house stands his large bronze **Venus Victrix**★.

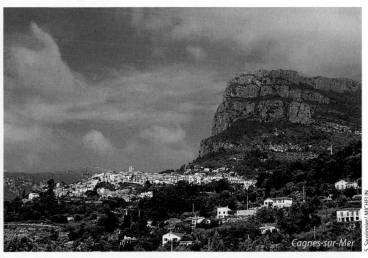

Cagnes-sur-Mer

S. Sauvignier/ MICHELIN

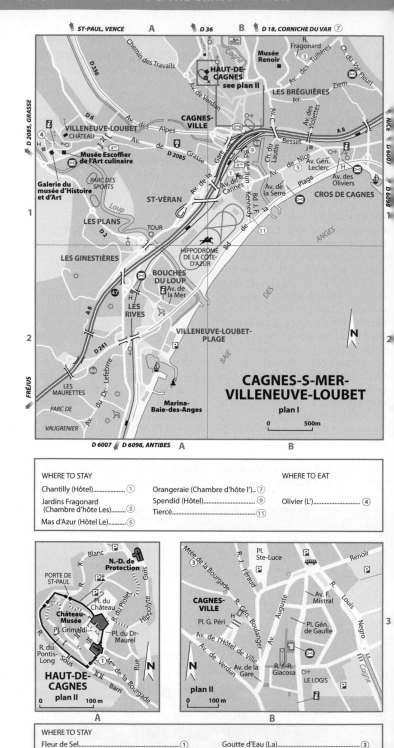

CAGNES-S-MER-
VILLENEUVE-LOUBET

plan I

0   500m

D 6007 — D 6098, ANTIBES — A — B

WHERE TO STAY

Chantilly (Hôtel)................... ①

Jardins Fragonard
  (Chambre d'hôte Les)......... ③

Mas d'Azur (Hôtel Le)........... ⑤

Orangeraie (Chambre d'hôte l')..⑦

Spendid (Hôtel)................... ⑨

Tiercé................................ ⑪

WHERE TO EAT

Olivier (L')........................ ④

HAUT-DE-
CAGNES
plan II

0   100 m

CAGNES-
VILLE

plan II

0   100 m

WHERE TO STAY

Fleur de Sel..①   Goutte d'Eau (La)..③

Renoir at Les Collettes

Pierre-Auguste Renoir was born in Limoges, but went to Paris as a young man, where his talents soon developed under the Impressionists. From 1882 he made several visits to Provence with Cézanne and, in 1900, with his wife and son Jean, who later became a film director. In 1907, his reputation universally established, Renoir settled permanently at Les Collettes in Cagnes-sur-Mer. His last years were saddened by the death of his wife, his sons being wounded in the First World War, and the inexorable progress of his illness, which confined him to a wheelchair and paralysed his right hand. In August 1919, after having received many honours and exhibitions in the major museums of the world, his work was officially accepted by the Louvre, in Paris. On 2 December 1919, just before his death, he was still at work, painting a bouquet of anemones.

Chapelle Notre-Dame-de-Protection

🔼 *Access up Montée du Château.*
🕐 *Open Tue afternoon as part of the "Medieval Village" tour, departure from Pl. du Château.* ⟳*No charge (tour 3€).* 📞*04 93 20 61 64. www.cagnes-tourisme.com.*

The Italianate porch and bell tower of this chapel inspired Renoir. The apse is decorated with 16C frescoes attributed to Andrea de Cella. A 17C altarpiece of the Virgin of the Rosary is in the north chapel.

🚗 DRIVING TOURS

The Baous and the Corniche du Var★
Round trip of 32km/20mi – about 1hr15min (excluding the ascent of the Baou of St-Jeannet).

▷ *From Cagnes take Avenue Auguste-Renoir and D 18 north to La Gaude.*

La Gaude
From the ridge above the River Cagne, La Gaude, which owes its prosperity to vineyards and flower cultivation, now houses research centres in the fields of data processing and horticulture. The 14C castle in the St-Jeannet district is attributed to the Templars.

▷ *At Peyron take the D 18 north through orchards and vineyards.*

St-Jeannet
The charming village occupies a remarkable **position**★ on a terrace at the foot of the Baou of St-Jeannet. Behind the church on the left a "Panorama" sign points to a terrace offering a **view**★ of the peaks *(baous)* and the coastline.

Baou de St-Jeannet★★
The signposted path starts from Pl. Ste-Barbe by Auberge St-Jeannet.
🔼 *2hr round trip.*

Also known as the Baou des Blancs, this sheer cliff 400m/1 312ft high dominates the village. From the top *(orientation table)* a huge **panorama** ★★ extends from the Esterel to the Alps.

▷ *Return to D 18 towards La Gaude. Turn left onto D 118.*

Centre d'Études et de Recherches IBM
The huge buildings on the left of this Research Centre, consisting of two opposing Y-shapes raised on concrete pillars are a good example of architecture harmonising with its natural surroundings.

Corniche du Var★
This scenic road clings to the hillside on the west bank of the Var, with a clear view of the river valley and Nice hinterland. The steep slopes of the valley are covered with flowers and olive groves.

St-Laurent-du-Var
Until the County of Nice passed to France in 1860, the Var formed the frontier with

the Kingdom of Sardinia. Locals usually forded the river, often on another man's back. The first permanent bridge was built downstream in 1864. Near the mouth of the River Var, a vast lake, pro-tected by a dyke, has been developed into a yachting harbour (over 1 000 moorings).

▷ *Return to Cagnes by N 7.*

ADDRESSES

🛏 STAY

🍽 **Hôtel Chantilly** – *31 Rue Minoterie.* 𝒸*04 93 20 25 50. 20 rooms.* 🅿. ⊑*8€.* This hotel housed in a villa behind the racecourse offers modest comfort at reasonable prices. Clean rooms in a verdant setting and a relaxed, family atmosphere.

🍽 **Hôtel Le Mas d'Azur** – *42 Avenue de Nice.* 𝒸*04 93 20 19 19.* 🅿 *15 rooms.* ⊑*7€.* Just off a main road, in an 18C building, this hotel has small, tidy rooms. Lush, flowery setting and breakfast terrace.

🍽🍽 **Chambre d'hôte L'Orangeraie de la Baronne** – *66 chemin du Maoupas, La Gaude.* 𝒸*04 92 12 13 69. www.orange raie.fr.* 🅿 *4 rooms.* ⊑. *Restaurant*🍽🍽. Located in the heart of a fruit and citrus orchard, this bed & breakfast has four spacious, simply decorated rooms with air conditioning. There is also an organic restaurant serving dinner nightly, a swimming pool and bike rental.

🍽🍽 **Les Jardins Fragonard** – *12 Rue Fragonard.* 𝒸*04 93 20 97 12. www.babazur.com. 3 rooms.* ⊠. *Restaurant*🍽🍽. A peaceful park planted with Mediterranean species forms the heavenly backdrop to this 1925 bed and breakfast. The large rooms are decorated in the Provençal spirit with rattan furniture, modern bathrooms.

🍽🍽 **Hôtel Splendid** – *41 Bd. du Maréchal Juin.* 𝒸*04 93 22 02 00. www. hotel-splendid-riviera.com.* 🅿. *26 rooms.* ⊑*9€.* A quiet, modern hotel in the centre of town. Although somewhat dated, rooms are comfortable and most rooms face the inner courtyard.

🍽🍽 **Hôtel Tiercé** – *33 Bd. Kennedy.* 𝒸*04 93 20 13 89. 23 rooms.* 🅿 ⊑*10€. Closed 25 Oct–29 Nov.* The bright and tidy rooms in this modern hotel face the sea or the hippodrome next door. Air-con, WiFi.

🍽 EAT

🍽 **L'Auberge du Palmier** – *34 Av. de Nice (N 7).* 𝒸*04 92 02 86 05. Closed Aug, Sun eve, Mon.* Once the haunt of General de Gaulle, this charmingly decorated inn is known for its couscous dishes and Oriental tea room.

🍽🍽 **La Goutte d'Eau** – *108 Montée de la Bourgade, Le Haut-de-Cagnes.* 𝒸*04 93 20 81 23.* After climbing the steep, cobbled alleys, you reach this small restaurant serving simple fare. The sun-blessed terrace welcomes you in fine weather.

🍽 **L'Olivier** – *4 Pl. Verdun, Villeneuve-Loubet.* 𝒸*04 93 20 85 11.* Pleasant restaurant serving traditional cuisine.

🍽🍽🍽 **Fleur de Sel** – *85 montée de la Bourgade.* 𝒸*04 93 20 33 33. www. restaurant-fleurdesel.com. Closed Thu eve, Wed.* A rustic little restaurant next to the church with Provençal decor and an open kitchen, where you can watch the chef whip up seasonal specialities.

🏃 SPORT AND LEISURE

Water Sports – Cagnes-sur-Mer has 3.5km/2.2mi of pebble beaches, including several private beaches, where you can dine or rent *chez longue*s. It's possible to water-ski, wakeboard, jet-ski and parasail in season at Tampa Beach *(between the Madrague and Neptune restaurants;* 𝒸*04 93 20 17 46).*

Hippodrome de la Côte d'Azur – 𝒸*04 92 02 44 44. www.hippodrome-cotedazur.com.* ⊚*4.50€.* This famous racecourse is the backdrop to many equestrian events between December and March, as well as in July and August.

🎭 EVENT

Fête Médiévale Haut-de-Cagnes – A medieval festival takes place in the village the 1st weekend in August.

Cannes★★

Alpes Maritimes

Star of the Côte d'Azur, Cannes became known as early as 1834 for its mild climate, making it the preferred winter salon of the world's aristocracy. Framed to the west by the red rocks of the Esterel and across the bay by the forested Îles de Lérins, this beautiful setting forms the backdrop to the palm-lined beaches of La Croisette and the world-famous Cannes Film Festival.

A BIT OF HISTORY

Cannes, the coastal watchtower – After Ligurian and Roman settlements (42BC), in the 10C a small village grew at the foot of Mont Chevalier (aka Le Suquet) named Canoïs, after the reeds *(cannes)* from the surrounding marshes. In 1131, the Count of Provence gave the settlement to the abbots of Lérins, who built fortifications to protect the fishermen against attacks by the Saracens. The town was also defended by the Templars and later the Knights of Malta.

Lord Brougham and the birth of the resort (1834) – Cannes was just a small fishing village of 4 000 inhabitants when the Lord Chancellor of England (1830–34), Lord Brougham, halted here on the way to Nice in 1834 due to a cholera outbreak in Provence. The wealthy traveller fell in love with the village, so he built himself a house there, soon followed by the English aristocracy, who exchanged the winter fogs of London for the Mediterranean sunshine.

Many famous French writers loved Cannes, including the Provençal poet **Frédéric Mistral,** Prosper Mérimée (who died there in 1870), and Guy de Maupassant, who anchored his yacht in the bay between 1884 and 1888 while writing *Sur l'Eau (On the Water)*.

Cannes Festivals – The festivals hosted by the city of Cannes are world famous. **The International Film Festival** is the most glittering artistic gathering on the Riviera. Other popular events include,

▶ **Population:** 70 610.
Michelin Map: 341 D6; local map: *see Massif de l'ESTEREL*
Info: Palais des Festivals – 1 Bd. de la Croisette. ✆04 92 99 84 22. www.palaisdesfestivals. com. Train station: Ailé Est of the Gare SNCF. ✆04 93 99 19 77. www.cannes.fr. Le Cannet: Av. du Campon. ✆04 93 45 34 27. www.lecannet.com.
Location: The most interesting areas of Cannes are between the RN 7 and the sea. The centre of the action is at the Old Port and Palais des Festivals. The old town extends from here up the hillside of Le Suquet; Upscale shops, hotels, and the beaches extend east along Boulevard de la Croisette. A tourist train covers the main sights.
Parking: Parking on the street is metered and only allowed for two hours maximum. Large parking garages *(fee)* can be found around the port, market, and the train station.
Don't Miss: The colourful Marché Forville, the fortified monastery ruins on the Île St-Honorat, the spectacular yachts in the Old Port, or the sandy beaches of La Croisette.
Timing: You'll need a full day to enjoy the sights of Cannes. Visit the Marché Forville and Lérins islands in the morning, then shop or hit the beach afterwards.
Kids: The car-free Île Ste-Marguerite and Fort Vauban are the perfect place to let the kids run loose.

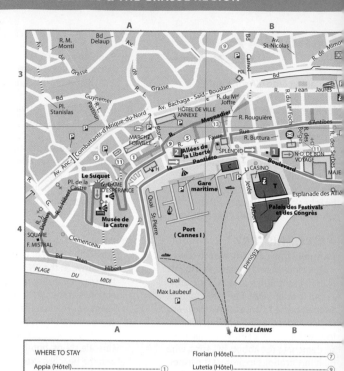

of course, **The Cannes Film Festival** (*see p87*), the prestigious regattas, the International Record and Music Market (MIDEM), and the International Market for Television Programmes.

🚗 DRIVING TOURS

1 EXPLORING CANNES: SEAFRONT★
30min

Boulevard de la Croisette★

Residents enjoy strolling along this elegant seaside promenade in winter, bordered by palms and gardens. Luxury hotels and chic boutiques line the front and side streets as far as Rue d'Antibes. At the top end of La Croisette, east of the port, stands the ultramodern **Palais des Festivals et des Congrès** and casino. Known as 'The Bunker', the building comprises a 2 400-seat auditorium, theatre, broadcasting studios and the Office of Tourism.

Between the conference centre and the gardens lies the **Allée des Stars**, an avenue of 200 tiles with handprints of movie stars who attended the Film Festival. Farther east on the opposite side of the road, beyond the Majestic Hotel, stands a private 19C mansion, **La Malmaison** (🕐 *open Jul–Sept Tue–Sun 11am–8pm (until 10pm Fri); Oct–Apr 10am–1pm, 2.30–6.30pm,* 🕐 *closed public holidays;* ⌚ *4€;* ℘*04 93 38 55 26; www.cannes.fr*). Once part of the Grand Hotel, it now houses the municipal cultural service and art exhibitions. Nearby the Hôtel Noga-Hilton incorporates the façade of the former Palais des Festivals, pulled down in 1988 after serving as the venue for the Cannes Film Festival for 40 years. Further on is the Belle Epoch Carlton Hotel, the Art Deco Martinez Hotel, and the modern Port-Canto.

▷ *Proceed east along Bd. de la Croisette to Pointe de la Croisette.*

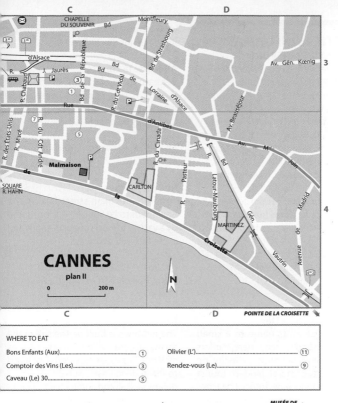

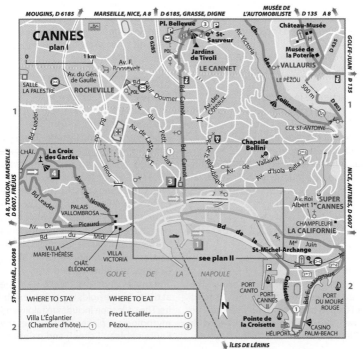

PRACTICAL INFORMATION
TOURS AND TRANSPORT
Bus – *Gare routière, Pl. de l'Hôtel-de-Ville.* 𝄞*04 93 39 11 39. www.rca.tm.fr.* TAM buses operate between Cannes and Nice, with direct airport service.

Train Station – *SNCF Gare de Cannes.* 𝄞*0 892 35 35 35. www.ter-sncf.com/paca.* This train station is served by SNCF trains, the TGV, and the local TER trains (service between Mandelieu-La-Napoule and Vintimille).

Trans Côte d'Azur – *3 Quai des Îles.* 𝄞*04 92 98 71 30. Closed Nov–Jan.* ☜*11€ (5.50€ children). www.trans-cote-azur. com.* Regular service to the Île Ste-Marguerite (15min), plus seasonal tours to l'Île de Porquerolles, Monaco, Saint-Tropez, etc.

Pointe de la Croisette★
This point owes its name to a small cross which used to stand there. It offers splendid views of Cannes, the Iles de Lérins, and the Esterel. Modern tourist developments include artificial beaches and the Palm Beach Casino complex,. Beyond Palm Beach is a splendid **view**★ of Golfe-Juan and Cap d'Antibes.

▷ *Follow the Avenue Maréchal-Juin and Rue d'Antibes back into town.*

Quartier de la Californie
This district consists of luxurious villas, the majority dating from the 19C, set in magnificent gardens.

There are stunning examples of extravagant architecture with exotic, quirky features: pagodas and Moorish minarets, façades surmounted by turrets and colonial villas.

② OLD CANNES AND THE PORT
1.5hr

The Harbour
Between the Palais des Festivals and Le Suquet lies the Old Port with its rows of fishing boats and luxury yachts. The west side of the harbour is lined with shops and restaurants. To the far south-

west is the embarkment for trips to the Îles de Lérins (☜*see Addresses*).

Allées de la Liberté
Beneath the plane trees, overlooking the port, is a large square where an early morning flower market takes place and locals play *pétanque*.

▷ *Take Rue Félix-Faure and Rue Rouguière to Rue Meynadier.*

Rue Meynadier
Formerly the main street linking the new town to Le Suquet, it is bordered by a variety of local speciality shops and some fine 18C doorways.

▷ *Go to Le Suquet via Rue Louis-Blanc, Rue Félix-Faure and Rue Mont-Chevalier.*

Le Suquet
The old town is built on the site of the former Canoïs village on the slopes of Mont Chevalier. Rue Perrissol leads to Place de la Castre surrounded by a defensive wall and dominated by Notre-Dame-d'Espérance, built in the 16C in Provençal Gothic style. The old bell tower leads to a long tree-lined terrace, offering a fine **view** of the town, port and Île Ste-Marguerite.

SIGHTS
Musée de la Castre★★
Le Suquet. ◷*Open Tue–Sun Apr–Jun and Sept 10am–1pm, 2–6pm; Jul–Aug 10am–7pm; Oct and Dec–Mar 10am–1pm, 2–5pm.* ◷*Closed public holidays.* ☜*3.20€, free the first Sun of the month.* 𝄞*04 93 38 55 26. www.cannes.fr.* The 11C Cannes Castle, built by the Lérins monks to watch over the harbour, houses substantial collections of archaeology and ethnography from the Mediterranean Basin and the Middle East as well as Primitive art from Africa, Oceania, the Americas and Asia.

The small Cistercian Chapelle Ste-Anne at the entrance holds temporary exhibits. The collection includes religious and mythological pieces (works from the Fontainebleau School) and paintings of Provence and Cannes by 19C and 20C artists.

Room 4 looks out onto the 12C square watchtower (22m/72ft), **Tour du Suquet**, where temporary photographic exhibitions are held. From the top there's a panoramic **view**★ of La Croisette, Îles de Lérins and the Esterel hills.

▷ *Follow Rue J.-Hibert and Rue J-Dollfus to reach Square Frédéric-Mistral.*

Chapelle Bellini

61 bis Av. de Vallauris; from the Av. Poralto, turn left onto the chemin du Parc-Fiorentina. ♿ ◷ *Open Mon–Fri 2–5pm, Sat–Sun by request.* ✆ *No charge.* ℘ *04 93 38 61 80.*

This chapel was part of the sumptuous Tuscan palace "Villa Fiorentina", built in elaborate Baroque style at the end of the 19C for the Balkan nobility. The coat of arms of Count Vitali decorates the west face. The interior retains several works by the last owner, the Cannes painter Bellini (1904–1989).

Église Orthodoxe St-Michel-Archange

40 Bd. Alexandre-III.

Since Empress Maria Alexandrovna, wife of Czar Alexandre III, had taken to spending the winter months in Cannes, it was necessary to build a church large enough to accommodate her court. It was inaugurated in 1894. The richly ornamented interior contains remarkable icons (one which represents **St Michael the great captain**) and banners from the Russian imperial family.

The church's choral group is particularly renowned for its interpretations of the liturgy. The crypt (◷ *closed to the public*) contains the bodies of members of the imperial family who died in exile and of the white Russian general Youdenitch who beseiged Petrograd in 1919.

Opposite the church, and slightly to its right, in Alexandra Square, is the **Chapelle Tripet-Skryptine**, a neo-Byzantine building which was the first Russian Orthodox church in Cannes.

[3] **LE CANNET**
♿ *See map of Cannes.*
▷ *Leave Cannes by Bd. Carnot.*

Sheltered from the wind by a circle of wooded hills, Le Cannet, at an altitude of 110m/361ft, complements the climate of Cannes. The artist **Pierre Bonnard** (1867–1947) spent the last years of his life painting views of Le Cannet from the Villa Le Bosquet (Avenue Victoria).

Le Vieux Cannet

The old town is reached by Rue St-Sauveur *(mostly pedestrian)*, lined with 18C houses with unusual façades and pleasant shady squares linked by alleyways. At no 19 a blank façade has been covered with a mural by the artist Peynet representing *Les Amoureux (The Lovers)*. Further on the left is the little 15C **Chapelle St-Sauveur** *(108 Rue St-Sauveur)*, sheltered behind a large lime tree, with a pediment decorated with polychrome mosaics. Inside the chapel are more mosaics, decorated wooden panels and stained-glass windows by the artist **Théo Tobiasse** (b. 1927).

Place Bellevue offers a superb view of Cannes and the Îles de Lérins. The old **Calvys Tower** (12C) still stands nearby, as well as the taller **Danys Tower** (14C). Both have fine façades topped with machicolations. There is an amusing fresco dedicated to the founding families of Le Cannet on one wall. The Jardins de Tivoli can be reached from the Hôtel de Ville via the pedestrian Rue Cavasse, passing luxurious 1900 villas.

Chemin des Collines★

This is a particularly attractive, if dizzying, road along the flanks of the hills above Cannes, with fine views over the Gulf of La Napoule and Lérins Islands.

▷ *Continue east to the Col St-Antoine.*

On the left in Avenue Victoria sits the **Villa Yakimour** (◷ *private property*), an Oriental residence given by the Aga Khan to his wife Yvette Labrousse (Yakimour is derived from their initials and *amour*, meaning love).

► Continue to Vallauris over the Col de St-Antoine, then left onto D 803.

Vallauris 👍 See VALLAURIS

Golfe-Juan★ 2km/1mi southeast of Vallauris by D 135. 👍 see GOLFE-JUAN. On returning towards Cannes on N 7, the road skirts the hills of Super-Cannes while on the horizon can be seen the Îles de Lérins and the red Massif de l'Esterel; the **view**★ is at its best at sunset.

► Return to Cannes along the seafront (Bord du Mer).

4 LA CROIX DES GARDES★
Round trip of 8km/5mi (steep climb).

► Leave Cannes on Av. Dr-Picaud. Turn right on Bd. Leader. 100m/110yd beyond the entrance to the Pavillon de la Croix des Gardes, turn right onto Av. J-de-Noailles and park the car 100m/110yd further on in.

🚶 Take a footpath to the top of the hill (alt 164m/538ft), where a strategically placed cross 12m/39ft high has given name to the lookout post since the 16C. From the foot of the cross there is a marvellous **panorama**★ over Cannes, the Îles de Lérins, the Esterel and, in clear weather, the St-Tropez peninsula.

► Continue along Avenue J.-de-Noailles to return to Cannes.

Îles de Lérins★★
👍 See Îles de LÉRINS.
Allow half a day's walk.

ADDRESSES

🏨 STAY

🛏 **Le Chanteclair** – 12 Rue Forville. ℘04 93 39 68 88. Closed 19 Nov–20 Jan. 15 rooms. 🍽 ⚌6€. After walking through a building, you will discover this friendly hotel, offering a selection of variously priced rooms depending on the level of comfort. Pleasant inner courtyard where breakfast is served.

🛏 **Hôtel Florian** – 8 Rue du Cdt-André. ℘04 93 39 24 82. www.hotel-leflorian.com. 20 rooms. ⚌6€. A family-run hotel between the train station and the Palais des Festivals, on a semi-pedestrian street of the old town.

🛏 **Hôtel Lutetia** – 6 Rue Michel-Ange. ℘04 93 39 35 74. 8 rooms. ⚌6€. A simple and comfortable hotel on a quiet side street, with air conditioning, Provençal decor and close proximity to the train station.

🛏 **Hôtel National** – 9 Rue du Maréchal-Joffre. ℘04 93 39 91 92. 17 rooms. ⚌8€. The main advantage of this hotel is its location near the Palais des Festivals and the sea. The white and grey air-conditioned rooms with tiled bathrooms are on the small side, but clean and carefully maintained.

🛏🛏 **Chambre d'hôte Villa L'Églantier** – 14 Rue Campestra. ℘04 93 68 22 43. 3 rooms. 🍽. ⚌. Impressive white villa dating from 1920, surrounded by palm trees and other exotic species. The large, peaceful rooms are extended by a terrace or a balcony.

🛏🛏 **Hôtel Appia** – 6 Rue Marceau. ℘04 93 06 59 59. www.appia-hotel.com. Closed 20 Nov–28Dec.31 rooms. ⚌7€. Practicality takes precedence over comfort in this downtown hotel where the well-kept, small rooms are air-conditioned and soundproofed.

🛏🛏 **Hôtel Festival** – 3 Rue Molière. ℘04 97 06 64 40. www.hotel-festival.com. 14 rooms. ⚌8€. Recently renovated family-run hotel walking distance from the Croisette and Rue d'Antibes shopping area. Rooms have air-con, soundproofing and WiFi, marble bathrooms and minibar. Jacuzzi and sauna available for guests.

🛏🛏 **Hôtel Le Mistral** – 13 Rue des Belges. ℘04 93 39 91 46. www.mistral-hotel.com. Closed 20 Nov–28Dec. 10 rooms. ⚌8€. A new boutique hotel with modern decor, just behind the Palais des Festivals. Rooms have air-conditioning, WiFi and a safe.

⍩ EAT

🍽🍷 **Aux Bons Enfants** – *80 Rue Meynadier. ✆No phone. 🗓 Closed Aug, Sat eve off season, Sun.* An old-fashioned cantina near the Forville market serving ratatouille, grilled anchovies, aïoli, stuffed sardines, etc. Wines by the pitcher and a friendly family atmosphere.

🍽🍷 **Le Caveau 30** – *45 Rue F.-Faure. ✆04 93 39 06 33. www.lecaveau30.com.* Large restaurant comprising two dining rooms done up in the style of a 1930s brasserie. The terrace overlooks a shaded square. Fish and seafood are house specialities.

🍽🍷 **Le Comptoir des Vins** – *13 Bd. de la République. ✆04 93 68 13 26. Closed Tue eves, Sat lunch, Sun–Mon.* This handsomely stocked wine boutique leads to a colourful dining area where light snacks can be served with a glass of wine.

🍽🍷 **Le Rendez-Vous** – *35 Rue F.-Faure. ✆04 93 68 55 10.* A chic bistro with an Art Deco-style ceiling, serving fish, seafood and other Mediterranean-flavoured dishes.

🍽🍷🍷 **Fred L'Écailler** – *7 Pl. de l'Étang. ✆04 93 43 15 85. www.fredlecailler.com.* A large neon sign marks the entrance to this rustic-style restaurant whose walls are draped with fishing nets. Fine selection of freshly caught fish and seafood.

🍽🍷🍷 **L'Olivier** – *25 Av. Beauséjour. ✆04 93 68 86 86. www.novotelcannes. com.* Pleasant, sunny decor, view of the litchens and Mediterranean dishes on the menu.

🛍 SHOPPING

Marché de Forville – *closed Mon in low season.* Stalls displaying fresh regional produce.

Shopping streets – *Rue Meynadier*: tempting window displays of food and craftwork in a lively pedestrian area. Rue d'Antibes: luxury clothes and luggage.

Cannolive – *16 Rue Vénizelos. ✆04 93 39 08 19. Closed Sun, two weeks in Dec.* This shop boasts an incredible choice of Provençal products to take back home: household linen, tapenades, crockery, santons, soap, and even Lérina liqueur from the nearby islands.

🍸 NIGHTLIFE

L'Amiral – *73 Bd. de la Croisette. ✆04 92 98 73 00. www.hotel.martinez.com.* Attached to the Martinez Hotel, this bar is by far the most popular meeting place along the coast. It owes its reputation to the head barman and to Jimmy, the American pianist (every evening from 8pm).

Le Bâoli – *Port Pierre Canto, Bd. de la Croisette. ✆04 93 43 03 43. Closed Sun–Tue, Mon–Fri off season.* The hottest night spot in Cannes with beachfront views over the bay, this bar-restaurant-nightclub with the exotic decor can host up to 1 500 jetsetting partygoers in high season.

🏃 LEISURE ACTIVITIES

For sailing, deep-sea diving or water-skiing, contact the tourist office or visit www.france-nautisme.com.

Beaches – Not all the beaches on La Croisette charge a fee (details of prices are listed at the top of the steps), or belong to a hotel (located opposite). There are also three free beaches, one of which is located behind the Palais du Festival. The other public beaches lie west of the old port, on Boulevard Jean-Hibert and Boulevard du Midi, at Port Canto and on Boulevard Gazagnaire beyond La Pointe.

Ponton Majestic Ski Nautique – *Bd. de la Croisette. ✆04 92 98 77 47. majesticskiclub.online.fr. Closed Nov–Mar.* If you want to get away from the bustling crowds, try your hand at water-skiing or parascending.

CALENDAR OF EVENTS

Cannes Film Festival – *🎬see p87.*
International Film Festival – Ten days in May; free open-air cinema retrospectives on the beach (official screenings open to accredited professionals only). *www.festival-cannes.org.*
Nuits Misicales du Suquet – End of July; classical concerts on the esplanade in front of the Église du Suquet. *✆04 92 99 33 83.*

Gourdon★

Alpes Maritimes

Gourdon "the Saracen" was built on the remarkable site of a rocky spur more than 500m/1 640ft above the River Loup. The village's old houses have been restored and converted into boutiques and artist worshops.

VISIT

The Village★

Close to the carparks, the **Saint-Pons Chapel** (12C), rests within a **medieval garden** of Mediterranean plants. The ramparts lead to Place du Portal then to the village, animated by the local galleries and artisans. Take Rue des Ecoles to the Sainte-Catherine Chapel and the **oldest house** of Gourdon *(la maison du Chevalier)* whose carved wooden door is surmounted by a beautiful sundial. The Eglise Saint-Vincent (1C–12C) contains the tombs of several lords of Gourdon. There is a magnificent panorama from the small church square overlooking the Loup River, which emerges from the upper gorge and winds its way to the coast, seen in the distance.

Château★

The castle, built in the 13C on the foundations of an old Saracen fortress and restored in the 17C, mixes architectural

▶ **Population:** 437.
🖢 **Michelin Map:** 341 C5.
🗎 **Info:** Mairie, Pl. de l'Église. ℘04 93 09 68 25. www.gourdon-france.com.
◖ **Location:** The secluded Alpes-Maritimes village is found 14km/8.7mi northeast of Grasse on D2085, then D 3. Gourdon can also be reached by a scenic route through the Gorges du Loup leaving from Vence.
🅿 **Parking:** All roads lead to a parking area just below the village. The village is accessible by foot only.

features from the Saracens (vaulted rooms), 14C Tuscans, and the Renaissance (doorway at the far end on the main courtyard).

Musée Historique

Ground floor of the chateau. ◷*Open daily Jun–Sept 11am–1pm, 2–7pm; Oct–May Wed–Mon 2–6pm.* ⊚*4€.* ℘*04 93 09 68 02. www.chateau-gourdon.com.* The entrance hall contains a fine collection of arms and armour. The imposing fireplace in the dining room is 14C and the furniture 16C and 17C.

Gardens at Château de Gourdon

B. Kaufmann/ MICHELIN

In the drawing room is an Aubusson tapestry, a secretaire which belonged to Marie-Antoinette, a *Self-Portrait* by Rembrandt and a fine 1500 painting from the Cologne School: **St Ursula**. The chapel contains a 16C triptych, a *Descent from the Cross* from Rubens' studio, a *Golgotha* by the Flemish School and a polychrome wood sculpture of St Sebastian by El Greco.

The guard-room contains a collection of 16C and 17C oriental arms. In Henry IV's Tower, the documents on show bear the Royal Seal; an opening in the floor reveals the former dungeon.

Musée des Arts Décoratifs et de la Modernité

First and second floors.
Guided tours (1hr) Jul–Aug; Sept–Jun by request. 10€. 04 93 09 68 02. www.chateau-gourdon.com.

This collection brings together some of the best examples of decorative arts and furniture design from the 1920s to the 1930s, including examples from the Union des Artistes Modernes (UAM). The rooms are arranged to look like vintage apartments: from the Art Nouveau room to the Art Deco room, with pieces by Eileen Gray, Mallet-Stevens, etc.

ADDRESSES

▯/ EAT

Au Vieux Four – *Rue Basse (in the village).* 04 93 09 68 60. *Closed Sat, weekday eves off season.* *Reservations recommended.* This is the perfect stopping-place to round off your visit of the village. The young couple who run the place prepare delicious Provençal food and grilled meat in an open fireplace before your eyes. Simple, refreshing decoration and reasonable prices.

Taverne Provençale – *Pl. de l'Église.* 04 93 09 68 22. *Closed 3–28 Jan, mid-Nov–mid-Dec, Wed off season.* Settle on the terrace and admire the superb views of the heights beyond Nice, as well as those of the Mediterranean. This Provençal bistro serves French cuisine according to tradition: trout, *coq au vin*, guinea fowl with mushrooms.

Local Specialities

From the surrounding forests of cork-oaks and chestnut trees comes the raw material for the manufacture of bottle corks and the production of sweet chestnuts sold under the name *Marrons de Luc*. In the autumn, **Chestnut Festivals** are organised to celebrate the harvest. Local markets are held on Wednesdays and Sundays. The chestnut festival runs late Oct–late Nov. Other towns also celebrate the chestnut during November, such as Cagnes-sur-Mer, Valdeblore, Guillaumes, Fontan and Roquebrune-Cap-Martin.

Gardens

Guided visits (1hr) Jul–Aug daily 3pm, 5pm; Apr–Jun and Sept by request for groups of over ten people only. 4€. 04 93 09 68 02.

The terraced gardens were designed by Le Nôtre in the 17C, and laid out on three levels. They are now part of a botanical garden centre, preserving typical flora of the Pre-Alps.

⬜ SHOPPING

Sainte-Catherine – *Rue des Écoles.* 04 93 09 68 89. www.sainte-catherine.com. Gourmet food lovers will find their happiness in this delicious-smelling boutique stocked full of herbs and spices, original jams, jellied fruits and plenty of regional mustards, vinaigres, honey and olive oil.

La Source Parfumée – *Rue Principale.* 04 93 09 20 00. www.galimard.com. A boutique of scented candles and perfumes blended by request in the old distillery, sold at wholesale prices. Also tours of the flower fields (3€).

Grasse★

Alpes Maritime

The perfume capital of France is nestled at the foot of a high plateau overlooking the fragrant plains, where the flowers that have made the town's fortune are cultivated. The blue sea off the coast of Cannes can be seen from the modern town, while the boutiques and perfumeries are found in the narrow alleys of the old Provençal town below.

A BIT OF HISTORY

In the Middle Ages, Grasse was a tiny republic, administered by a council whose members called themselves "Consuls by the Grace of God". Raymond Bérenger, Count of Provence, put an end to this independent existence in 1227. Thanks to its mild climate, the town later became a popular winter resort, hosting the estranged Princess Pauline Bonaparte in 1807–1808 (her brother. the Emperor, would pass through the town on 2 March 1815, on his way to Paris after his escape from Elba Island). Queen Victoria spent several winters in Grasse at the Grand Hotel.

A KALEIDOSCOPE OF FRAGRANCES

The Perfume Industry

Grasse had long specialised in leather work when perfumed gloves came into fashion in the 16C. This was the beginning of the perfume industry. The great *parfumeries* were born in the 18C and 19C and still enjoy an international reputation.

There are three manufacturing processes: distillation, *enfleurage* and extraction. **Distillation** is the oldest process. Flowers and water are brought to boiling point in a still. In the 18C **enfleurage** was invented, a labor-intensive process using animal fats to obtain a pomade. The latest process is **extraction** by which the flowers yield their perfume in its most concentrated form using solvents. The essences produced in

▶ **Population:** 48 801.

⏱ **Michelin Map:** 341 C6.

🏛 **Info:** Palais des Congrès, 22 Cours H.-Cresp. ℘04 93 36 66 66. www.grasse.fr.

◐ **Location:** Grasse is located 17km/10.5mi northwest of Cannes on the N 85, leading past the industrial and residential zones into the heart of the old town *(vieille ville)*. The most interesting part of Grasse is in the pedestrian streets between cours Honoré-Cresp, Boulevard du Jeu-de-Ballon and Place du 24 Août.

🅿 **Parking:** There are five parking garages in the centre *(from 1.10€–1.40€/ hr; open 24hr)*, including Place du Cours Honoré Cresp, Place de la Foux and at the Hôtel de Ville. ℘04 92 60 91 17.

◉ **Don't Miss:** The Musée International de la Parfumerie brings to light the town's main industry.

🕐 **Timing:** Plan on half a day for the old town, starting off with a visit to the perfume museum before taking a free tour of one of the perfume makers. Then explore the streets of the old town, or a hike around the surrounding countryside for some excellent panoramic views.

♣ **Kids:** The Grottes de St-Cézaire are popular with children.

Grasse, which are the base material of the perfume industry, are used locally or sent to Paris where the great perfume houses blend them according to secret formulas. The Grasse perfume industry has now diversified into the production of food flavourings.

PRACTICAL INFORMATION

Guided Tours – There are several themed guided tours of the town, its history, its perfumeries and artists in English from July to September.
🛈 *Enquire at the tourist office or visit www.vpah.culture.fr.*

TRANSPORT

Buses – *Bus station at the Notre-Dame-des-Fleurs car park, Pl. de la Buanderie.* 📞*04 93 36 37 37.* The city is served by 16 lines, which also go to Nice and Cannes.

Petit Train Touristique – *Runs Apr–Sept Mon–Sat 10am–6pm.* ⬜*6€ (3€ children 3–12).* Guided, commentated tours *(45min)* from Cours Honoré-Cresp to the heights of Grasse and the Parc de la Princesse-Pauline on a small tourist train.

SNCF Train – There is newly reopened train service between Grasse and Nice via Cannes. 🛈 *www.regionpaca.fr or www.grasse-riviera.com.*

Musée International de la Parfumerie★

2 Blvd. du Jeu-de-Ballon. 🕐*Open Jun–Sept daily 10am–9pm, Oct–May Wed–Mon 11am–6pm.* ⬜*3€.* 📞*04 97 05 58 00. www.museesdegrasse.com.*
After four years of renovations, this wonderfully modernised museum unites three buildings under a glass atrium. The exhibits cover more than 3 000 years in the history of perfumemaking throughout the world.
Among the 50, 000 pieces in the collection from Guerlain, Patou, Lanvin, and Chanel include different kinds of perfume vessels, flasks, scent bottles, boxes, chests and even travel accessories belonging to Marie-Antoinette.

Parfumeries

🅿*Visitor parking.* ♿*See the Addresses for addresses and admission times.*
There are several perfume manufacturers in Grasse (also known as *parfumeries* or *usines*) which give free guided tours of their perfume-making process, such as Fragonard, Molinard and Galimard. Try to visit on weekdays when the workers can be seen making the *eau de toilette* and scented soaps on sale in the boutiques.

Flower Fields

🛈 *Information at the tourist office and at perfume manufacturers' reception.*
In spring and summer, Fragonard and Molinard will take you on tours of their lovely flower fields. The **Domaine de Manon** *(Chemin de Servin, 7km/4.3mi from Grasse;* 📞*04 93 60 12 76)* allows access to its rose garden (May–June) and jasmine fields (July–November).

👣 WALKING TOUR
THE OLD TOWN★

Allow 1hr.
The houses of old Grasse are the colour of the sunset: red ochre, orange, yellow, pink ... and sometimes grey, since many of the villagers have abandoned the historic centre for more modern housing in the valley.

▶ *Leave the car in the car park on Cours Honoré-Cresp and take Rue Jean-Ossola, continued by Rue Marcel-Journet. Turn right on Rue Gazan and walk until you reach Pl. du Puy.*

"Nose" at work
B. Kaufmann/ MICHELIN

Cathedral Notre-Dame-du-Puy

Pl. du Petit-Puy. ○*Open Mon–Fri 9.30am–11.30am, 3–6pm.*

The 10C cathedral was restored in the 17C and the double staircase at the entrance, with its wide stone handrail, and the two crypts were added on in the 18C. The high narrow nave, with heavy pointed rib-vaulting, marks the beginning of the Gothic style in Provence. In the south aisle there are three **paintings**★ by Rubens (*The Crown of Thorns, Crucifixion* and *St Helen in Exaltation of the Holy Cross*). There is a fine **triptych** attributed to Louis Bréa depicting St Honoratus and a rare religious painting by Fragonard, *The Washing of the Feet.*

Place du 24-Août

From the far side of the square you can admire the chevet and bell tower of the cathedral. There is a fine **view** eastwards over the Grasse countryside. Close at hand is the Clock Tower (Tour de l'Horloge).

▷ *Turn left onto Rue de l'Évêché.*

Place de l'Évêché

At the centre of Place de l'Evêché stands an elegant three-tiered **fountain**. At the tiny Place de la Poissonnerie, follow the street of the same name to Place aux Herbes, where the colourful Grasse market takes place.

Picking rose petals

D. Pazery/ MICHELIN

▷ *Go along Rue Courte, turn left on Rue Droite, then right onto Rue Amiral-de-Grasse to Pl. aux Aires.*

Place aux Aires

This square used to be used by local tanners. At no 33 is the **Hôtel Isnard**, an attractive town house built in 1781.

▷ *Leave the square on your left and exit the old town via Bd. du Jeu-de-Ballon, and down to Pl. du Cours.*

Place du Cours★

This fine terraced promenade offers a charming **view**★ over the countryside.

Gardens of Grasse

Jardin de la Princesse Pauline

Access via Av. Thiers, Bd. Alice-de-Roth-schild and Bd. de la Reine-Jeanne.
Stay to the left and look for the signs.

This grove of oaks that Napoleon's sister adored during her winter stay here is now a large ornamental garden with **panoramic views**★ of Grasse, the Massif du Tanneron, the Esterel and the coast *(viewing table).*

Parc Communal de la Corniche

Access as above; then turn a sharp left on Bd. Bellevue and then right on Bd. du Président-Kennedy.

🚶*30min round trip.* At the bend, a path to the right *(sign)* leads to the edge of the steep Pre-Alps of Grasse. From the lookout point, the **view**★★ extends from the Baou of St-Jeannet to the coast and from the Tanneron mountains to the peaks of the Esterel.

SIGHTS

Musée d'Art et d'Histoire de Provence★

2 Rue Mirabeau. ○*Open Jun–Sept daily 10am–6.30pm; Oct–May Wed–Mon 10am–12.30pm, 2–5.30pm.* ○*Closed in Nov and public holidays.* *4€ (no charge first Sun of the month in winter).* *04 93 36 01 61.* *www.museesdegrasse.com.*

This museum, set in an 18C mansion called "Petit Trianon", provides a remark-

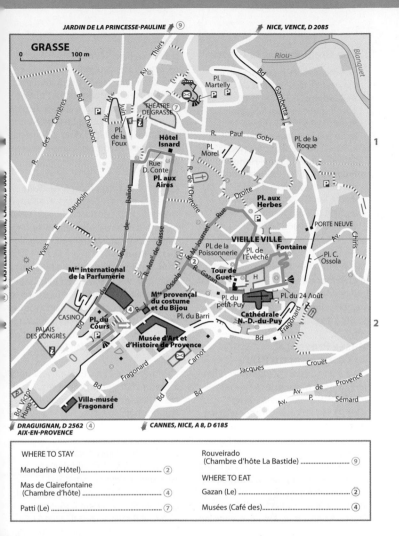

able compendium of the art and history of eastern Provence.

The ground floor displays pottery (18C–19C) from Apt and Le Castellet, and paintings by 19C Provençal artists (Chabaud, Camoin). In the basement are the mansion's reconstructed kitchens, Provençal nativity scenes and an archaeological section evoking the daily life of local people from Prehistoric times to the late Middle Ages.

Villa-Musée Fragonard

Same times and charges as the Musée d'Art et d'Histoire de Provence.

Jean-Honoré Fragonard took refuge during the Revolution in this elegant country house, which now displays a broad spectrum of his works: original drawings and etchings, sketches, paintings, *Landscape with Washerwomen*, *The White Bull* and *The Three Graces*.

Musée de la Marine

Villa Fragonard. Open Jul–Sept daily 10am–7pm; Oct–May Mon–Fri 10am–noon, 2–5pm. Closed public holidays. No charge. 04 93 40 11 11. The Marine Museum retraces the distinguished career of **Admiral de Grasse**, who was born at Bar-sur-Loup (*see*

The Great Artists of Grasse

Two children of Grasse excelled in the arts and letters. **Bellaud de la Bellaudière** (1532–88), a soldier-poet inspired by Rabelais and Petrarch who briefly revived the Provençal language in literature between the troubadours (12C) and Mistral (19C). **Jean-Honoré Fragonard** (1732–1806), although the son of a tanner and glove-maker, left for Paris to learn art as a young man, and won the Prix de Rome by the age of 20.

VALLÉE DU LOUP: Driving Tour), and his involvement in the American War of Independence. Among the 29 models are 18C sailing ships, a Maltese galley, and the flagship *La Ville de Paris*.

Musée Provençal du Costume et du Bijou

2 Rue Jean-Ossola. ○*Open daily 10am–1pm, 2–6pm; Nov–Easter Mon–Sat 10am–1pm, 2–6pm.* ◎*No charge.* ℘*04 93 36 44 65. www.fragonard.com.*
These private collections housed in an annexe of the Fragonard perfumery focus on women's clothing during the 18C. Peasants' robes, weavers' skirts and middle-class finery are on show alongside a series of crosses and curious ornaments made out of sea fossils *(étoiles de Digne)*. A fine, interesting presentation in which all the exhibits are genuine, except for the aprons.

DRIVING TOURS

Préalpes de Grasse★★
Round trip of 104km/65mi – about 5hr.

▷ *From Grasse take Bd. Georges-Clémenceau and turn left onto D 11.*

After crossing the Plateau Napoléon, the road rises towards Cabris offering fine **views** of the Grasse countryside.

Cabris★
🚹 *9 Rue Frédéric-Mistral.* ℘*04 93 60 55 63. http://cabris.site.voila.fr.*
This charming village occupies a magnificent site on the edge of the Provençal plateau, looking out over the Grasse countryside to Lac de St-Cassien and the sea *(20km/12mi)*. The village has long been a favourite haunt of writers and artists.

Church
○*Open during Sun service, 10.30am.*
The 17C church contains a painted wooden pulpit and a fine rustic altarpiece under the gallery. Behind the altar hangs a copy of a Murillo painting.

Castle Ruins
From the defensive wall and terrace is a superb **view**★★: southeast to Mougins and the hills running down to Le Cannet, out to sea over La Napoule Bay to the Îles de Lérins, south beyond Peymeinade to the Esterel, and westwards to the Lac de St-Cassien (◔*orientation table).*

▷ *Towards St-Cézaire, a small twisting route (on the right) passes close to the "9 Puits de la Vierge" nine wells of Roman origin.*

Grottes de St-Cézaire★
Outside the village de Saint-Cézaire. ○*Guided tours (40min) Jul–Aug 10.30am–6.30pm; Jun and Sept 10.30–noon, 2.30–6pm; Feb–May and Oct 2.30–5pm; Nov Sun 2.30–5pm.* ◎*7€ (4€ children 6–12).* ℘*04 93 60 22 35. www.lesgrottesdesaintcezaire.fr.*
Discovered by accident in 1888, the caves are hollowed out of the limestone and remain at a constant temperature of 14°C/57°F. Both the stalactites and the stalagmites are remarkable for the variety of their shapes – toadstools, flowers, animals – and their reddish colour, ascribed to the presence of iron oxide in the rock.

St-Cézaire-sur-Siagne
From its site dominating the steep Siagne Valley, the walls and towers of this interesting village testify to its feudal past. A marked path from the church leads to a **viewpoint** *(viewing table).*

Leaving St-Cézaire, take a left onto the narrow D 105, direction Mons.

Gorges de la Siagne

The road runs up through the rich vegetation in the deep gorge cut into the limestone by the waters of the Siagne. After crossing the river (from the bridge, **view** up and down the gorge), turn right onto the D 656, which is a very steep and narrow road.

After meandering steeply above the gorge, the road broadens out into a colourful rock circus before entering a wooded valley which brings it to the plateau.

At the crossroads turn left onto D 56.

Sources de la Siagnole

30min round trip.

On the right beyond the bridge a path leads to a very pleasant spot where several Vauclusian springs rise to form the River Siagnole. A bit further, a sign indicates the remains of a Roman aqueduct at **Roche Taillée**, still in use. There is a lovely **view**★ eastwards towards Grasse.

Return to the D5 and drive north. Turn left onto the road to the cemetery (signposted "Grotte Baume Obscure"). Continue beyond the cemetery for 2km/1mi to a large car park opposite a shelter built over the ticket office.

♣♣ Souterroscope de la Baume Obscure

Augioguided tours (1hr) May–Jun and Sept Mon–Sat 10am–6pm, Sun and public holidays 10am–7pm; Jul–Aug daily 10am–7pm; Oct–mid-Dec and Feb–Apr daily 10am–6pm. ⊕7.65€ (3.80€ children). ℘04 93 42 61 63. www.baumeobscure.com. A warm sweater and shoes with non-slip soles advised. Narrow passages.

The cave consists of an underground network of galleries, which remained undiscovered until 1958 because the long, narrow tunnels leading to them put off early explorers. The tour of the cave covers 500m/547yd and takes visi-

tors down 50m/164ft to the **Galerie du Pas de Course**, where the temperature is a constant 14°C/57°F.

St-Vallier-de-Thiey

☐ 10 Pl. de la Tour. ℘04 93 42 78 00. ☐ Park at Place du Grand-Pré (except on market day on Fri in summer) or Pl. St-Roch (Fri market autumn–spring).

This medieval village, once a Roman stronghold, is situated in the middle of a fertile plateau at the foot of the Pre-Alps. Its Romanesque church, old seigneurial château and ancient houses attest to the historical heritage of this village.

Church

The 12C Romanesque church, restored in the 17C, has a lovely 13C nave with pointed barrel vaulting and houses two Baroque altarpieces. The bell tower is decorated with arcading, a remnant from the original construction, and surmounted by a 19C campanile.

From St-Vallier-de-Thiey to Gourdon

30km/19mi – allow 2hr.

Leave St-Valliers-de-Thiey and take N 85 towards the Pas de la Faye, then D 5 to the right. After going through a pass, Col de Ferrier, the road overlooks the valley of Nans. Leave the main road, taking D 12 leading off to the right (sign "Caussols").

The **Plateau de Caussols**★, sitting at an average altitude of 1 000m/3 281ft, is itself enclosed by higher land. It is one of the rare examples of karst relief in France. The plateau features dolines, swallowholes and chasms where the limestone was eroded by rainwater. *Walkers should take care when near these pits and chasms, especially in rainy weather.* A particularly spectacular example of this feature can be seen by taking the small road to the right, leaving the centre of the sprawling village of **Caussols** to the east. The narrow road crosses the plateau diagonally to reach **Les Claps**★ (Provençal for "rocks"), a remarkable rock chaos. Some stone dwellings *(bories)* indicate human inhabitants. Turning around to face the plateau gives a view of the domes of the CERGA Observatory.

▷ *Return to D 12 and follow it for 2km/1mi towards Gourdon. 2km/1mi after Caussols on D 12, a road leads off to the left signposted "St-Maurice – Observatoire du CERGA". After passing the houses, continue past the sign "Route Privée," which indicates the entrance to the CERGA property.*

Observatoire de Calern
2130 Rte. de l'Observatoire. ⊙*Open Tue–Sat 7am–11pm.* ∞*9€ (reservations recommended).* ℘*04 93 85 85 58. www.astrorama.net.*
The **Plateau de Calern** (1 300m/4265ft) is home to the various installations and equipment of the CERGA Observatory, specialised in geodynamic and astronomical research. Teams work with interferometers (for measuring diameters of stars), the Schmidt telescope, and astrolabes.

▷ *Return to D 12 towards Gourdon.*

The road continues to the eastern edge of the plateau and then descends into Gourdon. There is a lovely **view**★ of the Loup Valley from the first big bend.

Gourdon★
See GOURDON.
The first major bend in the road on the way to Gourdon reveals a magnificent **view**★ of the Vallée du Loup (*see Vallée du LOUP*).

ADDRESSES

⌂ STAY

GRASSE
⊖ **Bastide La Rouveirado** – *22 chemin des Colles, Chateauneuf-Grasse.* ℘*04 93 77 78 49. www.larouveirado.com. 5 rooms.* ⊑*8€.* This modern bed and breakfast is hidden among evergreen oaks near Opio. Rooms have direct access outside to the pool and gardens through French doors. Simple decor yet comfortably appointed.

⊖⊖ **Hôtel Le Patti** – *Pl. Patti.* ℘*04 93 36 01 00. www.hotelpatti.com. 73 rooms.* ⊑*8€. Restaurant*⊖⊖. This 18C hotel in the old town is decorated in charming Provençal style with wrought-iron beds and patina'd walls. Rooms have air conditioning, WiFi and stereo. Provençal products for sale in the boutique, and Mediterranean cuisine in the restaurant.

⊖⊖ **Mandarina Hôtel** – *39 Av. Y.-E.-Baudoin.* ℘*04 93 36 10 29. www. mandarinahotel.com. 31 rooms.* ▯. ⊑*8€. Restaurant*⊖. Overlooking the city of Grasse, peace and quiet are guaranteed in this hotel, with lightly decorated rooms and pretty views of the coastline. Provençal fabric adds a lively touch to the dining room.

⊖⊖⊜ **Chambre d'Hôte Mas de Clairefontaine** – *3196 Route de Draguignan, Val du Tignet, 10km/6mi southeast of Grasse on Route de Draguignan/RD 562.* ℘*04 93 66 39 69. http://masdeclairefontaine.online.fr. 3 rooms.* ⊟. ⊑. A stone cottage surrounded by a terraced garden dotted with umbrella pines and reeds is the charming backdrop to your stay at this bed and breakfast. The rooms are tastefully appointed and excellent service. Grounds include a terrace shaded by a century-old oak tree and swimming pool.

CABRIS
⊖ **Chambre d'Hôte Mme Faraut** – *14 Rue de l'Agachon.* ℘*04 93 60 52 36. Closed 15 Oct–1 Apr.* ⊟. *5 rooms.* Nestled in the old quarter, this hotel fronted by a yellow façade offers simply decorated rooms painted in white. Pretty views of St-Cassien Lake and the Esterel Massif from the lounge and some of the bedrooms.

ST-VALLIER-DE-THIEY
⊖ **Villa Quercus** – *2 Chemin Blaqueirette, at the edge of the village, across from the pharmacist's shop.* ℘*04 92 60 03 84.* ⊟. *4 rooms.* The main advantages of this villa are its big shaded garden, home to a swimming pool, and its pleasing covered terrace

for summer breakfasts. The rooms display an interesting medley of decorative styles. Fully equipped kitchen at residents' disposal.

♀/ EAT

GRASSE

🍽🍽 **Le Gazan** – *3 Rue Gazan. Closed Dec–Jan, Mon–Thu eves off season, Sun.* *℘04 93 36 22 88.* Two delightful dining rooms with rustic furniture, linked by a spiral staircase, provide the setting for a succulent meal seasoned with local olive oil and aromatic herbs. Located in the old quarter of Grasse.

🍽🍽 **Café des Musées** – *1 Rue Jean Ossola. Closed Sun Oct–Mar. ℘04 92 60 99 00.* A chic tea room and café across from the Musée Provençal, serving light dishes for lunch such as beef carpaccio, smoked salmon, goats cheese salad and homemade tarts. There's also a fine selection of local wines.

🛒 SHOPPING

Palais des Olives – *1 Bd. du Jeu-de-Ballon. ℘04 93 36 57 73. www.palais-des-olives.com. Closed two weeks in Jan and Nov, Sun–Mon.* Traditional Provençal-style boutique featuring high-quality olive oils from Grasse and around the world, local olives, and organic products.

Le Moulin de la Brague – *2 Rue de Châteauneuf, Opio. ℘04 93 77 23 03. www.moulin-opio.com. Closed Mon morning Oct–Mar, Sun.* For six generations the Michel Family has preserved this rare working olive mill (part of which dates back to the 15C). The pretty boutique sells olive oil, tapenades, honey, jams, pottery, soaps and fabrics.

PARFUMERIES

Usine Fragonard – *20 Bd. Fragonard. ℘04 93 36 44 65. www.fragonard.com.* Perfume has been made here since 1782. Introductory course on "The Essence of Aromas" *(Absolus Aromatiques)* by request.

Fragonard-La Fabrique des Fleurs – *Carrefour des Quatre-Chemins, Route de Cannes. ℘04 93 77 94 30.* A modern perfume factory on the edge of Grasse, with tours and a aromatic flower and herb garden.

Parfumerie Molinard – *60 Bd. Victor-Hugo. ℘04 93 36 01 62. www.molinard.com. Closed Oct–Mar. ⊛No charge.* Traditional Provençal perfume house founded in 1849. Visitors are explained the successive stages in the making of a perfume. There are also courses on how to create perfumes *(fee)*.

Usine Galimard – *73 Route de Cannes (going towards Mouans-Sartoux). ℘04 93 09 20 00. www.galimard.com. ⊛Guided tours year round. ⊛No charge.* Created in 1747, the free tours include the perfume museum, labs, workshops and boutique.

Galimard-Studio des Fragrances – *5 Route de Pégomas, Rond Point des 4 Chemins. ℘04 93 09 20 00. www.galimard.com. Course (2hr) on perfume-making. Open by appointment Mon–Sat.* Make your own fragrance with the help of a real "nose" from Grasse (they keep your "formula" on file in case you want to order more).

🎭 ENTERTAINMENT

Casino – *Bd. du Jeu-de-Ballon. ℘04 93 36 91 00. www.casino-grasse.com.* Come here to indulge in a spot of gambling (roulette, blackjack). The café is open from 8.30pm to 2am. There are musical evenings and package formulas available (casino, dinner, transport).

CALENDAR

GRASSE

Rallaye de Grasse – April.

Exposition Internationale de la Rose – Over 30 000 cut roses on display in bouquets in mid-May.

Fête du Jasmin – First weekend in August.

Women's Festival on Ste-Agathe Day during the first weekend in February.

St-Pierre Festival towards the end of June.

Local festivities in honour of **Our Lady** on 15 August.

Juan-les-Pins★
Alpes Maritimes

Juan-les-Pins is one of the Riviera's most lively summer resorts, known for its jazz festival, numerous nightclubs and endless stretch of sandy beaches. Protected by the Cap d'Antibes and Pointe de la Croisette, the bay enjoys a mild climate and easy access to Cannes and Antibes.

- **Michelin Map:** 341 D6.
- **Info:** 51 Bd. Charles-Guillaumont, Juan-les-Pins. ℰ04 92 90 53 05. www.antibes-juanlespins.com.
- **Location:** Technically part of the same municipality, Juan-les-Pins is connected to Antibes on the east by the Cap d'Antibes (℮see ANTIBES), and to the west by Golfe-Juan, along the RN 7 or the coastal N 98. The train station is only a few blocks from the beaches.
- **Parking:** Parking spots are difficult to find in summer, but typically can be found by the station (gare) or along the beach (fee).

A BIT OF HISTORY
The "Swing" Era
The thriving musical nightlife of Juan-les-Pins began during the 1920s with the arrival of the first American tourists, who revolutionised the atmosphere of the resort with their exuberance: they sunbathed on the beaches, water-skied and listened to unfamiliar music called jazz. Frank Gould founded the first summer casino, frequented by the likes of Cole Porter, Douglas Fairbanks, Mary Pickford and Mistinguette. After the Liberation, Sydney Bechet brought music back to the town, and the first jazz festival took place in 1959, a year after his death, attracting names like Louis Armstrong, Count Basie, Duke Ellington, Dizzy Gillespie and Miles Davis.

RESORT LIFE
The pines and heavenly sandy beaches make this resort one of the most attractive on the French Riviera.
The Promenade au Soleil, running between the landing-stage and the casino, is full of restaurants, open-air cafés and nightclubs. During the day you can admire the architecture of many hotels and private homes built in the 1920s and 1930s (ask at the tourist office for the map).

Beaches
The pines grow right down to the gently sloping beach of Juan-les-Pins, a superb stretch of fine sand some 2km/1mi long and sheltered from the winds. There are several private and public beaches all around, dotted between the ports of Golfe-Juan and Juan-les-Pins.

Beach at Juan-les-Pins

Parc Exflora

Off the N 7 in the direction of Golfe-Juan. ⏱Open daily Sept and Mar–May 9.30am–7pm; Jun–Aug 9.30am–9.30pm; Oct–Feb 9.30am–5pm. ✆04 92 90 53 05 (tourist office).
Set within a vast olive tree orchard are the many different incarnations of Mediterranean gardens from antiquity to the 19C. The settings include a Roman garden, a palm tree garden, a labyrinth, a winter garden and an oasis overlooking the sea.

ADDRESSES

STAY

⌂ **Hôtel Cécil** – *Rue Jonnard. ✆04 93 61 05 12. www.hotelcecil-france.com. Closed 3 Nov–Jan. 21 rooms, half-board. ⌂6.50€* A handsome, traditional residence converted into a hotel in 1920. The smallish, impeccably kept rooms are laid out over three floors. Dinner is served out on the terrace in summer. Situated in the town centre, yet not far from the beach.

⌂ **Hôtel Ste-Valérie** – *Rue de l'Oratoire. ✆04 93 61 07 15. www.juanlespins.net. Closed mid-Oct–early Mar. 26 rooms. 🅿. ⌂23€.* Just off a quiet street, this hotel has carefully kept, air-conditioned rooms with terraces or balconies overlooking pretty gardens where breakfast is served on warm days. Outdoor pool.

EAT

⌂ **Le Capitole** – *26 Av. Amiral-Courbet. ✆04 93 61 22 44. Closed Dec.* Only the shelves remain in this former grocery shop, converted to a smart restaurant serving traditional fare.

⌂ **L'Amiral** – *7 Av. Amiral-Courbet. ✆04 93 67 34 61. Closed 8–15 Mar, 1–19 Jul, 29 Nov–6 Dec, Mon.* Small, family-run business providing tasty local cuisine on prettily decorated tables in a modern, friendly setting. If you like couscous, go on Thursday, but book first!

EXCURSIONS

Cap d'Antibes★

10km/6mi. Allow 2hr.
see ANTIBES: Driving tours.

Massif de l'Esterel★★★

96km/60mi. Allow half a day.
See Massif de L'ESTEREL.

Massif du Tanneron★

56km/34.7mi. Allow 1.5hr.
See Massif du TANNERON.

⌂ **Bijou Plage** – *Bd. Guillaumont. ✆04 93 61 39 07. www.bijouplage.com.* Locals and tourists alike flock to this beach restaurant on the road to Golfe-Juan. The menu pays tribute to *bouillabaisse* and other fish dishes. It also has a private beach and water sports facilities.

NIGHTLIFE

Eden Casino – *Bd. Édouard-Baudoin. ✆04 92 93 71 71. www.partouche-casino-juan-les-pins.fr.* Seaside casino with traditional table games and 180 slot machines, restaurant and themed bars.

Le Crystal – *Av. Gallice. ✆04 93 61 02 51. Closed 15 Nov–20 Dec, Mon off season.* First opened in 1936, this was a family brasserie housed in a small hut where sheep would come to graze. Today the popular club is hemmed in between the Casino and a host of other bars and discotheques.

LEISURE ACTIVITIES

Water Sports – Ask at the tourist office about beaches offering water skiing, wind surfing, scuba diving and paragliding.

Visiobulle – Leaves from the Embarcadère Courbet, opposite the Maison du Tourisme. *✆04 93 34 09 96. www.visiobulle.com. Closed Oct–Mar. Booking recommended in Jul and Aug. ⌂12€ (6€ children).* This glass-bottomed boat offers views of the sea depths right up to the tip of Cap d'Antibes, which cannot be reached by land.

Îles de Lérins★★
Alpes Maritime

Surprisingly tranquil despite their proximity to the bustling city of Cannes, the wooded Îles de Lérins offer visitors a fine panorama of the coast from Cap Roux to Cap d'Antibes, and the chance to explore the fortress on Ste-Marguerite and an ancient keep of the old fortified monastery on St-Honorat.

A BIT OF HISTORY
The Island in Antiquity
In ancient times the Île Ste-Marguerite was a Roman port called **Lero**, after a Ligurian hero. Excavations near Fort Royal have uncovered houses, wall paintings, mosaics and ceramics dating 3C BC–1C AD, while various wrecks and port substructures have been found off the coast.

VISITING THE ISLANDS
Île Ste-Marguerite★★
The larger of the two islands, Ste-Marguerite is 3km/2mi long and 900m/1 000yd wide, separated from the mainland by a shallow channel. The island belongs to the State except for the Domaine du Grand Jardin in the south.

Botanical Nature Trail
Many broad paths flanked by explanatory panels on Mediterranean flora cut through the forest to provide charming

- **Michelin Map:** 341 D6.
- **Info:** Palais des Festivals, 1 Bd. de la Croisette, Cannes. ℘04 93 39 24 53. www.cannes-on-line.com.
- **Location:** The islands can be reached by Cannes (*see Practical Information*), or on your own boat (just drop anchor in one of the coves).
- **Timing:** Allow at least half a day to visit both islands.

walks. Starting from the landing, follow the marked trail around the side of the fort. Then join the Eucalyptus Walk, which leads to the Domaine du Grand Jardin, cutting across the length of the island. The Allée Ste-Marguerite returns to the landing.

The cliffs are fairly steep making it difficult to reach the shore, but there is a path that skirts the edge of the entire island *(2hr walk)*.

Fort Royal
Open Tue–Sun Apr–Jun and mid-Sept–Oct 10am–1.15pm, 2.15–5.45pm; mid-Jun–mid-Sept 10am–5.45pm; Nov–Mar 10.30am–1.15pm, 2.15–4.45pm. Closed public holidays. 3.20€; no charge first Sun of the month. ℘04 93 38 55 26. www.cannes.com.

Coastline of Île Ste-Marguerite

PRACTICAL INFORMATION
REACHING THE ISLANDS (FROM CANNES)

To the Île Ste-Marguerite – *Cie Trans Côte d'Azur, Quai Laubeuf, Cannes. ℘04 92 98 71 30. www.trans-cote-azur.com.* Regular shuttle service, 4–8 departures daily depending on the season. Excursions to Monaco, St-Tropez, etc.

To the Île St-Honorat – *Société Planaria, Quai Laubeuf, Cannes. ℘04 92 98 71 38. www.cannes-ilesdelerins.com. ⊗11€ round trip (5.50€ children).* Regular shuttle service throughout the year.

ON THE ISLANDS

On the Île Ste-Marguerite – No hotels, only restaurants and cafés. Visitors are advised to bring food and water supplies for the day.

On the Île St-Honorat – The whole island is occupied by the monastery. A restaurant and boutique are run by the monks. Bicycles are forbidden and tourists are expected to dress appropriately.

The fortress was built by Richelieu and reinforced by Vauban in 1712 with a monumental entrance on the west side. The disgraced Maréchal Bazaine was imprisoned in the building on the left (1873–74) until his escape to Spain. From the terrace there is an extensive **view**★ of the coast. Behind Bazaine's quarters are the prisons and old castle.

Prisons

The entrance hall gives access to the museum *(right)* and the prisons *(left)*. On the right is the cell of the Man in the Iron Mask *(☾see box)*. The cells opposite were occupied by six Protestant pastors, imprisoned after the Revocation of the Edict of Nantes (1685). A Huguenot memorial recalls the Wars of Religion.

Musée de la Mer

The Marine Museum exhibits archaeological finds excavated in the fort and offshore, including a 1C BC Roman galley, 10C Saracen ship, a fine collection of Roman and Arab ceramics. There are also exhibits on pleasure boating and regattas.

Île St-Honorat★★

St-Honorat (1.5km/1mi long, 400m/437yd wide) is the private property of the monastery, but walking and bathing are permitted. Some of the land is culti-

---

The Riddle of the "Iron Mask"

In 1687 the fortress of Ste-Marguerite, a state prison, received the famous "Man in the Iron Mask", a character, who, according to Voltaire, wore a mask with a chinpiece which had steel springs. There are many theories about the identity of this man. He is said to have been an illegitimate brother of Louis XIV, a secretary who had tricked the "Sun King", an accomplice of Madame La Brinvilliers the poisoner, a black page who had an affair with Queen Maria Theresa, and even the son-in-law of a doctor whose autopsy of Louis XIII revealed the king's inability to father a child.

An even wilder theory maintains that a lady companion to the Man in the Iron Mask gave birth to a son who was taken away to Corsica. Entrusted (*remis de bonne part* in French – *di buona parte* in Italian) to foster parents, this child is said to have been called "Buonaparte" and to have been the great-grandfather of Napoleon.

When the man charged with guarding the Man in the Iron Mask obtained the post of Governor of the Bastille in 1698, his prisoner went with him and died there in 1703.

Brotherly Love

In the 4C St Honoratus settled on Lérina, the smaller of the two islands, and founded a monastery which was to become one of the most famous and powerful in all Christendom. Women were banned from the island, so his sister Marguerite set up a convent on the neighbouring island, where Honorat could come see her regularly.

In 660 St Aigulf founded the Benedictine Order in the monastery. Raids by pirates and the arrival of military garrisons were not favourable to monastic life, so by 1788 the monastery was closed. In 1859 the monastery once more became a place of worship and in 1869 it was taken over by Cistercians from Sénanque Abbey.

vated by the monks, who make a liqueur called Lérina, but the rest is covered by a fine forest of umbrella and sea pines, eucalyptus and cypress trees.

Island Tour★★

🚶 *2hr.*

Starting from the landing, an attractive shaded path follows the coastline. Occasionally veering inland, it offers views of the island, its cultivated fields and forest paths, as well as Île Ste-Marguerite and the mainland.

Ancien Monastère Fortifié★

🕐*Open daily Jun–Sept 8am–6pm; Oct–May 8.30am–5pm.* 🎟*2.50€; no charge off season.* 📞*04 92 99 54 00. www.abbayedelerins.com.*
The remarkable high 'keep' of this old fortified monastery on the southern coastline was built in 1073 by the Abbot of Lérins to protect the monks from Saracen pirates. The **cloisters** with pointed arches and the 14C and 17C vaulting (one of the columns is a Roman milestone) enclosesquare courtyard covering a rainwater tank paved with marble. The upper gallery houses the chapel of the Ste-Croix. From the platform with its 15C battlements and crenellations is a **view**★★ extending over the coastline.

Monastère Moderne

Only the church is open to the public.
🕐*Open daily 8.30am–6pm.*
🎟*No charge.* 📞*04 92 99 54 00. www.abbayedelerins.com.*

The early buildings (11C–12C) occupied by the monks have been incorporated into the "new" 19C monastery. Seven ancient **chapels** scattered about the island were used by anchorites, monks who prayed in the privacy of their retreat. Two have retained their former appearance, **La Trinité**, situated to the east, and **St-Sauveur** in the northwest.

ADDRESSES

🍴 EAT

🍽🍷 **L'Escale** – *Ste-Marguerite (Island).* 📞*04 93 43 49 25. Closed Oct–Mar, eves Jul–Aug.* Views of Cannes and the Cap d'Antibes from this enchanting restaurant and its long beachfront terrace. Buffet and seafood platters.

🍽🍷 **La Tonnelle** – *St-Honorat (Island).* 📞*04 92 99 18 07. www.tonnelle-abbaye delerins.com.* Views of Ile Ste-Marguerite from the large terrace (heated in winter) of this new-ish opened restaurant. Gourmet French cuisine and snacks accompanied by wines and liqueurs made on the island.

🛒 SHOPPING

CISTERCIAN SOUVENIRS
Boutique de l'Abbaye de Lérins – *Île St-Honorat.* 📞*04 92 99 54 00. www.abbayedelerins.com. Closed early Nov–Dec.* This shop attached to the Cistercian abbey sells wine, honey, lavandin and the famous liqueur *Lérina*.

Vallée du Loup★★

Alpes Maritimes

The Loup begins at an altitude of 1 300m/4 250ft in the Pre-Alps of Grasse. The gorge it cuts through the mountains on its journey to the Mediterranean is one of the most beautiful natural sights of Haute-Provence, framed by several picturesque perched villages.

> 🕭 **Michelin Map:** 341 C/D5/6.
> ▷ **Location:** In following the Loup, you'll pass through countryside dominated by orchards of olive, then citrus trees, and finally even snow-capped peaks. These driving tours, starting from Vence (🕭*see VENCE*), lead you through both the high and low valleys of the scenic river.

🚗 DRIVING TOURS

Gorges du Loup★★

56km/35mi – allow one day. From Vence take D 2210 northwest. 🕭*See map p225.*

Tourrettes-sur-Loup★

🛈 *5 Rte. de Vence.* ✆*04 93 24 18 93.* *www.tourrettessurloup.com.*

🅿 *Park outside the village and follow the pavement to the central square.*

This is violet country, where the flowers are cultivated under the olive trees. The fortified village stands on a rock plateau above a sheer drop, with its outer houses forming the rampart. It is also a lively arts and crafts centre.

Old Village★

Enter this medieval village through the belfry gate in the south corner of the main square and follow the Grande Rue, a steep, paved street lined with shops where artisans can be seen plying their trade. It leads to the old walls, with superb views of the surrounding landscape. Walk up the other side and re-enter the square.

At Place de la Libération stands a **church** with a 15C nave. Behind the high altar stands a Gallo-Roman altar.

Chapelle St-Jean

🕙*Open Apr–Sept.* ✆*04 93 24 18 93.* This chapel was decorated in 1959 with naïve frescoes. On the far wall are John the Baptist and St John the Divine, symbolising the link between the Old and New Testaments.

The road loops round the attractive village of Tourrettes-sur-Loup before passing the limestone fissures of the Loup Valley. The perched village of **Bar-sur-Loup**★ (🕭*see overleaf*) comes into sight, followed by the tiny hamlet of **Gourdon** (🕭*see GOURDON*) clinging to its promontory.

Pont-du-Loup

The Draguignan–Nice railway line, which crossed the entrance to the Gorges du Loup, was blown up by the Germans in 1944; the viaduct ruins are still visible.

▷ *Exit the village, turn right onto D 6.*

The road runs through the splendid **Gorges du Loup**★★, cut vertically through the Grasse mountains, with huge, gaping holes, smooth and round, hollowed out of their sides. Just before the second tunnel, in a semicircular hollow, the **Cascade de Courmes**★ spills down onto a mossy bed (40m/130ft).

▷ *Park your car after the third tunnel.*

Saut du Loup

🕙*Open Jul–Oct daily 10am–7pm.* ☞*1€.* ✆*04 93 09 68 88. www.cascade-sautduloup.com. Restaurant, snack bar.* Amid lush vegetation, a huge megalith marks the entrance to the Saut du Loup, an enormous cauldron shaped by prehistoric marine and glacial erosion. The **Cascades des Demoiselles** waterfall

Gorges of the Vallée des Loups

B. Kaufmann / MICHELIN

gushes down through a strange setting of petrified vegetation.

▷ *Just before the bridge, Pont de Bramafan, take a sharp left onto D 3.*

As the road rises to Caussols Plateau there are continual **views**★ down into the depths of the gorges with a particularly breathtaking **view**★★ where an overhang has been built out from a sharp right-hand turn *(signposted)*.

Le Bar-sur-Loup★

🛈 *Pl. F.-Paulet.* ℘*04 93 42 72 21. www.lebarsurloup.fr.* 🅿 *Park at Place des Carteyrades, near the tourist office.*
Nestled between the River Loup and its tributaries, Le Bar enjoys a privileged hillside **site**★ surrounded by terraced orange trees, jasmine and violets. The tranquil medieval village features a well-preserved castle dungeon and significant religious artworks.
The narrow streets of the old town, winding round the massive 16C castle with its four corner towers and ruined keep, are best visited on foot.

Église St-Jacques le Majeur

👁 *Closed indefinitely for restoration work.*
Embedded in the stonework at the foot of the bell tower is a Roman tombstone.

Gourdon★

👁*See GOURDON.*
Interesting drive downhill from Caussols plateau along D 3.

La Colle-sur-Loup

A picturesque village in the plain where fruit and flowers are cultivated. The main street shops sell Provençal antiques.

St-Paul-de-Vence★★

👁*See ST-PAUL-DE-VENCE.*
Beyond St-Paul the **view** extends to the foothills of the Pre-Alps of Grasse.

▷ *Return to Vence by D 2 and D 236.*

Haute Vallée du Loup★

47km/29mi – about 2hr.
Leave Vence by D 2 going northwest.
The road descends a green valley and from the Pont de Bramafan, the D 3 suddenly emerges into the **upper Loup Valley**★, a beautiful stretch of country with superb views both before and after Gréolières.

Gréolières

This is a perched village at the southern foot of Mont Cheiron; to the north are the extensive ruins of Haut-Gréolières. To the south are the remains of an important stronghold.
The **church**, which has only one aisle, has a Romanesque façade and a squat bell tower. On the left *(upon entering)* stands a 15C silver-gilt processional cross and a fragment of a 16C retable of John the Baptist. Opposite stands a 14C wooden statue of the Virgin and Child. The finest work (high on the right) is the **retable of St Stephen**★ by an unknown artist with Christ and his Apostles on the predella (15C).
West of Gréolières the road climbs above the village and then snakes westward along the side of the gorge passing in and out of brief tunnels and beneath huge rock spurs of fantastic shapes and sizes. More than 400m/1 312ft below flows the River Loup.

Clue de Gréolières★
Popular with canyoners, the rift was formed by a tributary of the Loup, its bare slopes pitted with giant holes and spiked with curious dolomitic rocks. The road emerges from the rift onto a broad plateau, Plan-du-Peyron.

▶ *In Plan-du-Peyron turn right onto D 802, a road flanking Mont Cheiron.*

Gréolières-les-Neiges
Alt 1 450m/4 757ft. 🚠 *Ski-lift,* ☏*04 93 59 70 02.*
The resort, which lies on the north face of Mont Cheiron, is the most southerly of the Alpine ski stations. It is welll equipped (14 lifts, 25 runs, 30km/18.6mi of cross-country trails), easily accessible and attracts crowds of local skiers.

▶ *Drive back via Col de Vence (♿ see VENCE: Excursions) or via the Gorges du Loup.*

ADDRESSES

🏨 STAY

🛏 **Auberge de Courmes** – *3 Rue des Platanes, Courmes.* ☏*04 93 77 64 70. aubergedecourmes.com. 5 rooms.* 🍴. *6€. Restaurant*🍴🛏. This recently renovated local inn on the square of a tiny hamlet dominating the Loup Gorges offers five small rooms and a welcoming dining area. Outstanding views of the mountains, facilities for hiking and rambling and a peaceful atmosphere.

🛏 **Chambre d'Hôte La Cascade** – *635 Chemin de la Cascade, Courmes.* ☏*04 93 09 65 85. www.gitedelacascade.com. 6 rooms.* 🏊. *Meal* 🛏. Guest house with swimming pool near the waterfall of Courmes. The original building, now enlarged and restored, has six tidy rooms particularly suitable for nature lovers and WiFi.

🛏🍴🏊 **Chambre d'Hôte Mas des Cigales** – *1673 Rte. des Quenières, 2km/ 1mi from Tourrettes, Rte. de St-Jean.* ☏*04 93 59 25 73. www.lemasdescigales.com. 5 rooms.* 🍴. Handsome villa surrounded by a leafy garden. From the terrace running alongside the pool, you can look down onto a small waterfall, a tennis court and, in the far distance, the sea. Air conditioned rooms are charmingly decorated.

🍽 EAT

🛏🍴 **Le Médiéval** – *6 Grand Rue, Tourettes.* ☏*04 93 59 31 63. Closed 15 Dec–15, Wed–Thu, eves Nov–Mar.* While strolling the charming village streets

you'll find this family-run restaurant with the rustic dining room. Traditional, hearty French cooking without surprises nor big prices.

🍴🏊🍴 **La Jarrerie** – *8 Avenue Amiral-de-Grasse, Le Bar-sur-Loup.* ☏*04 93 42 92 92. www.restaurant-la-jarrerie.com. Closed Jan, Wed lunch, Tue.* Housed in a wing of a former 17C monastery, this restaurant provides first-rate cuisine in a majestic setting: visible beams, huge fireplace, stone masonry. Large reception hall and a pleasantly shaded summer terrace.

🛒 SHOPPING

Confiserie des Gorges du Loup (Florian) – *Pont-du-Loup. www.confi-serieflorian.com. Guided visit of the sweet manufacturing 9am–noon, 2–6.30pm (0am–6.30pm in summer). Boutique open noon–2pm.* Candied fruits, citrus jams, sugared flowers and preserves made with rose, jasmine, violet and chocolate, all made on site.

CALENDAR
Fête de l'Oranger – Every Easter Monday the villagers celebrate the annual orange blossom harvest, with plenty of *vin d'orange*.

Fête des Violettes, Tourettes – Every first or second week in March (according to the flowering season), a two-day festival with a Provençal market, tours of the flower fields, and a huge violet parade through the village.

Mandelieu-la-Napoule

Alpes Maritimes

In the Middle Ages, Mandelieu was a small fishing harbour called Epulia, but today it is famed throughout the region for its lovely mimosa trees. The pretty bay and the River Siagne, bordered by lush plains and beaches further downstream, make this town a highly popular resort year round.

THE SEASIDE

Three scenic beaches (of which two are private) run along the bay, offering impressive views of the area.

The Port La Napoule can accommodate 1 140 pleasure craft, while the smaller Port de la Rague has 688 moorings.

A coastal path *(1km/0.6mi)* connects the two.

Panoramic Tour★

Leave from the post office by Rue des Hautes-Roches. 45min round trip.

This pleasant walk winding its way up Colline de San Peyré affords fantastic views★ over the Tanneron, La Napoule Bay, Cannes and Cap d'Antibes.

Along the Siagne

A trail follows the River Siagne from the centre of Mandelieu *(behind the Salle Olympie)* all the way to the sea.

▶ **Population:** 20 200.

Michelin Map: 341 C6; local map: *see Massif de l'ESTEREL.*

Info: 340 Rue Jean-Monnet. ☎04 992 97 99 27. www.ot-mandelieu.fr.

▶ **Location:** Lying at the foot of the Esterel and Tanneron Massifs, Mandelieu sits on the coast 8km/5mi west of Cannes on the N 98.

Parking: There are several free parking areas near the casino and along the coastline in La Napoule.

SIGHT

Château-Musée

Av. Henry-Clews, La Napoule.
Open Mon–Fri Feb–Nov 10am–6pm; Nov–Jan 2–5pm, Sat–Sun and public holidays 10am–5pm. Guided tours (45min) ⊚6€. ☎04 93 49 95 05. www.chateau-lanapoule.com.

Only two towers remain of the original 14C stronghold converted by the American sculptor Henry Clews and his wife, who was an architect. Located in an outstanding **site**★ at the foot of the Esterel corniche, the château offers a curious blend of Romanesque and Gothic styles enhanced by Oriental-like decoration. The public can visit the beautiful grounds, the salons, the cloisters and Henry Clews' studio.

ADDRESSES

🏠 STAY

⊖ **Corniche d'Or** – *Pl. de la Fontaine, La Napoule. ☎04 93 49 92 51. www.cornichedor.com. Closed Nov 29-Dec 16. 12 rooms. � 8€.* On a tiny square near the station, this modest hotel has simple rooms. Many have a small balcony, and two have a large terrace.

⊖ **Hôtel Villa Parisiana** – *Rue Argentière. ☎04 93 49 93 02. www.villaparisiana.com. 13 rooms. ⊆ 6.50€.* This Edwardian villa located in a residential area houses a congenial, family-style hotel with a treillised terrace, for a pleasant stay despite the proximity of the noisy railway.

🍴 EAT

⊖⊖⊖ **Le Marco Polo** – *Av. de Lérins, Théoule-sur-Mer. ☎04 93 49 96 59. Closed mid-Nov to mid-Dec, Mon off season.* Casual restaurant ideally situated on the beach, with rattan furniture and a terrace overlooking the Bay of Cannes. Salads at lunch, hearty dinner menus.

⭐ SHOPPING

MARKETS
Mandelieu – Place du Mail, Wednesday and Friday mornings.

La Napoule – Place St-Fainéant Thursday morning, and Place Jeanne-d'Arc on Saturday morning.

🏃 SPORT AND LEISURE

Domaine de Barbossi – 3300 Av. Paul-Ricard, San Estello. ☎04 93 49 64 74. A perfect outing for the whole family. Besides the tennis club, there are facilities for mountain biking, trampoline, miniature golf, pony rides and several playing areas for children. Red and rosé wines, produced and bottled on the estate, are available for sale.

Golf de Cannes-Mandelieu Riviera – Av. des Amazones. ☎04 92 97 49 49. An 18-hole golf course at the foot of the Esterel, with putting green and driving range. Club house restaurant.

CASINO

Pullman Cannes Mandelieu Royal Casino – 605 Av. du Général-de-Gaulle. ☎04 92 97 70 00. www.sofitel.com. Bar Blue-wave: 9am–2am. Piano bar: 7.30–10.30pm. Bar dancing: Sat–Sun 10.30pm–3am. Luxury establishment with a terrace and pool overlooking Cannes Bay features a casino, two restaurants, a nightclub and a piano bar with live music nightly.

CALENDAR

La Fête du Mimosa – Beginning of February. Ten-day festival and parade celebrating the mimosa blossoms.

Les Nuits du Château – In July and August the Cour d'Honneur hosts a summer festival of dance, concerts and theatre.

Mougins⭐

Alpes Maritimes

The old village of Mougins dominates the summit of a hilltop crowned by ancient ramparts and a 12C fortified entrance (known as the "Saracen Gate"). Restored houses and cobblestone streets corkscrew up the hill amidst lush greenery.

SIGHTS

Begin at **Place du Commandant-Lamy** *(map with commentary available at the tourist office)*, a festive square where restaurants and an ancient fountain are shaded by a giant elm.
Wander northwest, turn left towards **Place des Patriotes** which has a beautiful panoramic **view**⭐ over the coast *(orientation table)*.

Espace Culturel

Pl. du Commandant-Lamy. ◷Open Dec–Oct Mon–Fri 9am–5pm, Sat–Sun 11am–6pm. ◷Closed public holidays. ✎No charge. ☎04 92 92 50 42.

▸ **Population:** 19 361.
◔ **Michelin Map:** 341 C6.
🛈 **Info:** 15 Av. Ch-Malet. ☎04 93 75 87 67. www.mougins-coteazur.org.
◔ **Location:** Mougins lies between Cannes (6km/3.7mi) and Grasse (11km/7mi) on the N 85. The vestiges of the old ramparts, which date back to the town's fiefdom under the Lérins Abbots, mark the limits of the pedestrian-only Old Town.
🅿 **Parking:** Several parking areas can be found at the foot of the Old Town.

This former Chapel St-Bernardin of the White Peninents now houses the town hall, the Salle des Mariages, and the **Musée Maurice Gotlobb** (1885–1970), an artist who lived in Mougins from 1924–60. There is also an interesting retrospective of the history of Mou-

Village of Mougins

gins, including a section on the African explorer **Commandant Lamy**, born here in 1858.

Musée de la Photographie

Porte Sarrazine. ⊙*Open Jul–Aug daily 10am–8pm; Sept–Oct and Dec–Jun Mon–Fri 10am–6pm, Sat–Sun 11am–6pm.* ⊠*No charge.* ℘*04 93 75 85 67.* Located behind the church bell tower, this photography museum, on three floors, includes a lovely collection of old cameras, such as the **cidoscope**, numerous photographs of Picasso by his friend André Villers, and works by famous photographers such as Clergue, Doisneau, Duncan, Lartigue, Roth, Otero, Denise Colomb and Ralph Gatti.

EXCURSIONS
Ermitage Notre-Dame-de-Vie

6km/3.7mi east of Mougins by D 235 going northwest and D 35 east; after 2km/1mi turn right. ⊙*Open during Mass Sun mornings, 9am.*
The **site**★ is strikingly beautiful: the **hermitage** of Notre-Dame-de-Vie stands at the top of a long meadow bordered by

two rows of giant cypresses (on the right beneath the trees stands a 15C stone cross). The **view**★ towards Mougins is reminiscent of a Tuscan landscape. Picasso chose to spend his last years here, in the house just opposite.
The 17C **chapel**, roofed in colourful tiles, has three Gallo-Roman funeral inscriptions, and a collection of votive offerings.

▶ *A track suitable for motor vehicles leads to the D 3, which takes you back to Mougins.*

Étang de Fontmerle

▶ *3km/2mi by the D 35 towards the golf course, then at the round about take avenue de Grasse, and then turn right on the Promenade de l'Étang.*

This large pond was neglected for many years until it became a protected site for lotus flower cultivation, now the largest in Europe. See the flowers in bloom July to mid-September.

The Minotaur's Lair

As early as 1935 **Pablo Picasso** discovered Mougins in the company of Dora Marr and the photographer Man Ray. He and his wife Jacqueline settled in Mougins in 1961 and remained there until his death in 1973. They lived in the Notre-Dame-de-Vie district in the *mas* called L'Antre du Minotaure (The Minotaur's Lair), which became a creative workshop for artists.

Musée de l'Automobiliste★
5km/3mi southeast

▶ *From Mougins take D 234 northwest; turn right onto D 3 towards Cannes. Just before the motorway turn left onto Chemin du Belvédère, which becomes Chemin des Collines. At the second junction turn left onto Chemin de Ferrandou, then left again to cross over the motorway. Turn right onto Chemin de Font-de-Currault, which leads to the museum car park. The Car Museum is located next to the Aire Nord des Bréguières (service area on the north side) of motorway A 8; it can also be reached via the footbridge from the service area on the south side.*

🕐*Open Dec–Oct daily 10am–1pm, 2–6pm.* 🕐*Closed public holidays.* ⊘7€ (under 12s free). 𝄢04 93 69 27 80.
The concrete and glass façade of the futuristic building beside the motorway resembles a radiator. Two motoring enthusiasts, Adrien Maeght and Antoine Raffaelli have gathered a collection of vintage cars and more recent models, which are shown in rotation (about 90 at a time). All the famous makes in the gleaming display are in perfect working order: Benz (first serial model 1894), Bugatti (57, 1938), Ferrari, Hispano-Suiza, Delage, and Rolls Royce. The section devoted to racing cars, some of which have won Grand Prix competitions, contains a series of Matras from the years 1967 to 1974.

Mouans-Sartoux
3km/2mi northwest on the N 2085.
This town is made up of the medieval village of Sartoux, ruined by the Saracens, and the ancient fortress of Mouans that once protected the Route de Grasse. In 1588, Suzanne de Villeneuve, widow of a Huguenot, defended her village against the troops of the Duke of Savoy. After he razed the château despite a pact signed between then, Suzanne had him chased all the way to Cagnes, where he was forced to pay heavy reparations.

Espace de l'Art Concret★★
Château de Mouans. 🕐*Open daily Jul–Aug 11am–7pm, Sept–Jun Tue–Sun noon–6pm.* ⊘5€ *(no charge for temporary exhibitions).* 𝄢04 93 75 71 50. *www.espacedelartconcret.fr.*
In a pretty park, the 19C Château de Mouans hosts temporary contemporary art expositions as well as the **Albers-Honegger Collection** in a green-yellow concrete cube building on the premises. An exceptional collection of Abstract, Cubist, Minimalist and design arts.

ADDRESSES

🛏 STAY
😊😊 **Hôtel du Val de Mougins** – *95 Av. du Marechal-Juin.* 𝄢04 92 28 37 77. *www. val-de-mougins.com. 23 rooms.* �œ7.50€.
This family-run establishment on the Route Napoléon, at the foot of Old Mougins, has air-conditioned rooms decorated with pretty linens, many with balconies. The quietest rooms face the mountain behind the hotel.

🍴 EAT
😊 **La Broche de Fer** – *427 Av. St-Basile, Rte. de Valbonne.* 𝄢04 92 92 08 08. *www. labrochedefer.com Closed mid–end Feb, Oct 22–Nov 6 and Wed.* On the route towards Valbonne, this restaurant on four levels has been charmingly decorated in the true Provençal spirit. Main specialities are grilled and roast meats.

😊😊 **L'Amandier de Mougins** –*Pl. du Vieux Village.* 𝄢04 93 90 00 91. *www. amandier.fr. Closed 15–26 Nov.*
A 14C press has been converted into a ravishing inn with a vaulted dining area and a tiny terrace that is invariably booked for both lunch and dinner. It has earned a well-deserved reputation thanks to its attractive setting, its homey cooking and its warm, congenial welcome.

😊😊 **Brasserie de la Méditerranée** – *Pl. du Vieux Village.* 𝄢04 93 90 03 47. *Closed 4–20 Jan, Tue Nov–Mar.* This bistro on the village square has a fine terrace overlooking the main street. The menu presents Provençal specialities made with fresh local produce.

St-Paul-de-Vence★★

Alpes Maritimes

From afar, the first view of St-Paul-de-Vence looks like a bucolic film set, the epitome of the fortified towns that once guarded the Var frontier. Perched on a rocky spur behind well-preserved ramparts, it has kept much of its medieval appearance, while becoming one of the most visited villages in France for its contemporary art scene.

WALKING TOUR
MEDIEVAL ALLEYS
Rue Grande

Rue Grande is the main street *(closed to traffic)* running the full length of the village. Many of the arcaded 16C and 17C houses bearing coats of arms are now artists' studios, antique shops, and art galleries. Don't miss the urn-shaped **fountain** in the square with its vaulted washing place.

> *Climb up the stepped street above the fountain. Take the first right and then the first left to the church.*

Church

This 12C Gothic building with 17C vaulting and an 18C bell tower has a painting attributed to Tintoretto of Ste Catherine of Alexandria, 17C choir stalls in carved walnut, and a chapel adorned with a Madonna of the Rosary (1588) with Catherine de' Medici in the crowd. The **treasury** is rich in 12C to 15C pieces: statuettes, processional cross, reliquar-

- ▶ **Population:** 3 336.
- ⟳ **Michelin Map:** 341 D5.
- ▤ **Info:** Maison de la Tour, Rue Grande. ℘04 93 32 86 95. www.saint-paul devence.com.
- ▶ **Location:** The village is 4km/2.5mi south of Vence on the D 2. Enter through the north gate. A square machicolated tower houses the tourist office *(Syndicat d'Initiative),* together with a permanent exhibition of modern paintings. In high season the narrow streets of the village are completely packed with pedestrian tourists.
- ⓟ **Parking:** Park the car in one of the car parks provided at the entrance to the village, before passing through the north gate.

ies, a 13C enamel Virgin and Child, and a parchment signed by King Henri III.

Donjon

The **keep** opposite the church currently houses the town hall.

> *Return to Rue Grande and continue down to the south gate.*

Ramparts★

From the bastion of the south gate, overlooking the cemetery, there is a superb **view** of the Alps and the coastline. The ramparts remain much

---

Illustrious Visitors

After a period of prosperity in the Middle Ages, the village declined in the 19C to the benefit of Vence and Cagnes. It was "rediscovered" in the 1920s by painters such as Signac, Modigliani, Bonnard and Soutine who used to meet in a café, which has since become the sumptuous Auberge de la Colombe d'Or, its walls covered with paintings as in a gallery. Other artists were to follow suit – sculptors, illustrators, writers and entertainers – making St-Paul a famous Riviera landmark. The village was once a great favourite among celebrities from the silver screen, such as the couple Simone Signoret and Yves Montand.

View of the town

S. Sauvignier/ MICHELIN

as they were when built (1537–47) by François I. Follow them around counter-clockwise using the parapet walk where possible.

SIGHTS
Fondation Maeght★
Chemin des Fumerates. Permanent collection closed during temporary exhibitions. ⏲*Open daily Oct–Jun 10am–6pm; Jul–Sept 10am–7pm.* ◉*11€.* ☎*04 93 32 81 63. www.fondation-maeght.com.*
This modern art museum located northwest of St-Paul was designed by **José Luis Sert** in true Mediterranean style using white concrete and rose-coloured bricks. Its two buildings divided by a court adorned with sculptures by Giacometti house a collection of modern art exhibited in rotation. Works by Braque, Chagall, Léger, Kandinsky, Miró, Giacometti, Bonnard, Hartung, and Alechinsky, as well as works by artists of a younger generation (Adami, Garache, Messagier, Viallat).

Musée d'Histoire Locale
Pl. de l'Eglise. ⏲*Open Dec–Oct Wed–Sat and Mon10am–noon, 2–5pm.* ◉*3€.* ☎*04 93 32 41 13.*
Eight illustrated scenes with life-size figures depict the stages marking the village's history, which often mirror those of Provence itself, from the arrival of the Count of Provence, Raimond Bérenger V, in St-Paul in 1224. An exhibition of photographs of famous people who have stayed in St-Paul adds a contemporary note to this historical display.

ADDRESSES

🛏 STAY
⊜⊜ **Les Bastides de St-Paul** – *880 chemin Blanquières, D 336.* ☎*04 92 02 08 07. www.bastides.fr.fm.* 🅿. *20 rooms.* ⊑*10€.* Set just off a main road, this colourful farmhouse inn has spacious, soundproofed rooms. In the garden is a shamrock-shaped swimming pool.

⊜⊜ **Hostellerie des Messugues** – *Quartier des Gardettes, by Route de la Fondation Maeght 2km/1mi.* ☎*04 93 32 53 32. www.messugues.com. Closed Nov-Easter.* 🅿. *15 rooms.* ⊑*12€.* Just below the Maeght Foundation, in a lush and peaceful garden, lies this big Provençal villa surrounded by vines. The upstairs rooms are larger and slightly more comfortable. Do not miss the heated pool and its small island.

🍴 EAT
⊜ **Chez Andréas** – *Western ramparts.* ☎*04 93 32 98 32.* Settle on the delightful terrace of this restaurant and sip a *pastis* as you admire the setting rays of the sun. A tastefully decorated dining room, with salads, the day's special and a choice of local wines.

⊜ **La Cocarde de Saint Paul** – *23 Rue Grande.* ☎*04 93 32 86 17.* In the main street at the heart of St-Paul, this restaurant-tea shop will seduce you by its artful blend of Mediterranean colours. Excellent cuisine and homemade pastries.

⊜⊜ **La Ferme de St-Paul** – *1334 Route de la Colle.* ☎*04 93 32 82 48. Closed 31 Oct–26 Dec.* Tastefully restored old farmhouse boasting a superb decor: Provençal overtones, wooden beams, mahogany furniture, wrought-iron accessories and fine crockery. Quality cooking and interesting menu, where fish takes pride of place. Charming terrace and antique shop.

Café de la Place – *Pl. du Général-de-Gaulle.* ☎*04 93 32 80 03. Closed Nov–Dec.* This café, set up on the main square where villagers like to congregate and play pétanque, is at the heart of life in St-Paul. It belongs to the legendary Colombe d'Or Hotel *(located opposite)*, once the property of the actor Yves Montand.

🛒 SHOPPING

MARKETS
Marché d'Yvette – Fruit and vegetable market every Tuesday, Thursday, Saturday and Sunday beneath the wash-house at the village entrance

Flower Market – Fresh flowers beneath the wash-house at the village entrance, every Saturday morning.

Regional Products – Provençal market on Place de Gaulle every Wednesday morning.

🏃 LEISURE
Walking itineraries– The tourist office has a map of four self-guided walking and hiking itineraries of the old town and nearby historical sites.

Massif du Tanneron ★
Alpes Maritimes

Far from the beaten path and yet easily accessible from Cannes, the Massif du Tanneron lies to the north of the Esterel, with the rounded contours and rock formations characteristic of the Maures. From mid-January to March, the countryside is covered in brilliant displays of yellow mimosas.

⬡ **Michelin Map:** 341 C6.
◗ **Location:** Situated halfway between the Lac de St-Cassien and La Siagne, the Massif du Tanneron is separated from the Esterel to the north by a valley through which the N 7 and Provençal motorway run.

🚗 DRIVING TOUR

From Cannes to Mandelieu
56km/35mi – allow half a day.

◗ *From Cannes take N 7 west towards Fréjus. For a description of the route as far as the Logis-de-Paris crossroads* ⬡*see* 2 *Massif de l'ESTEREL.*

Then turn right onto D 237 which offers **views** of La Napoule Bay and Mont Vinaigre. Beyond Les Adrets de l'Esterel the view extends to the Pre-Alps of Grasse. The road crosses the Provençal motorway before skirting St-Cassien Lake.

Lac de St-Cassien

◗ *Turn right onto D 38.*

The road rises through a pine wood with **glimpses** of the lake, the dam and the mountain peaks on the horizon. Near the hamlet of Les Marjoris the road winds over mimosa-clad slopes down to the River Verrerie.

◗ *Before reaching Tanneron village, turn right onto a steep narrow road.*

Mellow Yellow

The Mimosa tree was introduced into the Mediterranean region from Australia in 1839, and has since invaded the slopes of the Tanneron Massif and brought financial success to the region. There are three main varieties. Silver wattle *(mimosa argenté)* has bluish-green bushes that blossom in winter and can be seen thriving on the terraces west of Cannes; indeed the small trees are cultivated and the bright yellow flowers sold both in France and abroad; blue-leaved wattle *(mimosa glauque)* is characterised by its greyish pendant twigs and is used for decorative purposes; thirdly, the most common variety in Provence is four-seasons wattle *(mimosa des quatre saisons)*, which grows in huge swathes and flowers all year round. The leaves are light green and the delicately fragrant pale yellow balls are a familiar sight in many parks and gardens of the Riviera.

Chapelle Notre-Dame-de-Peygros★
Alt 412m/1 352ft.
From the terrace of the Romanesque chapel, there is a fine **panorama**★ of the Lac de St-Cassien and Grasse.

◇ *Turn left after passing Tanneron.*

Auribeau-sur-Siagne★

◇ *7km/4.3mi – leaving from the Val-Cros crossroads (alt 296m/971ft).*

A twisting road between banks of mimosa leads up to the charming 12C village. Pass under the 16C Porte Soubran gateway and stroll through the stepped, narrow streets. The old houses huddle around the **church** which contains a 15C silver-gilt and enameled reliquary and a 16C chalice. From the church square the **view** encompasses the Siagne Valley, Grasse and its ring of mountains. Take the stepped streets (Degrés de l'Église and Degrés Soubran) leading to Porte Soutran, the fortified gateway.

◇ *Return to the D 9 (towards Pegomas), then the D 109 towards Mandelieu-la-Napoule. the D 309 towards Tanneron, and go left onto the D 138.*

Road to Mandelieu★★
The drive through the mimosa down a steep hill to Mandelieu-la-Napoule has **views**★★ of the Esterel, La Napoule Bay, Cannes and the Îles des Lérins, the Siagne Valley, Grasse and the Pre-Alps.

◇ *Return to Cannes by D 92 and N 98 along the seafront.*

ADDRESSES

⌂ STAY

◇ **Auberge de Nossi-Bé** – *66 Rte. du Village, Auribeau-sur-Siagne. ℘04 93 42 20 20. www.nossi-be.net. Closed Nov, Tue. 6 rooms. ⊊ 7.50€. Restaurant⊝⊝.* Appealing stone house with a terrace commanding superb views of the valley and wooded heights near La Siagne. Smallish but well-kept rooms in the rustic tradition. French cuisine.

⌂ SHOPPING

Vial Bernard – *Les Carreiros, Tanneron. ℘04 93 60 66 32.* This honey producer's domaine, surrounded by 10ha/25acres of mimosa, eucalyptus, and citrus trees, has hives on site, in the Mercantour and in the Alps. Honey can be tasted and purchased on the premises. Other honey/wax products also for sale.

HIKING
The Grand Duc forest has three hiking trails beginning at the picnic area. *Information available from the tourist office in Mandelieu.*

Valbonne

Alpes Maritimes

This *vallis bona*, or "happy valley" has been occupied since Antiquity, the village growing from what was once an abbey. Today its tidy grid of picturesque streets, lovingly restored, is home to art galleries and chic boutiques. A colourful Provençal market takes place every Friday morning.

SIGHTS
Old Village

Map available at the tourist office.
The village was reconstructed by the Lérins monks in the 16C, with the houses serving as the raparts. The **main square** with its 15C–17C arcading and old elm trees is an attractive backdrop to the lively cafés and restaurants.

Church

South of the village on the Brague River.
In 1199 the Chalais Order founded an abbey, which is now the parish church. Its form of a Latin cross with a square chevet is typical of the austere Chalais buildings. The abbey houses an interesting **Musée du Patrimoine** (⚬*open Tue–Sun Jun–Sept 3–7pm; Oct–May 2–6pm; ⚬2€; ℘04 93 12 96 54; www. abbyvalb.org*) that enlightens visitors on the area's heritage with tools, costumes, a reconstituted kitchen and bedroom.

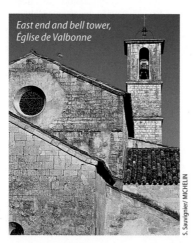

East end and bell tower, Église de Valbonne

S. Sauvignier/ MICHELIN

- **Population:** 12 114.
- **Michelin Map:** 341 D6.
- **Info:** 1 Pl. de l'Hôtel-de-Ville. ℘04 93 12 34 50. www.tourisme-valbonne.com.
- **Location:** Valbonne is situated between Grasse (11.5km/7mi) and Biot (9km/5.6mi) on the D 4.
- **Parking:** The village itself is a pedestrian zone, with several large free-parking areas to the west and south of the town.

ADDRESSES

⌂ STAY

⚬⚬ **Château de la Bégude** – *Opio, 2km/1mi northeast of Valbonne by Rte de Biot. ℘04 93 12 37 00. www.opengolfclub. com/begude. Closed 16 Nov–19 Dec. 35 rooms. ⚬. ⚬19€. Restaurant ⚬⚬.* A luxurious 17C manor with pool on the site of the Opio-Valbonne golf course. It combines the pleasures of old stone with the modern conveniences of the 21C. The restaurant is also used as a club-house and bar for golfers.

⌂ EAT

⚬⚬ **Auberge Fleurie** – *Rte. de Cannes, 1.5km/0.6mi by the D 3. ℘04 93 12 02 80. Closed 6 Dec–12 Jan, Mon–Tue.* Choose between the dining room or the outdoor veranda to enjoy the generous helpings of imaginative and carefully prepared cuisine with dishes such as duck pâté with aubergines (eggplant).

FOREST HIKES
⚬ *9km/5.6mi.*
A scenic, wooded path runs along the Brague River between Valbonne and Biot village, accessible from the bridge by the church. The Parc Valmasque, accessible from the Sophia-Antipolis Technology Park has 20km/12.4mi of trails under the pines.

Vallauris
Alpes Maritimes

The traditional craft of pottery in this 16C village was in decline when Picasso gave it a new breath of life, transforming it into an internationally recognised ceramics centre.

SIGHTS
Château-Museum★
Pl. de la Libération. ◷*Open Wed–Mon 10am–noon, 2–6pm (winter until 5pm).* ⊛*3.25€.* ✆*04 93 64 16 05.* *www.vallauris-golfe-juan.fr.*

A rare example of Renaissance architecture in Provence, this former Lérins priory with pepper-pot towers houses three museums. The Romanesque chapel of the former priory was decorated in 1952 by Picasso with the composition, *War and Peace.*

The **Musée de la Céramic** is one of the rare ones in France to display collections of contemporary cermics, including works by Picasso (plates, dishes, vases), traditional Vallauris ceramics, Art Nouveau, Art Deco and 1950s creations.

The **Magnelli Beques**t is devoted to the Florentine artist **Alberto Magnelli** (1888–1971), who spent most of his life in France.

Musée de la Poterie et de la Céramique
21 Rue Sicard. ♿◷*Open May-Oct 9am–6pm, Sun and holidays 2–6pm; Feb-Apr 2–6pm.* ⊛*2€.* ✆*04 93 64 66 51.*

Located in a working pottery studio, this museum shows how clay was worked in the first half of the 20C. In the neighbouring streets are pottery shops and workshops *(ateliers de céramique).*

Espace Jean-Marais
3 Av. des Martyrs-de-la-Résistance. ♿◷*Open Jul–Aug daily 10am–12.30pm, 2–6.30pm; Sept–Jun Tue–Sat l0am–12.30pm, 2–5.30pm.* ⊛*1.50€.* ✆*04 93 63 46 11. www.vallauris-golfe-juan.fr.*

In the old gallery of the artist-actor Jean Marais are sculptures, paintings

and ceramics inspired by the universe of Jean Cocteau films in which he played *(Beauty and the Beast, Orphée).*

🚗 DRIVING TOUR
57km/35mi – allow one day.

Route Napoléon
The route as far as Col de Valferrière is described here. The continuation north of the route is described in the *Michelin Green Guide to the French Alps.*

The Route Napoléon – Napoleon's Road – follows the route taken by the Emperor on his return from exile in Elba, from the point where he landed in Golfe-Juan to his arrival in Grenoble.

The new road was opened in 1932. Commemorative plaques and monuments bear the flying eagle symbol inspired by Napoleon's remark: "The eagle, bearing the national colours, will fly from steeple to steeple until he reaches the towers of Notre-Dame."

◷ *Leave from Golfe-Juan*

Golfe-Juan
It was on the beach of Golfe-Juan that Napoleon and his army of 1 100 men landed from the island of Elba on

---

▶ **Population:** 30 561.
♿ **Michelin Map:** 341 D6.
🚻 **Info:** Sq. 8-Mai-1945. ✆04 93 63 82 58. Golfe-Juan annexe: Vieux-Port, ✆04 93 63 73 12. www.vallauris-golf-juan.com.
◉ **Location:** Attached to the same municipality as the seaside resort of Golfe-Juan *(2km/0.9mi on the D 135)*, the modern town of Vallauris stretches out eastwards of the Old Town and its château.
🅿 **Parking:** Park above the château or next to the tourist office.

Napoleon's Road

After landing at Golfe-Juan on 1 March 1815, Napoleon and 700 loyal troops, preceded by an advance guard, made a brief overnight stop at Cannes. Wishing to avoid the Rhône area, which he knew to be hostile, Napoleon headed towards Grasse in order to reach the Durance Valley by way of the Alps. Beyond Grasse the small column had a difficult time proceeding along the mule tracks. They halted at St-Vallier, Escragnolles and Séranon, from which, after a night's rest, they reached Castellane on 3 March. The next day (4 March) the party lunched at Digne, and halted that evening at Château de Malijai.

Napoleon lunched in Sisteron on 5 March and left the town in an atmosphere of growing support for his cause. Once more on a coach road he arrived that night at Gap, where he was given an enthusiastic welcome. On 7 March he reached La Mure, only to find royalist troops from Grenoble facing him at Laffrey. They ended up joining the emperor en masse, and that same evening he entered Grenoble with thousands at his side to shouts of: "Long live the Emperor!"

1 March 1815 (*see Route NAPOLÉON*). This fishing port developed in the second half of the 19C by exporting local ceramics. With its 3km/1.8mi of fine sand and large choice of water sports, Golfe-Juan is now a popular summer resort.

The road winds round the west face of Super-Cannes hill, facing the Lérins Islands and the Esterel Massif.

Cannes★★
See CANNES.

▷ *From Cannes take N 85 to Mougins.*

The road rises above the town and the sea past the perched village of **Mougins★** (*see MOUGINS*).

Mouans-Sartoux
See MOUGINS.
On leaving Mouans-Sartoux, the road reveals Grasse spread out across the mountain slope ahead.

Grasse★ *See GRASSE.*
▷ *From Grasse take N 85 northwest.*

The road skirts "Napoleon's Plateau" where he halted on 2 March outside the town. Pass through the Provence Plateau and then the Pre-Alps of Grasse. The route crosses three passes in succession: **Col du Pilon** (782m/2 566ft),

Pas de la Faye (981m/3 218ft) and **Col de Valferrière** (1 169m/3 805ft), where the view south is magnificent.

Col du Pilon
From the southern slope there is a **view★★** of La Napoule Bay.

St-Vallier-de-Thiey
see ST-VALLIER-DE-THIEY.
As the road climbs to Pas de la Faye there are some very fine **views★**.

Pas de la Faye★★
Similar **view** to that seen from Col du Pilon. Those travelling south over the pass suddenly discover the Mediterranean and the Riviera coastline below.

▷ *1km/0.6mi before Escragnolles, by a gas station, a road to the Belvédère de Baou Mourine branches off to the left.*

Belvédère de Baou Mourine★
1km/0.6mi plus 30min on foot round trip. 🚶 *Path marked with red arrows.* Here you'll arrive at a terrace **viewpoint★** over the Siagne Valley. After Escragnolles, where Napoleon made a brief halt, there are fine views to the south.

▷ *For an alternative route to Cannes via Grasse described in reverse order see GRASSE: Driving Tours.*

ADDRESSES

♍/ EAT
◷◷ **Nounou** – *On the beach at Golfe-Juan. ℘04 93 63 71 73. www.nounou.fr. Closed Nov–Mar.* Regional cuisine and seafood specialities are on the menu at this landmark seaside restaurant open since 1928.

CERAMICS
Tour of traditional pottery workshops – *Closed Sat–Sun.* ◷*No charge. Information at the tourist office ℘04 93 63 82 58.*

Pottery classes – *Espace Grandjean, Bd. des Deux-Vallons. Closed winter, Sat–Sun in summer. ℘04 93 63 07 61.* Pottery classes for kids and adults at the fine arts school (10, 20 or 30 hours).

CALENDAR
Fête de la Poterie – This pottery fesitval takes place on the second Sunday in August.

Biennial International Festival of Ceramic Art – *℘04 93 64 34 67, http://biennale.vallauris.free.fr.* Even-numbered years July to mid-October.

Vence★
Alpes Maritimes

Vence is a picturesque old market town, favoured by artists and art galleries. The wines from the surrounding stony hillsides (La Gaude, St-Jeannet) are highly regarded.

A BIT OF HISTORY
An Episcopal Town – Vence was an important Roman town, then became a powerful episcopal seat under the Christians, home to bishops St Veranus (5C) and St Lambert (12C), and the Italian prince Alessandro Farnese, who became Pope Paul II (16C). During the Wars of Religion, Vence surivived a siege by the Huguenot Lesdiguières in 1592. The victory is celebrated each year at Easter.

Bishop Godeau (17C) – The memory of Antoine Godeau has remained vivid throughout the region. He began as the oracle of the House of Rambouillet, in great demand among cultured society ladies *(les précieuses)* because of his wit, his fluency and his rich and ready poetical vein. Richelieu made him the first member of the French Academy. At the age of 30, Godeau took holy orders and became Bishop of Vence. He took his new role seriously, repairing his cathedral and introducing various industries (perfumery, tanning and pottery) that would bring prosperity to his poor and primitive diocese.

- **Population:** 18 931.
- **Michelin Map:** 341 D5; local map: *see NICE.*
- **Info:** Pl. du Grand-Jardin. ℘04 93 58 06 38. www.ville-vence.com.
- **Location:** Vence sits on a hillside 10km/6mi inland, between Nice and Antibes.
- **Parking:** Three parking garages can be found west of the village.

◖◖ WALKING TOUR
◖ *Start from Pl. du Grand-Jardin.*

A large ash tree at **Place du Frêne** was supposedly planted for the visit of François I and Pope Paul III in 1538.

Old Town
The old town was enclosed within elliptical walls pierced by five gateways. Skirt the 15C square tower adjoining the château to reach the Peyra Gateway (1441), one of the five that enclosed the old town. Today the village bustles with artists, craftsmen and boutiques.

Place du Peyra★
The striking square with its gushing fountain in the form of an urn (1822) was the forum of the Roman town.

◔ *From the south side of the square take Rue du Marché and turn left to Pl. Clemenceau, site of the cathedral.*

Ramparts

Leave the cathedral (& *see Sights*) through the east door onto Place Godeau, overlooked by the square tower with its parapet. At the centre stands a Roman column erected to the god Mars. Take Rue St-Lambert and then Rue de l'Hôtel-de-Ville to reach the 13C Signadour Gateway and turn left.

The Orient gateway was opened in the 18C (the date 1592 carved on a stone refers to the siege during the Wars of Religion). Boulevard Paul-André follows the line of the ramparts, where several narrow stepped streets branch off to fine **views** of the foothills of the Alps. Re-enter the old town through the Gothic Lévis Gateway (13C) and walk up Rue du Portail-Lévis between handsome old houses to Place du Peyra.

SIGHTS
Cathedral
Pl. Clémenceau.

The Roman temple of Mars and a 5C Merovingian church originally occupied the site. The present church was begun in the Romanesque style, with Roman inscriptions on the Baroque façade dedicated to the emperors Elagabalus and Gordian. The tomb of St Lambert is in the second chapel *(right)*. A 5C Roman sarcophagus of Veranus is in the third chapel *(right)*. The north aisle contains a handsome carved doorway with Flamboyant Gothic rose windows and a 16C retable of angels. The baptistery contains a mosaic by Chagall. The **organ loft** is an unusual feature: the singing desk and **choir stalls**★ have risers, elbow rests and misericords by Jacques Bellot, a sculptor from Grasse (15C).

Chapelle du Rosaire (Chapelle Matisse)★
466 Av. Henri-Matisse. ◔*Open mid-Dec–mid-Nov Tue–Thu 10am–11.30am.* ◈*3€.* ℘*04 93 58 03 26.*
"Despite its imperfections I think it is my masterpiece... the result of a lifetime

devoted to the quest for truth." This was Henri Matisse's opinion of the chapel which he had designed and decorated between 1947 and 1951. From the outside it resembles an ordinary Provençal house. Inside everything is white except for the stained-glass windows and the mural compositions, a play of black lines on a white background. The gallery contains studies made by Matisse for his finished designs.

Château de Villeneuve – Fondation Émile Hugues
2 Pl. du Frêne. ◔*Open Tue–Sun 10am–12.30pm, 2–6pm.* ◈*5€.* ℘*04 93 58 15 78. www.museedevence.com.*
The 17C castle of the Barons of Villeneuve incorporates a 13C watchtower. Thematic exhibitions of contemporary and 20C artists such as Matisse, Dubuffet, Dufy and Chagall, inspired by the time they spent in Vence.

🚗 DRIVING TOUR

Routes des Crêtes★★
Round trip 59km/37mi – half a day

◔ *Leave Vence by D 2210, going northeast towards St-Jeannet.*

The road skirts three peaks – Baou des Blancs, Baou des Noirs and Baou de St-Jeannet – and provides a long, leisurely **view**★ of St-Jeannet.

Gattières

This perched village looks out over vineyards and olive groves to the Var Valley. The charming Romanesque-Gothic **church** contains a naïve painted sculpture of St Nicholas and the three children he revived *(right of chancel)*.

◔ *Leave Gattières by D 2209.*

Carros

The old village occupies a remarkable **position**★ huddled around the castle (13C–16C). Just below the village a rock bearing traces of an old mill has been made into a terrace: **panorama**★★.

The road from Carros to Le Broc provides magnificent **views**★ of numerous hill villages and of the Var.

◌ *Follow the D 1.*

Le Broc
This hill village has a fountain (1812) in the arcaded square and a 16C **church** (◌ *guided tours by request x; ℘04 92 08 27 30*) decorated by the modern painter Guillonet. From the village there is a fine view of the Var Valley. The road overlooks the confluence of the Esteron and the Var before turning west into the Bouyon ravine.

Bouyon
Every part of the village offers a **view**★ of Mont Cheiron *(alt 1 778m/5833ft)*, the Var and Esteron valleys and the Alps.

◌ *South of Bouyon the road (D 8) passes through Bézaudun-les-Alpes to Coursegoules.*

Coursegoules
Perched on a rocky spit at the foot of Mont Cheiron, the tall houses rise above the ravine of the nascent River Cagne. The Jaboulet workshops established in this tiny village are famous for their santons, said to be the most beautifully crafted in the region.

◌ *Take D 2 southeast to Vence.*

The road runs through barren countryside behind the River Cagne.

Col de Vence★★
Alt 970m/3 182ft. Just south of the pass, a fine **panorama**★★ opens up to the peaks east of the Var as far as Mont Agel, along the coast from Cap Ferrat, past the Baie des Anges, Cap d'Antibes and the Lérins Islands to the Esterel. To the north, the white slopes of Mont Cheiron stand out dramatically.

⚑ **Hike** *From the pass to St-Jeannet. 4hr.* After the Col de Vence, a trail to the left leads to St-Jeannet via the GR 51 footpath, stretching alongside the Cagne.

ADDRESSES

🛏 STAY

⊖⊜ **Hôtel Mas de Vence** – *539 Av. E.-Hugues. ☎04 93 58 06 16. www.azurline.com/mas. Closed Dec–Jan. 41 rooms.* 🅿. ⊊*9€.* A modern Provençal-style hotel with ochre walls overlooking the main route into town, a covered terrace and wimming pool. Air conditioned rooms have free WiFi.

⊖⊜ **Hôtel Miramar**– *167 Av. Bougearel. ☎04 93 58 01 32. www.hotel-miramar-vence.com. Closed 17 Nov–12 Dec. 18 rooms.* 🅿. ⊊*12€.* In a pretty, 1920s house with a pink façade overlooking the valley, this hotel has charming, flower-themed rooms.

⊖⊜ **Le Vieux Couvent** – *37 Av. Alphonse-Toreille. ☎04 93 58 78 58. www.restaurant-levieuxcouvent.com. Closed 15 Jan–15 Mar, Thu night off season, and Wed.* The stone vaulted ceilings of this former 17C chapel provide a unique setting for this restaurant serving regional specialities.

⊖⊜ **Villa Roseraie** – *Rte. de Coursegoules. ☎04 93 58 02 20. www.villaroseraie.com. Closed Dec–Jan. 14 rooms.* 🅿. ⊊*13€.* A 1900 villa is the setting for this tastefully appointed hotel in which the small rooms are cool and attractive. Tempting outdoor pool. Pretty terrace adorned with sculptures.

⊖⊜⊜ **Hôtel Diana** – *79 Av. des Poilus. ☎04 93 58 28 56. www.hotel-diana.fr. 28 rooms.* 🅿. ⊊. In the heart of Vence, with an open-air Jacuzzi, solarium and fitness room, this stylish hotel has panoramic views. Some rooms equipped with kitchenette.

⊖⊜⊜⊜ **La Tour de Vence** – *310 Chemin du Baou-des-Noirs, on the road to St-Jeannet. ☎04 93 24 59 00. www.latourdevence.com. Closed Nov–Dec.* ⊠. *5 rooms.* 🅿. ⊊. Restaurant ⊖⊜. Constructed entirely from stones from a Burgundian monastary, this luxurious bed & breakfast overlooking the valley is equipped with a swimming pool, pétanque court, tennis, and spacious guest suites tastefully decorated.

🍽 EAT

⊖ **Le Pêcheur de Soleil** – *1 Pl. Godeau. ☎04 93 58 32 56. www.pecheurdesoleil.com. Closed Nov–Feb.* This restaurant in the medieval quarter of Vence has an astounding choice of homemade pizzas, freshly baked in an open oven, and served in a rustic dining room.

⊖⊜⊜ **L'Armoise** – *9 Pl. du Peyra. ☎04 93 58 19 29. www.larmoise.com. Closed Sun eve, Mon, Tue lunch off season.* A tiny seafood restaurant overlooking the pretty square. Try the house bouillabaisse.

⊖⊜⊜ **Auberge des Seigneurs** – *Pl. du Frêne. ☎04 93 58 04 24. Closed 2 Nov–14 Mar, Sun–Mon.* Handsome 17C mansion at the entrance to the medieval district. The rustic setting with its thick wooden tables is alleviated by the refined silverware.

🛒 SHOPPING

MARKETS
Flowers and regional produce – This market takes place from Tuesday to Sunday on Place du Grand-Jardin and Place Surian.

CALENDAR
Fête de Pâques – Coinciding with Easter (end of March to early April) celebrations, this festival commemorates the village victory over the Hugenot siege during the Wars of Religion, 1592, with parades, music and dancing.

"Les Nuits du Sud" – Music Festival, mid-July to early August.

Fête Ste-Elizabeth – Village patron saint festival, first weekend in August.

Moyen Pays Fête – Traditional Folk Festival, beginning of October.

Villeneuve-Loubet

Alpes Maritimes

Villeneuve-Loubet embodies the contrasts of the Côte d'Azur: an old village coupled with a modern seaside resort. Sitting on the banks of the Loup River, the medieval castle and its surrounding village are bordered on the coast by a vast beach, which includes a modern marina.

> ▶ **Population:** 14 104.
> ☙ **Michelin Map:** 341 D6.
> 🖪 **Info:** 16 Av. de la Mer. ℘04 92 02 66 16. www.ot-villeneuveloubet.org.
> ▶ **Location:** Located on the coast between Nice and Antibes.

THE OLD VILLAGE

Follow the charming sloping alleys to the foot of the 13C **Villeneuve Château** (🚶 *guided tours 1st and 3rd Sun;* ≋*5€, map of the village with commentary, available at the tourist office*). Property of the Villeneuve family with a 9C keep, the castle was restored in the 19C. The Truce of Nice was signed here in 1538 to end the Italian Wars between François 1re and Charles V of Spain.

🚶 **The Riverbanks** *2km/1mi*
This hike goes from the village along the banks of the Loup River.

SIGHTS

🏛 Musée Escoffier de l'Art Culinaire★

3 Rue Escoffier. ◷*Open Jul–Aug 2–7pm Wed, Fri 10am–noon, 2–7pm; Sept–Oct and Dec–Jun Sun–Fri 2–6pm.* ◷*Closed public holidays.* ≋*5€ (child 2.50€).* ℘*04 93 20 80 51. www.fondation-escoffier.org.*
In the native house of Auguste Escoffier are the personal souvenirs and objects of this ambassador of French cuisine. Ustensils of his time, a Provençal kitchen reconstituted, a collection of miniature cars (used for dining room service) and1 500 menus from 1820 to today, illustrate the chef's art of cooking.

Musée d'Histoire et d'Art

137 Rue de l'Hôtel-de-Ville. ◷*Open 9.30am–noon, 2–6pm, Sat 9.30am–noon, Sun 11am–1pm.* ◷*Closed public holidays.* ≋*No charge.* ℘*04 92 02 60 39.*

PRACTICAL INFORMATION

NATURE WALK

🚶 The Vaugrenier Natural Park *(access by the RN 7)* stretches over 100ha/247 acres with both prairie and forest areas. There are 6km/3.7mi of trails and a small wetland marsh for observing waterfowl.

TOURS

The Balade Gourmande combines a tour of the village, a visit to the Musée Escoffier and a special surprise tasting. *Contact the tourist office (above)*

Called the Concrete Mountains by some, the Marina-Baie-des-Anges has been recognised by the Ministry of Culture as a 20C heritage site. It's up to you to decide. Take a guided tour. *Contact the tourist office (above).*

This museum is devoted to great 20C conflicts that involved France: two World Wars, the wars of Indo-China (1945–54) and Algeria (1954–62), interventions in Chad and Zaire (1969–84), Lebanon (1982–87), and the Gulf War (1991). Temporary art exhibitions *(first floor)*.

The Birth of Peach Melba

Native of Villeneuve, the illustrious cook Auguste Escoffier (1846–1935) made his name in Nice, then Paris in the Petit Moulin-Rouge before forging a reputation in the deluxe hotel he created with César Ritz. He could create personalised dishes that would delight (e.g. the Peach Melba, in honour of a professional singer of the same name). His trademarks were innovation, lightness, simplicity and quality.

NICE, THE RIVIERA AND MONACO

Nice and Monaco are the uncontested stars of the French Riviera, the headliners who never fail to impress or draw a crowd. Nice's seaside Promenade des Anglais and Monte-Carlo's majestic casino have been the stuff of legend since the late 19C, when the arrival of the railway also brought with it the throngs of summer and winter tourists eager to see this millionaires' playground of fast cars, private yachts, and palace hotels. Of course, one doesn't have to break the bank to enjoy this part of the French Riviera, where the roads winding between coastal resorts and precariously perched villages offer panoramic views and scenes of stunning natural beauty. Important vestiges of Roman, Greek and Medieval structures enrich the architectural heritage, and a vibrant arts and music scene continue to enhance the cultural character of this dynamic region for the millions of visitors who still flock to its sunny shores.

Highlights

1 Hike the breathtaking coastal path around the **Cap Ferrat** (p286)

2 Tour the villa and gardens of the **Villa Ephrussi de Rothschild** (p285)

3 Enjoy the scenic drive along the famous **Grande Corniche** (p330)

4 Place your bets at the Belle Époque **casino in Monte Carlo** (p302)

5 Taste the traditional Niçoise socca at the **Cours Saleya market** (p327)

Almost Not French

This part of the French Riviera is, historically speaking, hardly French at all. The counts of Provence held much of the southeastern region throughout the centuries, but Nice and the surrounding villages spent more time in the hands of the Sardinian House of Savoy, from their secession from Provence in 1388 until they were purchased by Napoleon III in 1860. Monaco's Grimaldi lords purchased their own principality from the Genoese in 1308, and although independently ruled, have been under the French 'protection' since 1861 when they sold off their towns of Menton and Rocquebrune. Not only has the architecture, cuisine, and even language of the Niçoise, Monégasques, and their neighbours been strongly influenced by their colourful and diverse Italian roots, it has also contributed to the fiercely independent character of the people throughout the region.

Not Just for Tourists

Nice and Monaco may owe their international prominence to the lucrative tourism industry, but today the region has become an important business centre for scientific research and high-tech

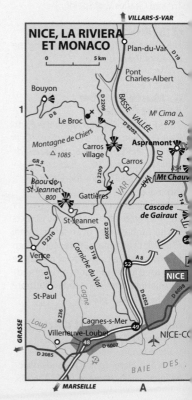

development, too. With the encouragement of local governments, an arguably enviable setting, and a pool of qualified graduates from local universities, many international companies have opened offices and small start-ups have flourished. The region's many hotels, international airport, and top-notch restaurants make it the ideal place for business conferences, which take place throughout the year. While some corners of the French Riviera are virtually closed down in the winter months, Nice and Monaco never stop moving.

Villa Ephrussi-de-Rothschild
J.Malbure/MICHELIN

Time to Celebrate

With such a colourful past and a good dose of Italian genes in their blood, the Niçoise, Monégasques and their neighbours sure know how to celebrate in style. The month of February is the best time to join in the festivities, when the 16-day Carnival takes over the streets of Nice, and mountains of lemons, oranges, limes and grapefruits decorate the processions for Menton's week-long Fête du Citron. In May, Monaco's Grand Prix attracts the biggest crowds who come from around the world to watch the Formula 1 cars racing through the centre of Monte-Carlo.

Beaulieu-sur-Mer★

Alpes Maritimes

This fashionable resort, sheltered from the north winds, is one of the warmest spots on the Riviera. This oasis of peace and quiet is centred around the Baie des Fourmis and exotic gardens of *Petite Afrique* along Boulevard d'Alsace-Lorraine.

WALKS
Sentier du Plateau St-Michel★★
2hr round trip – stiff climb.
Starting north of Boulevard Édouard-VII, the path leads up the Riviera escarpment to the plateau, affording wonderful views from Cap d'Ail to the Esterel.

Promenade Maurice-Rouvier★
1hr on round trip.
This remarkable promenade runs parallel to the Mediterranean shore from Beaulieu to St-Jean-Cap-Ferrat, passing fine white villas in beautiful gardens and amazing views of the Riviera coastline.

SIGHT
Villa Grecque Kérylos★★
Audio tour. Open Feb–Nov daily 10am–6pm; Dec–Jan Tue–Sun 10am–6pm, Mon 2–6pm. 8.50€. 04 93 01 45 90. www.villa-kerylos.com.
This faithful reconstruction of a sumptuous Greek villa of ancient times was

▶ **Population:** 3 720.
◉ **Michelin Map:** 341 F5; local map: *see Corniches de la RIVIERA.*
ℹ **Info:** Pl. Georges-Clemenceau. 04 93 01 02 21. www.ot-beaulieu-sur-mer.fr
◐ **Location:** Hugging the coastline between Nice and Monaco, Beaulieu sits right next to Villefranche The best way to get there is by the Basse Corniche (*see Corniches de la RIVIERA*).
🅿 **Parking:** The best places are around the port, behind the Hôtel de Ville. For walking along Promenade Maurice-Rouvier, leave the car along Avenue Blundell-Maple.

A Love Story

In 1891 this small harbour was discovered by the American press tycoon **Gordon Bennett**, who immediately fell in love with it. He offered to finance the building of a pier but the proud local fishermen declined his offer. However, the winding corniche road linking Beaulieu to Villefranche was his doing and it still bears his name.

Villa Grecque Kérylos

J. Malburet/MICHELIN

conceived by the archeologist Théodore Reinach in 1902, and bequeathed to the Institut de France in 1928. On a **site**★ reminiscent of the Aegean, the villa stands in lush gardens overlooking the sea.

ADDRESSES

🛏 STAY
🍽 **Le Sélect** – *1 Rue André-Cane and Pl. Général-de-Gaulle. ℘04 93 01 05 42. www.hotelselect-beaulieu.com . Closed Jan. 19 rooms. ⊆6.50€.* Housed in a handsome residence, this hotel with Provençal decor offers air-conditioned rooms with large beds and well-equipped bathrooms.

🍴 EAT
🍽🍽 **Le Marco Polo** – *On the marina. ℘04 93 01 06 50. Closed late Nov– mid-Dec, Tue–Wed Oct–May, Wed–Thu morning Jun–Sept.* Whether they are served on the radiant veranda or the terrace facing the marina and its luxury yachts, the dishes here all pay tribute to the Mediterranean, centring on fish, seafood and pasta. Attractive, reasonably priced menus.

🏃 LEISURE ACTIVITIES
Beaches – Small pebble beaches are well sheltered from the northerly winds, enjoying a southern exposure. They are located on either side of the marina: Baie des Fourmis beach and Petite Afrique au Nord beach.

Cap Ferrat★★
Alpes Maritimes

Tucked between Villefranche and Beaulieu, the lush vegetation and dramatic cliffs of the prestigious Cap Ferrat peninsula hide luxurious villas, including the spectacular Villa Ephrussi. Some of the best views of the coast can be had from the Sentier Littoral and St-Hospice Point.

▶ **Population:** 2 103.
🕹 **Michelin Map:** 341 E5; local map: *see Corniches de la RIVIERA.*
🛈 **Info:** 59 Av. Denis-Semeria. ℘04 93 76 08 90. www.ville-saint-jean-cap-ferrat.fr.
▶ **Location:** Also known as St-Jean-Cap-Ferrat (St-Jean being the name of the actual town), the peninsula is accessible by the narrow Bas Corniche, along the coastline.

SIGHTS
Villa Ephrussi-de-Rothschild★★
🕓*Open daily Feb–Oct 10am–6pm; Nov–Jan 2–6pm, Sat–Sun 10am–6pm. ☜10€. ℘04 93 01 33 09. www.villa-ephrussi.com.*
This villa was bequeathed to the Institut de France in 1934 by the Baroness Ephrussi de Rothschild. It stands in an incomparable **setting**★★★ of nine magnificent gardens, such as the Spanish garden and the Stone garden, on the narrow neck of the peninsula, with views of Villefranche and Beaulieu.

Musée Île-de-France★★
🔎*Guided tours only. ☜3€.*
The villa that houses this museum was built in the Italianiate style soon after 1900 to hold the furniture and (pre-

dominantly 18C) works of art that the Baroness collected throughout her life. Visitors can see the private apartments (bedroom, boudoir, Sèvres dining room) of Madame Ephrussi, medieval and Renaissance artworks and furniture, and the Impressionists' Gallery of landscapes by Monet, Renoir and Sisley.

Gardens★★
Magnificent grounds (7ha/17 acres) surround the villa, with themed French, Italian, Japanese and Spanish-style gardens of marble statues, fountains and both Mediterranean and exotic flora.

Cap Ferrat

👥 Zoo

♿🕐*Open daily 9.30am–5.30pm (Jul–Aug until 7pm).* 🎫*15€ (child 11€, under 3 free).* ☎*04 93 76 07 60. www.zoocapferrat.com.*

The grounds that once belonged to Leopold II of Belgium have been converted into a **tropical garden** and 3ha/7-acre zoo with 350 species of animals and exotic birds. Chimpanzee performances several times per day.

Cap-Ferrat Peninsula★★

10km/6mi – about 1hr.
🚶 *2hr, leaving from the port of St-Jean, arriving at the tourist office.*
This footpath winds along steep cliffs of the peninsula for a tranquil escape.

St-Jean-Cap-Ferrat★

Once a fishing village, St-Jean is now a quiet resort, its old houses overlooking the harbour of pleasure yachts.

The stepped street south of Boulevard de la Libération leads to a **viewpoint★** with of Èze, Mont Agel and the Italian Alps.

🚶 *1hr round trip from the port of St-Jean.*
The Promenade Maurice-Rouvier★ runs along the coast to Beaulieu.

Pointe St-Hospice

A pleasant stroll up between the private houses, past an 18C prison tower, leads to a 19C chapel. From the chapel there is a good **view★** of the coast and inland from Beaulieu to Cap Martin.

Plage de Passable

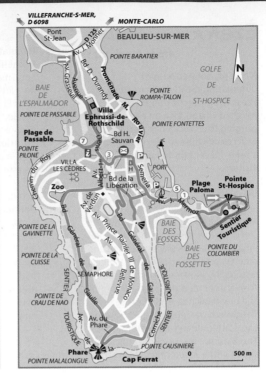

ST-JEAN-CAP-FERRAT

WHERE TO STAY

Brise Marine
(Hôtel)...................... ①

Panoramic (Le).......... ③

WHERE TO EAT

Capitaine Cook.......... ⑤

Plage
de Passable.............. ⑦

ADDRESSES

🏠 STAY

⊜⊜⊜ **Hôtel Brise Marine** – *Avenue Jean-Mermoz.* ℘*04 93 76 04 36. www. hotel-brisemarine.com. Closed Nov to Jan 18 rooms.* ⊒*14€.* Located in a quiet street, this charming house is reached through lush grounds. Superb views of the bay and Cap Ferrat. Book the rooms in the villa, rather than the annexe.

⊜⊜⊜ **Hôtel Le Panoramic** – *3 Avenue Albert Ire* ℘*04 93 76 00 37. www.hotel-lepanoramic.com. 20rooms.* ₱⊒*12€.* Every room in this hotel has sea views and a balcony. Decor is old fashioned but cosy, with a charming exotic garden and free parking.

🍽 EAT

⊝⊝ **Capitaine Cook** – *Avenue Jean-Mermoz.* ℘*04 93 76 02 66. Closed Nov 8–Dec 26, Thu for lunch and Wed.* Lying half-way between Paloma beach and the marina, this family-style restaurant serves traditional cuisine with a strong emphasis on fish and seafood.

⊝⊝ **Plage de Passable** – *Chemin de Passable.* ℘*04 93 76 06 17. Closed mid-Oct–Mar.* Beach restaurant located in Villefranche port on the way to St-Jean-Cap-Ferrat Peninsula serves salads, pizzas, pasta and seafood. Enchanting spot sheltered by pines and palms.

🏃 LEISURE ACTIVITIES

Beaches – There are several galet" (smooth stone) beaches in Cap Ferrat. **Plage de Passable** facing Villefranche, **Plage Paloma** facing Beaulieu, **Plage du Cro des Pins** near the port, and a beach at the **Pointe St-Hospice**.

287

Èze★★

Alpes Maritimes

A quaint, isolated hamlet dominating the Riviera coastline, Èze is the perfect example of a perched village. Like an eagle's nest clinging to its rocky outcrop 427m/1 410ft above the sea, the stunning site★★ never fails to impress visitors.

SIGHTS

A 14C double gateway with crenellations and a sentry walk leads into the steep, narrow streets of the **medieval village**★, in some places stepped and other places running beneath tastefully restored boutiques and artists' studios. At every corner are flowers, fountains and breathtaking views of the sea .

The **church** was rebuilt in the 18C with a Classical façade and a two-storey tower. The Baroque interior contains a fine statue of the Assumption (18C) attributed to Muerto and a 15C font.

Chapelle des Pénitents-Blancs
Carriera Plana.

The simple 14C chapel is decorated with enameled panels illustrating the life and death of Christ and the Virgin. To the left is a Crucifixion, an early example of the Nice School; on the high altar an unusual Catalan crucifix, dating from 1258,

- ▶ **Population:** 2 932.
- & **Michelin Map:** 341 F5; Local map: *see Corniches de la RIVIERA.*
- **Info:** Pl. du Général-de-Gaulle. ℘04 93 41 26 00. www.eze-riviera.com.
- ▷ **Location:** Between Nice and Monaco, Èze is accessible by RN 7 – Moyenne Corniche (& *see Corniches de la RIVIERA*).
- **Parking:** There are two parking areas *(next to the tourist office)* where you'll need to leave your car before climbing up to the village. Parking is also available at the two perfume houses, for clients only (& *see Addresses*).

where Christ is smiling; on the left a 14C statue the Madonna of the Forest, with the Child holding a pine cone.

Jardin d'Eze
Rue du Château. ◷*Open winter 9am– 5.30pm; summer 9am–8pm.* ◷*6€ (children under 11 free).* ℘04 93 41 26 00. www.eze-riviera.com.

Many varieties of succulents and cacti flourish in the gardens crowned by the

Èze viewed from the Jardin Exotique

D. Pazery/ MICHELIN

Tales of a Highwayman

After attacking and plundering the coaches and horsemen passing within their reach, Gaspard and his band would hide in a cave on the side of Mont Vinaigre. The bandit had a soft spot for elegance, wearing a splendid red costume, studded with jewels and silver buttons and buckles.

He was eventually arrested in an inn near Toulon and broken on the wheel in 1781 at the age of 25. His head was nailed to a tree on the road, which had been the scene of his many escapades.

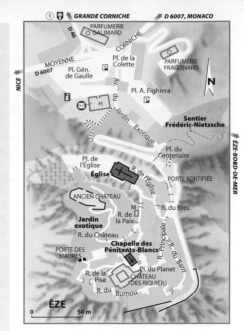

WHERE TO STAY

Hermitage du Col d'Èze (Hôtel de l')..①

remains of a 14C château. The terrace has a splendid **panorama**★★★.

EXCURSIONS
Astrorama
Take D 46 to the Col d'Èze (⊙ see Corniches de la RIVIÈRA, circuit ①).

ADDRESSES

🏨 STAY
⊜⊜ **Hôtel Hermitage du Col d'Eze** – *2.5km/1.5mi by D 46 and Grande Corniche. ℘04 93 41 00 68. www.ezehermitage. com. 14 rooms. 🅿. ⊒8€.* An elegant and peaceful hotel with its splendid terraces, overflow pool and sea views. Rooms are elegantly decorated, with air conditioning and free WiFi.

Sentier Frédéric-Nietzsche★
🏃*About 2hr round trip.*
Nietzsche thought out the third part of his masterpiece *Thus Spoke Zarathustra* on the picturesque mule path, which leads through pines and olive groves to the seaside resort of Èze-Bord-de-Mer.

FRAGRANCES
Parfumerie Fragonard – ♿🐾*Guided tours (30min) daily Feb–Oct 8.30am– 6.30pm; Nov–Jan 8.30am–noon, 2–6pm. 🐾No charge. ℘04 93 36 44 65. www.fragonard.com.* This annexe of the Grasse perfumery displays the various stages in the manufacturing of essential oils, perfumes and soaps. Boutique on-site.

Parfumerie Galimard – *Pl. du Général-de-Gaulle. ℘04 93 41 10 70. www.galimard.com. 🐾No charge.* Founded in 1747, this perfume house gives free tours of its manufacturing and small museum. Products are on sale in the boutique.

Levens

Alpes Maritimes

Perched at an altitude of 600m/
1 968ft, the medieval village streets
of Levens are a pleasant place to
stroll amongst the ancient houses
and fountains.

🥾 WALKING TOUR
THE OLD VILLAGE

Place de la République opens onto an
attractive public garden, its shaded
terraces overlooking the valley, and the
curved façade of the Baroque Chapelle
des Pénitents-Blancs. In Rue du Docteur-
Faraud, the Chapelle des Pénitents-Noirs
presents a fine collection of works of art,
many displayed in the crypt.

▷ *Go up Rue Masséna.*

After the Masséna family house (1722)
are the surviving ramparts and the **Maison du Portal** (*⏰open Sept–Jun Sat–Sun
2.30–5.30pm; Jul daily 2.30–6.30pm; Aug
daily 10am–noon, 2.30–6.30pm; ⚠no
charge; ✆04 93 79 85 84; www.lamaison-
duportal.fr)*, which houses the sculptures
of Jean-Pierre Augier and temporary
exhibitions.
At Place de la Liberté a vaulted passageway leads to the heavily restored
church.

▷ *Take the path on the left.*

The **view**★ extends over the Var, the
Vésubie, and the high mountains.

Celebrating Liberty

In 1621, the people of Levens were
tired of paying taxes to their feudal
Lord Grimaldi, and destroyed the
château. Ever since, on the Festival
of St-Antonin (early September),
everyone in the village jumps off
a symbolic stone in Place de la
Liberté to celebrate their escape
from tyranny.

▶ **Population:** 3 700.
♿ **Michelin Map:** 341 E4;
   local map: *see NICE*.
🏛 **Info:** 3 Pl. Paul-Olivier.
   ✆04 93 79 71 00.
📍 **Location:** Levens is
   19km/12mi north of Nice
   on the D 19. At the summit
   of the village, you'll find
   an open swimming pool.
🅿 **Parking:** Follow Levens-
   Centre, bearing left as
   you climb the hill, until
   you reach the municipal
   parking *(three levels)*.

EXCURSIONS
Duranus

8.5km/5.2mi from Levens on D 19 north.
The road overlooks the deep Gorges de
la Vésubie (*⏰see Vallée de la VÉSUBIE*)
from a great height, with a glimpse of
the chapel of Madone d'Utelle *(left)* high
in the mountains. Duranus, a pretty village surrounded by orchards and vineyards, was founded in 17C by the people
of Rocca-Sparviero, a ruined village at
Col St-Michel.

Saut des Français★★

At the northern end of Duranus is
Frenchmen's Leap, commemorating
Republican soldiers who were hurled
over the edge in 1793 by guerillas from
the Vésubie Valley. Utelle and its chapel
overlook the dizzying vertical drop.

ADDRESSES

🛏 STAY

🍴**La Vigneraie** – *Rte. St-Blaise, Levens.*
✆*04 93 79 77 60. Closed 9 Oct–11 Feb.
18 rooms.* 🅿. *⛔8€. Restaurant ☺☺.*
This family-run, country-style inn and
restaurant is known for its generous
home cooking and comfortable, if
basic, rooms. Large bay windows in the
dining room offer views over the green
countryside.

Menton★★

Alpes Maritimes

Menton is a coastal resort famous for its annual lemon festival and mild climate. The picturesque old town is framed by mountain cliffs and terraced citrus and olive groves.

A BIT OF HISTORY

Early history – Evidence of a human settlement in the Palaeolithic Era was discovered from excavations near the Italian frontier, but the name Menton was only first mentioned in 1261, when purchased by the Grimaldis of Monaco in 1346. Together with Monaco it oscillated between the protection of France and Sardinia, until it was permanently attached to France in 1860.

Modern town – In the late 19C and early 20C Menton benefitted from the popularity of the Riviera among the European aristocracy who came to nurse their health or simply enjoy the mild winters. Today, tourism and light industry make Menton a lively, cosmopolitan city, while the old town and vast green spaces have been preserved.

⬤ WALKING TOUR
THE OLD TOWN★★
Allow 2hr.

Rue St-Michel

This pedestrian street linking the old and new towns is bordered by boutiques and orange trees. **Place aux Herbes**, frames the seaside view with coloured paving stones, decorative colonnade and a fountain. Note the splendid Belle Epoch façades: former Hôtel d'Orient *(1 Rue*

☺ A Bit of Advice ☺

Many pedestrian streets in Menton are decorated with traditional mosaics made with smooth *galets*, or river stones, which are colourful yet a bit uncomfortable to walk on. Be sure to have thick-soled shoes if you plan on doing a lot of walking.

▶ **Population:** 27 655.
⬤ **Michelin Map:** 341 F5; local maps: *see Excursions, NICE and Corniches de la RIVIERA.*
▣ **Info:** Palais de l'Europe, 8 Av. Boyer. ✆04 92 41 76 76. www.villedementon.com.
⬤ **Location:** Menton is the last coastal town before the Italian border, about 30km/18.6mi east of Nice on the Corniches *(⬤see Corniches de la RIVIERA).* For those interested in getting there faster on a less scenic route, take the A 8.
▣ **Parking:** Most of the public parking places are around the port; all require payment, whether they are parking garages or metered street parking.
⬤ **Don't Miss:** The colourful parades during the annual Lemon Festival *(Fête du Citron)* in February, the pictuesque streets of the old town *(vieille ville)*, and the scenic views from the Cap Martin.
⬤ **Timing:** Allow at least a half day to walk around the pedestrian streets of the old town and the Promenade du Soleil, and visit one of the sights such as the Musée des Beaux-Arts. A full day would include a trip to the beach, a hike along the Cap Martin or a driving excursion inland to Gorbio or Castillon.

de la République); Winter-Palace *(20 Av. Riviera)*; Riviera-Palace *(28 Av. Riviera)*; covered market *(Quai de Monléon).*

⬤ *At Pl. du Cap, go up the Rue Logettes to the Rue Longue.*

View of Menton by night

Rue Longue

This was once the main street of Menton, formerly called Via Julia Augusta.

Parvis St-Michel★★

Access by the Chanoine-Gouget ramps.
At the top of the steps is a charming square in the Italian style framed by Baroque façades, overlooking the sea.

"Artium Civitas"

This inscription on the front of the town hall declared Menton's ambition to be a city of the arts. Art exhibitions are held throughout the year at the Palais de l'Europe. The **Chamber Music Festival** enjoys an international reputation with world-famous guest artists. There are flower carnivals throughout the summer, but the most famous festival is the **Fête du Citron**, held in the Biovès Gardens since 1929. The event calls for more than 100t of citrus fruit – oranges, lemons, grapefruit and kumquats – which is used to cover decorative metal frames erected in the gardens to illustrate a different theme each year. The festival closes with a procession of floats decorated with citrus fruit.

The square is paved with a mosaic depicting the Grimaldi arms.

Façade of the Chapelle de la Conception★

The façade of this chapel of the White Penitents (1685, restored in the 19C) has statues of the theological virtues.

Basilique St-Michel-Archange

🕐*Open Mon–Fri 10am–noon, 3–5pm; Sat–Sun 3–5pm.* ☎*04 93 35 81 63.*
This is the largest and finest Baroque church in the region. Its two-tier **façade** in yellow and pale green reflects a variety of architectural motifs. The tower (15C) on the left, which belonged to an earlier building, was crowned with an octagonal campanile with a glazed tile roof in the 17C, and the great Genoese-style campanile (53m/174ft) was added in the 18C. Local artists such as Puppo and Vento contributed to the decoration of the side chapels. Above the handsome 18C choir stalls is the **altarpiece of St Michael** (1569) by Manchello. The exuberant Baroque high altar is crowned by St Michael slaying the Devil.

▷ *Climb the steps to the Rue du Vieux-Château, leading to the cemetery.*

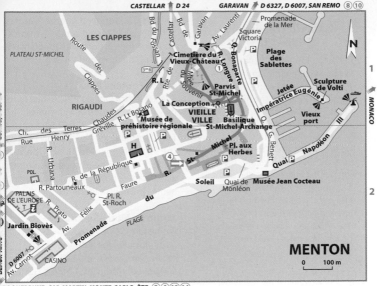

Cimetière du Vieux-Château

This international cemetery, laid out in the 19C on the site of the former medieval castle, has terraces with tombs arranged by religion or nationality. The cemetery is a souvenir of the time when Menton welcomed rich residents from all over the world. Among the celebrities from this era are Russian princes, the uncle and aunt (Delano) of Franklin D Roosevelt, and rugby founder William Webb Ellis. From the southern corner of the English graveyard there is a beautiful view★ of the old town and the sea.

THE SEAFRONT AND BEACHES★★

▶ *Start from the Casino Municipal.*

Promenade du Soleil★★

The wide promenade facing the sea follows the shore beneath the old town.

Old Port

The harbour, used by local fishermen and tourists alike, is flanked by the **Jetée Impératrice-Eugénie** and **Quai Napoléon-III** and its lighthouse. The far end of the port, home to Volti's sculpture of St Michael, commands pleasant **views★** of old Menton. In the distance you can admire the Italian coastline.

Plage des Sablettes

The gravel beach is dominated by Promenade de la Mer and **Quai Bonaparte**. From the top, there is a nice view of the old quarter. A huge flight of steps leads up to the church of St-Michel.

Garavan

This luxurious residential suburb of the town, running between Promenade de la Mer and Boulevard de Garavan, has many examples of the eclectic architecture of the Belle Epoch (like the Fondation Barriquand-Alphand, d'Abel

Katherine Mansfield (1888–1923)

This writer from New Zealand spent a year in Menton from spring 1920. Her delicate health caused her to choose Garavan and she moved into the Villa Isola-Bella *(now in Avenue Katherine-Mansfield)*.
In this peaceful haven she wrote five of her best works including *The Stranger, The Chambermaid, The Girl*. Writing in her diary, she said: "The house faces the sea; on the right is the old town with its little port and pepper plants growing on a tiny quay... This old town... is the loveliest place I have ever set eyes on."

Gléna on Boulevard de Garavan). The marina can accommodate boats up to 40m/132ft. The pretty 17C Baroque **Chapelle St-Jacques** houses a municipal gallery of contemporary art.

GARDENS OF MENTON★

The choice of tropical species and the unusual layout of these gardens reflect the fertile imagination of the foreign residents who have come here to stay over the past century.

Serre de la Madone

74 Rte. de Gorbio ⏱*Open Tue–Sun Apr–Oct 10am–6pm; Dec–Mar 10am–5pm.* ⏱*Closed public holidays.* ✆*8€.* ✆*04 93 57 73 90. www.serredela madone.com.*
This private garden created between 1924 and 1939 was purchased by the Conservatoire du Littoral in 1999. Its *palazzo* and restored gardens feature rare plants, a Moorish garden, a rock garden, and antique garden statues.

Jardin du Val Rameh★

Chemin de St-Jacques. ⏱*Open Apr–Sept daily 10am–12.30pm, 3-6.30pm; Oct–Mar Mon–Fri 10am–noon, 2–5pm.* ✆*5€.* ✆*04 93 35 86 72.*
These grounds arranged around the English Val Rameh Villa in the 1930s are now part of the Musée d'Histoire Naturelle

of Paris. The terraced garden features 700 species of Mediterranean, tropical and sub-tropical flora, with magnificent views of the town and the sea.

Jardin Fontana Rosa

Avenue Blasco Ibañez. ✆*Guided tours only with the Maison du Patrimoine, (1.5hr).* ✆*5€.* ✆*04 92 10 97 10.*
This unusual residence, built in 1924 by the Spanish novelist **Blasco Ibañez**, stands out because of its porch adorned with ceramics paying homage to leading names in Spanish literature.

Jardin de Maria-Serena

Promenade Reine-Astrid. ✆*Guided tours only with the Maison du Patrimoine (2hr).* ✆*5€.* ✆*04 92 10 97 10.*
Supposedly built by Charles Garnier (architect of the Paris Opera), this garden is known for its extensive collection of palm trees and views over Menton.

Jardin Biovès

Next to the tourist office.
These beautiful gardens in the town centre are bordered by palms and lemon trees, planted with flowers and ornamented by fountains and statues (*Goddess of the Golden Fruit* by Volti).

Oliveraie du Pian

Bd. de Garavan. Also accessible from a staircase in the Val Rameh gardens.
This olive grove is planted with more than 500 olive trees over 100 years old.

SIGHTS
Musée des Beaux-Arts (Palais Carnolès)★

Access by Av. Carnot, 3 av. de la Madone. ⏱*Open Wed–Mon 10am–noon, 2–6pm.* ✆*No charge.* ✆*04 93 35 49 71.*
This former summer residence of the princes of Monaco was built in the 17C in the spirit of the Grand Trianon of Versailles. After heavy remodelling in the 19C it was restored by the Danish architect Georg Tersling and decorated with frescoes on antique themes. The original stuccowork and gilding have survived in the Grand Salon de Musique and the Salon Bleu.

The first floor is dedicated to the collection of **early religious art** by French, Italian and Flemish masters, including Bréa, da Vinci, Luini and Orsi. There are also modern works by Suzanne Valadon, Kisling and Camoin.

A collection of **contemporary and modern work** is housed on the ground floor, including works from the Wakefield Mori Collection (Picabia, Forain, Dufy), contributions from various Biennales de Peinture (up to 1980) and gifts from artists.

Musée Jean-Cocteau

Quai Napoléon-III. ()*Open Wed–Sun 10am–noon, 2–6pm.* 3€. 04 93 35 49 71.

This 17C bastion, built by Honoré II of Monaco, was restored and converted into a museum by Cocteau, the 'Prince of the Poets', in 1957. The artist designed pebble mosaics in traditional Menton style on several themes and wrought-iron display cases. In the entrance hangs an Aubusson tapestry, *Judith and Holophernes*, which Matisse described as the "only truly contemporary tapestry".

Hôtel de Ville

17 Rue de la République. ()*The hall decorated by Jean Cocteau is open Mon–Fri 8.30am–12.30pm, 1.30–5pm.* 1.50€. 04 92 10 50 20. www.villedementon.com.

The **salle des mariages**, where marriages are celebrated, is decorated with paintings by Jean Cocteau. The artist also chose the furniture for the entrance and drew Mariannes (symbol of the French Republic) onto the two big mirrors.

Musée de Préhistoire Régionale

Rue Lorédan-Larchey. ()*Open Wed–Mon 10am–noon, 2–6pm.* ()*Closed public holidays.* No charge. 04 93 35 84 64.

This museum was opened in 1909 in a building specially designed by the architect Adrien Rey. It houses collections from local prehistoric sites, reconstructions of the interiors of Menton houses during the 19C, and a poster gallery

commemorating the golden age of Menton from 1870 to 1914.

Église Orthodoxe Russe

Rue Morillot, access by Av. Carnot. *Guided tours 4th Sat of each month Sept–Jun at 2.30pm.* 5€. 04 92 10 97 10.

The Russian Orthodox Church (1892) was designed by Georg Tersling, a Danish architect. Although its small size would be more suited to a chapel, the interior is lavishly decorated with murals by Prince Gagarin and many icons.

DRIVING TOURS

Menton to Roquebrunne-Cap-Martin

L'Annonciade★ *6km/3.7mi.*

From Menton take Av. de Verdun then Av. de Sospel, following the signs to the left up a steep, narrow road.

The 17C **chapel** has been a centre for pilgrimages to the Virgin since the 11C. From the terrace (225m/738ft) there is a panorama★ of the coastline.

Gorbio★ *9km/5.6mi.*

Leave Menton by the D 23 north to Gorbio, a narrow winding road.

The Gorbio Valley, with its flowers, olives and pines, and luxury residences, contrasts with the stark appearance of the village, perched on its wild and rocky site★. For the feast of Corpus Christi, the villagers organise a very attractive parade, known as the **Procession des Limaces**, in which everyone carries a snail shell filled with olive oil and lit by a little wick. Behind the church is a fine **viewpoint** across to Bordighera Point.

Ste-Agnès★ *13km/8mi – about 45min.*

From Menton take Av. Carnot north, turn right onto Cours René-Coty, Av. des Alliés and Rue Castagnins (D 22).

The road is uphill all the way with views of the Gorbio Valley. Bear right at **Col St-Sébastien** (alt 600m/1 969ft) which has a particularly picturesque **view**★ of Ste-Agnès. Located barely 3km/2mi from the sea, yet at an altitude of 780m/2 559ft, the village is the highest on the coast.

The picturesque cobblestone streets of the village, lined with craft shops, include Rue Longue and the vaulted Rue des Comtes-Léotardi. A rocky path leads from behind the graveyard to the ruins of the castle and a marvellous **panorama**★★.

Fort Maginot de Ste-Agnès

At the village entrance, turn towards the parking Sud, and park the car on the left near the fort. ☝*The interior is chilly.* ☝*Guided tours (1hr) Jun–Sept Tue–Sun 10.30am–noon, 3–7pm.* ☝4€. ☎04 93 35 84 58. www.sainteagnes.fr. This imposing building, camouflaged by the overhanging rocks surrounding it, was built between 1931 and 1938 as part of the Alpine Maginot Line. Its firing slots are equipped with 81mm mortars and 75/135mm guns faced southeast over Menton Bay. The barracks, deep in the cliff, still house an electric generator, a neutralisation room and kitchens. The tour of the fort gives an insight into life

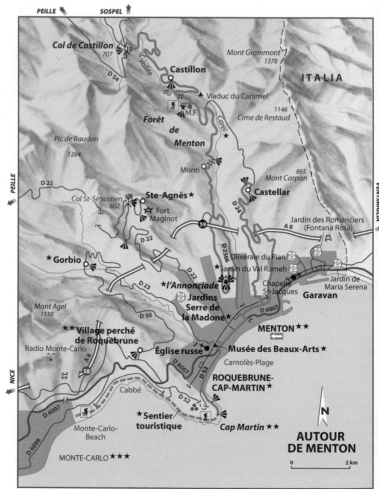

in such strongholds during the Second World War. Outside, set slightly downhill, a platform overlooking the intricacies of the Provençal motorway affords a marvellous **view**★★ of the coast from Bordighera in Italy to Cap Martin.

Castellar – *13km/8mi – about 45min.*
◗ *Take Rte. de Castellar north.*

Castellar is an attractive hilltop village and a popular place for hiking (it lies at the crossroads of the GR 51 and 52 trails). Its parallel streets are linked by covered alleys. There is a good **view** from the terrace on Place Clémenceau.

◗ *On the return drive, follow the same route for 2.5km/1.5mi, then turn right on the "Chemin du Mont-Gros".*

Roquebrune-Cap-Martin★ –
&*See ROQUEBRUNE-CAP-MARTIN.*

Col de Castillon Road
21km/13mi – about 1.5hr
◗ *Leave Menton by Av. de Verdun running into Av. de Sospel.*

The road riding over Col de Castillon – also called Col de la Garde – makes its way through a break in the ridge of hills running parallel to the coast. After passing under the motorway, the D 2566 climbs, twisting and turning up the beautiful **Vallée du Careï**★ beneath the ridges of the Franco-Italian border. After leaving the hamlet of Monti, the road skirts Menton Forest, with fine views.

Forêt de Menton
🔼 *1hr round trip.* To the left of the forest refuge a marked path leads to a **view**★ *(viewing table)* of the coast. The road soon passes the **Caramel Viaduct**, formerly used by the tramway between Menton and Sospel.

Castillon
On the right lies the new village of Castillon, a model of rural planning, built halfway up the hillside in the Provençal style. The village was reconstructed twice: after the earthquake of 1887 and after the bombardments of 1944. Its main district overlooking the village is occupied by artisans, painters and sculptors. From the summit are **views** of the Careï Valley and the sea.

◗ *After the village, the road to the Sospel Valley leads off to the left, plunging in and out of tunnels following the tracks of the old tramway. The road leading off to the right soon brings you to the pass.*

Col de Castillon
Alt 707m/2 320ft. The **view** to the north takes in the Bévera Valley with the Peïra-Cava and Aution peaks in the distance. To the left D 54 takes a picturesque route to Col St-Jean. From here the road drops gradually down into the Merlanson Valley. The forest is gradually replaced by olive groves and terraced vineyards. First the stronghold on Mont Barbonnet looms into sight, followed by the town of Sospel and the surrounding heights.

ADDRESSES

🏠 STAY

◗ **Hôtel de Londres** – *15 Av. Carnot. ℘04 93 35 74 62. www.hotel-de-londres. com. Closed Nov–15 Jan. 27 rooms. ⊡10€. Restaurant* ◗◗◗. This hotel near the coast features soundproofed rooms of varying sizes, appointed with either rustic or modern furniture and WiFi. Pleasant terrace.

◗◗ **Hôtel Paris Rome** – *79 porte de France. ℘04 93 35 70 35. www.paris-rome.com. Closed Nov–Dec. 22 rooms. ⊡12€. Restaurant* ◗. Run by the same family for a century, this rustic Provençal hotel and restaurant offers themed package stays and friendly welcome.

◗◗ **Hôtel L'Aiglon** – *7 Avenue Madone. ℘04 93 57 55 55. www.hotelaiglon.net. 29 rooms.* 🅿. *⊡10€. Restaurant*◗◗◗. This hotel is in a beautiful villa with garden terrace and swimming pool. Elegantly appointed rooms with WiFi. Fine dining restaurant.

◎◎ **Hôtel Chambord** – *6 Av. Boyer. ℘04 93 35 94 19. www.hotel-chambord. com. 40rooms.* 🅿. 🍴*10€.* Modern, sound-proof hotel near the Palais de l'Europe and casino. Breakfast served exclusively in the rooms.

◎◎ **Hôtel Prince de Galles** – *4 Avenue General de Gaulle. ℘04 93 28 21 21. www.princedegalles.com. 64 rooms.* 🅿 🍴*11.50€. Restaurant◎◎.* Formerly the HQ for the Monaco palace guards, this hotel has all of the modern comforts and views over the sea. The Petit Prince restaurant has a large garden terrace.

◎◎ **Hôtel Princess et Richmond** – *617 Promenade du Soleil. ℘04 93 35 80 20. www.princess-richmond.com. 46 rooms.* 🅿. 🍴*11€. Restaurant◎.* This seaside hotel features a smooth pebble beach and rooftop solarium and Jacuzzi. Some rooms face the sea, all have air conditioning, WiFi and classic contemporary decor.

◎◎◎ **Hôtel Napoléon** – *29 Porte de France. ℘04 93 35 89 50. www.napoleon-menton.com. 43 rooms.* 🅿. 🍴*14€. Restaurant◎◎.* Elegant, contemporary hotel right on the beach. Air-conditioned rooms; ones facing the sea have pretty teak balconies. The beachside restaurant has grilled fish, barbeque meats and ice cream desserts.

🍽 EAT

◎◎ **Auberge Pierrot-Pierrette** – *Pl.de l'Église, Monti. Closed Dec–15 Jan, Mon. ℘04 93 35 79 76.* In a tranquil hamlet perched on the hills above Menton, this family-run restaurant surrounded by gardens serves hearty Provençal meals.

◎◎ **A Braijade Méridiounale** – *66 Rue Longue. ℘04 93 35 65 65. www.abraijade.com. Closed 6–12 Jan, 15 Nov –5 Dec, Wed, lunch Jul–Aug.* Hidden in an alley of the old quarter, this homey restaurant provides Provençal dishes and grilled meats at very reasonable rates. Pretty dining room with visible stonework, beams and a fireplace.

◎◎ **La Cantinella** – *8 Rue Trenca. ℘04 93 41 34 20. Closed Jan, lunch in Aug, Tue.* The Sicilian owner delights in sharing his Mediterranean-infused cuisine in a friendly, laid-back atmosphere.

🛒 SHOPPING

Lemons – Many shops in Menton pay tribute to this sunny fruit by selling a wide range of produce made or flavoured with lemons: tarts and pies, gingerbread, wine, jam, soaps, etc.

Marchés – *Open daily in the morning.* Covered market on Quai de Monléon. Careï market at the top of the Biovès Gardens, beneath the railway bridge.

Confitures Herbin – *2 Rue du Vieux-Collège. ℘04 93 57 20 29. www.confitures-herbin.com. Kitchen tours Mon, Wed, Fri 10.30am. Shop closed Sat–Sun.* An impressive range of mouthwatering jams made on the premises of this family business? There's also different types of honey, vinegar, confit and mustard.

🚶 SPORT & LEISURE

Sports – La Promenade de la Mer is where most of the sports and recreation companies are found, including scuba diving, sailing, tennis and windsurfing clubs.

🎢 Koaland – *Av. de la Madone. ℘04 92 10 00 40. Closed Oct–May, Tue.* Leisure park for children and the younger generation with a miniature golf course.

CALENDAR

Fête du Citron (Lemon Festival) – Two weeks in February-March *(around Mardi Gras)*. Book at least two months in advance for this popular event.

Chamber Music Festival – In August on the esplanade of the Église St-Michel. This prestigious event is attended by talented soloists and conductors from around the world.

Monaco★★★

The Principality of Monaco, a sovereign state overlooking the Mediterranean between Nice and the Italian border, perfectly captures the essence of the Côte d'Azur with its rococo palaces, lush gardens, world-famous casino and glamorous royal family. Luxury hotels, exclusive shopping boutiques, and the annual Formula 1 Grand Prix make this a popular jet-set destination.

A BIT OF HISTORY

The Grimaldi family – Monaco was inhabited in prehistoric times and later became a Greek settlement and a Roman port, but its real place in history begins with the Grimaldi dynasty. **François Grimaldi**, expelled from Genoa during a family feud, captured Monaco in 1297 disguised as a monk with with his men. But François didn't hold it long, and it was only in 1308 that another Grimaldi bought the domain of Monaco from the Genoese. Since then the Grimaldi coat of arms (bearing two armed monks) has always been carried by the royal heirs.

A turbulent history – The history of Monaco has been fraught with family and political dramas. In the 16C Jean II was killed by his brother Lucien, who in turn was assassinated by his nephew; in 1604 Honoré I was thrown into the sea by his subjects. Monaco was subjected to foreign occupation: by the Spaniards from 1524 to 1641; by the French from 1641 to 1814; by the kingdom of Sardinia from 1815 to 1861. Menton and Roque-brune, which originally belonged to the Principality, were bought in 1861 by Napoleon III, with the annexation of Nice.

The Monégasques

There are just over 7 000 native Monégasque citizens in the Principality, all exempt from taxes and military service. They are not, however, permitted to gamble in Monaco's casinos.

▶ **Population:** 32 020.

♽ **Michelin Map:** 341 F5; local map: *see Corniches de la RIVIERA*.

ℹ **Info:** 2A Bd. des Moulins. ℘00 377 92 16 61 66. www.visitmonaco.com.

▶ **Location:** The 197ha/487 acres making up the Principality are divided into five districts: Monaco-Ville, the old town on The Rock (*La Rocher*); Monte-Carlo, with its luxury shops and casino; the busy La Condamine port; the new district of Fontvieille to the east; and the beaches of Larvotto to the west.

🅿 **Parking:** Parking garages (free for the first hour) can be found at Place du Casino and the Parking des Pêcheurs in Monaco-Ville. Access to the Rock (Le Rocher) is permitted only to vehicles with local (06) licence plates.

🖋 **Don't Miss:** The interior of the Monte-Carlo Casino and Opéra, the winding streets of old Monaco-Ville leading to the Prince's Palace and the panoramic views from the hillside Jardin Exotique.

🕒 **Timing:** Count on at least a half day to see the best of Monaco, or a full day if you plan on shopping or going to the beach. Start in Monaco-Ville, which has the most attractions and souvenir shops in one area. The casino tables don't open until 5pm.

👪 **Kids:** Child-friendly museums include the Collection des Voitures Anciennes and the aquariums of the Musée Océanographique.

PRACTICAL INFORMATION

TELEPHONE

To telephone Monaco from France, dial 00 followed by 377 (code for Monaco) and then the 8-digit telephone number.

CURRENCY AND POSTAGE

Monaco uses euros just like France, but it has an independent postal system. All letters mailed from within the Principality must have Monégasque stamps.

TOURS AND PUBLIC TRANSPORT

BUS: C.A.M. – ℘00 377 97 70 22 22. *www.cam.mc. Service every 10min from 7.30am–8.30pm.* ⬭*Tickets 1€ each or 3€ for day pass.* Five regular bus lines that loop around the Principality. Maps available at the tourist office.

TAXI: Two main **taxi** stands are located near the casino and at the train station. ℘00 377 93 50 56 28 or 00 377 93 15 01 01.

TOURIST TRAIN: Monaco Tours – *Av. St-Martin, in front of the Musée Océanographique.* ℘00 377 92 05 64 38. *www.visitmonaco.com. Operates 10.30am–5pm. Closed Jan, 15 Nov– 26 Dec.* ⬭*6€.* This small tourist train in Monégasque colours makes 30min round trip journeys around the Principality.

BOAT TRIPS: Aquavision – *Compagnie de Navigation et de Tourisme de Monaco, Quai des Etats-Unis.* ℘00 377 92 16 15 15. *www.aquavision-monaco. com. Daily departures Apr–Oct.* ⬭*11€ (child 8€).* Glass-bottomrd boat trips affording views of the sea depths, and marine fauna and flora (55min).

HELICOPTER: Héli Air Monaco – *Héliport de Monaco, Fontvieille.* ℘00 377 92 05 00 50. *www.heliairmonaco.com.* Regular daily service (6min) every 15min between Monaco and the Aéroport de Nice-Côte d'Azur. Also 10min sightseeing tours of Monaco and daily flights between Monaco and Fréjus.

Birth of Monte-Carlo – The first casino was an unremarkable establishment in Monaco-Ville itself, set up in 1856 by the Prince, who was short of funds. Only in 1862 did the casino move to its own premises in Monte-Carlo where it remained in humble isolation for several years. The arrival of **François Blanc**, director of the casino and spa in

Bad Hamburg, brought success. Within a few years the casino became fashionable and the surrounding land was covered with luxurious residences.

A thriving economy – To accommodate the influx of visitors attracted by the gambling tables and tax concessions, Monaco began to put up buildings at a

View of Monaco from the Grande Corniche

S. Sauvignier/ MICHELIN

furious pace. Once all the available space had been occupied the shoreline was extended into the sea, providing 22% more land (the Fontvieille district).

Tourism remains the main activity, however Monaco now has conference facilities rivalling those of Cannes and Nice. At Fontvieille light industry is being encouraged, and around 40 international banking institutions make Monaco a player in the financial world.

Original and revolutionary town-planning – Since the 1980s a new urban plan has been developed to satisfy the growing residential and service requirements: the future of property in Monaco would seem to lie underground. All the new access roads are now linked to the French network by deep tunnels. Connections between districts are facilitated by groups of automatic elevators or escalators. Behind the façade of some of Monaco's luxury hotels are access ramps to large public car parks hollowed out of the rock.

🚶 WALKING TOUR
THE ROCK★★
Tour: allow 3hr. Park in Parking des Pêcheurs and take the elevator.
Crowned by the old town of Monaco-Ville and its ramparts, the Rocher de Monaco jutts 800m/875yd out to sea over the bay. The town is so pretty that it resembles a studio set: neat little 18C houses with their salmon-pink façades, squeezed in along quaint alleyways. This is the medieval heart of the Principality, home to some of its most popular sights, including the **Musée Océanographique** (*see Discovering Local Flora and Fauna*) and Prince's Palace . On the car park terraces, near the Musée Océanographique, is **Monte-Carlo Story** (*open daily Jul–Aug 2–6pm; Sept–Jun 2–5pm; closed Nov–25 Dec; 7€; 00 377 93 25 32 33*) a multiscreen production retracing the history of the Grimaldi dynasty and the development of the Principality.

▷ *Take Av. St-Martin through the Jardins St-Martin, to the cathedral.*

Quiet square on the Rock
Allison M. Simpson/MICHELIN

Cathédrale
The neo-Romanesque cathedral was built with white stone from La Turbie on the ruins of the church of St-Nicolas between 1875 and 1903. The royal family tombs are located in the ambulatory. The cathedral has a collection of **early paintings from the Nice School★★**. There are two alterpieces by Louis Bréa: **St Nicholas** in the ambulatory.

▷ *Follow Rue de l'Eglise to Rue Emile de Loth, then left at Pl. de la Mairie to Rue Princesse-Marie-de-Lorraine.*

Chapelle de la Miséricorde
This chapel's classic pink and white façade was built in 1646 by the Black Penitents. The **Recumbent Christ** by the Monégasque sculptor Bosio is carried through the old town on Good Friday.

▷ *On leaving turn right onto picturesque Rue Basse to Pl. du Palais.*

Place du Palais★
This vast square, ornamented with cannons given to the Prince of Monaco by Louis XIV, is bordered to the northeast by a crenellated parapet from which there is a **view** of the harbour, Monte-Carlo and the coast as far as the Bordighera headland. To the southwest is the **Promenade Ste-Barbe**.

Palais Princier★

Open Apr 10.30am–6pm; May–Sept 9.30am–6.30pm; Oct 10am–5.30pm. 7€. 00 377 93 25 18 31. www.palais.mc

The palatial home of the Grimaldi family was built in the 17C in place of the original 13C Genoese fortress. The formidable perimeter is built into the vertical rock, with battlemented towers.

A monumental doorway with the Grimaldi arms adorns this robust-looking ensemble. The tour leads visitors through the Hercules Gallery decorated with 16C and 17C frescoes, and the Throne Room and the state apartments where official receptions are held.

Follow the Rampe Major through 16C, 17C and 18C gates down to Pl. d'Armes.

LA CONDAMINE

30min.

In the Middle Ages this term applied to cultivable land at the foot of a village or a castle. Nowadays La Condamine is the commercial district and port stretching between the Rock and Monte-Carlo.

Port Hercule

Prince Albert I commissioned the harbour, with its luxury yachts and terraced promenade. From the northwest corner of the harbour a valley separating La Condamine from Monte-Carlo runs under a viaduct to the church.

Follow the Bd. Albert I to the passage leading to Pl. Ste-Dévote.

Église Ste-Dévote

St Devota was martyred in Corsica in the 3C when, according to tradition, the skiff carrying her body to Africa was caught in a storm and guided by a dove to the shores of Monaco.

Changing of the Guard

The tightly choreographed changing of the guard takes place daily on Place du Palais at 11.55am.

The Grimaldi Family Today

In July 2005, the 47-year-old Prince Albert II of Monaco succeeded his father, Prince Rainier III, who died in April 2005 after ruling the Principality for 56 years. Albert and his sisters (Princesses Caroline and Stéphanie) lost their mother, the Hollywood actress Grace Kelly, in a car accident in 1982. The Prince's single status and his sisters' rocky relationships are closely followed in the European tabloids.

In the Middle Ages relics of the saint were stolen by sailors. But the thieves were caught and their ship razed – a legend which has given rise to the ceremony which takes place every January 26 when a ship is burned in the church square, followed by a procession.

Follow Rue Grimaldi, a popular shopping street, to the Rue Princesse Caroline, and finish at Pl. d'Armes.

MONTE-CARLO★★★

1.5hr.

Monte-Carlo is a name famous throughout the world. It brings to mind high-stakes gambling as well as the majestic setting of its palaces, casinos, luxurious shops and exotic gardens.

Place du Casino

Place du Casino is the centre of the action, where the Café de Paris and the Hôtel de Paris flank the **casino** *(see Sights)*, surrounded by beautiful gardens. Around the back of the casino is a fine **terrace**★★ overlooking the sea, with views reaching Italy.

Le Casino de Monte-Carlo

Forbidden to anyone under 18 years of age. Slots and European gaming rooms open from 2pm (noon on weekends); blackjack tables open from 5pm. Closed when the last person leaves. 10€ Public rooms, 20€ private rooms. ID/Passport required. 00 377 92 16 20 00. www.casinomontecarlo.com.

This impressive building comprises several sections built between 1878 and 1910. The oldest sections, designed by **Charles Garnier**, architect of the Paris Opera House, make up the seafront façade and the Opera-Theatre, once home to Diaghilev's Ballet Russe.

Avenue Princesse Grâce

Beyond the sleek Grimaldi Forum are the luxurious beaches of **Larvotto Plage**. Here you'll find boutiques, cafés and restaurants overlooking the beach. Swimmers will find two anchored diving platforms and many colourful fish inhabiting the underwater nature reserve.

Musée Napoléonien et des Archives du Palais★

Pl. du Palais. ○*Open Tue–Sun Apr 10.30am–6pm; May–Sept 9.30am–6.30pm; Oct 10am–5.30pm; Dec 10.30am–5pm; last entry 30min before closing.* ⊛*4€.* ℘*00 377 93 25 18 31. www.palais.mc.*

One wing of the Palace is devoted to a museum on Napoleon, including geneological charts showing how the Bonapartes are related to the Grimaldi princes. There are many of the Emperor's personal souvenirs and documents.

The upper floor is devoted to the history of Monaco, with the charter granted by Louis XII recognising the Principality's independence on display.

Nouveau Musée National de Monaco★

17 Av.Princesse Grâce. ○*Open daily Jul–Sept 10am–7pm.* ⊛*6€ (child 3.50€).* ℘*00 377 93 25 18 31. www.nmnm.mc.*

The New National Museum, housed in a charming villa built by Charles Garnier and fronted by a rose garden dotted with sculptures (formerly home to the collection of dolls and automata), has, since 2009, hosted temporary exhibitions on the history and culture of the Principality *(on the first floor).*

Terrace of the casino

D. Chapuis/MICHELIN

Collection des Voitures Anciennes★

Fontvieille. ⅌○*Open daily 10am–6pm.* ○*Closed 25 Dec.* ⊛*6€ (child 3€).* ℘*00 377 92 05 28 56. www.palais.mc.*

About 100 old vehicles and carriages from the royal collection are on display. On the first level are the barouches used by Prince Charles III. Next is the De Dion Bouton (1903), the first car owned by Prince Albert I, a Rolls Royce Silver Cloud given by Monégasque tradesmen to Prince Rainier on his wedding day in 1956, and a 1952 Austin London taxi converted for Princess Grace. The 1929 Bugatti (winner of the 1st Grand Prix) and a 1989 Ferrari F1 (600hp) have pride of place in the hall dedicated to Formula 1.

Musée Naval

Fontvieille. ⅌○*Open 10am–6pm.* ⊛*4€.* ℘*00 377 92 05 28 48. www.musee-naval.mc.*

The hundred exhibits in this museum are the cream of the royal collection of model ships, including models built by Prince Albert I in 1874, and a remarkable **gondole impériale** made in 15 days for the inspection of Napoleon I at Anvers.

MONACO MONTE-CARLO

0 _____ 200 m

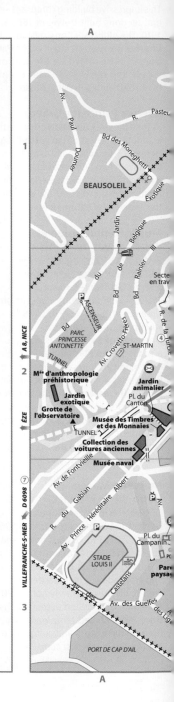

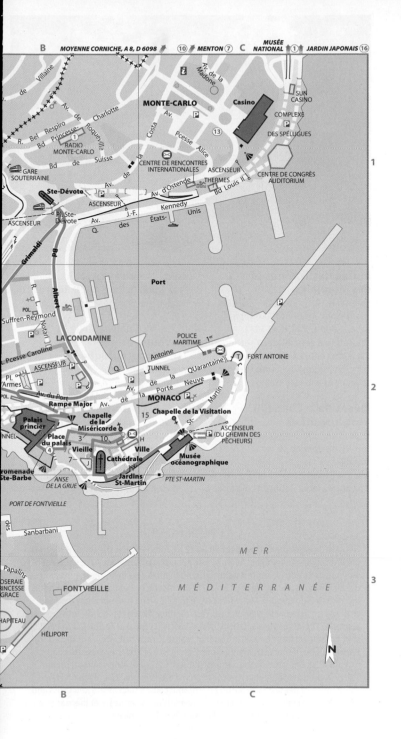

SUN CASINO

MONTE-CARLO

Av.

Casino

COMPLEXE

DES SPÉLUGUES

13

de Villaine

de

R. Bel Respiro

Bd   Pcesse

RADIO MONTE-CARLO

1

Bd   de   Suisse

Av. de Roqueville

Charlotte

Av.

Costa

Pcesse

Alice

de

la

CENTRE DE RENCONTRES INTERNATIONALES

Av. de la Madone

GARE SOUTERRAINE

ASCENSEUR

ASCENSEUR

THERMES

Bd Louis II

CENTRE DE CONGRÈS AUDITORIUM

Ste-Dévote

Av.

Pl. Ste-Dévote

Av.   J.-F.   Kennedy

Q.   des   États-   Unis

Av. d'Ostende

ASCENSEUR

Grimaldi

Bd

Port

Albert

R.

POL

Suffren-Reymond

Notari

1er

LA CONDAMINE

POLICE MARITIME   1er

Antoine

FORT ANTOINE

Pcesse Caroline

ASCENSEUR

Q.

TUNNEL

de   la

QUarantaine

Pl.   T   Armes

Av.   de   Porte   Neuve

St-   Martin

POL

Av. du Port

de

MONACO

Rampe Major   Av.

Chapelle de la Miséricorde   3

15   **Chapelle de la Visitation**

ASCENSEUR (DU CHEMIN DES PÊCHEURS)

Palais princier

Place du palais   4

10

H   St-

Vieille   **Ville**

NNEL

7

Cathédrale

Jardins St-Martin

Musée océanographique

romenade Ste-Barbe

ANSE DE LA GRUE

PTE ST-MARTIN

PORT DE FONTVIEILLE

Sanbarbani

des

M E R

Papaline

OSERAIE PRINCESSE GRACE

FONTVIEILLE

M É D I T E R R A N É E

HAPITEAU

HÉLIPORT

N

1

2

3

B   C

Grand bac 2000, Musée océanographique de Monaco

©M. Dannino Musée océanographique de Monaco

Musée des Timbres et des Monnaies

Fontvieille. ♿🕐*Open daily Oct–Jun 10am–5pm; Jul–Sept 10am–6pm.* 🎫*3€.* ✆*00 377 93 15 41 50.*

Housed in a very modern setting, this museum contains stamps made in the Principality together with the Princes' collections and rare stamps.

Musée de la Chapelle de la Visitation

Pl. de la Visitation. ♿🕐*Open Tue–Sun 10am–4pm.* 🎫*3€.* ✆*00 377 93 500 700.*

This 17C Baroque chapel houses the rich Barbara Piasecka-Johnson collection of sacred artworks. Of particular interest are works by Zurbarán, Rubens and the Italian Baroque masters.

LOCAL FAUNA AND FLORA

👥 Musée Océanographique★★

Av. Saint-Martin. ♿🕐*Open Jul–Aug 9.30am–7.30pm; Apr–Jun and Sept 9.30am–7pm; Oct–Mar 10am–6pm.* 🎫*13€ (child 6–18 years 6.50€).* ✆*00 377 93 15 36 00. www.oceano.mc.*

The Oceanographic Museum and Research institute overlooks the Mediterranean from an impressive cliff (80m/262ft) on the Rock. Founded in 1910 by marine research enthusiast

---

Princess Grace

Grace Kelly was born in Philadelphia on 12 November 1929, the third of four children. After studying at the New York Academy of Dramatic Arts, she began working as an actress for television and the theatre. Her first breakthrough in the cinema was the movie *High Noon* (1952), in which she played a young bride married to Gary Cooper. Many films were to follow but her name has remaine-closely associated with that of the British director Alfred Hitchcock, for whom she starred in *Dial M for Murder* (1954), *Rear Window* (1954) and *To Catch a Thief* (1955), shot entirely on location in the South of France. Grace Kelly was introduced to Prince Rainier of Monaco at the Cannes Film Festival and they were married in April 1956. She gave birth to three children, Caroline, Albert and Stéphanie. The new princess soon won the affections of the Principality's residents. She spent much of her time supporting charitable causes such as the Red Cross and AMADE, an organisation set up to help developing countries. Her life was to end tragically in 1982 when her crashed off the Grande Corniche.

Before Laying a Bet

Stroking the knee of the equestrian statue of Louis XV in the entrance of the Hôtel de Paris before heading into the casino is said to bring the gambler good luck. Admission is free to the slot machine rooms in the casino, in the Café de Paris (also on Place du Casino), and at the Sun Casino (in the Fairmont Hotel, 12 avenue des Spélugues). During the summer season (July–mid-September) gambling takes place in the Salles des Palmiers of the Sporting-Club de Monte-Carlo. Gaming tables usually require a fee of 10€–20€ to play.

Prince Albert I to house his scientific collections dating back to 1885, it has one of the most impressive **aquariums**★★ in Europe, with more than 4 500 fish representing 400 different species of tropical fish, sharks, turtles, and live coral reef from the Red Sea. The **Salle d'Océanographie Zoologique**★, also known as Salle de la Baleine, contains the skeletons of large marine mammals. A cinema shows films made by the legendary Jacques-Yves Cousteau, who was director of the museum from 1957–88. From the second floor terrace *(lift)* is a magnificent **view**★★ of the coast.

Jardin Exotique★★

52 Bd. du Jardin-Exotique. ⏰*Open mid-May–mid-Sept 9am–7pm; mid-Sept–mid-May 9am–6pm.* ⏰*Closed 19 Nov, 25 Dec.* ⊚*6.90€ (combined ticket with Grotte de l'Observatoire and Musée d'Anthropologie Préhistorique).* ☎*00 377 93 15 29 80.*

This exceptional collection (900 varieties) of cacti, some more than a century old, clings dramatically to the cliffs above Monaco, cascading down a steep rock face with huge candelabra-like euphorbia, giant aloes, "mother-in-law cushions" and Barbary figs. Down 279 steps is the **Grotte de l'Observatoire**★, adorned with stalactites and stalagmites. Tools and Prehistoric animal bones excavated at the site are on display in the **Musée d'Anthropologie Préhistorique**★ *(access through the Jardin Exotique)*. The Rainier III Gallery contains regional collections including animals which once roamed the Riviera before the climate changed, such as reindeer, mammoths and cave bears and even hippos.

Jardin Japonals★

Av. Princesse Grace. ♿⏰*Open 9am–dusk.* ⊚*No charge.* ☎*00 377 93 15 22 77. www.palais.mc.*

Jardin Exotique

©Photononstop/Tips Images

In the contemporary surroundings of the Larvotto district this garden provides a calm green oasis beside the sea. The garden (7ha/17 acres), which is designed according to Shintoist principles has a tea room and **Jardin Zen** for contemplation.

♙♙ Jardin Animalier

Fontvieille. ◐*Open Jun–Sept 9am–noon, 2–7pm; Mar–May 10am–noon, 2–6pm; Oct–Feb 10am–noon, 2–5pm.* ◎*4€ (child 2€).* ℰ*00 377 93 25 18 31.* The zoo terraces, on the southwest face of the Rock, present a large and varied collection of mammals, reptiles, exotic birds and numerous monkeys.

Parc Paysager

Fontvieille.
In this park plant species from all over the world are clustered around a charm-ing lake. Nearby lies the **Princesse Grace Rose Garden,** with more than 4 000 bushes belonging to 150 different rose varieties.

Coastal Path to Cap Martin★★

🚶 *3hr round trip leaving from Monte-Carlo, preferably in the afternoon – local maps* ۍ*see MENTON and Corniches de la RIVIERA.*
Tourists wishing to take a shorter route can drive to the train station of Roque-brune-Cap-Martin and join up with the path running below. On the left of the Monte-Carlo Beach Hotel, follow the steps down between two villas.

For a description of the walk in the opposite direction, ۍ*see ROQUEBRUNE-CAP-MARTIN: COASTAL PATH.*

ADDRESSES

⌂ STAY

▱▱ **Hôtel de France** – *6 Rue de la Turbie. Near the train station.* ℰ*00 377 93 30 24 64. www.monte-carlo.mc/france. 26 rooms.* ▱*9€.* Charming, sound-proofed rooms decorated in Provençal hues and a modern breakfast lounge enhanced with metal and wood furniture.

▱▱ **Hôtel Miramar** – *126 Av.. du 3-Septembre, Cap d'Ail.* ℰ*04 93 78 06 60. www.montecarlo.mc/hotel-miramar-capdail. 25 rooms. Closed Feb.* 🅿. ▱*7.50€.* A good-value family-run hotel in the neighbouring village of Cap d'Ail. Rooms have WiFi; some face the sea.

▱▱▱▱ **Novotel Monte Carlo** – *16 Bd. de la Princesse Charlotte.* ℰ*00 377 99 99 83 00. www.novotel.com. 218 rooms.* 🅿. ▱*16.50€.* A stylish, modern hotel in the heart of Monaco with all of the latest amenities, including heated pool, fitness centre, bar and restaurant.

🍴 EAT

▱ **Le Bistroquet** – *Galerie Charles III, Av. des Spélugues.* ℰ*(00 377) 93 50 65 03. www.mcpam.com.* Lively restaurant and bar with a heated terrace facing the casino gardens. Serves a combination of bistro fare and French classics, wines by the glass. Lve music Fri–Sat evenings.

▱▱ **Castelroc** – *Pl. du Palais.* ℰ*00 377 93 30 36 68. Closed 15 Dec–19 Jan, Sat .* The terrace under the trees with a view of the palace makes a lovely setting for meal of Mediterranean specialities.

▱▱ **La Maison du Caviar** – *1 Av. St-Charles.* ℰ*00 377 93 30 80 06. Closed Sat lunch, Sun.* This prestigious house has been serving choice caviar to Monaco residents for the past 50 years. In an unusual setting made up of bottle racks and wooden panelling, you can also purchase salmon and foie gras.

▱▱▱ **Café de Paris** – *Pl. du Casino.* ℰ*(00-377) 98 06 76 23 . www.monte carloresort.com.* An elegant and chic brasserie with terraces overlooking the casino square and the sea. Seafood and traditional French dishes, as well as light salads and sandwiches.

⊜⊜⊜ **Loga** – *25 Bd. des Moulins.* ☎*(00-377) 93 30 87 72. www.leloga.com. Closed Sun.* A friendly family-run establishment popular with the locals, serving traditional regional cuisine, daily specials on the slate board.

⊜⊜⊜ **Petrossian** – *11 Av. Princesse Grace.* ☎*(00-377) 97 77 00 24 . www.petrossian.fr. Closed Sun–Mon.* The romantic dining room of this caviar house is decorated in luminous shades of white and mother-of -pearl. Specialities focus on fresh seafood to complement the caviar, as well as gourmet foie gras and rare vodkas.

☺ NIGHTLIFE

Casino de Monte-Carlo – *Pl. du Casino.* ☎*00 377 92 16 20 00. www.casino-monte-carlo.com.* This is Europe's leading casino, with over a million euros in profits, attributed to gambling and not to slot machines as is the case in other casinos. The gambling salons and lavish dining hall Le Train Bleu, decorated in the style of the Orient-Express, are truly impressive.

La Terrasse (Bar du Vistamar) – *Square Beaumarchais.* ☎*00 377 92 16 40 00. www.montecarloresort.com.* This famous bar has been patronised by many celebrities, such as Onassis and Maria Callas. Its superb terrace affords beautiful views of Monaco harbour. The specialities of the house are American cocktails, particularly those made with champagne!

Sass Café – *11 Av. Princesse-Grace.* ☎*00 377 93 25 52 00. www.sasscafe.com.* Exclusive bar-restaurant with a cosy atmosphere where members of the local jet set drop in for a fancy vodka or champagne cocktail before meeting up at Jimmy'z.

Le Jimmy'z – *Quai Princesse-Grace.* ☎*00 377 92 16 22 77. www.sportingmonte carlo.com.* It would be unthinkable to leave Monte-Carlo without having paid a visit to the legendary Jimmy'z. Formal evening wear is expected in this small but select club where the rich and wealthy love to congregate, whether they come from banking, advertising, fashion, or entertainment world.

Stars'N'Bars – *6 Quai Antoine-1.* ☎*00 377 93 50 95 95. www.starsnbars.com.* This is a popular American bar where the ambience is slightly more relaxed than in the Principality's other establishments. Stars'N'Bars caters for a younger clientele eager to drink beer, eat a hamburger or two, play billiards, surf on the internet and dance the night away.

☺ ENTERTAINMENT

Le Cabaret – *Pl. du Casino.* ☎*00 377 92 16 36 36. www.montecarloresort.com. Shows mid-Sept–mid-Jun Wed–Sat from 10.30pm; bar/restaurant open from 8.30pm.* This cabaret, run by the Monte-Carlo Casino, presents nightly flamenco, jazz or pop concerts.

☺ SHOPPING

All the famous fashion brands have boutiques in Monte-Carlo. Shops specialising in traditional goods are to be found in the narrow streets of the Rock *(Le Rocher)* opposite the palace.

CALENDAR

Monte-Carlo Rally – Held every year since 1911 at the end of January.

Feast of Ste-Dévote – Monaco's Patron Saint feast, January 27.

Sciaratù Carnival – Monégasque festival during the week of Mardi Gras.

Spring Arts Festival – Art, music, theatre and dance festival throughout April .

International Tennis Masters Series – Held every April.

Monaco Grand Prix – every May in the streets of the Principality on a winding circuit (3.145km/2mi).

Monte-Carlo Golf Open – On the hills of Mont Agel every June.

National Day of Monaco – Picturesque procession on the Rocher and other cultural spectacles 19 November.

Nice★★★

Alpes Maritimes

The Italian charm of Nice, capital of the Côte d'Azur, is immediately apparent in the colourful baroque buildings of the Old Town and the flavorful Niçois cuisine. Nothing epitomizes the French Riviera more than a stroll along the Promenade des Anglais, where the fresh sea air and shining sun are as inevitable as the traffic jams and exhaust fumes.

A BIT OF HISTORY

From the Greeks to the House of Savoy – Excavations at Terra Amata (*see Sights*) reveal evidence of a human settlement in Nice 400 000 years ago, although the first Greek settlement, the Ligurian trading-post of Nikaia, wasn't founded until the 4C BC. Later, the Romans concentrated their colonisation efforts on Cimiez (Cemenelum), whose splendour eventually overshadowed the little Nikaia.

Barbarian and Saracen invasions, however, reduced Cimiez to nothing, and Nikaia, (now called Nice) returned to prominence under the Counts of Provence in the 10C.

In 1388, Nice and its hinterland seceded from the politically divided Provence, whose lords were at the brink of civil war, and joined Savoy. Except for a few short interruptions, Nice belonged to the House of Savoy until its restoration to France in 1860.

Catherine Ségurane – In the 16C François I and his Turkish allies launched military operations in 1543 against the County of Nice. According to local tradition, Catherine Ségurane was bringing food to a soldier on the ramparts when the Turkish assault began. She flung herself forward at the Turks who appeared at the top of the wall, knife in hand, and hurled several attackers into the moat below, seized a flag and put fresh courage into the men of Nice. The attack was contained and a statue was erected to Catherine by her fellow citizens.

▶ **Population:** 347 060.

Michelin Map: 341 E5; local maps: *herein and Corniches de la RIVIERA*.

Info: 5 Promenade des Anglais. ℘0 892 707 707 (0.34€/min). Train Station Annex: Av. Thiers. www.nicetourisme.com.

Location: The Old Town is wedged between the Château Hill (east), the seaside Promenade des Anglais and the Promenade du Paillon green belt. West of this promenade is Place Masséna, surrounded by shopping streets. To the east of the Château Hill is the old port and Cap de Nice. On the hills to the north are the museums and gardens of Cimiez district. **Getting around** on foot is not difficult, but for Cimiez or the port consider using the city bus or take a double-decker bus sightseeing tour. (*see Practical Information*).

Parking: Car parks can be found all over town, at the market and near the port. There are no free spots, even on the streets.

Don't Miss: Winding streets and market of the Old Town; sunset views from Château Hill; Cimiez's Gallo-Roman ruins.

Timing: You could easily spend a week in Nice, but if you have just one full day, start on the seafront and the Old Town, then visit Cimiez and one or two of the major museums.

Kids: Children will enjoy the merry-go-round at the Jardin Albert I or the playground in the park at the top of the Château Hill.

PRACTICAL INFORMATION
SIGHTSEEING AND TOURS

Since 1 July 2008, entrance to Nice's municipal museums and galleries is free.

Guided tours – *Centre du Patrimoine , 75 quai des Etats-Unis. ℘04 92 00 41 90.* Tours of the Old Town *(2hr)*. ⌨*3€.*

Nice Riviera Pass – A 1-, 2- or 3-day sightseeing pass with free entry to many sights, guided tours, and shopping and dining advantages in the greater Nice area, from 24€–54€. Available at the tourist office or online at www.frenchrivierapass.com.

⌨ **Petits Trains Touristiques** – ⌨*Tours (40min) Apr–Sept 10am–6pm (Jun–Aug until 7pm); Oct–Mar 10am–5pm. Closed mid-Nov–mid-Dec, 1–15 Jan.* ⌨*7€ (3€ child under 9). ℘06 16 39 53 51. www.petittrainnice.com.* Departures from the seafront at the Jardin Albert I. Tours of the Old Town, port, Château Hill with commentary in English.

Nice le Grand Tour – *Departures every 30 minutes.* ⌨*20€ (children 5€). ℘04 92 29 17 00.* Double-decker, open top bus tours with commentary in English (90min), departing from the Jardins Albert I. Hop-on-hop-off the 14

different stops from Promenade des Anglais, Cimiez, and the Port.

Trans Côte d'Azur – *Quai Lunel. ℘04 92 00 42 30. Operates Mar–Apr Tue–Wed, Fri and Sun 11am, 3pm; May–Oct Tue–Sun noon, 4pm; www.trans-cote-azur.com.* ⌨*15€ (children 4–10 years, 9€).* Guided tours *(1hr)* of the coast of Nice, the Bay of Villefranche and Baie des Anges. Reservations a must.

PUBLIC TRANSPORT

Bus/Tram – The Ligne d'Azur network *(10 Av. Félix-Faure; ℘0 810 061 006; www.lignedazur.com)* includes buses for the city of Nice and its suburbs, and a new tram line in central Nice.
Tickets 1€ each, or 4€ for an unlimited 1-day pass *(includes airport buses 23, 98, and 99).* The TAM network *(Gare routière, Promenade du Paillon; ℘04 93 85 61 81; www.rca.tm.fr)* has service to cities such Antibes, Cannes and Grasse.

TER Train – *SNCF Gare, Avenue Thiers. ℘0 891 70 30 00. www.ter-sncf.com/paca.* Local train service to Draguignan, Fréjus, St-Raphaël, Cannes, Antibes, Menton Vintimille, Monaco. The Nice-Cuneo line crosses the Bévéra and Roya valleys.

Bonaparte in Nice – The County of Nice became the Département of Alpes-Maritimes during the Revolution, when it was re-attached to France following occupation by French troops in 1792. In 1794 Bonaparte, then General of Artillery in the army, lived at no 6 in the street which now bears his name, where he was arrested after the fall of Robespierre. In 1796 he stayed in Nice again, on Rue St-François-de-Paule, on the way to his commander-in-chief post in Italy. He had married Josephine only a few days earlier and it was from Nice that he wrote the well-known letter: "My darling, anguish at our parting runs through my veins as swiftly as the waters flow down the Rhône ..." At the fall of the Empire in 1814, Nice was handed back to the House of Savoy under the Treaty of Paris.

Two local heroes: Maréchal Masséna (1758–1817), son of a wine merchant, became, under Napoleon, a Maréchal de France, Duke of Rivoli and Prince of Essling. Considered a military genius, after Napoleon he was the general most esteemed by Wellington.

Giuseppe Garibaldi (1807–82), one of the principal authors of the Italian Revolution in 1860, had an extraordinarily turbulent political and military life in Europe and South America. A great friend of France, he commanded a brigade of the French Army in 1870.

Plebiscite – As a result of the 1858 alliance between France and Sardinia (House of Savoy), Napoleon III undertook to help the Sardinians drive the Austrians out of the provinces of northern Italy. In 1860 the Treaty of Turin

© Corbis

Nice Carnival★★

King of the Carnival!

The **Nice Carnival**★★★ is one of the biggest celebrations in the region, with two weeks of parades, confetti battles, fireworks and masked balls *(veglioni)*. The **floral parades**, or *batailles de fleurs,* offer a picturesque spectacle and attract huge and excited crowds, drawn by the colourful fruit and flowers.

The tradition dates back a long way in Nice, with references as long ago as 1294, on the occasion of the visit of the Count of Provence, Charles II. Nice Carnival has always been a welcome diversion from social tensions and conflicts, which were constantly breaking out as a result of Nice's geographical location and disputed ownership. Until the end of the 18C, the carnival took place after the Lenten fast in the form of local festivities in the old part of the city.

After a break of several years, caused by the wars of the Revolution and the Empire, the first parade of carnival floats took place in 1830 in honour of the royal visit of King Charles Félix to Nice and the return to Sardinian sovereignty. The modern form of carnival dates back to 1873, with the establishment of the various stages of the festivities and the setting of a different official theme every year.

Carnival-going families from Nice belong to long lines of tradition verging on outright dynasties. Each "stable" of carnival floats has its own characteristics. On average, about one tonne of papier-mâché is used in the making of each float. Famous painters from this area have also played their part in enriching the carnival decorations.

The festivities begin with the triumphal entry of "Sa Majesté Carnaval" about three weeks before Shrove Tuesday, or Mardi Gras. An effigy of the King of the Carnival is later ceremonially burned to mark the end of the carnival season. During the intervening period celebrations are in full swing, with parades of carnival floats accompanied by people in costumes sporting huge comical heads made of papier-mâché.

between Napoleon III and the King of Sardinia, Victor Emmanuel II, stipulated that Nice be returned to France "without any constraint on the will of the people". The plebiscite was an overwhelming victory for France: 25 743 in favour, 260 against. The entry of French troops and the ceremony of annexation took place on 14 June 1860. The regions of Tende and La Brigue were to remain Italian territory for 87 years until the treaty of 10 February 1947 allowed France to extend its natural frontiers to the Alps.

"L'École de Nice" – At the beginning of the 1960s Nice became one of the most lively artistic centres in Western Europe. Unlike the painters who, during the first half of the century, worked in total seclusion, the new wave combined life and art. At the instigation of **Yves Klein**, who repositioned painting within a purifying process (vacuum, monochrome paintings symbolising the sky, fire, etc.) and **Arman**, who elevated everyday accessories to the level of art, the 'New Realists' gave a distinctive impulse to modern art in Nice. Other Nice School artists: Martial Raysse, Sosno, Verdet, Chacallis, Venet and Ben (*see Musée d'Art Moderne et d'Art Contemporain, p319*).

Nice Today – Since 1860 the development of Nice, which then counted 40 000 inhabitants, has been remarkable. Thanks to the railway, Nice became the most popular resort town in France, and a prosperous commercial trade city. It's now the fifth largest city in France.

WALKING TOURS
THE SEAFRONT★★
Allow 2hr.

▷ *Begin from the intersection of Bd. Gambetta and Promenade des Anglais. See the map for parking.*

Promenade des Anglais★★
Closed to traffic one Sunday per month.
This wide promenade, facing due south and flanking the sea along its entire length, provides wonderful views of the Baie des Anges. Until 1820 access

to the shore was difficult but the English colony, numerous since the 18C, undertook the construction of a coastal path which now carries its name.
Although taken over by six lanes of traffic, the promenade has retained its mythical aura, with many legendary buildings overlooking the sea: the Ruhl Casino and Hotel Méridien (1973), the 1930s Palais de la Méditerranée, the **Hôtel Negresco**, a striking Belle Époque structure (c. 1900) and the Musée Masséna. Avenue de Verdun skirts the **Jardin Albert I**, an oasis of greenery surrounding a fountain, *The Three Graces*, sculpted by Volti.

Place Masséna
Started in 1815 in the Italian style, the buildings form an architectural unit in red ochre with arcades at street level. The north side of the square opens into Avenue Jean-Médecin, the main shopping street. Rue Masséna and Rue de France form the axis of a pedestrian area where you'll find smart shops, cinemas, cafés and restaurants.
At the corner of the Jardin Maréchal-Juin, surrounded by fountains, sits Tête Carrée (Square Head) by Sacha Sosno, housing the Louis-Nucéra Library.

The Port
For 2 000 years ships simply tied up at the foot of the Château Hill. A deep-water port was excavated in 1750 under the Duke of Savoy. Place Île de Beauté, a square facing the port, has houses embellished with porticoes and pretty façades from the 19C.
Today Nice harbour is a busy maritime centre frequented by fishing boats, yachts, Corsican ferries, luxury liners and merchant ships. Stroll through the flea markets at the Quai Lunel, then return to the Promenade des Anglais.

OLD NICE★
After enjoying a whiff of the misty sea air, turn to the old quarter of town and set off for the Baroque district of Nice, hemmed in between the Château Hill and Rue des Ponchettes.

Aerial view of the Old Nice

Cours Saleya

Once the elegant promenade of old Nice, this picturesque pedestrian street, lined with shops and restaurants, is now home to the famous **flower and vegetable market**. Note the the yellow façade of the **Caïs de Pierla Palace**, where Picasso lived in a small room facing the sea between 1921 and 1938.

Chapelle de la Miséricorde★

2 Pl. Pierre-Gautier. ◷*Open mid-Sept–Jun Tue 2.30–5pm.*

This fine example of Niçois Baroque belongs to the brotherhood of the Black Penitents. It was built in 1740 by Vittone according to the plans of the famous 17C Italian priest-architect Guarini. Inside, angels circle the gilded beams and faux-marble columns. Two primitive Niçois **retables★** in the sacristy represent the Virgin of Mercy: one by Jean Miralhet (1429) and the other by Louis Bréa (1515), containing Nice's earliest portrayal.

▷ *Turn left onto Rue de la Poissonnerie.*

Chapelle de l'Annonciation

◷*Open 8am–noon, 2.30–6pm.*
✆*04 93 62 13 62.*

The chapel is known locally as the **Chapelle Ste-Rita**, an Italian saint still venerated in Nice, as the armfuls of flowers and pyramids of candles at her altar *(left on entering)* and in the sacristy clearly show. The interior is a lavish illustration of local Baroque **decoration★** with altars and rails inlaid with marble, sumptuous altarpieces, painted and coffered vaults and fine panelling.

▷ *Continue straight ahead then take a right on Rue de la Place-Vieille, then take a left.*

Église St-Jacques or Gésu★

◷*Open by request* ✆*04 93 92 01 35.*
Built as a chapel in the 17C, this church is reminiscent of the Gesù Church in Rome.

Midday Cannon

Each day at noon a short cannon shot can be heard. This custom was introduced by a visiting Englishman, Sir Thomas Coventry, who grew tired of irregular meal times. He offered to buy and maintain a cannon for the town so that each day a shot could be fired at noon from the castle hill. The tradition continues, but the cannon was replaced by an explosive device.

The general effect is highly ornate, with 164 painted and 48 carved cherubs. The ceiling is painted with scenes from the life of St James. The **sacristy**, formerly the chapter house, contains 14 huge ,walnut cupboards (1696) displaying the church treasures.

▷ *The Rue du Jésus (across from the church) leads to the Rue Ste-Réparate and the cathedral of the same name.*

Cathédrale Ste-Réparate

Pl. Rossetti. ℘*04 93 92 01 35.*
○*Open Mon–Sat 9am–noon, 2–6pm, Sun 3–6pm.*
Built in 1650 in honour of Nice's patron saint, who was martyred in Asia Minor at the age of 15. The church is topped by an 18C bell tower and a magnificent dome of 14 000 glazed tiles that stands out on the Nice skyline. The **interior**★ is a riot of Baroque plasterwork and marble. The high altar and choir balustrade, adorned with heraldic imagery, are of marble.

▷ *Proceed along Rue Rossetti opposite and take the third left turning into Rue Droite.*

Palais Lascaris – Musée de la Musique

15 Rue Droite. ○*Open Wed–Mon 10am–6pm* ⌖*Guided tours Fri 3pm.* ⊜*Museum no charge; tou 5€.* ℘*04 93 62 72 40.*
This Genoese-style palace, influenced by local tradition, was built in 1648 by J B Lascaris, a descendant of the counts of Ventimiglia. On the ground floor a pharmacy from Besançon (1738) has been reconstructed to display a fine collection of flasks and tripods.
A grandiose balustraded **staircase**★ is decorated with 17C paintings hanging in rockwork niches and 18C statues of Mars and Venus. Private apartments display 18C ceilings, painted medallions framed in stuccowork and Louis XV woodwork inlaid with silver.
A group of **salons** in Empire style, directly inspired by the Piedmontese château at Govone, has bay windows looking out on to the sea. The **first floor**

has a collection of Primitive Niçois, Italian, Flemish and Spanish works.
A collection of 18C instruments acquired in 2009 have become the **Musée de la Musique** on the second floor.
There is also a fine collection of arms and armour (14C–18C) and exhibitions of great Niçois citizens, the Revolution and the Empire (represented by a precious sketch of Bonaparte by David), the history of Nice illustrated by watercolours, a fine model of the town in 1890 and an interesting collection of aristocratic and bourgeois costumes (19C).

Place St-François

This square is home to the local fish market. Stuck to a house on the corner of Rue Droite and Rue de la Loge is a cannon ball which dates from the siege of Nice by the Turks, allies of François I (1543). Continue along lively Rue Pairolière, where several places serve *socca*, a local speciality (⌖*see p320*).

Place Garibaldi

This attractive square with the yellow ochre arcades was laid out at the end of the 18C in typical Piedmont style. It marks the northern limit of the Old Town and the beginning of the new, and was the start of the royal route to Turin in the 1700s (which is where the Café de Turin got its name). A statue of Garibaldi stands proudly among the fountains and greenery. The 18C **Chapelle de Saint-Sépulcre** on the south side of the square belongs to the Brotherhood of Blue Penitents, with a Baroque interior decorated in different shades of blue.

▷ *From Pl. Garibaldi, take Rue Neuve past the Café de Turin to the church of St-Martin-St-Augustin.*

Église St-Martin-St-Augustin

1 Pl. Sincaire. ○*Open Tue–Fri 9am–noon, 2–5pm.* ℘*04 93 92 60 45.*
This is the oldest parish in Nice, dating back to 1510. It is the site of Garibaldi's baptism as well as a mass performed by the Augustinian monk, Martin Luther, before the Protestant Reformation. The church has a fine Baroque **interior**★

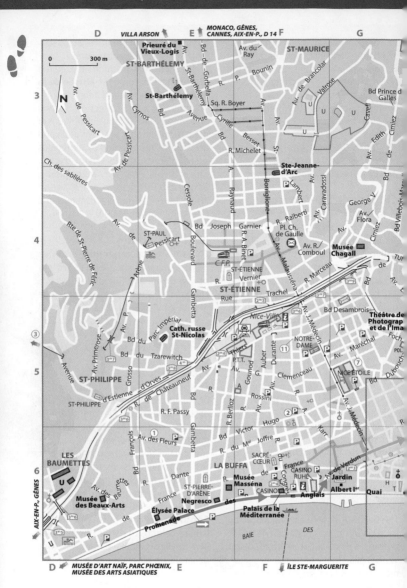

with a Pietà. Outside the entrance is a low relief sculpture that pays tribute to the local heroine Catherine Ségurane.

> *Follow the steep steps to the Château Hill along Rue St-Augustin and Rue de la Providence.*

Château Hill

This 92m/302ft high hill, arranged as a garden walk, was where Nice's fortress stood until it was destroyed in 1706 by Louis XIV's army. From the wide platform on the summit there is a sweeping **panorama**★★ *(viewing table)*. Below the terrace is an artificial waterfall. On the eastern side the **foundations of an 11C cathedral** (apse and apsidal chapels), on top of Roman and Greek foundations, have been uncovered. Walk around the ruins to the northwest corner of Château Hill where there is a **bird's-eye view** of the roofs of Nice and the Baie des Anges.

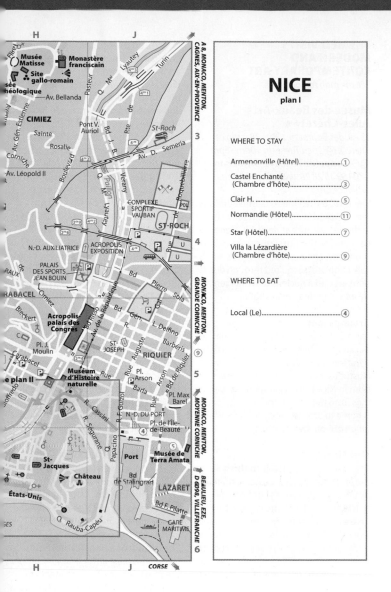

H   J

Eliseo ✕
Musée Matisse
Monastère franciscain
Site gallo-romain
sée héologique
— Av. Bellanda
CIMIEZ
Av. Gén. Étienne
Sainte
Pont V. Auriol
St-Roch
Corniche
Rosalie
Av. Léopold II
A 8, MONACO, MENTON, CAGNES, AIX-EN-PROVENCE
Pasteur
Lyautey
Turin
de
Av. D. Semeria
3
COMPLEXE SPORTIF VAUBAN
ST-ROCH
POL
N.-D. AUXILIATRICE
ACROPOLIS EXPOSITION
U
U
PALAIS DES SPORTS JEAN BOUIN
RAUX
Ormeto
Bd
Pierre Sola
MONACO, MENTON, GRANDE CORNICHE
4
RABACEL
Breckert
Acropolis- palais des Congrès
Gen.
L. Delfino
Barbéris
9
Carabacel
Pl. J. Moulin
ST-JOSEPH
Auguste
RIQUIER
MONACO, MENTON, MOYENNE CORNICHE
plan II
Muséum d'Histoire naturelle
R. Cassini
Guzori
Rue
Pl. Arson
Arson
Bd de Riquier
5
R. Ségurane
Barla
Rue
Pl. Max Barel
Papacino
N.-D. DU PORT
Pl. de l'Ile- de-Beauté
4
St- Jacques
Port
Musée de Terra Amata
5
BEAULIEU, EZE, D Ø D98, VILLEFRANCHE
Château
Bd de Stalingrad
LAZARET
États-Unis
Bd F. Pilatte
Q. Rauba-Capéu
GES
GARE MARITIME
6
H   J   CORSE

NICE
plan I

WHERE TO STAY

Armenonville (Hôtel)..........................①

Castel Enchanté
(Chambre d'hôte)............................③

Clair H. ....⑤

Normandie (Hôtel)...........................⑪

Star (Hôtel)......................................⑦

Villa la Lézardière
(Chambre d'hôte)............................⑨

WHERE TO EAT

Local (Le)..④

○ *Steps lead down from a chapel on the left. Continue to Tour Bellanda.*

Tour Bellanda

Despite its appearance, this imposing circular bastion only dates from the 19C, when it was built as an identical replacement for one of the towers of the citadel destroyed in 1706.

The composer Hector Berlioz (1803–69) lived here during his time in Nice, which he wrote of enthusiastically: "Here I am in Nice, breathing the warm, balmy air... Here life and happiness come running swiftly to greet me, music folds me into her arms, and the future smiles on me..."

THEMED VISITS
MODERN AND
CONTEMPORARY ART
See the map for locations.

Musée des Beaux-Arts Jules-Chéret★★

33 Av. des Baumettes. Bus 38 (stop at Chéret). ⏰*Open Tue–Sun 10am–6pm.* ⏰*Closed public holidays.* ⌨*No charge.* 📞*04 92 15 28 28. www.musee-beaux-arts-nice.org.*

Since 1928 the Fine Arts Museum has been housed in an 1878 residence built in the Renaissance style of 17C Genoese palaces for the Russian princess Kotschoubey. The museum displays a rich collection of art acquired through donations around a nucleus of works sent to Nice by Napoleon III in 1860.

Ground Floor

The galleries on the ground floor contain Italian Primitives, the important artistic dynasty of the **Van Loo** (whose most illustrious member, **Carle Van Loo**, was born in Nice in 1705) and official paintings from the Third Republic. The patio is home to *Bronze Age* by Rodin and *Triumph of Flora* by Carpeaux.

First Floor

The main staircase leads to the hall on the first floor which was used originally by musicians because of its acoustics. It is now adorned with the works of **Jules Chéret**, the inventor of modern posters, who died in Nice in 1932. This floor is dedicated to art of the second half of the 19C and early 20C, including works by Orientalists, an original plaster cast of *The Kiss* by Rodin, a series of works by the pre-Impressionist Félix Ziem, ceramics by Picasso, and a Van Dongen gallery housing the Fauvist's major works.

Musée Matisse★★

164 Avenue des Arènes. Bus 15, 17, 20, 22, 25 (stop Les Arènes/musée). ♿⏰*Open Wed–Mon 10am–6pm.* 🚶*Guided tours available.* ⏰*Closed 25 Dec, 1 Jan, Easter Sunday, 1 May.* ⌨*4€, tours 3€.* 📞*04 93 81 08 08. www.musee-matisse-nice.org.*

In 1670, on the site of a hut *(cabanoun)* buried in the ancient remains of Cimiez, a folly in Genoese style was built, its façades decorated with coloured pebble-dash and *trompe-l'œil* paintings and extended by balustraded terraces. Its owner, the Consul of Nice, named it Palais de Gubernatis. In 1950, when it was *in extremis*, the town of Nice saved it from being divided up and rechristened it **Villa des Arènes**. Since its redevelopment in 1993, it has housed the Musée Matisse.

A large composition of cut-out gouaches, *Flowers and Fruit,* which is Henri Matisse's last work (1953), greets visitors at the entrance. About 30 canvases illustrate the progression of the artist from the timid attempts of his early works in 1890. **Drawings** from his many different periods are also on display, including 30 sketches for the mural *The Dance* (1933). Matisse's activity as a sculptor is also well represented by 54 of the total of 62 **bronze sculptures** he produced during his lifetime.

Dotted around the museum are his personal belongings, his furniture and his private art collection, all of which are often depicted in his paintings.

Musée Marc-Chagall★★

Av. du Docteur-Ménard, Cimiez. Bus 15 (stop at Chagall). ♿⏰*Open Wed–Mon May–Oct 10am–6pm; Nov–Apr 10am–5pm.* ⌨*7.50€ (free first Sun and EU citizens under 26).* 📞*04 93 53 87 20. www.musee-chagall.fr.*

The result of Chagall's donation to France, this museum built in 1972 houses the most important permanent collection of the painter's works. It is built partly in glass and hidden among the trees on a hilltop in Cimiez. His poetical lyricism is visible in all **17 canvases** which make up the 'Biblical Message', an uninterrupted endeavour lasting 13 years (1954–67). There are also several sculptures by the artist. Note the series of 39 gouaches painted in 1931 after his return from Palestine. Some of the themes were taken up again in his larger canvases, 105 etchings and engravings for the Bible edited by Tériade in 1956.

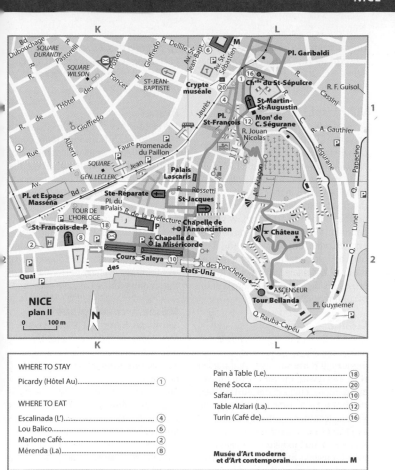

NICE
plan II
0   100 m

Musée d'Art Moderne et d'Art Contemporain★★

Promenade des Arts. ○*Open Wed–Mon 10am–6pm.* ○*Closed 1 Jan, Easter Sunday, 1 May, 25 Dec.* ◎*No charge.* ℘*04 93 62 61 62. www.mamac-nice.org.* Designed by Yves Bayard and Henri Vidal, the Museum of Modern and Contemporary Art is made up of four square towers with roof-top terraces linked by glass passageways. On the parvis, between the museum and the theatre, stands a monumental stabile by Alexander Calder.

The collections present French and American avant-garde art movements from the 1960s to the present. Both these countries were developing parallel art movements based on similar experiences. In France these ideas were often nurtured by artists living on the Riviera. In the 1960s the American **Pop Art** movement and the French **Nouveau Réalisme** (◎*see Klein below*) attempted to express the reality of daily life in a modern society of consumerism and popular culture. While Pop artists Andy Warhol, Roy Lichtenstein and others appropriated objects belonging to mass culture, the New Realists, more derisive, sought inspiration from those same objects as symbols of modern life, by collecting or breaking them (Arman), compressing them (César), capturing them under glass (Spoerri), or wrapping them (Christo).

A section of the museum is devoted to the French painter **Yves Klein** (1928–62), whose monumental work, *Wall of Fire,* is located on the roof-top terrace.

The museum also holds works by other artists of the Nice School such as Bernar Venet, Sacha Sosno, Gilli, Jean-Claude Fahri, Robert Malaval, Chubac...

Villa Arson

20 Av. Stephen Liégeard. Bus 4, 7 (stop at Fanny). ◐*Open Wed–Mon 2–6pm (Jul–Aug until 7pm).* ◑*Closed between exhibitions.* ≋*No charge.* ☎*04 92 07 73 73. www.villa-arson.org.*

The Villa Arson is in the northern part of the city, set in a Mediterranean garden on the hill of St-Bartholomew with a panoramic view of the Baie des Anges. The 18C villa, influenced by the Bauhaus architectural movement, houses the École Nationale Supérieure d'Art, an artists' residence and a national centre of contemporary art.

CIMIEZ

Allow 3.5hr. See the city map. Bus 15 also goes there (stop at Arènes).

Cimiez hill is the sophisticated part of Nice, filled with elegant town houses and gardens. But long before it was settled by the French and visited by Queen Victoria (commemorated by a statue at the top of Boulevard de Cimiez), the Romans called this hilltop 'Cemelenum'. In 2C there were at least 20 000 Romans living here. Many vestiges of their city can still be seen today.

▷ *Starting from Pl. Jean-Moulin, behind the Acropolis, drive west along Bd. Carabacel and follow the route marked on the plan.*

Arènes

The ellipse-shaped amphitheatre, which is only 67m/220ft by 56m/184ft, could hold 4 000 spectators. Traces remain of the gangways and of the sockets on the external façade, which held the posts supporting a huge adjustable awning *(velum).* The amphitheatre was designed for spear contests and gladiatorial bouts but not for animal fights. Traditional festivals take place here all year round *(Fêtes des Mai, Fêtes des Cougourdons)* and there are live jazz performances in the summer *(⌕see Calendar of Events).*

Musée Archéologique

160 Av. des Arènes. ⟁◐*Open Wed–Mon 10am–6pm (last entrance 1hr before closure).* ≋*No charge.* ☎*04 93 81 59 57. www.musee-archeologique-nice.org.*

The collections include finds excavated at Cimiez and around Nice, as well as donations. There are ceramics and bronzes from the great Mediterranean civilisations (Greece, Etruria, Roman Africa) and artefacts such as the superb **mask of Silenus**★ salvaged from shipwrecks. Ligurian and Roman arte-

---

Socca

The day started early in those days in the Nice bar where my uncle and I enjoyed our *socca*. The ingredients include chick-pea flour, olive oil and salt beaten into a smooth mixture in a large copper pan. It is baked in a wood fire oven, a cooking time based on exact calculation or long experience and a speedy hand in cutting the cake into pieces when it is served. Socca will not wait; it must be eaten piping hot – seasoned with pepper.

The recipe has never changed. This is the same *socca* that used to be delivered all over the town. It was put in a box with a zinc lid and the trays in the delivery vans were kept warm with charcoal heaters. Nothing was more satisfying to labourers, office workers, women shopping or anyone else overcome by the desire for a little something in the morning. It is the same socca which the dockers, who had knocked back a laced coffee at 5 o'clock, used to consume in the bars of Nice at half past six. It was their breakfast.

Louis Nucera
Chemin de la Lanterne (1981)
Published by Éditions Grasset

Ruins of the baths, Site Archéologique Gallo-Romain and Musée Matisse in the background

J.Malbrunet/MICHELIN

facts include the Bronze Age statue of a warrior from Mont Bégo, Iron Age items from perched strongholds or *oppida*) and milestones (1C) from the Via Julia Augusta. Roman civilisation is represented through examples of daily and public life, a display of imperial coins, as well as representations of Cimiez.

Site Archéologique Gallo-Romain★

Same as the Musée Archéologique.
Steps lead down into the *decumanus maximus* (the main east–west street of a Roman town) with its central drain and shops. To the left are the **North Baths**. for high-ranking Romans. On the eastern side are the latrines. The northern building contains the **cold bath** *(frigidarium)*; it was vaulted and its dimensions (10m/33ft high by 9m/30ft wide) give an idea of the huge scale of the northern baths (the warm room and the hot rooms built above the **underground stove** or *hypocaust*), and the public rooms, partially excavated. On the other side of the main street are the less elaborate but fully equipped **East Baths** for the general public, which can be viewed from a walkway. The western end of this street opens into the *cardo maximus* (main street running north–south) which returns to the Matisse Museum. On the left-hand side are the **West Baths**, for women only. The structure is quite well preserved, although it

was used as a cathedral in the 5C. The choir, in the *frigidarium*, contains traces of an altar and a stone seat.

◯ *Cross the public olive tree gardens to Pl. du Monastère.*

Place du Monastère

A twisted column of white marble, rising in the square in front of the church, bears a **Calvary** dating from 1477. On one side is the crucified seraph, who appeared before St Francis and imprinted the stigmata of the Passion on his body. Nearby in the Cimiez **cemetery** are buried the Fauvist painters Raoul Dufy and Henri Matisse. The latter's tomb lies in an olive grove to the north of the wall.

Monastère Franciscain★

The Franciscans, who in the 16C took over the buildings of a former Benedictine monastery founded in the 9C, have restored and considerably enlarged the abbey church.

Église Sainte-Marie-des-Anges

Pl. du Monastère. ◯*Open Sept–Jun.*
℘*04 93 81 00 04.*
The church possesses three **masterpieces**★★ by the local artist Louis Bréa, illustrating the Nice School. To the right of the entrance stands a **Pietà** (1475), and although it is an early work, it is undoubtedly one of his most perfect

creations. The arms of the cross and the stiff body of Christ emphasise the horizontal perspective, while the gold background reveals glimpses of a landscape. Weeping cherubs cluster round the Cross, while the lonely figure of Mary holds her son on her knees. Quite different but of equal beauty is the **Crucifixion** by the same artist, on the left in the choir. The **Deposition** in the third chapel, which is also attributed to Louis Bréa, complements the Cruxifixion and adheres to Renaissance principles: the figures aligned obliquely on the body of Christ are counterbalanced by the vertical lines of the landscape.

Musée Franciscain

Open Mon–Sat 10am–noon, 3–6pm. Closed public holidays. No charge. 04 93 81 00 04.

The **museum** recalls the work of the Franciscans in Nice from the 13C to the present day. The social and spiritual message of the Franciscans is proclaimed through documents and works of art (frescoes, engravings, sculptures) in a restored section of the old monastery.

Monastery Gardens★

On the south side of the monastery there are terraced gardens with flower beds and lemon trees looking down on the Paillon Valley from a **viewpoint** over Nice, the castle and the sea, Mont Boron and the observatory. A copse of cypress and holm oak marks the site of the former Ligurian *oppidum*.

NICE'S RUSSIAN HERITAGE

Around the middle of the 19C, after Empress Alexandra Fedorovna, the widow of Tsar Nicolas I, had settled in Nice, many wealthy Russian aristocrats chose this city as their favourite place of residence. These "eccentrics", as the locals would call them, re-created the atmosphere of their native country on the Riviera, hiring the services of architects who combined the Slav spirit with Mediterranean influences. Baron Von Dewies, who designed the Russian railway system, commissioned the building of the Gothic **Château de Valrose**

(Science Faculty of Nice University) and set up an isba from Kiev on his huge estate. At the west entrance to Nice, not far from the railway, the **Château des Ollières** features an impressive keep flanked by four turrets. The nearby **Palais Kotschoubey** houses the Musée des Beaux-Arts. Two other notable examples of Russian architecture are the **Palais Impérial** and the **Résidence Palladium** on Boulevard Tsarévitch.

Cathédrale Orthodoxe Russe St-Nicolas★

Open daily Mar–Apr and Oct 9.15am–noon, 2.30–5.30pm; May–Sept 9am–noon, 2.30–6pm; Nov–15 Feb 9.30am–noon, 2.30–5pm; Closed Sun morning and Russian Orthodox holidays. 3€. 04 93 96 88 02. www.acor-nice.com.

With its six gilded onion domes and its façade of ochre brick, the **Russian Orthodox cathedral** lends an exotic touch to the Nice skyline and symbolises the importance of the Russian colony on the Riviera. It is the largest Russian religious building outside Russia, built to accommodate the frequent visits of the Russian nobility.

The domes are coated with fine gold leaf and the mosaic icons on the façades were handmade by Russian artists. The inauguration took place in December 1912. At the entrance to the choir is a sumptuous **iconostasis★**, bringing together the finest examples of Russian religious art, taken from the church of Jaroslav and the church of St Basil the Blessed in Moscow. At the end of the park on the left a **Byzantine chapel** is dedicated to Tsarevich Nicolas, the son of Tsar Alexander II, who died of an illness here in 1866.

SIGHTS
Musée des Arts Asiatiques★★

In Parc Phœnix, near Nice-Côte-d'Azur airport. Open Wed–Mon 10am–5pm; May–mid-Oct 10am–6pm. No charge. (fee). 04 92 29 37 00. www.arts-asiatiques.com.

Delicately poised on the lake in Phœnix Park, this dazzling construction in white

Studios de la Victorine: the Story of Film-Making in Nice

With the dawn of cinema, Nice provided film-makers with the ideal ingredients for their future success: almost constant light and sunshine, the sea and the presence of magnificent hotels as natural backdrops.

Louis Feuillade, who made *Fantômas*, was one of the first to spot the potential of the area; the roofs of the Hôtel Négresco passed into cinematic posterity in the Fantômas-Judex chase.

The 'azure cinema' really took off in 1920 when a large unoccupied estate west of the town centre, La Victorine, was acquired by the fabulously rich Hollywood producer Rex Ingram, who had launched Rudolf Valentino and Roman Navarro. He produced the epic *Mare Nostrum*, to promote his new studios. For the following ten years La Victorine studios saw both French and European film-makers prosper, then changes in public tastes brought another decade of inactivity.

The Armistice of 1940 caused French cinema to seek refuge in Nice (Abel Gance, Prévert, Carné). In 1943 the filming of *Les Visiteurs du Soir* revived the production of large-scale films in Nice. In 1944 came *Les Enfants du Paradis,* the greatest production at La Victorine, co-produced by Marcel Carné and Jacques Prévert, with Arletty and Jean-Louis Barrault. The reconstruction of *Boulevard du Crime* in the middle of the Second World War required more than 30t of scaffolding and nearly 3 500sq m/4 186sq yd of fencing for the sets, as well as 2 000 extras, who were recruited in Nice. The worsening of the economic situation temporarily brought a halt to Nice's creativity. The post-war years were good, but were followed by a lull. Nowadays, a revival of filming seems to be underway.

marble presents sacred and traditional objects coming from several Asian countries. The building was designed by the Japanese architect **Kenzo Tange** in 1998.

The exhibits share the history of Buddhism through a series of stone Buddhas, illustrating 4C Gandhara and 12C Khmer art. On the ground floor, each gallery is devoted to a specific civilisation: China, Japan, Cambodia and India.

Parc Phœnix★

405 Promenade des Anglais.
&. ⓒ*Open daily Apr–Sept 9.30am–7.30pm; Oct–Mar 9.30am–5.30pm.*
◈*No charge.* ✆*04 93 18 03 33.*
This vast botanical garden (over 7ha/17 acres) inaugurated in 1991 is organised by theme and contains over 2 000 plant species from all over the world, grouped with their corresponding animal life.
The "Île des Temps Révolus" (Island of Bygone Times), in the middle of a big lake, takes visitors back into the past with a display of living plant fossils: cycads, ginkgo biloba, tree ferns, etc.

An aviary houses a colourful collection of parrots and other tropical birds, and the wadi-oasis reconstitutes part of an oasis in the Sahara.

The **giant greenhouse**★, known as the "Green Diamond", is a tropical hot-house covering 7 000sq m/75 300sq ft beneath a 25m/82ft high roof in which seven climates of varying temperatures and hygrometry are housed. Next door are the carnivorous plants and the butterfly house.

Outside, a 'Great Aztec Pyramid' displays what goes on beneath our feet, regarding both plants and animals that live underground.

Musée d'Art Naïf Jakovsky★

Av. du Val-Marie. Leave the town centre by Promenade des Anglais. ⓒ*Open Wed–Mon 10am–noon, 2–6pm.*
◈*No charge.* ✆*04 93 71 78 33.*
Housed in the elegant Château Ste-Hélène, the Anatole Jakovsky Bequest comprises 600 canvases illustrating the amateur talents of many countries. The Croatian artists include Generalic,

Rabuzin, Kovacic and Petrovic. Among the French are Bauchant, Vivin, Vieillard, Restivo and Crociani, and more dream-like paintings by Vercruyce and Lefranc. There are also works by Italians, Swiss, Belgians and from the Americas.

Musée Masséna★

35 Promenade des Anglais. Museum: ○*open Wed–Mon 10am–6pm; Gardens: open Jun–Sept 9am–8pm; Oct–May 9am–6pm.* ○*No charge.* ℘*04 93 91 19 10.*

This museum surrounded by gardens was built in 1898, It was modelled on Italian residences of the First Empire and was made after plans by Georg Tersling and the Niçois A Messian for Victor Masséna, great-grandson of the Marshal. In 1919 his son André gave it to the town.

In 2007 the new exhibit rooms opened, featuring the **chronological history of Nice** from the 19C to the 1930s presented on two floors. A restored library on the top floor houses over 30 000 photos and 3 000 maps.

Acropolis-Palais des Congrès★

1 Esplanade Kennedy. ℘*04 93 92 82 35. www.nice-acropolis.com.*

This enormous convention centre (74 000sq m/88 503sq yd) resembles a majestic vessel anchored to the five robust vaults spanning the River Paillon. It was designed by a group of local architects. Contemporary works of art displayed both inside and outside the building include works by Volti *(Nikaia),* Vasarely, Arman *(Music Power),* César *(Thumb),* Paul Belmondo, Moretti *(Louis Armstrong)* and Cyril de la Patellière *(Mediterranean Tribute).*

Théâtre de la Photographie et de l'Image

27 Bd. Dubouchage. ○*Open Wed–Mon 10am–6pm.* ○*No charge.* ℘*04 97 13 42 20. www.tpi-nice.org.*

Formerly known as the Théâtre de l'Artistique, this exhibition space dedicated to photographic images, benefits from the interesting architectural aspect of the building. A documentation centre contains a collection of photographs of Nice and the region.

♣♦ Muséum d'Histoire Naturelle

60 Bd. Risso. ○*Open Tue–Sun 10am–6pm.* ○*Closed some public holidays.* ○*No charge.* ℘*04 97 13 46 80. www.mhnnice.org.*

Nice's first museum, the Natural History Museum houses a curious collection of 7 000 casts of fungi, alongside an exhibition of minerals.

♣♦ Musée de Terra Amata

25 Bd. Carnot. ○*Open Tue–Sun 10am–6pm.* ○*No charge.* ℘*04 93 55 59 93. www.musee-terra-amata.org.*

An excavation site where an open hearth and human footprint were found in the hardened limestone is reproduced on the ground floor of the museum. Bones, stone tools and traces of fire mark one of the earliest human settlements known in Europe. Articles, drawings, maps and a full-scale reconstruction of a shelter made of branches illustrate the life of the Achuelean hunters some 400 000 years ago (early Palaeolithic).

Prieuré du Vieux-Logis

59 Av. St-Barthélémy. ○*Guided tours (1hr, 3€) by reservation Fri 3pm.* ℘*04 93 88 11 34.*

A medieval home has been reconstructed within a 16C farm and richly supplied with works of art, 14C to 17C furniture and items from everyday life (note the outstanding kitchen). There are numerous statues including a 15C Pietà from Franche-Comté.

Église Ste-Jeanne-d'Arc

11 Rue Gramond.

This is a modern concrete church designed by Jacques Droz with an ellipsoidal porch as its main doorway. The belfry wreathed in flames rises to 65m/215ft. Inside, the soaring vaulting is striking. The Stations of the Cross frescoes are by Klementief (1934).

ADDRESSES

🏨 STAY

Au Picardy Hôtel – *10 Bd. Jean-Jaurès. ℘04 93 85 75 51. 🍴 11 rooms. 🛏3€.* Between the train station and Old Nice, this friendly, family-run hotel has basic rooms, small, yet soundproofed.

Clair Hotel – *23 Bd. Carnot, Impasse Terra Amata. ℘04 93 89 69 89. 10 rooms. 🛏7.50€.* This converted schoolhouse near the archaeological museum has rooms all on one floor (in the old classrooms) and a Mediterranean garden terrace, where breakfast is served in the summer. Quiet neighbourhood, friendly, family-run atmosphere.

Hôtel Armenonville – *20 Av. des Fleurs. ℘04 93 96 86 00. www.hotel-armenonville.com. 12 rooms. 🅿. 🛏10€.* At the end of a passage in the old Russian district of Nice, this retro hotel built in 1900 has charming rooms decorated with antiques. WiFi, garden, air conditioning and free parking as well.

Hôtel de Normandie – *18 Rue Paganini. ℘04 93 88 48 83 . www.hotel-normandie.com. 44 rooms. 🛏7€.* Practical location a few steps from the train station, with typical Niçoise decor. Rooms are simple yet well-equipped, and there's free WiFi and a hot meal distributor in the lobby.

Star Hôtel – *14 Rue Biscarra. ℘04 93 85 19 03. www.hotel-star.com. 24 rooms. 🛏6€.* Small hotel close to the Étoile shopping centre, offering simple accommodation with air-conditioning and free internet access.

Chambre d'hôte Castel Enchanté – *61 Route St-Pierre-de-Féric. ℘04 93 97 02 08. www.castel-enchante.com. 🍴. 4 rooms. Closed mid-Nov–mid-Mar. 🛏.* A beautiful 19C villa on the hills above Nice, with a huge terrace surrounded by orchards. Rooms are lovingly decorated by Jacques and Martine, who also serve their homemade jams at the breakfast buffet.

Chambre d'hôte Villa la Lézardière – *87 B.d de l'Observatoire. ℘04 93 56 22 86. www.villa-nice.com. 5 rooms. 🅿. 🛏.* Perched on the Grande Corniche, this Provençal-style villa has great views over the Alps. Personalised bedrooms, some with kitchenettes. Also a large pool and enclosed garden.

🍴 EAT

Salade niçoise, socca, pan-bagnat, poutine, tourte aux blettes, beignets de fleurs de courgettes … to experience the best in local cuisine, look for the restaurants displaying the label "Cuisine Nissarde". A guide to these restaurants is available for free at the tourist office.

Lou Balico – *22 Av. St-Jean-Baptiste. ℘04 93 85 93 71. www.loubalico.com.* Three generations of the same family have been serving classic Niçois dishes in this cosy dining room, adorned with a piano and guest book with signatures from around the world.

Marlone Café – *4 Rue de l'Opéra. ℘04 93 85 96 15 . www.marlonecafe.com. Closed Mon.* A gourmet refuge just off Place Masséna, with traditional meals and comfortable, thoughtfully decorated dining room.

Le Pain à Table – *3 Rue St-François-de-Paul (cours Saleya). ℘04 93 62 94 32. www.lepainatable.com.* Sit at one of the communal wooden tables and order fresh breads with spreads, salads, open-faced sandwiches and brunch on the weekend.

Réné Socca – *2 Rue Miralhéti . ℘04 93 92 05 73 . 🍴 Closed Mon.* The most popular "Nissart" restaurant in town. Follow the line, order your food and sit at one of the long tables with your meal. Don't miss the *socca*, cooked fresh in the wood-fired oven, the *pissaladière*, and stuffed courgette blossoms.

Safari – *1 cours Saleya. ℘04 93 80 18 44. http://restaurantsafari.fr.* A trendy address overlooking the market at Cours Saleya, this restaurant has a beautiful terrace, and local specialities including a large selection of fish and seafood. Great for people watching.

La Table d'Alziari – *4 Rue François-Zannin. ℘04 93 80 34 03. Closed 9–20 Jan, 4–9 Jun, 2–6 Oct, 4–15 Dec, Sun–Mon.* Unpretentious family restaurant set up in a small alley of the old district. Typical dishes from Nice and the Provence area, chalked up on a slate, are served in a homey decor, with wines recommended by the owner.

L'Escalinada – *22 Rue Pairolière.*
04 93 62 11 71. www.escalinada.fr.
Closed mid-Nov–mid-Dec. Nestled in the old quarter, this charming restaurant offers attractively presented regional cuisine in a spruce dining room with rustic overtones. Friendly service.

Grand Café de Turin –
5 Pl. Garibaldi. 04 93 62 29 52.
This brasserie, which is over 200 years old, has become an institution in Nice. It serves seafood dishes à la carte at reasonable prices throughout the day. Pleasant, welcoming setting, although a bit noisy on the terrace.

Le Local – *4 Rue Rusca. 04 93 14 08 29.* Minimalist decor for this deli-restaurant specialising in Neopolitan and Sicilian dishes such as the *antipasto del mare.*

La Mérenda – *4 r. Raoul Bosio F.*
04 93 14 08 29. Uncomfortable stools, no telephone and credit cards are not accepted. Despite all of this, crowds flock to La Mérenda every day to sample its authentic Niçois cuisine!

NIGHTLIFE

Casino Ruhl – *1 Promenade des Anglais.*
04 97 03 12 22. www.lucienbarriere.com.
The casino boasts 300 slot machines and has facilities for French and English roulette, blackjack, stud poker, etc. American bar. Live cabaret performances on Fridays and Saturdays (except July–August). Bring photo ID.

Le Relais – *Hôtel Negresco, 37 Promenade des Anglais. 04 93 16 64 00. www.hotel-negresco.com.* The sumptuous decoration of this bar belonging to the legendary Negresco Hotel has remained the same since 1913: Brussels tapestry (1683), 18C paintings, replicas of the wall lamps adorning the Ballroom in Fontainebleau. Piano bar every evening.

La Trappa – *Rue de la Préfecture and Rue Gilly. 04 93 80 33 69. Closed Sun–Mon.* A lively tapas bar with deep, comfortable settees and red walls awaits you at La Trappa, open since 1886. Sip a Cuban cocktail while you listen to Latin American music (DJ weekends). Friendly atmosphere and local wine list.

SHOPPING

Most shops in Old Nice are closed on Mondays.

Shopping streets – The streets surrounding the Cathédrale Ste-Réparate have many shops selling typical Provençal articles: fabrics *(Rue Paradis and Rue du Marché)*, arts and crafts *(Rue du Pont-Vieux and Rue de la Boucherie)*, olive oil and *santons (Rue St-François-de-Paul)*.

Alziari – *14 Rue St-François-de-Paule.*
04 93 85 76 92. www.alziari.com.fr.
Closed Sun–Mon. One of the best addresses in town for olive oil and regional specialities.

La Maison de l'Olive – *18 Rue Pairolière.*
04 93 80 01 61. Closed Mon. Marseille soaps made from pure olive oil, lotions and scents for the body and home, and regional products such as dried tomatos, lemon jam, marinated capers and olives, and Provençal herbs and spices.

À l'Olivier – *7 Rue St-François-de-Paule.*
04 93 13 44 97. Every brand of French olive oil with the AOC label is sold in this boutique, originally opened in 1822, in Nice since 2004. Also a fine selection of elegant glassware, dishes, tablecloths.

Confiserie Auer – *7 Rue St-François-de-Paule. 04 93 85 77 98. www.maison-auer.com. Closed Sun.* A gorgeous vintage boutique selling sugared fruit and crystallised flowers from the Nice region, as well as chocolates, and *calissons* from Aix.

Confiserie Florian – *14 Quai Papacino, on the Port. 04 93 55 43 50. www.confiserieflorian.com. Guided tours of the factory 9am–noon, 2–6.30pm.* Sugared fruit, lemon, orange and grapefruit preserve, chocolates and sweets, crystallised petals and delicious jams made with rose, violet and jasmine blossom.

Maison Poilpot – Aux Parfums de Grasse – *10 Rue St-Gaétan. 04 93 85 60 77. Closed Mon.* This traditional perfumery produces more than 80 different fragrances, including popular Mediterranean scents such as mimosa, rose, violet and lemon.

L'Art Gourmand – *21 Rue du Marché, Old Town.* ℘*04 93 62 51 79.* This Old Nice boutique has many treats available to go or eat in: nougats, *calisson*, sugared fruit, cookies, pastries, ice cream and northern France specialities. There's a tea room on the mezzanine decorated with murals.

Fenocchio – *2 Pl. Rossetti, Old Town.* ℘*04 93 80 72 52. Closed Nov–Jan.* This famous ice cream and sorbet maker has some of the most amazing flavours, from avocado and sun-dried tomato to honey and pine nut. With almost 100 flavours to choose from, you'll have to go back more than once!

Maison Poilpot – *Aux Parfums de Grasse, 10 Rue St-Gaëtan.* ℘*04 93 85 60 77. Closed Mon, two weeks in Nov, lunch in holidays.* This artisan perfume maker propses 80 different scents (lavender, mimosa, rose, violet, lemon).

MARKETS

Marché aux Poissons – The fish market is on Place St-François Tue–Sun 6am–1pm.

Marché aux Fleurs – The flower market is on the Cours Saleya Tuesday–Sun 6am–5.30pm.

Marché aux Fruits et Légumes – The colourful food market on the Cours Saleya takes place Tue–Sun 6am–1.30pm.

Marché de la Libération – Locals' food market from the Avenue Malausséna to Place Charles-de-Gaulle.

Marché aux Puces – Flea market on Place Robilante Tue–Sat 10am–6pm.

Marché de la Brocante – Antique market on Cours Saleya Mon 7.30am–6pm.

LEISURE ACTIVITIES

Beaches – The Baie des Anges covers a 5km/3mi stretch of coastline with smooth pebbles *(galets)*. There are many public beaches placed under close surveillance, and 15 private beaches hosting sporting activities.

Hiking – *14 Av. Mirabeau.* ℘*04 93 62 59 99. www.cafnice.org. Office open Mon–Fri 4–8pm.* CAF (Club Alpin Français) organises one-day hiking tours across the Nice hinterland and Mercantour Park leaving from Nice.

Galet beach of Nice

S. Sauvignier/MICHELIN

Skiing – *www.guideriviera.com.* The nearby skiing resorts of Auron (℘*04 93 23 02 66*) and Valberg (℘*04 93 02 52 27*), which are only a 2hr drive away, are undoubtedly among the main attractions of the Nice area.

CALENDAR OF EVENTS

There are many traditional festivals throughout the year. Ask at the tourist office for a complete schedule.

Nice Carnival – This colourful, extravagant event invariably attracts large crowds every year. Festivities take place around Shrove Tuesday *(Mardi Gras)* and last for a fortnight. They include processions, floats, firework displays, costume balls and battles where showers of flowers and confetti are thrown!

Cougourdons Festival – Cougourdons are gourds that have been dried and painted. The city of Nice pays homage to these curious vegetables in early April.

Fête de la Mer et de la St-Pierre – A festival celebrating the sea and St-Peter on the port and Quai des Etats-Unis the last weekend in June.

Nice Jazz Festival – The former Roman amphitheatre is the prestigious backdrop for the jazz festival that is held in Nice the last two weeks of July, attended by leading performers from all over the world. ℘*0 892 707 407.*

Fête de la San Bertoumiéu – A festival of traditional arts and crafts, regional foods and entertainment in the Old Town the first weekend in September.

Crèche Vivante Lou Presèpi – A living nativity scene with people and animals, at Place Rossetti the week of Christmas.

Peille★

Peille's Ligurian name (Pilia) means "on the naked and grassy heights" is fitting for this Medieval village, perched dramtically above olive groves and rocky ravines.

◆ WALKING TOUR

From the 13C **Tower**, at the edge of the D 53, follow the steps going down the rocky Rue de la Sauterie, with its intersecting staircases and arched passages, until you arrive at Place A. Laugier.

On the right, the Rue Centrale leads to the Town Hall, housed under the dome of the **13C Chapelle Saint Sébastien**. You can also admire the former **Hôtel des Consuls**, also known as the "Palace of the Magus Judge", with its coupled windows and archways.

Behind the **Gothic fountain**, under a house, two half-arches lean against a Roman pillar. The right leads to the Rue Lascaris and towards the war memorial, where you'll find a superb view. The left opens onto **L'Arma**, the oldest part of the village.

The **Musée du Terroir** evokes the local customs through objects, furniture, tools and clothing donated by the inhabitants (◷ open Sat–Sun 2–5pm; ⊜ no charge; ℘04 93 91 71 71, town hall).

▷ **Population:** 2 243.
 Michelin Map: 341 F5.
 Info: Pl. Carnot. ℘04 93 79 89 37. www.peille.fr.
◐ **Location:** Peille is 11km/7mi north of La Turbie on the D 53; 11km/7mi northeast of Peillon on the D 53; 25km/15.5mi northeast of Nice on D 2564 an D 53 or D 6098 and D 53.
▣ **Parking:** There is only one public parking area at the entrance to the village.

Pelhasque: a Local Dialect

Some of the older inhabitants of this quiet village still speak *Pelhasque*, a local variation of the *Nissart* dialect (from Nice).

Church

Flanked by an elegant lombard bell tower in a pyramid shape, the 12C church is made up of two coupled chapels. On the left upon entering is a retable with 15 compartments made by Honoré Bertone in 1579. On the right is a representation of Peille as it looked in the Middle Ages. Ste-Anne is featured on the 14C fresco.

Peille

Peillon

H. LeGac/MICHELIN

Peillon★

Alpes Maritimes

Set back on a narrow spur overlooking the Paillon Valley, Peillon is a spectacular village of strict architectural unity imposed by the need for a highly strategic defensive system.

VISIT
Village

Virtually untouched since the Middle Ages, the village has few streets but many steep steps and covered alleys between the flower-decked houses huddled against each other. The 18C **Eglise St-Sauveur**, with its octagonal lantern, crowns the village. Inside are 17C and 18C paintings and an 18C wooden statue of Christ. There's a magnificent panoramic **view★** from the Plaça dei Gleia (place de l'Église) of the Esterel and St-Martin valley (orientation table).

Chapelle des Pénitents-Blancs

◷*Open by request Mon–Fri 9am–noon. A timed lightswitch on the outside allows you to see the frescoes through the bars.* ℘04 93 91 98 34.
The chapel's most interesting feature are the **frescoes★** by Giovanni Canavesio. At the far end is the Crucifixion with St Antony and Ste Petronella. On the walls and ceiling are scenes from the Passion, in particular the Flagellation and Judas' Kiss, vividly portrayed. On the altar stands a Pietà in painted wood.

▸ **Population:** 1 322.
◔ **Michelin Map:** 341 F5; local map: *see NICE*.
▸ **Info:** Mairie (Town Hall). ℘04 93 79 91 04.
▸ **Location:** A maze of vaulted passageways, the village of Peillon is easily reached from Nice (◔*see NICE: Driving Tour* ④).
▸ **Parking:** Park alongside the road going into the village.
▸ **Don't Miss:** A guided tour of the town's church and chapel, advance reservations a must.

▸ You can still walk along the old Roman road from Peillon to Peille *(2hr)*.

ADDRESSES

◸ **STAY**

◸ **Annexe Lou Pourtail** – *Entrance at l'Auberge de la Madone.* ℘04 93 79 91 17. *Closed 10 Oct–20 Dec. 6 rooms.* ◷14€. *Restaurant* ◷◷◷. At the foot of the village, this old cottage inn is full of charm: whitewashed walls, high vaulted ceilings and country furniture. Regional cooking served in the rustic dining room or on the garden terrace.

Corniches de la Riviera★★★

Alpes Maritimes

Between Nice and Menton the mountains plunge sharply down to the sea. Running along these heights are three famous routes: the Grande Corniche, the Moyenne Corniche and the Basse Corniche Inférieure. The first, which climbs to 450m/1 476ft, affords the most spectacular views; the second, offers beautiful vistas along the shore; and the third provides access to all of the chic coastal resorts.

- **Michelin Map:** 341 F/G5.
- **Info:** Cap d'Ail tourist office: 87bis Av. du 3-Septembre. ℘04 93 78 02 33. www.cap-dail.com
- **Don't Miss:** The Grande Corniche has the best panoramic views.
- **Kids:** Check out the stars from Astrorama.

🚗 DRIVING TOURS

1 GRANDE CORNICHE★★★
MENTON TO NICE

31km/19mi. Allow 3hr.
The Grande Corniche, built by Napoleon along the route of the ancient Via Julia Augusta, passes through La Turbie above the Principality of Monaco. Breathtaking views along the road leading to the perched village of Roquebrune.

▶ *From Menton take Av. Carnot and Av. de la Madone (N 7) going west. Either bear left onto D 52 to Cap Martin or continue uphill (N 7) bearing right onto D 2564 to Roquebrune.*

Roquebrune-Cap-Martin★
See ROQUEBRUNE-CAP-MARTIN.
▶ *Continue on the D 2564 westwards.*

Le Vistaëro★★
From nearly 300m/1 000ft above the sea is a marvellous **view**★★ extending out over Bordighera Point, Menton, and, immediately below, Monte-Carlo Beach. Further inland is the Alpine Trophy.

La Turbie★
See La TURBIE. The Grande Corniche reveals distant **views** of Cap Ferrat and then of Èze village as the road reaches its highest point at 550m/1 804ft. In Pical

a stone cross on the left commemorates Pope Pius VII's return from exile in 1814.

Col d'Èze
Alt 512m/1 680ft. Extended **view** to the north over the mountains and valleys. Mont Bastide, on the left, has been a Celto-Ligurian *oppidum* and a Roman camp.

▶ *On leaving Col d'Èze towards Nice, turn right on the road going up signed "Parc Départemental de la Grande Corniche-Astrorama".*

Astrorama
La Trinité. ⏰*Open Mar–Oct Fri–Sat (Tue–Sat in Jul–Aug) 7pm–11pm.* 💶*9€ (child under 25, 7€).* ℘*04 93 85 85 58. www.astrorama.net.*
After a series of hairpin bends, the road reaches a plateau which is home to an old defensive gun battery, now home to an astronomy research and observation centre.

▶ *Park at the foot of the Fort de la Revère (⚬closed to the public).*

Parc de la Revère
From the base of the fort there is a superb **panorama**★★ over the whole Var coast as far as Italy.

Belvédère d'Èze
1.2km/0.7mi beyond the pass, opposite a small café, is a wide panoramic **view**★★ of the Tête de Chien, Èze and the sea below, Cap Ferrat, Cap d'Antibes, Lérins islands, the Esterels, and the Alps.

Col des Quatre-Chemins

A short way beyond the pass (alt 327m/1 037ft) one can see the Alps through an opening made by the Paillon Valley. Soon the road descends steeply offering a wide **view**★ of the Pre-Alps, and then of Nice and the Cap d'Antibes.

▷ *Enter Nice from the east by Av. des Diables-Bleus.*

② MOYENNE CORNICHE★★ NICE TO MENTON

31km/19mi. Allow 2hr.

Shorter and less winding than the Grande Corniche, the Moyenne Corniche is a modern road built between 1910 and 1928. It tunnels through the larger mountain chains and provides the only access by road to Èze.

▷ *Leave Nice by Pl. Max-Barel on N 7 heading east. Look for the designated roadside parking areas provided at all the best viewpoints.*

Views of the town, the Château Hill, the port and the Baie des Anges give way to views of the Esterel chain and the chalky mountains of Grasse to the southwest.

Col de Villefranche

Alt 149m/489ft. From a bend in the road soon after the pass, Villefranche-sur-Mer harbour and Cap Ferrat come into sight.

Just before entering a 180m/200yd-long tunnel, there is an extraordinary **view**★★ of Beaulieu, Cap Ferrat, Villefranche-sur-Mer, Nice and Cap d'Antibes. After the tunnel, the old village of Èze comes into view, perched high on its rock against the backdrop of Tête de Chien (alt 556m/1 880ft).

Plateau St-Michel★★

▷ *2km/1mi from N7. After the tunnel turn right onto the narrow D34, which climbs back over the tunnel for 2km/1mi to a terrace car park.*

Walk up to the viewing table on the edge of the plateau (371m/1 271ft). The **panorama**★★ extends from the tip of Cap d'Ail to the Esterel.

Èze★★ ♿ *See Èze.*

Beyond Èze the Moyenne Corniche circles the rocky escarpments of Tête de Chien and brings into sight new panoramic views overlooking Cap Martin and the Bordighera headland in Italy. At the entrance to Monaco bear left onto N 7, which skirts the Principality and offers remarkable **views**★ of Monte-Carlo, Cap Martin, the Italian coast.

Beausoleil

This resort forms part of the Monte-Carlo conurbation although it is officially on French territory. Its houses, reached by stepped streets, project from the slopes of Mont des Mules like balconies.

▷ *Bear left onto D 53.*

Mont des Mules★

🚶 *1km/0.6mi plus 30min round trip along a marked path.* From the top there is a fine **panorama**★ *(viewing table).*

▷ *Return to N 7 which passes below the Vistaëro before joining the Basse Corniche at Cabbé.*

Cap Martin★★ ♿ *See ROQUEBRUNE-CAP-MARTIN*

③ BASSE CORNICHE★★ NICE TO MENTON

33km/21mi – about 6hr.

The Basse Corniche was conceived as long ago as the 18C by a prince of Monaco. Work was undertaken by the Empress of Russia in 1857 and completed in 1881. The road, running at the foot of the mountain slopes and following the contours of the coast, serves all the Riviera resorts.

▷ *From Nice take Bd. Carnot, N 98, heading southeast.*

The road skirts the base of Mont Boron with **views**★ of the Baie des Anges, Cap Ferrat, Villefranche-sur-Mer port, Èze and Tête de Chien in succession.

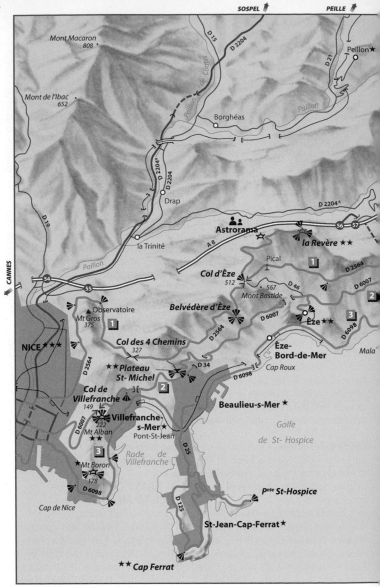

Villefranche-sur-Mer★
See VILLEFRANCHE-SUR-MER.

Cap Ferrat★★
See CAP FERRAT.

Beaulieu★
See BEAULIEU.
As the road skirts Cap Roux, there is a view across the water to Cap d'Ail.

Èze-Bord-de-Mer
The resort lies beneath the cliffs below Èze-Village. As the road hugs the rocky coast, Cap d'Ail is in full view.

Cap d'Ail
The elegant properties of Cap d'Ail cover the lower slopes of the Tête de Chien down to the sea.

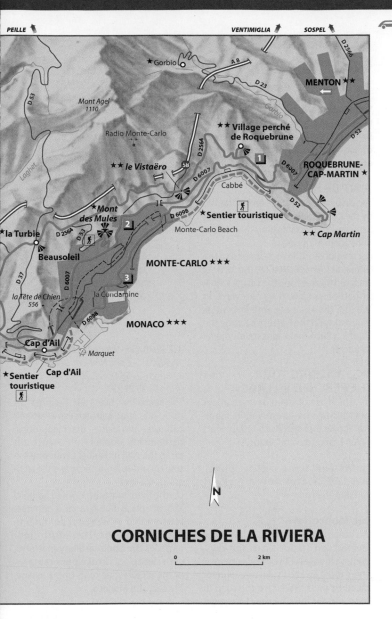

CORNICHES DE LA RIVIERA

0   2 km

Coastal Path of Cap d'Ail★

1hr round trip. On the east side of the station, descend the steps into a tunnel that comes out on a road. Turn left and at Restaurant La Pinède, take another flight of steps on the right down to the sea.

A coastal footpath running eastwards skirts the rocks at the foot of Cap d'Ail. To the west lie Beaulieu, Cap Ferrat and Monaco Rock. The footpath ends on Marquet beach. You can take the road into Monaco.

Monaco★★★

See MONACO.

The road joins the Moyenne Corniche at Cabbé.

Cap Martin★★

See ROQUEBRUNE-CAP-MARTIN.

Roquebrune-Cap-Martin★

Alpes Maritimes

This pretty resort covering the Cap Martin extends along the coast below the perched medieval village of Roquebrune and its Carolingian-era castle keep.

A BIT OF HISTORY

The castle was built at the end of the 10C by the Count of Ventimiglia to stop the Saracens from establishing themselves once again in the area.

For several centuries it belonged to the Grimaldis (&see MONACO). The fortress enclosed the keep and the village within its battlements, with six gateways. In the 15C the keep became known as the castle and the fortress became the village, which maintains its medieval character.

☞ WALKING TOUR
THE PERCHED VILLAGE★

1hr. The maze of steep covered alleys and stairways has preserved its medieval appearance despite the influx of art galleries and souvenir shops.

◐ Start on Pl. de la République, then cross the Pl. des Deux-Frères to the Rue Grimaldi, then turn left.

Rue Moncollet★

This street, long and narrow, has many covered and stepped passageways. Medieval houses with barred windows, where those invited to join the seigneurial court once lived, face the road in front, while at the back they lie against or are cut right into the rockface.

◐ Rue Moncollet leads into Rue du Château. Go left to see the keep. After crossing the "flowered enclosure," you enter the ancient keep.

Donjon★

Pl. William–Ingram. ◐*Open daily Apr–Jun and Sept 10am–12.30pm, 2–6.30pm; Jul–Aug 10am–12.30pm,*

- ▸ **Population:** 13 067.
- ⚲ **Michelin Map:** 341 F5; local maps: *see MENTON: Excursions and Corniches de la RIVIERA.*
- ℹ **Info:** 214 Av. Aristide-Briand. ℘04 93 35 62 87. www.roquebrune-cap-martin.com.
- ◖ **Location:** Roquebrune village sits on the Grande Corniche above Menton and the resort of Roquebrune-Cap-Martin.
- ℙ **Parking:** Parking is available at the village entrance.
- ☺ **Don't Miss:** Nature lovers should hike the coastal path on the Cap Martin.

3-7.30pm; Feb–Mar and Oct 10am–12.30pm, 2–6pm; Nov–Jan 10am–12.30pm, 2–5pm. ☜*3.70€.* ℘*04 93 35 07 22.*

The keep (26m/80ft) has 2–4m/6–12ft thick walls fitted with defensive features: cannon embrasures, machicolations, battlements, loopholes etc. Steps leads up to the Hall of Feudal Ceremonies, a small guard-room, a prison and the archers' dormitory.

On the third floor are furnished baronial apartments, a dining room, a primitive kitchen and a bedroom containing ancient weapons. The fourth floor includes the upper artillery platform, with sweeping, circular **panorama**★★ of the picturesque roofs of the village, the sea, and Monaco.

◐ Return to Rue du Château and then turn left on Rue de la Fontaine .

Olivier Millénaire

On the Chemin de Menton (200m/219yd beyond the end of the village) you'll find a 1 000-year-old **olive tree**, said to be one of the oldest trees in the world.

◐ Return to Rue du Château (left).

Roquebrune-Cap-Martin

B. Kaufmann/MICHELIN

Église Ste-Marguerite

The fairly plain Baroque façade masks the original 12C church, which has undergone many alterations over the years. Inside are two paintings by a local painter, Marc-Antoine Otto (17C).

▷ *If you return to Rue de la Fontaine and turn right into the cemetery, you'll find the sarcophagus (square J, no 3), where Le Corbusier rests eternally, designed by the architect himself.*

TOURING THE RESORT
Cap Martin★★

With its magnificent estates, Cap Martin is the wealthy residential suburb of Menton. A massive tower of feudal appearance rises at the centre, formerly the old beacon, now converted to a telecommunications relay station. At its foot lie the ruins of the 11C basilica of St-Martin, built by the Lérins island monks and destroyed by pirates in 1400. From the road along the eastern shore is a marvellous **view**★★ of Menton in its mountain setting and the Italian coast. There are several beaches below the old village at Cabbé and Carnolès to the east.

Le Cabanon de Le Corbusier

☞ *Guided tours Tue and Fri 10am by appointment at the tourist office.* ☞*8€. ℘04 93 35 62 87.*
This 'cabin', where the architect lived, is still an object of curiosity for the uninitiated visitor and a point of reference for the study of architecture. "I have a château on the Riviera which measures 3.6m by 3.6m/12ft by 12ft. It is wonderfully comfortable and pleasant", confided Le Corbusier. It has a deceptively plain exterior; inside, a corridor is decorated with a fresco painted by the architect. Furniture is multipurpose and the windows are for light and ventilation.

Coastal Path★

🅿 *Av. Winston-Churchill car park at the end of Cap Martin. A sign "Promenade Le Corbusier" near a restaurant marks the start of the footpath.* 🥾 *4hr round trip.*
A coastal footpath runs from Cap Martin to Monte-Carlo beach westwards

Traditional Processions

For the past 500 years a procession, representing the principal scenes of the Passion in six tableaux, is held on 5 August for 2hr. The **Procession of the Entombment of Christ**★ is held at 9pm on Good Friday with a train of some 60 people walking through the village streets representing Roman centurions and legionnaires, disciples carrying the statue of Christ, and holy women. The town is decorated with lighted motifs recalling the symbols of the Passsion and illuminated countless tiny lights formed by snail and sea shells filled with olive oil.

round the headland. A series of steps and inclines skirts the grounds of private properties through wild vegetation.

ADDRESSES

🏨 STAY

Hôtel Alexandra – *93 Avenue Winston Churchill. ℘04 93 35 65 45. www.alexandrahotel.fr. 40 rooms. ☐. ⊊10€.* A beachside hotel typical of the 1960s/1970s, make sure to request upper floor rooms facing the sea.

> *A flight of steps on the right crossing the railway line provides a shortcut back to Carnolès beach via the town hall.*

🍽 EAT

La Roquebrunoise – *12 Av. Raymond-Poincaré. ℘04 93 35 02 19. www.laroque brunoise.com. Closed Nov–Dec, Mon except Mon eve Jul–Aug, lunch Tue–Fri.* This pretty pink house on the edge of the village has a country-style dining room. The food is unpretentious and tasty; a terrace overlooks the sea and the château.

La Turbie★

Alpes Maritimes

The hilltop village of La Turbie *(alt 480m/1 575ft)*, **built in a pass on the Grande Corniche, is most famous for its Alpine Trophy, a masterpiece of Roman art.**

A BIT OF HISTORY

When Caesar died, the Alps was occupied by unconquered tribes who posed a constant threat to communications between Rome and its possessions in Gaul and Spain. **Augustus** ended this by extending Roman rule into the Alps. In 6 BC the Senate and the Roman people commemorated the victory with the erection of the trophy on the Via Julia Augusta. There is only one other Roman trophy still standing (in Romania).

WALKING TOUR
> *Start from Av. Général-de-Gaulle.*

You'll see a 19C fountain, built at the end of a Roman aqueduct. Below, from the southwest corner of Place Neuve, is a fine **view**★ of the coast.

Rue Comte-de-Cessole
Pass through the West Gate, climbing past medieval houses to the Trophy. A house on the right bears a plaque with verses Dante dedicated to La Turbie.

▶ **Population:** 3 155.
Michelin Map: 341 F5; local maps: *see NICE and Corniches de la RIVIERA.*
Info: Pl. Detras. ℘04 93 41 13 99. www.ville-la-turbie.fr.
Location: La Turbie is on Grande Corniche at the base of the massive Tête de Chien promontory above Monaco.

Église St-Michel-Archange
Light switch in the chapel on the right. The 18C church is a fine example of the Nice Baroque style, with paintings attributed to J-B Van Loo and Veronese.

▶ *Return to the Rue de Cessole.*

At the top of the hill, make sure you take a look at the Trophy (*see Visit*), then go back towards the Rue Droite, passing under the East Gate. Bring your camera to capture the great **panoramic views**★★★ of Monaco, the Italian Riviera, Èze, and the heights of Mont Agel to be had from the terraces here.

VISIT
Trophée des Alpes★
&🕐*Open Tue–Sun mid-May–mid-Sept 9.30am–1pm, 2.30–6.30pm; mid-Sept–mid-May 10am–1.30pm, 2.30–5pm.* ⊚5€. ℘04 93 41 20 84.

The **Alpine Trophy** was built with local white stone. in the Middle Ages it was converted into a defensive structure.

Later it served as a source of building stone, reducing it to a ruined tower and a pile of rubble. Patient restoration has rebuilt the Trophy up to about 35m/115ft high, but a large part of it has been left untouched. The **museum** recounts the story of the Trophy and its restoration.

Villefranche-sur-Mer★
Alpes Maritimes

Villefranche is a fishing port and holiday resort encircling one of the most beautiful harbours in the Mediterranean, with a deep bay where cruise liners and warships can lie at anchor. The town has preserved its 17C character in its port, citadel and picturesque streets lined with sherbet-coloured houses.

A BIT OF HISTORY
The Origins of Villefranche – The town was founded in the 14C by the Count of Provence, Charles II of Anjou, nephew of St Louis. Between its cession to Savoy in the late 17C and the excavation of the harbour in Nice in the mid-18C, Villefranche was the major port of the Savoyard and Sardinian states.

The Congress of Nice – In 1538, the Congress of Nice was convened by Pope Paul III to bring peace between François I and Charles V. The Queen of France, sister of Charles V, went to see her brother, whose ship was moored at Villefranche. Charles, giving his hand to the Queen and followed by the Duke of Savoy and lords and ladies of his suite, advanced majestically to the jetty from the ship, when the gangway collapsed. The Emperor, the Queen and the Duke, soaked and dishevelled, were pulled ashore by onlookers. The peace of Nice lasted for barely five years.

▸ **Population:** 6 610.
& **Michelin Map:** 341 E5; local map: *see Corniches de la RIVIERA*.
🛈 **Info:** Jardin François-Binon. ℘04 93 01 73 68. www.villefranche-sur-mer.com.
◖ **Location:** Located 6km/3.7mi east of Nice on the Basse Corniche. Rue du Poilu is the main street in a network of narrow alleys, some of which are stepped or vaulted.
🅿 **Parking:** There is parking (absolutely packed in summer) around the citadel and the old port.

From Naval Base to Zoological Station – After the Crimean War, in 1856, Villefranche harbour was used by the Russian military fleet, deprived of access to the Mediterranean via the Bosphorus. They would also use it as a home base for the Imperial nobility on holiday. In 1893 a team of Russian scientists from Kiev replaced the soldiers to conduct oceanographic research until the 1930s when the premises were reclaimed by the Université de Paris, who established a marine zoology station.

Église St-Michel
6 Rue Baron-de-Brès.
This Italian Baroque church contains 18C altarpieces and, in the north transept, a 17C crucifix carved with impressive realism from the trunk of a fig tree by an unknown convict.

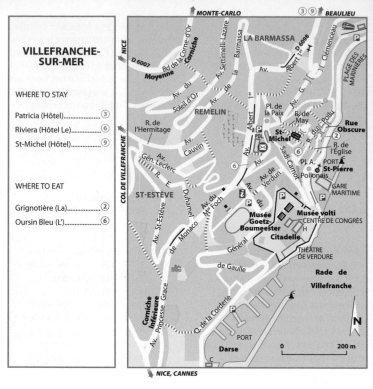

VILLEFRANCHE-SUR-MER

WHERE TO STAY

Patricia (Hôtel)..................③

Riviera (Hôtel Le)..............⑥

St-Michel (Hôtel)...............⑨

WHERE TO EAT

Grignotière (La)..................②

Oursin Bleu (L')..................⑥

Harbour (Darse)
Once a military port where galleys were built and manned, this is now a marina for yachts and pleasure boats.

SIGHTS
Chapelle St-Pierre★
Open Tue–Sun mid-Mar–mid-Sept 10am–noon, 3–7pm; mid-Sept–mid-Nov and mid-Dec–Mar 10am–noon, 2–6pm. 2€. 04 93 76 90 70.
This chapel was decorated with frescoes in 1957 by **Jean Cocteau**. His theme, the life of St Peter, is illustrated by simple realistic scenes. There are also some secular scenes celebrating the young women of Villefranche and gypsies.

Citadelle
Open daily Jun–Sept 10am–12.15pm, 2.30–6pm, Sun 3–6.30pm; Oct and Dec–May 10am–noon, 2–5.30pm, Sun 2–6pm. No charge. 04 93 76 90 70.
This stronghold was constructed in 1560 by the Duke of Savoy to guard the port.

Admired by Vauban, it was spared Louis XIV's destruction of Nice's defences. Restored in 1981, it now comprises the town hall, the former chapel of St Elmo used for temporary exhibitions, and an open-air theatre. The casemates of the citadel house a collection of **submarine archaeology** exhibits from the wreck of a sunken 16C Genoese ship excavated in the Villefranche harbour in the 1980s. The citadel is also home to three museums (same hours as the citadel).

Musée Volti★
The main courtyard of the citadel and the surrounding vaulted casemates provide an admirable setting for a collection of sculptures by Antoniucci Volti, a citizen of Villefranche of Italian origin.

Musée Goetz-Boumeester
The main collection was given to the town of Villefranche by the painter-engraver **Henri Goetz** (1909–89). There are about 100 works signed by Picasso, Miró, Hartung, and Picabia.

Villefranche-sur-Mer

B. Kaufmann/MICHELIN

Collection Roux
This is an exhibit of ceramic figurines displayed in small tableaux evoking everyday life in the Middle Ages and during the Renaissance.

ADDRESSES

🛏 STAY

🛏 **Le Riviera** – *2 Av. Albert-1.* ℘*04 93 76 62 76. www. hotelrivieravillefranche.com. Closed Jan. 26 rooms.* ⊂*9.50€.* Unpretentious, prettily restored hotel lying on the Corniche Inférieure. Some rooms afford views of the sea. Agreeable rooftop terrace for summer breakfasts.

🛏 **Hôtel Patricia** – *Av. de l'Ange-Gardien via the Corniche Inférieur.* ℘*04 93 01 06 70. www.hotel-patricia.riviera.fr. Closed Nov –Dec.* 🅿. *13 rooms.* ⊂*7.50€.* Despite the close proximity of the train tracks, this hotel is well-placed just a few steps from the beach. The rooms are tastefully decorated, ones on the upper floors have views of the sea.

🛏 **Hôtel St-Michel** – *2000 Av. Olivula.* ℘*04 93 01 80 42. www.hotel-saint-michel.com. 35 rooms.* ⊂*8.50€.* Located in the peaceful residential hills above the town, this hotel has recently renovated rooms in the main building and larger ones in the annexe, some with kitchenettes. Wifi available.

🍽 EAT

🍽 **La Grignotière** – *3 Rue du Poilu.* ℘*04 93 76 79 83. Closed Mon–Sat lunches, Wed eve off season.* This restaurant makes a point of serving hearty meals made with fresh ingredients of excellent quality. Follow the locals and tuck into a gargantuan dinner of French and Mediterranean dishes.

🍽🍽 **L'Oursin Bleu** – *11 quai Courbet.* ℘*04 93 01 90 12. Closed 10 Jan–10 Feb, and Tue off season.* The charming nautical decor and large aquarium complement this popular port-side seafood restaurant.

TOURS

Guided tours – Guided tours of the town *(1hr45min)* on Wednesdays at 10am. ⊜*5€*; breakfast and a guided tour of the village on Fridays April–September. *8€. Reserve at the tourist office.* ℘*04 93 01 73 68.*

Tourist Train – *La Rafale. Operates 15 Apr–Oct.* ⊜*6.50€ (child 3€).* ℘*04 93 09 40 60.* Departures from Place Wilson for round trip tour *(1hr)* of the village with commentary.

THE PRE-ALPS OF NICE

Although part of the Alpes-Martimes administrative department, and therefore grouped with the French Riviera, the mountains and valleys north of Nice have their own distinct character. There are no fancy casinos or palace hotels, no beaches or yachts and few examples of the conspicuous wealth found along the coast. Modest inns and humble perched villages welcome visitors who come to admire the flora and fauna, to enjoy the outdoor sports, to see the rich religious art treasures found in many of the churches, or to simply get away from the crowds and summer heat found elsewhere on the Riviera. And, while the deep ravines and vertiginous peaks make for impressive panoramic vistas, the narrow, winding roads require attentive drivers as they hairpin up and down the mountains, and through the often icy or even snow-covered forest roads.

Highlights

1 15C frescoes in the **Chapelle Notre-Dame-des-Fontaines** (p354)

2 Prehistoric engravings in the **Vallée des Merveilles** (p357)

3 Stunning views from the **Madone d'Utelle Panorama** (p369)

4 Rafting or canyoning on the **Bévéra River in Sospel** (p361)

5 Drive the Authion or Col de Braus Road in the **forest of Turini** (p366)

Nature Close-Up

These hinterlands running along the Italian border at the foot of the Alps don't quite meet the sea, but their proximity contributes to the unique mix of Mediterranean and Alpine landscapes. Olive groves and Maritime pines eventually give way as elevation rises to oaks, firs, spruces, and Swiss pines, as well as flowering plants such as edelweiss and saxifrage. The rivers, notably the Roya and Bévéra, have cut deep into the valleys on their way to the sea, creating fascinating rock formations and waterfalls as the snow melts on the pre-Alpine peaks. Much of this natural beauty is protected in the Parc National du Mercantour, which, partnered with the bordering Parco Naturale della Alpi Marittime in Italy, is home to the prehistoric engravings in the Vallée des Merveilles, over 200 rare plant species including wild orchids, and many endangered or rare animals including grey wolves, golden eagles, ibex and bearded vultures.

Sporting Activities

The uniquely rugged character of this landscape provides ample opportunities for sports enthusiasts of all abilities. There is a variety of trails for hikers, some

Breil-sur-Roya

F. Bayer / MICHELIN

which follow sections of the national GR *(Grand Randonnée)* trails, with several refuges providing food and shelter. Rock climbing is also popular, particularly teamed with the *via ferrata* routes, which traverse some of the deeper canyons. For water sports fans, Sospel and Tende host many river rafting and canyoning companies, which provide proper equipment and seasoned guides in the summer months.

Of course, the hinterlands of Nice also attract visitors in the winter season to a handful of slopes in La Colmiane-Valdeblore, Camp d'Argent in the forest of Turini, and Peira-Cava near Lucéram. Regardless of the season, anyone setting out into the wild should check the local weather reports and be sure to dress and pack accordingly for inclement weather.

Religious Heritage

There are no large monasteries in this part of the French Riviera, but the mountain passes and perched villages house a surprising number of Gothic chapels with 14C frescoes, Italian-style churches with their distinctive bell towers, and many rare artworks by Louis Bréa, Giovanni Baleison, and altarpieces from the Nice School. Many of these churches and chapels are only open during services or on request where noted, so be sure to call ahead before making a long journey to avoid disappointment.

The Return of the Bearded Vulture

The bearded vulture, a magnificent bird with a huge wingspan (2.8m/9.6ft), indeed the largest Alpine bird, is an example of a European endangered species. Its numbers were greatly reduced in the 19C in the Alps, although it survives in the Pyrénées and Corsica. This bird, has a curious way of life: alternating between soaring flight and perilous aerobatics, it flies over the steep, sloping pastures looking for the carcasses of chamois and sheep from which it takes the large bones (up to 3kg/6.6lb). It then drops the bones from a great height onto rocks in order to shatter them, hence their nickname 'bone-breaker' *(casseur d'os)*. It used to be looked on as the natural assistant of the shepherd.

The reintroduction of bearded vultures as chicks into the Parc du Mercantour (at Roubion) in 1993 was crowned with success. It takes eight years for the birds to reach maturity after, which they can live for around 40 years.

In 1996 five birds were released in the southern Alps and 60 throughout the Alps in an extensive international reintroduction programme, the only one of its kind.

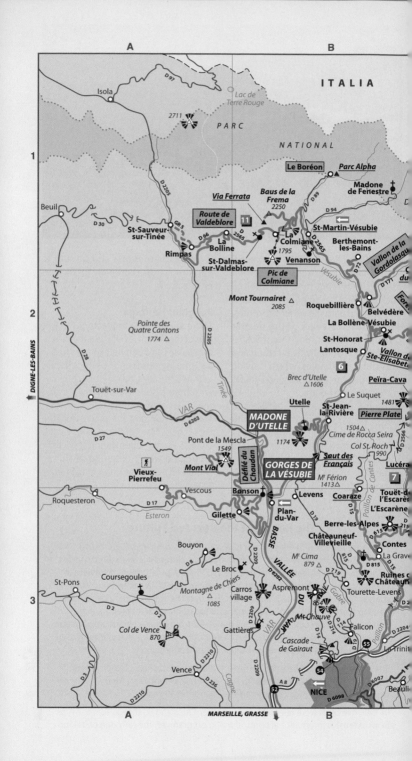

L'Arrière Pays Niçois

The hinterlands of Nice, often the least-explored region of the French Riviera, are made up of dramatic clifftop villages and peaks with panoramic view, accessible by dangerous winding roads, sometime with over a dozen successive hairpin turns, and often covered in snow most of the winter. But those who brave the journey are rewarded with breathtaking sites of natural and manmade beauty.

Info: Tourist offices at Gilette Val d'Esteron &04 92 08 98 08, www.esteron.fr; at l'Escarène &04 93 79 62 93, www.escarene.fr; or at Contes &04 93 79 13 99, www.ville-contes.fr.

Location: The Arrière Pays lie in the mountains and valleys north of Nice, towards the Alps, along the Italian border.

Don't Miss: Views from the Plateau St Michel or Mont Alban.

🚗 DRIVING TOURS

1 LES DEUX MONTS★★
Round trip of 11km/7mi – about 45min.

▷ *Leave Nice from Pl. Max-Barel on N 7, Moyenne Corniche, going east. After 2.5km/1.5mi turn right onto a forest road. 1km/0.6mi further on turn left onto a signposted path to the fort.*

Mont Alban★★
Alt 222m/728ft. A footpath circles up to a splendid **view★★** of the coastline: to the east lie Cap Ferrat, Cap d'Ail, the Bordighera Point and the Tête de Chien. To the west lie the Baie des Anges. The massive 16C fort bastions and watch-towers can be admired only from the outside.

▷ *Return to the fork and proceed straight ahead to Mont Boron.*

Mont Boron★
Alt 178m/584ft. From the mountains there are **views★** extending over the Villefranche harbour and along the coast to Cap d'Antibes. On the horizon can be seen the mountains around Grasse and the Esterel range.

▷ *Return to Nice along the Corniche Inférieure (N 98).*

16C fort of Mont Alban

©Guy Thouvenin/Robert Harding

2 PLATEAU ST-MICHEL★★
Round trip of 19km/12mi – about 1hr.

⊳ *Leave Nice going east along Avenue des Diables-Bleus and the Grande Corniche (D 2564).*

Look back to enjoy views of Nice and the Cap d'Antibes. Ahead lie the fort of La Drète and Mont Agel further back.

Observatoire du Mont-Gros
The private road to the Nice observatory leads off to the right of the Grande Corniche. ⌖ *Guided tours (1.5hr) Wed and Sat 2.45pm, Sun 2pm, 2.45pm, 3.30pm. ⌖6€. ℘04 93 85 85 58. www.astrorama.net.*
This famous international centre for astronomical research was founded in 1881 by the scientific patron Bischoff-heim. Charles Garnier oversaw the architecture, while Gustave Eiffel built the metal frame for the great dome (26m/85ft in diameter). This houses an astronomical telescope called the 'great equatorial'. It is 18m/59ft long with an optical diameter of 76cm/30in and was for a long time the largest instrument of its kind in the world

⊳ *Bear right on D 34 and park the car in the car park after 500m/547yd.*

Plateau St-Michel Viewpoint★★
A viewing table identifies the coastline from Cap d'Ail to the Esterel.

⊳ *Continue along D 34 and then bear left onto the Moyenne Corniche (N 7).*

After a long tunnel there is a marvellous **view**★ of Beaulieu, Cap Ferrat, Villefranche-sur-Mer, Nice and Cap d'Antibes. The road winds round above Villefranche harbour. After Col de Ville-franche, Nice with its castle hill, the harbour and the Baie des Anges comes into sight.

⊳ *Return to Nice via Pl. Max-Barel.*

3 TOUR OF MONT CHAUVE★
Round trip of 53km/33mi – allow half a day.

⊳ *From Nice take Avenue du Ray north; turn sharp right on Avenue de Gairaut, D 14, towards Aspremont and after passing under the motorway (2km/1mi) bear right following D 14 and then turn left following the signs.*

Cascade de Gairaut
In two great steps the waters of the Vésubie Canal tumble down into a basin. From the chapel terrace there is a beautiful **view** of the town.

⊳ *Return to D 14.*

Soon afterwards there are views to the left of Nice, Mont Boron and Cap d'Antibes, and towards Aspremont the **view** extends to the Var Vally.

Aspremont
The village, built to a concentric plan, perches prettily on its hilltop site. The **church** (⊘*closed between services*) has a Gothic nave decorated with frescoes. On the left is a painted wooden Virgin and Child. Above and behind the church once stood the castle, now destroyed. From the terrace that overlooks the town is a **panorama**★ comprising several hill villages, Cap d'Antibes, the hills beyond Nice and Mont Chauve.

⊳ *On leaving the village, take D 719 over a little pass, Col d'Aspremont, between Mont Chauve and Mont Cima to the rich basin of Tourrette-Levens.*

Tourrette-Levens
Circled by mountains, this village on the Salt Route clings to a knife-edged rock. The 18C **church** (⊘*open by request ℘04 93 91 00 41*) has a carved wooden altarpiece, also 18C, of the Virgin between St Sylvester and St Antony (behind the high altar). A short walk through the village to the partially restored château and the Maison des Remparts which shelters the **Musée des Métiers Traditionnels** (⊘*open Wed–Sun Apr–Sept 2.30–6pm;*

Sanctuaire Notre-Dame-de-Laghet

Oct–Mar 2–5.30pm; no charge; 04 97 20 54 60) exhibiting over 6 000 tools arranged by trade in reconstituted workshops.

▷ *Return to D 19 turning left into the Gabre Valley, then right on D114.*

Falicon
This typical Niçois village huddles on a rocky outcrop among olive groves. Illustrious guests including Queen Victoria were attracted to the village on account of its delightful surroundings.
The **church** (○*open Mon–Fri, visits on request at the town hall* 04 92 07 92 70), which was founded by the Benedictines of St-Pons, has a square belfry and a façade in trompe-l'œil. In the nave is a beautiful 17C Nativity framed in gold. Climb up the stairway to the left of the church and turn right onto a path leading to a terrace for a **view** ★ of Nice.

▷ *Return to D 114 on the left. At the chapel of St-Sébastien turn right onto D 214, a narrow road, to Mont Chauve. Leave the car at the end of the road.*

Mont Chauve d'Aspremont
Alt 854m/2 802ft.
⬆ *30min on foot round trip.*
"Chauve" means bald, and the mountain lives up to its name. A disused fort stands on the naked summit offering a magnificent **panorama**★★: the snow-clad Alps and the Nice hills, and the coast from Menton to Cap Ferrat. On a very fine day Corsica is visible.

▷ *Return to D 114 turning left; 2km/1mi further on turn sharp right onto D 19. Go under the motorway; 1km/0.6mi later there is a right-hand turning up to St-Pons.*

Église St-Pons★
The Benedictine abbey of St Pontius was founded during Charlemagne's reign and played an important part in local affairs for 1 000 years. The church, rebuilt in the 18C, stands on a headland above the Paillon Valley, its graceful silhouette and Genoese campanile visible from all sides. The interior plasterwork is richly decorated.

4 THE TWO PAILLONS★
Round trip of 90km/56mi – allow 1 day.
The Paillon de l'Escarène emerges from the northeast of Col St-Roch, whereas the Paillon de Contes springs from the slopes of Rocca Seira to the northwest. They meet at Pont de Peille and flow into the sea at Nice. The suggested route goes up one valley and down the other with detours at Peille and La Turbie.

▷ *Leave Nice by Blvd J.-B.-Verany and Route de Turin, D 2204 going north. In La Trinité bear right to Laghet.*

The road goes up the verdant Laghet Valley. The Roman road from La Turbie to Cimiez was on the opposite bank.

Sanctuaire Notre-Dame de Laghet
& ○*Sanctuary open 7am–9.30pm. Museum open in summer 3.30–5.30pm;*

open Wed–Mon May–Oct 3.30–5.30pm.
≪No charge. ℘04 93 41 50 50.
www.sanctuaire-laghet.cef.fr
The sanctuary, founded in 1656, is
a pilgrimage centre for France and
Italy. Innumerable votive offerings,
touching and amusing in their naivety,
cover the church and cloisters. The
best of them are displayed in the little
museum on Place du Sanctuaire.

▷ *The road winds through olive groves
to the Grande Corniche; turn left.*

La Turbie★ (≪see La TURBIE)
▷ *Leave La Turbie on D 53 with its
views of the sea. On the left of the road
is the Chapelle St-Martin.*

Église St-Martin-de-Peille
⚬━ Currently closed for restoration.
℘04 93 91 71 71.
The church stands in a secluded but
beautiful setting of olive-tree clad
mountains. It is a modern structure of
very simple design, with plastic windows and the trunk of a giant olive tree
used as the altar.
The road winds round the lower slopes
of Mont Agel before descending to
Peille. Near the last tunnel there is a
fine **view** of Peille village.

Peille★ (≪see PEILLE)
▷ *Join Paillon Valley at La Grave. After
2.5km/1.5mi turn left onto D 121 which
climbs to the eagle's nest of Peillon.*

Peillon★★ (≪see PEILLON)
▷ *Return to D 21 and turn right.*

The village of Peille comes into view on
the slopes of Mont Castellet (right).

Gorges du Paillon★
The route crosses a lush, wooded ravine.

L'Escarène
Built at the junction of the road to the
resort of Peïra-Cava and the beginning
of the hairpin bends leading up to Col de
Braus, this large town stretching along
the bottom of the Paillon Valley was an
important staging post on the Salt Road
from Nice to Turin (*Route du Sel – ≪see
SOSPEL*).

Église St-Pierre★
This 17C church, flanked by two chapels
of the Black and White Penitents, is the
work of the Niçois architect Guibert.
On the road to Col de Turini, the imposing mausoleum dedicated to the Ist Division France Libre, inaugurated in 1964 by
General de Gaulle, commemorates the
sacrifices and battles of the Liberation at
the end of the Second World War.

▷ *Take D 2204 south to Col de Nice
and turn right onto D 215.*

Berre-les-Alpes
The village boasts a charming site at
an elevation of 675m/2 215ft. From the
cemetery there is a **panorama**★ of the
Pre-Alps of Nice and the sea.

▷ *Return downhill on the same road
bearing right onto D 615.*

The drive winds its way through chestnut and olive groves.

Contes
Originally a Roman settlement, the village is built on a rocky promontory that
dominates the River Paillon de Contes
like a ship's prow.
The south chapel of the church contains a remarkable altarpiece by an
artist belonging to the Nice School
(1525). The central panel representing
Ste Madeleine has disappeared but the
predella★ illustrates her life.
Bordering Paillon (*on D 15, in the direction of Coaraze*) is a site with two mills:
a 13C oil press still in use by the village
(*Dec–Mar*), and a 14C iron forge where
large farming tools were made until
1958. You can visit the forge and a reconstituted 19C country kitchen (⊙open
Dec–Oct Sat 9.30am–12.30pm, 2–5pm;
≪2€; ℘04 93 79 00 01).

▷ *Take D 715 to La Grave; cross the
Paillon and take D 815.*

The road winds uphill through pines and olives above the Paillon, until the rocky outcrop of Contes and Berre-des-Alpes are seen below.

Châteauneuf-Villevieille
The village on the site of a Ligurian settlement, later a Roman camp, overlooks the Paillon de Contes Valley. The 11C Romanesque church, **Madone de Villevieille** is decorated with festoons and Lombard bands. The interior was restored in the 17 with ceiling frescoes. Behind the high altar, a fine plaster altarpiece frames a 15C wooden statue of the Virgin and Child.

The deserted ruins of medieval walls and towers (🚶 *2km/1mi, 30min round trip*) make a strange spectacle against the rocky landscape. The village people hid up here in the Middle Ages during attacks. From the top of the bluff there is a sweeping **panorama**★.

▷ *Go back to D 15, which leads to Nice via the Paillon Valley.*

5 VALLÉE DU VAR AND VALLÉE DE L'ESTERON
66km/41mi – allow half a day.

▷ *Leave Nice by Promenade des Anglais, which becomes Promenade Corniglion-Molinier. Return to N 98, then turn right towards Plan-du-Var.*

The N 202, which hugs the east bank of the Var, allows quick access to the Nice hinterland. In a landscape composed of flower beds and vegetable plots, of vineyards and olive groves, the hill villages stand out one by one: on the west bank Gattières, Carros and Le Broc; on the east bank Aspremont and Castagniers at the foot of Mont Chauve, followed by St-Martin-du-Var and La Roquette-sur-Var. The **view**★ includes the snow-capped Alps on the horizon.

▷ *Cross the river over Pont Charles-Albert and take D 17 to Gilette.*

The site of the village of Bonson, on an impressive rock spur high above the river on the west bank, comes into view followed by Gilette, nestling in a cleft.

Gilette
From Place de la Mairie follow the arrows up to the castle ruins for an impressive **view**★ of the *corniche* roads, the Var Valley and the Pre-Alps of Nice.

There is a pleasant walk, bordered by acacias and plane trees, below the castle with fine views of the hill villages – Bonson and Tourette-du-Château – and of the Alps to the north.

▷ *From Gilette take D 17 north up the Esteron Valley; 2km/1mi beyond Vescous turn right onto a narrow road which climbs to Vieux-Pierrefeu.*

Vieux-Pierrefeu
Alt 618m/2 028ft. The village is reserved for pedestrians. Austere and proud, Vieux-Pierrefeu is a handsome perched village with beautifully restored stonework throughout. High above the Esteron Valley, this former Roman signalling post (Petra Igniaria) was a link in the chain that ran from Hadrian's Wall on the border between England and Scotland to Rome used to transmit optical messages.

The church just down the road in Pierrefeu has been converted into a picture gallery called the **Musée "Hors du Temps"** (🕐*open with two days' advance notice at Town Hall;* ⊕*2€;* ℘*04 93 08 58 18*). This small museum houses a unique collection of paintings on the theme of Genesis, with the work of 40 contemporary artists including Brayer, Carzou, Folon, Erni, Vicari, Villemont and Moretti. On the drive down D 17, you'll see views of the Var Valley, Bonson and La Roquette, perched on its rock.

Bonson
Built on a remarkable **site**★ on a rocky spur high above the Var Valley, Bonson offers an exceptional **view**★★ from the church terrace of the Vésubie springing from its gorges and meeting with the waters of the Var, the Défilé de Chaudan

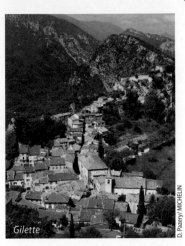

(👆 see p349). This famous, wooded area was razed by fire in 1994 that destroyed everything up to the village edge.

The **church** contains three beautiful Primitive paintings from the Nice School. On the back wall there is a **retable of St Antony**, where the figure of Ste Gertrude, who was invoked against the plague, is identified by the great rats climbing up her shoulders. In the south aisle is a **retable of John the Baptist**, attributed to Antoine Bréa (the centre panel has been spoiled by overpainting). At the high altar, in a Renaissance frame, is a **retable of St Benedict★**, including the figure of Ste Agatha clutching her wounded breasts.

Mont Vial★
20km/12.4mi from Bonson.

▷ *Take D 27 west towards Puget-Théniers.*

The picturesque road twists and turns along the flank of the hill with attractive glimpses of Gilette. After Tourette-du-Château take the road going sharply down to the right which winds to Le Vial ridge before reaching the summit (1 549m/5 082ft, *U-turns possible*). An impressive **panorama★★** will reward those who have made the effort of climbing up.

▷ *Return to Bonson by the same route.*

The road loops down to Pont Charles-Albert, giving beautiful **views★** of the Var Valley. Cross the bridge and turn left onto N 202. North of Plan-du-Var cross the River Vésubie where it joins the Var. The road to the right climbs up the Gorges de la Vésubie (👆 see Vallée de la VÉSUBIE).

Défilé du Chaudan★★
The defile, which is named after the little village of Chaudan at its southern end, has been created by the Var, which has worn a deep, narrow and winding channel through the rocks. The road follows the course of the river in and out of every bend and through four tunnels.

Gilette

D. Pazery/ MICHELIN

At the northern end, at **Pont de la Mescla**, the River Tinée flows into the Var.

▷ *Go back to Nice on N 202.*

⑥ VÉSUBIE VALLEY
👆 *See Vallée de la VÉSUBIE*
Plan-du-Var to the Madone d'Utelle
St-Jean-la-Rivière to St-Martin-Vésubie

⑦ TURINI FOREST
👆 *See Forêt de TURINI*
The Authion★★
Vallon Ste-Élisabeth★
Col de Braus Route★★

⑧ COL DE CASTILLON ROAD
👆 *see MENTON: Pass Road*
Menton to Sospel

⑨ COL DE BROUIS ROAD
👆 *See SOSPEL: Outings*
Sospel to La Giandola

⑩ SAORGE AND BERGUE GORGES
👆 *See SAORGE: Driving Tours*

⑪ ROUTE DE VALDEBLORE
👆 *See ST-MARTIN-VÉSUBIE: Driving Tour*

⑫ ROUTE DES CRÊTES
👆 *See VENCE: Driving Tours*

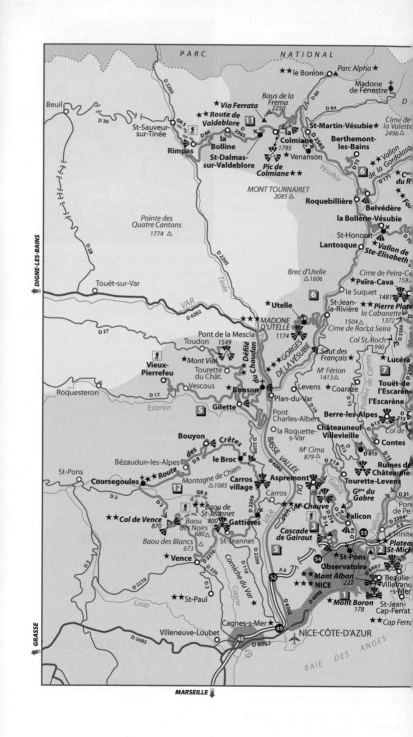

TORINO

D 2604

45 △
' CLAPIER
Cade de
'Estrech
Fontanalbe

Casterino

Roya

★ Tende

★ la
Brigue

D 143

Mt SACCAREL
2200 △

2935 △
Baisse de Valmasque
△ 2872
Mt Bégo

D 91

St-Dalmas-
de-Tende

D 43

Levense

N.-D. des-
Fontaines ★★

Vallées des
Merveilles
2685 △
ME DU DIABLE

Granile

HAUTE VALLÉE DE LA ROYA

M E R C A N T O U R

l'Authion ★★
Pte des
3 Communes ★★
2082

89

D 68

★ Gorges de Bergue ★

D 6204

Fontan

Mon
aux Morts

★★ Gorges
de Saorge

Saorge ★★

10

Cabanes
Vieilles

07
de Turini

la Giandola

Roya

ITALIA

Vallée
Turini
de

Mt Mangiabo
△ 1801

Nervia

ulinet

D 2204

879

9

Brell-s-Roya

N.-D- de
la Menour

Col de Brouis ★

D 2566

Col du
Perus

Col de
Vescavo

Piène-Haute

D 6204

Cascade

Mt 654
Agaisen
△ 745

477

ges du
iaon ★
de
us 02

St-Roch

Olivetta

Bevera

A
D 2566

847

Fort Suchet

7

642

Sospel ★

8

Col St-Jean

707

Col de Castillon

S 20

Roya

ue de Braus

Castillon

Gorges
pation

Forêt de Menton
Col des
Banquettes

Viaduc du Caramel

Peille ★

4

Ste-
Agnès

Monti

Vallée du
Carei

Castellar

A 10

GENOVA

GENOVA

SAN
REMO

Gorbio

D 23

A 8

59

S 1

Ventimiglia

eillon

Mont Agel
1110 △

D 53

Roquebrune

2566

St-Martin-de-Peille

MENTON ★★

N.-D. de
Laghet

Cap Martin ★

57

D 6007

Cap Martin ★★

la Turbie

MONTE-CARLO ★★★

ze ★★

Cap-d'Ail

MONACO ★★★

M E R   M É D I T E R R A N É E

ARRIÈRE-PAYS NIÇOIS

0   5 km

N

Breil-sur-Roya
Alpes Maritimes

Breil lies below the summit of l'Arpette (1 610m/5 282ft), astride the Roya River, a few miles from the Italian border, giving the town an Italian look and feel. The town is known for fishing and water sports.

VISIT

The old village consists of picturesque streets with traces of the ramparts and ancient gateways. The Renaissance **Chapelle Ste-Catherine**, which hosts regular art exhibitions, stands south of the parish church.

Sancta-Maria-in-Albis

Pl. Brancion. ◷*Open daily 9am–noon, 3–6pm.* ℘04 93 04 42 19.
The vast 18C church with its carved doors (1719) and Baroque interior is adorned with an ornate 17C **organ loft** of carved and gilded wood, and an early **altarpiece** (1500) left of the chancel.

Écomusée du Haut-Pays

Gare de Breil. ◷*Open Jun–Sept 10am–noon, 2–5pm.* ℘04 93 04 42 75. ☞2€.
The old Breil train station has been transformed into a railway museum featuring an old steam train, a tramway, trolley, and working model trains.

PRACTICAL INFORMATION
TOURS
Self-Guided Tours – The tourist office provides a detailed map for exploring the village as well as three hiking intineraries promising "fascinating and panoramic views".
TRANSPORT
Access by train: The Italian and French rail links from Nice and Vintimille towards Cuneo and Turin pass by the stations of Breil (Roya-Bévéra), Sospel and Tende. A particularly scenic trip. 👥 In summer take the "Train des Merveilles," which has live commentary of the route (℘*see Planning Your Trip*).

▶ **Population:** 2 092.
 Michelin Map: 341 G4; local map: *see NICE.*
 Info: Pl. Bianchéri. ℘04 93 04 99 76. www.breil-sur-roya.fr. Office du tourisme de la Vallée de la Roya. ℘04 93 04 92 05. www.royabevera.com.
 Timing: Breil is situated on the main road from Ventimiglia to Turin, via the Col de Tende pass, 23km/14mi from Sospel.

ADDRESSES

🏠 STAY

☞ **Le Roya** – *Pl. Biancheri.* ℘04 93 04 48 10. *13 rooms.* ☞7.50€. This hotel, on the left bank of the Roya, stands out because of its brightly coloured façade. Simple, unadorned rooms and roomy bathrooms await you here. We recommend the rooms overlooking the mountain or the river.

🤸 LEISURE ACTIVITIES

A.E.T. Nature – *392 Chemin du Foussa.* ℘04 93 04 47 64. www.aetcanyoning.com. Open daily by reservation.
This company organises hikes, *via ferrata*, rafting, and a camping refuge for up to 20 *(reservations required)*.

Roya Évasion – *11 Blvd Rouvrier.* ℘04 93 04 91 46. www.royaevasion.com. Closed Sat–Sun in Sept–Jun, Nov–Mar.
For canoeing, rafting, hiking and mountain biking excursions. Equipment for hire.

La Brigue★
Alpes Maritimes

Part of Italy until 1947, La Brigue is a charming mountain village among the vineyards in the Levense Valley, with views of Mont Bégo. Known as a centre of Primitive Niçois artworks, the village has preserved the ruins of the castle of the Lascaris Lords, local rulers from the 14C to the 18C.

·♣· WALKING TOUR
OLD VILLAGE
At the foot of the 14C chateau ruins are a number of medieval houses with green schist rooftops. Some of the houses are built over arcades; others have carved lintels, often with a heraldic detail (*particularly Rue de la République*). Place Vieille commands a fine **view** of Mont Bégo.

To the right of the parish church stand two Penitents' Chapels: the 18C **Chapelle de l'Assomption** with its Baroque façade and graceful Genoese bell tower; and to the left the **Chapelle de l'Annonciation**, also Baroque on a hexagonal plan, with a collection of ecclesiastical ornaments.

Collégiale St-Martin★
This parish church has a fine late 15C square Romanesque bell tower and a doorway framed in the Antique style (1576) with an older (1501) green schist lintel. The 17C organ was repaired in the 19C. The white marble font is crowned by a painted and gilded baldaquin.

The church contains a remarkable collection of **Primitive paintings from the Nice School**★. Chapels along the south aisle contain a Crucifixion with saints and donors comparable with Louis Bréa's in Cimiez, an altarpiece of St Martha recounting the legend of her arrival at Marseille on a boat, a rare realist painting by Bréa of the Sufferings of St Elmo, and a fine altarpiece of the **Adoration of the Child**, also by Bréa. On the north side, the first chapel contains a triptych of the Italian Fuzeri of **Our Lady of the Snows** (1507) with its 18C Baroque frame.

▶ **Population:** 630.
🚲 **Michelin Map:** 341 G3; local map: *see NICE*.
🈂 **Info:** 2 Av. du Général De-Gaulle. ℘04 93 79 09 34. www.labrigue.fr. Vallées Roya-Bévéra. ℘04 93 04 92 05. www.royabevera.com.
▶ **Location:** Located inland from Nice in the Roya Valley. Arrive via St-Delmas-de-Tende, crossing the Roman bridge over the river, for the best view of Mont Bégo.
🕐 **Timing:** Allow 2–3hr to explore La Brigue and its sights.

🏃 Local Trails
Ask for the maps from the tourist office. The "Chemin des Oratoires" from la Brigue to St-Dalmas-de-Tende *(1hr)*. Nature Interpretation Trail between La Brigue and Notre-Dame-des-Fontaines *(1.5hr)*.

EXCURSION
Chapelle Notre-Dame-des-Fontaines★★
4km/2.5mi east on D 43.
🕐*Open Jun–Sept Mon, Wed and Fri–Sat 2–5pm, Sun 2–6pm; Oct–May by request at tourist office.* ◉*1.50€.*

La Brigue

B. Kaufmann/MICHELIN

Jesus Questioned by Pilate by Giovanni Canavesio

Painted Chapels of the Nice Hinterland

Scattered in the valleys of the Roya, the Paillon and the Basse-Tinée, many medieval chapels contain superb frescoes designed to teach the Scriptures:

◆ Coaraze, St-Sébastien
◆ Lucéram, Notre-Dame-de-Bon-Cœur and St-Grat
◆ Peillon, Pénitent Chapel
◆ St-Dalmas-Valdeblore Church
◆ Venanson, St-Sébastien

There are also several modern successors worthy of note: Matisse in Vence, Cocteau in Villefranche and Tobiasse in Le Cannet.

Set alone in the Mont Noir Valley near Mont Bégo and overlooking a mountain stream, the chapel of Notre-Dame-des-Fontaines is a pilgrimage site on a former sanctuary dedicated to water.

The nave was added to the 12C chancel in the 14C, then raised in the 18C with seven clerestory windows. The exterior is unadorned, but the interior is ornate, with striking **frescoes**★★★. The chancel panels were discovered in 1950 under a coat of wash. They were painted in 1451 by **Jean Baleison**, master of the Gothic style, depicting the Four Evangelists (on the vault), the Resurrection of Christ and the Virgin's Assumption (on the walls). The nave was decorated in the same period by the Renaissance Primitive **Giovanni Canavesio** (1420–early 16C), in his exuberant Gothic-inspired style.

ADDRESSES

HIKERS' REFUGE

◎ **Le Pra-Réound** – *On D 43 outside the village after the Maison Adapeï.* ℘*04 93 04 65 67. Closed 20 Nov–1 Mar. 6 rooms.* 🍴. ⊘*6€.* Hikers will appreciate this small refuge located at the entrance to a picturesque mountain village. Motel-style rooms with terraces face the snowcapped peaks. Fully equipped kitchens are available for a quick meal.

Lucéram★

Alpes Maritimes

The pretty village of Lucéram, perched dramtically on a steep rock below the Cime du Gros Braus mountain peak, is known for its colourful roof tiles and an exceptionally rich collection of religious art.

VISIT
Medieval Village★

▷ *On Pl. Adrien-Barralis, follow the arrows to the church (église).*

A maze of stepped streets, Gothic houses and vaulted alleyways make up the medieval town. From the church terrace one can look down over Lucéram, and beyond the hills to the sea.

Église Ste-Marguerite

🕓*Open Tue–Wed 10am–noon, 2–7pm, Sun 2–7pm.* 👄*Guided tours, contact the tourist office* ℘*04 93 91 60 50.*
The interior of the simple 15C church was remodelled in the 18C with elaborate plasterwork. The **altarpieces★★** form the most complete group attributed to the Nice School. In the south transept is the **altarpiece of St Antony** framed in Flamboyant Gothic panellinq. Behind the high altar, the **altarpiece of Ste Margaret,** divided into 10 panels, is by Louis Bréa: around the central figure are Mary Magdalene *(bottom left)* and St

▶ **Population:** 1 228.
🕭 **Michelin Map:** 341 F4; local map: *see NICE.*
🛈 **Info:** Maison de Pays de Lucéram, Pl. Adrien-Barralis. ℘04 93 91 60 50.
▷ **Location** 21km/14mi northeast from Nice.
🅿 **Parking:** Available at both ends of the village, near the fire department and close to the post office.

Michael *(top left).* Three fine altarpieces by the Bréa School are in the nave. The **treasury**★ comprises some remarkable pieces: a silver statuette of Ste Margaret (1500), a finely engraved 14C reliquary, a statue-reliquary of Ste Rosalie from Sicily, two candlesticks and an alabaster Virgin (16C).On the left of the entrance stands an unusual Baroque Pietà in painted wood and to the left of the chancel another one in plaster on cloth dating from the 13C.

Chapelle St-Grat

1km/0.6mi to the south on D 2566, on the left at the exit of the village, before the tunnel. Follow the path down on foot.
This chapel is decorated with frescoes attributed to **Jean Baleison.** Beneath a triple Gothic canopy are the Virgin and Child who is holding a dove, St Grat bearing the head of John the Baptist

Lucéram

B. Kaufmann/ MICHELIN

Noël des Bergers★

Each year shepherds from the neighbouring mountains make their offering of lambs and fruit to the church to the strains of fife and tambourine music.

and St Sebastian in elegant attire with an arrow in his hand.

Chapelle Notre-Dame-de-Bon-Cœur

2km/1.3mi northwest on D 2566, park on the left, then 15min on foot. Interior visible through the bars.
The frescoes, attributed to Baleison, are interesting despite some shoddy repainting. In the porch are *Good and Bad Prayer* and the martyred St Sebastian. In the chapel is the *Adoration of the Shepherds*, the *Adoration of the Magi* and scenes illustrating the life of the Virgin.

ADDRESSES

EVENT
Circuit des Crèches – *Ask for information at the tourist office.*
In December-January, over 400 nativity scenes (crèches) are displayed in the caves and streets of Lucéram and Peïra Cava. A shepherd's procession and mass in Provençal take place Christmas Eve.

Vallée des Merveilles★★
Alpes Maritimes

At the foot of **Mont Bégo** (alt 2 872m/9 423ft) lies a region of glacial lakes, valleys, rocky cirques formed during the Quaternary Era, cut off by the scarce roads and harsh mountain climate. In this dramatic landscape is the Vallée des Merveilles, part of the **Parc National du Mercantour**, and famous for the thousands of Prehistoric rock engravings found there.

Access Routes
There are two different ways of getting to the Vallée des Merveilles, but all require a good hike:

◗ *Take the N 204 up the Roya Valley to St-Dalmas-de-Tende, then D 91 to Casterino and follow one of the footpaths:*

🚶 *3hr.* Lac des Meches to the Arpette area and the Refuge des Merveilles

🚶 *2.5hr.* Casterino refuge to the Fontanalbe refuge and the Fontanalbe district

◆ **Michelin Map:** 341 F3/4.
🛈 **Info:** Parc National du Mercantour, 23 Rue d'Italie, Nice. ✆04 93 16 78 88. www.parc-mercantour.eu. Maison du Parc National à Tende. ✆04 93 04 67 00. www.tendemerveilles.com. Roya-Bevera Office du Tourisme www.roya bevera.com.
◗ **Location:** The whole of the site known as the Vallée des Merveilles consists of seven distinct regions around Mont Bégo: the Vallée des Merveilles itself, which is the largest area; the Vallée de Fontanalbe, which is narrower; the Valmasque, Valaurette, Lac Sainte-Marie, Col du Sabion and Lac Vei del Bouc areas which contain only a few scattered carvings.
⊛ **Don't Miss:** The open-air museum engravings.

◗ *From Belvédère to St-Grat (◆see Vallée de la VÉSUBIE) and the footpath to Pas de l'Arpette.*

Magic Mountain

The engravings reveal the preoccupations of the Ligurian people who lived in the lower valleys and made pilgrimages to Mont Bégo, which they believed had divine powers. The engravings have five themes: horns, arms or tools, anthropomorphs, geometric figures and other unidentified images. The mountain cult was linked to that of the bull; drawings of horns and bovine creatures feature in half the engravings. Ploughs and harnessed animals suggest that agriculture was practiced, and crisscross patterns may represent parcels of land. There are many representations of weapons matching those excavated on nearby archaeological sites. The rare human figures have been given names: Christ, the Wizard, the Chieftain, the Dancer. Others, of a more enigmatic nature, are open to interpretation such the Tree of Life at Fontanalbe (*guided tours only*).

B. Kaufmann/MICHELIN

Over 600km/373mi of marked trails cover the area, including sections of the GR 5 and GR 52A trails which circle the Mercantour National Park and cross through the Vallée des Merveilles. There are also trails which lead to Authion, Boréon and to the Madone de Fenestre (*see Vallée de la VÉSUBI and Forêt de TURINI*). The engravings can be visited from June to September (*see Addresses for guided tour information*).

A BIT OF HISTORY

The Engravings

The name Bégo is derived from an Indo-European root which means the sacred mountain *(Be)* inhabited by the bull-god *(Go)*. The region of Mont Bégo is an **open-air museum** comprising over 40 000 engravings.

Although they were discovered and identified at the end of the 17C, it was not until 1897 that they were studied systematically by the British scholar Clarence Bicknell. In 1947, when the region became part of France, more intensive research was carried out by a team working under Henry de Lumley, which spent 30 years recording every engraving within a wide area of 12ha/30 acres.

Cut into the rock face worn smooth by glacial erosion 15 000 years ago, the linear engravings date from the Gallo-Roman period through the Middle Ages to the present. The most interesting ones to the archaeologists date back to the early Bronze Age (c. 2800 BC–1500 BC). A stippling technique was used by juxtaposing tiny dots punched in the rock face with flint or quartz tools.

The Mercantour National Park

Created in 1979, it covers 68 500ha/170 000 acres in the Alpes-Maritimes and Haute-Provence. Once part of the hunt-

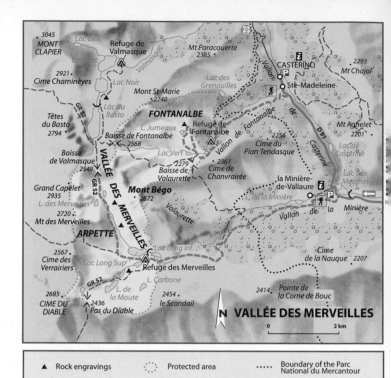

VALLÉE DES MERVEILLES

▲ Rock engravings   ⋯ Protected area   ⋯⋯ Boundary of the Parc National du Mercantour

ing grounds of the kings of Italy, it's now twinned with the Parco Naturale delle Alpi Marittime across the border. These two parks work together to protect their natural and cultural heritage.

⚓WALKS
VALLÉE DES MERVEILLES

◐ *10km/6mi north of St-Dalmas-de-Tende by D 91. Leave the car at Lac des Mesches.*

🏃 *8hr.*
Take the signposted footpath *(3hr on foot)* to the Refuge des Merveilles and then to Lac Long, the starting point for a guided tour of the Arpette area *(2hr round trip).*
It is possible to spend the night at the refuge (reservation necessary), and then the following morning, walk up the Vallée des Merveilles as far as the Baisse de Valmasque *(about 2.5hr).* Return by the same route to reach the car park in the late afternoon.

Fontanalbe

◐ *12km/7.4mi north of St-Dalmas-de-Tende by D 91. Park in Casterino.*
🏃 *5hr. Easier walking than the first hike; ideal for families.*
Start south of Casterino by the information panel *(sign: Fontanalbe),* taking the wooded path west and continuing to the refuge *(about 1hr).* Bear left of the refuge building and continue to Lac Vert *(about 45min),* the starting point for self-guided tours of the Sentier du Découverte *(1.5hr round trip).* For a guided tour of the engravings continue along the side of the lake to the guides' hut at **Lacs Jumeaux.**
By staying overnight at the Fontanalbe refuge it is possible to climb the foothills of Mont Bégo as far as the Baisse de Fontanalbe (alt 2 568m/8 423ft) – fine views of the three lakes in the Valmasque Valley. It is possible to continue towards the Valmasque Refuge or to return to Casterino by the outward route.

PRACTICAL INFORMATION
HIKING IN THE VALLÉE DES MERVEILLES

Important: these sites are at high altitude (1 600-2 500m/5 429-8 202ft), certain preparations are advisable: good physical stamina, mountain boots and warm clothing for protection from cold and rain. Storms are frequent and sometimes violent, so it is wise to listen to the weather forecast. Study the route in advance on Map 1/25 000 – Vallée de la Roya – published by the Conseil Général des Alpes-Maritimes.

REGULATIONS AT THE SITES

Basic Guidelines: The main regulations are symbolised by the signs shown below (*see box at bottom of map, left*). Violations of these regulations, detected by the official park guides, are punishable by heavy fines.

Visiting the Engravings: Although the Bronze Age rock engravings are protected for most of the year by a covering of snow, in recent years they have suffered considerable damage, inflicted intentionally or unintentionally by human visitors. To prevent such defacement the trustees and the officers of the Parc National du Mercantour have limited public access to the Arpette and Fontanalbe sectors only. Visitors may only enter these areas accompanied by the guides who are on duty at the sites daily throughout the summer season.

For the Vallée des Merveilles – *Depart from the Refuge CAF des Merveilles. Jul–Aug 8am, 11am, 1pm, 3pm; Sept Mon and Fri–Sun; Jun Sat–Sun 8am, 1pm.* 10€.

For the Vallée de Fontanalbe – *Open 8am from the Refuge de Fontanalbe, 11am and 2pm from the Pont du Lac Vert; Jul–Aug daily; Sept Mon and Fri–Sun; Jun Sat–Sun.* 10€.

Within the National Park

No domestic animals, no fires, no camping within an hour of the park boundaries and no disposing of waste within the boundaries. Refreshments and accommodation are available from the two refuges. Advance reservations highly recommended.

OFFICIAL GUIDES

Merveilles, Gravures & Découvertes– *10 Montée des Fleurs, Tende.* 06 86 03 90 13 or 04 93 04 89 72. Registered mountain guides of the Mercantour National Park for hikes and tours of the engravings.

Destination Merveilles – *10 Rue des Mesures, Villeneuve-Loubet.* 04 93 73 09 07. www.voyages-randonnees.com. Organises various outings and hiking tours in the Vallée des Merveilles.

Association des Guides, Accompagnateurs et Amis des Alpes Méridionales – *St-Martin-Vésubie.* 04 93 03 26 60. Guides specialising in the Vallée des Merveilles.

REFUGES

Refuge de Fontanalbe – 04 93 04 89 19. *Closed mid-Sept–mid-Jun.* Accommodation and snacks available on-site. Reserve well in advance in season.

Refuge des Merveilles – 04 93 04 64 64 or 04 93 04 69 22 (off season). *Open Jun–Sept, call for off season reservations* 04 93 62 59 99. www.cafresa.org. Accommodation and half-board on-site. Reserve one night in advance.

Saorge★★
Alpes Maritimes

The stone-covered houses and proud belfries of the church and chapels of Saorge cling to the steep slopes of a natural amphitheatre where the Roya Valley broadens out. Saorge was originally a Ligurian settlement and then a Roman colony.

> **Population:** 431.
> **Michelin Map:** 341 G4; local map: *see NICE.*
> **Info:** Mairie (Town Hall). ℘04 93 04 51 23. www.saorge.fr.
> **Location:** Saorge is located 11.5km/7mi north of Breil-sur-Roya.
> **Parking:** Park at the north entrance of the village.

🚶 WALKING TOUR
THE OLD TOWN★

The stepped and twisting streets make an interesting walk past 15C houses. On the far side of the square, go straight, then right and right again to reach a terrace offering a beautiful **view**★ into the Gorges de la Roya.

Église St-Sauveur
The south nave of this 16C church has an 18C canvas depicting Elijah with the Virgin and Child, a fine Renaissance tabernacle, a 15C font beneath a painting by a local artist (1532), and a Virgin in gilded wood beneath a canopy (1708).

> *Leave from the southern end of the village, bearing right at the road fork.*

Madonna del Poggio
○━*Private property.*
The early Romanesque building has a soaring **belfry** with six rows of Lombard bands. This is the oldest religious build-ing in the Roya Valley. The return to the village offers a fine **view** of Saorge and terraced olive groves.

> *Take a sharp right at the road fork towards the monastery.*

Couvent des Franciscains
○*Open Wed–Mon Apr–Oct 10am–noon, 2–6pm; Nov–Mar 10am–5pm.*
🚶*Guided tours (1hr) 10.30am, 3pm.*
⊙5€. ℘04 93 04 55 55.
The 17C Franciscan convent, reinhabited by the monks in 1969, is set among olive trees. The Baroque-style church has a bell tower capped by a bulbous roof of coloured tiles.
Small **cloisters** are decorated with unrefined but pretty paintings on pious themes. From the terrace is a splendid **view**★★ of Saorge and the Roya Valley.

Saorge

DRIVING TOUR

Saorge Gorges and Bergue Gorges

39km/24mi. Allow 4hr.
See local map for Nice.

Breil-sur-Roya

See BREIL-SUR-ROYA.
Leave Breil-sur-Roya to the north by N 204.

The road to Col de Brouis (*see SOSPEL*) forks off to the left.

La Giandola *See SOSPEL.*

Gorges de Saorge★★

The road follows the river's every curve in narrow *corniche* style beneath overhanging rocks. At the end of the gorges,

there is a view between two rock cliffs of the extraordinary **setting**★★ of Saorge built in curved tiers, on a hillside clad in olive trees.

Gorges de Bergue★

Beyond Fontan, the road ascends gorges cut through red schist where the rock appears deeply coloured and foliated. The valley widens out into the St-Dalmas-de-Tende Basin (*see TENDE*).

ADDRESSES

🍴 EAT

Le Bellevue – *5 Rue L.-Périssol. 04 93 04 51 37. Closed Mon eve, Tue.* Interrupt your tour of the covered alleys and settle in the cheerful yellow dining room with its ceiling enhanced by wainscoting. Panoramic views of the village and the Roya Gorges.

Sospel★

Alpes Maritimes

This mountain village straddling the Bévéra was once the capital of the County of Ventimiglia in the 13C. Later it became a stopping point along the **Salt Road** *(Route du Sel)* linking Turin, capital of the Kingdom of Sardinia, to the coast. Today its old houses and olive groves, surrounded by high mountains, create a picturesque backdrop for hiking, canyoning and river rafting.

🥾 WALKING TOUR
THE OLD TOWN★

A map of the village is available at the tourist office.

Right Bank

The church and arcaded houses frame Place St-Michel. The oldest house (Palais Ricci) to the right of the church bears a plaque recording Pope Pius VII's stay in 1809.

▶ **Population:** 3 394.
Michelin Map: 341 F4; local map: *see NICE.*
Info: Le Pont-Vieux, Sospel, *04 93 04 15 80.* www.sospel-tourisme.com. Vallées Roya-Bévéra. *04 93 04 92 05.* www.royabevera.com.
Location: Sospel lies 19km/12mi north of Menton on narrow, winding roads.

Église St-Michel

Open daily 9am–noon, 2–5pm.
At the time of the Great Schism this church was a cathedral. The Romanesque bell tower with Lombard bands flanks an imposing Baroque façade. The interior decor is pure Baroque: huge altarpieces, *trompe-l'œil* frescoes, and gilding. In the north apsidal chapel the **Immaculate Virgin**★ is one of François Bréa's most accomplished works.

Old bridge of Sospel

Old Streets

To the right of the parvis, large stairways lead to the ruins of a Carmelite convent, now almost hidden by vegetation. Carry on to reach the remains of some fortifications, including a huge 15C corner tower and, further on, a semicircular arched gateway. Go through this gateway and follow a stairway to **Rue St-Pierre**, which runs on from the cathedral parvis. The road, lined by arcades, leads to the square behind the *mairie* (town hall).

Old Bridge★

The toll tower on the 11C bridge, rebuilt after The Second World War, now houses the *Syndicat d'Initiative* (tourist office) and, in season, an information centre about the Mercantour National Park.

Left Bank

Cross the old cobblestone bridge to Place St-Nicolas with its old houses and 15C fountain, the oldest in the village. Rue de la République to the right once housed a host of small businesses and enormous cellars used as warehouses by passing merchants before they settled their toll at the bridge. The houses along this road feature beautifully carved stone lintels (nos 14, 15, 23 and 51). The picturesque and narrow Rue des Tisserands leads to the 17C Ste-Croix Chapel.

EXCURSIONS
Fort St-Roch★

1km/0.6mi south of the village, on D 2204 to Nice; turn right after the cemetery (signed). ⊙*Open Jul–Aug Tue–Sun 2–6pm; Apr–Jun and Sept–Oct Sat–Sun and public holidays 2–6pm.* ≈*5€.* ℘*04 93 04 00 70.*

This fort was part of the Alpine Maginot Line of fortifications built in the region during the 1930s. An underground town 50m/164ft deep, it could survive for up to three months without contact with the outside world. The tour covers underground galleries, the kitchens, an electricity generating station, an operations block, the firing stations, a small cinema and artillery rooms, as well as the periscopes which enabled the inhabitants to view their surroundings.

Piène-Haute via Col de Vescavo★

9km/5.6mi – allow half a day.
▶ *From Sospel take D 2204 east. After 2km/1mi turn right onto a road signed "Piène-Olivetta". After 4km/2.5mi D 93 reaches Col de Vescavo (alt 478m/1 568ft). The road then crosses the border to the Italian village of Olivetta. Follow D 193 to the left.*

The road continues to climb up to the charming little village of **Piène-Haute**, in solitary splendor on an outcrop 613m/2 011ft in altitude. The best place to park is on the esplanade at the entrance to the village. Before setting off downhill on foot, admire the **view**★ of the old houses huddled side by side below the castle ruins. The church, on a rise, has a beautiful carved belltower and an unusual red marble altarpiece. Above the village, by the castle ruins, are splendid views of the Roya valley.

HIKING TOURS
Botanical Trail

◗ *The path is below D 93 to the right towards the Olivetta frontier post. Go down the slope from the road towards the railway, then turn left under the bridge. A signpost near a ruin marks the start of the botanical footpath.*

🚶 *1.5hr on foot round trip.* This delightful footpath, marked with boards detailing the plants to be seen, goes through a wood of young oak trees, scrubland which was once cultivated in terraces, and a holm oak wood.

Mont Agaisen

◗ *7km/4.3mi by car and then From Sospel take the road beside the post office that climbs up the north bank of the Bévéra. After 1.5km/1mi, turn right and follow a road uphill towards Serres des Bérins.*

🚶 *1.5hr on foot round trip.* On entering the Bérins district, take the surfaced road on the right, heading south. After a short stretch through some woods, the old

Papal Revenge

When Napoleon had the pope driven out of the Papal States annexed to the Empire, Pius VII had him excommunicated from the Catholic Church.

army road reaches the first small forts of the fortified complex of Mont-Agaisen (⊶ *closed to the public).* Leave the car in any free space along the road.

On the path that leads to the summit (alt 745m/2 444ft) is the occaisional casemate or firing turret. To the south at the edge of the summit is a large metal cross and a good view of the village, the Bévéra Valley and Mont Barbonnet. There are other viewpoints on the summit, towards Col de Brouis and north towards the valley dominated by the bare peak of Mont Mangiabo (alt 1 801m/5 909ft).

🚶 *3hr.* The more experienced ramblers can opt for a variation on this excursion, leaving from the village and undertaking it entirely on foot. In this case, they should leave from the Groupe Scolaire overlooking the village and follow the path leading off to the right, marked *"GR 52 – Mont Agaisen".*

The track merges with the GR 52 (red and white blazes) for about 1km/0.6mi. Turn left onto a surfaced road at the junction, and follow it uphill for another half a mile or so until you reach the first

Village of Piène-Haute

S. Sauvignier/MICHELIN

The Salt Road

Owing to its essential role in the preservation of meat and the tanning of hides, salt has always been of considerable interest to tradesmen. Provençal salt-works have supplied Piedmont since the Middle Ages. The salt was unloaded from sailing barges in Nice and transported by mule to Turin through the Col de Braus, Col de Brouis and Col de Tende via Sospel and Saorge. This strategic highway became known as the Salt Road (Route du Sel). Now embellished with works of modern art, it is still the main highway between the Riviera and Piedmont.

military ruins and rejoin the itinerary described above.

DRIVING TOUR

9 COL DE BROUIS ROAD
21km/13mi – about 1hr.
See local map: NICE.

This road is an extension of the Col de Braus Road (*see Forêt de TURINI*) towards Turin, formerly known as the "Salt Road".

▷ *From Sospel take D 2204 east.*

There is a view to the rear over Sospel guarded by the Fort du Barbonnet.

Col du Pérus
Alt 654m/2 146ft. The road runs just above the deep Bassera ravine.

Col de Brouis★
Alt 879m/2 884ft. This pass takes its name from the heather-like shrub that thrives in the area, known as brouis. The monument above the car park on the right commemorates the last French attack of April 1945 against the German forces, who had been driven back into the valleys. A broad **view** ★ opens up of the peaks on the far bank of the Roya. The road descends to La Giandola.

La Giandola
Attractive mountain hamlet with a Renaissance church tower.

▷ *Return by the same itinerary; it's also possible to take a detour via Breil-sur-Roya (see BREIL-SUR-ROYA) or go back through the Vallée de la Roya, to Saorge, 5km/3mi away (see SAORGE).*

ADDRESSES

STAY

Hôtel des Étrangers – *7 Bd. de Verdun. 04 93 04 00 09. www.sospel. net. Closed Nov–Mar. 27 rooms. 8€. Restaurant.* This unpretentious hotel-restaurant makes a great base for exploring the area. Swimming pool. Local produce used in the restaurant.

SHOPPING

The village is known for its production of honey and its handcrafted objects made with olive wood.

Markets – Place Gianotti on Thursdays and Place de la Cabraïa on Sunday

mornings (especially honey and goat's cheese). There is a market selling regional produce on St Michel's Day (29 September).

LEISURE ACTIVITIES
ABC d'Air – *04 93 21 11 39. www.abcdair.fr. 70€.* The summit of Mont Agaisen overlooking the village is a perfect starting-point for paragliding, affording fine views of the valley below.

Hiking – A list of all the hiking paths starting from the village is available from the tourist office. There are also facilities for exploring the neighbouring countryside on horseback.

Tende★
Alpes Maritimes

Tende (alt 816m/2 677ft) has a breathtaking Alpine **setting** on the banks of the Roya, beneath the steep rockface of the Riba de Bernou. Its tall, shingle-roofed houses seem to be stacked on top of one another. Tende is a starting point for trips to the Vallée des Merveilles (*see Vallée des MERVEILLES*).

SIGHTS
Old Town★
Most of the houses, some dating from the 15C, are built in a maze of narrow streets with the local stone of green and purple schist. Note the Renaissance bell-towers on the chapels of the Black and White Penitents. From above the town on the site of the old castle, the **view**★ looks down onto the village.

Collégiale Notre Dame-de-l'Assomption
Open daily summer 9am–6pm; winter 9am–5pm.
This 15C collegiate church was built on the orders of Honoré Lascaris (Count of Tende) with green schist, except for the Lombard tower capped with a pretty little dome. The Renaissance style doorway is flanked by two Doric columns resting on two lions, inspired by Romanesque Art. The inside is divided into three aisles by thick, green schist columns. The Lascaris lords are buried here.

▶ **Population:** 2 025.

Michelin Map: 341 G3; local map: *see NICE.*

Info: Av. 16-Septembre-1947, ℘04 93 04 73 71. www.tendemerveilles.com. Vallées Roya-Bévéra, ℘04 93 04 92 05. www.royabevera.com.

Location: The old town huddles below the château ruins on the left bank of the Roya River. Tende, full of dizzying switchbacks all the way up to its peak, was once part of the Old Salt Route for Cuneo and Turin.

Musée des Merveilles★
Av. du 16-Septembre-1947, opposite the Customs Office. Open Wed–Mon Sept–Apr 10am–5pm; May–Jun and Sept–mid-Oct 10am–6.30pm; Jul–Aug daily 10am–6.30pm. Closed 12–24 Mar, 13–25 Nov, public holidays. No charge. ℘04 93 04 32 50. www.museedesmerveilles.com.
The history of the Vallée des Merveilles and its inhabitants is illustrated in this museum, centring on three themes: relief models and animations show the regional geology; archaeology forms a major exhibit with dioramas reconstructing daily life in the Bronze Age, many casts of the carvings, the original

Old town, Tende

B. Kaufmann/ MICHELIN

Changing Borders

When the county of Nice was attached to France, the Italian King Victor-Emmanuel II managed to keep the upper Roya Valley for his hunting excursions! At the end of the Second World War, the peace treaty with Italy, confirmed on 12 October, 1947 by a plebiscite, finally ended this situation, and the upper valleys of the Roya, Tinée and Vésubie, were attached to France, thus aligning the border naturally along the waterways.

stela known as *chef de tribu* and objects discovered during excavations.

EXCURSION
St-Dalmas-de-Tende

This attractive resort, once the main frontier post on the road linking Nice to Cuneo, is a good jumping-off point for excursions into the Vallée des Merveil-les, with facilities for cycling, riding, skiing and hiking.

La Brigue★
6.5km/4mi southeast. ♿ *See La BRIGUE.*

Granile
▶ *10km/6mi to the south. Go towards Casterino (D 91), turning left after 1km/0.6mi. After 5km/3mi, park just outside the village at Granile.*

This seemingly isolated village on the side of a mountain has an unusual appearance of mountain houses decorated with wooden balconies and stone slabs roofs. There is an impressive view of the Gorges de la Roya.

▶ *Return to St-Dalmas-de-Tende and continue up the valley.*

The apple trees in the meadows contrast with the rock-strewn olive groves in the regions around Sospel and Breil.

ADDRESSES

🛏 STAY
◉ **Le Prieuré** – *Rue Jean Médecin, St-Dalmas, 4km/2.5mi south of Tende by N 204.* ☎*04 93 04 75 70. www.leprieure.org. Closed Mar. 24 rooms.* 🅿. ⌷ *8€. Restaurant*◉◉. Tastefully restored former priory containing large, well-kept rooms decorated with locally made furniture. The vaulted dining hall opens out onto a pleasant patio. The menu offers Mediterranean cuisine. Sit down under the arbour on the terrace and admire the sight of Mont Bego.

🍽 EAT
◉ **Auberge Tendasque** – *65 Av. du 16-Septembre-1947.* ☎*04 93 04 62 26. Closed two weeks in Feb, Tue and Thu eves Jun–Oct.* This modest restaurant sits within walking distance of the fascinating Musée des Merveilles. Good provençal cuisine. Reasonable prices.

🏃 SPORT AND LEISURE
Lucien Bérenger – ☎*04 93 04 77 85. www.berengeraventures.com.* Professional mountain guide, abseiling, rock-climbing, canyoning and more.

Via Ferrata – Rope bridges and vertiginous canyon crossings using special mountain-climbing equipment, the course itself is quite demanding (*5hr*), but you can also opt for the shorter version (*2.5hr*). *Map of the course and tickets available at the tourist office.* ⬤*3.50€ (children 12–18 years 1€).*

Ski – Fans of the slopes can find the nearest ski resorts across the Italian border at Limone *(accessible by train).* Cross-country skiing and snowshoeing can be found in Casterino. *For information contact the tourist office.*

Forêt de Turini★★

Alpes Maritimes

The huge forest of Turini is unusual, since its trees are generally found in more northerly latitudes. The lower slopes are covered with maritime pines and young oaks, but higher up there are maple, beech, chestnut, spruce, larch and pines.

- ⏱ **Michelin Map:** 341 F4; local map: see NICE.
- ▶ **Location:** Situated in the Nice hinterland 15.5km/ 9.6mi from Menton, the forest covers 3 500ha/ 1 350acres between the Vésubie and Bévéra valleys.

 **DRIVING TOUR**

7 L'AUTHION★★

Round trip 18km/11mi from Col de Turini – allow 45min.
The Authion road passes through magnificent mountain scenery. ⏱*The roads are usually blocked by snow in winter.*

Monument aux Morts

The Authion Massif has twice been a backdrop to military action. In 1793 the Convention's troops fought here against the Austrians and Sardinians, and in 1945 the Germans were driven out. Panoramic **view**★ from the memorial.
Continue along D 68 bearing right at the fork to Cabanes Vieilles, an old military camp. The road runs through Alpine pastures with **views**★ of the Roya Valley.

▶ *Turn right by another monument onto a track, which leads (500m/547yd) to a platform.*

Pointe des Trois-Communes★★

At this altitude (2 082m/6 830ft) there is a marvellous **panorama**★★ of the peaks in the Mercantour and Nice Pre-Alps.

▶ *Return to D 68; at the war memorial take the road back to Col de Turini.*

7 VALLON DE STE-ÉLISABETH★

Round trip 15km/9.3mi from Col de Turini – allow 1hr.
The road (D 70) winds northwest cutting its way between the mountain peaks overlooking the Vésubie tributary.

Gorges de Ste-Élisabeth

This rugged gorge cuts a savage gash in the concertina-like folds in the rock.

▶ *Soon after the tunnel, stop at the Chapelle St-Honorat.*

St-Honorat Viewpoint★

The view extends from the terrace by the chapel over the perched village of Bollène, the Vésubie, and the Mercantour peaks.

La Bollène-Vésubie

This pleasant village stands at the foot of a mountain peak, Cime des Vallières. The road winds down into the Vésubie Valley on the D 2565 *(towards Nice)*, with breathtaking views.

7 COL DE BRAUS ROAD★★

Round trip 76km/47mi leaving from Col de Turini – allow one day.
The drive to Peïra-Cava passes through the thickest part of Turini Forest.

Cime de Peïra-Cava★★

1.5km/1mi – plus 30min on foot round trip.
🧗It's an easy climb to the top *(follow the lift),* where you'll have panoramic **views**★★ of the Vésubie Valley and the peaks on the Franco-Italian frontier.

Peïra-Cava★ *Alt 1 450m/4 757ft.*

This summer resort and winter sports centre is perched on a ridge between the Vésubie and Bévéra valleys.

▶ *Beyond the village a sharp right turn leads to a car park, then walk 50m/55yd.*

La Bollène-Vésubie.

Pierre Plate★★

This peak provides a **panoramic view**★★. Return downhill to D 2566 and in La Cabanette turn left onto D 21. The road descends through steep bends with magnificent **views**★.

▶ *D 21 continues to Lucéram.*

Lucéram★

See LUCÉRAM.
▶ *South of Lucéram D 2566 descends the Paillon Valley to L'Escarène.*

L'Escarène

See NICE [4]: Les Deux Paillons.
From L'Escarène D 2204 climbs northeast up the Braus Valley to Sospel.

Touët-de-l'Escarène

The route passes through this charming little village with a Baroque church.

Clue de Braus

This rift that opens up beyond Touët village is short but impressive. From St-Laurent (hamlet) one can reach the Braus waterfall (⏱ *15min*).
The D 2204 winds around 16 hairpin bends before climbing to **views**★ from the Nice observatory to Cap d'Antibes.

Col de Braus

Alt 1 002m/3 287ft.
Beyond the pass the road descends through 18 bends offering extensive **views**★★ of the Bévéra Valley.

Col St-Jean

At Col St-Jean, between the dwellings on the left, an old army road leads off **Fort Suchet**, built 1883–86.

Sospel★ *See SOSPEL.*

The D 2566 climbs northwest through the forest up the **Bévéra Valley**★. There is a beautiful waterfall on the right.

Gorges du Piaon★★

The *corniche* road runs beneath an overhang of rock high above the bed of the stream, strewn with huge boulders.

Chapelle Notre-Dame-de-la-Menour

An oratory marks the beginning of a path that provides a good view of the valley and the gorge. A great flight of steps leads up to the chapel, which has a two-storey Renaissance façade. The route passes through the charming village of Moulinet before returning through the forest to the Col de Turini.

ADDRESSES

🛏 STAY

🍽🍽 **Les Chamois** – *Turini (Col de).* ℰ04 93 91 58 31. www.hotel-les-chamois.com. *15 rooms.* Ideally situated to observe the Monte-Carlo rally as it passes over Col de Turini. Mountain-style restaurant with terrace. Pleasant accommodation; some with balconies.

Utelle★

Alpes Maritimes

An isolated village at an altitude of 800m/2 625ft, projecting like a balcony over the Vésubie Valley. Once the most important town between Tinée and Vésubie, Utelle still has much of its original character and ruined fortifications.

▸ **Population:** 685.
Michelin Map: 341 E4; local map: *see NICE.*
Info: Town Hall ℘04 93 03 17 01. www.vesubian.com.
Location: Utelle is outside the gorges of the Vésubie Valley (left at St-Jean-la-Rivière). Be cautious on the hairpin bends leading to the village.

SIGHTS
Église St-Véran★
This 14C church altered in the 17C has an elegant Gothic porch with carved panels illustrating the legend of St Veranus in 12 tableaux.

A **carved wooden altarpiece**★ depicts scenes from the Passion. There is an altarpiece of the Annunciation (Nice School) above the first altar in the north aisle and a 13C Recumbent Christ below the altar in the south aisle.

Chapelle des Pénitents-Blancs
The chapel near the church contains a carved wooden altarpiece of the Descent from the Cross by Rubens.

EXCURSION
Madone d'Utelle Panorama★★★
6km/3.7mi southwest.
The sanctuary of the Madonna of Utelle, founded in 850 by Spanish sailors who had survived a storm, was rebuilt in 1806. Pilgrimage tributes take place on August 15 and September 8.

A short distance from the chapel stands a viewing table (alt 1 174m/3 852ft) covered by a dome. You'll enjoy a breathtaking **panorama**★★★ over a wide expanse of the Alpes-Maritimes *département* and the Mediterranean.

Vallée de la Vésubie★★

Alpes Maritimes

The Vésubie valley, one of the most beautiful above Nice, has a forested Alpine landscape in the upper valley, Mediterranean climat terraced with vines and olive trees in the middle valley, and below St-Jean-la-Rivière the river torrent has created a deep gorge with dramatic vertical walls.

Michelin Map: 341 E4; local map: *see NICE.*
Info: Pl. Félix-Faure, St-Martin-Vésubie. ℘04 93 03 21 28. www.vesubian.com.
Location: The Vésubie, an eastern tributary of the Var, is formed by two torrents: the Madone de Fenestre and the Boréon, near the Italian border.

🚗 DRIVING TOUR

Plan-du-Var to St-Martin-Vésubie
110km/68mi – about 5hr.

◗ *D 2565 follows the narrow, winding Gorges de la Vésubie★★★. In St-Jean-la-Rivière turn left onto the road (D 32) which climbs towards Utelle.*

La Madone d'Utelle★★★
See UTELLE.

Vallon de Gordolasque

Make a U-turn at St-Jean-la-Rivière and turn left onto the D 2565.

Beyond St-Jean-la-Rivière, the valley squeezes between bluffs of rock, skirting the foothills of the Brec d'Utelle.

Lantosque

This tiny perched village has a canyoning via ferrata course *(2hr)* which crosses the Gorges of Lantosque *(contact the Mairie for information, 04 93 03 00 02)*.

Roquebillière

This little town has been rebuilt six times since the 6C due to rock falls and floods. The last landslide in 1926 left some of the austere old houses and the 15C church on the west bank. Located in the new town, the **Église St-Michel-du-Gast** is a combination of Romanesque and Gothic styles.

On leaving Roquebillière-Vieux turn right onto a road to Belvédère (D 71).

The picturesque road winds up the **Vallon de la Gordolasque**★★ between Cime du Diable (Devil's Peak) and Cime de la Valette.

Belvédère

The **site**★ of this charming village overlooks both the Gordolasque and the Vésubie. From the terrace behind the mairie (town hall) there is a **view**★ of Roquebillière-Vieux below backed by Tournairet Mountain, of the Vésubie to Mont Férion and Turini Forest. The road (D 171) continues up the valley past massive rocks and tumbling waterfalls, including the **Cascade du Ray**★ where the river divides into two waterfalls.

Cascade de l'Estrech★

The road ends near a path *(1km/0.6mi of mountain track)* that leads to the beautiful Estrech waterfall flowing down from a **cirque**★★ of snow-capped mountains.

Return to D 2565; turn right on D 72.

Berthemont-les-Bains

This therapeutic spa has naturally sulphrous waters of 30°C/86°F used as long ago as Roman times. As the road climbs, the valley changes to a landscape of chestnuts, pines and green pastures which has earned the region round St-Martin-Vésubie the title of "Suisse Niçoise" (Nice's Switzerland).

ADDRESSES

STAY

Auberge du Bon Puits – *Le Suquet, 5.5km/3.4mi south of Lantosque towards Nice. 04 93 03 17 65. Closed Dec–Easter, Tue except Jul–Aug.* This roadside inn made with local stone stands on the banks of the Vésubie. The dining hall features visible beams and an open fireplace. There are a few rooms as well as an ornamental park with ponies and a playing area for children.

St-Martin-Vésubie★

Alpes Maritimes

St-Martin-Vésubie stretches out along a rocky cliff between the Boréon and Madone-de-Fenestre streams. Encircled by summits and alpine greenery, the town known as "Switzerland Niçoise" is a popular summer **mountaineering centre**.

 **WALKING TOUR**

▷ *Start under the plane trees in Pl. Félix-Faure.*

Rue du Docteur-Cagnoli

A narrow street bordered by Gothic houses with handsome porches and lintels runs north-south through the town. Several 14C houses survived the fire of 1487 (Maison du Coiffeur).

Chapelle des Pénitents-Blancs

The chapel has a carved façade, a bulb-shaped bell tower and, below the altar, a recumbent Christ with cherubs holding instruments of the Passion.

▷ *From Rue Dr-Cagnoli turn left into Rue du Plan to Pl. de la Frairie.*

- ▶ **Population:** 1300.
- **Michelin Map:** 341 E3; local map: *see NICE.*
- **Info:** Pl. Félix-Faure. ℘04 93 03 21 28. www.saintmartinvesubie.fr.
- **Location:** Located 71km/ 44mi north of Nice on the D 2565.
- **Parking:** Park to the northwest of the entrance to the old town.

Place de la Frairie

From the terrace overlooking Madone de Fenestre Torrent is a **view** of the gushing river and nearby mountains, Cime de la Palu and Cime du Piagu. The church is behind the square.

Church

This Roman building beautifully decorated in the 17C features a richly dressed 12C statue of the Madone de Fenestre. On the last Saturday in June, it's carried in procession to a mountain sanctuary (℘*see Excursions*) where it remains until September. The second chapel's left-hand aisle houses two panels from an altarpiece attributed to Louis Bréa. From the terrace is a partial **view** of the Boréon Valley and Venanson village.

A Mountaineering Pioneer on the Riviera

The Chevalier Victor de Cessole (1859–1940), a member of an old Nice family, took to climbing late in lifewhen his doctor recommended exercise and fresh air. He enrolled in the new Club Alpin Français when he was already in his thirties, and became a compulsive mountaineer, climbing successively the highest peaks in the Alpes-Maritimes (Mont Clapier, Mont Gélas) and setting several records in the Massif de l'Argentera.

His recommended walks, described in illustrated brochures, are forerunners of the guide books of today. His activities earned him the presidency of the Club Alpin Français, a position which he held for 40 years, and enabled him to inaugurate and organise the chain of mountain refuges. In 1901 he opened the Nice refuge above Madone de Fenestre. He initiated the first skiing competitions and is considered to be the founder, in spirit at least, of Beuil, the oldest resort in the area. His interest in nature led him to establish the first measures for the protection of wildlife in the region – the banning of the picking of *Saxifraga florulenta*, now the emblem of the Parc du Mercantour.

EXCURSIONS
Venanson★
4.5km/3mi.

▶ *Leave St-Martin-Vésubie by the Boréon bridge and take D 31 south.*

The village square standing on a triangular rocky outcrop 1 164m/3 819ft high commands a good **view**★ of St-Martin and the Vésubie Valley.

Chapelle St-Sébastien
🕐 *Open by request at the restaurant La Bella Vista.* ✆*04 93 03 25 11.*
This 15C chapel is considered one of the most complete examples of Art Niçois, with the interior covered in **frescoes**★ by Baleison. At the far end beneath a Crucifixion, St Sebastian is pierced by arrows; on the side walls and the ceiling, scenes from the saint's life.

Parish church
Pl. de l'Eglise.
On the left of the entrance is a triptych of the Virgin and Child, flanked by St John and St Petronella. At the high altar a Baroque altarpiece (1645) of the Coronation of the Virgin features the donor.

Le Boréon★★
From St-Martin-Vésubie take D 2565 8km/5mi north up Le Boréon's west bank. The resort stands on a superb site (1 500m/4 201ft) on the southern edge

of the Parc National du Mercantour by the **Cascade du Boréon**★ where the river drops 40m/130ft down a narrow gorge. Le Boréon is the starting place for forest walks, up to the high peaks and mountain lakes. By car you can reach the Vacherie du Boréon *(2.5km/1.5mi east).*

Vallon de la Madone de Fenestre
12km/7.4mi east – about 30min. From St-Martin, take Avenue de Saravalle.
The road climbs rapidly up the Madone Valley between Cime du Piagu and Cime de la Palu, crossing and re-crossing the river. The road ends in a rugged rock **cirque**★★ much appreciated by mountaineers. Caïre de la Madone, huge and pointed, rises nearby, and the slopes of **Cime du Gélas** (3 143m/10 312ft), covered with frozen snow, dominate the northern horizon on the Italian border. The **Madone de Fenestre** chapel is a place of pilgrimage, which in summer houses the statue of Our Lady of Fenestre. In September it is returned to St-Martin-Vésubie in solemn procession.

🚗 DRIVING TOUR

Route de Valdeblore★★
29km/18mi. Allow 2.5hr.

▶ *North from St-Martin by the D 256.*

The road linking the valleys of the Tinée and the upper Vésubie passes through the Valdeblore district, a mountainous region of pastures and wooded slopes. Before the tunnel is a fine **view**★ over Vésubie Valley and St-Martin.

La Colmiane
This ski resort in the Col St-Martin (alt 1 500m/4 921ft) consists of chalets and hotels dotted among the pines.

▶ *At Col St-Martin turn left onto a narrow road which leads to the ski-lift.*

Le Boréon waterfall, St-Martin-Vésubie

E. Baret/ MICHELIN

The Return of the Wolf

In 1995 the presence of a pack of eight wolves *(canis lupus)* was confirmed in the Parc du Mercantour. The return of the wolf (from the Abruzzi in Central Italy where the wolf population is estimated at more than 500) is a sign of ecological health in the area. The Parc du Mercantour conducts a campaign of awareness and education with shepherds who now pen flocks at night and use sheepdogs (the Pyrenean Patou) to prevent wolf attacks.

Pic de La Colmiane★★
Ski-lift to the summit. Jul–Aug daily 10am–6pm (Sat–Sun only Sept–Jun). 2.50€. 04 93 02 83 54.
From the top is an immense **panorama** ★★: south over the Vésubie Valley and Turini Forest; east over the Mercantour; north and west over the Baus de la Frema to Mont Mounier with Valdeblore in the foreground.

Via Ferrata du Baus de la Frema★
At the pass, turn right opposite the minigolf (sign "Via Ferrata"). There is plenty of space to park on the way up the slope. The Via Ferrata begins at the end of the car park. Open Jun–Sept. 3€. 04 93 23 25 90. www.colmiane.com.
This recent development, directly accessible by car, offers ideal facilities for learning rock-climbing and overcoming vertigo. There are three routes graded blue, red and black according to their difficulty. The first course takes at least 1.5hr. Those looking for big thrills will particularly enjoy crossing the footbridge (35m/115ft long; 50m/164ft above ground level).

St-Dalmas-de-Valdeblore
Have a stroll through the winding alleys of this village before visiting the Romanesque **Ste-Croix church**. Striking with its pyramidal Alpine-style bell tower, stout buttresses and Lombard bands on the chevet. Above the high altar there is a polyptych by Guillaume Planeta of St Dalmas, St Roch and the Evangelists. In the north aisle is an altarpiece of St Francis attributed to André de Cella. Behind an altarpiece of the Rosary (17C) in the south apsidal chapel are the partial remains of some very old frescoes.

West of La Bolline turn right on D 66.

Rimplas
The curious **site**★ of this village on the edge of the cliff (1 000m/3 281ft high) is striking. From the chapel, dedicated to Mary Magdalene, there is an extensive **view**★ of the Tinée Valley, Bramafan Valley and the Valdeblore villages.
*2hr round trip. A nice and easy trail leads down into **St-Sauveur-sur-Tinée** by the GR 5, northwest of the village.*

By the road, follow the Valdeblore by the D 2565, then la Tinée by the D 2205, right for St-Saveur, left for Nice.

ADDRESSES

STAY
La Châtaigneraie – *04 93 03 21 22. www.raiberti.com. Closed Oct–15 May.* *37 rooms. 5€. Restaurant.* Pleasant accommodation nestling in a peaceful park with pool and WiFi. Ideal for those who wish to go climbing or hiking in the Parc du Mercantour.

SHOPPING
Markets – Tuesday, Saturday and Sunday on Place du Marché *(summer season)*.

SPORT & LEISURE
Ski – Le Boréon has 30km/18.6mi of cross-country ski trails.

INDEX

INDEX

INDEX

INDEX

🛏 STAY

🍴 EAT

MAPS AND PLANS

A map reference to the appropriate Michelin map is given for each chapter in the Discovering The French Riviera sections of the guide.

COMPANION PUBLICATIONS

Michelin Maps

Motorists who plan ahead will always have the appropriate maps at hand. Michelin products are complementary: for each of the sites listed in The Green Guide, map references are indicated which help you find your location on our range of maps.

To travel the roads in this region, you may use any of the following:

♦ the regional map at a scale of 1:200 000 **no 528**, which covers the main roads and secondary roads, and includes useful indications for finding tourist attractions.

This is a good map to choose for travelling in a wide area. At a quick glance, you can locate and identify the main sights to see. In addition to identifying the nature of the road ways, the map shows castles, churches and other religious edifices, scenic view points, megalithic monuments, swimming beaches on lakes and rivers, swimming pools, golf courses, race tracks, air fields, and more. You may also consult **Michelin maps nos 340 and 341**.

And remember to travel with the latest edition of the **map of France no 721**, which gives an overall view of the region of Provence, and the main access roads which connect it to the rest of France. The entire country is mapped at a 1:1 000 000 scale and clearly shows the main road network.

Michelin is pleased to offer a route-planning service on the Internet: **www.ViaMichelin.com.** Choose the shortest route, a route without tolls, or the Michelin recommended route to your destination; you can also access information about hotels and restaurants from *The Michelin Guide*, and tourist sites from *The Green Guide*.

Bon voyage!

MAP LEGEND

	Sight	Seaside resort	Winter sports resort	Spa
Highly recommended	★★★	♨♨♨	✳✳✳	♯♯♯
Recommended	★★	♨♨	✳✳	♯♯
Interesting	★	♨	✳	♯

Selected monuments and sights

◉ ⇨	Tour - Departure point
⛪ ⛩	Catholic church
⛪ ✝	Protestant church, other temple
✡ 🕌	Synagogue - Mosque
🏛	Building
▪	Statue, small building
✝	Calvary, wayside cross
◎	Fountain
●—●—■	Rampart - Tower - Gate
✕	Château, castle, historic house
∴	Ruins
◡	Dam
✿	Factory, power plant
☆	Fort
⋂	Cave
▭	Troglodyte dwelling
⩊	Prehistoric site
▾	Viewing table
Ⓥ	Viewpoint
▲	Other place of interest

Abbreviations

A	Agricultural office (Chambre d'agriculture)	**P**	Local authority offices (Préfecture, sous-préfecture)
C	Chamber of Commerce (Chambre de commerce)	**POL.**	Police station (Police)
H	Town hall (Hôtel de ville)	🛡	Police station (Gendarmerie)
J	Law courts (Palais de justice)	**T**	Theatre (Théâtre)
M	Museum (Musée)	**U**	University (Université)

Sports and recreation

🏇	Racecourse
⛸	Skating rink
≋ ▨	Outdoor, indoor swimming pool
🎥	Multiplex Cinema
⛵	Marina, sailing centre
⛺	Trail refuge hut
▱—▪—▪	Cable cars, gondolas
▱—┼┼┼	Funicular, rack railway
🚂	Tourist train
◆	Recreation area, park
🎢	Theme, amusement park
Ψ	Wildlife park, zoo
⊛	Gardens, park, arboretum
⊜	Bird sanctuary, aviary
🚶	Walking tour, footpath
☺	Of special interest to children

Special symbol

🏖	Beach

Additional symbols

🛈	Tourist information	✉	Post office
═══ ═══	Motorway or other primary route	☎	Telephone
❶ ❶	Junction: complete, limited	✉	Covered market
▭▭ ══	Pedestrian street	⋅✕⋅	Barracks
Ɪ═══Ɪ	Unsuitable for traffic, street subject to restrictions	△	Drawbridge
▦▦▦ ─ ─ ─	Steps – Footpath	ʊ	Quarry
🚆 🚉	Train station – Auto-train station	✕	Mine
🚌 🚏	Coach (bus) station	Ⓑ Ⓕ	Car ferry (river or lake)
─┼─	Tram	🚢	Ferry service: cars and passengers
Ⓜ	Metro, underground	⛴	Foot passengers only
🅿	Park-and-Ride	③	Access route number common to Michelin maps and town plans
♿	Access for the disabled	Bert (R.)...	Main shopping street
		AZ B	Map co-ordinates